THE
INTELLECTUAL DEVELOPMENT
OF
Voltaire

THE
INTELLECTUAL
DEVELOPMENT OF
Voltaire

Ira O. Wade

PRINCETON, NEW JERSEY

PRINCETON UNIVERSITY PRESS

1969

This book has been composed in
Linotype Granjon

Printed in the United States of America
by Princeton University Press, Princeton, New Jersey

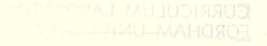

To M. H. W.

Ton souvenir en moi luit comme un ostensoir

CONTENTS

Introduction   ix

Part I. *The Poet*

   1. Early Training   3
   2. Voltaire's Literary Masters   23
   3. Voltaire's Ancestors in Lyric Poetry   44
   4. Poetry and Anti-poetry   82
   5. The Poet and His Art   93
   6. The Poet as Free-thinker   120

Part II. *The Civilization of England and Its*
         Meaning for Voltaire

   1. Voltaire in England   149
   2. The Publication of the *Henriade*   156
   3. Voltaire's Observations of England:
      The *Correspondence*   161
   4. Voltaire's Observations of England:
      The *Notebooks*   166
   5. Voltaire's Literary Activities   173
   6. The Impact of the English Experience   180
   7. Interlude, 1728-1734: The Results of the
      English Experience   187
         a. *Histoire de Charles XII*
         b. Shakespeare and Voltaire's Tragedies
         c. *Le Temple du goût*
         d. *Les Lettres philosophiques*
   8. From Poet to Philosopher   240

Part III. *Cirey: The Reeducation of Voltaire*

   1. Cirey   253
   2. Mme du Châtelet and Voltaire   265
   3. Voltaire and Frederick   292
   4. The Diversity of Activity at Cirey   329
   5. 1738-1739, The Revolution of a Human Mind   367
   6. Controversy   401
   7. Voltaire and the Science of 1738   428

CONTENTS

8. Voltaire and History   451
9. Biblical Criticism   511
10. The Meaning of the Cirey Experience   564

Part IV. *The Philosopher*

1. Voltaire and the Philosophers   573
   a. Pascal, Descartes, Newton, Locke
   b. Bayle
   c. Leibniz, Spinoza, Malebranche
2. Voltaire's World   720
3. Philosopher, "Philosophe," Free-thinker, or Poet?   755
4. Voltaireanism and the Life of the Spirit   768

Conclusion   775

Bibliography   789

Index   797

INTRODUCTION

IT SEEMED when I first undertook this work that its execution would be simple. I wished merely to trace the intellectual biography of a man with whom I had spent the greater part of forty years. I judged that it would be necessary only to unite in some consistent way the modest investigations of Voltaire which I had been pursuing with the important studies which others had published, thereby arranging in coherent fashion our knowledge about the intellectual activities of the author of *Candide*. I quickly learned, however, that things are not so simple as I had thought. The sheer mass of Voltaire studies during the past sixty years—since Lanson's remarkable little biography in 1909—is terrifying. In the *Studies on Voltaire and the Eighteenth Century*, which began just fourteen years ago, there are already over sixty volumes dealing to a greater or lesser extent with Voltaire. If one adds to this staggering corpus the work produced elsewhere by such Voltaire scholars as Messrs. Pomeau, Brumfitt, Besterman, Perkins, Bottiglia, Naves, Gay, and many others of the previous generation—Torrey, Morehouse, Crowley, Havens, Dargan, Mornet, and Hazard—the results will appear overwhelming. Certainly, he who attempts to construct a synthesis of Voltaire's thought does not have any reason to complain about the lack of material, nor about its quality either.

The first problem I had to consider is what constitutes the reality of an author—not his descriptive reality, which we can always capture without difficulty by depicting his activity in a linear manner, but rather his inner reality. I have assumed that the latter consists in the thoughts he has, the way he expresses those thoughts, and the way he interprets them in action. In the strictest sense, a man is what he thinks, what he says, and what he does. Yet there is no interval between these apparently consecutive operations: reality is all these things, plus an awareness that they are present simultaneously. A man is what he thinks, what he thinks is what he says, and what he says is what he does, and together these activities constitute his reality, his meaning, his being. I have further assumed that these spontaneous operations of thinking, saying, and doing are organic, that they unite at any given moment to create a personality, a "moi," which is aware of its being and its possibilities. This "self" also understands that it has to make every effort to be coherent. Nothing prevents it from developing in time along with other "selves" to form the organized personality of a group, a personality likewise organic and unified. Finally, I have assumed that what nurtures this "self" is experience of the surrounding world, which offers to each person a challenge and elicits from each a response which we are all too prone to call a reaction. Properly speaking, every event is an influence which, when digested, invites action rather than re-action, which is merely a passive response. The more active the com-mitment to the possibilities of living is, the richer is the life of the "self."

Our particular interest in this essay lies in the multiple possibilities which Voltaire's experience offered him. Strictly speaking, we wish to show what Voltaire was as a creative human being after he had been subjected to the various vicissitudes of living. These changes can come from the external world, from others who have lived or are living in that world, and from thoughts which they have had or actions to which these thoughts have led them. We have to remind ourselves continually that although we live by thinking—thinking in the broadest sense of the term—we also live with thoughts. To get at the individual, therefore, we have to examine scrupulously the ideas producing the movement of thought, the coherent way in which predecessors and contemporaries organize these ideas, and, lastly, the organization the individual creates within himself out of these heterogeneous intellectual forces. If, as we believe, man molds his existence as he produces a work of art, we have to try to pene-trate it in the same way we try to probe the work of art, by continu-ally analyzing its structure in order to discover its inner form.

The individual, fortunately, does not have to spend too much time inquiring into the origin or the evolution of the process, for it un-furls so easily and effortlessly that, if he were to pay no attention whatever to his position in the movement, or even if he were to re-fuse to insist upon an awareness of the phenomena with which he is involved, reality would continue on its merry way nonetheless. Thus, the simplest fact of life is that each man can become engaged with reality, thereby making it the inner reality of the "self," or can just as well ignore it. The result is that coherence, continuity, and consistency can be either the sources of real existences, organically arranged, or merely absurd possibilities. The factors which distinguish between the two alternatives are consciousness and will.

The man whose inner reality we should like to penetrate here was not inclined to quibble about these matters. Although where others were concerned he drew sharp distinctions between what was truth and what was apparent truth, he would accept no such nonsense with respect to his own life. In every sense, *his* being was *his* thinking, *his* saying, *his* doing, and, because action was for him the be-all and end-all of existence, he wrapped that being in eighty-four years of perpetual intellectual motion. Nor was he often confused by *his* incoherence or *his* lack of continuity. He probably did not have unlimited faith in many things, but he did act—as he said that every man must—as if he were free and, in doing so, asserted unequivocally the power of the human mind to shape life consistently, coherently, and continuously. Providing an example which was to him by no means modest, he used his keen intelligence to mold his own life down to the smallest detail. I doubt that there was ever a man who calculated each move he made as thoroughly as did Voltaire. We shall try, in a more modest fashion, to see what it all amounted to.

In spite of this attitude, however, Voltaire was really no better at distinguishing between truth and seeming truth in the matter of his own life than anyone else. I suspect even that he often used the resulting confusion to attain his own ends. Yet his life did have one dominant characteristic: an intense mobility. Voltaire seems to have been constantly on the move: from one place to another—from Paris to Sceaux, to Ussé, to Richelieu, or to Sully, and from France to England, to Holland, to Germany, or to Switzerland; from one kind of work to another—from poetry to a historical or philosophical treatise, from a treatise to a play, from a play to an epic, from an epic to a mock-epic; from one preoccupation to another—from aesthetics to religion, to politics, to economics, to morality, to metaphysics; and even from one idea to another—from Newtonian attraction to free will, to good and evil, to kinetic energy, to equality.

This extreme mobility, which was typical of the age as well as of Voltaire, gave rise to three other characteristics: clandestinity, humanism, and the search for new art forms. These three characteristics, likewise symptomatic both of Voltaire and of his time, had one thing in common: they were all concerned with the imbalance between the old and the new, between "préjugés" and "rapports," between beliefs and scientific knowledge, between form and content. The desire of men in this age was for a life of organic unity, in which all the parts of life would have a reasonable place in the whole. But the actual state of affairs was such that these parts could have no fixed position: the whole situation had become fluid, and movement had become just as essential to being as unity. This mobility, of course, produced an impossible situation, for it was always undoing the unity or at least rendering necessary another kind of unity.

The result was clandestinity, a masking of one's intentions in order to achieve certain unified ends—a tendency I have noted in my introduction to *Micromégas*. Every major work of Voltaire from *Œdipe* to *Zadig*, with the exception of the drama, was a clandestine work, and sometimes the drama also was masked. After 1750, major and minor works alike were published anonymously, or penned under a pseudonym, or attributed to some other writer. Not only was their authorship concealed, but their contents likewise were disguised under a style which we call wit. We still struggle to ascertain what the date of composition of a Voltaire work was in our attempt to understand its genesis; and we debate endlessly the question of what Voltaire meant by an idea (*l'Infâme*, for example) or what can be learned from his contradictions, his ironies, his wit. This mask was created and developed so consistently that we often adopt Voltaire's seeming truth as truth, to the detriment of our understanding of the man. We are, of course, fooled at times by all artists, but with Voltaire clandestinity was a preconceived plan, so artfully enacted that we are almost willing in his case to accept that old statement of Malagrida that "God gave man speech to conceal his thoughts." Strangely enough, however, Voltaire who, looked at rationally, undoubtedly devised this technique as a means of outwitting his public, so that that public would be encouraged to sharpen its wits and thereby create its own clandestinity, actually developed it to the point (in *Candide*, for instance, or with Spinozism) where he used it to deceive himself. This aspect of *Candide* in its relationship to Voltaire I have previously attempted to interpret in *Voltaire and Candide*.

Another characteristic derived from Voltaire's mobility was his humanism. Here the key idea was that the continuity of life depends upon an infinite series of life experiences, that, although the source of our being derives from our awareness of ourselves, this awareness itself is dependent upon our activities. What Voltaire envied in the man from Saturn was the large number of senses which he possessed and the infinite number of new insights which these senses made available to him. Voltaire's curiosity, which he exhibited at every turn, led him to make a true effort to augment his relationships with the world as a means of increasing his knowledge of the universe and deepening his awareness of himself. He was convinced, as were all his contemporaries, that this seizing of the universe and of one's self (what we have come to designate as "penetrating reality with consciousness") is not only the source of a vital personality but the origin of human power. The important word here is "human." For, as Voltaire and his time understood it, to be human not only requires an ability to grasp the way one's inner, vital mechanism performs but demands an effort to pursue a maximum functioning of that mechanism in order to create ever more important possibilities for living dynamically. This simple faith in knowledge as power is a mark of Voltaire's humanism. This humanism does not deny that the origin of man rests in God; on the contrary, it really affirms that man's beginning can lie only in God. It asserts, rather blandly, that God gave man reason, the assumption being that, once having received that gift, man is responsible for making the most of it. There is in it, too, a steady conviction that this goal can be reached, that, even though progress be not as swift as one might wish, yet with a judicious effort and a certain amount of good will some headway can be made. This is the humanism which Voltaire, in the spirit of his time, espoused.

This creative activity, the application of knowledge to the expression of human possibilities, led to a final characteristic—the constant search for new art forms. The starting-point here, as with every Enlightenment event, was the increase of knowledge. This augmentation brought about a situation where some former content—called "préjugés"—had to be discarded because it could no longer stand the scrutiny of reason. The newly acquired knowledge also had to adjust itself to the other "true" knowledge—called "rapport"—with which it had to be integrated. Consequently, every new acquisition upset the vital unity which had been achieved and entailed not only a destruction but a restructuring and a reforming of another organic unity. Sometimes this process was so common that we pay scant attention to it, as when Voltaire abandoned his dominant interest in lyric poetry and acquired an interest in dramatic poetry. More important was the change that came about in 1738 when Voltaire announced his intention to shift from poetry to philosophy. And a more noteworthy event still occurred when, to make amends for the breakdown of all seventeenth-century art forms, he created a new form of expression in the *conte philosophique*. This process, which is nothing but a constant movement from structure to form, affects not only artistic forms but other vital forms as well. That is to say, a modification in one category of life will entail a restructuring and a reforming of all the other categories. Since it is understood that the human mind has the responsibility for this reshaping, we undertake to follow its peregrinations, not so much for psychological purposes—although they are not lacking in importance—as for vitalistic reasons.

It is not easy, though, to trace the making of an intellectual life as diffuse as Voltaire's. In the first place, his was a particularly long life, and this longevity complicates matters. We usually divide it into periods: the young Voltaire (1694-1725), Voltaire in England (1726-1729), Cirey (1734-1749), Potsdam (1750-1753), Geneva (1755-1759), Ferney (1759-1777). Our custom has been to characterize this reality as a series of geographical experiences, often at the expense of a central focus or at the risk of failing to establish either continuity or consistency. It is quite common for a volume to be devoted to only one period or, at best, to several periods. There are those who, realizing the difficulty of achieving focus in this matter, have established it first and reconstructed the activities of Voltaire around it; usually, it is either the poet, the dramatist, the critic, or the philosopher to whom we are introduced. In this scheme, Voltaire appears either as a man of letters or as a thinker, the conclusion ordinarily being either that the man of letters prevented the thinker from achieving any significant thought or that it was the philosopher who kept the poet from attaining superiority in poetry. We rarely understand that there was for Voltaire a natural continuity from poetry to philosophy; we almost always regard these aspects of Voltaire's activity as in opposition to each other. In general, we feel that he must have been either artist or thinker and that, whenever he turned from one field of endeavor to the other, it was a clear indication of a deficiency or a defeat, or at least a confession of weakness. Accordingly, we are apt to explain that he became a philosopher because he became aware of his shortcomings in poetry and turned to thought as an inferior activity. Even then we have difficulties because, when we seek to define what kind of philosopher he was, we are forced to ask ourselves whether he was not simply a literary critic, expounding his thoughts upon the art of poetry, or whether he was indeed a thinker, attempting to organize his apprehension of the universe in some systematic way.

When we realize that he cannot be classed with the great philosophers of the world any more than he can with the great poets or dramatists, artists or critics, we are tempted to ask what the directing motive of all this thought was: was it scientific, aesthetic, religious, moral, political, or social? Did he have the deep interest in the development of natural science that was characteristic of his time, and did he aspire to become one of its leaders? Did he attempt to interpret the universe in the light of new scientific discoveries, hoping to achieve metaphysical insight into truths hitherto unknown? And did he apply these fresh thoughts upon nature and humanity to the artistic interpretation of man? Or, on the contrary, did he reduce all this thinking to "la morale," as he himself claimed? Or, with this reduction of scientific, religious, metaphysical thinking to "la morale," did he transform the political, economic, social approach to life and offer mankind a new goal?

All these questions have been broached by first one and then another Voltaire scholar. Yet, with few exceptions, only one aspect of the subject has been taken into consideration, without much attention paid to the other aspects. That is, the question we ask is: in what field was Voltaire's contribution to the thought of his time greatest—in science, in religion, in politics, in ethics, in aesthetics, or in still some other category of learning? And nearly always we answer that it was in one or another of these realms without showing what relation that area of learning has to the other fields which held some interest for Voltaire also. Thus, we have some really excellent works on Voltaire's religion, or Voltaire's politics, or Voltaire as historian, or "le goût" of Voltaire, or any of the areas of thought or life with which he was concerned, but we have few which display a real effort to show the relationship between any one of his preoccupations and all the others. The reason for this neglect is clear: Voltaire's interests were so diverse, so all-embracing, and his competence seems to us to have been so limited and questionable at times, that we often lose the thread of continuity which ran through all these activities or decide that there was in them much that was unorganized, ill-directed, insignificant, or incoherent. Indeed, we know of only one critic—Lanson—who has tried to gather all these manifestations of Voltaire into one coherent picture. That is why his *Voltaire* remains after half a century the most satisfactory presentation of the whole of Voltaire. In spite of the excellence of that work, however, the knowledge we have of Voltaire still seems inorganic, unmotivated, scattered, and unproductive.

We have sometimes attempted to avoid this difficulty of fragmentation by employing a motivational concept to serve as a focus: Voltaire, man of justice; Voltaire, genius of mockery; Voltaire, philosopher; Voltaire, man of taste. These attempts have not been unsuccessful; some of them have, in fact, been extraordinarily important, as we shall show. In general, though, they have only gained their success at the expense of a failure to grasp the whole vital expression of Voltaire. Try as hard as we may, this approach ultimately produces an image that is disjointed, lacking in proportion, and riddled with contradictions.

More recently, with the excellent Besterman edition of the correspondence now available, some of us dreamed of constructing an intellectual biography. We thought that, if we could bring together the pertinent letters, we should be able to discover which of Voltaire's predecessors and contemporaries had a lasting effect upon him, which works left the greatest mark, and which ideas he considered paramount. We judged that we could, by sifting these works, these predecessors, these ideas, and the letters which record significant events, bring them into perspective and thereby gain some insight into the motives underlying Voltaire's activities. This method of proceeding appeared all the more attractive in that the responsibility would devolve upon Voltaire to relate himself through his letters to his goals and his meaning, and our part of the task would become merely organizational; as long as we held to some order, such as the chronological, and extracted only the essential details from that order, it seemed possible to grasp the evolution and the coherence of his development, as well as the relationships between the parts. The chief difficulty in pursuing this method stemmed from the amount of effort it would have taken to exhibit separately the importance of these innumerable parts. We would have had to stop time and again to inquire into the significance for our author of Newton, Locke, Mandeville, Chaulieu, Mme du Châtelet, Frederick II, or the Abbé de Saint-Pierre, plus a host of lesser individuals. Or we would have had to revert to the problems of influence and inquire what effects such works as the *Principia,* the *Essay concerning Human Understanding,* and myriad others, great and small, had upon the development of Voltaire's thought.

These difficulties are not peculiar to the study of Voltaire; investigation of any important figure in the past would offer the same reasons for hesitation and the same complexities. After all, everyone's life is governed by the categories of living. We must all exist in the realms of religion, science, aesthetics, politics, and economics, within a social order structured by morality. All must adapt to conditions which we designate as good and evil. And all must live with a developing "self," that "arrière-boutique," as Montaigne called it, where every man can withdraw and ponder his situation and determine what he must do to give meaning to his life. Everybody must arrange these categories in such a way as to give major priority to some and relative priority to others or, at any rate, must create with them a viable framework which will offer him the maximum satisfactions in living. Everybody must submit to the weight of tradition, to the momentum of the activities which have originated in the past and still continue, though in modified form, in the present. So, too, must each person submit to those who, in his opinion, have best interpreted life in his terms, whether they be of the past or of his own generation. Everybody must therefore immerse his present existence in the stream of history and associate himself with the movements which seem important to him and with the people who have something to say about their importance. The stream may be small and the people of consequence few, but still we must use them according to our abilities and desires. Finally, we must use what they have created: the works they produced, the organizations they built, the tendencies they initiated, and the goals they set. What we are and what we think, say, and do are made up in part of what other people have been and what they have thought, said, and done—plus the way we put this heritage to use.

Voltaire is like everybody else in this respect. He must be studied by the critic in the context of the tradition in which he stood, with an awareness of predecessors who had meaning for him and of contemporaries who shared his intellectual task. He must be seen in a perspective which encompasses his complete personality, which permits him to be viewed as a man trying to live, in his own way, a full life and trying, therefore, to integrate its many aspects in order to impart to it coherence, unity, harmony, and meaning. We shall find him to have been in many respects less complicated than others, especially certain of his contemporaries. He profited greatly from groups that preceded him and, to a lesser extent, from individuals also. But he often chose to follow individuals who were representative of groups—Chaulieu, for instance, whom he regarded as having summarized the whole current of libertine Horatian poetry. He had a way of explaining, to those who were willing to listen, his problems of integration, and he disclosed clearly at times, particularly in his correspondence, how he understood a problem and what plan he intended to pursue in attacking it.

The general outlines of Voltaire's intellectual biography are therefore clearly visible. They must be viewed, however, in the light of the situations in which Voltaire found himself. We shall make every effort to discover the essential features of these prime situations, and we shall spare no energy in attempting to bring these factors together in some systematic way, not so much to show the impact of the milieu upon the personality of the artist as to map out the way the artist in his desire to penetrate his reality with consciousness distilled therefrom his own "inner reality." We shall want to trace, as accurately as we can, not only the elements which entered into that reality but also the means whereby Voltaire seized those elements coherently and, in the expressive metaphor of Kafka, "like a little ball."

For the moment, however, it is only the general condition which interests us. Voltaire appeared on the scene when the glory of France was being eclipsed by the rise of England. The preceding epoch had distinguished itself as one of the four great eras of humanity; Voltaire himself placed the age of Louis XIV alongside the age of Pericles, the age of Augustus, and the age of the Medici in Renaissance Florence. But, in reality, only the first twenty-five years of Louis XIV's reign represented the climax of that glory, the crowning point in the development of the Renaissance in Europe.

What brought about that magnificent achievement was, first, science and philosophy and, then, arts and letters. Both underwent phenomenal development in Europe during the seventeenth century, and at the moment of greatest advance in modern civilization lay thought and beauty of expression. In each of these areas France played a dominant role. It furnished far more than its quota of scientists and philosophers and gathered unto itself as well scientists and thinkers from all parts of Europe. In the field of the arts it not only contributed its share but surpassed all others. It reigned supreme, too, in religious, political, and military affairs. Paris was the cultural center of Europe. To it came many of the outstanding figures of the day, including Leibniz and Locke, and from it the glory of French culture radiated throughout Europe, into the realms of England, Germany, and Austria. It stood as a symbol of the final triumph of Latin civilization over the Germanic.

Then disintegration set in, and from 1685 to the end of his reign Louis XIV saw his boundaries restricted, his political and economic hegemony constantly challenged. Arts and letters started to show signs of exhaustion; inner strains, particularly in the areas of science, philosophy, and religion, began to appear. The disruption was greatest in religion, which suffered from innumerable quarrels that immeasurably weakened the Catholic Church. In the meantime, leadership in science and philosophy shifted from France and the continent to England: Newton and Locke overshadowed Descartes, Leibniz, and Spinoza. Literature, too, languished now that the great writers of 1660 had all departed from the scene. Molière had died, Racine had retired from the stage, and Boileau was engaged in a silly dispute with Perrault and Fontenelle over the merits of ancients and moderns. Bossuet was caught up in a fight with Fénelon over quietism, in an argument with Richard Simon over biblical criticism, and in an interminable discussion with Leibniz over the union of the churches. Everywhere appeared disharmony, disunion, disintegration. Jansenists quarreled with Jesuits, and both in turn clashed with Protestants; conflicts arose between religion and philosophy and free-thinking, between the ancients and the moderns, between poetry and prose, between the poet and the geometer, between reason and grace. Clearly, the position of France as the leader of Europe was being challenged by the achievements of England in the political, the economic, the scientific, the philosophical, and even the artistic spheres. The great advance, however, was won in England by yielding to the tone of France, and eventually English thought, English art, and English power were filtered throughout Europe by way of Holland, Switzerland, and France.

Such was the larger context in which the glory of France rose (1660-1685) and fell (1685-1715). The decline was brought about by a weakening or a diminution of all those things which had sustained this glory: politically, Louis XIV encountered a series of defeats, which diminished his power and ruined his economy; socially, the nobility was drained by the wars, by the economic and political disasters, and by the breakdown in morals; religiously, there had been a move to create a unity which succeeded only in producing a continual schism, both within and without the Catholic Church. Religion and politics, which in the previous era had supported each other, now broke apart and yielded to science and philosophy. But the greatest weakness of all developed in the arts, which in the quarrel of the ancients and the moderns saw their whole foundation challenged.

It was at this point that Voltaire, appearing upon the scene, made his decision to be a poet. He prepared himself by adopting Horace, Virgil, and Lucretius as his guides, along with a whole line of free-thinking Horatian poets from Théophile de Viau to Chaulieu. But Voltaire was steeped also in the great writers of Louis XIV's age: Molière, Corneille, and especially Racine and Boileau. The ideal poet as Voltaire conceived him would be a combination of Horace and Virgil tempered by Racine and Boileau, and he would write for a society which appreciated the Chaulieus and the La Fares. It was precisely the times, however, that would not tolerate the ideal poet: owing to the quarrel of the ancients and the moderns, poetry became discredited. Geometry overruled all, and the youngster whose one ambition was to be a poet found himself in a world which was rapidly becoming anti-poetic. Voltaire opposed the current for twenty-five years. Between 1713 and 1738 he struggled to renew the poetic flame. This struggle involved not only the creation of poetry but the formulation of a body of poetic theory, for the dogma of classicism was now being shattered in the name of modernity and new forms had to be discovered. What caused the most difficulty was the doctrine of modernity. The basic idea was that the discoveries of science should be allowed to replenish the content of art, but it was felt in England to be just as basic that the content of thought be deemed superior to the expression of art. Voltaire in his English experience learned two things: the necessity for harmony in the elements of a civilization in order to guarantee its vitality, and the present superiority of science and philosophy over arts and letters. He was fully aware of his incompetence both in the analysis of an organic civilization and in the fields of science and philosophy. He was therefore forced to reeducate himself, to supplant the "poetry and nonsense" he had learned at Louis-le-Grand by more substantial subjects like metaphysics, physics, history, biblical criticism, and philosophy. This was the challenge of Cirey, and in responding to it Voltaire was compelled literally to reconsider the elements of a civilization (seen in the context of history) and the categories of life (viewed in the light of the relationship between thought and art). In the course of this vast undertaking Voltaire was led to create a totally different world.

It is the making of this world that is the core of this study. It is our contention that Voltaire, more than anyone else, effected it, but the really important point is that he did not bring it about single-handed. There was always a close coordination between his response to the conditions of his time and that of his contemporaries. Sometimes, as we shall see, he actually seems to have fallen behind them, at which point he would strenuously set to work to readjust his position and place himself once more in the vanguard of the Enlightenment. And he finally had to accommodate his response to the response of those who also were men of power. Eventually, we shall be faced with the problem of his ultimate success and the success of his age, and we shall have to consider then what constitutes victory or defeat when one human mind of consequence brings about a total revolution in the direction of thought.

PART I

THE POET

Un poète, c'est de Voltaire; et puis qui
encore? De Voltaire; et le troisième? De Voltaire;
et le quatrième? De Voltaire.[a]

Le vrai poète est, à ce qui me semble,
celui qui remue l'âme et qui l'attendrit; les
autres sont de beaux parleurs.[b]

1. EARLY TRAINING

SAINTE-BEUVE URGED that the critic grasp his author at the first moment of his productive life. This is not an easy task, however, since there are so many first moments through which an intelligent author passes before he is ready to create. In a way, the whole youth of Voltaire was a preparation for that moment. It was in many respects an undistinguished period, but it gained for young Arouet a reputation which now seems out of all proportion to his intellectual and literary achievements.

The era preceding Voltaire's birth had witnessed a magnificent rise in the power of France. The hegemony she had thereby come to exercise over the rest of Europe, however, was soon disputed, in all spheres of life, by England. As a result, the great flowering of French civilization which extended throughout the first half of Louis XIV's reign was followed by a decline not only in the country's political and military might but in all the other manifestations of its vitality as well. It was during this latter part of Louis's reign that Voltaire passed his youth. The spectacle that unfolded before his eyes in these years was bleak indeed: the defeats of the military, the withdrawal of the French boundaries in the face of the coalition arrayed against the King, the *débâcle* of the nation's fiscal policies, and the increasing misery of the lower orders of society altogether constituted an environment little suited to inspire optimism. Added to this gloomy picture were the interminable religious quarrels, as well as the results of the expulsion of the Protestants and the persecution of the Jansenists, of which Voltaire must likewise have been aware.

The glory of the age, however, had been founded upon the excellence of the arts and the achievements of science. In letters, in painting, in architecture, and in philosophy the century had found means of expressing its apparently inexhaustible energy. But now these pursuits, too, were suffering eclipse, especially in France. The great writers of the earlier period were disappearing, while those who arose to fill the void could not match the caliber of their predecessors. Nor did they share the same interests. For, whereas

ª *Neveu de Rameau*, Garnier edn., p. 483.
ᵇ Voltaire, *Dictionnaire philosophique* (M. XVIII, 572).

the earlier writers had attempted to achieve distinction in drama, especially by their eloquence, those of Voltaire's day seemed more interested in ideas and in the spirit of reform. The excellence of literature had given way to its utility. Even in the formal genres there appeared to be a loss of momentum, as both science and philosophy in France showed signs of weakening. The great thinkers now were the English; those who won acclaim in France were the freethinkers, rather than the thinkers.

Of the great writers of the classical period, Pascal was the first to die, in 1662, although his important work for the Enlightenment, *Les Pensées*, did not appear until later, in 1670, the same year in which Spinoza's *Tractatus* was published. Molière departed from the scene next, in 1673. Racine, after *Phèdre* (1677), withdrew from the stage, only to return for the Saint-Cyr performances of *Esther* (1689) and *Athalie* (1691). In 1699, following twenty-two years of relative silence, he too died. La Fontaine, meanwhile, had passed away four years earlier, while La Rochefoucauld had already been gone for nineteen years and Corneille, who came to the end of a long and wearisome old age in 1684, almost as long. Thus, by 1685, only Boileau and Bossuet among the great French writers of this period remained to carry on the classical tradition: Boileau deeply involved in the defense of classicism in the quarrel of the ancients and the moderns before the onslaughts of the Perraults, the Saint-Sorlins, and the Fontenelles; and Bossuet engaged with equal ardor in the defense of the Catholic faith against the attacks of Leibniz, Richard Simon, Fénelon, and the rising deists. By 1711, both of these stalwart defenders of the century had succumbed, too—Bossuet in 1704, Boileau in 1711.

Of those who took the places of the departed, there were undoubtedly some of a superior order: La Bruyère, for instance, whose *Caractères* (1688) deserves to be ranked among the great works of Louis XIV's reign, and Fénelon, whose *Télémaque* (1699) richly merits the popularity it enjoyed. In 1696, however, La Bruyère joined the host of those who had expired, and Fénelon, caught up in the religious quarrels of the time, was both discredited and banished from court. Bayle, who himself died in 1706, and Fontenelle were the most productive writers during this period. One devoted himself particularly to the popularization of science, the other to the popularization of philosophy: with his *Eloges des académiciens* Fontenelle endeavored to write a history of science of the preceding epoch, while Bayle intended his *Dictionnaire historique et critique* as a kind of history of philosophy from earliest times to the present. Within the domain of literature proper, the outstanding essayist was undoubtedly Saint-Evremond, the writer perhaps most representative of the age; yet in his exile he was completely out of touch with the literature of France. Poetry, meanwhile, could only boast of Chaulieu and La Fare, the last of the seventeenth-century Horatian poets, who, following Théophile de Viau, had continued throughout the century to pour forth their libertine verse. Also imbued with the spirit of libertinage were the utopian novels which appeared during this period: Foigny's *La Terre australe connue* (1676), Vairasse's *Histoire des Sévarambes* (1677-1679), Fénelon's *Télémaque* (1699), Gilbert's *Histoire de Caléjava* (1700), Lahontan's *Mémoires sur l'Amérique septentrionale* (1703), and Tyssot de Patot's *Voyage et avantures de Jacques Massé* (1710). In fact, after 1700, all that remained of the splendid century in literature was an accumulation of mediocre, lyric, libertine poems and a strong run of utopian novels, accompanied by an overwhelming amount of voyage literature and an ever increasing number of deistic treatises. Many of the tracts were, moreover, frankly reformist. Fénelon's *Mémoire au Roi* (1710) and Le Sage's *Diable boiteux* (1707) and *Turcaret* (1709) were composed with this aim in mind, and even Saint-Simon, who was now writing, though not publishing, leaned in this direction.

Thus, the young Voltaire entered upon his career just when France was passing through a turbulent period of decline. Most of the great writers who had been the pride of France in the preceding era had already passed from the scene, and literature had come to be regarded no longer as an object of aesthetic reverence but as an instrument for reform. The world in which Voltaire came of age in 1719 was one where discouragement and degeneration were rampant, where hypocrisy and a strong current of journalism were the earmarks of literature. The medium that exhibited the greatest vitality was political, social, and religious free-thinking, expressed in terms of satire. Indeed, it was this free-thinking which dominated the circles in which Voltaire lived and moved. Saint-Evremond, in London, had become its high priest. It overran the voyage literature, especially that dealing with China, much pseudo-oriental fiction, the deistic treatise, free verse, and even the journalistic essay. If Bayle was the intermediary who assembled it in the *Dictionnaire* and the *Nouvelles de la république des lettres*, Voltaire was the one who carried it into the Enlightenment. That, however, was not his original ambition; what he desired to do above everything else was to revive the great glory of French letters. It was a worthy ambition for a young man just out of the leading *lycée* of the time and surrounded by fellow students who represented some of the foremost families of France.

Voltaire reached literary maturity between the years 1719 and 1723, that is, between the tragedy *Œdipe* (1719) and the epic poem *La Ligue* (1723), with the philosophical poem *L'Epître à Uranie* at an intermediate point (1722). These works, along with the light verses (odes, satires, and epistles) which flourished from 1712 to 1724, constituted Voltaire's literary production during what we customarily call his early period. Coinciding with the last half of the Regency (1715-1723), this period played a role in Voltaire's life similar in importance to the position the Regency years occupied with respect to the century as a whole. For, just as the Regency period set the tone for the rest of the eighteenth century, so Voltaire's works of 1719-1723 were destined to lay the foundations for his long literary career.

In some peculiar way, though, these writings seem not only to represent the initial outburst of Voltaire the poet but also to summarize all the energies of his early years. Indeed, this preoccupation with poetry did not cease with the period of his youth (1694-1725). Between the inauguration of his career as a poet in 1712 and the shift toward philosophy in 1738, Voltaire served the muse of Horatian verse, epic verse, and drama, and was considered to be outstanding in each of these realms. This superiority in poetry, of course, gave him the right to be the arbiter of literary taste, but only because he believed superior taste to be grounded in the writing of superior verse. The esteem in which he was held as a poet extended even beyond the years 1712-1738. In 1770, after Voltaire's interest in the field, no longer paramount, had yielded to other activities he considered of greater importance, Lacombe, in the "Avertissement" of his *Poétique de M. de Voltaire*, saluted him as a "génie heureux et fécond" who had combined all the talents of Horace,

Virgil, Sophocles, Euripides, Menander, Terence, Anacréon, and Ovid. The Patriarch, he added, had excelled in the epic, drama, and light verse and had always placed the precepts alongside the masterpieces.

These activities were conditioned by three dominant ingredients in Voltaire's youthful development, which deserve to be analyzed with some care: his family background, his literary training at Louis-le-Grand, and his experience at the Temple. Each of these influences had an unquestioned role in shaping the intellectual and artistic character of the young Arouet, who within the short span of four years displayed in no uncertain fashion his ambition to become France's foremost lyric, dramatic, and epic poet.

The family background is relatively easy to delineate,[1] although it is difficult to assess its importance. François Marie Arouet was born in Paris on 21 November 1694, the son of François Arouet and Marguerite Daumart. The Arouets were originally natives of Poitou, some of them having lived in the little village of Saint-Loup, others in the neighboring village of Airvault, only a stone's throw away. Airvault was a "seigneurie" whose "seigneur," in the days of Voltaire's youth, was very old and without heirs—a situation the young man was to take advantage of at the time he changed his name. Arouet's ancestors have been traced back to the Renaissance. Most were of bourgeois stock: tanners, tradesmen, and, in general, members of the lesser bourgeoisie, although occasionally a public official or a notary could be found among them. By the end of the seventeenth century, they had risen in the social scale. Arouet senior was by profession a notary, whose clientele included some of the aristocrats of the time. Saint-Simon, for instance, records in his *Mémoires* that the older Arouet administered his father's estate. Arouet also had as clients several of the members of the Temple. The family at the time of Voltaire's birth was connected socially with well-known personages: a Richelieu had been godmother to Armand, a Châteauneuf was godfather to François. There is a suspicion, derived largely from anecdotes, that the Arouets knew Boileau, but the claim seems rather unsubstantiated. It is true, however, that they cultivated an interest in literature, probably through the father's

[1] G. Chardonchamp, *La Famille de Voltaire, les Arouet.*

business connections with the Temple—although gossip has always been eager to attribute a poetical strain to the mother because of her associations with Rochebrune. The family of six—Armand (the oldest child), Cathérine, Marie, François, and the two parents—was comfortably situated, though not wealthy; it was still rising in the social scale, but with discretion.

Very little is known about the Daumarts. There does exist evidence that Mme Arouet possessed properties in the environs of Paris —the house at Châtenay, for instance—and this has led some to infer that she was perhaps a bit higher in the social scale than her husband. There are, furthermore, those who would see in the name "d'aumard" a title of lesser nobility. In reality, though, we still know practically nothing about this side of the family.

In 1701, Marguerite Daumart died, leaving the young François to be cared for by his sister Cathérine. The boy's attachment to his sister was apparently quite strong; her death in 1727 left him broken-hearted. But he had only contempt for his brother Armand, whom he frequently referred to as his "Janséniste de frère." Some biographers, however, persist in seeing resemblances between the two brothers in spite of this antipathy.

Attempts have been made to stress the religious leanings of the family and to see in these tendencies the source of young Arouet's religious preoccupations. At the time of François's birth, the struggle between the Jesuits and the Jansenists was at its climax; between 1694 and 1704, when the youth entered the Jesuit school of Louis-le-Grand, the political persecution of the Jansenists was intense. It has been suggested that the father, being of a profession noted for its partiality toward Jansenism, must have been drawn toward the group. After all, the argument runs, had he not sent his elder son to Saint-Magloire, an Oratorian school, and were not the Oratorians considered allies of the Jansenists in their struggle with the Jesuits? Moreover, was not Armand's conduct in the Frère Pâris affair, in which he was ultimately implicated, an indication of Jansenism in the Arouet family? Professor Pomeau, for one, has weighed this evidence, noting that there were, in reality, two Jansenisms, one an orthodox religious sect and the other a social group distinguished by its sympathy for Jansenism rather than by any active participation in its excesses. This "Jansénisme bourgeois," he concludes, was very widespread and the Arouet family might well have identified itself with the movement. What is significant in all this speculation, however, is not that some members of the family *could* have become allied with the group but that some of them actually *did* espouse Jansenism.

At the same time, it is often pointed out that, having sent his elder son to a Jansenist-oriented school, Arouet senior balanced matters neatly by sending his younger son to a Jesuit institution—the inference being that he must not have had any strong feelings one way or the other about the two groups. It probably is true that he selected the schools more because of their popularity and the social advantages they opened to his sons than because of any partiality he might have felt toward the groups themselves. It just happened that, in the 1680s, the schools superior in these respects were run by the Jansenists, whereas, in 1704, they were run by the Jesuits. The choices Arouet senior made, then, indicate an indifference to dogma and a bourgeois inclination to obtain the best social relations for his children. Thus, it seems reasonable to conclude that the open quarrel between the two groups had more effect upon the youth than any family persuasion, although one might with equal force argue that Voltaire inherited his indifference to both groups from his father.

We must not, however, overlook an obvious fact in the evolution of ideas that was taking place between 1685 and 1720. When Louis XIV assumed full control of the throne in 1660, he set about to arrest the growth of both skepticism and free-thinking in order to restore dignity and balance to orthodox religion. So well did he succeed that, as Professor Lanson has remarked, France was splendidly, if not profoundly, religious during at least the first half of his reign. The religious quarrels and the political persecutions of religious groups—Protestants, Jansenists, Quietists—that occurred during the second half, however, undoubtedly introduced uneasiness into religious affairs and encouraged a renewal of the skeptical, free-thinking current which had previously been suppressed. Leibniz was scarcely exaggerating when he insisted that the great danger was the establishment, not of deism, but of atheism, and Bossuet's statement that an assault was being organized against Christianity in the name of Cartesianism only confirmed these fears. Whether the Arouets took an active role in this resurgence of free-thinking is beside the point; what is important to realize is that they could not very well have ignored it. Consequently, there arises this additional possibility, that the relative indifference of Voltaire's father to the quarrels of the Jansenists, Jesuits, and Quietists may have been the result of the developing free-thinking of the time. This skepticism, then, may have had a greater impact upon the youth than any family preoccupation with religion. But, of course, the factors that enter into the formation of a personality are so complex, particularly in the early stages of life, that we can never be too sure that we have found them all or weighed accurately the ones we have found.

One version of this view has been suggested by Pomeau. While admitting the presence in the Arouet family of leanings toward Jansenism (albeit a Jansenism of a "bourgeois" type, in reality nothing more than a straw-man Jansenism), he nonetheless concludes that Voltaire, in spite of the association of Armand and a cousin, Archambault, with the "Convulsionnaires," was firmly anti-rigorist and anti-Jansenist even in his early years. This assertion, if it could be verified, would do much to justify the claim that free-thinking influenced Voltaire in his youth.

The argument does not, however, entirely square with the evidence we already possess. Gazier's article, "Le Frère de Voltaire," for example, clearly shows that Voltaire inquired into some of the events involving Jansenists in 1722 and, indeed, expressed in verse his sympathy for those Jansenists who were being persecuted by the political authorities. Moreover, there seem to be no reasons to doubt the veracity of the statements contained in Voltaire's letter to Mme de Bernières to the effect that he had investigated with some care the miraculous cure of a certain Mme Lafosse, even though the tone of the letter does leave room to question the sincerity of his inquiry. One can hardly neglect, either, the interest that Voltaire showed in the unjust persecutuion of the Bishop of Senez, and, although it is still uncertain (notwithstanding Gazier's assurances) whether Voltaire wrote the *Jansénius*, it seems impossible to cast doubt upon the authenticity of his open-minded investigation of this incident. Gazier, of course, while substantiating the event, questions Voltaire's motives, maintaining that his interest was really either a hypocritical gesture intended to placate his Jansenist brother or simply a pose with no religious significance whatsoever. In spite of his scholarly objectivity, which here wears a little thin, the last thing Gazier seems to want to admit is that Voltaire in his early years could have been even momentarily a partisan of the Jansenist cause. Pomeau, who has probed with extraordinary perspicacity the religious psychology of the young Voltaire, also regards any such suggestion as unthinkable. Still, it is not impossible that Voltaire, as a member of a religious-minded bourgeois family in an age of intense religious ferment, with a mind undoubtedly motivated by much curiosity and even at this early date by a certain sense of justice, could have had his reasons for inquiring into these events. More important than the actual inquiry and the concern for justice the move to undertake it conveyed, however, is the latent evidence of the unsettling effect the persecutions had upon Voltaire's attitude. To one earnestly trying to get at the truth, it would have been only natural to respond either by defending one side against the other, by assuming indifference to all these squabbles, or even by revolting against the source of the trouble. And, indeed, there is reason to believe that Voltaire's reaction followed all three lines. It is true, though, that he did in time become anti-Jansenist, adopting what Pomeau calls so aptly "un fanatisme retourné."

The important fact to note in connection with this aspect of Voltaire's early development, however, is less his anti-royalist, anti-religious, anti-rigorist attitude—which, after all, was in no way consistent during this period of his life—than his persistent preoccupation with the problems of the beneficent monarch, the nature of religious feeling, and the constitutive sources of moral action. It is fairly easy to record Voltaire's repeated statements upon these matters, and usually we end up doing so, at excessive length, with the aim of proving that the poet was much more of a thinker during the early years before his journey to England than anyone has hitherto suspected and that, in reality, the young Voltaire was already a deist—as Pomeau's statement (*La Religion de Voltaire*, p. 78) that *Le Vrai Dieu* was Voltaire's first deistic work suggests—a critic of the *Ancien Régime*, and a propagandist for the free expression of the passions. We assume naturally that these opinions constituted the germs of all the attacks Voltaire subsequently leveled against royalty, *l'Infâme*, and the moral law. But the assumption, even though it probably does contain some measure of validity, is really premature. The first observation to make is that the young Voltaire exhibited a surprising tendency to discuss religious problems as if he were taking a fundamental interest in religion. The epistles he wrote in verse during this period have been scanned for evidence of free-thinking by Lanson, Ascoli, and Pomeau, but no trace of it has been discovered. If one could forget the nature of the thought and concentrate for a moment upon the subject matter, one would find that what really concerned Voltaire at this time were problems of religious dogma as seen in a free-thinking context: the existence of God, the immortality of the soul, free will, grace, and tolerance. That he offered certain tentative solutions which were unorthodox is secondary to the fact that he was deeply preoccupied with serious religious questions. It is possible, as we have seen, that he received the initial impetus in this direction from his family. But it is more probable that he derived it from his milieu, for, curiously enough, this preoccupation with religion and religious problems that gripped Voltaire in the years 1719-1723 was particularly strong throughout the Regency period in general.

The second ingredient in Voltaire's early training that exercised a marked influence upon his intellectual development was the group of his teachers at Louis-le-Grand. It was the education he received at this Jesuit school that was mainly responsible for his choice of a career, as well as for the manner in which he decided to pursue it. In his early correspondence with Fyot de la Marche, Voltaire charged that the Jesuits had actually encouraged him to consider a life as a member of the order, but he was probably just exaggerating. Although it is true that the staff of teachers was on the lookout for good recruits, it is by no means certain that the young Arouet would have been deemed an attractive candidate. The importance of Louis-le-Grand, as far as Voltaire was concerned, lay elsewhere. The good Jesuits Tournemine, Olivet, Lejay, Tarteron, and Porée strove to form their students into cultivated men of the world. The basis of this education was the *Litterae humaniores*; Thoulié's purism expressing itself in devoted teaching of Cicero's style, Porée's love of the drama inspiring his training in the analysis of dramatic art and in the composition and presentation of drama, Tarteron's veneration of the Roman satiric poets—all were major influences in developing the student of Louis-le-Grand into a man of taste. It is hardly surprising, then, that the three outstanding traits of Voltaire's literary talents turned out to be his devotion to the purity of language, his dedication to the art of drama, and his inimitable satiric expression. His Jesuit masters performed their task well, though no doubt they had only to stimulate the growth of qualities Voltaire already possessed in germ before attending the school.

The young Arouet, despite his protestations and witticisms ("je savais du latin et des sottises"), appreciated the superior wisdom of his teachers. At a later date, he regretted that they had not taught him either his country's laws or its interests in the international field and nothing of mathematics or philosophy ("Education," *Dictionnaire philosophique*). It was only then that "Latin and nonsense" loomed as great defects in his education. At other times he could write with more fairness: "Of all the teaching orders, the Jesuits are those who best understand *belles-lettres*, and they have always succeeded in the teaching of oratory and poetry" (*Temple du goût*, ed. Carcassonne, p. 86). It is significant that young Arouet, during the first half of his long life, endeavored to court his former teachers' approval of his literary works by presenting copies to them: the *Henriade*, *Œdipe*, and *Mérope* to Porée; *Œdipe* and *Mérope* to Tournemine; *Zaïre* and *La Mort de César* to Olivet. His correspondence with Olivet especially is marked by a continual expression of admiration and esteem, but letters to other teachers also are filled with personal tributes of gratitude for their valued training. Even though some of this effusion was undoubtedly flattery, particularly in the period when Voltaire unashamedly solicited their support for his effort to be admitted into the French Academy, much of it derived from a genuine respect for their criticisms, a deep desire to be commended by those whom he esteemed, and a sincere feeling that their criticism of his literary endeavors could aid him in improving his writing.

Naves (*Le Goût de Voltaire*, pp. 150ff.) has pointed out that the Jesuits always attempted to mingle the study of belles-lettres with the study of religion. This program would have appealed to the young Voltaire, who seems from the beginning to have possessed an interest in both. In the *Ratio studiorum*, the teaching of belles-lettres, indeed, occupied the place of foremost importance. Even in 1706, when Jouvancy published the *De ratione discendi*, a preeminent position was still assigned to the knowledge of languages and the perception of the sciences which could be best acquired through rhetoric and poetics. In the *Candidatus rhetoricae*, Jouvancy was even more explicit: there humane letters are divided into grammar, humanity, and rhetoric, which are designed, according to the prospectus, to inculcate respectively correctness of speech, elegance, and eloquence. To attain these ends, the student must be endowed with four natural gifts for the practice of belles-lettres: *intellectus*, or understanding, which includes both "genius" and talent; imagination; *affectus*, or sensitivity; and taste (*judicium conciliumve*), defined as the personal discernment whereby we feel deeply and recognize with discretion the good and the beautiful in nature and in the arts. All education tends to the formation of this discernment: its objective is to train the student to unite the purity of his taste, which is a rational quality, with its delicacy, which is a refinement of his sensitivity. The desired result can be obtained, said Jouvancy, by studying a text extracted from a work and analyzed as a unit. The lesson thus becomes an exercise and, at the same time, an interpretation, an imitation, an amplification, and is supposed to develop memory, judgment, and imagination.

Ascoli ("Voltaire," p. 676) has stated that Voltaire learned his literary art in the Jesuit school at Louis-le-Grand, and Voltaire himself acknowledged that his teachers had instilled in him elegant and sure taste, solid classical culture, and a well-grounded knowledge of Greek and Latin masterpieces. His apt response to their training is evident in all of his critical work from the *Lettres sur Œdipe* to his literary articles in the *Questions sur l'Encyclopédie*. His definition of taste, his analysis of the merits and defects of a work of art, his insistence on proper balance between imagination and sensibility, between discernment and judgment, and his emphasis upon that taste which instinctively perceives correctness of speech, as well as elegance of expression and eloquence of presentation, may be attributed in great part to his development of the lessons he learned at an early age from these Jesuit masters. Ascoli infers that the Jesuits also guided their young prodigy in his reading of the great works of French literature. For this claim we have less evidence, but it is certain that the training he received in the classics prepared him to deal as well with the perfections and faults of his own country's literature.

Although all of Voltaire's teachers did their part to implant in him an unerring taste, there was one whose contribution was particularly significant—Father Tarteron. For it was he who introduced to the pupil that writer of antiquity thought to be the supreme exponent of this taste—Horace—and thereby fired in the youth an ambition to emulate, if not to surpass, that poet in the art of poetry. Strangely enough, Father Tarteron is not as well known as other of Voltaire's Jesuit teachers. Pierron, for example, does not mention him at all in his book on *Voltaire et ses maîtres*. Beaune (*Voltaire au collège*, pp. xcviii-xcix), however, notes that, according to J. B. Rousseau, it was Father Tarteron, by far the senior instructor in the Jesuit Institut at Louis-le-Grand, who put into Voltaire's hands Horace and Juvenal, carefully expurgated *ad usum juventutis*, and was struck by his pupil's "surprenantes dispositions pour la poésie." Beaune points out further that Jérôme Tarteron (who died in Paris at the age of 75) published French translations of Horace, Perseus, and Juvenal. Pomeau (*Religion*, pp. 38, 46) repeats a part of Beaune's note and adds that Tarteron was the spiritual director of the future Président Hénault (see *Mémoires*, p. 13). Naves (*Goût*, p. 47) states simply that Tarteron translated Juvenal and Perseus. Tarteron also figures in the list of authors in Voltaire's *Siècle de Louis XIV* (M. XIV, 139), where the following comments appear:

> Tarteron (Jérôme), jésuite. Il a traduit les satires d'Horace, de Perse, et de Juvénal, et a supprimé les obscénités grossières dont il est étrange que Juvénal, et surtout Horace, aient souillé leurs ouvrages. Il a ménagé en cela la jeunesse, pour laquelle il croyait travailler; mais sa traduction n'est pas assez littérale pour elle; le sens est rendu, mais non pas la valeur des mots. Mort en 1720.

Voltaire no doubt had a first-hand acquaintance with his professor's translations. He possessed his own copy (still in his library at Leningrad) of Tarteron's *Traduction des Satyres de Perse et de Juvénal* (Paris, 1698), and, although he apparently did not have the translation of Horace (at least, it is not now in his library), he seems to have known it well enough to have scrupulously avoided it after a first acquaintance or to have abandoned it when other and better editions appeared.[2]

It is evident that from his school days, when his teachers first introduced him to Horace and the classic satiric poets, the young Arouet was encouraged to devote himself to satiric poetry and to take Horace, especially, as his example. But Voltaire's attachment to these poets was not confined to his youth. Indeed, throughout his long life Voltaire held them in high esteem, reserving for Horace his greatest admiration. The number of editions of Horace, Juvenal, and Perseus in Voltaire's library published from 1770 on is itself an indication that, even in the last decade of his life, Voltaire still retained an active interest in the Roman satiric poets.

There were good reasons, of course, why Horace occupied so prominent a position in the teaching of the Jesuits at Louis-le-Grand and why the young Arouet proved so receptive to his influence. Marmier, who has recently published an excellent work on the impact which the Roman poet had upon the literary public of the seventeenth century,[3] notes that there was always a strong rapport between the Latin poet, who sang in measured verse the life of the Golden Mean, and the French genius. It is easy to see in Horace the very qualities which had persisted throughout the history of French literature: the sense of proportion, the desire for clarity of thought, the precision of expression, the tendency to banter, the disposition for lightness and airiness even to the point of superficiality, and the inclination toward satire, founded more on mischievousness than on malice. And no one was more typically French in these respects than Voltaire. In addition, the French had developed with surprising consistency the taste for moralizing, particularly when it could be done without an appeal to ponderous systems of thought. Morality

---

[2] The Leningrad collection contains: *Œuvres d'Horace en Latin et en Français*, avec des remarques critiques et historiques. Par Mr. Dacier. 4e édition. T. 1-10. Amsterdam, 1727; *Q. Horatii Flacci Poemata*, ex castigationibus observationibusque Bentleii, Cuningamii et Sandonis emendat. Londini, J. Nourse, 1740; *Essai de traduction de plusieurs odes d'Horace* (S.L.) 1746; *Odes d'Horace, traduites en vers français*. Avec des notes par M. Chabannes de Maugris. Livre 3e. Paris, 1773. Voltaire also had two other editions of Perseus and an additional translation of Juvenal: *Satyres de Perse*, Traduction nouvelle par M. Carron de Gibert. Amsterdam, 1771. *Satyres de Perse*, . . . par M. Sélia. Paris, 1776. *Satyres de Juvénal*, . . . par M. Dusaulx. Paris, 1770.

[3] J. Marmier, *Horace en France, au dix-septième siècle*.

for them, as for Horace, was a part of day-to-day living, and, as such, it was tinged with both epicureanism and stoicism—with both the yearning to savor the joys of existence while they are still present and the commonsense, hardheaded firmness of character which comes from the struggle to survive. Even Horace's limited lyricism, regulated with the same sort of precision as his code of ethics, could appeal to a people who had always looked with displeasure at any attempt to exceed the boundaries of the social order and with some fear of all conceptions of life which attribute the highest values to unrestrained energy and to the fullest expression of feeling. The apportionment of just the proper amount of thought and feeling, with a strict insistence that there always be a predominance of thought, and the desire that the finished product should exhibit delicacy rather than beauty, qualities rather than any supreme quality, taste rather than enthusiasm, were as fundamental to the French as they were to Horace. More than any other poet of antiquity, Horace turned poetry into a philosophy. His verse, whether it took the form of ode, epistle, or satire, was designed to sing forth praise of the good life, to reveal the possibilities it offered for happiness while not ignoring its inevitable but endurable discomforts, to criticize those things and those people who render its full enjoyment difficult, and even to suggest moral legislation which would increase its joys and create for future generations equal opportunities for pleasure. Here, too, with his finest achievement, the identification of art with the pursuit of life itself, Horace shared common ground with the French. And, again, there was in this respect no more typical Frenchman than Voltaire.

Thus, it was perfectly natural that the social and intellectual atmosphere into which the young Arouet was born was imbued with a predominantly Horatian spirit. Horace, whose *De Arte poetica* had had such a direct influence upon the formation of the classical doctrine, had become a model for the lyrical poets from Théophile de Viau to Chaulieu. In fact, of all the writers of antiquity who up to that point had had a primary effect upon the development of poetry in France, Horace, Virgil, and Lucretius were by far the most influential, and there could be little doubt that, of these three, the one who at that time carried the greatest weight was Horace. Chaulieu, for example, in his introduction to his volume of poetry, explained that, as lyric poetry was then showing a tendency toward poetic elegance rather than toward Horatian content, he felt it desirable to employ the Horatian procedures as a means of giving an added vitality to his verse. The extent of the Roman's hold upon the poets of the late seventeenth century, as well as upon the public, can be measured also by Boileau's desire to become the French Horace. The young student at Louis-le-Grand, himself familiar with these signs of a powerful force at work, could hardly help being cognizant of the fact that he had arrived in a society which strongly appreciated the qualities of Horace and saw them all renewed in the master critic Boileau.

The third important ingredient in Voltaire's youthful development was the Temple, the town residence of the Duke of Vendôme, who by tradition was the leader of the Knights Templars. The Temple was one of the literary centers of France during the closing years of Louis XIV's reign and the period of the Regency. It was characteristic throughout the whole century for the lyric poets to assemble in some salon. Thus, in the early days of the first Regency, a group to which Chapelle belonged met with Gassendi at Luillier's. Mme Deshoulières and Dehénault had been the leaders of those who congregated at the Duchess of Bouillon's, while La Fontaine, who had often visited the Temple, was the cynosure of Mme de la Sablière's salon. The Duke of Nevers played host to a similar gathering, which, incidentally, had formed a "cabale" with the devotees of the Duchess of Bouillon against Racine.

Sainte-Beuve, in an article published in the *Revue des deux mondes* (1839, pp. 198-204) entitled "Une Ruelle poétique sous Louis XIV," pointed to the existence of a school of poets at the end of the seventeenth century and the beginning of the eighteenth for whom, in certain essential respects, the age of Louis XIV never existed. According to his testimony, this school, which came into being in the age of Louis XIII—or, more precisely perhaps, in the first Regency (1643-1660)—and extended to the second in 1715, began with Saint-Evremond and ended with La Motte and Fontenelle. Its poetic style resembled closely the first manner of La Fontaine. During the glorious days of Boileau and Racine, its members withdrew to the Hôtel Bouillon, to the Nevers's, and to the Deshoulières's. Distinguished by an unconcern for the great masterpieces of the time, its most curious trait was that it stood at the same time behind and ahead of its day. The group was both "précieux" and "hardi" or, as Sainte-Beuve says, eager "de mêler dans son bel esprit un grain d'esprit fort." Its principal writers showed free-thinking tendencies, in morality as well as in poetic taste, and strongly espoused free-thought in religion. Bayle, Sainte-Beuve adds, found them very congenial and tried to find a place for them in his *Dictionnaire*.

The Temple was one of these poetic assemblies that Sainte-Beuve attempted to define. Its leading poet was Chaulieu, who acted as a kind of business manager for the Duke, besides serving as his laureate, and extended the activities of the Temple to Anet and Sceaux, where Voltaire was a frequent visitor. Chaulieu was ably seconded by La Fare. There were as well many others whose names now bring to mind only one or two poems but who in their day enjoyed a respectable measure of poetic renown; among the more outstanding were Malézieu, Courtin, Châteauneuf, and Ninon de Lenclos, whom rumor associated with Châteauneuf but who, in fact, was just as closely connected with Saint-Evremond, with whom she carried on an extensive correspondence, and with La Fontaine, who was a devoted member of the group.

It was there that Châteauneuf, Voltaire's godfather, introduced the youth in 1706, in the early days of Louis-le-Grand. Until 1723, the Temple was, in effect, Voltaire's poetic home. Chaulieu himself took charge of guiding the fledgling poet, serving as his mentor until 1720. It was he, as we shall see, who in a series of poems entitled *Trois façons de penser sur la mort* gave to his young ward the theme for the *Epître à Uranie*, Voltaire's outstanding work in the area of lyric, free-thinking poetry. Actually, all of the themes Voltaire used in his poetic writing derived from Chaulieu. Coming at the end of the long line of libertine poets who extended throughout the seventeenth century, Chaulieu in a way combined for Voltaire not only their themes but their poetic tendencies as well.

True disciples of Lucretius and Horace, these poets rejected the orthodox interpretation of religion, treating the Reformation and the Counter-Reformation with an indifference that amounted to impertinence, and united, probably in large measure without knowing that they were doing so, the naturalism of the Paduans with the epicureanism of Gassendi. Their thinking ran parallel to that of

Giordano Bruno, Vanini, and Cremonini; one hardly knows whether it should be called illuminism or naturalism, since they insisted as much upon the animism as upon the atomic structure of matter and, whenever the occasion presented itself, stressed the similarities between man and the animal world alongside their atomistic view of the universe. They sang, too, of the inevitability of death and repudiated the notion of the immortality of the soul. They counseled the enjoyment of simple pleasures, but, sensitive to the fleeting passage of time, reconciled to the impossibility of ever achieving the stability necessary to prolong these pleasures, they assumed a stoic attitude toward life—albeit a very diluted version of the philosophy of Seneca. Hence, they were inclined to mingle the sternness of Lucretius with the lightheartedness of Epicurus and the resignation of Seneca. Equally followers of Horace, who also had espoused a combination of epicureanism with stoicism, they adopted a tone that was ironical and, above all, satiric. The subject-matter of their poems, moreover, was broader than might be expected, for it included not only a fair amount of political, as well as social, satire but even some debauchery and drinking songs.

Throughout the seventeenth century there can be found an almost limitless number of these libertine poets, extending from Théophile de Viau to Chaulieu. We shall want to examine in due course those who seem to have led directly to Voltaire: Théophile de Viau, Des Barreaux, Blot, Dehénault, Mme Deshoulières, Saint-Evremond, and the early La Fontaine. All of them were skeptical, free-thinking, satiric imitators of Horace—"libertins," in the true sense of the term. Possessed of a finely honed sensitivity for epicurean pleasures, all of them were nevertheless prepared to meet the misfortunes of life with a more stoic response. And, finally, all of them saw in the art of poetry the refined expression of the art of living. This was the poetic tradition that Voltaire inherited at the Temple from his friend Chaulieu, who in this respect acted as intermediary between the lyrical voices of the seventeenth century and the youth so anxious to join that "aimable" choir. But it must be noted that, if Chaulieu and the group assembled at the Temple in a way exemplified the whole long line of free-thinking poets by gathering together all their themes and poetic mannerisms, it was not for poetry alone that they deserved the recognition they received;

as Sainte-Beuve pointed out, the free-thinking of these poetic ancestors of Voltaire so appealed to Bayle that he purposely set aside
a place for each of them in his famous *Dictionnaire*.

It was, then, these three influences—family, Louis-le-Grand, and
the Temple—in conjunction with the circumstances of the time,
particularly the religious discussions, that first turned the young
Voltaire toward a career in letters and began to encourage in him a
certain seriousness of thought. There was not, to be sure, complete
harmony between these forces and the circumstances that conditioned their effect. There never is when a personality is being
formed. Thus, while the family nurtured its "bourgeois" Jansenism
and occasionally took a more intimate interest in Jansenist activities
during periods of intense Jansenist-Jesuit controversy and violent
religious persecution, the Jesuits at Louis-le-Grand concentrated on
the cultivation of literary taste, particularly through instruction in
the satiric and dramatic literatures of the past. Their aim was to
implant morality in man as a means of fostering his religious aspirations. Classic literature was, in their opinion, an excellent device for
preparing the "gentleman." The poets assembled at the Temple,
on the other hand, though they had literary interests which over-
lapped those of the Jesuits at Louis-le-Grand, promoted a different
interpretation of them. The poetry they produced was basically the
same as the poetry of the Jesuits, but they viewed that poetry instead
with the eyes of the libertine, free-thinking poets whose vision they
had inherited. Still, the frequenters of the Temple shared with the
Jesuits a common heritage in Horace, Lucretius, Perseus, and Juvenal, and for both the fundamental objective of study lay in the
cultivation of taste and the creation of the good life.

The natural focus of Voltaire's poetic interest was thus centered
on the Latin poets—Horace and the satirists, Virgil, and Lucretius—
and on the imitators of these poets throughout the seventeenth century in France—Théophile de Viau, Des Barreaux, Blot, Dehénault,
Mme Deshoulières, Chaulieu, and La Fare. To these solid ancestors
of French classicism and the line of irregular libertine poets they
spawned, however, must be added certain particular influences—all
of them classical French writers—who seem to have early attracted
Voltaire's attention. Four of them were of great importance to him
as literary models: Boileau, Corneille, Racine, and the early La Fon-

taine. Yet, significantly, though these writers formed an indispensable part of the literary tradition with which Voltaire identified himself, they, too, could ultimately be linked with the primal influence of Horace.

2. VOLTAIRE'S LITERARY MASTERS

ONCE HAVING CHOSEN poetry as a profession, Voltaire proceeded to select from among the vast number of his predecessors those to whom he could accord a sincere respect to serve as his literary models. There were four of these intimate poetic friends—two from classical antiquity, Horace and Virgil, and two from the preceding age of Louis XIV, Boileau and Racine. Curiously, juxtaposition of these two pairs reveals a certain parallelism: Horace and Boileau were the master critics, who had the same poetic ideal; Virgil and Racine were the master poets, who had the same poetic qualities. For Voltaire, these four represented the very acme of the poetic art.

HORACE

We have already seen how Voltaire was introduced to Horace. Both at Louis-le-Grand and at the Temple he encountered men who expressed the highest regard for the Roman satirist. The two undoubtedly most responsible for providing him with this introduction were Tarteron, his teacher, and Chaulieu, his model. Having accepted the Roman as his master, the aspiring young poet turned to the translations of Horace by his teacher. This version, however, Voltaire found defective, and he soon switched to Dacier's, which he knew at least by 1714, even before his departure from the *lycée*. In the *Bourbier*, an early satiric poem directed at La Motte, Voltaire refers to

> Anacréon, Virgile, Horace, Homère,
> Dieux qu'à genoux le bon Dacier révère.

We should not take this reference too seriously, however; in the *Siècle de Louis XIV*, Voltaire conceded that Dacier was more learned than elegant as a writer, adding that his translation and notes had value. Dacier's translation of the *Odes* of Horace, he remarked (M. XXIII, 419), was more faithfully rendered than Desfontaines's translation of Virgil, more instructive and more scholarly in its notes, albeit totally lacking in gracefulness, harmony, and imagination.

It is not surprising that the young Voltaire, living in a society so fond of Horace, guided by his professors at Louis-le-Grand, and assisted by the translations of Tarteron and Dacier, should have finished by adopting Horace as his model poet. René Bray, in his *Formation de la doctrine classique en France*, has pointed out that, although Aristotle was looked upon as the founder of the classical doctrine, it was Horace who served primarily as the defender of the classical position and who, in fact, was best known. The author of the *De Arte poetica* enjoyed wide prestige because of his theory of literary criticism and even much later shared in Aristotle's importance and fame. Naves (*Goût*, p. 75) has noted that, as the lay public replaced scholars in determining reading trends, Horace became the sole master who, thanks to his urbanity, gave the tone to French politeness. His reading public was very large. Dacier's translation went through five editions between 1681 and 1733, and Tarteron's, first published in 1685, was republished in 1708 and reedited in 1738.

In his preface to the ten-volume translation, Dacier attempted to give an explanation for Horace's popularity. Horace, in the eyes of this scholarly critic, was the poet who had profited most from philosophy, filling his *Odes* with important moral maxims and metaphysical truths. His aim had been, not to dispute with philosophers, but to render poetry more useful and worthy of its origin. His poetry, rightly interpreted, was capable of forming taste, shaping morals, and establishing a critical viewpoint. His lyrical verse was seasoned with philosophical insights; his *Satires* and *Epistles* offered a complete and perfect course in ethics.

Already, in the preface to his first edition, Dacier had outlined six general points to be borne in mind by readers of Horace: the historical situation of each poem, the beauty of its language, the strength of its words, the propriety of the epithets, the precision of its figures of speech, and the sense of its allegories. He further insisted that complete comprehension of each poem requires an exact knowledge of the geography, historical events, and characters with which it deals. The reader, he said, also must have keen discernment, taste fostered by sound knowledge of the great classical works, a facile critical sense, extraordinary delicacy, and great penetration. In short, the editor was making rigid demands on the interpreter, requiring that he be animated by the same spirit that had inspired the poet. This insistence that the reader must have the taste, the imagination, and the skill to become an equal of the poet was topped by a second and even more stringent prerequisite: to become a Horatian poet, the reader would have to learn how to merge satiric tone with poetic expression and with thought. Already the foundation was being laid for the view that the poet must at the same time be a satirist and philosopher, though he must be a poet first of all.

It was, then, the influence of his teachers and the popularity of the Roman poet among cultivated people of his time that spawned in Voltaire the deep respect he had for his chosen mentor. But there were more personal reasons for this predilection, too. In Voltaire's opinion, Horace represented poetic perfection; he was a classical writer of most exquisite taste, a model of judgment, philosophy, and even of conduct. Indeed, Voltaire was quick to identify his own turn of mind with that of the Roman satirist, who became not only the source of his inspiration but also the symbol of his poetic ambitions. It was no mere idle compliment Chaulieu paid the young Arouet when he wrote:

> Que j'aime ta noble audace,
> Arouet, qui d'un plein saut
> Escalades le Parnasse,
> Et tout d'un coup, près d'Horace
> Sur le sommet le plus haut
> Brigues la première place.

Voltaire himself, when he wished to flatter, would liken his correspondent to the Roman poet. Sending the *Défense du Mondain* to the Maréchal de Saxe (circa 15 January 1737), he enclosed this note: "Je vous cite Horace qui vivait dans le siècle du plus grand luxe, et des plaisirs les plus raffinés. Il se contentait de deux demoiselles ou de l'équivalent; et souvent il ne se faisait servir à table que par trois laquais; *coena ministratur pueris tribus*." In October 1737, he wrote Frederick, comparing him to the satiric poet and to Maecenas; at the beginning of November 1737, he called him "élève de Socrate et d'Horace, et d'Euclide." In a letter to Vauvenargues, dated 3 April 1745, Voltaire remarked: "Vous pourriez, monsieur, me dire comme Horace: *Tam rarò scribis, ut toto non quater anno.* Ce ne serait pas la seule ressemblance que vous auriez avec ce sage aimable: il a pensé quelquefois comme vous dans ses vers; mais il me semble que son cœur n'était pas si sensible que le vôtre" (B. 2869). The compliment was sometimes, in turn, addressed to Voltaire. Thus, Algarotti wrote to him that Virgil and Horace were "confratelli vostri" (B. 3152); likewise, Frederick declared that Horace was Voltaire's "devancier" (B. 3530) and that Madame du Châtelet had "un génie, digne d'Horace et de Newton" (B. 624).

Throughout his long career Voltaire was to quote often from other writers of antiquity. But Horace remained his favorite, and Voltaire's admiration for him never diminished, as these remarks from a letter to Darget (4 December 1752) clearly show:

Scit genius, natale comes qui temperat astrum. Je vous assomme toujours de citations d'Horace. On ne le cite guère à Fontainebleau et à Brunoy. . . . C'est pourtant le meilleur prédicateur que je connaisse; il est prédicateur de cour, de bougre, et de bon goût; et surtout du repos de l'âme. Il sait *quid te tibi reddat amicum.* Il savait vivre avec Auguste et Mécène; et sans eux, il avait son Sabine comme M. de Valori a son Estampes. Vous n'etes pas encor *ruris amator,* vous, Monsieur le courtisan: *miraris fumum et opes strepitumque Romae.* . . . Et toujours Horace: *Quod petiit spernit, repetit quod nuper omisit.* Vous m'allez envoyer promener, me traiter de pédant: cependant vous m'avez paru assez content de mon dernier sermon dont ce philosophe voluptueux et libre m'avait fourni le texte.

One might, indeed, accuse Voltaire of pedantry, were it not for the fact that he did not cite his poetic mentor in order to impress or even to provide an excuse for meditating and expatiating upon some deep moral problem. He admired Horace, rather, for having condensed vitally important moral and philosophical thoughts in the clearest and most concise of forms. From his days at Louis-le-Grand, Voltaire seems to have stored in his memory these finely chiseled verses, which recall the way of wisdom and decorum in the activities of everyday life. Throughout his voluminous correspondence these snatches of the Roman satirist seem to rise naturally from the experiences being discussed. They serve both as an introduction to the experiences and as a conclusion to be drawn from them; and their ready appropriateness to the simple, human quality of events, their elegance in evoking the eternal desires and serene responses of man, their pithy conciseness, and their sharp, witty, ironic repartee establish a mood which is genteel, cultivated, carefree, and happy. Hence, it is easy to understand why they recur so frequently in the immense correspondence of the eighteenth-century poet. In a letter to D'Argental, dated 14 July 1738, for instance, Voltaire writes: "Si le public devenu plus dégoûté que délicat à force d'avoir du bon en tout genre, ne souffre pas qu'on égaie des sujets sérieux, si le goût d'Horace et de Despréaux est proscrit, il ne faut donc plus écrire" (B. 1486). Here Horace is viewed as the guarantor of the furtherance of literary excellence. Elsewhere he is seen as the great comforter in time of stress. Writing to Thiériot on 18 March 1746, Voltaire acknowledges: "J'ai lu Horace pour me consoler" (B. 3037).

Horace became Voltaire's guide, consoler, model, and counsellor. From the early lessons with Tarteron when the poetic flame was first fanned in him to the final decade of the seventies when it had all but died away, Horace accompanied the poet Voltaire as Virgil had accompanied Dante. Naves has attempted to assemble Voltaire's quotations from Horace: there are one hundred and thirty-nine different citations, more than from any other poet, including Virgil. Seventy-three are taken from the *Epistles*. Voltaire was especially fond of Horace's *Epistle* I, 4: "Albi, nostrorum sermonum candide judex." Practically every verse of this epistle is quoted somewhere, and a number of verses are cited more than once. The quotations present some forty-five different themes or attitudes toward life, seventeen of which constitute pervasive motifs of Voltaire's philosophy; several of them recur as much as from five to twenty times.

From a study of these themes it is possible to grasp the nature of the Horace who accompanied Voltaire in his search for poetry. For the young Arouet, the Roman was the master of serenity in philosophy: his was "un épicurisme de cour." Voltaire found it easy to translate Horace's attitude into the facile life-style of the Regency and the early years of Louis XV's reign, when it was still thought possible that princes could be poets, and poets, princes. For at the heart of this style was a philosophy of the aristocracy, carefree, more worldly wise than serious, superficial rather than profound, more rational than sentimental, but just sentimental enough to take the edge off rationalism—the philosophy of a highly talented, closely organized society, a kind of poetic elite. Into this society Voltaire envisioned his friend moving with his ironic smile and serene counte-

nance. Sometimes the very perfection of the scene palls. In a letter
to Crousaz, dated 27 February 1746, Voltaire wrote: "Horace a beau
dire: *Principibus placuisse viris non ultima laus est*. Horace est trop
courtisan: il était bien loin de la vertu des Romains" (B. 3032). On
occasion, the French disciple adopted a somewhat severe tone in
speaking of his master. To D'Argens he remarked that *Satire* I, v, is
a "plat ouvrage," a "méchante pièce," although, true to the Horatian
credo, he attenuated this judgment by seeing in it "de petits traits
qui ont fait fortune" (B. 4309). One has a right to rebel from time to
time with a "boutade," but rarely did Voltaire assert himself in this
way. The most famous instance is Pococurantè's judgment of the
Roman satirist, which has the merit of using Horatian techniques to
condemn Horace, Pococurantè himself being almost a perfect Horace as he was conceived in the eighteenth century (Morize, *Candide*,
p. 189):

—Oserais-je vous demander, Monsieur, dit Candide, si vous n'avez pas
un grand plaisir à lire Horace?—Il y a des maximes, dit Pococurantè, dont
un homme du monde peut faire son profit, et qui étant resserrées dans
des vers énergiques se gravent plus aisément dans la mémoire. Mais je
me soucie fort peu de son voyage à Brindes et de sa description d'un
mauvais dîner, et de la querelle de crocheteurs entre je ne sçai quel
Pupilus, dont les paroles, dit-il, *étaient pleines de pus*, et un autre dont les
paroles *étaient du vinaigre*. Je n'ai lu qu'avec un extreme dégout ses vers
grossiers contre des vieilles et contre des sorcières, et je ne vois pas quel
mérite il peut y avoir à dire à son ami Mécenas, que s'il est mis par lui
au rang des Poëtes Liriques, il frapera les Astres de son front sublime.

Voltaire's moments of discontent with his cicerone were quite infrequent. Generally, he devoted his attention to celebrating Horace's
health, his renown, his favors at the court of Augustus, his freedom
of speech, his love of country life, and his retreat. He also spoke
highly of Horace's moral attitudes, tinged with a stoicism quite divorced from haughtiness and characterized by courage and dignity,
by perseverance in doing a task well, by fidelity to one's self, and by
contempt for the "canaille."

Voltaire was drawn to Horace, then, principally because of the
Roman's courtier philosophy and his attenuated moral stoicism, atti-
tudes which the young poet himself wished to cultivate. In Horace
Voltaire also found a master of taste (see Naves, *Goût*, p. 168),

whose vigilance, adherence to social standards, severity of judgment, and conformity of tone with talent were all, he felt, deserving of praise. Horace appealed to Voltaire by reason of precisely those qualities which made him attractive to the contemporary literary public. Voltaire sums them up in several articles in the *Questions sur l'Encyclopédie*: natural gracefulness, discriminating taste, an eternally modern spirit, extreme refinement of the intellect, and tremendous inspiration (as exhibited, for instance, in the *Poème séculaire*).

The resemblance between the two poets is so great that it is often difficult to determine whether the master instilled these qualities in his disciple or whether the inclinations of the disciple conditioned the admiration for his master. Naves (*Goût*, p. 168) notes, quite correctly, that Voltaire discovered in Horace a nature remarkably akin to his own, having similar tastes in literature and similar reactions to the phenomena of the time. Many are the critics who have seen the parallel between the Roman poet's retreat to his Sabine farm, *parvi contentus*, and the eighteenth-century Frenchman's withdrawal from court life to cultivate his garden. Both were attractively modern, skeptical without being unduly caustic, cultivated yet simple, more smiling than bitter, ironic but discreet; both were enlightened philosophers and men of unquestioned taste. Naves concludes: "Horace avait de quoi séduire le jeune habitué des cours galantes, le moraliste de *Zadig* and le jardinier des Délices; voilà pourquoi, pendant toute sa vie, Voltaire n'a pas cessé de chérir cet ancien ami et de murmurer ses vers, *versus secum meditari canoros*" (p. 168).

The resemblance is borne out in their styles, at least as far as lyric poetry is concerned; it is particularly striking in the satiric tone in which this poetry is cast. Dacier in his translation develops some interesting ideas about the nature of this satire. He explains that this literary form was original with the Latins. The word itself derived from *satur*, which means "plein" and refers to dyed wool; *satur color* then means "which has well absorbed the dye." *Satura* (adjective) became *satira* (adjective), which, with *lancem* understood, signifies a bowl filled with all kinds of fruit, that is, "des choses mêlées"—in other words, a "pot-pourri." Whether the etymology of the word is really such as Dacier describes it I cannot say, but its appropriateness as a characterization of Voltaire's writing should be obvious. For, in a way, the entire body of Voltaire's work can be broken down into miscellaneous writings—*Œuvres mêlées*. It is, in fact, a gigantic mixture of all sorts of satiric treatises, a genuine "pot-pourri." Actually there are, in the *Mélanges*, some fragments entitled *Pot-pourri*. It may be that the satiric spirit is by nature rambling, wide-ranging, necessarily fragmentary, and, above all, diverse and totally unorganized. Still, however multifarious, it always constitutes itself as an attack. It is startling to what extent Voltaire manifested, as did Horace, all its inner aspects.

In any event, when Voltaire's lyrical work is printed, it is usually divided into "odes," "satires," and "epîtres," with a section set aside for an unclassified number of poems designated "poésies mêlées," which comprise the *contes, stances*, epigrams, and all kinds of improvised verse. Since the first three were the characteristic genres of Horace's lyrical poetry, it is evident that Voltaire tried to pattern his verse after Horace's even in its outward structure. In all Voltaire wrote nineteen satires, twenty-one odes, and one hundred and thirty epistles, his work in each genre extending from the early part of his life to his very last years.

It was in keeping with Voltaire's character that he never renounced his devotion to the Roman poet once he had chosen him as his master. He even addressed one of his later epistles (1772) to Horace himself:

> Je t'écris aujourd'hui, voluptueux Horace,
> A toi qui respiras la mollesse et la grâce,
> Qui, facile en tes vers, et gai dans tes discours,
> Chantas les doux loisirs, les vins, et les amours,
> Et qui connus si bien cette sagesse aimable
> Qui n'eut point de Quinault le rival intraitable.

In this epistle Voltaire compared his life with the Roman poet's. Being Frederick's court poet he alleged, was better than being the court poet of Augustus, for Frederick at least was an authentic king, who did not owe his greatness to crime. One was less a slave at his court, too. The King had the delicate taste and the discreet refinement so characteristic of Horace. Besides,

> Nul roi ne fut jamais plus fertile en bons mots
> Contre les préjugés, les fripons, et les sots.

With the coming of Maupertuis and his "orgueil philosophique" to Frederick's court, everything had been spoiled:

> Le Plaisir s'envola; je partis avec lui.

Like the Roman, Voltaire too had a retreat—Ferney—which, he ventured to say, was more beautiful even than Horace's Tibur. There among a happy, free people he tried to preserve his own freedom:

> Je le suis en secret dans mon obscurité;
> Ma retraite et mon âge ont fait ma sûreté.

There, too, he developed his land, established his villagers, opened up factories, encouraged tolerance, and fought misery:

> J'ai fait un peu de bien; c'est mon meilleur ouvrage.
> Mon séjour est charmant, mais il était sauvage.

There, finally, he understood the greatness of his Roman master. Horace's philosophy, his moral, his mocking spirit of irony had taken on added meaning amidst the everlasting change. In the end, Voltaire averred, only the work of art survives:

> Ce monde, tu le sais, est un mouvant tableau
> Tantôt gai, tantôt triste, éternel, et nouveau.

> Tout passe, tout périt, hors ta gloire et ton nom.
> C'est là le sort heureux des vrais fils d'Apollon:
> Tes vers en tout pays sont cités d'âge en âge.

To the banal uniformity of the declining years of the Enlightenment, Voltaire contrasted the diversity of his idol's poetry:

> Sur vingt tons différents tu sus monter ta lyre;
> J'entends ta Lalagé, je vois son doux sourire;
> Je n'ose te parler de ton Ligurinus,
> Mais j'aime ton Mécène, et ris de Catius.

Admitting that he had lived longer than his Latin model but that his verses would certainly live less long, Voltaire promised to follow the lessons of his master:

> J'ai vécu plus que toi; mes vers dureront moins.
> Mais au bord du tombeau je mettrai tous mes soins
> A suivre les leçons de ta philosophie,

A mépriser la mort en savourant la vie,
A lire tes écrits pleins de grâce et de sens,
Comme on boit d'un vin vieux qui rajeunit les sens.

It was moderation, the golden mean, which now seemed to be the true lesson of life:

Avec toi l'on apprend à souffrir l'indigence,
A jouir sagement d'une honnête opulence,
A vivre avec soi-même, à servir ses amis,
A se moquer un peu de ses sots ennemis,
A sortir d'une vie ou triste ou fortunée,
En rendant grâce aux dieux de nous l'avoir donnée.

With these lessons, one could learn to face the end of life as a true gentleman:

Tu dus finir ainsi. Tes maximes, tes vers,
Ton esprit juste et vrai, ton mépris des enfers,
Tout m'assure qu'Horace est mort en honnête homme.

VIRGIL

The place of high honor that Horace occupied in Voltaire's scale of literary values was shared by a second Latin poet—Virgil. Naves (*Goût*, p. 168), who measures Voltaire's esteem for Virgil by counting quotations, notes some ninety-seven passages in the correspondence, with some twenty motifs, extracted not only from the *Aeneid* but from the *Eclogues* and the *Georgics* also. Voltaire celebrated in this Latin poet the same qualities he revered in Horace; Virgil, too, exemplified for him the ideal combination of poet and philosopher. But in Virgil it was the poet who practically always dominated the philosopher, even in the lyrics of the *Eclogues* and the *Georgics*. Voltaire, like all his contemporaries, never forgot Virgil's "Felix qui potuit," or "Macte animo," or the "Fortunatos nimium." But what he selected for praise was not so much the finely chiseled maxim, which distinguished the poetry of Horace, nor even its moral and didactic content, as the gracefulness and harmony of the verses, which, to be sure, were in perfect accord with the thought. Voltaire was especially impressed by the ability of Virgil to express in simple, natural, true terms a wide range of human emotions: proud, energetic passions, pathetic manifestations of sorrow and grief, the

feeling of sadness at the memory of the past (*O passi graviora,
. . . fuge crudeles terras*), the deep pain which arises from remembrance of happy moments that are gone (*et dulces moriens reminiscitur Argos*)—those profound human emotions which Dante understood so perfectly.

Voltaire admired not only the technical skill Virgil displayed in his masterful command of the instrument of his verse but also the facility with which he could, through his grasp of language, imbue the simplest event of everyday life with elegance. Horace, too, could achieve this effect. But, whereas Horace did so without dropping the tone of conversation, Virgil employed all his powers of eloquence to endow with dignity and nobility the slightest circumstance, raising it to heights of grandeur. Always, though, was his eloquence tempered by measure and harmony. Voltaire called it poetry adapted to the taste of civilization, and he placed the Roman poet above Homer because, for him, Virgil represented this fine flowering of civilization, which Homer had never known.

In the *Essai sur la poésie épique*, Voltaire stressed first of all Virgil's timidity, his gentleness, his modesty. He relates that the author of the *Aeneid* was so revered that on one occasion, when he appeared at the theatre where some of his verses were being recited, the audience arose and acclaimed him. Voltaire adds that the *Aeneid*, in spite of its defects, is the finest monument which has come down to us from all antiquity. Nevertheless, he emphasizes these defects. Virgil, he charges, has imitated Homer too closely and has failed to introduce epic action (this being the interpretation which he attributes to Horace's "molle et facetum"). Virgil has not provided a cast of characters, only Aeneas and a group of attendants; his last six books are inferior to the first six; the Latin war is dull and unmotivated, and Turnus overshadows Aeneas as the hero. Even so, Voltaire, like Pococurantè in *Candide*, maintains that the second, fourth, and sixth books approach perfection. The fourth, particularly, he praises highly for its sensitive expression of deep emotions; it is, he says, so filled with things of beauty that one would have to cite the whole book to bring them out.

When Mme du Deffand asked him if he preferred Pope to Virgil, Voltaire replied that there could be no comparison between the two; Pope, the poet of didactic, philosophic verse, did not deserve to be placed alongside Virgil, and, in any case, there was no way of measuring poetic epistles against an epic poem. As for the *Georgics,* Voltaire assured a M. Rosset, author of a poem upon agriculture, that they would always be the delight of poets, not because of the precepts Virgil taught or because of his flattery of Augustus, but because of his "admirables épisodes, de sa belle description de l'Italie, de ce morceau si charmant de poésie et de philosophie qui commence par ce vers: *O fortunatos nimium,* etc." (B. 17798). It is true, wrote Voltaire, that Virgil's observations on nature were as false as his praise of Octavius Caesar, that he had, for instance, assembled in his verses all the errors on the bees. Still, he concluded (M. XIX, 436), Virgil's poetry abounds in picturesque expressions which one could not even render in the current jargons of Europe.

BOILEAU

The French Horace was without a doubt Boileau, erstwhile neighbor of the Arouets in the Cour du Palais and the Cloître Notre-Dame, at least until he moved to his retreat at Auteuil. Voltaire might have met him in his last days, although it is unlikely that a young student in a Jesuit school would have had much opportunity to become acquainted with this well-known defender of the Jansenists. At all events, Boileau, who also wrote satires, epistles, and odes, as well as an *Art poétique,* was associated in Voltaire's mind with Horace as a master of elegance and taste.

In the list of writers beginning his *Siècle de Louis XIV,* Voltaire pointed out that the critic, after trying law and the Sorbonne, had devoted himself exclusively to cultivating his talent and thereby become the honor of France. His works had already been the object of so many commentaries, though, that whatever one might add would be superfluous; in the first edition of the *Siècle,* Voltaire merely stated that Boileau is "le plus correct de nos poètes." Voltaire repeated this compliment toward the end of his life in the *Epître à Boileau* (1769):

> Correct auteur de quelques bons écrits
>
> ....
>
> Mais oracle du goût dans cet art difficile
> Où s'égayait Horace, où travaillait Virgile.

Here the encomium Voltaire bestows upon his idol is lavish indeed. Boileau is the greatest master of French verse, his most important contribution to this art being his insistence upon the purity of the language. Voltaire recalls (M. VII, 242) how he used to repeat with his fellow students at Louis-le-Grand two lines which should be the rule of all who speak and write:

> Sans la langue, en un mot, l'auteur le plus divin
> Est toujours, quoiqu'il fasse, un méchant écrivain.

They were made to understand, he adds, that the defects of language consist not only of solecisms and barbarisms but of obscenities, improprieties, insufficiencies, exaggerations, vulgarities, lack of imagination, harshness, pomposity, and incoherence of expression.

On this occasion, Voltaire's judgment happened to be very accurate. Boileau did, in fact, attempt to define the excellent in poetry in the 1701 edition of his works. Already, in the preface of the earlier edition (1666-1669), he had mentioned that his critics were accusing him of having borrowed his thoughts from Juvenal and Horace; but he had no desire to object to this accusation, for it was, he said, such an honor to be so linked with these illustrious predecessors that it would be very wrong to protest. Boileau affirmed this resemblance to Horace throughout his career; besides, it was a title which all his classical contemporaries accorded him without hesitation or reservation. It was in keeping with his image as the Roman's spiritual descendant that the French critic made an effort to define what is excellent in a literary work. To qualify, a work must possess a "certain agrément" and a "certain sel propre à piquer le goût général des hommes." This "agrément" and this "sel" must be recognized not only by the "connaisseurs" but by the common run of men as well. These qualities, said the critic, are more easily felt than described; the excellent is, hence, that indefinable something, that "je ne sais quoi." Nonetheless, the critic made so bold as to affirm that it consists principally in always presenting to the public true thoughts and precise expressions ("vraies pensées et justes expressions"). It was this view that justified Voltaire's designation of his predecessor as "correct auteur" and his insistence that Boileau could always express clearly and precisely exactly what he wanted to say. The seventeenth-century critic persistently maintained that a novel, brilliant, extraordinary idea is not one which no one has ever had before but one which everyone has had and which for the first time is presented in a lively, precise, new way ("vive, fine, et nouvelle"). Indeed, in his *Satire II, La Rime et la Raison*, Boileau advanced the idea that poetry, by insisting upon rime, had placed a constraint upon thought. This was, of course, the fundamental point in the quarrel of *La Géométrie* between Houdar de la Motte and Voltaire. The conclusions of Boileau were entirely different from La Motte's, however. For, although Boileau sincerely deplored the "tourment d'enchaîner rime et raison," he was at the same time convinced that the poet must ever struggle with his poetic demon— unless, of course, he happened to be a Molière, blessed with a "facilité de rimer." It was Boileau who said (*Satire II*, 53-56):

> Maudit soit le premier dont la verve insensée
> Dans les bornes d'un vers renferma sa pensée,
> Et donnant à ses mots une étroite prison;
> Voulut avec la rime enchaîner la raison.

So greatly did Voltaire prize this quality of precision that he conferred upon his predecessor some of his highest praise. He wrote that both Boileau and Racine had "un pinceau correct" and had said what they wanted to say without sacrificing in the slightest the harmony and purity of their expression (B. 461). Boileau's style was "doux et coulant" (B. 40), his verses "coulants et naturels" (B. 487). His *Art poétique* was more poetical than Horace's; moreover, he had given example as well as precept and, though it had been written in imitation of the Roman's, the copy was superior to the original. His *Epîtres* were beautiful and, at the same time, founded on truth. Voltaire naturally had reservations. He deemed the satires inferior to the epistles and charged Boileau with being unjust in his judgments. It was, for instance, wrong of Boileau to praise Segrais while ignoring La Fontaine, wrong to rank Voiture above Horace. His satire against women revealed that he was quite unacquainted with feminine brilliance and charm, having had no experience with mundane society. In a moment of pique, Voltaire even accused the French Horace of being nothing but an imitator (B. 2029):

> Dans ses tristes beautés si froidement parfaites.
> Il est des beaux esprits, il est plus d'un rimeur;

Il est rarement des poètes.
Le vrai poète est créateur.

A letter to Helvétius (B. 2343) contained a more balanced assessment: there Voltaire agreed with his correspondent that Boileau was lacking in strength and was devoid of any sublime traits. His imagination was anything but brilliant. It would consequently be an error to call him a sublime poet. To be sure, he had done well what he was equipped, and what he actually wished, to do. He had set in harmonious verses the play of the human intelligence. He was clear, consistent, smooth, successful in his transitions; he never soared, yet he scarcely ever sank to poor poetry. He had a firm grasp of the art of writing, respect for his language, a very logical arrangement of ideas, and a facile manner with which he carried the reader along. His greatest traits were a naturalness of style, which was a part of his art, and this apparent facility, which was the result of careful workmanship. Voltaire expressed a quite similar opinion in a letter to Thiériot, though this time with a slight note of disapproval: "Vous me reprochiez d'imiter Despréaux, et à présent vous voulez que je lui ressemble. Trouvez-vous donc dans ses épîtres tant de vivacité, et tant de traits? Il me semble que leur grand mérite est d'être naturelles, correctes et raisonnables, mais de la sublimité, des grâces, du sentiment, esce là qu'il les faut chercher?" (B. 1582)

Nonetheless, Voltaire not only admired the critic in Horace and Boileau but practiced in the same genre and strove for the same results: precision and elegance of speech, a union of the true and the beautiful, chiseled maxims, and a presentation of life in a manner at once ironic, serene, and philosophical.

RACINE

In addition to Horace, Virgil, and Boileau, there was in Voltaire's pantheon of honored writers a place reserved also for Racine. In the notice devoted to him in the *Siècle de Louis XIV*, Voltaire remarks that the great dramatist was not as good a philosopher as he was a poet. In the chapter on the arts in the *Siècle*, Voltaire ascribes Racine's greatness to his constant elegance. Echoing his evaluation of Boileau, Voltaire finds that the dramatist is "toujours correct, toujours vrai, qu'il parle au cœur." He was, Voltaire asserts, far superior to the Greeks and to Corneille in the understanding of the passions, and he

carried the harmony of poetry to its highest point. Voltaire enthusiastically proclaims that, after Virgil, Racine was the one who had
known the art of poetry best. Voltaire is lavish in his praise. It was
Racine, he says, who excelled in painting the passions. He was the
only tragic poet of his day whose genius had been directed by good
taste. His tragedies were perhaps the only ones since those of Aeschylus to be well structured from beginning to end. His grand merit as
a playwright consisted in saying exactly what was called for by the
circumstances in which he placed his characters and saying it with
simplicity, nobility, and elegance. Of all the world's poets, it was he
who knew best the human heart; he was, too, the only French poet
who spoke both to the heart and to the mind. Truth was predominant in his works. Indeed, Voltaire concludes, if anything could be
called perfect in this universe, surely it would be Racine's writing.

Voltaire's opinion of Racine's works—except for what he called the
"faible tragédie d'Alexandre"—was for the most part unusually
favorable. He was much impressed, for instance, by the character of
Pyrrhus in *Andromaque*. Boileau, it will be recalled, had disliked
Racine's portrayal because Pyrrhus's love was not sufficiently violent.
Voltaire observed that, on the contrary, "ces caractères indécis et
mitoyens ne peuvent jamais réussir, à moins que leur incertitude
ne naisse d'une passion violente, et qu'on ne voit jusque dans cette
indécision l'effet du sentiment dominant qui les emporte. Tel est
Pyrrhus dans *Andromaque*, caractère vraiment théâtral et tragique"
(M. XXXII, 288). *Britannicus,* on the other hand, he considered a
weak play: it did not draw tears, the roles of Britannicus and Junie
were undistinguished, some of the other characters were odious,
and there was a lack of "bienséance" in the conduct of the Emperor. He did find some merit in the play as a historical portrayal of
Nero's court, though, and he commented that the treatment of
all the characters was masterful and, as he said, "nécessaire." He
referred specifically to the beautiful portrayal of Burrhus and even
of Narcisse (B. 17758). He was willing to concede that *Bérénice* was
not a tragedy; along with many of his generation, he was inclined
to regard it instead as an elegy. In this opinion he was at one with
La Motte, who asserted that, with a subject as simple as this, one
would have to be extraordinarily gifted to sustain a whole work
merely with detailed poetic beauties. Unlike La Motte, however, Vol-

taire was aware that poetic treatment is much more important than adherence to a genre. True to his fundamental principle, Voltaire maintained that a great poet is one who can stir the soul; that effect, he felt, Racine certainly achieved in *Bérénice*.

His attention was attracted to *Bajazet* because of the exposition, which he called the "chef-d'œuvre de l'esprit humain." He was less enthusiastic about *Mithridate*; he considered the protagonist an insipid novel hero and judged there was too much French gallantry throughout the play. And Mithridate's action he condemned as lacking in "bienséance." Nevertheless, he did admit, as everyone else did, that the remark "Seigneur, vous changez de visage," though nothing in itself, was sublime in the circumstances in which it was said. In fact, he was prepared to argue that, if the play was badly conceived, the versification was almost perfect. *Iphigénie* was the greatest of plays, said Voltaire, who praised all the characters, declared that the heroine was better portrayed than in Euripides, and called it "le chef-d'œuvre de la scène" ("Art dramatique," *Dictionnaire philosophique*, M. XVII, 408). *Phèdre* was exceptional in that Phèdre's role was the most beautiful of all parts and her character the most dramatic that had ever been created. She was an "admirable caractère," the "chef-d'œuvre de l'art et cet effort de l'esprit humain." Her role from beginning to end was "ce qui a jamais été écrit de plus touchant et de mieux travaillé." *Esther* charmed him with the beauty of its style. Finally, *Athalie* he called the most perfect of French tragedies; it was the "chef-d'œuvre de la poésie."

Throughout his correspondence, from 1731 to the end of his life, Voltaire never ceased to express to his friends his deep admiration for the author of *Phèdre*. Opportunities were always arising for heralding the glory of the great dramatist. At one moment he would be engaged in comparing the author of *Athalie* with Corneille or with Shakespeare, at another moment he would be encouraging some critic—La Harpe or Blin de Sainmore perhaps—to bring out in detail the many perfections of Racine's writing. Or, finally, he would find occasion to pay his respects to his predecessor enthusiastically in letters to his friends.

From the beginning the two traits Voltaire most admired in Racine were "la poésie de style" and "les beautés de détail" (B. 404). This "poésie de style," it seems, comprised two main qualities: writing to Olivet, Voltaire asserted that great tragedy requires only that the characters be interesting and that the verses be "good," which he defines as "appropriate to the subject" (B. 9172). Voltaire had already long before, in a letter to Brossette (B. 461), celebrated the style of both Boileau and Racine. These were the only two poets, he wrote, who had "un pinceau correct," who had always used "des couleurs vraies," and who had never failed to copy nature faithfully. They had said what they wanted to say without ever endangering either the harmony or the purity of their verses. The quality of this style was characterized by what Voltaire called Racine's "douceur élégante" (B. 499). Voltaire once remarked to Blin de Sainmore that he did not know whether the French language was susceptible of a greater perfection than Racine had given it (B. 11543).

Constantly, he called Racine's plays admirable (B. 10072). Racine was the first writer who really had taste; yet he had never received the honor he justly deserved. He was certainly a great writer (B. 10600). His works, Voltaire wrote D'Argental, were filled with simple, natural expressions (B. 10606). Racine was truly great, Voltaire assured Voisenon, all the more because he had made no apparent effort to be so; the poet of *Athalie* was a perfect writer, all his verses were good, whereas Corneille had mustered only about two hundred which could qualify as excellent (B. 10941). Voltaire did not hesitate to call Racine the finest of the French poets (B. 13659). A letter to Olivet described him as the immortal, admirable, inimitable Racine (B. 13790); another, to Horace Walpole, referred to him as "l'excellent, l'illustre" Racine and spoke of his plays as being the most perfect of tragedies (B. 14179). Writing to Blin de Sainmore, Voltaire called Racine the poet of feeling (B. 13363); to Chabanon, he revealed that Racine was driving him to despair, "comme il va au cœur toujours tout droit!" (B. 14166) Racine's writing was rarely as tragic as it should have been, Voltaire admitted to Ximénes; still, it was always "intéressant, adroit, pure, élégant, harmonieux" (B. 13160).

Voltaire confessed to his friends that the further he progressed in his commentary on Corneille, the more he came to adore Racine. "Je vous confie," Voltaire wrote to Voisenon, "qu'en commentant Corneille, je deviens idolâtre de Racine" (B. 10228). To Mme du Deffand he exclaimed: "Racine m'enchante, et Corneille m'ennuie"

(B. 11133). Voltaire's admiration for his predecessor knew no bounds. No playwright before Racine, he often asserted, had produced any really superior plays, and the plays of later dramatists were always crammed with horrible defects. He felt, for instance, that Crébillon's plays "ne valent rien" in comparison with Racine's, and he even acknowledged that his own "ne valent pas mieux." To D'Argental he confided that Racine drove him to despair and that Crébillon, Campistron, La Grange-Chancel, and he himself were "gens excessivement médiocres" (B. 10229). He repeated the same remark to Cramer (B. 10241).

But it was not only the technical builder of verses he admired in Racine. It is true that he often defined the art of Racine in terms of the "douceur élégante," as when he wrote Vauvenargues (B. 2567) that Racine possessed always this "sagesse toujours éloquente, toujours maîtresse du cœur" which permitted him to say only what should be said and in the way that best fit the particular situation. Racine, moreover, had spoken of love "en homme," whereas Corneille had disfigured his play with the theme of love. Racine was preeminently the poet of taste, Voltaire wrote to Blin de Sainmore (B. 11238), and must be put in the foremost rank of authors; it was this taste which produced such true and interesting characters as the Acomats and the Burrhus. In another letter to Blin de Sainmore, Voltaire confessed that he attached more importance to the one character of Acomat than to all of Corneille's heroes. What was so exceptional in Racine's characters was that, in inventing all the "nuances" of these "beaux caractères," Racine had depicted them with such art and eloquence that he had displayed a perfect genius for character portrayal. Besides, he had observed all the rules "avec un art enchanteur"—not the silly Aristotelian restrictions, but those whose function is to promote purity of style, expression of true thoughts without bombast, presentation of characters with decorum, and depiction of the theme of love, passionate love, in a way which speaks to the heart (B. 11260).

Voltaire's enthusiasm for the author of *Athalie* burst forth time and again, always with the same note of veneration. Racine was "sage et correct." He did not go seeking "esprit" or "déclamations ampoulées." No one, Voltaire wrote Olivet (B. 12354), had ever carried the art of speech to such heights or given more charm to the

French language. To La Harpe, Voltaire repeated that Racine was always "dans la nature" (B. 17081). What made the seventeenth-century dramatist so superb, Voltaire explained to Chabanon, were the "détails qui vont au cœur" and produce tears in his audience. The situations and the maxims (*sentences*) had no value in themselves, for one could find these things anywhere. But the beautiful pieces of poetry which linger in the memory and which stir the depths of the soul, he said, assure Racine a perpetual immortality. In a letter to Saint-Lambert, Voltaire described Racine as a god who holds the hearts of men in his hand (B. 15082). It was in a letter he wrote to Sumorokow in 1769 that he summed up this admiration: "Je regarde Racine comme le meilleur de nos poètes tragiques, sans contredit, comme celui qui le seul a parlé au cœur et à la raison, qui seul a été véritablement sublime sans aucune enflure, et qui a mis dans la diction un charme inconnu jusqu'à lui. Il est le seul encor qui ait traité l'amour tragiquement . . ." (B. 14524).

From these opinions there can be derived not only some glimpse of the reasons why Voltaire was led to choose these four poets as his masters in the art of poetry but also a view of that art as Voltaire envisaged it. His goal, one feels, was not simply to be as great as each of these predecessors but to become so accomplished in the art of poetry that men would judge him superior to all four. Voltaire's ambitions were never modest; once he even felt that he could outdo both Racine and Shakespeare. When the *Henriade* appeared in England, he seemed sincerely convinced that he had surpassed all previous epic poets. He had no hesitation in affirming his intention of becoming that poet who would unite the greatness of Horace and Virgil with the excellence of Boileau and Racine.

What qualities would such an ideal poet possess? It seems clear that he would be skilled in blending thought with art or, as Boileau expressed it, "pensées vraies" with "expressions justes." He would know what to say in every poetic situation, and he would know how to say it correctly. In other words, he would be a combination of poet and philosopher, and the union of poetry and philosophy in his work would be so effected by the critical poetic judgment that it would be impossible to produce a more vital harmony between what is said and the expressive way it is put. That is not all, however. This poet would know, too, through his poetic intuition that he had created that harmony. His taste would be so attuned to that harmony that he could sense the slightest defect or the slightest beauty in the thought and the expression and feel it spontaneously. Voltaire's apprehension of art was, then, not modest, since he saw as its goal the same creative power which God gave to life.

3. VOLTAIRE'S ANCESTORS IN LYRIC POETRY

VOLTAIRE'S LITERARY MASTERS, in the sense that they represented the very acme of the poetic art, were Horace, Virgil, Boileau, and Racine. Together they became for the young student at Louis-le-Grand, and remained for him thereafter, not only models of poetic taste but, more explicitly, representatives of the great poetic genres: the epic, the drama, the satire, the epistle, and the ode. Together, by their precept and practice, they established for the young student the code of all that was superior in the art of poetry. The high esteem with which Voltaire regarded them did not, however, prevent him from uniting with a freer tradition which developed during the seventeenth century from Théophile de Viau to Chaulieu. Thus, while professing in the major genres of poetry a deep fidelity to his masters, in the minor genres he gave his devotion to the more irregular libertine poets of the seventeenth century. It is as if he wished to achieve a wide diversity in poetry, as he later attempted to do in thought. He was by no means content to be just the master of the epic, of the drama; he desired as well to be the outstanding poet of the more evanescent lyric poetry which expressed the yearnings, the desires, and the personal ambitions of day-to-day living.

There had been throughout the seventeenth century a whole mass of these poets who passed for "irregular." They were the free-thinkers in art who at the same time represented the free-thinkers in thought. They were very numerous in Italy, in France, and, particularly toward the end of the century, in England. In general, because of their frequent references to all the pleasures of love and of the flesh, they were thought even in their day to be writers given to debauchery. The center of this poetic libertinism was undoubtedly France; the model poet of the kind was certainly Théophile de Viau. Professor Adam has shown that there was formed around him a group of independent poets: Maynard, Boisrobert, Saint-Amant, and Tristan. All of them were distinguished by their impiety; in fact, they composed a collection of irreverent poems, which still exists in an Arsenal manuscript (3127) and which has not been published for obvious reasons. Adam admits that quite probably all of them were atheistically inclined and were libertine in spirit as well as in their actual moral lives. All of them, moreover, boasted of being modern, but in a way that went beyond the kind of modernity Malherbe and his group espoused. In reality, theirs was essentially an individualistic outlook. The distinguishing characteristic of their work was more a certain view of man than a literary doctrine.

Perhaps the most comprehensive presentation of their viewpoint is that which Théophile has given us in his pessimistic conception of man. Even in his love poems he portrays, as Adam states, the despair, the revolts, and the defeats of one who has submitted completely to his passions. His other poems, especially his elegies, progress still further in this direction. There he goes beyond the conventional banality of mundane gallantry and presents the pessimistic tragedy of the human condition in all its stark reality. He rejects the orthodox philosophy of his time, replacing it with the naturalism of the Italians, which he took from Giordano Bruno and his own contemporary Vanini. Although he admits the existence of God, it is a deistic God rather than the God of Christianity. Théophile insists upon the denial of Providence, too. But, if he seems unable to conceive either of the Christian God or of divine Providence, he does have a deep poetic feeling for the riches of nature, by which he means, not the phenomena of this universe, but rather its fertility. Once more, the concept comes from Bruno and Vanini, particularly from the *Spaccio* and the *De admirandis Naturae*. Adam calls this high regard for nature a pure naturalism. It is, of course, Paduan in its origin, but thoroughly imbued with a rigid determinism and a strong critique of man's nature, attitudes which recall Montaigne's point of view:

> Une nécessité que le ciel établit
> Déshonore les uns, les autres anoblit.
> (second satire)

Théophile did not, however, subscribe to a pure materialism. Man is a composite of matter, it is true, but in his formation, just as in the universe as a whole, there is at work a soul, a "divine flamme," a "doux flambeau." Man, at the same time, is subject to a blind destiny. Unrelated to the divinity, he is born of the elements of nature. Animals are superior to him in adaptation to environment. His reason, of which he boasts so much, is inconsistent; his desire is unstable; his standards of morality are all relative. He is far from being the king of the universe. He is but the product of blind forces of nature, a mixture of air and mud, under the complete sway of necessity. Though he thinks he is reasonable, he is led by his passions. Even love which he deems a noble, free activity, is really only a form of slavery and degradation.

To be sure, none of these ideas of Théophile's are organized. They originated, after all, in spontaneous outbursts of poetic fancy. But this is precisely one of the advantages of libertine poetry: it does not have to conform to anything outside of itself. That it was well understood by the later generations of the seventeenth century can be measured in a small way by the fact that Théophile's works went through ninety-three editions in the period between 1620 and the end of the century (see Adam, *Histoire*, I, 88).

For the poet, the one immutable law is change:

> Ce qui sert aujourd'hui nous doit nuire demain,
> On ne tient le bonheur jamais que d'une main.
> Le destin inconstant sans y penser oblige,
> Et, nous faisant du bien, souvent il nous afflige.

One can thus measure the distance between the orthodox norm and Théophile's view of this world. For the Christian God, Théophile has already substituted the power of nature; in the place of Christian Providence, he puts a kind of blind destiny. Nothing in nature gives evidence of intelligent thought. But there is a soul of the world, and man, too, has a soul. Neither can preserve man from his passions, his misery, his disgust. He cannot trust even his reason. Théophile proposes, though, that he follow nature and, in so doing, create himself:

> J'approuve qu'un chacun suive en tout la nature;
> Son empire est plaisant et sa loy n'est pas dure.
> Ne suivant que son train jusqu'au dernier moment,
> Mesmes dans les malheurs, on passe heureusement.
>
> Notre destin est assez doux,
> Et pour n'estre pas immortelle,
> Nostre nature est assez belle,
> Si nous savons jouyr de nous.

Much of this attitude, certainly the thought that the greatest joy of life comes from enjoying one's self, reminds one of Montaigne. But Théophile goes further than Montaigne, with the assertion that we can never be sure of survival after death:

> Servons à notre jeune vie;
> Aussi bien l'estre de la vie
> Au tombeau comme nous est mis,
> Et quel bon sens ou quelle estude
> Nous peut oster l'incertitude
> Du futur qui nous est promis.

Thus, the conclusion is not comforting. There is no universal reason, but only nature, infinitely diverse, never the same, as Leibniz will say. No tradition can be accepted, nor can one possibly practice conformity to the rules of society. All orthodoxy is to be rejected. There remains only one hope: to achieve one's own originality, one's own nature. That is what the aim of poetry is.[4]

Théophile combined in his poetry the tradition of Paduan naturalism as it was developed by Bruno and Vanini with the anti-rational, epicurean thought of Montaigne, particularly as it was presented in the *Apology*, to yield a poetic doctrine distinguished by its originality and by its insistence upon the power of individual poetic expression which lies within every man. This movement continued throughout the whole seventeenth century. It became, if one may dare use a paradoxical term, a tradition compounded of the early drinking songs, the political satires, the love songs, especially those of an erotic nature, and a mood which was drawn from Horace, Lucretius, Italian naturalism, and Montaigne. The line extended all the way from Malherbe to Voltaire; in fact, Voltaire's early poetry partook of this libertine, free-thinking current, after it had been renewed by a revival of Horace and Lucretius.

We can only trace briefly the way in which the movement developed. Gathered in the circle immediately around Théophile were, as we have seen, Boisrobert and Saint-Amant. One of those familiar with the group who happened to be an especial admirer of Théophile was Jacques Des Barreaux, who captured the title of prince of the seventeenth-century libertines. Des Barreaux had a great-uncle who

---

[4] The poems which contain the fullest expression of this thought are the first and the third satires.

had been burned at the stake, in 1574, for writing a work entitled *La Béatitude des Chrétiens*, which circulated clandestinely. Des Barreaux himself was a contemporary of Descartes's and actually attended the Jesuit school at La Flèche just after the philosopher. Tradition has it that he was a great admirer of Cremonini, as was Naudé, but we know little about his relations with the Paduan professor. He had a relatively lengthy life, surviving La Mothe and Patin by one year, dying, in fact, the same year as Molière, in 1673. He became acquainted with Théophile by chance but was not for that reason any less active in the group. Besides, he later became associated with Luillier and his friends, at whose gatherings Gassendi was a frequent visitor; to them, and perhaps to Cyrano and Molière as well, he is thought to have taught his epicurean philosophy. It is certain that Des Barreaux was deeply interested in philosophical, epicurean matters. Lachèvre treats with more than necessary profusion the relations between Théophile and Des Barreaux, as well as those between the latter and Marion de Lorme. These relations are perhaps symptomatic of a mind not of great importance, in spite of Lachèvre, to the free-thinking movement. At the end of his life, Des Barreaux retired to Châlons-sur-Saône and became converted.

Like all these poets, Des Barreaux celebrated the sufferings of love, "ce démon qui gouverne et la terre et les cieux." His poems, particularly those which date from his affair with Marion de Lorme, are distinguished by a simplicity and a naïveté which are not without charm. He was not a careless poet; in fact, he formed his verses with much attention, and the result often reminds one of the careful workmanship of La Fontaine, even to the point of suggesting at times a studied negligence. To this regard for expression is added a tone which is remarkably genuine:

> Je m'en vais à la mort, où toute la nature,
> Impuissante qu'elle est, se laisse évanouir:
> J'ay veu sous le soleil tout naistre et tout périr,
> Qui me dispenseroit de la même avanture?

Into this lyric poetry, however, is inserted a note which is less pure. Here is a "Couplet" that brings to view an activity which was to become very common as the century progressed and which was entirely typical of Voltaire and the Enlightenment:

> Nous sommes ici demi-douzaine
> Qui ne nous mettons guères en peine
> Du Vieux ni Nouveau Testament,
> Et je tiens qu'il est impossible
> De trouver sous le firmament,
> Des gens moins zélés pour la *Bible*.

Accompanying this impertinence is indifference, which Des Barreaux expresses in the Fronde:

> Et cette belle indifférence
> Assure ma neutralité
> Par tout le royaume de France.

It is, however, an indifference which quickly borders on egotism:

> Conservons avec soin la douceur de notre estre
>
> Car je jouïs encor des plaisirs de nature,
> Avec indépendance et pleine liberté.

He confesses, as nearly all his comrades did, to a disbelief in immortality:

> Je suis fort naturel, je ne veux point mourir,
> Mais je compte pour rien d'avoir perdu la vie.

Like all poets, Des Barreaux had his vision of the ideal life:

> Avoir l'esprit purgé des erreurs populaires,
> Porter tout le respect que l'on doit aux mystères,
> N'avoir aucun remords, vivre moralement.
>
> N'avoir pour l'avenir crainte ni espérance.

The objective, however, is to retain the maximum of freedom, and, in order to achieve this aim, one must restrict his desires. Des Barreaux's view of man, though not as thoroughly pessimistic as Théophile's, is nonetheless hardly encouraging. He calls man a "brave animal," attributing to him a long list of bodily activities but little reason: "Ce sont de beaux présents que te fait ta raison." He compares life to a point, a nothing in relation to something eternal. He finds man overwhelmed by his passions, much less happy than the wild beasts, and he judges that "nostre mal ne nous vient que de l'entendement." He looks forward to only a "sommeil éternel." Many of his poems, indeed, treat of an inexorable death:

Nos sens s'éteignent tous quand on vient à périr,
De l'âme avec le corps ne se fait point rupture.

In a lengthy article on Des Barreaux, Bayle maintains that, although others had often spoken of the poet as an atheist, it was certain that he had never gone so far as to deny the existence of God. Bayle admits that sometimes Des Barreaux did go rather far in his "petites chansons de débauche," but he insists that the poet was an "honnête homme," a man of honor, sound in heart and soul, and a good, generous, liberal friend. Frédéric Lachèvre, who in the first third of the twentieth century regarded all these libertine poets with extreme horror, stresses that Des Barreaux and Théophile had the same inclinations, the same ambitions, the same intellectual culture. He adds that Des Barreaux was the most complete model of a libertine in the seventeenth century, both in his morals and in his ideas: "ses sonnets matérialistes vont à l'extrême limite de l'incrédulité."

A second successor of Théophile was Jean Dehénault (1611-1682), son of a baker and a brilliant student at the Collège de Clermont, where both Chapelle and Molière likewise studied. Lachèvre suggests, without too much evidence, that his lack of a fortune drove him to Holland, England, and finally to Sicily. Returning to France without in any way having increased his resources, he cast about for a protector and at last was admitted to Condé's circle, where he met the future Mme Deshoulières. It was Dehénault who initiated her into poetry. In the meantime, Dehénault passed from Condé to Fouquet. One sonnet, L'Avorton, had given him a reputation which was hardly deserved. Fouquet had him appointed to a tax post at Saint-Etienne, but the disgrace Fouquet subsequently suffered meant for Dehénault the loss of the appointment and of the pension that he had received. Like La Fontaine, Dehénault remained faithful to the interests of his patron, though to no avail. And like Molière, he, too, produced a translation of Lucretius.

Bayle devoted an article to Dehénault in the second edition (1703) of the Dictionnaire historique. Most of it was composed by someone who had known Dehénault personally; Bayle, for his part, contented himself with quoting extracts from the memoir and adding his own comments here and there. The memoir records that the poet was "pretty famous in Paris whilst he lived, and is so still, though he has been dead these fourteen years." He was, the memoir continues, "a man of wit and learning, loving pleasure with refinement, and a debauchee with art and delicacy." But it also notes that he had the "worst turn of mind imaginable, that he pretended to be an atheist," and that he "made ostentation of his sentiments with a fury and affectation that were abominable." The writer of the memoir adds that the poet made a trip to Holland to see Spinoza. Dehénault himself is cited as the author of a little character sketch: "You know that I am a man wholly by myself, that I do not place my happiness in the opinion of others, that my errors are very different from those of all the world besides." The memoir goes on to observe that many of his verses are imitations of Seneca's choruses and that he was deeply infatuated with the problem of the mortality of the soul. As an example of this interest, the memoir quotes an original poem by Dehénault:

> Pour moi je ne suis point la dupe de la gloire,
> Je vous quitte ma place au Temple de mémoire,
> Et je ne conçoi point que la loi du trépas
> Doive épargner mon nom et ne m'épargner pas.
> Je me mets au-dessus de cette erreur commune,
> On meurt, et sans ressource et sans réserve aucune.
> S'il est après ma mort quelque reste de moi,
> Ce reste un peu plus tard suivra la même loi,
> Fera place à son tour à de nouvelles choses,
> Et se replongera dans le sein de ses causes.

Dehénault made a translation of the first part of Lucretius, the greater part of which he is supposed to have destroyed at the time of his death. We still have, however, a good portion of the beginning, ending with the famous line: "Tant la Religion peut enfanter de maux!" He was fully cognizant of the role religion played in the affairs of man. This particular quotation, incidentally, which has always been connected with Spinozism in the period that interests us here, was the line perhaps most often quoted from Lucretius in the clandestine essays as well as in the works of the eighteenth-century writers, who never seemed to tire of it. Dehénault also translated the song of the chorus of the second act of Seneca's *Troades*:

> Tout meurt en nous quand nous mourons,
> La mort ne laisse rien, et n'est rien elle-même;
> Du peu de temps que nous durons,
> Ce n'est que le moment extrême.

These are the two basic themes of Dehénault's writing: the deceitfulness of religion, and the mortality of the soul. To these two he eventually added a third, also from a chorus in a Senecan play (*Thyestes*): that man is a king who knows how to dominate his passions, limit his ambitions, and scorn the vulgar mob:

> Pour moy je mets ma seureté
> Dans une heureuse obscurité,
> J'évite en me cachant, et la haine, et l'envie;
> Je goûte le repos, et l'honneste loisir,
> Et je passe la vie
> Dans l'innocence et le plaisir.

These are the compensations for the sins, the suffering, and the deceptions of life; but, essentially, the great reality is death: "On meurt, et sans ressource, et sans réserve aucune."

There is, nonetheless, in Dehénault's poetry a side which is more modest, less pessimistic, and more moderate, and which was to become a part of the poetry of the Enlightenment. For, in spite of his denials and his profound detachment from the things of this world, Dehénault often praises the "douceur de vivre," particularly when enjoyed away from the bustle of the crowd:

> S'élève qui voudra par force ou par adresse,
> Jusqu'au sommet glissant des grandeurs de la cour;
> Moi, je veux, sans quitter mon humble séjour,
> Loin du monde et du bruit rechercher la sagesse.

He extols, as all these poets do, the freedom of love, but at the same time he accepts the counsel of moderation in the pursuit of pleasure that reason offers:

> Échappé des périls d'une ardente jeunesse,
> Et parvenu dans l'âge où règne la sagesse,
> Je m'étais résolu d'écouter la Raison
> Et d'être sage au moins dans l'arrière saison.

This resolution does not, however, prevent him from declaring in his *Elégie* that reason can scarcely be trusted; for that was also a general theme among these poets. Finally, in the *Consolation à Olympe*, he stresses the idea of Montaigne that nature is the best guide for the good life.

A third successor of Théophile was Claude de Chouvigny, Baron de Blot l'Eglise, a satiric poet who wrote light verses, poking fun in more or less scurrilous ways at his contemporaries, and especially at his patron Gaston d'Orléans, as well as the Queen and Mazarin. Blot achieved what is not present in the other poets around Théophile or, at any rate, what is not too apparent, for he combined political and personal satire with outspoken incredulity. It is evident that this poetry had its origin in the religious quarrels of the post-Renaissance era. Blot writes:

> Messieurs, accordez-vous,
> Huguenots et papistes;
> Morbleu, croyez-moy tous:
> Soyons francs athéistes.
> > Et allons!
> > Et allons!
> Je suis illuminé:
> Il n'en sera jamais ny sauvé ny damné.

This type of reaction must have been common in the first four decades of the seventeenth century, although it is doubtful that many outspoken examples of it could be found. Blot, however, does not rest content with merely recording his disbelief. Indeed, he pushes it to the point where it becomes total religious indifference:

> Qu'importe que tu sois papiste,
> Calviniste ou Luthérien,
> Mahométan, Anabaptiste,
> Ou de la secte de ton chien,
> Boy, f---, et n'offense personne:
> Ta religion est fort bonne.

This note is sounded frequently in Blot's poetry; evidently, the plurality of religions had left him with the definite impression that, since there are so many different sects, they must all be spurious:

> Je ne veux ny turban ny chappe,
> Je ne croy ny Mufti ny Pape,
> Par le sang bleu, je suis fort net;

> Je ne suis dervis ny apôtre,
> Mets un signe à ton cabinet,
> Que je ne croy ny l'un ny l'autre.

Cultivation of this incredulity, however, leads naturally to the abandonment of any loyalty toward a religion and to the devotion of one's self to epicurean pleasures, accompanied, as Horace had already stated, by as little trust as possible in the future:

> Dans les plaisirs, amis, soyons plongés,
> Tant que les jours nous seront prolongés.
> Pour ce que l'on vaut après le trespas,
> > Nous le saurons
> Et nous en parlerons
> Quand nous serons là-bas.

This indifference toward religion, with its more or less discreet invitation to pleasure, had since Horace's time been a manifestation of poetic license. With Blot there came to view additional reactions, which were to become very characteristic of Voltaire and the Enlightenment. Blot, for instance, explains that, since he will be persecuted if he is frankly a debauchee, he intends to become a hypocrite:

> Puisqu'enfin il faut que je quitte
> Ce beau titre de débauché,
> Je veux devenir hypocrite,
> Crainte qu'il me manque un péché,
> Et je prendray la contenance
> De quelque cagot d'importance.

In reality, he has an outspoken contempt for all the practices of religion:

> Je ne hante plus les sermons,
> Tous les docteurs je les méprise,
> Après ce qu'a dit Salomon
> Tout le reste n'est que sottise.

He condemns the sacraments:

> Je suis bougre de vieille roche,
> Qui n'auray jamais de reproche
> D'avoir usé de Sacrement.

> Morbleu, tous sept, je les méprise,
> Et pour le montrer hautement,
> Je consens qu'on me débaptise.

He confesses that he no longer accepts the Bible:

> Messieurs, encore un mot
> Avant que je me taise:
> Je ne suis pas sy sot
> De croire à la Genèse.

Finally, he contends that there is no hope either in this life or in a future life:

> Ce monde icy n'est que misère,
> Et l'autre n'est qu'une chimère.

> Amis, ma tristesse est profonde,
> Je ne croy point à l'autre monde.

From the documents at our disposal, it appears that the outspokenness of his views made Blot an exception. One wonders how he escaped difficulties with the authorities, unless by a more or less successful clandestinity. It is likely, however, that, even though Blot with his crude expression of incredulity may seem an exception, we would, if we possessed or examined carefully the anonymous poetic *Recueils* of the time, come upon a fair number of similar confessions.

Mme Deshoulières, whose character undoubtedly was above reproach, is of an entirely different order. Married at an early age to M. Deshoulières, a commander at Rocroy who was imprisoned on suspicion of irregular conduct, she remained faithful to him, actually sharing in his imprisonment. Even Lachèvre can find no fault in her behavior.

She was trained in the writing of poetry by Dehénault, but she appears to have possessed far more intelligence and poetic talent than her teacher. It is true that she imitated some of Dehénault's themes. Still, even in her imitations she tempered the extreme position of her teacher. None of the atheistic tendencies of which Dehénault boasted, for instance, shows in the work of his pupil. She did adopt his themes of the inevitability of death and the weakness of human reason, however.

In the *Réflexions diverses*, she stresses the theme of death:

Homme, contre la mort quoy que l'art te promette,
Il ne sauroit te secourir.
Prépares-y ton cœur, dis-toy, c'est une dette
Qu'en recevant le jour j'ay faite,
Nous ne naissons que pour mourir.

This was a well-worn theme dating from Villon's time, and Mme Deshoulières returns to it over and over, sometimes uniting it with the theme of false pleasures, or with that of pleasures which vanish all too quickly, or with the theme of vanity:

Que l'homme connoist peu la mort qu'il appréhende,
Quand il dit qu'elle le surprend!
Elle naist avec lui; sans cesse luy demande
Un tribut dont en vain son orgeuil se défend.

To this deep dread of death she adds the denial of immortality. It is perhaps her strongest sentiment. In *Les Fleurs*, she writes:

Quand une fois nous cessons d'être,
Aimables fleurs, c'est pour jamais.

We enter, she continues, into the "profond repos" from which Nature first drew us. Scarcely more than a slight memory of our name is preserved among men, and even then death, the great leveler, confuses the hero with the traitor. Mme Deshoulières concludes, however, with resignation, that life is not very desirable either:

Elle n'est qu'un amas de craintes, de douleurs,
De travaux, de soucis, de peines.

Those who have experienced human misery know well that

Mourir n'est pas le plus grand des malheurs.

Her other theme, also derived from Dehénault, is the weakness of reason, especially when it is combated by the passions. In *Les Moutons*, she speaks of "cette fière raison dont on fait tant de bruit" and assures us that it is not a "sûr remède" against the passions. Allied with this theme is her emphasis on the bitter after-effects of the passions:

De tant de passions que nourrit nostre cœur,
Apprenez qu'il n'en est pas une

> Qui ne traisne qu'après soy le trouble, la douleur,
> Le repentir, ou l'infortune.

She concludes that, even when reason penetrates the reality of things, it aims at the wrong objects:

> De ce sublime esprit dont ton orgueil se pique,
> Homme, quel usage fais-tu?
> Des plantes, des métaux, tu connais la vertu,
> Des différents pays, les mœurs, la politique,
> La cause des frimas, de la foudre, du vent,
> Des astres le pouvoir suprême!
> Et sur tant de choses savant
> Tu ne te connais pas toy-même!

There is, finally, in Mme Deshoulières's poetry a theme of incessant social revolt. It is expressed, for instance, against the "faux dévots," an echo of Tartuffe in which the hypocrite states: "Nous savons en vertu transformer tous les vices." Mme Deshoulières resents this type of social hypocrisy; she would, she declares, rather have commerce with an atheist than with a person whose professed piety is merely a sham. But, for the rest, her revolt is scarcely more than a mild poetic pose. She likes animals, flowers, solitude, and meditation—the things which pleased La Fontaine. All of her verse, as a matter of fact, is a sort of moral meditation on the nature of man. Usually, she harps upon the weakness of the human lot, the uselessness of fame, reputation, glory, and the vanity of human existence. She brings out how different man is in his search for happiness from animals, who are satisfied with a simple life. Man, too, she suggests, should take simplicity as the goal of his striving:

> Faible raison que l'Homme vante,
> Voilà quel est le fond qu'on peut faire sur vous!
> Toûjours vains, toûjours faux, toûjours pleins d'injustice,
> Nous crions dans tous nos discours
> Contre les passions, les foiblesses, les vices,
> Où nous succombons tous les jours.

Mme Deshoulières had her poetic circle, with Dehénault, Saint-Pavin, and others, organized around the Duchess of Bouillon. A later circle was organized around the Duke of Vendôme at the Temple. Its leader, Chaulieu, was ably seconded by La Fare. There were many others in the group—Malézieu, Courtin, Châteauneuf, to name a few—whose names now recall only one or two poems but who in their day could boast of having earned a fair share of poetic renown. The circle also numbered among its members Ninon de Lenclos. It was through this group that the young Arouet was initiated into contemporary poetry. Chaulieu, for one, made a lasting impression upon the youth, who was then still a student of Louis-le-Grand; Voltaire's *Epître à Uranie*, in fact, has much in common with Chaulieu's *Trois façons de penser sur la mort*. There are as well some striking resemblances between both Chaulieu's and La Fare's epicurean verse and other early poetry of the author of the *Henriade*. Thus, it is possible to follow an unbroken line of what have been called "poètes libres" from Théophile not only to Mme Deshoulières and La Fontaine but to Voltaire himself. Throughout this whole range of poetry one comes across the same themes, the same tone, the same gestures, and even from poet to poet the same versification. Professor Spink has noted that, in general, the poetry of those between Théophile and Mme Deshoulières was seldom published. He gives us the distinct impression that, being personal poetry, it passed from poet to poet until its effect was spent. And certainly there was a constant exchange of poetry among the poets of the time. But there was also, as Lachèvre has shown in a splendid bibliography (*Bibliographie des Recueils collectifs de poésies, 1597-1700*), a large number of collections in which these poems circulated. It must not be assumed, either, that they were not published in the *Œuvres* of the poets themselves. Even though some *Œuvres*, Des Barreaux's for instance, had only infrequent printings, others, like Mme Deshoulières's, went through numerous editions.

The truth is that, while in one sense all of these poets were followers of Théophile de Viau, in another sense they were also descendants of Lucretius and the *De rerum natura*. Voltaire understood the underlying motives of the movement when in the *Epître à Uranie* he referred to himself as a new Lucretius. These poets were also loosely connected with the rehabilitation of Epicurus as it was inaugurated by Gassendi.

One could name many more than the handful of poets we have considered. The Abbé de Choisy, Maynard, Lignières, and many others besides took advantage of the social conditions which allowed them to assemble in groups and share with one another their poetic interests. Mme Deshoulières's circle was, of course, only one of many such groups, which became increasingly numerous as time went on. Of them all, the Temple was historically the most important because of Voltaire's association with it.

The best introduction to Chaulieu is undoubtedly the informal foreword which he placed at the beginning of his collected poems (see *Œuvres de Chaulieu*, 2 vols., La Haye, 1774) in lieu of a formal preface. Chaulieu explains that a preface "sent un peu trop l'auteur." All his friends know, he says, that as a man of the world he has not cultivated his vanity enough to practice this method. He assumes that talents are a gift of nature which one should not boast of any more than of a mistress's favors. He insists that his readers should not be shocked at an apparent lack of decorum, or suspect libertinism on his part, because of things which a too vivid imagination has compelled him to write and which are not his real opinions. These poems are, he says, but an "amas confus des sentiments de mon cœur" occasioned by a joyful disposition, the pleasures of conversation, gallantry, or the desire to please his Prince and his friends, all of them as libertine as himself. Chaulieu then adds a very interesting explanation of his *Trois façons de penser sur la mort*: "C'est dans cette idée que j'ai composé les *Trois façons de penser sur la mort*. Il faut plaire aux esprits bien faits, disait M. Pascal; c'est à eux que je m'adresse ici, et je les conjure de ne me pas condamner sur les apparences, et de n'aller pas prendre pour mes opinions, ce qui n'étoit en effet que des Essais de poésie." Chaulieu tells us that he wrote the first poem in the spirit of Christianity, without being "dévot," the second in the spirit of pure deism, without being Socinian, and the third in the epicurean manner, without being impious or atheistic. This he had done just as he has sung of love and wine, "toujours voluptueux, et jamais débauché." And he concludes with a rather startling apology: "Ferme dans les principes de ma religion, je n'ai point prétendu dogmatiser le libertinage." Chaulieu confesses that Chapelle had been his master in poetry. He had observed, however, that, although Chapelle's light verses were extremely elegant, he had not sufficiently adorned or sustained them with moral reflections, maxims of a philosophical order, or high principles. Chaulieu declares that he has tried to remedy this weakness by imitating the poetic procedures of Horace "que je trouve en cela merveilleux, à mêler les réflexions les plus sérieuses sur la briéveté, et sur le néant de la vie, sur les misères de la condition humaine, et sur la fatale nécessité de mourir, aux peintures et aux idées agréables, de la molle volupté d'Epicure, et à cette jouissance du présent . . ." (*Œuvres,* 1774, p. 6).

Trained in the writing of poetry by Chapelle, Chaulieu had thus supplemented what he learned from his master with this great admiration for Horace, especially the Horace of the *Epistles.* His understanding of poetry, however, differed from the conception of Boileau, who had aspired to be the French Horace. The essence of poetry, for Chaulieu, consisted in uniting a facile and natural style with moral and semi-sentimental feelings. He did not believe, though, that there was any mechanical way of achieving the harmony he desired; it depended, rather, upon the delicacy of the ear and was a gift of nature. On the other hand, he did think that the themes of Horace, or Lucretius, or the free-thinking poets who had preceded him could be cultivated. Poetry, for him, thus turned out to be a charming music containing an artificial content and expressing an "aimable" character. It was this complex quality which made Chaulieu's poetry resemble rather closely, although in a lesser key, the poetry of La Fontaine, whom he knew and admired.

Adam, who has written a very perceptive introduction to Chaulieu's poetry, maintains (*Histoire,* V, 306) that it was from Chapelle, his teacher, that he learned that all is vain in man's life—honors, wealth, position—and that its only compensation is the joy of loving, which Chaulieu called "volupté." In reality, as we have seen, this position was held in common by all these seventeenth-century libertine poets. On the other hand, it is true that in Chaulieu there is a peculiarly personal note of melancholy, which arises from awareness of the frailty of human happiness: even the "volupté" which he celebrates flees all too fast, and our pleasures soon abandon us. In face of the destruction of all things in time, the poet counsels us to remain serene in spirit, to withdraw into solitude, to enjoy as much friendship as possible, and to resolve firmly to await the end in peace. In a general way, this attitude is not too unlike Saint-Evremond's, as we shall see.

It is summed up very concisely in the so-called *Trois façons de penser sur la mort*, to which the author alluded in his informal preface and which he had the astuteness to place at the beginning of his collected poems. In the first of these poems, after the fashion of Christians, Chaulieu draws the distinction, as Voltaire did in the *Epître à Uranie*, between the "Dieu vangeur," the "Juge rigoureux" presented by the rigorists whom he rejects, and the "Dieu bienfaisant," the "Dieu pitoyable," whom he accepts (*Œuvres diverses de M. L. de Chaulieu*, Amsterdam, 1733, p. 16):

> Mon cœur à ce portrait ne connaît point encore
> Ce Dieu que je chéris; et celui que j'adore,
> Ai-je dit, et Mon Dieu n'est point un Dieu cruel;
> On ne voit point de sang ruisseler son autel.

Chaulieu inveighs against the superstition imprinted in our hearts by "une faible nourice," who with ghosts and werewolfs, devils and hell, instills fear in us. To the "fantômes vains," "ces enfants de la peur," he opposes his reason:

> Ma raison m'a montré, tant qu'elle a pû paroître,
> Que rien n'est en effet de ce qui ne peut être.

He rejects the notion that God looks with disfavor upon his frailties:

> Je n'ai pu concevoir que mes fragilités
> Ni tous ces vains plaisirs qui passent comme un songe,
> Pussent être l'objet de tes sévérités. . . .

Chaulieu insists upon the pardoning God, the God of pity, who has granted him life by taking him from the bosom of matter. In reality, although he tries to leave the impression that it is the Christian God he is presenting and not the cruel God of the rigorists, the God he actually succeeds in picturing more nearly resembles the deist God, a forgiving, fatherly God who can be worshipped with confidence, free from terrors.

The second poem, after the fashion of deists, counsels the rejection of prejudices and the "imposture des vaines superstitions" fostered by feeble minds, who impute a crime to those who enjoy the good things of this life. The God of the first poem has become now what Pascal called the "Dieu des philosophes": He is a "Dieu moteur de tout," and His existence is proved by the doctrine of final causes. He is also the God of goodness. The poet now feels that good human acts toward one's neighbor are what are morally required of us all. Otherwise, we must enjoy our days as best we can:

> Ainsi on doit passer avec tranquilité
> Les ans que nous départ l'aveugle destinée;
> Et goûter sagement la molle oisiveté
> D'une paresse raisonnée.

Then, when the final moment comes, we can depart from this "triste lieu," confident that we will return into the bosom of nature or into the arms of God.

In the third poem, after the fashion of Epicurus, Chaulieu opposes to the inevitability of death the art of living happily. The poet here counsels a studied reaction to "le néant de la vie." He recalls that he has been brought into this life without having been consulted, that the ruling Powers have fixed the length of his days, and that he will depart without warning or consultation also. He asserts that there is no reason why his wisdom should not find ways to enjoy the life he has been granted. He advises us to steel our souls to the thought of death, which is, after all, only an "éternel repos," "un paisible sommeil," simply the end of life: "Aux pensers de la mort accoutume ton âme." There is nothing to be frightened of in death itself. The horrors of a dark abode, of demons, Hell, and flames, are all false. Death is followed neither by rewards nor by punishments; it is simply the end of our woes. The poet urges, after these "sages réflexions," that we devote ourselves to the enjoyment of "l'erreur des passions" and that we seek those amusements which distract us from our sufferings. Above all, we should await the end quietly, and, when it comes, we should, giving thanks to nature, return to it what we received. This is the lesson of Epicurus, "Cet esprit élevé, qui dans sa noble ardeur / S'envola par delà les murailles du monde," and freed poor mortals from their deathly fear by banishing from this world the gods, falsehood and error.

These are the reflections of the poet whom Voltaire constantly called "aimable." One would hardly consider them profound; and yet, upon second thought, they are probably more humanly profound than they would have been if they had tried to distill the essence of the great philosophies of the day. The themes, after all, are the major themes of Horace and Lucretius, and, if they are not expressed with the impeccable style of the one or the fierce vigor of the other, it is because the poet was living in an age when the pleasures of volupty were worth more than the poetry which celebrated them. Pascal saw this attitude in his predecessor Montaigne and pronounced the words "molle et lâche." There is notwithstanding in this undespairing despair, this constantly differing indifference, this lighthearted way of proffering facile answers to impossibly profound problems—the existence of God, the immortality of the soul, thinking matter, free will and grace, good and evil—a charm which conceals the emptiness of life and the hollowness of the poet (*Œuvres*, 1733, pp. 32-35):

> Volupté, viens à mon secours;
> Toi seule peux de ma vieillesse
> Bannir la fatale tristesse
> Qui noircit la fin de nos jours.
>
> Ainsi puissai-je mollement;
> Et d'une âme toujours égale,
> Profitant de chaque moment,
> Rencontrer mon heure Fatale:
>
> Où content de ne plus souffrir
> Cent maux dont elle nous délivre,
> Je cesse seulement de vivre,
> Sans avoir l'horreur de mourir.
>
> Surtout aimable volupté,
> Répand dans ma douce retraite
> Un esprit de tranquilité
> Qui calme mon âme inquiète:

Through these reflections shines the serenity of an epicurean voluptuary who has cultivated his epicureanism to the point of stoicism and who still in uneasy tranquility awaits the end (*Œuvres*, 1733, p. 49):

> Ainsi, pour éloigner ces vaines rêveries,
> J'examine le cours et l'ordre des saisons;
> Et comment tous les ans, à l'émail des prairies,
> Succèdent les trésors des fruits et des moissons.

Je contemple à loisir cet amas de lumière,
Ce brillant Tourbillon, ce Globe radieux;
Et cherche s'il parcourt en effet sa carrière,
Ou si sans se mouvoir il éclaire les Cieux.

Puis de là tout-à-coup élevant ma pensée
Vers cet Estre, du Monde et maître et Créateur,
Je me ris des erreurs d'une Secte insensée,
Qui croit que le hazard en peut être l'Auteur.

Ainsi coulent mes jours sans soins, loin de l'envie,
Je les vois commencer, et je les vois finir;
Nul remords du passé n'empoisonne ma vie;
Satisfait du présent, je crains peu l'avenir.

One wonders what these ideas and these circumstances might have become in the hands of an excellent poet. There are ways of getting at this question, but, when one is dealing with an excellent poet, usually one relegates problems concerning the history of ideas to a very minor position—rightly so, I think, since the creation of art is a unique and rare event in human life and since ideas do appear inordinately numerous, unorganized, and very often irrelevant. In this particular case, though, where we are dealing with the diffusion of ideas through literary means, it seems advisable that we not avoid an author because he is a "good," indeed, an "excellent" artist.

The general way of regarding the age of Louis XIV, it should be recalled, is to treat it—or, at any rate, the first half of it (1660-1685)—as a hiatus in the development of thought. According to this manner of looking at things, the free-thought of the first part of the century went underground while classicism—which is based on principles of order, restraint, and regularity—reigned supreme. Then, once the great classicists had had their day, free-thinking was resumed, and the preparation of the Enlightenment began. This view, assumed by all those who have undertaken to sketch the origins of the Enlightenment, was best expressed by Hazard at the conclusion of his *Crise de la conscience européenne* (II, 293). Only since 1935, just after Hazard, has there arisen any tendency to question it seriously.

In the first place, the erudite free-thinkers studied so brilliantly by Pintard lived and wrote in the classical period at least into the late seventies, and the works of those who had already disappeared were still being published and read. Furthermore, the secondary literature—the verse of the minor poets, the very popular travel literature, the imaginary utopian novel, the essay—not only continued the free-thought and the philosophic development but actually diffused them more widely and effectively, in *Recueils* and through the social groups, than in the first part of the century. Finally, the great classicists did not escape—nor did they apparently want to escape—this free-thinking movement. Indeed, of the four great ones, two—La Fontaine and Molière—have by many critics been closely identified with it.

The case of La Fontaine is very instructive.[5] We have always been led to believe that his distinguishing traits were naïveté, simplicity, and, above all, sincerity. There are, indeed, those who have stressed that he had, with childish simplicity, confessed all. Much of his charm comes from these confessions: who would ever think of questioning the deep faith of the conclusion of the *Deux Pigeons*, or *La Laitière et le pot au lait*, or many another fable? Practically everyone would agree with Maucroix that La Fontaine was a "bon garçon"—that is, as Gohin explains, "aimable et sympathique." But was he also, as Maucroix said, "fort sage et fort modeste"? Gohin complains that the portraits which Rigaud and the other painters left of La Fontaine are not in agreement. One might say the same about those who have attempted to penetrate his character. Only on one point is there any consensus: La Fontaine would submit to no constraint of any sort, not even to a self-imposed restraint. Clarac, referring to La Fontaine's short stay with the Oratorians, remarks that the strange thing about the episode is not that he so speedily withdrew from the group but that he ever consented to join it in the first place. No one would even dream of expecting La Fontaine to be consistent or well-disciplined; his "free" verses are the best portrait of his character. In all respects, he is the perfect example of Montaigne's definition of man: "Certes c'est un sujet merveilleuse-

<hr>

[5] See esp. A. Adam, *Histoire de la littérature française au XVIIe siècle*, IV, 7-70; H. Busson and F. Gohin, *La Fontaine, Discours à Madame de la Sablière*; F. Gohin, *La Fontaine, Etudes et recherches*, esp. Chaps. III ("La Fontaine et Montaigne"), IV ("La Fontaine et Gassendi"), V ("La Religion de la Fontaine"), and VI ("La Morale des *Fables*"); L. Petit, *La Fontaine et Saint-Evremond*, pp. 187-253; and P. Clarac, *La Fontaine par lui-même*, pp. 117ff.

ment vain, divers, et ondoyant." La Fontaine, in his portrait of himself in *Clymène*, remarked upon both his changeability and the
impossibility of knowing himself:

> Sire, Acanthe est un homme inégal à tel point,
> Que d'un moment à l'autre on ne le connaît point:
> Inégal en amour, en plaisir, en affaire;
> Tantôt gai, tantôt triste; un jour il désespère,
> Un autre jour il croit que la chose ira bien:
> Pour vous en parler franc, nous n'y connoissons rien.

Apparently, the difficulties which he himself experienced have been
noticed by others; Adam judges that La Fontaine, more than anyone, was "divers, secret, et déchiré." In those qualities he greatly
resembled the other great artists of his time, especially Molière and
Racine, and doubtless the three reflected all that was "douloureux"
in that age. It is true that he had some personal peculiarities—tendencies toward nonchalance, laziness, distraction, revery—which cannot often be found in his other contemporaries; they were a part of
his mask, along with a "lovable" disposition, which, he confessed,
embraced everything (". . . il n'est rien / Qui ne me soit souverain
bien, / Jusqu'au sombre plaisir d'un cœur mélancolique") and which
won for him the affection of everyone, whether child or scholar,
who had touched his verses. He was "amiable and charming"; no
one would begrudge him these epithets. And yet we grant them
cheerfully at a distance. Those who knew him more intimately had
other things to say.

There is no doubt, however, about his intellectual capacity or
about his alertness. Adam stresses that he was most attentive to political incidents, but he was just as keen when it came to philosophical matters and sharper still when a moral issue was involved. He
undoubtedly liked the pleasure which came from contemplation of
the simple things of life—flowers, odors, the peaceful sky, and,
above all, the wiles of his animals. Yet he did not rest content with
mere contemplation, for, as Taine has shown in his magnificent
study, this simple soul penetrated with unfailing accuracy and an
uncompromising irony the resemblances between the animal and
the human world. If it is true that he had at his command only a
minimum of Greek, it is also true, as Olivet testified, that he read his

Plato and his Plutarch "la plume à la main." In addition, he was remarkably well versed in Descartes as well as in Gassendi, as we shall see. He knew all the epicurean poets from Théophile to Chaulieu, a fact that does not appear so surprising once we realize that he seemed to be acquainted with all the poets from Homer to those of his own day. He was a faithful reader of Rabelais, but he was equally well acquainted with Boccaccio, not to mention all the fabulists who flourished from Aesop's time to his own—Phaedrus, Nevelet, Haudent, and many others.

Still, with all this learning, it is not easy to fit him into the intellectual currents of his time. He was a member of the Duchess of Bouillon's salon, where so many of the libertine poets gathered and where he is thought to have met Bernier. He was an enthusiastic follower of Molière after the presentation of the *Fâcheux*. He was on intimate terms with Saint-Evremond, with whom he carried on a regular correspondence. As we shall see, no one resembled Saint-Evremond more closely than La Fontaine so far as their opinions were concerned. He read avidly Rabelais, Marot, Bonaventure des Périers, and Théophile de Viau, from whom all the epicurean poets were descended. He was sheltered by Mme de la Sablière, who was interested in the exact sciences and whose uncle, Dr. Menjot, as well as Bernier, was in constant attendance at her group's meetings. The distinguishing characteristics of Mme de la Sablière's circle were its anti-Cartesianism and its interest, through Bernier, in Gassendi. Adam has noted that it was resolutely opposed to Christian stoicism and in favor of epicureanism, though not, of course, the debauched variety; all of the members of the group, even, or perhaps I had better say, especially Ninon de Lenclos and her correspondent Saint-Evremond, believed in the restricted happiness which comes from a moderate use of the passions. We should add that La Fontaine, along with these companions, especially Saint-Evremond, was an ardent admirer of Petronius and Ariosto and a devotee, as everybody in the seventeenth century was, of Horace. He knew his Lucretius well and became a worshipper of Ovid.

The result was a modest epicureanism, a skeptical, ironic approach to the organization of society, and a disarming gentleness in dealing with some of life's profoundest problems. It is certainly not this which gives us the greatest pleasure in reading the *Fables*, but, whether we like it or not, they are filled with social and political satire, to a point where Taine could see in them nothing more than a full portrait of seventeenth-century France. It was not, for La Fontaine, a question of reforming this society; rather, he seemed to take the stand that the wise man will arrange his life beyond the reach of society. It was a position like Montaigne's, so aptly put by Strowski: "Le sage ne vit que pour soi." For La Fontaine, like Montaigne, lent but did not give himself to society. His morality was realistic and lucid, as was that of all the libertines and Jansenists. He nonetheless counseled a withdrawal, an external submission, though without sacrifice of the internal freedom of the spirit. If he refused to become, as we say these days, "engagé," it was because he was convinced that our "engagement" would add nothing to the "branle du monde." He felt, moreover, that our relationship with nature is one of misunderstanding and ignorance. In the *Astrologue qui se laisse tomber dans un puits*, he points out that, although we may think we understand the mystery of life, all we really know is that we are here to live, not to know. The order and stability of the universe are established by laws, but we shall never completely comprehend them.

If the *Fables* of 1668 were social and political, those of 1678-1679 became more and more philosophical. Adam has stressed that their full import cannot be grasped unless they are viewed in the context of the philosophical controversy of the time. The center of this dispute was the salon of Mme de la Sablière, with Bernier, Menjot and the others, where the quarrel between Descartes and Gassendi broke out anew. There was already under way a full flowering of Gassendism. Bernier presented, between 1675 and 1678, his eight-volume abridgment of Gassendi's philosophy; a M. de Launay opened up a series of public lectures on Gassendi and published an *Introduction à la philosophie* and *Essais de la physique universelle*, which apparently found their way to Locke's library. Locke himself was in Paris at the time. It has been noted that the last six books of the *Fables* talk rather frequently about atoms and the vacuum.

The quarrel between Gassendists and Cartesians turned once more upon the problem of animal souls.[6] From 1672 on, there had been a

---

[6] See L. Rosenfield, *From Beast-machine to Man-machine*.

long line of works treating the subject: G. Pardies's *Discours de la connaissance des bêtes* (1672), Du Hamel's *De mente humana* (1672) and *De corpore animato* (1673), Dilly's *De l'âme des bêtes* (1676), and Lamy's *Discours anatomiques* (1675).

La Fontaine's first reaction to the Cartesian doctrine, expressed in his *Les Souris et le Chat-huant*, was one of complete opposition. This was, of course, a perfectly natural response for a fabulist who saw all kinds of analogies between the thoughts and actions of animals and those of humans. The very basis of La Fontaine's art, after all, lies in the identification of man and animal: that is, what powers of thought man has, animals have also; what social qualities man has, animals have too; what diverse traits of character man has, animals have likewise. The whole art of the fable is built upon resemblances between man and beast, and the conclusion—whatever characterizes man characterizes the beast also—is perfectly natural and logical. If man has a soul connected with thought, so does the beast. This belief was all the stronger in France—and, indeed, in Europe—because of the tradition. All of fable literature depended upon it. Moreover, Montaigne gave it, in the *Apology*, a complete backing. His whole argument against the exceptional powers of man's reason is founded upon a comparison between the cleverness and superiority of animals and the stupidities and limitations of man. The public could well appreciate the paradox, all the more since it had a particular moral value and received more or less official confirmation from scholastic thinking. The scholastics, indeed, granted to the animal a soul, which is the principle of life, albeit a mortal one inferior to the human soul. Montaigne's tendency to equate this soul with instinct and man's soul with intelligence, and the conclusion that the beast can do more, and do better, by instinct than man can do by intelligence, certainly suggested that, the animal soul being more efficient than the human, there was small justification for assigning permanence to the one and not to the other. Indeed, the paradox could be, and was, carried further. Animals had not been guilty of original sin, their way of knowing had not been perverted by their conduct. From these observations, it was easy to infer: (1) there was no real basis to the belief that man is more intelligent than the beast; (2) there was less basis still to the belief that reason is superior to instinct, even in man; and (3) it was manifestly unjust to grant immortality to the human soul and refuse it to the animal soul. These inferences led naturally to two conclusions: man would be better advised to trust his animal instincts than his understanding, his ratiocination, his logic, and his will; and, since animals are denied immortality, there can be no reason for assuming that man has an immortal soul either. These conclusions drawn from inferences based on a paradox are, humanly speaking, true conclusions. The only way one can call their validity into question is by using the very instrument which has been shown to be unworthy of trust, that is to say, the human mind, or by appealing to faith, a right which the animal can claim as well as man, or, lastly, by distinguishing between the animal soul and the human soul on the basis of their different natures. In this way, the simple discussion of a moot point lay at the foundation of the problems of knowledge and of the soul's immortality, two of the most important issues of the time. Eventually, even before the end of the century, the controversy involved the whole philosophy of materialism.[7]

For the time being, though, the major attention was given to the making of distinctions. Descartes inaugurated the whole movement with his remark in the *Cogitationes* (1619): "From the very perfection of animal actions we suspect that they do not have freewill." His initial public statements, however, occurred in the *Discours*. There he treated man's bodily machine as an organism which functions in a purely involuntary way, having no other source of movement than the heat of the heart, causing the blood and animal spirits to circulate through the system. Descartes added that the body of an animal operates similarly, so that a machine in the shape of an animal would be indistinguishable from the beast itself. Descartes explicitly granted sagacity to animals and specific talents, though he withheld from them both speech and reason: ". . . they are destitute of reason and . . . it is nature which acts in them according to the disposition of their organs." The conclusion he drew was that this lack of speech and of reason proves their mechanical nature and that this mechanistic quality, in turn, proves the lack

---

[7] A. Koyré, *Gassendi, 1592-1655, sa vie et son œuvre*, p. 61, notes that "il me paraît certain que, grâce à Bernier et à son abrégé, l'honnête homme de la fin du XVIIe siècle était beaucoup plus souvent gassendiste que cartésien." Koyré finds that Descartes's influence on his contemporaries was not very great.

of any soul, which, by definition, cannot be drawn from matter, extension, body, and which is, in fact, "of a nature wholly independent of the body." Froidmont immediately observed in a letter to Plemp that what Descartes said about circulation from the heat of the heart in animals could be applied just as easily to the human soul. Later, around 1640, Mersenne asked Descartes how animals can feel pain if they have no soul; Descartes replied that they in effect do not feel pain. Here he made the very important distinction between thinking and feeling: the former is the ability of thought to reflect upon itself, the latter is only the mechanical ability to perceive. Implied in this distinction is the view that perception is mechanical, while consciousness is reflection. This stand Descartes expressed more clearly in his reply to the objection that Hobbes had made to the *Méditations*. There Descartes pointed out that Hobbes, unlike himself, included as thought sensory perception unmixed with self-conscious reflection. As a matter of fact, the *Méditations* elicited a whole body of objections to Descartes's theory of animal mechanism. Arnauld, for instance, objected on general grounds. More particularly, Gassendi, like Hobbes, refused to accept Descartes's definition of thought. Essentially, Gassendi believed that thought is present in both man and beast but that the degree of thought in each is different. Many of the writers of the "objections" sided with Gassendi against Descartes in this matter. As a result, this criticism prompted Descartes to make his strongest statement upon animal mechanism: "However, not only have I asserted plainly that animals do not possess thought, as is here assumed, but I have given a most stringent proof of this, a proof which no one has hitherto refuted" (see E. Haldane and G. Ross, *The Philosophical Works of Descartes*, 1912, II, 244). Further, he stated even as late as 1648 to H. More that animals are lacking in speech—"not a single brute speaks"—and that it is in this difference that the true distinction between man and beast resides. Descartes specified particularly that he was not denying to animals either life (which he attributed to the heat of the heart) or sense (which he considered a simple bodily mechanism).

It is not our purpose to trace the various ramifications of the argument as it developed from Descartes's stand until it became a central preoccupation with La Fontaine. Mrs. Rosenfield has given us an ample bibliography of the movement and a very clear presentation of the various points of view. We are concerned, rather, with the role which the problem played in the development of thought and the way in which it was diffused through La Fontaine to Voltaire. We should recall that the controversy was particularly lively between 1672 and 1682, when the works of Pardies, Du Hamel, Dilly, Darmanson, and Lamy mentioned above were the centers of attention. The stand taken by each of these writers was conditioned by the general philosophy they represented. Pardies, a Jesuit with a predilection for scholasticism, offered a compromise between the positions of Montaigne and Descartes; he granted to beasts a "connaissance sensible" but refused them a "connaissance spirituelle." Du Hamel likewise granted them a "connaissance inconsciente," although he insisted more than Pardies did upon the distinction between perception and thought. Darmanson, as we have already seen, made the logical deduction that what we say about beasts must apply equally well to man. Gassendi had pointed out to Descartes in his *Objectiones* that this would inevitably be done. As for Gassendi himself, he had devoted a long section in his *Syntagma* to the subject. Briefly, his whole argument boiled down to the attribution to animals of a "material" soul, which he defined as a soul intermediate between matter and thought. This "material" soul, in Gassendi's opinion, was derived from the highly refined portions of his atoms.

It appears that La Fontaine was well acquainted with all these statements. Professors Jasinski and Busson in a series of articles[8] have discussed at great length La Fontaine's familiarity with them. Jasinski, in particular, shows that the poet was closely familiar with the Latin wording of long passages of the *Syntagma*, while Busson indicates that he was fully as well acquainted with long passages from Pardies's *Discours*. They disagree a little when it comes to deciding which writer should be given as the primary source; but they do agree (along with Gohin, also) that La Fontaine knew them all, as well as the points of view of his close contemporaries— Bernier and Dr. Menjot, for instance. Bernier, whose *Abrégé de la philosophie de Gassendi* was beginning to appear at this particular

[8] R. Jasinski, "Sur la philosophie de La Fontaine dans les livres VII à XII des *Fables*"; H. Busson, "La Fontaine et l'âme des bêtes."

time, not only was aware of Gassendi's explanation but had a point of view of his own, granting to animals a "connaissance imparfaite et grossière." Dr. Menjot, for his part, spoke of a "connaissance approchante du raisonnement." By and large, La Fontaine seems to have modified his view with the aid of Gassendi, who attributed to animals "quelque espèce de raisonnement" derived from their imagination. La Fontaine was, however, much more specific, for he granted them "le sentiment, la mémoire, fonctions corporelles" and "de l'esprit" and "la pensée" analogous to those of a child. The crux of all these distinctions, of course, resided in the general opinion that man possesses the capacity of reflection, that is, the ability of thought to turn back upon itself. All agreed that animals do not have this capacity and that humans do. Simply stated: "nous connaissons que nous connaissons."

La Fontaine summed up his views upon animal automatism in his *Discours à Mme de la Sablière.* The present way of interpreting these views is to note that he had shifted his position from what it had been at the conclusion of *Les Souris et le Chat-huant* (1675). There he very explicitly stated, after having related the incident in the fable, that "Cet oiseau raisonnait, il faut qu'on le confesse." He then defied any Cartesian to show that this event was the sole result of the action of a series of mechanical springs such as one would expect to find in a timepiece, the comparison being precisely Descartes's metaphor. La Fontaine concluded, rather categorically, that

> Si ce n'est pas là raisonner,
> La raison m'est chose inconnue.

To this he added, however, a note which is certainly as important as the fable itself: "Ceci n'est point une Fable, et la chose quoique merveilleuse et presque incroyable, est véritablement arrivée." What this means is that Bernier, in telling the story, had treated it, not as a piece of fiction, but as a real event. If it were mere fiction, all that would be required of it would be verisimilitude, and any conclusions would be based upon a likelihood, upon the appearance of things, upon the illusion of truth. But, as an event in the real world, it was subject to the demand laid upon any scientific experiment: the deductions drawn from the observations must have scientific validity. La Fontaine, however, continued his note: "J'ay peut-estre porté trop loin la prévoyance de ce hibou; car je ne prétends pas établir dans les bêtes un progrès de raisonnement tel que celuy-ci." What this means is that, after having offered the real experiment and asserted the scientific validity of the observation, the scientist La Fontaine withdrew and left the field to the poet La Fontaine, who had no pretensions whatever of insisting upon the details of the scientific conclusion. But there is still more to the note: ". . . mais ces exagérations sont permises à la poésie, surtout dans la manière d'écrire dont je me sers." This means, I suppose, that poets have to be liars, even when dealing with a scientific matter, in order to tell the truth. This is a clear-cut illustration of Descartes's own theory that poets can say things much better than philosophers because of their intuition and the force of their imagination. La Fontaine was merely claiming his right to express himself in this way, not modestly bowing out. He wanted it understood, though, that he was speaking with the authority of a scientist while claiming the exemption of a poet.

This is his position in the epistle to Mme de la Sablière which, significantly, he entitled *Discours*. This is not a fable either, although it is filled with fables. We should point out that we do not know the exact date of either poem, or even the relative dates of the two, although, in the arrangement which La Fontaine gave Books IX, X, and XI, the *Discours* (in IX) precedes the Fable (XI). This perhaps, is of some importance as far as a final statement of La Fontaine's position is concerned, particularly since *Les Souris et le Chat-huant* is the last fable of Book XI, coming just before the Epilogue. However, it is not necessary to push this point, because, in spite of appearances, there seems to be no justification for believing that the conclusions of the two poems differ.

The *Discours*, immediately after the introductory compliment to the lady, and having made the distinction between "la bagatelle" (poetry) and science, promises the same mixture of poetry and philosophy as that which appeared in the fable. This time La Fontaine arranges his argument in true philosophical fashion, beginning with a clear exposition of the Cartesian doctrine. This is followed by a set of clear-cut laboratory cases—the deer, the mother partridge, the beavers, and the Polish boubaks—all of them arranged scientifically, leading to a scientific conclusion. La Fontaine, the poet, then adds a fable, followed by his poetic conclusion.

The poet gives a fine presentation of a "certain philosophy" which others call "new" but which he calls "subtle, attractive, and bold." They say that animals are machines, moved by springs, having no freedom of choice, no feeling, no soul, but only a body. In their view, a beast resembles a clock which moves in measured steps, blind and aimless, in which one wheel moves another and that another, until finally the clock strikes. That is more or less what happens to an animal: the external object strikes a nerve which communicates with another, the sense picks up the communication, the impression is made. But how is it made? They say through mechanical necessity, without involving the passions or the will. The animal is stirred by what the ordinary man calls joy, sorrow, love, pleasure, pain; but they say that interpretation is not correct. What is the animal then? A clock. And what are we? Something else.

Here is how Descartes, that mortal man whom the pagans would have made a god, explains the phenomena: man has the gift of thought and knows that he thinks, whereas animals, even if they should think, could not turn the thought back upon the object or their own thinking. Descartes, however, denies even that animals think. "Vous n'estes point embarrassé de le croire, ni moy," La Fontaine adds. Still, there are cases which can be cited which indicate otherwise. La Fontaine here offers (1) "le vieux Cerf," who forces a young deer to take his place and uses hundreds of other tricks to elude the hunter and his dogs, (2) the mother partridge, who limps away from her defenseless young in order to draw the attention of dogs and hunter and, when she has done so and the young are out of danger, flies away, and (3) beavers, who have a society more highly organized than the primitive savages living in their land and who can build dams, bridges, and houses while the inhabitants "Vivent ainsi qu'aux premiers temps / Dans une ignorance profonde." La Fontaine draws a tentative conclusion at this point:

> Que ces castors ne soient qu'un corps vide d'esprit,
> Jamais on ne pourra m'obliger à le croire.

Then he hurries on to give his fourth example: the animals in Poland, who from one generation to another wage bloody wars against their enemies on the other side of the border—wars that are conducted according to well-laid plans.

La Fontaine yields the floor now to "le rival d'Epicure" (Descartes) and asks what his comment would be in these cases? The answer is clear: nature accomplishes all these feats by means of springs, memory is corporeal, nothing more is required. Images follow one another along the same paths without any need for thought. We, however, are determined by will, not by the external object and not by instinct. We possess an intelligent principle, distinct from the body, which is the supreme arbiter of all our movements. But, the poet asks, how do the bodies react? The instrument obeys the hand, but who guides the hand? What guides the planets? Is it some angel? What is certain is that some spirit lives in us and moves all our springs. The impression is made, but only man has it. But, says La Fontaine, how do you explain this fable? And he relates *Les deux rats, le renard, et l'œuf.*

The poet is now prepared to give his general conclusion:

> Qu'on m'aille soutenir après un tel récit,
> Que les bêtes n'ont point d'esprit.

He confesses that, were he the master, he would grant them the same amount of intelligence as children. They think, although they do not know they are thinking. He would allow them, not an advanced reason, but at least a reason superior to a set of springs. He would take matter and refine it, and would make it capable of feeling and judging, albeit imperfectly. To humans he would give two souls, one like the animal soul and the other a spiritual soul:

> Et ce trésor à part créé
> Suivrait parmi les airs les célestes phalanges,
> Entreroit dans un poinct sans en être pressé,
> Ne finirait jamais quoyqu'ayant commencé,
> Choses réelles quoy qu'étranges.

Being much stronger, man's reason would, he concludes, be more able to pierce the darkness of matter which envelops the other, less perfect soul.

La Fontaine's defense of the animal soul against Cartesian automatism and, indeed, against scholasticism once again brings to our attention his libertinism. Gohin has traced his relationship with Montaigne and Gassendi. Jasinski has drawn up a list of astonishing parallels between the poet and Bernier. Busson has shown how the author of the *Fables* was connected not only with Pardies and Du Hamel, who are really not suspected too much of libertinism, but also Guillaume Lamy, who was a follower of Gassendi and Epicurus. Petit has described the close relationship that existed between the fabulist and Saint-Evremond. Finally, La Fontaine's presence in the more or less libertine salons of the end of the century would lead us at least to suspect that we are dealing with a free-thinker.

It is well to note that, starting around 1670 and continuing into the eighteenth century, there was a revival of interest in Epicurus through a revival of interest in Gassendi. It is perhaps unwise to speak of a revival of Gassendi; at the present time we have sufficient documentation to indicate the continued influence of the *Syntagma* from its publication in 1656 on. Undoubtedly, as Adam has argued, this influence was felt among the scholars of Europe, not among the people at large. Around 1672, however, this influence began to spread among the general public. The chief cause of the diffusion was Bernier's *Abrégé de la philosophie de Gassendi*, published in eight volumes by 1678. Now that the ideas of the philosopher had become available in French, they seem to have enjoyed a rather wide circulation among the literary circles of the time. Epicurus, Democritus, and Lucretius, who were the sources of Gassendi's philosophy, also profited from the diffusion. La Fontaine was not the only poet to take a part in the movement; in fact, all the poets at the Duchesse of Bouillon's and the Duke of Vendôme's, especially Chaulieu and La Fare, were its fomenters. We have already indicated, though, that the development of "poésie libre" throughout the century, since the time of Théophile de Viau, was connected with the Epicurus-Lucretius current. What we have not pointed out is that, although there was a filiation between these poets and Epicurus and Lucretius, it is often very difficult to distinguish the moral aspects of epicureanism from the scientific aspects. Indeed, so strong was the classical influence in this "classical" period that Democritus often played as important a role as Epicurus and Horace had as much significance as Lucretius.

One of the lesser known contributors to this movement was the doctor Guillaume Lamy, who practiced his art in Paris from 1672 to 1682, just after Guy Patin. Lamy's first book, *De principiis rerum libro tres, in quorum primo proponuntur et refelluntur principia Peripateticum; in secundo Cartesiana philosophandi methodus atque de rerum principiis opinio rejiciuntur; in tertio Epicuri principia paululum emendata nova methodo stabiliuntur* (Paris, 1669), placed him squarely on the side of the free-thinkers, opposed to Descartes, whom he, like Voltaire, called a poet, not a philosopher. He was likewise dead set against all authority and tradition and, as can be seen in his lengthy title, closely allied to Epicurus. He accepted the Democritean dogma of atoms, declaring them indivisible; in short, he united Gassendi with Epicurus, Democritus, and Lucretius. He finally chose as his ultimate guide Gassendi, but with no great enthusiasm for Gassendi's defense of Christian dogma, and in his second book, the *Discours anatomiques* (1675), he espoused pure materialism. Bayle eventually made use of the work in his articles on Blondel, Patin, Anaxagoras, Ovid, and Castellan. Lamy was clearly anti-finalist and, in his study upon the soul, entirely epicurean. He nevertheless added thereto a discussion of the animism of the Stoics, which the sixteenth-century Italians had adopted along with the theory of a world-soul from Plato and Protagoras. But he rejected these theories. The theory he considered most satisfactory was the "subtle spirit" of rarefied atoms proposed by Gassendi: for those who wish to distinguish, between the souls of animals and the souls of men, a second soul for men which "la foi nous enseigne . . . immatérielle et immortelle, qui sort immédiatement des mains de la Divinité . . . , c'est elle qui est le principe de nos raisonnemens."

La Fontaine, who was familiar with Lamy, Du Hamel, Pardies, and Nicolas Denys, was also intimately associated with Bernier (indeed, they lived together at Mme de la Sablière's) and thus derived his own free-thinking both directly and indirectly from Gassendi. There can be no doubt, as Jasinski has said, that Gassendism constituted a sort of crossroads at the juncture of the seventeenth and eighteenth centuries. As a philosophy, it stressed the necessity of having a body of thought which could be reconciled with the Christian religion and which would, at the same time, insist upon human weaknesses and a morality of striving, since all are affected by original sin. But it expressed confidence, too, in the senses, in the physical body, the goodness of nature, happiness, and progress. In its development it had taken an anti-Cartesian position and insisted, in the rehabilitation of Epicurus, upon an atomistic universe containing a vacuum. Finally, it preached a hedonistic morality.

La Fontaine adhered publicly to Gassendism. In *Démocrite et les Abdéritains*, he states his belief that nature is composed of atoms; there, too, he accepts the vacuum as possible. Allusion is likewise made to atoms in *L'Horoscope*, where the poet talks of "des vides sans fin." He remarks upon the infinite plurality of worlds, too, in *Démocrite*. There is no doubt, then, that La Fontaine adopted without reservation the atomism of Gassendi.

In addition, Gassendi maintained that each world possesses its own soul and that each object (sun, moon, earth, precious stone, plant) is animated. Thus, as Gassendi explained, it was perfectly correct to talk about the souls of metals, plants, or stars, and even about a universal soul. La Fontaine also accepted this view in principle. In the *Discours*, he writes: "Cependant, la plante respire." And, in the *Discours à M. le duc de la Rochefoucauld*, he adds:

> La Nature
> A mis dans chaque créature
> Quelque grain d'une masse où puisent les esprits.

Gassendi, however, had to make a distinction between all these souls and the superior human soul. This he did by designating the human soul as "l'âme raisonnable" and all the others as inferior souls provided with differing degrees of desires and feeling, but of corporeal essence and consequently perishable. La Fontaine adopted this way of separating the corporeal souls from the spiritual souls. He even accepted Gassendi's description of how the corporeal souls are formed from the rarefied atoms.

Gassendi conceived of God as dominating all these atoms and souls. The proof of His existence is drawn from the marvels of nature. La Fontaine gives a specific case, not without humor, in *Le Gland et le Citrouille*:

> Dieu fait bien ce qu'il fait. Sans en chercher la preuve
> En tout cet univers, et l'aller parcourant,
> Dans les citrouilles je la treuve.

Having organized an atomistic universe and put in charge a providential Deity, Gassendi then explained the nature of man. He subscribed to the theory of the *tabula rasa*, that nothing exists in the understanding which is not first in the senses. He admitted the objectivity of sensitive qualities, but he believed nonetheless in an immaterial principle which dominates the facts of the senses. La Fontaine in the *Animal dans la lune* writes:

> Mon âme, en toute occasion,
> Développe le vrai caché sous l'apparence. . . .
> Mes yeux, moyennant ce secours,
> Ne me trompent jamais en me mentant toujours.

It was his answer to those who said that the senses could not be trusted as a guide to truth: in the final analysis, it is the reason which decides, although not without some collaboration between the reason and the senses.

Gassendi proclaimed the right of every man to happiness, but he prudently observed that religious felicity is superior to ordinary enjoyment and that an absolute happiness is impossible in this world. It behooves us, therefore, to assure ourselves of all the joys we can achieve. For that purpose he proscribes a severe morality and urged instead a "sagesse souriante." La Fontaine's *Fables* are full of this counsel. In *Le Loup et le chasseur*, for instance, he writes:

> L'homme, sourd à ma voix comme à celle du sage,
> Ne dira-t-il jamais: "C'est assez, jouissons"?
> —Hâte-toi, mon ami, tu n'as pas tant à vivre.
> Je te rebats ce mot, car il vaut tout un livre:
> Jouis.—Je le ferai.—Mais quand donc?—Dès demain.
> —Eh! mon ami, la mort te peut prendre en chemin:
> Jouis dès aujourd'hui. . . .

Voltaire is the heir to all these free-thinking poets. He repeats their themes: the inevitability of death, the mortality of the soul, the feebleness of human reason, the hopelessness of persecution, the necessity for human happiness, such as it is, and the desire for tolerance. He adopts all their tones: a mild and gentle resignation to the ennuis of existence, a modest seeking after pleasure while it is still possible, a satiric approach to human follies, a skeptical acceptance of the passing of all things. He mixes, as they do, the attitude of

Horace with that of Epicurus, with that of Seneca, and with that of Lucretius. He imbibes the spirit of his ancestors, particularly Montaigne, Saint-Evremond, and La Fontaine. It is hardly fair to speak of Voltaire's philosophical position at this time. What characterizes his poetry is rather a set of stylized attitudes toward life, taking their origin in certain classical poets and expressing themselves in the poetic themes of his free-thinking predecessors.

4. POETRY AND ANTI-POETRY

IT IS EASY to see that Voltaire had appeared upon the poetic stage at a moment in which all sorts of discussions concerning the art of poetry were taking place. There was under way a total re-evaluation of the poetic act itself, most fully expressed in the quarrel between the ancients and the moderns.[9] Involved in that quarrel were (1) the authority of the ancients' works of art, (2) the validity of rules drawn from those works to serve as guides to contemporary artists, (3) the relationships between the poet and his time, (4) the necessity for the poet to express the spirit of his time, but also (5) his desire to express himself, his intuition, his imagination, his inner sense of beauty, and (6), most important of all, the questions of what constitutes taste, what justifies a change in taste, and what role taste should play in creating and judging the poetic act. Simply put, the quarrel posed the problem of the opposition between the aesthetics of antiquity and modern rationalism, between the necessity of rules and the rights of the imagination, between the validity of reason and the spontaneity of taste, and, finally, between the geometrician and the poet.

The quarrel, for all its abstractness, embraced three solid issues, each of which possessed a unity of its own: (1) the relative merits of poetry and prose, (2) of ancient art and modern art, and (3) of the ancient epic and the desire for the creation of a modern epic. Into each of these issues was injected a discussion of the relative merits of reason and imagination. In short, the whole field of literature was concerned with three oppositions: ancient versus modern, imagination versus reason, poetry versus prose.

The concept which dominated the quarrel was change. From this concept was derived the conviction that, to be true, the poet has to conform to his time, not to a distant past. It was readily admitted that Homer had done this, but it was pointed out that Homer's time was very different from the age of Louis XIV. Between the two periods had come a whole long line of discoveries—gunpowder, the printing press, the astrolabe, and myriad others—which had

[9] See H. Rigault, *Histoire de la querelle des anciens et des modernes*; H. Gillot, *La Querelle des anciens et des modernes en France*; G. Lanson, *Histoire de la littérature française*; W. Folkierski, *Entre le classicisme et le romantisme*.

changed the world. Inventions had brought about new ways of living and new insights into nature, had given rise to new ways of thinking, new thoughts, new methods, a new morality. If the Greeks were brutal in their wars, it was because the age in which Homer lived was a barbaric age. If the morality of the *Iliad* was coarse, it was because the age was coarse. What had made tremendous strides since those days was reason, both in the methods whereby it learned to penetrate the secrets of nature and in the many ways in which it experienced, analyzed, and structured all phenomena. Moreover, the ancients, for all their poetic beauties, had been surpassed by modern poets. Coupled with the sense of change, then, was this pride in present-day achievements which had been made possible by the development of the human intelligence.

Thus, along with the concept of change came the worship of reason. It was proclaimed that, having liberated man's thought through the Cartesian method, reason would now liberate literature. We must recognize, it was urged, that antiquity represents the childhood of art, while modern times represent its maturity. Inventions in art are important, but development of those creations is more important still. No one seems to have condemned the naïveté of Voltaire when he hypothesized that, if Sophocles had lived in the age of Louis XIV, he would have been a superb dramatist and would have avoided all his dramatic errors. It was a commonly held opinion about all the ancients that it was their misfortune to have arrived too soon in the world to achieve greatness. La Motte sounded the note this way: "*L'Iliade* me paraît aussi éloignée de la perfection que l'auteur était propre à l'atteindre, s'il eût été placé dans les bons siècles." The prerequisite, of course, for reaching this perfection was, as Fontenelle pointed out, "la manière de raisonner." Already the formula was being developed that what one thinks is what one says, and does, and is.

In this way, the pride of present-day achievement expressed itself by celebrating the superiority of reason. It was this confidence which led to geometry in literature. In the terms of Boileau's doctrine, reason controls literature; in terms of geometry, reason is the inspiration of literature. It was now believed that reason gives the rule, the rule produces the work, and the work pleases—hence, that a strict relationship exists between reason, rules, the work, and the pleasing effect. There was thought to be a similar relationship with utility: the work pleases because it is useful, morally useful. According to the classical doctrine, reason deduces the rules from the great works of antiquity; now it was judged permissible to deduce new rules from old rules. Gravina described the procedure in a passage quoted by Naves (*Goût*, p. 16): "la raison poétique dont je traite, selon laquelle je rapporte la poésie grecque et ses règles à une idée éternelle de nature, peut concourir aussi à former de nouvelles règles."

There is some indication, however, that the intention of the writers was not to advocate the autonomy of reason in the poetic act. It was not planned that reason should be opposed, for instance, to imagination. La Motte defined an "enthousiasme réglé" in such a way that reason was understood as being an aid to enthusiasm: "un enthousiasme réglé est comme ces douces vapeurs qui ne portent qu'assez d'esprits au cerveau pour rendre l'imagination féconde, et qui laissent toujours le jugement en état de faire, de ses saillies, un choix judicieux et agréable" (quoted by Naves, *Goût*, p. 17). Marivaux spoke of a "désordre toujours sage." What occurred was the rise of the conviction that the science of letters would benefit the art of literature. In reality, it merely opened the way for an attack against the poetic art. At first, for example, it was discovered that Homer's comparisons detract from the central subject; then it was suggested that all ornaments depreciate a work of art. Saint-Evremond actually advised replacing them with thoughts. Then came the grand offensive against Homer led by La Motte, who condemned his "merveilleux," his gods, his heroes, his repetitions, and his style. La Motte drew from his condemnation an anti-poetic attitude: the sounds of a language are indifferent in poetry, it is the sense which attracts. Ideas are what give pleasure; what one seeks is "précision, clarté, agrément." In the face of this doctrine, Homer became completely discredited, and, with Homer, poetry itself was threatened.

The movement had been prepared over a long period of time: Naves quotes a debate between prose and poetry which dates from 1663. Boileau's "épître" to Molière stressed the difficulties of according rime and reason, while Fontenelle showed a skeptical indifference to poetry and eloquence in comparison with philosophy. Then came the treatises attacking poetry. Lefèvre's *De futilitate poetices* accused the art of both futility and immorality. It is futile, he said, because it cannot handle important subjects. He concluded that the cult of form injures the seriousness of the subject-matter. Le Clerc, in his *Parrhasiana*, charged poetry with falsehood, on the ground that it cannot be precise, clear, or true. Even Fénelon was persuaded that "la rime gêne plus qu'elle n'orne des vers." La Motte attempted a tragedy in prose and wrote an ode in prose. He commended, a bit maliciously, Mme Dacier's translation of Homer because it was in prose. Marivaux lauded La Motte because his style was not in his expression but in the ideas which he expressed. Fontenelle judged that a "poète si peu frivole [as La Motte], si fort de choses ne pouvait pas être un poète." De Pons declared that "l'art des vers est un art frivole," while Du Cestre d'Auvigny asserted that poetry is nothing but a "ridiculous arrangement of words."

The leading spirit of the crusade against poetry was beyond a doubt Houdar de la Motte, who was all the more effective because he was so eminently reasonable. La Motte wrote a *Discours sur la poésie* and a *Discours sur Homère*, which, along with his *Réflexions sur la critique*, contained the corps of his doctrine. In his opinion, poetry is differentiated from ordinary discourse first of all by a measured arrangement of words, to which are added fiction and figures of speech. The aim of all discourse being to make one's self understood, poetry is naturally defective in this respect, since it imposes a constraint which handicaps the clarity of expression. Moreover, it requires more effort and time to compose than the ordinary manner of speech. La Motte did not accord it any special merit either in revealing beauty or in teaching morality. In his opinion, it is equally apt to teach morality as to foster immorality. In one respect, it is naturally deficient, since it demands a constant use of the imagination rather than a "jugement sûr." He noted that it is filled with "images vives et détaillées" but that the reasonings in it are rare and superficial. This feature he attributed to the fact that its sole aim is to please by imitation. Although he granted that the first philosophers were poets, he denied the implication that poetry is in any way essential to philosophy. Enthusiasm he defined as a "chaleur d'imagination." He insisted that it should be guided by reason—the result being what he called an "enthousiasme réglé" (*Œuvres*, Paris, 1754, I, Part I, 28). It is by this mechanism, he claimed, that the poet attains the necessary precision, clarity, and truth.

La Motte set forth in the *Réflexions* a defense of this point of view: "L'esprit géométrique vaut bien l'esprit commentateur. Un géomètre judicieux ne parle que des matières qu'il entend: il examine les choses par les principes qui leur sont propres; il ne confond point l'arbitraire et l'essentiel; en un mot, il apprécie tout et range tout dans son ordre. Il n'y a point de matière qui ne soit sujette à la plus exacte discussion; l'art poétique même a ses axiomes, ses théorèmes, ses corollaires, ses démonstrations" (*Œuvres*, 1754, III, 162). In other words, just as Spinoza could arrange philosophy *more geometrico*, the critic could so arrange the poetic art. La Motte maintained that sound has no importance in poetry, that ideas alone are the source of our pleasure or displeasure. What the poet should seek is precision, clarity; what he should produce is "agrément," not harmony. What the reader seeks is the reasonable; everything else is superfluous. It is on these grounds that La Motte condemned Homer. Even though he translated or, rather, "adapted" him, he nonetheless considered Homer's gods immoral and his heroes inconsistent chatterboxes. In his eyes, Homer was repetitive, interminable in his descriptions, monotonous in his speeches, and the *Iliad* totally incoherent.

Voltaire protested vigorously against this geometrizing of poetry, especially in the 1730 preface to the *Œdipe*. While conceding, as Boileau had tacitly done in his "épître" to Molière, that rules in poetry are a constraint, he maintained—contrary to La Motte and the whole group of geometricians—that this constraint produces a beauty and elegance of expression which adds to the content of the work. He described poetry as "le charme de l'harmonie chantante qui naît d'une mesure difficile," an "éloquence harmonieuse," and retained a lingering memory of what it had been formerly while expressing a deep yearning for an eventual return of its former glory.

Voltaire adduced the universality of poetry as grounds for its defense. Never had there been a people who did not adopt poetry, either rimed or in rhythm. Even history was originally written in verse, and the founders of religion, the first legislators, the philosophers, as well as the historians, were all poets. To the allegation that poetry could not be sufficiently precise to carry the thought of these subjects, Voltaire replied that Virgil and Horace had united the precision of thought with the harmony of expression in classical language and that Boileau and Racine had done the same in French. Voltaire was revolted by La Motte's opinion that versification is a mechanical, ridiculous task. He condemned his statement that the only merit of poetry is in overcoming an added difficulty. Acknowledging that rime does not constitute the sole merit of poetry, Voltaire nevertheless insisted that the harmony which comes from a difficult measure does have a special charm. All arts, he added, have obstacles to their perfection.

The position of Voltaire, however, was not entirely secure. He agreed, in principle at least, with the moderns in that he, too, believed that the poet must be strictly of his time. He devoted himself without any hesitation to writing a "modern" epic, and, when he turned to drama, it was to write "modern" tragedies, even if the themes he adopted were ancient. Further, he granted that poetry imposes constraints upon expression and that, particularly in French poetry where the constraints were so severe, it was very difficult to achieve the harmony he desired. He even asserted that the French were the least poetic of all the Europeans.

In their way, these were arguments which could have been used by the geometricians. They were, however, supplemented by others which the geometricians would not have wanted to adopt. Thus, even while admitting that the restraints cause difficulties and often offer insurmountable obstacles, Voltaire counseled nonetheless, as Boileau did, a consistent poetic effort and a continual struggle to overcome these obstacles. He argued that, when the difficulties are resolved, the result is a rewarding beauty which prose can not match. His enthusiasm for poetry was, indeed, high: he called it the language of the gods, the music of the soul, and held that imagination is its essence. It is the charm of youth, and its charm consists in beautiful details. It is the kind of music that ennobles everything and augments the sphere of the slightest things. There is no true poetry which is not allied to great wisdom. It bestows upon the peoples who develop it great riches. Its perfection is always an infallible proof of the superiority of a nation in the arts of the mind. Moreover, it fixes the genius of the people and their language. Voltaire, imbued with his admiration for the great "modern" poets of the age of Louis XIV, was all but prepared to assert that poetry is the supreme test of civilization. He recalled, however, that it cannot succeed except insofar as it is the ornament of reason and that it cannot sustain it-self in French except by the perfection of its style.

Thus, as his affirmations show, Voltaire both supported the arguments of the moderns and at the same time opposed their conclusions. While granting the validity of their statements, he maintained that poetry is the supreme goal of art and is therefore worth all the effort and torture required to compose it. His defense of poetry was a sort of two-pronged declaration of independence: at the same time, he declared himself free both from the restraints of antiquity and from the dictates of those who would suppress the art of poetry because of the futility of these restraints. He did not, however, declare himself free from their rational analysis of the poetic art. He, as well as they, felt that success in the field demands a continual reflection upon the activities of poetry and a reasonable application of the rules derived from the works of antiquity. Poetry is first of all the art of writing verses. It is an ornamentation—a studied ornamentation which guarantees, when properly applied, beauties which prose cannot achieve. Consequently, the art of poetry is the writing of verse, while the science of poetry is the development of precepts which explain that art and create and foster taste; the whole act of poetry is, accordingly, the expression of the high mark of civilization. It is the "fine fleur" of the life of the spirit and can, properly understood and practiced, supplant and even replace another category of life.

Voltaire therefore presented himself as the defender of the art of poetry by writing poetry. This is why, from the very beginning, he concentrated on the broadest fields of the art, from lyric to epic to dramatic poetry. In a way, his intention was to present a gigantic demonstration of the immense variety in the art. This superabundance at first astonishes: there seems no end to the effort. Voltaire even announced that he was going to try to write an opera—and he actually did! Alongside the practice of poetry, he assumed a second task: that of setting forth by precept the nature of poetic enjoyment, the cultivation of taste, which he defined as knowledge of the beauties and defects in works of art.

It would seem reasonable to consult here the precepts he used to judge these works. This can be done by analyzing the commentaries which accompany his own poetic offerings: the *Lettres sur Œdipe*, the prefaces to the various plays, the *Essai sur la poésie épique*. We shall examine them carefully in connection with the works themselves. For the moment, we shall seek the underlying principles which Voltaire proposed as a basis for his adoption of poetry as a supreme act of civilization.

We can pass over lightly the poet's conviction, which we have already mentioned, that in the past philosophers, legislators, founders of religion, and historians were all poets. It is merely an extension of Descartes's assertion that poets are superior to philosophers, through intuition and the force of the imagination. Voltaire affirmed that the goal of the poetic act is good poetry, which he defined as that poetry in which the words are precise, the sense is clear and true, and there is not too much or too little of anything. These qualities, he conceded, are necessary in good prose, also; but verse must have in addition rhythm, swing, melody, and a restrained daring ("une sage hardiesse") in poetic figures of speech. The beautiful is only the true expressed clearly. Such expression is achieved by the happy choice of words and by the musical rhythm ("mélopée"). The most sublime thoughts are as nothing if they are badly expressed. Happily, said Voltaire, the genius of the French language is clarity and elegance, and French poetry permits not a single license, since it must move with the same clarity as prose and in the precise order of our ideas.

The supreme quality of poetry is truth, which was, he added, Boileau's highest poetic virtue. Nearly all his works possess this truth, which Voltaire, like Boileau, defined as a faithful copy of nature which can be discerned in history, in morality, in fiction, in maxims, in descriptions, and in allegories. He distinctly felt, though, that Boileau's *Equivoque* is not true. Another way of getting at truth is to see whether what the author says is in conformity with his age, his character, his social status. Voltaire believed that, to read an author with profit, one must always examine whether what is being said is true, that is, true in general, but also true under the circumstances in which it is said and true in the mouth of the speaker. Voltaire concluded that truth is always the first beauty of a work, and he insisted that "tous les sentiments de la *Henriade*, de *Zaïre*, d'*Alzire*, de *Brutus* portent les caractères de vérité sensible."

The writer has to strive for certain poetic effects. He must remember that each language has its own particular genius, formed partly by the genius of the people who speak it and partly by the construction of its phrases, according to the length or the brevity of its words. He should also keep in mind that there is a hidden logic in everything that is said, and even in the most violent of passions: without this logic, all speech is aimless and verses lose their inner meaning. Even "le bon sens doit animer jusqu'au délire de l'amour." To achieve this secret logic, one must work tirelessly over the expression. Voltaire felt that the poets of his time were not putting in sufficient work on their verses; they were not paying enough attention to the choice of words, nor were they struggling sufficiently against the difficulties. We must always remember, he urged, that only "la poésie de style" gives perfection to a poem and that "beautés de détail" sustain the works and pass them on to posterity.

The work of art, in addition to aiming for clarity, elegance, and simplicity, should attempt to attain naturalness and purity of expression, without which any work is bad. Voltaire was not very specific about what is required to achieve these qualities, but he noted that Sophocles had possessed them and confessed that he despaired of ever attaining the Grecian dramatist's "pomp" and his "really tragic magnificence" which stemmed from them. Finally, art and genius consist in finding everything in the subject and only in the subject, not in something outside.

Voltaire believed that the French excelled in light poetry, that is, the Horatian poem, whether epistle, ode, satire, epigram, or chanson. In a way, this affirmation does contradict what he had said elsewhere: that France is the least poetic of all races. But what he seems to have had in mind in the latter statement is the epic. Chansons he found to be abundant in France and really superior to those of Anacreon. They unite gaiety with "la morale," and formerly they gave much reputation to the poet; now, however, they are treated as "aimables bagatelles," written for pleasure rather than glory (Lacombe, *La Poétique de M. de Voltaire*, p. 523). What the poet requires to succeed in these "bagatelles" is finesse, which Voltaire defined as "délicatesse," the capacity to conceal and at the same time reveal a part of one's thought. In addition, he must have sentiment, harmony, and the astuteness not to mount too high or to descend too low, and especially not to draw out the poem. Above all, the poet must have "esprit," which Voltaire defined as a "new" comparison, an "allusion fine," a new sense attributed to a word or a new meaning suggested, or the art of opposing one thing to another or saying only the half which one thinks in order to have the other half divined. Voltaire insisted that in the light verses one cannot have too much "esprit." It is here that imagination plays its full role: "ces jeux de l'imagination, ces finesses, ces tours, ces traits saillans, ces gayetés, ces petites sentences coupées, ces familiarités ingénieuses qu'on prodigue aujourd'hui, ne conviennent qu'aux petits ouvrages de pur agrément."

The work of art is not only the responsibility of the poet but also the charge of the spectator. To seize it in its entirety, one must possess taste, which Voltaire defined as a spontaneous discernment, the ability to see beauties and defects. It is not sufficient to *see* the beauty; one must feel it in all its *nuances* and grasp them simultaneously. Taste is developed by acquaintance with the works of great artists, and in the nation it develops in proportion as great artists appear. It is acquired only by those who know how to feel: "Pour juger des poètes, il faut savoir sentir, il faut être né avec quelques étincelles du feu qui anime ceux qu'on veut connaître."

In conclusion, poetry as Voltaire understood it, like history, is an art, a science, and a philosophy. It is of concern to the artist, to the reader, and to the maker of civilization. Voltaire rather casually accepted the view that, in the making of a civilization, the artist, the reader, and the philosopher were more or less one and the same person. As a matter of fact, though, he came to make some significant distinctions between the three. Essential to all were the technique of creating "good" poetry, the possession of an adequate way of recognizing and distinguishing "good" poetry from "bad"—an awareness that Voltaire designated as "connaissance des beautés et des défauts" —and, finally, the role of the human mind in forming the proper taste for understanding and seizing spontaneously these beauties and these defects. In reality, Voltaire had some difficulty conceiving of the poet as distinct from the critic and the man of taste. In general, he admitted with some hesitancy that what the poet is striving to achieve in the making of "good" poetry is elegance, naturalness, harmony, simplicity. What he works with in order to produce these qualities are "pensées vraies" and "expressions justes": he has to struggle to be certain of the verity of the thought and the exactness of the expression. To succeed in these two tasks, he must carefully weigh, calculate, and ponder the thought to be expressed and ascertain its clarity, its precision, and its order; but he must also weigh, calculate, and ponder the sounds, the words, and the expressions which will exactly express this clarity, this precision, and this order. The qualities of elegance, naturalness, and truth will spring from the harmony between the "poésie de style" and the "beauté de détail." To know what to say and how to say it, given the circumstances, is what constitutes the real art of the poet. In accord with Dacier's analysis of Horace, Voltaire required that the reader perform all over again the steps of the creating poet. He is, in a sense, the critic-creator, delicately attuned to beauties and more sensitive to defects. The beauties he feels in the harmonious adjustment between characters and language, while he must feel in the "beaux caractères" a harmonious adjustment between what they say and the circumstances in which they say it. The one thing the reader finds intolerable is the low, the vulgar, the untrue. The one thing he finds superior to everything else is the appropriate, the simple, the natural. Most of all, he seeks a new way of expressing a simple, natural, human emotion, a new comparison, a new sense given to words.

There is, however, a critic who stands beyond the artist and the reader-critic: he is the man of taste who, from a constantly reiterated experience, or an endless comparison of experiences, or a continual search for new aesthetic experiences, has developed a spontaneous reaction to the great and beautiful creations of man. He can understand and appreciate simultaneously and justify his judgments rationally. He can even distinguish each one in the hierarchy of aesthetic values which go from the simple to the sublime. In a way, he is the philosopher of criticism, who knows not only that he understands beauties but why he perceives them so spontaneously. He is a very rare individual, indeed, as rare in the field of aesthetics as the saint in the religion of Jansenism. In his calling, which really is analogous in many respects to the vocation of the saint, he is not only poet and critic but also a divinely inspired poet-critic.

5. THE POET AND HIS ART

IN THE YEARS between 1715 and 1723, the young Voltaire, having
set out to become a poet, entered the field with a flourish which
carried him to the pinnacle of literary fame among his contemporaries. They understood the breadth of his poetic effort, and they
were prepared for the changes which he brought about. It was perfectly reasonable that he should adopt as his masters Horace and
later Virgil and follow as his models Chaulieu and La Fare and,
for a time, Jean-Baptiste Rousseau. It was more logical still that he
should absorb lessons from Corneille, Racine, and Boileau. For the
plan he consciously pursued—producing, first, satires, odes, and
epistles in imitation of Horace, then, the epic in imitation of Virgil,
and, finally, the tragedy in imitation of the Greeks, Corneille, and
Racine—could not have been more broadly or more intelligently
conceived. If anything, one might wish it to have been a little less
planned: some spontaneity would not have changed the nature of
the production, perhaps, but it might have injected an element
which would have counter-balanced the poet's cocksureness. As it
was, he and his contemporaries were in agreement that this production was excellent, all that one could hope for, very modern, very
Regency, very geometrical, too, very much in the spirit of the time.

Critics have often wondered where Voltaire acquired so extensive
a literary reputation before his trip to England. The answer is simple: he had become France's greatest and most renowned poet.
There is, indeed, every indication that he intended to remain so. It
is, as we shall see, with some difficulty that one can subscribe to Lord
Morley's famous dictum that Voltaire went to England a poet and returned a sage, but there is no doubt that he went to England a poet.
It is true that he did other things while in England, too, but if one
may judge by his *Notebooks*—and they should give some clue to his
intellectual preoccupations—he was still deeply interested in poetry,
not always of the best order. And, when he returned to France, it
was still with the intention of being France's foremost poet, particularly her greatest dramatic poet. This ambition undoubtedly continued throughout his life, although around 1738, as we shall see,
it was superseded by even greater ambitions.

One might expect that Voltaire's magnificent training in the classics, especially in Horace and Virgil, his keen interest in poetry already declared to his father, his consuming ambition to be a poet, and his lifelong activity in this field would have won him a place of high rank among the great poets of the world. Indeed, evidence from his contemporaries can be presented which would give him unquestioned leadership in the field of eighteenth-century poetry.

When, for instance, *La Ligue* appeared in 1723, Marais wrote in his *Journal* (ed. Lescure, III, 89):

Le poème de la Ligue, par Arouet, dont on a tant parlé, se vend en secret. Je l'ai lu: c'est un ouvrage merveilleux, un chef-d'œuvre d'esprit, beau comme Virgile; et voilà notre langue en possession du poème épique, comme des autres poésies. . . . On ne sait où Arouet, si jeune, en a pu tant apprendre. C'est comme une inspiration. Quel abîme que l'esprit humain! Ce qui surprend, c'est que tout y est sage, réglé, plein de mœurs; on n'y voit ni vivacité ni brillants, et ce n'est partout qu'élégance, correction, tours ingénieux de déclamations simples et grandes, qui sentent le génie d'un homme consommé, et nullement le jeune homme. Fuyez, La Motte, Fontenelle, et vous tous, poètes et gens du nouveau style. Sénèques et Lucains du temps, apprenez à écrire et à penser dans ce poème merveilleux qui fait la gloire de notre nation et votre honte.

Marais is not known as an uncritical admirer of Voltaire; he was ordinarily far from enthusiastic about the poet's activities. But just the fact that he was usually a severe critic makes this judgment all the more convincing. And, if that were not enough, his commendation can be found repeated by others in the *Mercure*, the *Journal des savants*, and the other literary periodicals of the time.

We should not conclude, however, that the popularity of the *Ligue* was restricted to Voltaire's French compatriots or that it was limited to the flurry occasioned by its first publication in France (1723) or in England (1728). One of the most eulogistic comments upon *La Henriade* appears in a letter written by the fourth Earl of Chesterfield to Philip Stanhope, his son, on 4 October 1752 (B. 4410):

I have never read the *Lusiade* of Camoens except in a prose translation, consequently, I have never read it at all, so shall say nothing of it; but the *Henriade* is all sense from the beginning to the end, often adorned by the justest and liveliest reflections, the most beautiful descriptions, the noblest images, and the sublimest sentiments, not to mention the harmony of the verse, in which Voltaire undoubtedly exceeds all the

French poets: should you insist upon an exception in favour of Racine, I must insist, on my part, that he at least equals him. What Hero ever interested more than Henry the Fourth, who, according to the rules of Epic poetry, carries on one great and long action, and succeeds in it at last? What description ever excited more horror than those, first of the massacre, and then of the famine, at Paris? Was love ever painted with more truth and *morbidezza* than in the ninth book? Not better, in my mind, even in the fourth of Virgil.

This is high praise, indeed, once more from a quarter usually more reserved and conservative. To equate Voltaire, in one stroke, with Racine, for his ability to compose harmonious verses, and with Virgil, for his ability to depict with truth and *morbidezza*—whatever that may mean—a scene of love, is more than generous.

These two examples of approval we have quoted could be supplemented by an almost limitless number of others (see O. R. Taylor, ed., *La Henriade*, I, 188-212). When the work appeared in England in 1728, for instance, three editions were brought out almost immediately. And, apparently, there were about sixty editions published during Voltaire's lifetime in France. Mornet, in his article "Les Enseignements des bibliothèques privées," found that 181 of the 500 private eighteenth-century catalogues he examined listed the *Henriade*, and the periodicals of the time remark upon its renown in Europe. Indeed, it was translated into practically all the European languages.

From the critics it received an interminable accolade. C. E. Jourdan called it a "pièce unique en son genre," adding that it was "l'une des œuvres les plus remarquables de la littérature française contemporaine." Vauvenargues insisted that it was "le plus grand ouvrage de ce siècle, et le seul poème, en ce genre, de notre nation." Prévost judged it "d'une beauté inimitable," while D'Argens thought it worthy to be classed with the *Iliad* and the *Aeneid*. Luchet, who wrote a life of Voltaire at the end of the century, spoke of it as "le poème le plus parfait qui soit dans la langue française." Aquin de Châteaulyon declared that, as long as the French language lasts, the *Henriade* will be read and admired. To Mme du Boccage, Voltaire was the "French Virgil." Buffon viewed the poem as "a civilized epic." D'Alembert stated that one can read the *Henriade* from cover to cover without becoming tired or being bored.

When one attempts to understand this widespread enthusiasm, however, the task becomes more difficult. Evidently, some of the more flattering remarks were prompted by friendship. There were critics, though, who saw in the excellence of the poem particularly attractive qualities. Thus, the philosophers as a whole were inclined to praise it for its outstanding philosophy; Diderot maintained that there was more philosophy in this poem than in the *Iliad*, the *Odyssey*, and all the other epics put together. The themes of this philosophy were varied: tolerance (Frederick II), condemnation of fanaticism and superstition (Marmontel), political and religious questions (Pagès de Vixouse). Condorcet attributed to its excellence a moral aim, leading to the condemnation of fanaticism, to the establishment of tolerance and to love for humanity. There were those who, like Marais, appreciated the poem not so much for the content of its thought as for the excellence of its poetry. And many others were conscious of the novelties in the poem but stressed also its poetic qualities, especially its harmonious versification.

There were, of course, some negative criticisms. Gauchat, among others, found the poem to be historically incorrect, while Bury accused the author of having favored the Protestants over the Catholics. There were already those—La Beaumelle, for example—who could not approve either Voltaire's political or religious views. Some objected to the poem's deistic tendencies, to its constant criticism of Rome, to its attacks against the priesthood. And some of the Protestants, for their part, found fault with Voltaire's treatment of the Protestants. Taken as a whole, though, the response to Voltaire's epic was as full and as enthusiastic, during the forty years following its appearance, as any that has ever been accorded a literary work.

This popularity of Voltaire's *Henriade* seems nowadays so excessive that present-day scholars, who are all too aware of the poem's lack of interest, have tried to find historical reasons for its appeal when it first appeared. One of the most persuasive arguments of this kind is that which Professor Taylor has given us in his recent critical edition of the *Henriade*. Taylor accepts the view that Voltaire first undertook the composition of his epic poem in the opening months of 1716, at which time the second phase of the quarrel between the ancients and the moderns, the quarrel over Homer, was still in full swing in literary circles. Voltaire, ever alert, saw an opportunity to take advantage of public interest in the quarrel by creating an epic adjusted to contemporary taste on a subject which could be expected to arouse more than moderate interest among the literary elite. It was only natural that, with this aim in mind, he should consider the activities of Henry IV, about whom Caumartin had discoursed, a fitting subject for a "modern" epic, at a moment when Homer was being so violently assailed as an "ancient" epic poet. This was a very peculiar situation for Voltaire to be in; here, at the very beginning of his literary career, he wants to be an imitator of Virgil and Horace but refuses categorically to have anything to do with Sophocles and Homer. No better indication of the change in contemporary taste can be found than this sudden abandonment of a Greek classicism for a Roman classicism in the name of a "modern classicism."

In addition, it is possible, as has been pointed out, that the analogy between the time of Henry IV and that of Philip of Orléans was strikingly apparent. The early years of the Regency, with its political unrest nurtured by the struggle between Orléans and Philip V of Spain, the unsettled condition of the nobility which still displayed some tendency to revolt, and the constant quarrels of religion over the *Bulle Unigenitus,* made more vivid still the "modern" aspect of the wars of religion at the end of the sixteenth century. We must not insist too much upon this analogy, though, which Taylor has traced so painstakingly and with such precision. Voltaire was so careful to plan his every step that we might be easily persuaded that the poem engendered enthusiasm because of its portrayals, through Henry IV, of the contemporary situation in 1715-1723, rather than because of any inherent epic worth. But we must not be too hasty in that direction either. Voltaire was just the sort of person who could derive an advantage from both tendencies. I would be easily convinced, however, that he counted more upon the popularity of the subject than upon his manner of executing it.

Indeed, there had appeared in Du Bos's *Réflexions critiques,* of 1719, an eloquent plea by the critic for some epic poet to undertake a poem with Henry IV as the hero. The passage (pp. 518-519) is so striking that Ascoli was prepared to accept it as the primary source of Voltaire's poem:

Qu'on fasse un poème épique de la destruction de la Ligue par Henri IV, dont la conversion de ce prince, suivie de la réduction de Paris, serait naturellement le dénouement. Un homme capable par les forces de son génie d'être un grand poète, et qui pourrait tirer de son propre fonds toutes les beautés nécessaires pour soutenir une grande fiction, trouverait mieux son compte à traiter un pareil sujet, dans lequel il n'aurait point à éviter de se rencontrer avec personne, qu'à manier des sujets de la fable, ou de l'histoire grecque et romaine. Au lieu d'emprunter des héros aux grecs et aux latins, qu'on ose donc en faire de nos rois et de nos princes. . . . Qu'on ose donc chanter les choses que nous avons sous les yeux, comme sont nos combats, nos fêtes et nos cérémonies. Qu'on nous donne des descriptions poétiques des bâtiments, des fleuves et des pays que nous voyons tous les jours, et dont nous puissions confronter pour ainsi dire, l'original avec l'imitation. Avec quelle noblesse et quel pathétique Virgile aurait-il traité une apparition de Saint Louis à Henri IV, la veille de la bataille d'Ivry, quand ce prince, l'honneur des descendants de ce saint roi, faisait encore profession de la confession de foi de Genève? Avec quelle élégance aurait-il dépeint les Vertus en habit de fête, ouvrant à ce bon roi les portes de la ville de Paris![10]

The important thing is not so much whether Du Bos suggested the theme of Voltaire's epic to him as the meeting of those two minds, which indicates that Henry IV had attained a popularity in public opinion which was wider than might be imagined. This popularity does suggest that there was a studied policy in the Regency to stress the attractiveness of "Le Vert Galant" and to point out analogies between Henry's and Orléans's liberalism, even to the extent of overstressing the previous persecution of the Protestants (Orléans planned, it will be recalled, their return to France) and a totally new international orientation toward England, rather than the previous, Spanish-oriented foreign policy. In all probability, the fact that Voltaire's poem abetted these practical, political considerations accounts for the interest which the Duke showed in its

[10] O. R. Taylor, *La Henriade*, I, 36, while admitting the unquestioned influence of Du Bos on the *Henriade*, does not accept the view that the critic furnished Voltaire with the plan for his epic. He holds, instead, that the author of the *Réflexions critiques* was well enough informed to have been able to describe the state of the *Henriade* at the time he penned his advice, that is, around 1718. Voltaire himself is responsible in the *Siècle* (M. XIV, 553) for the statement that Du Bos had had the idea for a poem on Henry IV since 1714.

composition and the relative mildness of the government authorities when it became impossible to give thorough approval to the poem.

More important than the political aspects surrounding the poem's publication, for our purposes here, are its literary aspects. It should not be overlooked that, although Du Bos had some official relationship with the government authorities, he was also certainly at the time France's foremost literary and artistic critic. His *Réflexions critiques sur la poésie et la peinture* (1719) was one of the outstanding documents in the intense literary debate which had been raging since 1700. It is not easy to grasp his theory of the epic in its entirety because of some apparent contradictions between his sense of history, which was relative, and his sense of taste, which was rather arbitrary. It has been pointed out (Lombard, *L'Abbé Du Bos*, p. 291) that his theory of the sixth sense actually justifies the taste of the ancients, rather than that of the moderns. It is nonetheless significant that in his treatise he envisaged not only a "modern" subject ("Le poète qui introduirait Henri IV dans un poème épique nous trouverait déjà affectionnés à son héros, et à son sujet") but a subject drawn from the history of the race; those subjects involving the history of other races were, in his opinion, to be rigidly excluded from the French epic. Du Bos even urged selection of a national subject which did not go too far back; in France, for instance, he recommended going no further than Charles VII. Moreover, he counseled the creation of a new epic language divorced from Greek figures of speech and ornaments, from what he calls "des phrases poétiques des anciens," and drawn instead from the genius of the modern poet. Although he sanctioned Christian "merveilleux" as a legitimate part of modern dress, he restricted as much as possible the role of allegory, advising that it be used with great discretion. Still, he judged that "modern" poetry could achieve distinct merit with the use of Christian miracles, which would add, if well employed, a sublime quality. Finally, he stressed that the absolutely indispensable factor, after all these precautions have been taken, is "la poésie du style," which he defines as the ability to instill "des sentiments à tout ce qu'on fait parler comme à exprimer par des figures, et à présenter sous des images capables de nous émouvoir, ce qui ne nous toucherait pas s'il étoit dit simplement en style prosaïque" (*Réflexions*, I, 264).

Voltaire paid his respects to Du Bos, whom he called a "homme de très grand sens." He did not fail to observe that the critic, in his *Réflexions critiques*, had judged that the destruction of *La Ligue* by Henry IV was the only true epic subject in all of French history —although here Voltaire was a bit summary, since Du Bos had also looked with some favor upon an epic celebrating Joan of Arc. Voltaire regretted, however, that Du Bos had not stressed that, all the paraphernalia used by the Greeks and the Romans being unsuitable to a "modern" epic, the possibilities of introducing new beauties into a French epic poem were considerably narrowed. All the same, he studied with great care the recommendations of Du Bos and adopted each one in the elaboration of his "modern" epic.

This enthusiasm for a modern, national, Christian epic ran counter to that part of the classical doctrine which stressed imitation of the ancients. In particular, it was strongly opposed to the Homeric epic. It is this situation which explains how Houdar de la Motte, the Abbé Pons, and especially Terrasson, all of whom were committed to a "modern" epic, came to launch a vigorous attack against the defects of Homer.[11] Consequently, the search for a "modern" epic became intimately connected with the attack against Homer, an attack inaugurated by La Motte, seconded by De Pons, and developed by Terrasson. These critics offered three reasons for condemning the *Iliad* and the *Odyssey*: the coarseness of the gods and the heroes, the interminable descriptions and the inappropriate comparisons, and the dull, monotonous depiction of the battles. The principles upon which their criticisms rest are (1) the impossibility of establishing the quality of a work upon the tradition and authority of a previous work and (2) the supremacy of reason over all powers of tradition. As La Motte expressed it: "L'esprit géométrique vaut bien l'esprit commentateur." Insofar as the world is embellished by the arts and perfected by "la morale," the stuff of poetry becomes more beautiful. Homer, the poet of barbarous times, who in his works lacks both those poetic embellishments and "la morale," is clearly inferior to Virgil, the poet of a more refined civilization. Terrasson, in his *Dissertation critique*, likewise rejected the authority and tradition of ancient epics because of these deficiencies, and tended to replace this authority by a more "scientific" approach. The

[11] La Motte, *Réflexions sur la critique*, Paris, 1715; De Pons, *Dissertation sur le poème épique*, Amsterdam, 1738; Terrasson, *Dissertation sur l'Iliade*, Paris, 1715.

principles of an art, he insisted, exist outside of all works of art, just as the principles of science exist outside of every particular phenomenon. This is not to say, of course, that rules cannot be formulated from the study of previous works. But, in general, the errors of early works are corrected by later ones. There follows in Terrasson's *Dissertation* a long series of rules which, though apparently scientific, are actually classical restrictions. As a matter of fact, Lombard (*L'Abbé Du Bos*, pp. 291ff.) has demonstrated that, in matters of rules and restrictions, there was little difference between ancient and modern. There was, though, no accord between ancient and modern thought when it came to the subject of the epic, or the nature and use of "le merveilleux," or the place of "la morale," or the conception of the hero, or the art of presentation, or the question of style. On each of these issues, the moderns drew distinctions between themselves and the ancients, taking their examples of defects from Homer: the brutality of Achilles, the barbarity of Ajax, or the cruelty of all the Homeric characters. The morality, they charged, is that of primitive societies, and the style is not at all sustained by the nobility of manners and customs.

Out of all this discussion arose the conception of an epic which, though evolved from the epic of Homer and Virgil, was entirely different in kind. What was desired now was an epic having a "morale" admirable in every respect, an ideal hero more or less in accordance with the idea of an "honnête homme," thorough documentation, a logical structure, all sorts of classical virtues, such as brevity, concentration, variety, elegance, and rapidity, and all this sustained by a harmonious and limpid versification (see Taylor, ed., *La Henriade*, I, 117).

Voltaire to a large extent shared these views and endeavored to support them. In the *Essai sur la poésie épique*, in spite of the homage he paid to Pope and his translation of the *Iliad*, he found much to criticize in Homer: lack of method in the composition, monotony of the descriptions, the inordinate length of the story, lack of a central character, barbaric heroes, and an absurd "merveilleux" (F.D. White, *Voltaire's Essay on Epic Poetry*, pp. 91-93). He disclosed his adherence to the moderns by repeating the criticisms of La Motte and his followers: Homer is unable to structure a satisfactory plot; his cantos are badly organized and bound together; there are all sorts of digressions, and, in addition to the long descriptions, there are all kinds of technical terms. The Homeric metaphor is wearisomely long and often not applicable to the subject. His repetitions are excessive, and his style is characterized by a long, interminable series of absurd epithets of an impossible vulgarity. The heroes themselves partake of this vulgarity, while the gods are both ridiculous and indecent.

Voltaire, along with his contemporaries, felt it deplorable that France, alone of all the European countries, had no epic. He cited the general European opinion that the French were incapable of creating a poem in this genre, even though they were superior in all other literary genres. But he rejected this opinion, offering a whole series of considerations to explain away the apparent deficiency. He asserted, for instance, that one of the reasons for France's inferiority in the epic was that those writers who had been preoccupied with the genre had never been among the great poets of the nation. The great writers—Corneille, Racine, Boileau—had never attempted an epic. *Télémaque,* which some apologists had offered as the French epic, he was unwilling to accept because, in the first place, it was in prose: it was, rather, a "roman moral," written in the style one would use to translate Homer. Voltaire even maintained that it would not have succeeded as an epic had it been written in poetry, because of the infinite number of details and the political and economic discussions.

One of the excuses advanced by the critics to account for the failure of the French to create an epic was the lack of sublimity in the French language. Voltaire gave some consideration to this point, also. He granted that Greek and Latin were more harmonious and poetic than the modern tongues, but he argued that French was more dynamic than Italian and more harmonious than English. Since there were epics in these two languages, it was evident, he concluded, that the weakness of French was no impediment to the creation of an epic poem. Nor did he accept the explanation of those who claimed that the use of rime in verse is a handicap to the writing of an epic; Tasso and Ariosto, he countered, had rimed their epics. He felt, nevertheless, that writing an epic was more difficult for a French poet than for any other because, of all the highly cultured nations, France was the least poetic. The difficulty was especially great at the time in which he was writing, since the "esprit géométrique" had become, he noted, a new restraint upon poetry. What one expected in French poetry was method and truth. Little by little, French taste had come to exclude the imagination required in epics. The pagan gods were deemed ridiculous: a poet who sang of saints would be severely criticized; and, if he dared introduce devils, he would be regarded with derision.

Voltaire explained that he had attempted to conform to the serious, exacting genius of the French and to the century in which he lived. He had therefore chosen an authentic, instead of a legendary, hero; he had described real wars, instead of imaginary battles, and had employed no fiction that was not an image of truth.

Thus, we can see that Voltaire, sensitive to the poetic as well as to the political and social conditions, was prepared to enter upon a field of poetry where the French had the reputation of being incompetent. He was ready to test his ability in that art by adopting a new conception of the epic and by exploiting it in his poem. He was careful to select a subject which would be popularly acceptable and to stress those factors in it which bore some analogy to the political, social, and religious circumstances of his time. His efforts thereby united the modern critics, the political leaders, the social elite eager for some new approach to art, and the liberal free-thinkers, who in their way were all representatives of these groups. He had thus played his chance of succeeding as intelligently as he could, and he had been acclaimed for his success by his contemporaries with surprising enthusiasm. There can be no question that Voltaire had done everything he could to win this acclaim, nor can there be any doubt that, at the time, he received it, it was genuine and very enthusiastic, so much so that one would be inconsiderate to oppose its judgment.

Nevertheless, it is true that, as the century progressed, the favorable judgment turned more and more into disapproval. There was a group of critics—Fréron, La Beaumelle, Clément, Linguet, Bury—who were in agreement that the *Henriade* had been vastly overrated. Specifically, they objected to the satiric intentions of the poet, noting that he had treated political and religious institutions with scant respect. They criticized the historical background of the poem and blamed Voltaire for offering a false portrait of the religious wars, in which he equated fanaticism with Catholicism. They did not restrict themselves, however, to decrying Voltaire's attitude toward his subject, for they found much to censure now in the literary domain as well. They pointed out that the poem did not at all conform to the classic conception of the epic. Some called it a "gazette rimée" or "versified history." They condemned the insufficiency of the "merveilleux" and attacked Voltaire's allegory as totally "invraisemblable." In addition, they found all sorts of flaws in the composition: the poem lacked unity of action, the structure was weak, the plot badly conceived. All now agreed that the work had been created without imagination. Its aesthetic merits were few, chiefly because the author had used the analytic procedures of the moralist and the historian. The depiction of the hero was insipid. The versification was quite faulty; it suffered from inaccuracy, forced, exaggerated expressions, vulgar, technical terms, and sections abounding in repetitions and antitheses. Trublet had already summed up this negative criticism: "Ce n'est point le poète qui ennuie et fait bâiller dans la poésie; c'est la poésie, ou plutôt, les vers." Finally, as the century approached its end and the poetic sensibility showed signs of turning away from classicism to romanticism, there were those who declared that what Voltaire lacked were true poetic qualities: imagination and sensibility. This was the view of Thomas, Le Jeune, and Chateaubriand. It was, perhaps, not held by the majority. Still, just as Voltaire had profited by the excessive praise of his followers until 1767, so he now suffered from the widespread condemnation of his enemies, who thereafter became increasingly vocal. There is a clear line of demarcation between the 1767 edition of the *Henriade* supervised by Marmontel, which met with enthusiastic commendation, and the 1769 edition supervised by La Beaumelle and, later (1775), by Fréron, which met with thorough condemnation. The *Commentaire sur la Henriade*, as the latter edition was called, was clearly the beginning of the end. There were, notwithstanding, some sixty more editions between 1775 and 1830. They did not prevent, however, a complete change in the general opinion. As Taylor concludes, everyone now agrees that the *Henriade* has all the qualities of the best philosophical and didactic poetry of the eighteenth century and all the elegance of the Regency; but it is not, for all that, epic or poetic.

The history of the rise and fall of the *Henriade* in the esteem of the public is so curious that twentieth-century critics cannot resist seeking its causes. Voltaire had expended much intelligence and energy in composing his work. He had selected the most popular subject conceivable, he had treated it so that there were definite analogies between the subject of the poem and the conditions of the Regency, and he had studied the treatises which had formulated what is required in the "new" epic and had followed each recommendation so scrupulously that it seemed impossible that he could fail, unless he were—something that seems altogether impossible— no poet at all. The enthusiastic reception given his poem over a forty-year period is eloquent testimony that he was, at least, a poet— unless one would like to argue that things had come to such a pass that Voltaire's public could not distinguish any more between "good" and "bad" poetry. We shall have to consider both of these possibilities later. For the moment, it is enough to point out that there were possible reasons for the poem's failure.

The first was Voltaire's complete fidelity to his models. In one sense, Voltaire had carried his scrupulousness too far. He had picked his subject too carefully, he had noted the analogies with his time too consistently, he had followed the rules of the "modern" epic too religiously. His greatest mistake was to heed Du Bos's final injunction too conscientiously. It will be recalled that the critic of the *Réflexions* had asserted that Virgil could compose this epic with the greatest "élégance." This is precisely what Voltaire attempted to do: in addition to adopting the plot suggested by Du Bos, the young poet also imitated the way Virgil would have treated the subject. The result was that the *Henriade* repeats, under circumstances which are entirely different, the scenes of the *Aeneid*. Like Aeneas recounting his experience to Dido, Henry IV relates his to Elizabeth. Like Aeneas, he engages in fierce battles and massacres. He delays his mission in the arms of Gabrielle, in imitation of Aeneas dallying at Carthage with Dido. Finally, he descends into Hell and is allowed to look into the future by one of his glorious ancestors. Voltaire could not have followed more closely the story of the *Aeneid* in writing his "modern" epic.

The situation having been taken from Du Bos and the handling of the incidents being but a repetition of the *Aeneid*, one might at least expect the composition to be Voltaire's. At first glance, it does seem to be his: the descriptions, particularly of the Saint-Barthélemy massacre and the episode of Jacques Clément, do have a certain grandeur, and the verses in these episodes are notable for their color and precision. But they, too, were derived from the past, from the great classicists of the seventeenth century, Corneille, Racine, and Boileau, and, in truth, their expression was as unoriginal as the subject and the episodes. Indeed, the two outstanding characteristics of the poem are its almost total lack of originality and its poverty of verbal invention. Only one aspect of it was original with Voltaire: the way in which the philosophy of tolerance is disengaged from the claptrap of unoriginal poetry.

It is therefore necessary to devote some attention to the content of the *Henriade*, which from the early days of Voltairean criticism has usually been treated under the rubric of propaganda. Both Lanson and Ascoli have noted Voltaire's evident intention to instill the idea of tolerance, especially religious tolerance, in his readers. In the early part of the nineteenth century, Tabaraud, in his *De la Philosophie de la Henriade* (Paris, 1824), endeavored to examine the work's philosophical content. He found that, in general, the poem is written in accordance with the principles of Catholicism but that Voltaire's incessant satire against the ministers of the Catholic religion appears inappropriate when he is celebrating the triumph of this same religion in Henry IV's conversion. Tabaraud added (p. 17):

Voltaire prétend que son poème ne respire que l'amour de la religion, et il se flatte de n'y donner à cet égard aucune prise à la censure. Il est vrai que les maximes philosophiques y sont distribuées avec plus de discrétion, ou du moins avec plus d'art, que dans plusieurs de ses autres ouvrages, et que le palliatif y est presque toujours mis à côté du mal. Mais toute l'adresse du poète n'a pu en couvrir tellement la teinte philosophique, qu'elle n'y soit souvent très-sensible.[12]

Tabaraud was not surprised at this philosophical tendency in the *Henriade*. After all, in his *Epître à Genonville*, Voltaire had spoken skeptically about the spirituality and immortality of the soul; in his *Epître au Duc de Sully*, he had ridiculed two of the Catholic

---

[12] Lanson suggested much the same thing when he talked about a "certain tour de philosophie hardie et provocante" (*Voltaire*, p. 91).

sacraments; in *Œdipe*, he had attacked the clergy; and, finally, in his *Epître à Uranie*, he had expressed at length his objections to the Christian religion. In the *Henriade*, he manifests indifference to all religions, but he is particularly animated against Catholicism, holding its clergy responsible for all the disasters of Henry IV's reign. He goes even further: the God he presents in the poem is a deist God, and the tolerance he preaches is nothing but indifference to all formal religions.

Taking such a stand is, of course, possible in philosophical poetry. But it is impossible in the epic. Indeed, Voltaire, in his *Siècle de Louis XIV*, in speaking of Boileau's poetry, says that it is necessary to distinguish carefully between what has become a proverb and what deserves to become a maxim, since maxims are noble, wise, and useful, composed for men of wit and taste, while proverbs are for the vulgar. In writing his poem for men of wit and taste and in trying precisely to avoid the vulgar, he was undoubtedly striving to produce the finely carved maxim which would be accepted by the elite society of the Regency.

One wonders how a poet with any knowledge of Homer, no matter how slight, could conceive of an epic written for the elite of a nation. Since the first principle of an epic is to embrace all life, all tones, all attitudes, all styles, an epic embracing but part of the race is necessarily condemned from the start to social restrictions even more critical than the poetic restrictions to which the lyric poet has to submit. On the other hand, while the *Henriade* could never have been an epic of the Homeric order under the social conditions and the poetic rules then prevalent—and, indeed, was never intended to be of the Homeric order—the very fact that it was written for a limited public and with a restricted set of conventions was largely responsible for its popularity. Enlarge the audience, even the French audience, eliminate the conventions, the *Henriade* would immediately sink into obscurity.

Still, there would have been something left, which, for want of a better name, may be called "human" maxims, maxims that are, in essence, philosophical. Here are a few examples which might be mistaken for propaganda. Consider this one on humanity and its relation "with" God:

> Les œuvres des humains sont fragiles comme eux;
> Dieu dissipe à son gré leurs desseins orgeuilleux,
> Lui seul est toujours stable, en vain notre malice
> De sa sainte Cité veut sapper l'édifice;
> Lui-même en affermit les sacrez fondemens;
> Ces fondements vainqueurs de l'enfer et des temps.

The poetry is certainly not as rich as in *Esther*, although, in all probability, it was from there that the poetic content took its origin. We quote another on the contradictions in human nature, since it also bears some comparison with scenes of carnage in the Racinian play:

> Ce que vous-même encor à peine, vous croirez,
> Ces monstres furieux de carnage altérez,
> Excitez par la voix des Prêtres sanguinaires,
> Invoquaient le Seigneur en égorgeant leurs frères;
> Et le bras tout soûillé du sang des innocents,
> Osaient offrir à Dieu cet exécrable encens.

Here is a maxim of enlarged dimensions which could easily embrace the bourgeois as well as the aristocratic spirit:

> C'est peu qu'un vain éclat qui passe et qui s'enfuit,
> Que le trouble accompagne, et que la mort détruit,
> Tous ces honneurs mondains ne sont qu'un bien stérile,
> Des humaines vertus récompense fragile.
> D'un bien plus précieux osez être jaloux,
> Si Dieu ne vous éclaire il n'a rien fait pour vous.

Some of these maxims even carry within them a deep pity. Witness, for example, the remarks of Henry IV in Hell:

> Hélas: s'écria-t-il, si dans ce lieu d'horreur,
> Des malheureux humains la foule est engloutie,
> Si les jours passagers d'une si triste vie;
> D'un éternel tourment sont suivis sans retour;
> Ne vaudrait-il pas mieux ne voir jamais le jour;
> Heureux s'ils expiraient dans le sein de leur mère,
> Ou si ce Dieu du moins, ce grand Dieu si sévère,
> A l'œuvre de ses mains avoit daigné ravir,
> Le pouvoir malheureux de lui désobéir.

And, finally, we have one that strikes an entirely modern note:

On voit la Liberté, cette esclave si fière,
Par d'invincibles nœuds en ces lieux prisonnière;
Sous un joug inconnu que rien ne peut briser;
Dieu sçait l'assujettir sans la tiranniser;
A ses suprêmes loix d'autant mieux attachée,
Que sa chaîne à ses yeux pour jamais est cachée,
Qu'en obéissant même elle agit par son choix,
Et souvent aux destins pense donner des loix.

We can see now why what was so enthusiastically acclaimed in Voltaire's day because it conformed to the spirit of the time became less and less attractive as that spirit changed. When an author writes a modern epic, he naturally runs the risk, when modern times change, as they inevitably must, of losing contact with subsequent eras. When he writes an epic for an elite, he runs the additional risk of losing appropriate contact with that elite when it is transformed into a different, and wider, group. There is something to be said in favor of writing for humanity, and even for eternity, in spite of the bombast that we now feel are ever-present in those words. Otherwise, what will happen is that only the part of the content appropriate to the changing conditions will be preserved and the author will be accused of using propaganda. Or, if he escapes this charge, he will have succeeded in composing only a philosophic or didactic poem in the framework of an historical narrative, not an epic.

Even before the *Henriade* was published under the title *La Ligue,* Voltaire busied himself with the composition of the *Œdipe.* It was the first of his ventures in the writing of drama, which he was destined to continue until the end of his long life. One of his final escapades was a visit to the Comédie Française to witness the performance of his last play, *Irène*; one of his unfinished works, *Agathocle,* was a play, too. He succeeded in writing over fifty plays, a number about equal to the combined production of Corneille and Racine, though not more than twenty-seven were tragedies. Not all of them were written in poetry, either, although none of the early ones, and only a relatively small number of the later ones, were composed in prose. It was perfectly normal that, having started by writing poetry inspired by Horace, he should turn to the epic actuated by the quarrel of Homer and inspired by Virgil and, thence, to drama under the influence of Sophocles and the inspiration of

Corneille and Racine. Indeed, it was to the writing of drama that the young Arouet was intent upon devoting the full measure of his poetic ability. His Jesuit teachers, especially Father Porée, had had their role also in the formation of the dramatic poet.

Voltaire requested the honor of dedicating his tragedy Œdipe to the Duke of Orléans in October 1718. Presented on 18 November, published at the beginning of 1719, it enjoyed great success, having a run of some forty-eight performances, thirty of them consecutive.[13] Bolingbroke wrote to Mme D'Argental on 4 February 1719, thanking her for procuring him a copy of the play. He confessed that he had heard it spoken of with great praise and ventured the remark that Voltaire's merit had been quickly recognized in spite of his youth, adding that his "coup d'essai passe pour un coup de maître" (B. 71).

Voltaire hurried a copy to J. B. Rousseau on 1 March with assurances of having regarded him always as his master. Rousseau responded on 25 March with rather profuse praise: "Ce qui m'a le plus surpris dans un auteur de votre âge c'est l'économie admirable de votre pièce, et la manière judicieuse et adroite avec laquelle vous avez évité les écueils presque inévitables d'une action aussi difficile à traiter que celle que vous avez choisie." Rousseau assured the young French author that he, like Sophocles, had evoked the curiosity of the audience and aroused its passions. Rousseau even complimented him for having understood the real spirit of tragedy. Whereas, said Rousseau, interpreters ordinarily attribute to Sophocles the intention of purging wrath and curiosity since these are the two defects of Œdipus, he, Rousseau, was convinced that Sophocles wished rather to show that men cannot avoid their fate and that, without the aid of the gods, their virtue and prudence are as naught. He concluded that the young poet had perfectly well portrayed this same intent and that all the ancients were perfect Jansenists (B. 73). To Brossette, Rousseau wrote with more restraint, conceding that there were fine passages in Voltaire's play, well-developed scenes, good lines, and interesting situations, but arguing that there were also defects.

[13] The enthusiasm generated in the public is evident in *Les Correspondants de la Marquise de Balleroy*, Paris, 1883, I, 370, 380, 383, 386; II, 9; and in P. Dangeau, *Journal*, Paris, 1854-1882, XVII, 418, 423, 436, 475-476. See also H. C. Lancaster, *French Tragedy in the Time of Louis XV and Voltaire, 1715-1774*, I, 54-56.

Sophocles's *Œdipe* was neither Corneillian nor Racinian, although apparently the young author had had these great writers in mind and had even imitated several of their lines. In a later letter to Brossette (29 April 1719), Rousseau averred that he found the work much finer than he had expected, that it had only a few flaws. He still approved Voltaire's conception of the character of Œdipus in that, unlike Sophocles, Voltaire had given him neither uncontrolled anger nor inordinate curiosity. Furthermore, the versification, he felt, was in general very beautiful, although there was some negligence in rime.

Voltaire published also the *Lettres sur Œdipe*, in which he attempted to compare his play with Sophocles's and Corneille's, his obvious intention being to show the difference between a modern and an ancient *Œdipe*.

It is very revealing to approach Voltaire's *Œdipe* through his commentary upon the original *Œdipus* of Sophocles. Some allowance must be made, I suppose, for the fact that the Greek dramatists had, as Voltaire said, fallen from their former position of high esteem and were either ignored or treated with contempt. Voltaire, it is true, has the grace to condemn this attitude and recommends the reading of Greek drama. If it is too full of errors to be approved, it is at the same time too full of beauty to warrant the scorn heaped upon it. Voltaire finds Euripides superior to Sophocles and even declares that, had the former been born in a more enlightened age, he would have been the greatest of poets, for he reveals consummate genius, despite the imperfections of his tragedies. His most praiseworthy feat, however, in the eyes of the critic, was inspiring Racine to such an extent that practically a whole scene of the French *Phèdre* turns out to be a word for word translation of Euripides. Voltaire adds, in typical fashion, that this is about the only beautiful and reasonable part of the whole Greek play.

Voltaire confesses having taken two scenes from Sophocles—the one involving the high priest and the other the two old men (the two shepherds)—and definitely leaves the impression that the remainder is not worth imitating. The defects he cites are all of a logical, or rational, order: contradictions, absurdities, idle declamations. He even gives a list of passages he has found revolting: for instance, the vanity of Œdipus in presenting himself when all the Thebans already know him, the high priest's fashion of introducing himself, the comparison of Thebes wracked by plague with a boat tossed by a tempest—a metaphor which Voltaire considers trite. He finds it ridiculous that Œdipus, who has been reigning so long a time, fails to know how his predecessor died. Even more absurd, to him, is the report of the one survivor of Laius's party, who announces that Laius was overpowered by a group of robbers when he knows perfectly well that Laius and his whole retinue were slain by one man. When Œdipus learns that there is one survivor, he fails to send for him immediately, although that is the most reasonable thing to do, and, when he does have him come, fails to ask him about the murder of Laius. This is all the more reprehensible, according to Voltaire, since the subject of the play is the vengeance of Laius's murder. Finally, the whole secret of Œdipus's birth is disclosed at the end of the second act and, again, at the end of the fourth, thus rendering the fifth act absolutely superfluous after the catastrophe of the fourth. Voltaire asserts that Œdipus's and Jocaste's ignorance of the past event is merely a contrived trick of the poet, who, in order to give his play the required length, stretches out to the fifth act a recognition scene already evident in the second and who, in order not to contravene the rules of the drama, violates all the rules of common sense (M. II, 24). This Œdipus, who can explain riddles, fails to understand the most obvious things. Sophocles is, moreover, he adds, totally deficient in the art of preparation.

Voltaire concludes by stating that we must not be too severe with these early dramatists. Sophocles's play is distinguished by the harmony of its verse (which the eighteenth-century critic could not read) and the "pathétique qui règne dans son style"—whatever that may mean. The youthful dramatist adds that we should not expect more than rough sketches in the early stages of an art and should therefore respect the genius of these authors, while blaming the imperfections of their plays; for, whereas their faults are attributable to their period, their beauties belong to them. He feels certain that, had they possessed the good fortune to live in the eighteenth century, they would have perfected an art which they could only invent.

One would have to look far to find a more stupid and more impertinent piece of literary criticism than this. Voltaire undoubtedly knew Aristotle's *Poetics*, Horace's *De Arte poetica*, and Boileau's *Art poétique*. But there is no sign that he had any interest in what these works said about tragedy, and it is very likely that he did not at this time have any notion of the import of their content. These *Lettres* try to give the impression that he had reflected upon the nature of dramatic art, but their close perusal leaves the reader with the conviction that he had given no thought whatever to it. Nowhere is there the slightest indication that he was concerned with what constitutes tragedy or even what role tragedy can play in the society which has created it. He was not the least bit concerned with what constitutes a tragic hero or what tragic irony is. He had a faint glimmer that there may be a tragic effect; he divined that it may be pity. But tragic purgation and the play as ritual were totally devoid of meaning for him. He would not have been willing to consider that *Œdipus* is the story of a man who goes in search of himself, relentlessly and unconditionally, that, as Sophocles's play unfurls, Œdipus, the greatest of men, becomes as nothing, and that only then is he fit to become a god. Voltaire was not conscious of the symbolism of sight, of the tension in the soul of a man who wants to know the truth and dreads to know it because he realizes that the truth destroys, of the paradox in human existence which drives a man to will his every act and at the same time to do everything to avoid the outcome, of the irony of a human situation in which one has the freedom to act but no freedom to choose, a freedom which carries with it utterly degrading responsibilities and which may lead one to become the vilest of men or a god without knowing why, or how, or even when. Voltaire understood nothing of these things, and yet he intended to write twenty-seven tragedies, which would, he sincerely thought, be distinguished, like Sophocles's *Œdipus*, by the harmony of the verse and the "pathétique qui règne dans son style."

Voltaire's criticism of Corneille's *Œdipe* reveals the same ineptitude he had shown in his criticism of Sophocles's play. To begin with, his point of view is totally negative. He firmly believes that criticism should be directed at the imperfection of great writers. He sometimes pronounces the word "beautés" but rarely gives a concrete example of beauty, whereas, if it is a question of defects, he becomes exceedingly specific. His opinion of Corneille's *Œdipe* is less favorable than his judgment of Sophocles's play, and he contemptuously remarks that, when Corneille is not sublime, he is far below mediocrity. As for the versification of the play, he deems it unworthy of discussion. Whereas many of the faults in Sophocles's play were due to lack of verisimilitude, many of those in Corneille's play may be attributed to lack of decorum—the role of Dircé, for instance. The whole episode of Theseus and Dircé, which has nothing to do with the play, has been invented, he says, in order to give movement and scope to the plot. According to Voltaire, the Greek custom of presenting dramatic incidents in all their simplicity, or rather their sterility, cannot be imitated by French playwrights. These subjects are difficult to handle, and, since they contain material barely sufficient for a scene or two, it is necessary to supplement these fearsome and moving events by uniting with them the passions which prepare the way for them. This observation is not original with Voltaire, for Racine had expressed the formula in his preface to *Bérénice*: "il suffit que l'action en soit grande, que les acteurs en soient héroïques, que les passions y soient excitées, et que tout s'y ressente de cette tristesse majestueuse qui fait tout le plaisir de la tragédie." Voltaire seems to have forgotten the part about the "tristesse majestueuse." At all events, he takes Corneille to task for having tried to enlarge the scope of his *Œdipe* by adding extraneous passions which are either too strong, and stifle the subject, or too weak, and kill the action. The young poet insists upon keeping to the subject, which is the slaying of Laius. When things are somewhat reversed in Corneille's play, the passion of Theseus becoming the central theme of the tragedy and the misfortunes of Œdipus only episodes, Voltaire is entirely confused. He can only conclude that Corneille was not familiar with Sophocles's play or, at least, held him in great contempt, since he borrowed nothing from him, either beauties or defects.

One would think that Voltaire, having so generously pointed out the defects of his predecessors, would have been able to avoid them in his own play. This, by his own admission, he did not do, although the defects he admitted he had a tendency to excuse. For him, the principal difficulty was the subject, since the Œdipus legend did not offer sufficient material to make a play. Logically, Œdipus should have recognized his guilt at the end of the first act.

At best, the material could be stretched over two acts. Since neither Sophocles nor Corneille had explained why Œdipus is so ignorant of his situation and so oblivious of the events around him, Voltaire flattered himself—although he was not sure—that he, at least, had explained away this difficulty in the dialogue. As a device for filling in the space of three acts, he used the legendary passion of Philoctetes for Jocasta, at the same time confessing it a considerable defect, for now he seemed to have two tragedies—one centering on Philoctetes, the other on Œdipus. Once having brought Philoctetes into the story, Voltaire felt it proper to assign him the position of hero—as, indeed, it was very fitting to do, seeing that Sophocles had, with Philoctetes, created one of the most brilliant static tragedies the world has ever known. Voltaire, unfortunately, invented only the role of suitor for this hero. Besides, bringing him into the story gives us two uninformed principal characters in the play, for Philoctetes knows no more about what is going on than Œdipus. Voltaire complained that this made his introduction to *Œdipe* very difficult, but he pretended to have solved the problem by studying the situation of Nicomède, which, he asserted, was similar to Philoctetes's, and Racine's introduction to *Bajazet*, which he deemed a superb performance.

Voltaire paid some attention also to the role of the chorus, having created one in his own play. He understood that the chorus is used either to discuss what has just happened in the entr'actes (an unnecessary function, in his opinion) or else to foretell what will happen (thus eliminating the element of surprise) or, finally, to discuss things irrelevant to the play (and, hence, superfluous). In the scenes themselves he considered the chorus even more misplaced, since it prevents the main actors from confiding in each other. Despite these objections, he created a chorus for his *Œdipe* only, as he said, to add more interest to the scene and more pomp to the spectacle. He gave the impression of wishing to use a chorus in the way Racine did in *Esther* and *Athalie*. He apparently had no intention of integrating it with the tragedy, as the Greeks had so superbly done. He only wished to add scenic effect to the work, and, in the last analysis, he regarded the chorus even in Greek plays as a useless survival of old Bacchic rites.

With these prejudices and an immaturity which accounts for

much of his impertinence, how could Voltaire have been expected to produce a work that would appeal to one of the most disciplined and sophisticated audiences that has ever existed? And yet his work did appeal to that audience.

It is impossible to find any standard of comparison whereby Voltaire's *Œdipe* can be measured against Sophocles's *Œdipus Rex*. The haunting beauty, the profound overtones of human mystery, the deep cry of human misery which Matthew Arnold discerned in the Greek work are totally lacking in Voltaire's false production. The horror produced by the presentation of an act so dreadful that no man dares gaze upon it coldly and dispassionately is nowhere felt in Voltaire's presentation. The simplicity and, at the same time, the world-shattering consequences of the deed are borne in upon us in the Greek play in a manner quite different from the geometrical schemings of the French counterpart. Suffering ennobles in Sophocles's play, while in Voltaire's version, even if it may be said to be present, it merely produces a command performance. The overpowering monstrosity of life, those hidden secrets springing from the depths of consciousness and impelling us to affirmations of self even when the annihilation of everything or the creation of everything is involved in that self, these things of which Racine could catch a vision in *Phèdre*, or Shakespeare in *Lear*, were totally incomprehensible to Voltaire.

And yet Voltaire's play was eminently successful, if success can be measured by its reception. Forty-eight performances attest to its popularity, and the praise of his contemporaries bears witness of its excellence. We have already noted that Jean Baptiste Rousseau, who did not normally dispense praise lavishly, admitted that it far exceeded his expectations. The career of a playwright never has begun more auspiciously, and in but few instances in the history of literature has it extended over a longer period of years, met with more triumphs, been more fiercely pursued, and ultimately been considered so mediocre.

We cannot assume, however, that, because Voltaire did not show any intimate knowledge of Aristotle's *Poetics*, Horace's *De Arte poetica*, or Boileau's *Art poétique* in his *Lettres sur Œdipe*, he was not interested in the nature of tragedy. There are few playwrights, I suspect, who, on the presentation of their first play, feel competent to pass judgment upon the nature of drama. Voltaire's mistake was discussing out of turn things which he was not ready to treat.

As a matter of fact, he was very interested in the art of the drama throughout his long life; he discoursed upon it, interminably, in the *Correspondence* as well as in the prefaces to the plays. When Lacombe edited the *Poétique de Voltaire* (1770) with the poet's blessing, he had a lengthy section (pp. 175-362) given over to excerpts from Voltaire's opinions about drama. We cannot dwell upon these ideas at length, but, if we are ultimately going to judge Voltaire's plays, it seems only fair to do so in his terms.

Voltaire was convinced that the theatre was one of the noblest inventions of the human mind and also one of the most useful ways of shaping manners and customs and of polishing morals. He insisted that the theatre had a special duty to correct morals. In his opinion, a play was one of the finest ways of teaching youth. Moreover, it was practically the only method of bringing sociable people together. Voltaire placed great weight upon this socializing tendency of the theatre: "Rien ne rend les hommes plus sociables, n'adoucit plus leurs mœurs, ne perfectionne plus leur raison, que de les rassembler pour leur faire goûter ensemble les plaisirs purs de l'esprit."

Voltaire nonetheless recognized some serious imperfections in the French stage of his time. In the first place, the physical arrangement of the stage made acting practically impossible. The play was thus reduced to a series of conversations, and action was suppressed. Voltaire regretted this shortcoming. He would have preferred a combination of English action with the wisdom, elegance, nobility, and decency of the French. It would be desirable, he urged, to develop more taste in the public for the beauties of drama. He agreed that the goal of all tragedy is to evoke terror and pity, and he distinguished three kinds: heroic, "terrible," and "attendrissante." He admitted that there were in French tragedy some almost insurmountable obstacles. It was very hard, for instance, to be precise and eloquent in French verse and equally difficult to bind together the scenes and to observe all the complicated rules of decorum. The factors which counted in a play were the beauties of the verses, the truth of the feelings, the "liaison" of the scenes, the dialogues, the sublime thoughts, and the emotions expressed. Voltaire concluded that, of the "plaire" and "toucher," which all the classicists accepted as the aim of drama, the "toucher" was the most difficult to achieve. "Le secret de toucher les cœurs, est dans l'assemblage d'une infinité de nuances délicates, en poésie, en éloquence, en déclamation, en peinture, et la plus légère dissonance en tout genre est senti aujourd'hui par les connaisseurs." The public had become, in fact, very sensitive to defects, even more sensitive to defects than to beauties. Voltaire accepted the Aristotelian definition of tragedy as the representation of an action, but he seemed to understand by it the more normal meaning of the word "action," rather than "act." He deemed the rules reasonable: they prevent defects and occasion beauties. The aim of dialogue, he held, consists in making the actors say what in reality they should be saying. To achieve this aim, the author must have the imagination to transform himself into each character. Moreover, in the dialogue there must be a "secret logic" which is the soul of all conversing.

Voltaire noted that the French had become most distinguished in the theatre, in the first place because they were highly socialized, but also because they had a high regard for pomp and the sublime. According to his interpretation, pomp is for the eyes, while sublime thought is for the soul. Still, he believed that, despite its merits, French tragedy was lacking in force: instead of terror, pity, and horror, it aroused tenderness, astonishment, and the milder emotions. He also felt it to be lacking in depth: although it was distinguished by the conversations and its "esprit de galanterie," it lacked a "degré de chaleur." Voltaire proposed the substitution of "peintures vivantes," "actions terribles et déchirantes," for the "déclamations." Finally, he judged the French theatre superior to the Greek in the art of developing the scenes, in the invention of the plot, and in the beauties of style. History had been substituted for fables, and politics, personal ambition, and jealousy had supplanted heroic actions. The French, he thought, were more skilled in the techniques of the theatrical art: in the introductory scenes, in the liaisons of the scenes, in the entrances and exits of characters, in the clash of sentiments, in the accuracy of speech, and in the purely invented plot. In all these respects, Racine was his model. Voltaire praised him for the art of verse and the use of language; he had nothing but admiration for Racine's "charmes de la poésie," the "grâces de sa diction," and the "douceurs de son éloquence sage."

In these terms, a place could be found in the theatre for Voltaire's *Œdipe* and, indeed, for the remainder of his dramatic works, too. In relation to their audience, distinguished by its desire to converse at length upon the permissible and the impermissible in drama, upon the real and the appearance of reality, upon the moral and the immoral, these plays were certainly quite adequate. *Œdipe* and Voltaire's subsequent drama were perfectly suited for the kind of analysis they were given, based on rules of judgment which emphasized the harmony of the verses, the technical aspects of the stage production, and the ways in which a character may be portrayed. Since beauty of detail is what the audience demanded and what Voltaire aimed to supply, there is no reason to condemn his plays for lacking in total effect or organic unity. In his own terms, he had tried, as he had with the epic, to produce what was demanded and to do so to the best of his ability.

6. THE POET AS FREE-THINKER

Although it was the avowed intention of Voltaire between 1715 and 1738 to become France's outstanding poet and although to all intents and purposes he did achieve that ambition, only to trade his poetic renown for one far greater, it would nevertheless be unwise to assume that he was, during these early years, giving his undivided attention to the art of poetry. In any event, practically all his biographers from Duvernet on have undertaken to present a Voltaire precocious in his unbelief, active in his opposition to Christianity, extremely anti-clerical, and ardently deistic. Only a few of them fail to note that he already had those tendencies before leaving Louis-le-Grand. Duvernet stresses that virtually all of his classmates at the Jesuit college, became, as he did, fervent deists, thereby implying either that the young Arouet was exceedingly active in making converts or that the Jesuits were exceedingly lax in doing so. Since Duvernet's day, scarcely a biographer has failed to repeat Elie Harel's story concerning Lejay's exasperation at the young Arouet and his prediction that his pupil would one day become the leader of deism.

By far the most detailed exploration into the development of Voltaire's thought in these early years is that undertaken by René Pomeau in *La Religion de Voltaire*. His inquiry into the forces, social and intellectual, which turned Voltaire away from orthodox Catholicism leads him to list first among them the latent Jansenism present in the Arouet family that found full expression through Armand, Voltaire's "Janséniste de frère." Voltaire himself was not entirely free from this influence and became involved, as we have seen, at least to the point of expressing in verse his deep respect for the Bishop of Senez. We have not sufficient evidence to measure the extent to which Jansenism attracted him, but very likely whatever interest he may have evinced was counteracted by the unquestioned influence of his Jesuit teachers. On this matter, too, our evidence is scant. Pomeau, on the strength of a letter Voltaire wrote to Fyot de la Marche, suggests that the teachers, recognizing the brilliance of their young student, encouraged him to enter the order but that he was uninterested in the invitation. This hypothesis is tenuous indeed. It would be more helpful if we knew to what extent these teachers introduced Voltaire to seventeenth-century thinkers and to philosophy in general. To this problem we have no possible solution. Pomeau, pointing to the liberalism in the Jesuit catechism and the optimism in the Jesuits' view of man, surmises that Voltaire at least played this liberalism and optimism against the rigorism of the Jansenists. Pomeau also stresses the existence of such works as Abbadie's *Vérité de la Religion chrétienne,* Bastide's *Incrédulité des déistes confondue,* and Le Vasseur's *Entretiens de la religion* and raises the possibility that the Jesuits might have recommended these to their pupil. There is, however, no evidence that Voltaire was familiar with any of these works at this time. The writings of Fénelon, also suggested by Pomeau, were more likely known to him.

A far greater force in directing his thought, as well as his poetry, seems to have been the society of the Temple, whose distinguishing mark was libertinism. Voltaire had been introduced to this group by his godfather, who is also thought to have taught him at an early age to recite the *Moïsade.* Among those frequenting the society, he appreciated particularly La Fare and Chaulieu. Indeed, Chaulieu's three poems entitled *Trois façons de penser sur la mort: La Première, dans les principes du Christianisme; La Seconde, dans les principes du pur Déisme; La Troisième, dans les principes d'Epicure et de Lucrèce* had perhaps more impact on the youthful Voltaire than any other influence of the Temple.

Chaulieu's three poems, it should be noted, sum up the libertine attitude to life as it had been developing from Montaigne's time to the opening years of the eighteenth century. They were cast, for poetic reasons, in a form indicating that there are three approaches to the problem of life and death—the Christian, the deist, and the epicurean. All three of these approaches had been amply discussed by the greatest of "libertins"—Montaigne. When compared with the great sixteenth-century author of the *Essays,* however, Chaulieu seems terribly diminished; his poetry has neither the force of the *Apology* nor the depth of *De l'Expérience,* and it has none of the *Essays'* richness of substance, none of the inherent creative power of Montaigne's skepticism. From the point of view of art, the result is disappointing. Assuming that Descartes is correct and that poets can always say things better than philosophers, we should expect Chaulieu's poems to be more condensed, tense, carefully structured, and certainly better formed. At best, they are a pale reflection of a literary giant. But they are nonetheless a historical summation of a whole century.

The poems contrast the libertine concept of God with the rigorist concept. Both concepts are declared Christian, but in reality one is rigorist and Christian—Calvinist and Jansenist, if you will—while the other is libertine and Christian. The God who is libertine and Christian is next placed in contrast with the deist God, the God of Nature, *Deus sive Natura*, the giver of moral law, of justice, of human possibilities. And, finally, the deist God, the moral God of the libertine, is placed in contrast with Nature, the Nature of Lucretius and Epicurus, in all probability the Nature of Descartes, Leibniz, and Spinoza, certainly the Nature of Gassendi. Chaulieu does not follow the order of history, but, after all, it is asking too much for poets to be historians, too. It is enough to expect them to be philosophers.

Again, in observing these three poems, we are impressed by the fact that they, perhaps better than any critical disquisitions, represent the mentality of the Temple habitué and the Regency libertine. The revolt against Catholic rigorism, the acceptance of a God of goodness and mercy, the perfect tolerance in balancing one of these concepts against the other, the insistence upon morality as the supreme gift of God and upon justice and friendship as the supreme blessings of morality, and, finally, the belief that the good life is heir to these things by virtue of the bounties of nature and that man hastens to profit from them—all these were elements of libertine philosophy, the result of crossing Horace the poet with Epicurus and Lucretius the philosophers. But Horace and Epicurus and Lucretius are just as fleeting as time itself. The striking thing about this philosophy is that it was as carefree, as "indifférente," as impertinent as was Watteau's "Indifférent."

Voltaire's whole intellectual attitude toward life at this time was summed up in these three poems of Chaulieu. Indeed, they impressed him so strongly that he all but took them over bodily. We have only to make a line-to-line comparison of the *Epître à Uranie* and the Chaulieu verses, taking note of similar, and sometimes even identical, expressions, to realize how greatly Voltaire was indebted to his old friend. In scanning the contemporary epistles and odes, we find repetition of the same themes: the *carpe diem*, the pleasures of the mundane, the values of friendship, belief in a God of mercy and goodness, indifference to dogma, dislike of rigorism, love of justice. Voltaire in 1722 gathered these themes into his *Trois façons* and called it the *Epître à Uranie*.

The Temple, along with its interest in Horatian poetry, best expressed for Voltaire by his old friend Chaulieu, was also interested in free-thinking in general and, indeed, through connections with some of its frequenters, laid claim to that outstanding representative of the free-thinkers, Saint-Evremond. Although he had spent his life in exile, either in Holland or London, from 1661 on, Saint-Evremond carried on a consistent correspondence with La Fontaine and with Ninon de Lenclos. Sainte-Beuve was among the first to point out the filiation: "De Montaigne et de Charron à Saint-Evremond et à Ninon et de Ninon à Voltaire, il n'y a que la main, comme on voit. C'est ainsi que, dans la série des temps, quelques esprits font la chaîne." (*Causeries du lundi*, Garnier edn., IV, p. 190)

Saint-Evremond was, as Sainte-Beuve called him, a "Montaigne adouci." Lanson has noted that he took a median position between rigid virtue and selfish interest. Indeed, he refused to believe in either extreme vice or extreme virtue; he considered man too mediocre to be extreme in anything. He counseled indifference to the Christian ideal of sacrifice and advised against paying too close attention to the problems of life. Man must get out of himself, forget his misery, and use his pleasures to palliate the pain of living; the "divertissement" which Pascal condemned, Saint-Evremond approved. Fully epicurean, he demanded an active, not a passive, seeking after happiness, judging it an individual matter. At the same time, he displayed scant interest in social bliss, although most of his life was spent in pleasant conversation in the salon of the Duchess of Mazarin. In religious matters, he was an unbeliever, but he was not vocal in his opposition. For him, reason and faith could have nothing to do with each other, since reason is unable to prove the existence of God or the immortality of the soul. He paid scant attention to the various conventicles, noting that what is common to all sects is morality. He urged tolerance and condemned all forms of persecution. And yet, though he counseled obedience to the laws of one's country, he expressed a certain contempt not only for the persecutor but also for the persecuted.

Voltaire knew of Saint-Evremond not only through the Temple but also through Desmaizeaux, his biographer, whom Voltaire called upon frequently in England. Desmaizeaux noted in his biography Saint-Evremond's desire to understand the nature of things and his assiduity in seeking out the scholars of his day. Already he had immersed himself in Montaigne and Descartes; he visited Gassendi, whom he found the most enlightened of philosophers and the least pretentious. In Holland he became acquainted with Spinoza, Heinsius, and Vossius. In the salon of the Duchess of Mazarin, he was thrown together with Saint-Réal, the historian who influenced Voltaire. The frequenters of this salon discussed all sorts of subjects: philosophy, history, religion, belles-lettres, and even gallantry. In the quarrel of the ancients and moderns, Saint-Evremond took the side of the moderns. Finally, he held in great esteem Bayle's *Dictionnaire*. Desmaizeaux added that he depicted himself as a voluptuary, neither superstitious nor impious; he inclined naturally to all pleasures, though he had much distaste for debauchery. He was loath to see and to expose the evil side of man but readily admitted that he found man and his follies amusing. In friendship he asserted that he was more constant than a philosopher.

Voltaire set aside a place in his catalogue of writers in the *Siècle* for Saint-Evremond and devoted an additional article to him in the *Lettres à Monseigneur*, but in neither article did he do justice to his predecessor. Voltaire did note that Saint-Evremond's philosophy and his works were well-known and that his *History of the Romans* was appreciated. Still, he found his verses detestable and denied that the deistic treatises attributed to him after his death in 1703 could have been composed by him. Finally, he rightly ascribed the famous *Entretien* of the Maréchal d'Hocquincourt to Charleval. And he concluded by condemning Desmaizeaux for filling Saint-Evremond's biography with ideas extracted from his works, thus tacitly admitting, I suppose, that he had read the biography and had been able to identify the sources of the ideas discussed.

One would think that Voltaire would have been more perspicacious and more enthusiastic, since Saint-Evremond was apparently one of the most popular libertine writers (fifteen editions up to 1703, twelve more between 1703 and 1753). By and large, he was the representative of the free-thinking "honnêtes gens," discreet in his pronouncements, modest in his assertions, but skeptical, ironic, almost genuinely indifferent to all the problems of life. Saint-Evremond was convinced that man seeks happiness, that pleasures prevent him from thinking about his misery, and that those pleasures which endure the longest are found by withdrawing from the world. A small company of "honnêtes gens," conversation, the reading and discussing of literature—these were his delights.

In many respects, Saint-Evremond wrote of the good life as a model "mondain." In the essay entitled *He who wishes to know everything, does not know himself*, he stressed that, in our desire to know what will become of us after death, we look to the philosophers for the answer, not realizing that they are as ignorant as everyone else about these things: Plato, Aristotle, Zeno, Epicurus contradict each other. Saint-Evremond noted that it is one of life's misfortunes that we can never know certain things. Philosophers who proclaim one view act contrary to their own opinions. Epicurus taught that everything is matter—even soul, spirit, mind—and that everything becomes corrupt and perishes; yet he acted as if he expected to survive this life. And Descartes, who talked of a substance which is purely spiritual, which thinks eternally, what did he prove, except that he had no proofs for his belief? Saint-Evremond concluded that reason must submit in all matters of faith.

Since it is impossible to know first principles or ultimate answers, we must console ourselves, he said, by seldom reflecting upon life and by endeavoring to escape our misery through our search for pleasures. Glory, success, love, and volupty, well understood and regulated, are great bulwarks against the rigors of nature and our afflictions. In an essay on the *Subjects to which an "honnête homme" may devote himself*, Saint-Evremond confessed that he preferred conversation to reading. Discussions upon theological matters he eschewed, since they had become "fort communes." Moreover, they elicited contradictory responses: an ordinary man who denied the existence of God was burned, while, in the Schools, scholars debated publicly the question of whether God exists. Hobbes, the greatest genius in England since Bacon, blamed Aristotle and his subtleties for the division of the Church. Saint-Evremond acknowledged that philosophy gives great freedom to the mind and that it leads to knowledge of the nature of things. He became aware, nonetheless, that there are so many contradictions among philosophers that the results of much speculation are useless. It was at this juncture that he visited Gassendi, who complained that he had a limitless curiosity and a limited intelligence. Turning to mathematics, Saint-Evremond found them surer, but too exacting. He respected mathematicians, but he believed we gain more from enjoying the world than from knowing it. He concluded that an "honnête homme" can concern himself only with "la morale," "la politique," and "les belles-lettres." "La morale" will teach him to govern his passions; "la politique" will instruct him in the affairs of state and in the regulation of his conduct in the passing events; and "les belles-lettres" will polish his understanding and inspire delicacy and charm.

In a *Discourse on Religion,* he conceded that we sometimes become so surfeited with libertinage that we crave to become "dévots." But there are difficulties: our opinions about supernatural things are often conditioned by our different temperaments. Besides, since reason has not established our beliefs, reason cannot justify changing them. Still, religious dogma is everywhere in dispute. Men can, however, agree concerning morals. The world is, in fact, in agreement on God's commandments to man and on the obedience which is His due: "Car alors Dieu s'explique à l'homme en des choses que l'homme connaît et qu'il sent." But, when it comes to mysteries, the human mind is incapable of understanding them.

These views are so closely in accord with those Voltaire expressed in his *Discours en vers sur l'homme* that one can hardly deny their importance. Yet, owing to the peculiar circumstances in which they were developed, it is difficult to determine whether they passed directly from Saint-Evremond to Voltaire or whether Voltaire absorbed them via the English moralists. Saint-Evremond undoubtedly derived them from the libertine Frenchmen from Montaigne to Bayle. His *Essay on Friendship,* for example, displays the same structure, the same ideas, and the same form as Montaigne's *De l'Amitié.* But Saint-Evremond developed these ideas in the free-thinking atmosphere of England. They were appreciated particularly by the English moralists Locke, Shaftesbury, and Mandeville and, most of all, by Pope; and, because of them, the French essayist was accorded the honor of being buried in Westminster Abbey. Whether Voltaire received them by way of England or came upon them before the English experience is thus a delicate question, and one which no critical analysis can ever answer.

At all events, it seems incontestable that Saint-Evremond's association with Saint-Réal modified his writing of history and that the two exercised considerable influence upon Voltaire. In the *History of the Romans*, Saint-Evremond confessed that he had tried to bring out the "divers génies" of the Romans: "Je me contenterai de suivre le génie de quelques temps mémorables, et l'esprit différent dont on a vu Rome diversement animée." He agreed with Fontenelle, Bayle, and Lenglet that, "pour connaître le génie des temps, il faut considérer les peuples dans les diverses affaires qu'ils ont eues." Curiously, he held war to be one of the most important of these affairs, whereas Lenglet and Espiard attached more importance to religion. Saint-Evremond, for his part, laid down the rule that historical events derive from human character and, therefore, the historian who best analyzes character will best understand historical events. He conceded that the study of character is difficult because of the complications of humors. Virtues which seem similarly present in two peoples turn out often to be very distinct virtues because of the different "humeurs" and "génies" of the peoples who possess them. Some of the difference, he said, is also due to the fact that the "génie" of a people frequently derives from their manners and customs.

Voltaire found all these suggestions helpful when he undertook his *Charles XII*. Earlier in his career, they must have been, though a distant guide, glimpsed by him through the eyes of his libertine friends. But I doubt that the young poet, so alert to the mode of the day, spent much time pouring over the *Essays* of his predecessor. He frankly avowed that Saint-Evremond's poetry was bad. Still, the author of the *Œuvres mêlées*,[14] with his reputation for being the model "honnête homme," the "mondain," the skeptical, satirical, ironical free-thinker, could hardly have failed to attract the attention of the young Arouet.

[14] Voltaire's library had one volume of the *Œuvres meslées*, Barbin, 1699, and nine volumes of the ten-volume *Œuvres meslées*, Paris, 1740, along with Desmaizeaux's biography. Apparently, Voltaire's acquaintance with Saint-Evremond was perfunctory until the Cirey period.

From 1718, after his release from the Bastille, until 1725, when the unpleasant episode with the Chevalier de Rohan began, Voltaire turned out an incredible body of writing. His activity was particularly intense between 1719 and 1723, the period embracing the *Œdipe*, the *Ligue* and the *Epître à Uranie*, not to mention other epistles and odes. Significantly, this period coincided exactly with the feverish traffic in clandestine manuscripts which circulated during the first part of the century. Boulainvilliers, who was in a way the center of this clandestine activity, died in 1722, one of the peak years of the movement. This short passage from the Cardinal de Bernis's *Mémoires*, quoted by Pomeau, reveals the character of the age: "Dès 1720, la corruption devint presque générale, on afficha le matérialisme, le déisme, le pyrrhonisme; la foi fut réléguée chez le peuple, dans la bourgeoisie et les communautés; il ne fut plus de bon ton de croire à l'Evangile" (*Religion*, p. 89). Evidently, it was at this time that Voltaire became acquainted with Lévesque de Pouilly: in a letter to Pouilly in 1739, he mentions having been fond of him for twenty years. Indeed, in 1722, he wrote a short note to Thiériot, urging him to pass by Pouilly's house in Paris and giving certain information about the latter's habits which clearly shows that he was familiar with them. It was during this period also that he knew Saint-Hyacinthe, who took part in the dragonnades and who was said to be the author of *Le Militaire philosophe*, one of the clandestine manuscripts written around 1711. Saint-Hyacinthe later became embroiled with Voltaire in the Desfontaines affair. In 1719, the only reasons for his association with Voltaire were his interest in clandestine manuscripts and his friendship with Lévesque de Pouilly and Lévesque de Burigny, who is also known to have dabbled in clandestine manuscripts. Lévesque de Pouilly and his brothers, Lévesque de Burigny and Lévesque Champeaux, were acquainted with Bolingbroke; in fact, Lévesque de Pouilly was at La Source when Voltaire visited Bolingbroke in 1724. Voltaire had a lasting regard for Pouilly. In 1742, he described him as a man of great learning, who was at the same time amiable, gentle, and easy in manner—not at all like a scholar. Even as late as 8 October 1749, Voltaire was singing his praises to D'Argental.

It was Bolingbroke, however, who not only served as the focus around whom these people congregated but who actually guided his

French friend along the path of philosophy. The problem of the extent of this influence still remains very uncertain. Hurn, for instance, apparently exaggerates it, while Torrey is inclined to minimize it. Certain critics point to the fact that the publication of Bolingbroke's works occurred too late (the five-volume Mallet edition of the *Philosophical Works* appeared in London in 1754-1755) for them to have had an appreciable impact on Voltaire. If one is to give any credence to Voltaire's notification "écrit vers 1736" on the *Examen important de Milord Bolingbroke,* the *Philosophical Works* certainly could not have influenced him. Nor could they have been of any great assistance in his other, particularly his historical, studies. However, recent discoveries about the publication dates of Bolingbroke's works have reopened the question of relationship. Even before Nadel's discoveries, Professor Dargan, in a review of Torrey's *Voltaire and the English Deists*, suggested that Torrey was too ready to assume an "anti" attitude toward the Bolingbroke-Voltaire relationship (see *Modern Philology*, XXIX [1931], 123). And Pomeau, citing Bolingbroke's letter of 27 June to Voltaire, first published in the *Collection of Autograph Letters and Historical Documents formed by Alfred Morrison* (1893), declares that the matter has now been settled: "Bolingbroke fut bien l'initiateur philosophique de Voltaire" (*Religion*, pp. 91-92).

Although much confusion still surrounds the question of the relationship between the two men, there is now some evidence that Bolingbroke did, at least, aid in turning the young Voltaire away from his flirtation with the general epicureanism and libertinism of the Temple toward a more serious consideration of philosophers and philosophy. In the letter just mentioned, Bolingbroke wrote: "Si vous lisez *l'Essay sur l'Entendement humain,* vous lisez le livre que je connois le plus capable d'y contribuer. Si vous n'y trouvez que peu de choses, prennez garde que ce ne soit votre faute. . . . Il est sûr que vous n'y trouverez pas les profondeurs de Descartes, ni le sublime de Mallebranche . . . on a découvert par exemple que Des Cartes dans la physique et Mallebranche dans la Métaphysique ont étez plutost poètes que philosophes." (B. 185) Bolingbroke added that these poetic flights of Descartes and Malebranche beyond the bounds of observation and geometry had been countered by Huyghens and Newton, who had proved that Nature acts quite differently. He urged his young friend to bring out "le grand fond de bien" bestowed upon him by Nature and to hasten to cultivate his judgment.

It is difficult to judge whether Bolingbroke's letter was just a general exhortation on the part of an older man to a young and promising admirer or whether it was intended as a specific plan for approaching the study of philosophy. It becomes all the more awkward to establish a fixed opinion in the absence of Voltaire's reply, which has not been preserved. However, there can be no doubt that Bolingbroke was the first of Voltaire's friends to exhort him to take a more serious approach to philosophy, and it may be inferred, also, that up to this point the poet had given scant thought to a thorough preparation in this field. There still remains the question to what extent Bolingbroke was capable of advising his young protégé. Voltaire saw in him a man of broad culture and great learning; such, at any rate, was the impression he gave in his enthusiastic report to Thiériot. At a much later date, when Sherlock was visiting him at Ferney, he expressed another opinion: Bolingbroke's works are like a tree having many leaves but little fruit. Modern criticism has made much of this later judgment.

From Bolingbroke's letter we may gather that Voltaire was being advised to turn his attention to Locke, Descartes, Malebranche, Huyghens, and Newton, particularly Locke and Newton. We may infer from it, too, that Voltaire already had some acquaintance with Descartes and Malebranche. W. H. Merrill, in his *From Statesman to Philosopher*, has raised the question of Bolingbroke's competence in philosophy, particularly with regard to his knowledge of ancient philosophy, contemporary philosophy, and deism. Among the works of ancient philosophers, it appears that the noble lord knew Ficino's translation of Plato, Dacier's translation of the *Phædo*, Plutarch's *De placitis philosophorum*, Cicero's *De Natura deorum* (and, indeed, practically all of Cicero's essays), Aristotle's *Metaphysics*, his *De Anima*, and the *De Historia animalium*. In addition, he seems to have had some acquaintance with Lucretius and Seneca. Among the moderns, he was most enthusiastic about and most familiar with Bacon. He had read Hobbes as carefully as Bacon, and he knew Locke thoroughly, especially the *Essay concerning Human Understanding*, which he recommended to Voltaire. On the other hand, he knew Newton only from secondary sources, such as Fontenelle's

Eloge (1728). By and large, he was much more familiar with English than with continental philosophers. He knew Descartes apparently through Daniel's *Voyage au monde de Descartes* and was dependent upon Daniel not only for his knowledge but also for his criticism of Descartes. Daniel's four points of attack—criticism of the *cogito*, objection to the principle of the soul's essence being thought, protest against the notion that animals are machines, and a critique of occasionalism—were all repeated by the English lord. Furthermore, he had not read Spinoza and, like many others who had no first-hand knowledge of his works, reacted to him violently. He showed no real knowledge of Leibniz either, although he quoted from him in discussing the Leibnizian criticism of Malebranche's doctrine. Since he had read Clarke thoroughly, he must have been well acquainted with the Leibniz-Clarke controversy. He was familiar with all the political theorists, from Grotius and Pufendorf to Selden. He appears to have known Malebranche exceedingly well, probably because of the latter's connection with Locke. But, of the continental philosophers, he was best acquainted with Bayle. Indeed, it is more than probable that his fundamental source for continental philosophy was Bayle's *Dictionnaire historique et critique*. From the above sampling we may reasonably assume that, if Bolingbroke rendered service to Voltaire in the field of philosophy, it was in directing him toward Locke and Newton and, more important still, in introducing him to Bayle.

The question of Voltaire's acquaintance with Bayle is even more perplexing than that of the Bolingbroke influence. The first reference Voltaire made to Bayle was in 1723 in connection with *La Ligue*, when he indicated that he had been using the *Réponse aux questions d'un provincial* to document his epic poem. But it is highly probable that he knew the author of the *Dictionnaire* long before that date, and, in fact, it is hard to understand how the young Voltaire could have avoided coming across the "philosophe de Rotterdam." There was, for instance, a reedition of the *Dictionnaire* in 1720, dedicated to the Regent. In 1722, Voltaire made his trip to Holland with Mme de Rupelmonde and apparently met Basnage, for at a later date he spoke of Basnage's deep devotion to Bayle. It is unlikely, too, that he could have frequented the milieu of the Temple so assiduously without knowing Bayle. And, at a still earlier date, his teachers, in their respect for a worthy opponent, may well have discussed the philosopher with their student. These conjectures, which are always repeated by Voltaire's biographers, are, it must be stressed, only conjectures. Even if they were true, they would not prove that Bayle had much influence on Voltaire, because real knowledge of Bayle can be obtained only by reading him, and, besides, the Rotterdam philosopher is so enigmatic that one cannot be assured even then of knowing him truly. Thus, even though it is not impossible that Voltaire had by 1724 heard Bayle discussed by the members of the Temple, as well as by Bolingbroke, it is unlikely that he had any clear understanding of his significance or any real acquaintance with his work until he started preparing the *Lettres philosophiques* (that is, in 1728 or 1729).

There are two remarks to be made concerning the influence Bolingbroke exerted over Voltaire. It should be recalled that the English lord was thoroughly versed in Malebranche's *Recherche de la vérité*. Voltaire, for his part, deemed the first part of the *Recherche* a masterpiece and confessed that he had thoroughly annotated the whole work. That Voltaire knew the *Recherche* is confirmed by a remark in a letter to Thiériot (27 June 1725): "Je vous envoierai la recherche de l'amitié au lieu de celle de la vérité. . . ." That he knew it well is revealed in another letter by his reference to "un exemplaire marginé de ma main il y a près de quinze ans" (M. XXXIV, 523). It is not unlikely that the English lord was the one who attracted the Frenchman's attention to the work.

The second remark is more problematical. Bolingbroke rejected, as Voltaire did in the *Epître à Uranie*, both the portrait of God presented in the Old Testament and the one presented by Paul in the New Testament (*Philosophical Works*, ed. Mallet, 217):

If God must appear to be the fountain of all good, and the sole author of all the happiness we can hope for; can any man now presume to say, that the God of Moses, or the God of Paul, is this amiable Being? The God of the first is partial, unjust, and cruel; delights in blood, commands assassinations, massacres, and even exterminations of people. The God of the second elects some of his creatures to salvation, and predestinates others to damnation, even in the womb of their mothers. The precept of the Gospel, Thou shalt love the Lord thy God with all thy heart, cannot refer to such a God as either of these.

It is unlikely that Voltaire used the Bolingbroke passage or that he even needed it. Chaulieu's poems were entirely ample for the young visitor at the Temple; in his conclusion to *Le Pour et le Contre*, for example, Voltaire followed Chaulieu's line of thought, rather than Bolingbroke's. In another place, however, Bolingbroke presented in very succinct terms the same conclusions as Chaulieu and Voltaire: "That the Christian law is nothing else than the law of nature inforced by a new revelation, every friend to Christianity admits, and the worst of its enemies dares not deny, though he denies the reality of the revelation" (*Works*, IV, 26). It is interesting to note that the same basic problem occurred both to the epicurean poet and to the English lord and that Voltaire, in one way or another, ran into both presentations.

Besides turning Voltaire toward philosophy and away from poetry, by introducing him to Locke and Newton and perhaps encouraging him to explore Malebranche and Bayle, Bolingbroke might have influenced him in 1725 with his own philosophical ideas. This possibility can be illuminated by a comparison of certain of their views—though, it should be stressed, such a comparison can be made only in a general way.

Bolingbroke, like Voltaire, accepted the proofs of the existence of God from final causes but was inclined to reject the ontological proofs proposed by Descartes. Like Voltaire, too, he insisted upon a general rather than a particular Providence, feeling that God regards his human creatures collectively, not individually. He consequently refused to accept the idea that man is the final cause of the world. However, contrary to Voltaire, he expressed no particular interest in the doctrine of rewards and punishments. He took the attitude that any system of particular Providences would make for an unjust belief in rewards and punishments and in predestination, that, indeed, it would produce complete disorder in the universe. The end result, he felt, would be a series of constant miracles until miracles ceased to be. Miracles as such Bolingbroke accepted; but he was opposed to the idea that they were wrought by God in order to establish the Christian religion, and, in fact, he was inclined to deny their evidential value. Taking this position was tantamount to admitting that miracles are possible but uselsss.

Of more importance than these cut-and-dried deistic views was

Bolingbroke's optimistic view of the nature of the world, which he derived from his conception of God's attributes. Voltaire at one time took a similar approach. From this standpoint God was conceived as all-wise and all-powerful; consequently, it was assumed that He had created a world so perfect that His intercession was no further needed. Bolingbroke asserted, along with Leibniz, that this is the best of all possible worlds. But, as has been pointed out, his reasoning was illogical. From the order and perfection of the universe he inferred the existence of an omniscient and omnipotent God, and then, turning about, he inferred from the wisdom of God that the world is perfect. His argument led him to the acceptance of the principle of plenitude and the "Great Chain of Being" theory, a theory to which Voltaire was also at one time favorably disposed, as was Leibniz. The English lord, in fact, carried the theory to the point where he conceded that there are many rational beings above man in the scale of being and that (as Voltaire admitted, too) other planetary systems may include inhabited worlds.

From these principles he deduced the existence of evil. At first, he, like Bayle, was attracted by the view of the Socinians, who posited two forces whose constant struggle for domination of this world produces either good or evil according to the force dominating at a given moment. In time, like Bayle, he came to regard this explanation as equivalent to the Christian doctrine of the devil. Bolingbroke, attempting to explain evil, stressed that "the seeming imperfections of the parts are necessary for the real perfection of the whole" and argued that evil does not conflict with God's goodness but rather with man's ideas of goodness, which are entirely different from God's. Moreover, man by nature exaggerates evil. "The real evils, that men suffer, are not in truth so great as they appear in these exaggerated representations of them." He found proof of this claim in the fact that few men ever commit suicide—an argument that Voltaire once presented. Bolingbroke, in keeping with his time, classified evil into physical and moral categories, finding the former relatively rare and explicable by the interplay of parts with the whole, the latter much more prevalent and attributable to the exercise of free will by mankind. These ideas resemble those of Leibniz and King; in all probability, they derived from King rather than Leibniz and were tinged with the general optimism of Shaftesbury and Locke. Bolingbroke himself is said to have denied that he knew Leibniz.

Like Voltaire, Bolingbroke could not find proofs justifying either acceptance or rejection of the doctrine of the soul's immortality. Arguments for immortality, he believed, could neither be deduced from God's justice nor be proved by metaphysical explanations of the soul's immateriality. Although he was inclined to accept the notion that the soul is mortal, he did attempt to evade the charge of being a materialist, especially one like Spinoza. He was primarily interested, however, in establishing a natural religion based on reason. Being reasonable, it would, he felt, appeal to all men; by nature ethical, it would be based on a universal law applicable to all times and places.

Thus, in 1724, when Bolingbroke was giving advice to Voltaire, he was concerned not so much with philosophy as with deism, viewed as a modified type of Christianity. Had he been more philosophical, he would probably have exercised no influence upon the young Frenchman. As it was, Voltaire was of a mind to listen, and the *Traité de métaphysique*, written a decade later, gives confirmation of the fact.[15]

Professors Ascoli and Lanson have undertaken to assess the philosophical position of Voltaire before his departure for England.[16] Both stress that he wished to be libertine and philosopher. Ascoli notes that the two sources of Voltaire's thought at this time were the epicureanism of Lucretius (especially in the Third Canto of *De rerum natura*) and the philosophy of the free-thinkers. Lanson remarks, more carefully, that the atmosphere in which the young Voltaire circulated was compounded of the libertine current extending from Montaigne (whom Voltaire knew at the time and greatly appreciated) to Saint-Evremond, Vairasse, and Lahontan and the philosophical movement generated by Locke and, especially, Fontenelle

[15] L. Foulet, *Correspondance de Voltaire (1726-1729)*, pp. xiii-xiv: "Bolingbroke est certainement l'Anglais que Voltaire a le mieux connu, c'est celui qui était intellectuellement le plus près de lui, et il est même douteux si aucun de ses contemporains, Anglais ou Français, a eu sur lui plus d'influence que l'ancien ministre de la Reine Anne."

[16] See G. Lanson, *Voltaire*, pp. 26-36; G. Ascoli, "Voltaire," XXV[2] (1923-1924), 16-27, 128-144.

and Bayle. All of this free-thinking spirit was a part of the Regency society which he frequented. Lanson sums it this way: "Oter à la raison la connaissance de Dieu et de l'immortalité qui sont déclarées avec un respect ironique matières de foi, aimer la tolérance, détester la persécution et la guerre civile par scepticisme, par urbanité, par humanité, régler la vie selon la nature par la raison. . . ." To this were added a tendency toward deism and a search for happiness in the actual present-day world.

Into this milieu stepped Voltaire, ambitious, eager to acquire prestige as France's leading lyric poet, dramatist, epic poet, and arbiter of taste. To be a "homme de lettres," "homme de goût," was the foremost ambition of the young student who sallied forth from Louis-le-Grand and who was adopted by the devotees of the Temple. In addition, Voltaire had a keen desire to enjoy to the fullest the pleasures of this brilliant society and an equally strong urge to penetrate the inner meaning of life. He would be both a "libertin" and a "philosophe," balancing in the realm of thought his activity in the field of art. His deep curiosity concerning life, sometimes approaching morbidity and carrying with it an almost demonic defiance, was at the same time carefree and serious. In all probability, however, Voltaire imbibed the spirit of the Regency without delving too deeply into the free-thinking literature at his disposal. He might have plunged into Fénelon, Saint-Evremond, Houtteville, Bayle, and Fontenelle, as Lanson suggests, but it is more likely that he spent his time with the classical writers of Louis XIV's time, the Roman satirists, Virgil, and Lucretius. Although there was an abundance of free-thinking literature available, the chances are very strong that he became acquainted with it only second-hand at the Temple and at Bolingbroke's. We have already remarked that Bolingbroke may have directed him to Bayle, Locke, and Malebranche, and it is probable that he studied, or began to study, these three philosophers in some consistent fashion. But it is more likely still that his English friend in the course of conversation instructed the young man in the elements of philosophy and gave him some insight into his own views.

The first thing to be noted concerning Voltaire's philosophical frame of mind in 1725 is that the tone of his writing is almost as important as the content. This is particularly true in the *poésies légères*, where he strives for an effect at the same time epicurean, in the Horatian sense, and Regency or modern. To the Abbé Servien, imprisoned in Vincennes, he writes:

> A son état mesurant ses désirs,
> Selon les temps se faire des plaisirs,
> Et suivre enfin, conduit par la nature,
> Tantôt Socrate, et tantôt Epicure.

And, by way of encouragement, he adds:

> Ne passons point les bornes raisonnables.
> Dans tes beaux jours, quand les dieux favorables
> Prenaient plaisir à combler tes souhaits,
> Nous t'avons vu, méritant leurs bienfaits,
> Voluptueux avec délicatesse,
> Dans tes plaisirs respecter la sagesse.

This tone of levity can quickly change to seriousness. Here is an extract from an epistle to another abbé, who has lost his mistress:

> Ce qu'on perd en ce monde-ci,
> Le retrouvera-t-on dans une nuit profonde?
> Des mystères de l'autre monde
> On n'est que trop tôt éclairci.

Following this serious note is a description of the joyful life:

> Quelques femmes toujours badines,
> Quelques amis toujours joyeux,
> Peu de vêpres, point de matines,
> Une fille, en attendant mieux:
> Voilà comme l'on doit sans cesse
> Faire tête au sort irrité;
> Et la véritable sagesse
> Est de savoir fuir la tristesse
> Dans les bras de la volupté.

To a lady, he gives this counsel:

> Les plaisirs ont leur temps, la sagesse a son tour.
> Dans ta jeunesse fais l'amour,
> Et ton salut dans ta vieillesse.

This theme of *carpe diem* is repeated over and over:

> Gondrin, songez à faire usage
> Des jours qu'Amour a conservés;
> C'est pour lui qu'il les a sauvés:
> Il a des droits sur son ouvrage.

The classical model of this Horatian theme is the *Epître XIII à Madame de G———:*

> Le plaisir est l'objet, le devoir et le but
> De tous les êtres raisonnables;

> ....

> La superstition, fille de la faiblesse,
> Mère des vains remords, mère de la tristesse,
> En vain veut de son souffle infecter vos beaux jours;
> Allez, s'il est un Dieu, sa tranquille puissance
> Ne s'abaissera point à troubler nos amours:

This carefree tone mingled with a note of gravity and a touch of disrespect is very characteristic of Voltaire's light poetry. From the point of view of philosophy, it should not be accorded any particular importance, since poets have always been impertinent, satiric, and epigrammatic; indeed, Voltaire's chosen model, Chaulieu, was distinguished by these very traits.

Voltaire had, however, a tendency to thrust his intellectual preoccupations into his verse, thereby making it philosophical poetry. It was not an invention of his; Lucretius, one of his models, had used the same medium for the expression of his thought, and it had been a fixed practice with Horace, his master. Moreover, from time immemorial, poets have understood that their art consisted in singing in measured tones the profound thoughts of a people. If the poet was a seer, it was because he fathomed the deep meaning of these thoughts and could shape them in golden words and harmonious expression so that they would imprint themselves in the soul of man and upon the spirit of a race. Poetry thus became a song, a song of joy, sung by man the creator, the maker, to God, his Creator, his Maker. The poet was restricted by all sorts of rules but, in reality by only two conditions: his trade as poet (his "métier," as the French said) and the harmony of structure and content (that is, the rhythm into which he cast his thought had to be his thought). And there had to be a proper balance between these two conditions. Any attempt to enhance the "métier" at the expense of the harmony could have led to disaster; so could have any desire to augment the harmony at the expense of the "métier."

If these simple guidelines are kept in mind, we may better understand the tenor of the movement in philosophy and poetry in the seventeenth and early eighteenth centuries from which Voltaire took his origin as poet and philosopher. The first point we should bear in mind is that the most magnificent developments in the civilization of the seventeenth century occurred precisely in the realms of philosophy and poetry. Simply put, in no age in Western Europe up to that time had there ever been more and better philosophers and more and better poets. Indeed, in the history of Western Europe there had never been an age distinguished at the same time by the excellence of its poetry and by the excellence of its thought. It is not surprising, then, that there eventually arose the question of who was superior, the poet or the philosopher.

We cannot trace here the way in which this problem was developed. We can, however, make three points which are very important for the understanding of Voltaire's position as poet. The first concerns the attitude Descartes took from the very beginning of his career toward the relative importance of poet and philosopher (M. Decorte, "La Dialectique poétique de Descartes," p. 109). In the *Olimpica*, one of his early works, Descartes wrote (*Œuvres*, Adam and Tannery edn. X, 217): "Mirum videri possit, quare graves sententiae in scriptis poetarum, magis quam philosophorum. Ratio est quod poetae per enthusiasmum et vim imaginationis. . . ." There can be no doubt that, in the opinion of the one who was to be known as the father of modern philosophy, poetry was superior to philosophy precisely because the poet had at his disposal two faculties—enthusiasm and imagination—which the philosopher could not use. Descartes, in a development of this thought, explained in what way these faculties made the poet superior (*Œuvres*, X, 217ff). The seeds of truth, he stated, are found in ourselves, as fire in rocks, and not in the outside world. Consequently, it is in our own souls that we must seek this truth. This we can do only by the use of that intuition which resembles more the imagination of the poet than the reasoning of the philosopher. This intuition stirs our doubts and fears and thereby delivers our spirit from the throes of our evil genius, by purifying it from the evil effects of pride and senses and by driving us to action in which we obey the good even before knowing what it is. This intuition profits from the relationship which exists between the signs of the imagination and the truths of the understanding, between the world of extension and the world of the spirit. It gives us a sudden insight into our existence and our imperfections and, at this moment of recognition of our nothing-ness, leads to a glimpse of God, the perfect Being who alone can ex-plain both our imperfections and our feeling of imperfection. It is at this point that we have our poetic vision of God, the Unchang-ing Will, the Creator of the order of things, of essences as of exist-ences, of the laws of thought as of the laws of nature, and, finally, of the Good, which is God himself, who leads all things to perfection.[17]

It was in this way that Descartes established once and for all, I suspect, the true relationship between poetry and philosophy. But Descartes was a philosopher, by profession interested in penetrating the reality of things with the understanding. He only retained that part of the poet concerned with developing the metaphorical ex-pression of that reality; that is, in some peculiar way, he retained the symbols of poetry, even though his primary intent was to pene-trate the reality of things with reason. The result was that he and all his followers—Spinoza, Leibniz, and Malebranche—became known by those who believed that philosophy was superior to po-etry as "dreamers" and "poets." It was precisely in this way that

[17] This passage is so crucial to the whole development of philosophy and poetry that I cannot resist quoting it in the Chevalier translation of the Latin:

Les semences de la vérité se trouvent en nous, comme le feu dans le silex, et c'est en nous, dans nos âmes qu'il la faut chercher,—grâce à cette intuition qui ressemble plus à l'imagination du poète qu'au raisonnement des philosophes: —une intuition préparée par le doute, qui délivre notre esprit du malin génie en le purifiant des sens et de l'orgueil, et par l'action, qui nous fait obéir au bien avant de le connaître;—une intuition qui use des liaisons naturelles que Dieu a établies entre les signes de l'imagination et les vérités de l'entendement, entre le monde de l'espace, et le monde de l'esprit; une intuition, enfin, qui nous révèle tout à la fois notre être et son imperfection, et qui dans cette marque en creux, saisit l'être même de Dieu, l'Etre parfait qui seul peut expliquer notre être imparfait et le sentiment de notre imperfection,—volonté immuable, fonde-ment de l'ordre des choses, des lois de notre pensée, comme des lois de la nature, des essences comme des existences, et finalement du Bien, qui est Dieu même, ce Dieu qui mène toute chose à sa perfection.

Voltaire regarded him, after being introduced to him by Boling-broke. But, instead of seeing poetry as an extension of philosophy that was superior to it, Bolingbroke and Voltaire, and undoubtedly the whole school of geometricians, viewed it instead as opposed, and inferior, to philosophy.

There are reasons why it was natural for them to have adopted this attitude. The most important is the change which philosophy itself was undergoing. Instead of being understood as the philosophy of first principles, which is certainly the way Descartes first con-ceived it, it quickly became identified with the philosophy of the external world, that is, of nature. This shift was brought about partly by the mathematizing of nature but even more by the tremendous growth in natural science, which all but overwhelmed the other branches of philosophy. Even Descartes himself came to think of his importance as a philosopher in terms of natural science. Poetry could treat of the philosophy of first principles, but it seemed to have difficulty in dealing with the new science, the new learning, and the new cosmology.

Some of this difficulty led to the quarrel of the ancients and the moderns. As rationalism developed, it split away from aesthetic taste or, rather, classical aesthetic taste. Reason could look forward with confidence to its ability to penetrate the truth of things, but it was not so easy to make that truth conform to the dictates of clas-sical taste. In this respect, Cartesianism really betrayed Descartes. The emphasis shifted from truth to the clarity of truth. The proper balance between the expression and the harmony of structure and content was upset. The new discoveries in physics, couched in mathematical language, became increasingly difficult to translate into verse; it will be readily understood that geometry in poetry was merely an attempt to confirm a situation which had developed in accordance with its own logic. In short, there was, as Boileau stated in his poem to Molière, an imbalance between reason and rime. As La Motte put it, there was no thought which could not be more clearly expressed, and consequently better expressed, in prose. As even Fénelon confessed, poetry was a constraint which impeded thought.

Thus, the rise of geometry, which pretended to give a greater clarity and accuracy to poetic expression, in effect led to a quarrel between poetry and prose which threatened poetry with extinction. The argument between Voltaire and La Motte was characteristic of a widespread discussion current in the realm of letters during the period from 1685 to 1730. La Motte urged more and more the use of prose even in the poetic genres, while Voltaire, who acknowledged that poetry placed a dreadful constraint upon the expression of thought, steadily maintained until 1738 that every effort should be made to overcome the constraint because the use of poetic expression added an additional beauty to thought. The result of this overly urbane argument, between a poet who did not think any longer that the poetic effort justified itself and his friend who found that much could not any longer be put into poetry but that such thought as could be couched in verse justified the effort, was the ultimate removal of the poetic act from its position of supreme importance.

For Voltaire, who concerns us here, the results were anything but beneficial. He was still committed to remaining a poet-philosopher in an age committed to becoming philosophical. With the Cartesian balance overturned, the very existence and purpose of poetry were put into question. The greater misfortune arose when the age clearly decided in favor of prose. Voltaire, who wanted to be a poet, also wanted to be strictly of his time. He therefore found himself torn between the urge to be poetic and the need to be philosophical. As usual, he tried to shape his career so that he could preserve versifying and at the same time satisfy the public need for clarity of expression and mobility of ideas. He undoubtedly thought that the solution lay, not in the abandonment of poetry and the adoption of prose, which was the course La Motte, and, indeed, all the active geometricians favored, but rather in the infusion of more philosophy, that is to say, modern ideas, into poetry, thereby creating a philosophical poetry.

It is customary to list Voltaire's ideas in the order in which they occur in the *Epître à Uranie*, the *Henriade*, and the *Œdipe*. This practice is quite sensible, although only the *Epître à Uranie* is a true philosophical poem and even it is philosophical solely by derivation, since it was first an epistle of the Horatian kind. We have already observed how closely it depended upon the three Chaulieu poems; here, following Ascoli's judicious remarks, we should also point to its dependence upon the Third Canto of Lucretius's *De rerum natura.* The problem, however, is not the poem's source, although that is not without interest, but rather the coherence of Voltaire's thought in these works. There are three oppositions in *Le Pour et le Contre*: the first between the God of the Old Testament and the God of the New; the second between the Christ of the New Testament and the God who predestines vast numbers of human beings to damnation; the third between the Christian God and the deist God. The first two are developed in sequence, the third from the other two. But the fundamental issue, philosophically speaking, concerns the existence of God, not the choice of one of these portraits. The positive affirmation is deism: the essential point is God's existence free from dogma, cult, priesthood, and sect. Ascoli is correct in saying that Voltaire, in this first philosophic poem, reached his definitive attitude toward Christianity. The God of Voltaire may be defined in terms of the Christian God, but in reality He incarnates all the qualities stressed by deists:

> La puissance, l'amour avec l'intelligence
> Unis et séparés composent son essence.

Not only is He the essence of power, love, and intelligence, but He is also a God of reason, law, and justice. Hence, His subjects are those who pay Him homage by virtuous living, and His children are those who have the spirit of justice.

Although Voltaire believed firmly in the existence of a just God and felt that His existence can be proved by the doctrine of final causes, he was uncertain about the immortality and the immateriality of the soul (*Epître XVII*):

> Mon esprit m'abandonne, et mon âme éclipsée
> Perd en moi de son être, et meurt avant mon corps.
> Est-ce là ce rayon de l'essence supreme
>   Qu'on nous dépeint si lumineux?
> Est-ce là cet esprit survivant à nous-même?
> Il naît avec nos sens, croît, s'affaiblit comme eux:
>   Hélas! périrait-il de même?
> Je ne sais; mais j'ose espérer
> Que, de la mort, du temps, et des destins le maître,
> Dieu conserve pour lui le plus pur de notre être,
> Et n'anéantit point ce qu'il daigne éclairer.

Here we see considerable hesitation, but the note of materialism has been struck. It is true, though, that the materialism is balanced by a pious hope. Some of this expression was no doubt due to prudence, and some to genuine uncertainty. This, too, was to be the definitive attitude of Voltaire, though from time to time during his long career he would play the proportions of this attitude differently, sometimes emphasizing a firmer materialism, particularly when he could attribute the position to another, sometimes showing a kind of vacillation supported by a personal hope (he himself often used the word "hope" when he was really disturbed).

As for the problem of free will, Voltaire had already attempted to give it a rational definition. He believed fundamentally in a God who was the creator of this universe and whose will intervenes in the world He has created. He also felt that he, personally, was free to act—and he gave great importance to this feeling. His first inclination was to accept the orthodox position, which asserted the two firm principles without attempting to explain how the two are united. This was certainly his stand in the *Ligue*:

> On voit la Liberté, cette esclave si fière,
> Par d'invisibles nœuds en ces lieux prisonnière....

This "explanation," however, does not explain. It is dangerously close to making God, who is goodness and power, the author of our evil actions. Voltaire felt the same hesitation as Bayle before the problem of evil:

> Si ce Dieu du moins, ce grand Dieu si sévère
> A l'œuvre de ses mains avait daigné ravir
> Le pouvoir malheureux de lui désobéir!

But he did not push beyond the initial position in spite of his dilemma: God is the creator of all things; man has the feeling of being free. Voltaire did not change this position during his visit to England. He did, with the reading of Locke, clarify it. Locke explained that the dilemma occurs because the question is treated theologically rather than philosophically. The problem is not whether the wishing is free, it is whether the power is free. If I can do what I wish, then I am free; but I cannot will to will. Voltaire would ultimately question this position also, in the *Philosophe ignorant*, but his position is not clear even then.

The final element relating to the coherence of Voltaire's thought at this time is the problem of ethics. In this category Voltaire was much more explicit than would at first appear. The great sin of man is injustice; God does not tolerate this sin. He requires "bonne foi," "bonté," "douceur." All of these are marks of Christian charity, which should be used toward others. Charity is the source of our love of justice, the voice of conscience which speaks in the hearts of all men at all times, at all places. It was implanted in our hearts by nature. Nature is therefore good. In following it, we cannot go astray, but we often do go astray. Morality is nonetheless universal; it is the origin of a complete tolerance, which is the source of freedom of conscience. Man is responsible for his actions before men, but he is responsible for his beliefs only before God. Voltaire had already been struck by this tolerance in Holland, which can be seen in his letter of 7 October 1722 to Mme de Bernières: "Je vois des ministres calvinistes, des arminiens, des sociniens, des rabbins, des anabaptistes qui parlent tous à merveille, et qui en vérité ont tous raison."

Voltaire's thought before his departure for England thus embraced ideas on the nature and existence of God, the immortality and immateriality of the soul, free will and determinism, and the nature of the moral law, that is "le bien et le mal moral." It is striking that these were precisely the philosophical problems he reconsidered in the *Traité de métaphysique* in 1734, after his return from England. It is even more striking that they are considered in the *Traité* in practically the same terms as they were in the period preceding the English journey. There are, to be sure, some differences: Voltaire's thoughts concerning these matters had not been collected in a coherent whole until the *Traité*; the treatment accorded the problem of free will was enriched in the *Traité* by Locke's shifting of the problem from theology to philosophy; in the section in the *Traité* upon moral good and evil, Voltaire, owing to his attachment to Mandeville, streamlined the theory of natural law and stressed more fully the relativity of morality; and, finally, there was an added metaphysical problem, that of thinking matter, taken from Locke.

Incorporated in Voltaire's poetic thought, particularly in the *Henriade*, before his trip to England was also a body of ideas on political philosophy—if one may dare call his thoughts by such a formal name. Voltaire maintained that the interest of the state is the supreme institutional interest. He favored the monarchical state, but he also had much admiration already for the republican form as he had observed it in Holland. The one principle upon which he insisted is that the state should respect freedom of conscience. He feared, however, that the church would be more likely to intervene in the affairs of state than vice versa. He therefore laid down the principle that the state should tolerate all sects and expressed the thought that a multiplicity of sects might be beneficial for religious tolerance. He required loyalty to the state on the part of all sects: the Protestants receive his commendation in the epic poem because they remained loyal to the king. If he preferred a king as a ruler, it was because he demanded a certain number of qualities which make of the king a father of his people. He could not conceive of sovereignty of the people; for the moment, the term held no meaning for him. He regarded ordinary people as ignorant and untrustworthy; they seemed to him servile imitators of the voices of the court, full of superstitions, fond of miracles, and inclined to fanaticism. He wanted a mediator between the ruler and his people, such as he found in the Parlement, which not only provided the connecting link between tyranny and rebellion but also acted as a defender of the nation against the Holy See.

These last ideas are extremely interesting, but not because they entered into the philosophical pattern of Voltaire's thought. Like all his ideas at this time, they were scattered throughout his poetry. Their main interest is the way they fit into the general pattern of seventeenth-century thinking upon political affairs. Ascoli makes the remark that he does not know what could have been the source of these ideas. One might venture the statement that they show some resemblance to the political ideas of Hobbes (which Voltaire could have heard about from Bolingbroke) and to those of Spinoza. To infer that they came from any other source than hearsay, however, would be risky indeed. It would not be too hazardous, though, to conjecture that all of Voltaire's so-called philosophy, before 1726, came to him by way of the free-thinkers. For it was that type of informal thinking to which a poet, particularly a Horatian poet, would naturally be constantly exposed.

PART II

THE CIVILIZATION OF ENGLAND AND
ITS MEANING FOR VOLTAIRE

1. VOLTAIRE IN ENGLAND

BEFORE ENTERING upon an analysis of Voltaire's intellectual journey to England, it is necessary to establish a chronological sequence of events leading to his departure and his return. The quarrel with Rohan which precipitated the trip took place at the Comédie Française on 28 or 29 January 1726. It has been conjectured that the beating administered by Rohan's hirelings to Voltaire occurred on 31 January or 1 February. It was reported by Marais to Bouhier on 6 February and inscribed in Marais's *Journal*, III, 392. On 5 February, Maurepas wrote to Hérault, the Lieutenant de Police, requesting him to collect information on the affair and to arrest those whom Rohan had engaged to administer the beating. On 15 February, Marais imparted to Bouhier the news that Voltaire was being snubbed by people at court. The *Daily Courant* for 3 March, quoting a *Nouvelle à la main* for 25 February, announced that Voltaire, having failed to obtain any satisfaction in France, had gone to England. The report was premature. On 7 March, Vernet told Turrettini that Voltaire was taking fencing lessons; on 23 March, Maurepas informed Hérault that Rohan would be in Paris on that date and urged him to arrange matters to prevent another quarrel between the Chevalier and Voltaire. Two days later, on 25 March, the Rohan family obtained a *lettre de cachet*. On 26 March, Voltaire was reported arrested; on the day following, he was again said to have left for England. In reality, Maurepas did not give Hérault the order for Voltaire's arrest until 28 March. It was not executed immediately since, on 2 April, Marais notified Bouhier that Voltaire had disappeared and, on 14 April, announced to the same correspondent that the poet was now in the vicinity of Paris. On 16 April, Daumart, Voltaire's relative, appealed to Hérault for assistance in moderating Voltaire's activity. Hérault disclosed his intention of executing the order which Maurepas had previously issued to him, and, on 18 April, he stated that Voltaire had been arrested. Voltaire sent a letter to Maurepas almost immediately, asking permission to go to England and requesting to be released from the Bastille. The request to go to England was repeated on 24 April; the order for his release was given on 29 April, and he was exiled to a distance of fifty leagues from Paris. On 30 April, Voltaire told Thiériot that he was to be taken to Calais on the morrow or on the day following. As it turned out, he obtained his release and departed for Calais on 3 May, according to the *Daily Courant* for 13 May. On 5 May, now at Calais, Voltaire wrote to Hérault in order to set the matter straight about his exile. On the same day, he announced to Thiériot his departure for London in "quatre ou cinq jours." Foulet surmises that he reached London on 15 May. Just how he apportioned his time thereafter is not entirely clear. To Thiériot, on 12 August, he confessed that he had made a secret trip to Paris to seek out his enemy, but without success. On 26 October, he acknowledged to Thiériot that he had gone back to England at the end of July "very much dissatisfied with my secret voyage into France both unsuccessful and expensive." This secret trip to France has some enigmatic aspects. Even as late as 25 June 1728, Voltaire was exhorting Thiériot: "but let nobody be acquainted with the secret of my being in France" (Foulet, *Correspondance de Voltaire*, p. 157). Just why he should caution Thiériot almost two years after the event is puzzling. The only way I can interpret this remark is to assume that Voltaire had already returned to France when the letter was written or else contemplated returning secretly right away. Thiériot was let in on the secret because Voltaire must have notified him that he was going to use his permission to return, which had been granted him over a year before, if he was challenged. Voltaire, however, did not leave England before August, because we have a letter dated August at Wandsworth. At all events, on 25 November 1728, Peterborough informed Towne that Voltaire had gone to Constantinople; but I suspect that it was said in a spirit of jest. In February 1729, Voltaire wrote to Thiériot, apparently from French soil: "I am here upon the footing of an English traveller" (B. 335). On 10 March, he announced that he intended to stay at Saint-Germain and, on 25 March, stated that he had now arrived there. On 9 April, Maurepas wrote, granting him permission to stay in Paris.

It is not easy, because of the uncertainty of some of the information, to calculate the length of Voltaire's stay in England. The period from 15 May 1726 to February 1729 covers about two years and nine months; however, to be accurate, one would have to deduct the length of the secret trip to Paris, which seems to have taken about a month, and perhaps the three months' leave which Maurepas granted Voltaire on 29 June 1727. This adjustment would reduce the period to two years and five months. If Voltaire left England in November 1728, as Peterborough said, at least three more months would have to be deducted. The total then would be two years and two months. Peterborough spoke of Voltaire's departure as if it had taken place sometime in the past. Foulet calculates that it must have occurred two months before Peterborough's letter to Towne. Taking this fact into account would give Voltaire exactly two years in England,[1] or—since the question whether Voltaire used the permit to return to France in 1728 is very problematical—two years and a quarter. It is well to keep this estimate in mind so that we may not be tempted to crowd too much activity into the English experience.

Voltaire had shown some interest in England before the Rohan affair, as Professor Baldensperger has demonstrated.[2] Some of it was fostered by his epic poem. Since he had planned the visit of Henry IV to Queen Elizabeth (Canto II of the *Henriade*) it was perfectly natural for him to take an interest in the country which, in a way, became an ally. Once having achieved in a literary way some sort of rapport with England, Voltaire made some move to attract the attention of the English ruler. It has been suggested that he was the "certain petit philosophe" mentioned by the English plenipotentiary in 1714. At all events, it is certain that, on the publication of *Œdipe* (1719), Voltaire requested that a copy be sent to George I, with a characteristic dedicatory epistle. In return, the King presented to the poet a gold medal and a watch.

Voltaire had also known some distinguished Englishmen before his trip. He was acquainted, for instance, with Lord Stair when the latter was ambassador to Paris in 1718-1719. Indeed, he read Stair extracts from his epic, and it was through him that he arranged to have a copy of *Œdipe* with some dedicatory verses transmitted to the King of England. Voltaire was acquainted also with Bishop Atterbury, who had been introduced to him by Thiériot. His closest

---

[1] Voltaire himself once said that his stay lasted two years. See Voltaire to Brossette, 20 November 1733: "Mais si vous aviez été deux ans comme moy en Angleterre . . ." (B. 661).

[2] F. Baldensperger, "Voltaire anglophile avant son séjour en Angleterre."

English friend, though, was undoubtedly Bolingbroke, who, with the appearance of *Œdipe*, had become an admirer of the French poet. Voltaire visited him at La Source where he also met Lévesque de Pouilly, whom he later declared to have been the first in France to know Newton. As we have seen, too, Bolingbroke wrote to Voltaire in 1724, counseling him to address himself to the study of Newton and Locke.

Voltaire's personal interest in England coincided with the general interest engendered by French and English political events since 1685. The first of these events was the Revocation of the Edict of Nantes. Since England, unlike France, had evolved as a Protestant country, it was to be expected that many of the evicted Protestants would elect to exile themselves in London. Indeed, they established a center around the Rainbow Coffee House and there organized a movement which consisted in translating, printing, and sending to France political and philosophical tracts and works. Three of these French Protestants of importance to Voltaire were Coste, the translator of Locke's *Essay concerning Human Understanding* (1700) and Newton's *Optics* (1720), Desmaizeaux, the biographer of Bayle and Saint-Evremond, and César de Missy, the political pamphleteer whose collection of international documents were very helpful to Voltaire in the 1740s. We have no way of knowing the specific details of these relationships in 1726-1729, however, since documentary evidence is lacking. Hence, we can only record that Voltaire was exposed to the activities of the Rainbow Coffee House and could have availed himself of this material if he desired to do so. We can show that at a later date, at Cirey, he actually did make use of it, but any assumption that it was of importance to him in the initial period of his English experience is purely speculative.

The second political event which encouraged Voltaire's interest in things English was the Anglo-French Alliance established after the death of Louis XIV. This alliance was forged to serve as a defense of the Regent against Philippe V of Spain and as a quasi-defense of George I against the Stuarts. Although it was devised by Dubois and Stair as a political move, it came more and more to be cultural in its effect. It was this cultural aspect which undoubtedly attracted Voltaire at this time and which explains the courtesy shown him by the British authorities during his stay in England. We can understand more easily the real meaning of the *Lettres philosophiques* if we keep this event in mind, since the original plan for writing them grew out of a need to introduce France's new ally to the French and, only secondarily, out of a wish to reform France.

In England, Voltaire continued his relationship with Boling-broke, who had now returned, actually giving the noble lord's ad-dress for his mail. Through this friendship he undoubtedly found opportunities to meet with the aristocracy, as well as the literary fig-ures of the day, but just how this arrangement was managed we do not know exactly. Horatio Walpole, the English ambassador in Paris, furnished the exile with some letters of recommendation; it was apparently through him that the French poet struck up an acquaint-ance with Bubb Dodington, the Maecenas of the day, and through Dodington he came to know Lord Peterborough. Bolingbroke, Dod-ington, and Peterborough offered the French poet the chance to get to know all the important writers of the time: Swift, Pope, Young, Gay, Congreve, and Cibber (who was later to become the poet laureate). The French poet seems to have been on very intimate terms with Swift; when the latter planned a trip to France, Voltaire furnished him with letters of recommendation to Dunoquet, Mor-ville, and M. de Maisons, and, when the *Henriade* was about ready, he requested Swift, then in Ireland, to secure some subscriptions for him among the Irish. The two writers were said to have lived to-gether over a period of several months at Lord Peterborough's. Vol-taire visited Pope at Twickenham and, on the occasion of Pope's acci-dent in 1728, expressed deep concern for his welfare. Young became so closely associated with him that he is thought to have corrected the French poet's two *Essays*. Finally, Voltaire visited Congreve and later related how the comic writer requested that he regard him, not as a playwright, but only as an English gentleman.

Voltaire also mingled in circles other than those of the aristocracy and the writers. The *Daily Journal* for 27 January 1727 announced that the poet had had an audience with the King, who had graciously received him. He was on very intimate terms with the Prince and Princess of Wales. He became most closely attached to Everard Falkener, a merchant who at a later time became ambassador to the Porte. He spent many months at Wandsworth, where Falkener lived, particularly in the early part of his sojourn when he was attempting to learn the language and feel his way around. It was through his friend Falkener that Voltaire got to know the merchant class. There is even some evidence that he had himself instructed in the Quaker religion by one Edward Higginson, a teacher. He arrived too late to know Newton, but he had an audience with Mrs. Conduit, Newton's niece, who, incidentally, told him the anecdote of Newton and the apple, which he subsequently publicized. He was closely associated with Dr. Clarke, Newton's friend, and was on friendly terms with Bishop Berkeley. He knew Chetwood, the prompter at Drury Lane Theatre, and is supposed to have spent some time in the prompter's box following the text of some Shakespeare performances. He even identified himself for a while with the French Protestant refugees at the Rainbow Coffee House, but only in passing. However, he did continue his association with Desmaizeaux, who, besides being the biographer of Saint-Evremond and of Bayle, was the editor of a very important collection of essays upon Leibniz and Leibnizianism.

It is well to try to understand the state of mind induced in Voltaire by the incidents which led to the English journey, even though this is a very difficult task to perform, since the only documents to aid us are the correspondence, the *Notebooks*, and the few indirect references Voltaire made to the situation. From the official correspondence it can be inferred that he was enraged by the injustice he suffered at the hands of Rohan but that he was even more incensed by the intolerable injustice meted out to him by his noble friends and especially by the government. Although he maintained his personal relations with Maurepas and Hérault on a courteous level, it does not take much imagination to sense that Voltaire must have been very near the point of exploding.

We have had enough experience with these trying moments in Voltaire's life to know his regular way of responding to them. His first reaction to all forms of unjust persecution was one of terror. Consequently, from the very first he was conscious, as are all intelligent men in similar circumstances, of making a poor showing. His next reaction was one of concealment, as if he wished as much to hide from himself as to withdraw from society. In this moment of clandestinity, Voltaire's senses would become extraordinarily acute, and, in something akin to cold rage, he would plan his every move. It was at such moments that Voltaire was at his most dangerous, because, although every reaction appeared to be genuinely reasonable and serene, and Voltaire himself seemed most ingratiating, beneath the surface lurked a wounded vanity, which could only be appeased by some act of destruction. The curious thing about this act of destruction was that the thing destroyed, seen from the angle of abstract right and wrong, always seemed to deserve its fate. Voltaire's executions were not always reasonable, or aboveboard, or even in many cases very dignified, but they were, as far as I can see, absolutely just—as just as the human mind can make them.

2. THE PUBLICATION OF THE *HENRIADE*

W E MUST NOT FORGET that Voltaire came to England with the intention of bringing out an edition of the *Henriade*. The English ambassador in Paris, Horatio Walpole, explained to Bubb Dodington on 29 May 1726 that "Mr. Voltaire, a French poet, who has wrote several pieces with great success here, being gone for England in order to print by subscription an excellent poem, called Henry IV, which, on account of some bold strokes in it against persecution and the priests, cannot be printed here . . ." (B. 287). Voltaire explained to Thiériot that he had intended to print the *Henriade* at his own expense in London but that the loss of his money on arriving had given him pause. He expressed some reluctance to try "the way of subscriptions by the favor of the court." Nevertheless, he did revert to the plan of taking subscriptions, at the same time bringing out a more modest octavo edition for the general public. The quarto edition appeared on 21-22 March 1728. It was dedicated to Queen Charlotte, the wife of George II, and was preceded by *An Essay upon the civil wars of France extracted from various manuscripts. And also upon the epic poetry of the European nations from Homer down to Milton*, December 1727.

It has generally been assumed that the two essays were devised as advertising pieces to prepare the British public for the published *Henriade*. Without some prior instruction, the English public would have been too unfamiliar with the subject of the *Henriade,* the civil wars in France, to take more than a passing interest in it. Since an epic is by definition the complete expression of a people's aspirations and the widest possible portrayal of its institutions and creations, there is always the possibility that a foreign people might be unable to enter into the spirit of the work. Voltaire could have met the difficulty in one of two ways. He could have so arranged his poetic presentation that it would transcend the psychology of the French and offer a picture of a universe comprehensible to all men. What humanity has ultimately admired in the *Iliad* is not the portrayal of Greek life or, as Renan said, Homeric life, but the deep, broad portrayal of human life or what Matthew Arnold called "human misery." Had Voltaire been capable of transmitting a sense of that human misery, as Pascal, Racine, or Molière could have done, he would have had no need to accompany his epic with explicit commentary. Since he was unable to do this, he had no choice but to acquaint his public with the details of the French civil wars.

The exigency of writing a French epic for an English audience thus created a poetic difficulty. Voltaire attempted to solve it by instructing the English in those aspects of French civilization which underlay the events described in the *Henriade* and in the nature of those artistic requirements of the French which had to be explained in order to prepare the foreign audience for the proper appreciation of his artistic production. To properly grasp the artistic values of a foreign work of art, the reader had to be prepared historically and aesthetically. He had to be informed of the country's historical events and trained in its aesthetic taste. The author, too, had to broaden his perspective, since he was forced to study the relationship between history and the epic, as well as the nature of the epic in the various countries. Two very important ideas resulted: (1) there are no universally valid rules for a literary form, and (2) a work of art takes its origin in the history of the country of its birth. Both ideas were to play an important role thereafter.

Voltaire's two essays were certainly composed with these two necessities in mind. But the importance of these requirements for him and, indeed, for the Western Europe of his day lay elsewhere. In a way, they were a product of the quarrel over Homer, and the *Henriade* was, as Voltaire maintained, a "modern" epic. It was, in other words, the presentation of an action local in character for the enjoyment of the members of that locality only, who enjoy it because it is written in their language and is the expression of their mores, institutions, and aspirations. For others to appreciate the real values of this work of art, they had to be instructed in the events, mores, language, institutions, and aspirations of the foreign people with which it dealt. Voltaire's experience in England had already taught him that there is a correlation between the way a people talks, the way it acts, and the things it expresses. In these two essays he was merely attempting to instruct one of these peoples in the habits and expressions of another.

These considerations are at the basis of the views concerning epic poetry which Voltaire proposes in the second essay. From the first he seems opposed to rules and definitions in epic poetry. It is easy to see why he adopts this attitude, since there is no point in telling a foreign audience that a work of art can be comprehended only by applying a set of arbitrary rules. Voltaire also objects to defining epic poetry by citing Homer. He speaks of those "who mistake commonly the beginning of an art, for the principles of the art itself, and are apt to believe, that every thing must be by its own nature, what it was, when contriv'd at first" (White, *Voltaire's Essay on Epic Poetry*, p. 81). Voltaire understands very well that the *Henriade* cannot be compared with the *Iliad*; it is something entirely different. His position is that poetry is a constantly changing art: "The same fancy which hath invented poetry, changes every day all its productions, because it is liable itself to eternal vicissitudes" (p. 82). An epic, for him, is a "discourse of some great action," which "ought to be grounded on judgement, and embellish'd by Imagination" (p. 83). Voltaire adds that what belongs to good sense constitutes the heritage of all nations. Nowhere does it occur to him that an epic is the song of a people, that it is valuable precisely because all of us take part in that song, that judgment and common sense have nothing to do with poetry (he has already forgotten that the poet is superior to the philosopher because he transcends judgment and common sense), and that, where there is no mystery, there is no poetry.

Curiously enough, what Voltaire is defining is not the epic, but history. The same is true of his attempt to give the general requirements for an epic. All nations except England require in an epic "unity of action, attended by variety; an action which should be *great* and strike us with awe; an action which should be *interesting*, because we delight in being moved; finally one which is *entire*, so that our minds may be wholly satisfy'd" (p. 84). These Voltaire calls the great and eternal laws of the epic; they are the *sine qua non* of the genre. On the other hand, episodes and style vary from nation to nation and depend upon taste, which also varies from nation to nation. There is a common taste, of course, which consists in the perception of beauty, but what is considered beautiful will vary from people to people. This national taste will be founded on custom. Voltaire concludes that there is no fixed concept of what an epic is: the only thing which can be done is to take a survey of all the different poems of that kind which have succeeded in different

ages and in different countries. He rejects all ideas of slavish imitation of the ancients. We should be their admirers, not their slaves, he
says. We differ from them in language, in religion (the great basis
of epic poetry), and in inventions. Consequently, he implies, we
should differ from them in our concept of epic poetry, too. Voltaire,
appealing to judgment and common sense, calls upon the epic poet
to make use of the recent discoveries: "The Invention of Gun-pow-
der, that of the compass, that of printing, so many arts besides newly
emerg'd into the world, have alter'd the face of the universe; and an
epic poet, being surrounded with so many novelties, must have but
a small share of genius, if he durst not be new himself" (p. 87). This
passage is strikingly like the *Invention* of André Chénier, so many
years later. Voltaire conceives of an art as subject to the rise and fall
of events and to those petty circumstances which spring from living.
It is the critic's task to follow the progress of an art and to "pursue
it through its various changes." He should be competent to point
out its beauties and its faults, and he should ignore all rules, making
his own rules from the various examples he has before his eyes.
Once more we see that Voltaire is already a literary historian, with
the emphasis upon the historian. A historian with a strong tendency
to morality, he actually submits that morality is the aim of poetry
and states that he cannot understand why the poet should be forbid-
den to intersperse his descriptions with moral maxims and useful
reflections.

There is no use belaboring the point. What Voltaire was talking
about in this essay was not poetry, but history in verse; what he was
seeking was to teach history by example, and he really believed that
this verse should be modern, as if modernity had anything to do
with poetry. Although he still censured La Motte for advocating the
abandonment of poetry for prose, in reality he had done practically
the same thing, the only difference being that he continued to write
verse which he thought was poetry. These are incidents in the activities of writers which deserve neither praise nor blame. But, in place of
the art which Voltaire had now lost, he had taken hold of two other
arts, at least in embryo: the art of history and the art of analyzing
civilization.

It nonetheless remains true that, having set out to sell the *Henriade*
to the British people, Voltaire did a magnificent job with three simul-

taneous editions, one of them a deluxe subscription edition. It is the only success we are sure Voltaire achieved during his sojourn, but it was, in fact, the avowed reason for the trip. Once having completed the task, in the early months of 1728, Voltaire began to give some thought to his return. Yet he remained for at least three months more. What was the reason for this delay? We do not really know. Voltaire's sojourn in England is, indeed, one of the most difficult periods in his life to elucidate. The only period approaching it in obscurity is the span of two or so years which Voltaire spent in and around Alsace after his fiasco at Berlin. About the best we can do, then, is to construct a biography from the remarks of the people with whom we know he associated and from the references he made to his experiences in his correspondence, his *Notebooks*, and, at a later time, in his published works.

3. VOLTAIRE'S OBSERVATIONS OF ENGLAND: THE *CORRESPONDENCE*

THE CORRESPONDENCE of Voltaire during those two years and three months, however, is not very revealing. It does permit us to sketch the details of his comings and goings, and it does give us a fairly good view of his relationship with the authorities; but it furnishes only a very meagre insight into his state of mind and tells us virtually nothing about his relationships with the English. One of the reasons for this dearth of information is that Voltaire deliberately ceased corresponding with his French friends, a resolution that in due time, after his return, he came to regret.[3] From the point of view of his intellectual biography, then, the material is very slim. Fortunately, he did write from time to time to Thiériot, and there are a couple of letters to Des Alleurs, also.

To Thiériot, he wrote on 12 August 1726: "Je sai que c'est un pays où les arts sont tous honorez et récompensez, où il y a de la différence entre les conditions, mais point d'autre entre les hommes que celle du mérite" (B. 291). This first impression, which, incidentally, was one of the strong points made in the *Lettres philosophiques,* was hardly more than a general expectation. Voltaire even voiced the common opinion of the British held in France at the end of the previous century: "C'est un pays où on pense librement et noblement sans être retenu par aucune crainte servile" (B. 291). And he added that, if he followed his own inclination, he would establish himself in London, with the sole intention of learning how to think.

On 26 October 1726, he informed Thiériot that he intended to send him two or three poems by Pope. He designated him the best poet in England and, as far as he was concerned, the best in all the world. Voltaire commented further that he regarded the *Essay on Criticism* as superior to Horace's *De Arte poetica* and the *Rape of the Lock* as superior to Boileau's *Lutrin.* "I never saw so amiable an imagination, so gentle graces, so great varyety, so much wit, and so refined knowledge of the world, as in this little performance." Since

[3] Voltaire to Thiériot, 31 March 1729: "Cependant j'ay été trois ans sans luy écrire comme à tout le reste du monde. On n'a pu arracher de moi que des lettres pour des affaires indispensables" (B. 339).

the *Notebooks* contain attempts to translate passages from Pope, it is certain that Voltaire had a genuine interest in the poet.

In the same letter, Voltaire arrived at a fixed opinion concerning the English. It is evident that he was making every effort to designate their inner reality. In the first letter to Thiériot after his arrival, the English traveler had started with the conventional French opinion of the British. That he had made some progress in the two months since is clear from his remarks in the letter of 26 October 1726. After a vague reference to the strong spirit of this unaccountable nation, Voltaire declared: "You will see a nation fond of their liberty, learned, witty, despising life and death, a nation of philosophers." Voltaire was now prepared to begin that long study of comparison of English and French traits: "not but that there are some fools in England, every country has its madmen. It may be, French folly is pleasanter, than English madness, but by God English wisdom and English Honesty is above yours." Voltaire promised to acquaint Thiériot one of these days with the character of this strange people. His insistence upon the mixture of wisdom and folly in the English is further described in his letter to Des Alleurs of 11 April 1728: "I assure you again that a man of Y^r temper would not dislike a country, where one obeys to the laws only and to one's whims. Reason is free here and walks her own way, hippocondriaks especially are well come. No manner of living appears strange; we have men who walk six miles a day for their health, feed upon roots, never taste flesh, wear a coat in winter thinner than y^r ladies do in the hottest days. All that is accounted a particular reason, but taxed with folly by no body." This keenness of observation on Voltaire's part was to stand him in good stead when he came to compose the *Lettres philosophiques*. It almost led him, as we know from some fragments of the *Lettres philosophiques* which we possess, to give a picturesque presentation of the English.

From the correspondence we also learn that one of the aims of Voltaire's early activities was to get some command of the English language. This task he undertook in the conviction that one cannot understand a people if one does not have some command of the language they speak. He believed also that embodied in the spoken language is the peculiar genius of a people, which can be grasped only after one has understood the inner mechanism of the speech.

To Richard Towne, Voltaire wrote on 23 July 1728: "the language of a free nation as yours is the only one that can vigorously express what I have but faintly drawn in my native tongue" (B. 331).

In addition to this interest in the English spirit and character and in the relationship between the language and the spirit of a people, Voltaire made certain references which disclose some acquaintance with English authors and their works. We have already mentioned his interest in Pope's poetry, both critical and satirical in content. It was only natural that he should seek out the English poet who most resembled him. The correspondence gives but little indication of this relationship, however. On the occasion of Pope's accident, Voltaire sent him a letter of sympathy, and there seems to have been a letter requesting Pope to translate some verses of the *Henriade* into English. Otherwise, the only reference I find to Pope is contained in a letter to Swift, where the French poet stated that he had not seen Pope during the whole winter of 1727-1728. As for Swift himself, the correspondence discloses a greater degree of intimacy and, possibly, a greater literary interest. When Swift announced his intention of crossing over to the continent, for example, Voltaire wrote for him letters of introduction to Dunoquet, M. de Morville, and M. de Maisons. On the publication of the *Essay on Epic Poetry* and the *Essay on the Civil Wars in France*, Voltaire sent a copy to Swift, requesting that he seek subscriptions from Ireland. And, when Thiériot was looking for some English work to translate, Voltaire recommended to him *Gulliver's Travels*. When he procrastinated, Voltaire urged him to complete the translation: "C'est le Rabelais d'Angleterre comme je vous l'ay déjà mandé. Mais c'est un Rabelais sans fatras et le livre seroit très amusant par luy-même, par les imaginations singulières dont il est plein, par la légèreté de son stile, etc. quand il ne seroit pas d'ailleurs la satire du genre humain" (B. 300). Thiériot, having missed the opportunity of translating *Gulliver's Travels*, asked to be sent *The Improvement of Human Reason or The Self-Taught Philosopher*. This work was unknown to Voltaire. When Thiériot persisted in seeking a work to translate, the French poet advised him to wait a few months for Pemberton's *A View of Sir Isaac Newton's Philosophy*. Although the book did not appear until 1728, Voltaire spoke as if he were already acquainted with it, perhaps from the announcements which preceded its appearance: "This book is an easie, clear and regular explanation of Sir Isaac Newton's philosophy, which he undertakes to make palatable to the most unthinking men. It seems the man intends to writ chiefly for y^r nation" (B. 307). The only other English work Voltaire took up in the correspondence is the third volume of Pope's and Swift's *Miscellanies*.

This analysis of the correspondence for the period of Voltaire's stay in England brings out only two aspects of his activities. First, he became interested in what gives a nation its personality, what we would call nowadays its "civilization." He attempted to analyze the English character, to deduce, as well as he could with his little experience, the "esprit" of the nation, and to see that "esprit" in as coherent a way as possible. With this desire to penetrate the reality of English civilization, he combined a second, but correlated interest. Always the poet, always the literary artist, he endeavored to become acquainted with the outstanding writers in England, and, in doing so, extended that acquaintance to those who were considered great but were not contemporary. Here, too, he united a preoccupation with the personality of a nation to an interest in its letters.

One of the great values of a literature is that it expresses the civilization of the time. Voltaire noted that each country of Europe has its distinct personality and its distinct literary expression; indeed, each has also a peculiar genius to its language. There is, finally, a correlation between the language, the literature, and the civilization they express (quoted by C. Dédéyan, *Voltaire et la pensée anglaise,* p. 22):

"Vous sentez dans les meilleurs écrivains modernes le caractère de leur pays à travers l'imitation de l'antique: leurs fleurs et leurs fruits sont échauffés et mûris par le même soleil; mais ils reçoivent du terrain qui les nourrit des goûts, des couleurs, et des formes différentes. Vous reconnaîtrez un Italien, un Français, un Anglais, un Espagnol à son style, comme aux traits de son visage, à sa prononciation, à ses manières. La douceur et la mollesse de la langue italienne se sont insinuées dans le génie des auteurs italiens. La pompe des paroles, les métaphores, un style majestueux, sont, ce me semble, généralement parlant, le caractère des écrivains espagnols. La force, l'énergie, la hardiesse, sont plus particulières aux Anglais; ils sont surtout amoureux des allégories et des comparaisons. Les Français ont pour eux la clarté, l'exactitude, l'élégance: ils hasardent peu; ils n'ont ni la force anglaise, qui leur paraîtrait une force gigantesque et monstrueuse, ni la douceur italienne, qui leur semble dégénérer en une mollesse efféminée."

This conception of different "génies" Voltaire could have derived from any number of traveler's books, but he probably got it from Bolingbroke. "Cet homme," Voltaire wrote "... a trouvé ... le moyen de tout apprendre et de tout retenir. Il sait l'histoire des anciens Egyptiens comme celle d'Angleterre. Il possède Virgile comme Milton; il aime la poésie anglaise, la française, et l'italienne: mais il les aime différément, parce qu'il discerne leurs différents génies" (M. I, 77). At all events, this way of defining the particularism of individuals belonging to different countries constituted a new approach to the analysis of the traits of a country. More original still was the idea that the "génie" of a country lies in its way of expressing itself in language.

4. VOLTAIRE'S OBSERVATIONS OF ENGLAND:
THE *NOTEBOOKS*

IN ADDITION to the evidence furnished by Voltaire's correspondence, we now have substantiating evidence presented in the *Notebooks*. There are two of these *Notebooks* which are regarded as specifically English *Notebooks*, but, in fact, there are English references in all the *Notebooks*. Scholars have known about them for a long time, but no one seems to have studied them for the light they can throw upon the problem of Voltaire's ability to penetrate the reality of the English or the further problem of the meaning of the English experience for the French poet. Professor Torrey, in his article "Voltaire's English Notebook," has noted that in the first of these two *Notebooks*, now known as the *Little Leningrad Notebook*, there is a relatively large number of selections from the English poets, particularly from Pope and Dryden. There are one or more selections also from Swift, Rochester, Waller, Denham, Johnson, and Gay. None come from Shakespeare, and only one from Milton. Of prose extracts, the largest number are from Addison. Torrey points out that there is much concern with religion in this *Notebook* and that the content is a kind "of political, anti-clerical, whiggish deism." Yet Voltaire shows no familiarity with the philosophical deists. As for the source of this material, Torrey observes only that much of it apparently comes from Addison's *Spectator* and Bysshe's *British Parnassus or Art of Poetry*, while some of the political material is drawn from the *Independent Whig*. Torrey proffers no conclusion to these abbreviated remarks. But it is evident that this *Notebook* indicates that Voltaire was still pursuing the interests that had absorbed his attention in France before his trip to England: poetry, religion, and, to a lesser extent, the relation of state and church. For the rest, he was interested in getting acquainted with the foibles of the English. Bysshe provided sustenance for his enthusiasm for poetry, Addison material for his observation of British manners and customs.

There are two or three additional remarks which may be made. Voltaire, as was his wont, was quick to gather up any story he heard and to relate it in English in the same succinct manner he used in

French. We should note in this connection that the *Notebook* is as much a practice-book in English as it is a commonplace book. There is only one reference in it to an English philosopher (a remark about the *Reasonableness of Christianity*) and no mention whatever of an English deist. It contains several interesting remarks about England and Englishmen: England is the meeting-place of all religions; there is nothing more difficult than to be qualified for English society; a king is necessary in England to preserve the spirit of liberty; the English tongue, formerly barbarous and barren, is now rich and harmonious. These kinds of observations, greatly multiplied, and obviously extracted to a large extent from Addison's *Spectator* or Steele's *Tatler*, were to become the raw material for Voltaire's portrait of England. Of much greater importance, since it shows the technique Voltaire used in getting acquainted with a foreign country and the frame of reference in which he would cast the product of that technique, is this observation (*Notebooks*, ed. Besterman, I, 34):

In England everybody is publik-spirited—in France everybody is concerned in his own interest only. An English (man) is full of thoughts, french all in miens, compliments, sweet words and (loves) curious of engaging outside, overflowing in words, obsequious with pride, and very much self concerned under the appearance of a pleasant modesty. The English is sparing of words, openly proud and unconcerned. He gives the most quick birth, as he can, to his thoughts, for fear of losing his time.

We can summarize all this discussion in a few words. Voltaire, seen through the first English *Notebook*, was chiefly concerned with continuing the activities of his Parisian life. Though transplanted in a foreign atmosphere, he investigated to the best of his ability the English poets and addressed himself seriously to a study of the English language. In addition, he devoted some attention to the picturesque aspects of English life, in which he had become intrigued by reading Addison's sketches. There is some evidence that he had become aware that one has to proceed methodically to grasp the unity of a foreign atmosphere and to organize its diverse elements into a meaningful experience. His attempt to locate this unity in the notion of "public spirit" bespeaks a considerable imagination and an uncommon ability to see, beneath the surface of events, a national trait. His effort to contrast the characteristics of one people with those of another, particularly the English with the French, had now already begun. It is, of course, one of the most natural ways to get acquainted with a foreign country.

We cannot be so sure at what time the second English *Notebook*, now called the *Cambridge Notebook*, was composed, nor even that it was a genuine English *Notebook*. Of course, some weight can be given to the fact that Voltaire continued here the copying of English poems—more, it seems, because of their keepsake quality than because of their intrinsic poetic worth. It could possibly be argued that Voltaire copied down the numerous selections from Tasso while he was putting the finishing touches on the *Henriade* or the *Essay on Epic Poetry*. The exercises in English composition noticeable in the first English *Notebook* continue to some extent here, too, but they are much less evident, and there are very few of them in comparison with the number of items in French.

There are some definite reasons for believing that the notes of this *Notebook* were composed after Voltaire's return from England. The quatrain *Pr Mgr le c. de Clermont* (*Notebooks*, I, 69), was published in a letter to Mlle de Guise dated (by Besterman) August 1731 (B. 412). It seems improbable that the verses written for Mlle de Guise could have been composed very long before this date. The *Vers à corriger dans Erip* could not have been composed before 1731 and probably were not written before 1732; they were never incorporated into the play. The *Réponse à Mr de Tressan* was sent in a letter on 3 August 1732 (B. 490). Finally, the notes published under the rubric *To my lord Bolingb.* were collected in the *Cambridge Notebook* (*Notebooks*, I, 82-84) as material for the dedication of *Brutus* to Bolingbroke; they could hardly have been assembled before 1731. All of these extracts indicate that Voltaire composed a good part of the present *Notebook* after his return from England, and, since these passages are not successive in the manuscript, it seems fair to assume that the intervening passages belong to the same period.

Although the *Cambridge Notebook* cannot tell us very much about Voltaire's activities in England, it can give us some clue to what change came over Voltaire after his return to France. The information has to be pressed rather hard, and, as always in the case with notes, it is not very firm. Such as it is, however, it is not devoid of interest. To begin with, the one passage (I, 52) quoted from Shakespeare is *not* from that author. Moreover, it appears that the various poems quoted as Rochester's are not always readily attributable to that poet. As for the philosophers, Voltaire inserts a note to record that Leibniz and Newton "invented the same truths." And, he adds, so did Galileo and Maetius (I, 53). A quotation from Hobbes—"Words are the money of fools and the counters of wise men"—shows some knowledge of that philosopher, although the quote is not entirely accurate (I, 54). Newton also receives some attention, while Bacon is credited with the discovery of attraction. Voltaire mentions in a note that he chooses to side with Newton against Descartes, for whatever good he may get from it. He compares himself to a man who, having left a sum of money to say masses, prescribed that the rest of the money was to be used for something else if it happened that the masses did not produce the desired effect. In another note he states that, "en fait d'esprit, il y a des Newtons et des Fontenelles, comme en fait de corps il y a des Hercules et des Milons." Such references show that Voltaire was aware of Newton's existence but that his knowledge of him did not extend much further at this moment. Still, an additional note shows that he was beginning to understand Newton's place in the development of the laws of attraction: "Avant Kepler tous les hommes étoient aveugles, Kepler fut borgne, et Newton a eu deux yeux" (I, 63).

Actually, Descartes receives much more attention, though often of a negative sort, than Newton. The usefulness of Newton's discovery does not seem as yet to have impressed Voltaire. His general attitude seems to be in the remark: "Quand même l'attraction serait vraye, il n'en résulterait pas le moindre avantage, pas le moindre secours dans les méchaniques. Cependant Neuton a passé sa vie à rechercher cette découverte, et des miliers d'hommes à l'aprendre" (I, 65). In contrast, he credits Descartes with having been the first to discover the cause of refraction (I, 66). And elsewhere he remarks that it was Descartes who found out how to perfect the telescope, although Newton found out why it cannot be further perfected (I, 72). Voltaire has a tendency to liken Descartes to Aristotle: "Aristote veut aussi bien que Descartes qu'on examine la figure et le mouvement des parties et cependant tous deux se sont trompez, car après avoir dit qu'il faloit payer en bonne monoye, ils ont payé en jettons" (I, 65). An important analysis of Descartes appears under the rubric "Erreurs de Descartes dans le livre de l'homme." Voltaire contradicts Descartes's assertion that the heart is more open when it is contracted, that the liver and the spleen are "caillebots" of blood, and that the digestive fluid goes from the "mesoraiques" to the liver. He objects to Descartes's statement that all movements tend to follow a straight line; if there is a plenum, Voltaire reasons, movement can only follow a curved line. He disagrees, too, with the Cartesian explanation that saliva comes from the vapors of the stomach. He does concede that Descartes's proposition, taken from Aristotle, that the principle of life is in the heart is probably correct, but he adds that practically everything true in his philosophy comes from Aristotle. Innate ideas, animal mechanism, the propagation of light by emission, and the Cartesian principles Voltaire condemns as "billevesées" (I, 66-67). He notes, finally, this time with apparent approval, Descartes's claim that man's memory, appetites, and passions depend on his organs, "ne plus ne moins qu'une montre."

As might be expected, this attempt to grasp the positions of Descartes and Newton forced Voltaire to explore, if only in a very desultory way, his own views on the nature of things. The resulting pronouncements are very interesting. Voltaire writes that "God cannot be proved, nor denied, by the mere force of our reason." He asserts: "We do not know what a soul is, we have no idea of the thing, therefore we ought not to admitt it" (I, 67). He compares the *Entretiens sur la pluralité des mondes* of Fontenelle with the *Cosmotheoros* of Huyghens: "On trouve même dans Mr. Huguens les agréments qu'on admire dans F, par exemple le caractère des peuples des différentes planettes, mais non pas les compliments à la marquise." Even with his aroused interest in science and philosophy, though, he still clings to former preoccupations which seem to him more essential. After comparing Newton and Fontenelle, he adds: "On a bau prouver le mouvement de la terre, la nature de l'arc en ciel, l'impénétrabilité de la matière, la foy ne subsiste pas moins. La découverte des antipodes n'a servi qu'à leur porter notre relligion" (I, 57). He is still sensitive to the relations of poetry and philosophy; he notes that "parmy nos français les esprits d'agrément sont peu solides, et nos raisoneurs sont presque tous sans grâce. Chez les romains le philosophe étoit poète. Lucrèce parloit à l'imagination et à l'esprit" (I, 60).

There are two interests Voltaire manifests which should be noted because of the tremendous importance they assumed in his later work. The first is an interest in history. It shows itself in Voltaire's attempt to formulate some sort of opinion concerning Daniel and Mézeray. It is also apparent in his attempt to gather facts on the formation of French institutions: for example, "tiers ordre de l'état, commença états généraux sous Phil. le Bel; Au procez du duc d'Alençon, les présidents commencent à avoir la préséance; Le roy Jean acorde une charte pareille à celle de Jean sans terre, mais inutile" (I, 58).

The second interest—in philosophy—is of considerable philosophical importance because it represents a point of view Voltaire holds in common with Pascal: "Je ne sçaurois comprendre ce que c'est que la matière, encore moins ce que c'est qu'esprit" (I, 74). Voltaire, however, develops this attitude in a way which Pascal would not under any circumstances have approved. The result is a sort of intellectual blueprint, which will serve Voltaire throughout the remainder of his life:

S'il y a un dieu, s'il n'y en a point, si le monde est fini ou infini, créé ou éternel, arrangé par intelligence ou par loix phisiques, encor moins par hazard.
Je ne saurois comprendre
        comment je pense,
        comment je retiens mes pensées,
        comment je remue.
Les premiers principes aux quels mon existence est attachée sont tous impénétrables. Ce n'est donc pas cela qu'il faut chercher mais ce qui est utile, et dangereux, au corps humain,
les loix par les quels il se meut, non p^r quoy il se meut, l'art d'augmenter les forces mouvantes, non les principes du mouvement.
Savoir comment je puis guérir la dissenterie, non, si le ventre est formé avant le cœur ou le cœur avant le ventre.
Tâcher de rendre une terre fertile, non rechercher comment le blé peut croître.

The essential points to bear in mind about the second so-called English *Notebook* can be summarized briefly. To begin with, whereas the first *Notebook* dates from 1726-1727, it is very likely that the second one dates from 1731-1732. It therefore reveals the shift that had occurred in Voltaire's preoccupations between the early part of his sojourn in England and his return to France. One difference is perhaps not very significant: clearly, Voltaire had become more interested in erotic poetry. More important is the fact that he was still interested in poetry and particularly attracted to drama. And more significant still is the number of references to philosophers: Bacon, Leibniz, Descartes, Newton, Hobbes. The quality of the references does not show that Voltaire had any particularly deep acquaintance with these philosophers. But it is clear that Voltaire was at least now aware of a Newton-Descartes quarrel. There is every indication that Voltaire, having selected to side with Newton in the quarrel, although he was not yet very enthusiastic about the English philosopher, was now thoroughly convinced that there were substantial errors in Descartes's philosophy. And it is certain that, before taking this stand, he had studied, if only superficially, a fair number of Descartes's works. This experience brought about a great change in Voltaire's orientation. He now openly made statements which gave evidence of his thorough interest in philosophical subjects and actively set about to draw up a program for the study of philosophy, which has every appearance of being a miniature *Traité de métaphysique*.

5. VOLTAIRE'S LITERARY ACTIVITIES

How all this new experience affected Voltaire cannot be clearly discerned from his *Notebooks*, from his correspondence, or from the usual periodical comment by others who follow the day-to-day living of a distinguished poet. The reason is that Voltaire, during the two and a quarter years he was in England, led a rather clandestine life. We have already noted that he willfully cut off all correspondence with his French friends, excepting only the letters to Thiériot and a few to Des Alleurs. The remainder of his correspondence during the actual time of his sojourn was devoted in large measure to keeping the record straight with the authorities. Altogether, it is the most meagre portion of the rich collection of Voltaire's correspondence. In the 102 volumes (in Besterman's edition) needed to contain the epistolary output of his eighty-four years, the letters from the English period take up less than 100 pages of one volume. This poverty of material can certainly be blamed in part on Voltaire's determination to cut off his relationships with his former associates, and it can probably be traced also to his desire to acquire a certain anonymity, since his rise to fame had brought him such misery. But the real explanation, I feel, is that Voltaire was actually overwhelmed by his English experience and was working extremely hard, even in England, to turn it into something positive.

It is not easy, because of the clandestinity of Voltaire's actions, to get at this positive thing. We do know, though, that Voltaire began to assemble materials and actually composed parts of three works while he was in England. Foulet, in Appendix IX ("Quels ouvrages Voltaire a-t-il rapportés à Paris?") of his *Correspondance de Voltaire,* has attempted to seek the necessary evidence that these works were begun before the return in 1728 or 1729. He notes that, in February 1729, Voltaire promised to show Thiériot some new things in his portfolio. The assumption is that these new things were works which he had composed or sketched while in England.

The first of these works was the *Histoire de Charles XII*. The assumption is substantiated for this one by Voltaire's own statement: "cette histoire fut principalement composée en Angleterre, à la campagne, avec Mr. Fabrice, Chambellan de George Ier, électeur de

Hanovre." Indeed, Voltaire added further that some of the information he incorporated into his history had been given to him in 1727 by the Duchess of Marlborough and that it had been confirmed by Bolingbroke (M. XVI, 226). Foulet believes that work on the history was well advanced before the projected return to France, to the extent that Voltaire felt he could send his manuscript to M. de Maisons in 1728. This latter date, however, is not too firmly established. All we know for sure is that Voltaire in 1729 requested M. de Maisons to return the manuscript.

The second work Voltaire began in England was the tragedy *Brutus*, which he appears to have started writing in the summer of 1728, while residing at Falkener's. He seems to have composed only the first act at this time; evidently, he did not feel competent enough yet to write a play in imitation of Shakespeare.

The third work inaugurated during the English sojourn was the *Lettres philosophiques*. Since it was, above all, a clandestine work in every sense of the word, we have to use a good deal of ingenuity in order to state with any precision when it was begun and just how it was developed. Both Foulet and Lanson have proposed solutions to this problem. Their answers, however, are based upon divergent arguments.

Foulet believes that Voltaire must have composed the work sometime during the last half of 1728 and the early months of 1729, when he was in hiding in Normandy. The gist of his argument in support of this conclusion is that only during this period could Voltaire have found the time to assemble his material and work it into a coherent draft. Indeed, considering how active Voltaire was between 16 April 1729 and 10 March 1731—that is, between his return from England and his trip to Rouen to see to the publishing of *Charles XII*—there seems to be no room for so large an enterprise as the *Lettres philosophiques*. Nor could the subsequent three and a half months spent in bringing out *Charles XII* in Rouen have been devoted to the *Lettres*, for, shortly after the Rouen journey, Voltaire began to talk of the *Lettres* as if they were then in their final form and needed only a month or so more to be put in definitive shape. Thus, Foulet argued, it could only have been during the last months of 1728 which he spent in England and the early months of his return in 1728-1729, while he was in hiding in Normandy, that Voltaire had the time to spend on this project.

Lanson, in the introduction of his admirable edition of the *Lettres philosophiques*, admits that it is possible, and even probable, that Voltaire began his work in England at the end of 1727 or the beginning of 1728, taking notes, sketching some letters, and writing some passages in final form. But he judges it impossible that the larger number of letters were written in 1728 "dans la maison de notre cher et vertueux Falkener." Instead, he concludes: "Le travail principal de la rédaction se placera donc, autant que j'en puis juger, entre 1729 et 1731; sans doute fut-elle interrompue par d'autres travaux" (*Lettres philosophiques*, I, xxxix). Lanson's principal argument in support of this conclusion is taken from the internal evidence of many of the letters, which indicate by reference to works and events a late, rather than an early, composition. Three of the letters (XVIII, XX, and XXII), for instance, contain the words "ici" or "en France"; it is assumed, therefore, that they were written in 1729, at the earliest. The second letter refers to a passage in Niceron's article on Malebranche, which did not appear until 1729. At first glance, Letter VII seems to have been written between 1727 and 1729; but, in the composition of the letter, Voltaire used Whiston's *Mémoires*, which appeared only in 1730. It is clear that Letter IX was composed before 8 May 1730, the date of Townsend's resignation as Minister of State, but there is no way of finding out how much before. Letter XI includes a reference to a volume of the *Lettres édifiantes*, published in 1731. Letter XII is contemporary with the *Sottise des deux parts*, which came out in 1732. Letter XIX dates from 3 December 1730, after Cibber had become poet laureate. Letter XX makes a reference to the visit Lord Harvey paid Voltaire at the end of 1729. Letter XXII announces a translation of Du Resnel which appeared in 1730. Letter XXIII must date from 1730, too, because of a reference to Mlle Lecouvreur's death. Only Letter XIV, according to this way of dating, can reasonably be assigned to 1728, because it contains the statement "l'an passé, 1727."

It should be noted, however, that, even though the bulk of this evidence points to composition at a later date than the sojourn in England, it merely constitutes a presumption, rather than positive proof, for it was always possible for Voltaire, after the initial composition, to add references whenever he wished up to the beginning of 1733. Since we know that he spent time from November 1731 to the beginning of 1733 revising, recasting, and retouching the *Lettres,* the evidence presented here is by no means incontrovertible. Nor can one accord too much importance to the assertion that the *Lettres* must have been composed in an earlier period because Voltaire had more free time to devote to them in that earlier period than he did in the subsequent period, which was so crowded that he could not have found the necessary time to work upon them. One could argue, with some show of reason, that, when he had the free time, he did not have the necessary information and that, when he had the necessary information, he could always have arranged to allocate to the enterprise the necessary time.

A truer picture of the situation is obtained if the opinions of Foulet and Lanson are united—as, indeed, the latter to some extent attempts to do. In reality, between the opinion of Lanson—that the important work on the *Lettres philosophiques* was done in 1729 and 1731—and the opinion of Foulet—that it was done in England in the second half of 1728 and during the period of the Normandy seclusion in the fall of 1728 and the early winter of 1729—there is not as much difference as would appear at first, all the more since Lanson concedes that Voltaire may have conceived of his work in the last months he spent in England, in which case he would certainly have begun to assemble his material and may actually have composed passages which entered into the finished product. What both scholars are saying, each in his own way, is that the *Lettres philosophiques* were composed over a long period of time extending from June 1728 to the beginning of 1733.

Looking at the matter in this perspective, we can venture an alternative solution. It is evident that one of the main reasons why Voltaire remained in England after the publication of the *Henriade* is that he wanted to assemble more information for his *Lettres philosophiques*. It is also apparent that he could not gather all his material during those six months, so he had to wait until a fairly long time after his return before he considered himself well enough prepared to begin writing. Undoubtedly, what he lacked most was philosophical material, which could not be as easily gathered in England as that dealing with manners and customs, institutions, and perhaps literature.

This hypothesis seems to accord with all we know about the conditions surrounding the inception of the work. What evidence we have about the initial stages, the early discarded plan, the bits about Voltaire's early experience in England, and his attempt to organize the presentation of England around the generating idea of "contradiction"—which is a perfectly normal way of viewing a foreign country in the initial stages of becoming acquainted with it—indicates that Voltaire committed himself to the work while he was still in England.

The prefaces offer some additional confirmation of the validity of this last remark. The preface to the English translation states, for instance, that the work was composed "entre la fin de 1728 et environ 1731." Thiériot's French preface, on the other hand, states that it was written "depuis 1728 jusqu'à 1730." Volume IV of the *Œuvres* (1746) gives the date as "vers 1727." Moreover, Voltaire wrote to Thiériot that he should mention in the preface that "ces lettres vous ont été écrites pour la plupart en 1728." And he added, "vous ne direz que la vérité," since, in fact, they were written at that time at Falkener's. Because they were not addressed to Thiériot, however, there has been an inclination to reject the other part of the sentence. It is nonetheless true that, in a letter to Thiériot, Voltaire did promise to write him about that strange land England. However that may be, there is really no reasonable excuse for rejecting Voltaire's insistence on the early date, at least as far as the inauguration of the *Lettres philosophiques* is concerned.

Foulet's remarks are totally sound, but they should be supplemented by Lanson's. In the period following the publication of the *Henriade* and the *Essays* and ending at the termination of the Normandy seclusion—that is, from February 1728 to February 1729—Voltaire did have free time to devote to work upon the *Lettres philosophiques,* even if he used some of this time to engage in the composition of *Charles XII* also. Indeed, it was the freest period he had between the publication of the *Essays* and the *Henriade* and the publication of the *Lettres philosophiques.* But we must insist that he did not have at this time the wherewithal to make the letters "philosophiques." It was perfectly logical, nonetheless, that, having sold

French civilization to the British public, he should begin to think of selling English civilization to the French public.

Once the project had been decided upon, Voltaire had two ways of proceeding: he could discuss English arts and letters, and the political and social institutions of the country, or he could describe the manners and customs of the people in the light of his own experiences, giving what he called "une idée générale du peuple." But he became immediately aware of two difficulties: first, these "idées générales" are contradicted by too many exceptions; and, second, a foreigner ordinarily does not know the country well enough to establish "idées générales." "Il ne voit que la façade du bâtiment; presque tous les dedans lui sont inconnus" (*Lettres philosophiques*, II, 256). It is not an easy matter to penetrate the "génie" of a country, and Voltaire was quick to recognize the difficulty.

Nevertheless, this seemed to have been Voltaire's purpose in the initial stages of his composition. In the "Projet d'une lettre sur les Anglais," as it is now called, which was beyond doubt the earliest of the *Lettres philosophiques*, Voltaire insists that the only way one may gain the right perspective on a foreign people is to learn the language of that people and converse continually on all sorts of subjects with all classes. To really know the English, one must have the leisure to learn to speak the English language, to converse freely with Whigs and Tories, dine with a bishop, sup with a Quaker, attend the synagogue on Saturday and St. Paul's on Sunday, listen to a sermon in the morning and go to a play in the afternoon, move from the court to the stock exchange, and refuse to be put out by the coldness of English ladies. This, in his opinion, would be the best preparation for the task, and even then a man so prepared would be very likely to fall into many errors. Voltaire experimented with this method in this trial letter, trying to focus the whole experience upon the idea of contradictions brought about by change. The result was a charmingly informal presentation, but its picturesqueness invalidated the content. Voltaire subsequently abandoned this scheme. The reason often given is that it had already been used in Muralt's *Lettres sur les Anglais et sur les Français* and was being used by Prévost in his descriptions of England. But it is doubtful that Voltaire was swayed in his decision by either circumstance. There is, in fact, nothing in Muralt to compare with the freshness, sprightliness, and impertinence of Voltaire's trial lettter, and Prévost had not yet begun his description of England when Voltaire experimented with it. It is more likely that he abandoned the method because he was unable to penetrate with it beyond the façade into the inwardness of the people, just as he had said in the introduction. It is lucky for us, however, that he made the experiment, because, if we are forced to conjecture when we discuss the date of the composition of most of the *Lettres*, we can date this one fairly accurately. Voltaire refers to three specific events: the impressment, the four treaties on the miracles of Christ (Woolston), and the poor bookseller who was pilloried for having published a translation of *La Religieuse en chemise* (Curll). The agitation to reform the impressment took place in April-May 1728; the condemnation of Curll occurred on 23 February 1728; and the *Fourth Discourse* of Woolston was published on 14 May 1728. This is, for a work of Voltaire, fairly good evidence that, by the middle of 1728, he was well on his way in preparing himself for the *Lettres*, although he still had a long way to go before they could be published. (See H. Brown in *Mélanges Besterman*, 1968.)

Even if this evidence has not been too rigorously interpreted, we have nevertheless been able to deduce that Voltaire had planned very early in his English experience a project for understanding, interpreting, and sharing with the French public that experience. The first step of that plan consisted in getting acquainted with the language and deducing from it the "génie" of the people who used it. The second step, if one may trust the rather flippant statement we have just summarized from the "Projet d'une lettre," was to converse with all kinds of people on all sorts of subjects. It was beyond a doubt this unique way of collecting his material which gave to the *Lettres philosophiques* not only their conversational style but their sprightliness. It also explains why Lanson often found it necessary to seek, not the printed source of Voltaire's statements, but the public opinion of the matters about which his statements were made. Voltaire's third step became an earnest inquiry into the ideas of the writers and thinkers of England. It was this third step, to be sure, which required of Voltaire so much more time before he felt himself ready to publish the *Lettres philosophiques*.

6. THE IMPACT OF THE ENGLISH
EXPERIENCE

T HE FINAL POINT to settle concerning Voltaire's stay in England has to do with the difference between the intellectual baggage he took to England and the intellectual baggage he carried back with him to France. The natural assumption to make is that the difference was due to the influence which England had upon the French traveler. It is not always easy, however, to measure this influence. For one thing, many of the ideas brought back may not have been revealed until much later. Then, too, national pride enters into the calculation. Ever since Lord Morley stated succinctly that "Voltaire left France a poet, he returned to it a sage," this matter has been debated back and forth as if the national honor was at stake in both countries. But, as the debate has developed, the nuances which Morley gave to his pithy statement have been neglected. "Before his flight," he continued, "though we do not know to what extent he may have read such history as was then accessible, he had been actively productive only in the sphere of the imaginative faculties, and in criticism of the form and regulation proper to be imposed upon them. When he returned, while his poetic power had ripened, he had tasted of the fruit of the tree of scientific reason, and, what was not any less important, he had become alive to the central truth of the social destination of all art and all knowledge" (*Voltaire*, p. 58). These two statements, beautifully balanced and nuanced in Morley's superb English, modify completely the original absolute statement, by their admission that we do not know to what extent Voltaire was versed in the history of modern thought before his journey (an ignorance which was almost total in Morley's day, and has been only partly remedied in our own), that he was engaged in imposing upon such thought as he controlled a poetic form (which was also true, although he still continued for some time to be preoccupied with this activity after his return, as we shall see), that his poetic power had ripened (which means that he returned to France a better poet than when he went to England, although this was not the point which Morley was trying to make), and, finally, that this improvement in poetry was unimportant in comparison

with his newly acquired interest in scientific things and the usefulness to which both art and knowledge can be put (which means that
Voltaire acquired in England a new interest, which he added to
the interests he had already developed, and that he learned from the
practically minded English that social utility is the goal of all intellectual and artistic life).

Morley's view of Voltaire as a French poet before his trip to England and as an English philosopher after his return, which is the
abstract way in which it is usually presented, has been supported in
general by English biographers who have undertaken to discuss the
matter anew.[4] The presentation of the view is never as categorical as
it seems, however. Ballantyne, for example, concedes that there was
a serious side in the works of Voltaire before his trip, the inference
being, I suppose, that what is serious is philosophical, not poetic.
Ballantyne comes close to contradicting himself, though, by insisting that it was England which developed this serious, that is, philosophical side of Voltaire. Still, seen in a modest sort of way, and
without insisting too much upon his terms, his explanation of Voltaire's intellectual evolution does not appear too unreasonable.

It was J. Texte, in his *Jean-Jacques Rousseau et le cosmopolitisme
littéraire* (pp. 68-72), who first attempted to refute Morley's claim.
To the French critic, it seemed that only someone with a singular
ignorance of Voltaire's seriousness before his trip to England would
venture such a statement. Texte counters Morley's claim with the
argument that the Voltaire of 1752 was not essentially different
from the Voltaire of 1726. He develops this argument with a tena-
city which borders upon passion. He affirms that it is not necessary
to assume that the trip to England was a turning point in Voltaire's
life, and he hazards the guess that Voltaire's life would have unfolded
as it did even if he had not gone to England. Practically the whole
Voltaire, he adds, was already in the *Œdipe*; what little more was
needed to round him out could have been found in the *Lettres
persanes* and in the long line of his French ancestors: Jean de
Meung, Rabelais, Montaigne, Gassendi, Descartes, La Mothe le
Vayer, and especially Bayle and Fontenelle. The unfortunate thing

[4] See J. C. Collins, *Bolingbroke, a Historical Study, and Voltaire in England*; A. Ballantyne, *Voltaire's Visit to England, 1726-1729*, pp. 325-327; C. B. Chase, *The Young
Voltaire*, p. 232.

about Texte's argument is its tendency to state everything in absolute terms, which makes it difficult to reconcile to the simple truths of practical living. It is not true that the Voltaire of 1752 was essentially the Voltaire of 1726; it is not true that Voltaire would have been in 1752 what he was in 1726 had he not gone to England, simply because he did go to England; it is not true that a person of Voltaire's intellectual mobility and genuine curiosity, and even poetic imagination, could go to England or any other country and not be changed by his experiences.

In general, those French biographers who have dealt with Voltaire after Texte have been inclined to be less peremptory and more flexible in their judgment. Their tactic usually consists in summarizing the intellectual content of Voltaire's poetic production down to 1726 and in placing this content into the milieu of the Regency. Two assumptions are implicit in their approach. One is that, although Voltaire's free-thinking, which is generally equated with philosophy, was not very broad prior to his trip, it was already founded upon the long, rich tradition of free-thinking and needed only time to develop. The usual conclusion is that given by Ascoli and Lanson. Ascoli writes in the *RCC* (XXV², 143-144):

Nous avons du moins clairement vu que sur l'ensemble des questions métaphysiques, morales, et sociales, l'esprit de Voltaire, loin d'être une table rase, présentait avant son départ pour l'Angleterre un ensemble d'idées assez nettes et définies. Bien plus, nous avons pu voir, par les rapprochements que nous avons multipliés chemin faisant, que si les opinions de Voltaire se sont modifiées par la suite, sous d'autres influences, elles n'auront en général fait qu'évoluer dans le sens où elles tendaient déjà à se diriger: sur bien des points même, Voltaire mûri et vieilli, gardera ses convictions de jeunesse.

This means that Voltaire had, before going to England, a coherent set of opinions, which he expressed in the poetic medium he was using at the time, and that these opinions now ran upon other opinions, expressed in another medium, and became modified, but not distorted. Perhaps Lanson, in his usual succinct way, has best summarized the effect of England upon Voltaire: "L'Angleterre a mûri, armé, excité Voltaire: elle ne l'a pas fait" (*Voltaire*, p. 36). Foulet, however, has made what seems to me the most judicious statement of all, at any rate for one undertaking to assess the intellectual development of Voltaire during his sojourn in England (*Correspondance de Voltaire*, p. x):

Il découvre l'Angleterre et la littérature anglaise, il lit, observe, admire et critique, il s'instruit et il désapprend, il approfondit ce qu'il soupçonnait, il développe ce dont il avait l'instinct, il compare, note, recueille des matériaux. C'est tout un prodigieux travail qui s'accomplit en lui et dont on verra plus tard les résultats.

This means that Voltaire consistently continued his development which he had begun in France, seized every opportunity to enhance and broaden his interests, as he always did, made every effort to profit by new experiences in the new country, and, above all, compared these new experiences and this new country with his former experiences and the country he left. It was perfectly normal that he acted this way, for he was always inordinately alert, active, and curious.

After these perceptive statements of Ascoli, Lanson and Foulet, it would seem that not much could be added, except a few more details, to summarize the effects of the English experience. And yet I cannot help but feel that these general statements of Morley, Ascoli, Lanson and Foulet, in spite of the elements of truth each contains, the excellence and precision each manifests in its formulation, and the concise way each is expressed, do not present the whole problem, or even cast it in the right perspective. It is perfectly true that Voltaire, before going to England, held, and expressed in his poetry, "philosophical" views concerning the nature and existence of God, the immortality of the soul, free will, moral good and evil, and the relationship between the church and the state. We have shown that these problems, not treated too philosophically, to be sure, were wrapped in a general epicureanism and a mild, gentle stoicism, resembling, along with a touch of Lucretius and Seneca, the Horatian approach to life and, above all, the attitude of that long line of free-thinking Horatian poets which extended from Théophile de Viau to Chaulieu. Moreover, the Horatian influence he encountered in the "libertin" poetry of his predecessors he must have encountered likewise in the English poets whose acquaintance he now made. The kind of lyric poetry prevalent in both countries was typically Horatian, both satiric in attitude and epicurean-stoic in tone with a concern for what Boileau called "pensées vraies" and "expressions justes." We must remember that Pope was no less a Horatian than Boileau. English classicism, in fact, was not unlike French classicism. English thought, which Voltaire deemed so superior to French thought and which had, thanks to Newton, Locke, and the Royal Academy, assumed a position of superiority over all continental thought, actually had developed from the magnificent outburst of seventeenth-century European thought. One need only review the European sources of both Newton and Locke to realize how European Newton was and how French Locke was. As a matter of fact, the best way of acquiring a synthesis of that thought, both scientific and ethical, would be to read Bayle (and probably Fontenelle) rather than Newton and Locke. Finally, as Professor Bonno has demonstrated, there had been between England and France, long before Voltaire's sojourn in England, many fruitful intellectual contacts.

The conclusion seems incontrovertible that Voltaire, like every traveler to a foreign land, saw what he wanted to see. But, although for propaganda purposes his observations had some importance, that is not really the crux of the matter. He made every effort to find out what the significance of his experience in England was and did not rest until he had persuaded his compatriots that this knowledge which he had acquired had a peculiar relevance for them, too. That is why we are really forced to examine bit by bit the influence of every English writer, English work, and English idea upon Voltaire, and, once having come to some sort of conclusion about its impact upon him, we are then constrained to see how all these particular influences united to give Voltaire a whole new understanding of the meaning of civilization.

Consequently, since the general assessments of Ascoli, Lanson and Foulet, we have tried to know more about the relationship of Mandeville to Voltaire, especially in regard to the content of the *Défense du Mondain*, something more about the effect of Pope upon the philosophical poetry (*Le Mondain, Discours en vers sur l'homme, La Loi naturelle*), a good deal more about the impact of Bolingbroke upon Voltaire's development in philosophy, and something about the contribution of Pope, Bolingbroke, and Shaftesbury to his elaboration of philosophical optimism. Despite much effort, we have learned but little about what meaning Shakespeare had for Voltaire, and that little does not seem to be as consequential as it ought to be. In fact, we have now assigned to Dryden the role in drama we once wanted to give to Shakespeare. We know what Voltaire said about Milton, but we still do not know what Milton meant to him. In reality, just what significance the field of English literature had for Voltaire is, in spite of these additional details, not very clear. It is hard to understand how these writers, along with a whole raft of others (Rochester, Lady Montague, Pryor, Young, Congreve, and even Addison), matured, equipped, or excited Voltaire as a man of letters. It can be argued that English letters awakened some curiosity in him, and we shall endeavor eventually to weigh its extent. But it can also be affirmed that, although it undoubtedly broadened Voltaire and offered him some noteworthy novelties, it was less significant than one would have a right to expect.

In the field of ideas (scientific, moral, philosophical, and political), on the other hand the impact of the English experience seems to have been very great. Newton, Locke, and, to some extent, Hobbes and Bacon appear not only to have unveiled for Voltaire new areas of knowledge but to have played a critical part in turning him toward other considerations. This phenomenon was undoubtedly what Lord Morley was trying to point up when he placed it in the poet-philosopher context, which for the moment, as far as it concerned Voltaire, was inappropriate, since his excitement was fostered by the novelties which he witnessed, rather than by any temptation to reorient his life from letters to philosophy. What challenged Voltaire's curiosity the most was the acquaintance with a new civilization. England as an organic culture, rather than English philosophy or English letters, offered to Voltaire an opportunity for maturing, equipping himself, and reorienting himself. It was this factor which opened up to him a whole new approach to life, and he was intelligent enough to analyze it advantageously and to ask the proper questions concerning its significance. What excited him was how a nation of thinkers were able to organize in every sphere of life a dynamic, organic civilization. He was already prepared to accept that what a man thinks is what he is as a personality and that what he is as a personality is what he does. Now he suddenly discovered also that what a nation thinks is what the personality, the spirit, of a nation is and that this spirit drives on to create a dynamic way of life which, when organically developed, offers a "new" harmonious civilization. Voltaire had never been aware of this possibility, not even in Holland, and he was extremely curious to know how it worked.

7. INTERLUDE, 1728-1734:
THE RESULTS OF THE ENGLISH
EXPERIENCE

VOLTAIRE RETURNED from England with the intention of publishing a work upon the manners and customs of that country. He was determined that the work would not be a picturesque description but a philosophical penetration of the civilization. This represented a new approach to the inner reality of a people, and, to carry it out, he fashioned a method which clearly analyzed what he thought to be the significant elements of the civilization and gave them an organic meaning. It is probably true that the work was also envisaged as propaganda on the part of an author who saw in England the qualities he deemed admirable in a people and who noted their lack in his own country. Voltaire stressed those qualities so vigorously that never between 1734 and 1789 were there lacking Frenchmen to urge their cultivation in France. It was in this sense that he deserves a place of primacy in the merging of English with French (or continental) civilization. In claiming primacy in presenting this or that English trait or idea, Voltaire was, as Bonno has shown, exaggerating, but it is undoubtedly true that he was the first to introduce effectively into his country both a coherent view of England and Anglomania. That, in itself, is important and suggests that the merging of two civilizations requires the intervention of some superior force or energy, such as that which Voltaire furnished in order to complete the merging wrought by others. It must not be thought, however, that Voltaire, having produced this effect, moved on to other fields in characteristic fashion, abandoning Anglomania himself. It should be recalled here that, after undertaking an intellectual or artistic enterprise, Voltaire would often reduce that enterprise in priority yet would never abandon it altogether. Therefore, we shall have to return in due time to consider Voltaire's Anglomania throughout his life.

For the moment, we shall concentrate on the other enterprises Voltaire brought back from England, either in his head or in some moderately advanced state of composition. There were four of these undertakings: the writing of history, exemplified in the *His-*

toire de Charles XII; the introduction of Shakespearean drama in French classical tragedy, exemplified in *Brutus, Eryphile, Zaïre,* and *La Mort de César*; the composition, publication, and revision of *Le Temple du Goût* (1733-1735); and the publication of the *Lettres philosophiques*.

The mere chronological listing of these activities will indicate how terribly full the years 1729-1734 were. It is clear that, soon after his return, Voltaire was certain that *Charles XII* was all but ready for publication. In fact, he was so convinced that the work was in its definitive form that, little suspecting the difficulties he would encounter with his informants and with the censors, he began talking to Thiériot about the portion of the royalties he wished him to have from the "bookseller who will bargain for the Swedish King's life" (Foulet, *Correspondance de Voltaire*, No. 67). It is certain that preparation of the work was well advanced: an announcement in the *Mercure* of May 1729 (p. 973) referred to its forthcoming publication in two duodecimo volumes. But Voltaire went through a whole long series of consultations, with M. de Brancas, M. de Croissy, La Mottraye, and eventually Villelongue. The task of putting the finishing touches on *Charles XII* extended throughout 1729, and perhaps throughout 1730. On 30 January 1731, Voltaire wrote to Cideville: "Je voudrais faire imprimer à Rouen une *Histoire de Charles XII*, roi de Suède, de ma façon. C'est mon ouvrage favori, et celui pour qui je me sens les entrailles de père." An edition, which appeared in Paris just before this letter, had been seized. Voltaire now arranged clandestinely to have an edition published in Rouen. On 10 March 1731, he left Paris for a three-and-a-half month's sojourn in Rouen. There he was occupied with the preparation of the edition, which appeared finally in October 1731.

In the meantime, before the end of February 1729, he took up anew *Brutus*, already started in England. On 12 August 1729, in a letter to Thiériot, Voltaire noted: "voici la première prose que j'ai écrite depuis huit jours, les alexandrins me gagnent." Obviously, he had returned to *Brutus*, and by December he was prepared to present his play. But he had second thoughts, because of a plot which he feared against the work. He withdrew this version from the Comédie Française, worked upon it during much of 1730, and presented it only on 11 December 1730. It was published in the early months of 1731, accompanied by a long *Discours sur la tragédie à Milord Bolingbroke*. Just previously, Voltaire had published an edition of *Œdipe*, this time with a fairly long introduction in which Voltaire combats the ideas of La Motte on tragedy and on the use of prose. In the same year, he brought out a new edition of *Mariamne*. But the work which occupied his constant attention during practically all of 1730 was the *Henriade*. It is perhaps not exaggerating too much to say that the same urge which had driven Voltaire to England, that is, the desire to bring out an edition of his epic poem, drove him back to France. It seemed ridiculous to him, even before he undertook to return, that a French poem written for a French audience should be withheld from that audience just because of censorship. Finally, after arduous efforts on Voltaire's part, the *Henriade* appeared in November 1730, with the tacit permission of the censors, if one may trust the statement Voltaire made to Cideville. Both the *Henriade* and *Brutus* were published by Voltaire himself. About a month after his departure for Rouen, a paper merchant, Jacques Chauchat, brought judgment (4 April 1731) against the poet for failure to pay for the paper he had furnished, as he said, "pour l'impression de ses livres intitulez l'anriade et Bruttus qu'il a composez et qu'il fait imprimer par luy-meme" (see Foulet, *Correspondance de Voltaire*, p. 303). In addition to his other works, Voltaire had "mis dans son cadre" *Eriphyle* and written *La Mort de César*. In the meantime, he composed a long letter to the *Nouvelliste du Parnasse,* corrected an edition of his works for Amsterdam, and prepared *Brutus* for a new edition "revue et augmentée de plusieurs scènes nouvelles." He revised the *Essay sur la poésie épique* and decided to bring out another edition of the *Henriade*, this time with the *Essay*. Finally, he proposed to bring out an edition of his tragedies.

The year 1732 was equally as crowded as 1731. In May, Voltaire prepared to publish *Eriphyle*, but the play was not a success and he turned to something else. On 29 May, he told Formont that he had written an act of *Zaïre*. The finished play was presented at the Comédie on 13 August. In September, he tried to recast *Eriphyle* and *La Mort de César* and to revise *Charles XII* for a new edition in Holland. It is evident that Voltaire was scurrying around from one project to another as if he still had no focus to his life and as if he did not have a single moment to lose. A careful analysis of his four principal activities will show, nonetheless, that he was acting only after the most deliberate planning.

Beuchot states that the *Histoire de Charles XII* was composed in 1727 and 1728 (*Œuvres*, XXIV, i). Thus, in his opinion, it was essentially a product of the English sojourn. Foulet (*Correspondance de Voltaire*, p. 196) confirms this dating to the extent of pointing out that Voltaire, in his letter of 2 April 1729 to Thiériot, seems on the point of bringing out the "Swedish king's life": "You must have a hundred crowns beside from Bernard, and as much from the bookseller who will bargain for the privilege of the Swedish king's life. . . ." Besides, as Foulet has also pointed out, Voltaire is full of recommendations to Thiériot concerning *Charles XII*: "I hope M. de Brancas will instruct me on the particularities which he knows concerning the late King of Sweden. . . ." "You may go to the Swedish ambassador . . . ," he prompts his friend, and he provides him with a list of inquiries: whether Count Piper had a hand in having the King declared a major at sixteen; what role the Queen-grandmother played after this event; what sort of government was established in Sweden after the King's arrival in Turkey. "I beg of you to see M. de Croissy," he urges, giving his friend a correspondingly long list of questions concerning the European scene at the time of Charles XII: what the Pretender's interest in the King was; whether France had any intention of helping the Pretender and Charles; what Baron Goertz's plan concerning the Pretender and the Empire involved. It is obvious that Voltaire was busy revising his manuscript and was eager to get the details correct. Foulet believes that the manuscript was near its final form and notes that M. de Maisons had already received it long before the first of April 1729, when Voltaire was seeking its return. Foulet surmises that it was sent to the Président in 1728, probably from England. Finally, Voltaire himself wrote that "cette histoire fut principalement composée en Angleterre, à la campagne, avec M. Fabrice, chambellan de George 1er, électeur de Hanovre, roi d'Angleterre, qui avait résidé sept ans auprès de Charles XII, après la journée de Pultava" (M. I, 87). In a note in 1738, Voltaire wrote more specifically still: "l'auteur écrivait en 1727" (M. XVI, 226). Most specific of all was his letter to the *Journal des savants:* "De même, me trouvant à la campagne en 1727 avec M. de Fabrice qui avait passé sept années auprès de Charles XII, il me conta des faits si extraordinaires que je ne pus résister à l'envie qu'il m'inspira de les écrire" (B. 2426).

If the manuscript was prepared in 1727 and 1728, and if it was brought back to France in so finished a state that Voltaire thought it warranted publication, it is evident that he was quickly undeceived. This is shown in the way he handled Villelongue's material, which was written in February and March 1730 (B. 360 and 362). This material was worked into the text, then, a year after the work was presumed to be ready. In all probability, however, the same thing happened in the case of *Charles XII* that usually occurred with Voltaire's works: a draft which he deemed ready for publication underwent severe revisions before it was published.

Even with these clarifications, the genesis of the *Histoire de Charles XII* remains shrouded in mystery. Brumfitt, in *Voltaire Historian*, has given us a short sketch, consisting mostly of a set of probabilities, of the way in which Voltaire was led to a consideration of history from the time of the *Henriade*. Work on the *Henriade* probably introduced its author to Mézeray, De Thou, and Bayle. Bayle's *Dictionnaire* was probably the source of much information. Brumfitt, following Haxo ("Pierre Bayle et Voltaire avant les *Lettres philosophiques*") suggests that it was through Bayle that Voltaire first made contact with the problems of history. The trouble with all these probabilities is that, having very meagre documentation on Voltaire at the time he was composing the *Henriade* (since it, too, had its clandestine aspects), we are reduced in large part to conjecture. We do have one bit of information, however. Voltaire, in 1722, wrote Thiériot with great enthusiasm that he had been impressed with Bolingbroke's knowledge of ancient and modern history. Since there are difficulties in showing Voltaire's interest in Bayle at so early a date, our best guess so far is that Bolingbroke was the first of Voltaire's acquaintances to turn him toward history. Voltaire, however, claims to have shown some interest in Charles XII as early as 1717, when he had met Baron Goertz at the home of the banker Hogguers. Once again, we are driven to draw an inference from a fairly unsubstantial surmise, because, even after his return from England, Voltaire was still inquiring into the role played by Baron Goertz. In accordance with the letter to the *Journal des savants* which we have mentioned above, Voltaire seems to want us to believe that it was Fabrice who inspired him to write about the extraordinary feats of Charles, just as it was Caumartin who had inspired him to record the exploits of Henry IV. It is this remark that leads Brumfitt to view the two works as closely allied, both being concerned with the biographical aspects of an outstanding individual and both being primarily conceived as works of art.

It is true that Voltaire was struck by the resemblance between history and drama. While he was engaged with *Charles XII*, he was equally preoccupied with historical drama, and we actually have in his correspondence, though at a later date, the expressed conviction that history should be related in the same form as a play: an introduction to set the stage, the development of the complications of the plot, until a climax is reached, and then the unraveling of the plot. It has often been pointed out that *Charles XII* fits admirably this dramatic conception of history. Brumfitt finds that the tone, as well as the hero, is tragic and that Charles is indeed a victim of *hubris*. Voltaire portrays him as fearless and extraordinarily bold, calling him from the beginning a mixture of greatness and madness, and eventually referring to him as "moitié Alexandre, moitié Don Quichotte." Voltaire is a little obsessed by his daredeviltry; he finds it hard to point up the fact that, though the Swedish King was overly proud and a great visionary, he was a poor strategist. Voltaire avoids trying to delve into his psychology, possibly because he could not well enter into this sort of person. In this respect, he is better in dealing with Charles's great enemy, Peter the Great. He understands a King who schemes for the good of his people better than he understands one who fights for his personal glory.

The book is not only attractive because of its conception of history as art. The *Petit Larousse* has expressed in a most succinct way the outstanding quality of the work: "modèle de narration vive, claire, et objective." In fact, when a severe indictment was brought against *Charles XII*, it was concluded that it read like a novel. This was not a distorted view: Voltaire had assembled the oral testimony of eyewitnesses insofar as he could. They had naturally, as anyone involved in telling a story, endeavored to give a lively, personal flavor to the events. Anecdotes abound, as they always do in Voltaire's histories, since he believed that one gets some deep insight into events through them. In fact, he felt that anecdotes are to history what metaphors are to epic poetry. It is easy to see how the work is organized, with the art of story-telling (so acutely developed by Voltaire at a later moment) employed at every opportunity to artistic advantage. It has even been shown that, stylistically, the events are related superbly by a constant switch in tense structure.

To see how the technique works, one would have to take the sources—such as Villelongue, for instance—and study how Voltaire has transformed what is a pedestrian account, written without much regard for timing, rhythm, or dramatic effect (although there is some effort to achieve dramatic effect), into a narrative in which all these qualities are superbly utilized. This is what Brumfitt calls "humanist history," and it is here exhibited at its best: the hero dominates the social scene, action dominates the interpretation of events, and, though harangues are suppressed, conversations and *bons mots* are retained, and anecdotes, as we have said, play a large role.

It would be a mistake, however, to think that there is nothing more to *Charles XII* than the art of story-telling and the techniques of style. Voltaire aimed to give it an interpretation. He recalls that history is a witness, not a flatterer, speaks with some impertinence about how kings may profit by reading these exploits which they will want to avoid, and divides kings into good kings (Louis XII for the love he bore his people, Francis I for the arts and sciences he gave his, and Henry IV for the conquest he made of his heritage by knowing how to conquer and to pardon), bad kings (whom Voltaire prudently refrains from naming), and those in between, who resemble both tyrants and the good kings but are more closely connected with the tyrants. He remarks that these latter are the most appealing to the public, which is wont to regard with admiration those who have done ill in a brilliant way. Otherwise, kings are so common, they are usually so mediocre, their enterprises have been so undistinguished, and their treaties, wars, and alliances are so numerous that posterity will be crushed beneath all this meaningless material. It is evident that the Republican Voltaire, who had just passed through his English experience, is still speaking. But there is more to this: the Voltaire who is speaking had been listening to Bolingbroke, precisely the one who had made popular, if he did not invent, the notion that "history teaches by example." History really depicts, or should depict, those who have produced a great revolution or those who, having been depicted by some great writer, stand out above the crowd. Voltaire presents his two characters, Charles and Peter, as "les personnages les plus singuliers qui eussent paru depuis plus de vingt siècles." He concedes that, of the two, Peter was by far the greater man but asserts that the example of Charles, who ruined his country by his love of conquest, would be of inestimable utility to some princes, "si ce livre leur tombe par hasard entre les mains."

More important than the paltry lesson of humility a prince may learn from the book is the lesson a country may learn in the making of its own civilization. Voltaire, just as later in the *Lettres philosophiques*, tries to show not only that history teaches by example but that the true historian will learn how to analyze what comprises the force of a country, what contributes to its grandeur, and what brings about its downfall. The contrast of Sweden and Russia juxtaposes the monarch who ruins his country with the monarch who enlightens his. Peter is celebrated throughout the first book as the maker of civilization, while Charles is portrayed as the destroyer. But the philosophy of the author extends further. A country's civilization depends upon its geography, its climate, its arts, its population, its industry, and its institutions. Peter had understood that, to be great, Russia had to learn how to turn all these elements to its advantage. And he had learned something more: that a country can be educated to its civilization. Reform is possible. Voltaire was destined to learn this lesson even better than Peter the Great.

Voltaire went over to England with an epic poem which he published and sold to the British; he came back with a history which bore artistic resemblances to that epic and which he published and sold to the French. In both works he had built upon a traditional foundation, but in each something else had been added: art had been added to history in the *Henriade* in England, while history had been united with art in the *Histoire de Charles XII* in France. So far, all the record shows is that Voltaire was a man of letters with a high sense of literary form and a great power of literary expression, who had been able both to broaden the literary form to include history and to sharpen the expression by reverting to prose. He had not, however, renounced poetry for prose, nor had he abandoned literature for ideas. He had merely enlarged poetry with narrative prose and enriched the formal genre of the epic by historicizing it with ideas.

This achievement can be seen more clearly in the way he treated the theatre. At the time of his arrival in England, Voltaire aspired to become the foremost epic and the foremost dramatic poet, after having been acknowledged the leading Horatian poet of light verse. The Horatian strain he elaborated through his association with Pope, but it was the literary critic Horace, not the writer of epistles, odes, satires, and *poésies mêlées*. In the field of lyric poetry, I do not really see that Voltaire brought back anything more than he took. However, in balancing Pope against Swift, he did learn that prose was a much more effective mode for satire in contemporary times than poetry. But he did not yet abandon satire as a Horatian form of poetry; he merely appreciated how satire could be just as appropriately conveyed in artistic prose as in artistic poetry. It was not until later, though, that he actually came to use it.

For the moment, what he thought might be more immediately serviceable was anything he could learn from Shakespeare and the English theatre. Even before leaving England, Voltaire was committed to adapting Shakespeare to the French stage or, at least, adapting what he thought would be useful aspects of Shakespeare and English tragedy to the classic French tragedy. Foulet has already noted (*Correspondance de Voltaire*, pp. 297ff.) that among the works Voltaire brought back from England was at least the draft of a tragedy entitled *Brutus*. Indeed, he wrote to Bolingbroke in 1731 that *Brutus* was born in England while he was in seclusion at Wandsworth with Falkener (in 1728), that he composed the first act in English prose, and that he often had discussed with Bolingbroke the play he was developing. Foulet surmises that it must have been well advanced before Voltaire left England and that he must have completed it in French during his retreat in Normandy.

Voltaire, it should be noted, deemed this tragedy of *Brutus* the one most appropriate to the English stage, and he expressed surprise that the English had never made use of this theme. However, there was an English *Brutus* by Nathaniel Lee and, strikingly enough, one by Voltaire's old Latin teacher and still a third by Mlle Bernard.

The theme seems to have been connected in Voltaire's mind, not with any of these predecessors, but with the general conception he held of the love of liberty which, in his opinion, was "bien Anglais." Love of liberty, hatred of tyranny, and heroism before the natural passions were certainly associated in his mind with what was essential in the British character. That he transported the play to Rome, however, was due to the classicism which was fundamentally his own tradition. His idea of placing upon the stage the Roman Senate, with the senators all garbed in red robes, was a dramatic effect which he thought was "bien Shakespearien." He justified it, however, with reference to the last acts of *Rodogune* and *Athalie*.

The play was accompanied by the usual discursive essay, this time a lengthy *Discours sur la tragédie* addressed to Lord Bolingbroke. Voltaire had just put out, in January 1730, a reedition of *Œdipe* with a fairly long preface in which he returned to discussions which he had had with La Motte before his sojourn in England. These discussions turn upon the use of prose instead of poetry in tragedy and upon the necessity of the three unities. On the first point, Voltaire still maintains that poetry adds rhythm, harmony, and elegance to a tragedy. He notes that the English, and the Italians also, use poetry to enhance their literary works. In fact, he adds, poetry, far from being a barbaric custom invented in comparatively recent times, as La Motte stated, constantly found favor with the Greeks and the Romans. It has always flourished in France; Italy and England have never thought of abandoning it. Voltaire still concedes that poetry increases the difficulty of artistic expression, but he sturdily maintains that its advantages are such that it cannot be suppressed. His defense is conducted with vigor: poetry has been and always will be cultivated by all peoples; the first philosophers, legislators, founders of religions, and historians were *all* poets. He then adds a sentence of supreme significance, his profession of faith as a poet still (M. II, 55):

Il semble que la poésie dût manquer communément, dans de pareils sujets [that is, philosophy, legislation, religion and history], ou de précision ou d'harmonie: mais, depuis que Virgile et Horace ont réuni ces deux grands mérites, qui paraissent si incompatibles, depuis que Mm. Despréaux et Racine ont écrit comme Virgile et Horace, un homme qui les a lus, et qui sait qu'ils sont traduits dans presque toutes les langues de l'Europe, peut-il avilir à ce point un talent qui lui a fait tant d'honneur à lui-même?

The "homme qui les a lus" is naturally La Motte, but Voltaire is more thinking of himself as the heir of this tradition than he is talking of La Motte.

Voltaire likewise defends the three unities. They are still "ces sages règles du théâtre," they are "bonnes et nécessaires," they are beginning to be respected by other nations than the French; even in England, they are becoming more rigorously observed than in France. Voltaire returns to Aristotle's definition in their defense; a play is "the representation of an action." Nature itself has taught us this precept; we are even shocked to see two events in a painting. For the same reason, the unity of place is essential, because a single action cannot take place in several spots at the same time. The unity of time is joined closely and naturally to the other two rules. "Je ne suis point venu à la comédie pour entendre l'histoire d'un héros, mais pour voir un seul événement de sa vie," Voltaire remarks. In a moment of liberality, he is willing to extend the twelve-hour day to twenty-four hours; but abuses must not be tolerated, he maintains, for otherwise "nous verrions en peu de temps des pièces telles que l'ancien *Jules César* des Anglais." The unities not only prevent defects, they make for real beauties.

These views are assembled here to show that, in many respects, the Voltaire who went to England was the same as the one who returned to France. This is a distorted interpretation, however, even in regard to the theatre. If the preface to the 1730 *Œdipe* is placed alongside the *Discours sur la tragédie*, which appeared about a year later (*Brutus* was performed in December 1730 but published in 1731), a great change can be seen to have occurred. Voltaire still prattles about the necessity of rime and about the difficulties of French versification. He still maintains that "nous ne pourrons jamais secouer le joug de la rime; elle est essentielle à la poésie française"—all the more essential since French poetry lacks many of the devices of other languages, such as long and short syllables, enjambement, and innate harmony of syllables. He is still opposed to tragedies in prose. Tragic theatre will doubtless always require poetry, and the French will require in addition rime. They will have to struggle to avoid having it restrict thought, they must demand that the thought be neither trivial nor "recherchée," they must require the same precision, the same clarity, the same purity in poetry as in prose, and so on. Voltaire asserts that the English theatre is full of defects, that it cannot boast a single good play, even though there are splendid scenes. English plays are totally lacking in purity of diction, regularity of dramatic development, propriety in action and style, elegance, and all the other fine things which distinguish the French theatre. But they do have something in addition to admirable scenes: they are full of action.

This is precisely what Voltaire thinks is lacking in the French theatre. Instead of action, the typical French play consists of a collection of beautiful elegies and is often handicapped by excessive delicacy of taste. The French, Voltaire charges, are afraid to risk novelties, their stage is altogether inappropriate for the performance of tragedy, and the spectators on the stage make action practically impossible. The scenery, often unsuitable to the play, creates stage conditions which make what action there is seem ridiculous. Voltaire still hesitates to counsel the extremes to which the Greeks and the English go in representing horrible actions on the stage; he shudders at the thought that the stage can become a scene of carnage. Yet he hazards the guess that there are scenes which appear horrible and disgusting to the French but which, "bien ménagées, représentées avec art, et surtout adoucies par le charme des beaux vers, pourraient nous faire une sorte de plaisir dont nous ne nous doutons pas." He holds firmly to the conviction that the rules of the unities must be upheld and that those of decorum must not be breached.

In reality, then, Voltaire on his return was still fundamentally a classical playwright, he would, it is true, have liked to adapt to the French tragedy the action of the English, and he would have liked to get away from love as a theme. But he had no desire to give up either the elegance, the harmony, or the charm of poetry which he felt the French possessed by right.

Voltaire did set to work to develop the action of Shakespeare in his own writing, however. *La Mort de César* had been sketched at Wandsworth in 1727 but was not completed until 1731 (Voltaire to Thiériot, 30 June 1731). Both Lamare's "Avertissement" and Voltaire's preface stress that, although the work was begun as a translation of the famous scene in which Marc Antony confronts the rabble, the author abandoned the translation and remade a *Mort de César* which, curiously enough, he offers as portraying "le génie et le caractère des écrivains anglais"—obviously, because of its monstrous nature, which Voltaire does not fail to point out. But it becomes more curious when this "génie" of the English is equated with the freedom which is the characteristic of the Romans as well as the English. Voltaire evidently felt that he might be criticized for the ferocity Brutus shows toward his own father (he accepted the legend that Caesar was Brutus's father). To obviate this charge, Voltaire states that this was a well-known trait of Brutus's character. What saves all this nonsense is Voltaire's insistence that the whole play is "dans le goût anglais."

In spite of all this assurance and self-assurance, it is evident that what attracted Voltaire's interest in the first place was the spectacle (and the animation) of the Antony scene. Dédéyan (*Voltaire et la pensée anglaise*, p. 32) insists that what Voltaire admired was the horror, the tragic emotion, and the large panorama of history but that he failed to see the irony of Caesar's death in the name of a liberty which does not produce freedom. Voltaire judged excessive the action which followed the death of Caesar. The spectacle of Caesar's dead body on the stage was, for him, the ultimate dramatic effect. He failed completely to see that, for Shakespeare, the unity of the play did not lie in Caesar's death but in Brutus; hence, all he could grasp in the play was spectacle and movement. That he was uneasy about its effect can be seen in the fact that, although it had been written as an experimental play in 1731, he did not dare risk presenting it on the stage of the Comédie Française until 1743.

In his next play, *Eriphyle*, Voltaire undertook to recreate the spectacle of the ghost which Shakespeare used in *Hamlet*. Dédéyan even sees in the Voltaire play the actual theme of *Hamlet*, but it must be confessed that the resemblance between the two plays is at best slight. When presented on 7 March 1732, it was ill received. Voltaire nevertheless repeated the experiment in 1748 with *Sémiramis*.

Voltaire made another experiment in 1732 with *Zaïre*, which resembles *Othello*, at least insofar as the jealousy theme is concerned. Voltaire took great pride in the simplicity of this play. It must be acknowledged, however, that the jealousy theme, the "Turquerie," and the imitations of Dryden make it more complicated than the author realized. Voltaire was determined to add another Shakespearean element to his work, too. Carried away by the historical plays of the English dramatist, the Frenchman gave the whole setting a historical flavor to bring out the glories of France in the crusades. This element he tried to introduce again in *Adélaïde du Guesclin*, but this time the audience rejected the innovation. It was repeated in the *Duc de Foix* almost two decades later and was said to have succeeded.

When one comes to sum up the immediate impact of Shakespeare on Voltaire, it is not easy to distinguish between actual imitation, general impressions, and changing attitudes. The first statement which seems justified is that Voltaire was very much attracted to the bard of Avon. The attraction was both favorable and unfavorable. There were things which he deemed surprisingly brilliant and others which he thought unbelievably vulgar. In general, he concluded that there were many more vulgar than brilliant things. He also indicated in all his pronouncements that the beauties of Shakespearean drama were incorporated in particular scenes, never in entire plays, and were attributable to the two qualities of action and spectacle. I know of no place where he found them in the strength of diction or the powers of thought, or in the shattering beauty of the expression. I know of no place where he seemed to comprehend the total effect of a Shakespearean play, or even where he made any effort to comprehend a play as an organic entity. It was, unfortunately, not his way of understanding literature. He often said that the beauties of literature were particular beauties, that they were always seen in details. And, even in his own plays, he seems never to have gotten beyond the beauties of detail. All of his negative criticism down to *Zaïre*, as far as the theatre is concerned, is also based on detail. He will tell you that such and such a play is monstrous because ... (and he will cite what he thinks is a defect of detail). However, there is this difference between his positive and negative criticism: the negative leads to some general condemnation, whereas the positive rarely, if ever, leads to any general approval.

The result is that when we are dealing with his own opinion of Shakespeare, we have to content ourselves with a mere listing of the scenes or actions he approved in particular plays. In *Julius Caesar*, for instance, he approved what Dédéyan calls "une décoration pompeuse et animée" and "une exposition immédiate et pressante." In other words, he was attracted by the Senate scene or the rabble scene, and what he liked in them were the red robes, the animation, the boisterousness of the action, and the parliamentary setting. He liked to think that this was all "so English" as well as "so Roman," particularly here where—he thought—the theme was liberty versus tyranny. Consequently, in his *Brutus*, he tried to take this theme "so English" and "so Roman" and present scenes in a vivid setting, with much animation and noisy spectacle. In *La Mort de César*, he attempted to achieve the same kind of effect in some of his scenes, but he also felt attracted to *Julius Caesar* because it was a play of male action and, hence, different from French plays which were either "salon" conversations or madrigals of love. Thus, in Shakespeare's *Caesar*, the actors shout for liberty, as in Racine's *Bérénice* they sigh for love; Shakespeare is concerned with the most profound aspects of politics, and this theme is presented on the English stage with the greatest ferocity. It is true that Voltaire for once had tried to analyze, at least in theory, the total effect of a Shakespearean play. But, when he tried to imitate it in an effort to secure this effect, it turned out that this was not Shakespeare's desired total effect at all—nor Voltaire's either.

Hamlet had, for him, one scene of amazing consequence, the scene of the ghost. This, he felt, is the sort of thing that can strike terror into an audience. In a way, it is just a matter of spectacle. Voltaire undertook in *Eryphile* to produce the same effect. The only other thing he admired in the play was Hamlet's soliloquy, which he translated; it is not easy, however, to determine from the translation what in the soliloquy attracted his attention. It can be fairly stated that, whatever it was, it was not the brilliance of the diction, nor the harmony of the expression, nor the depth of the thought. Anyway, he found the ghost more attractive. But his experiment did not succeed, both because his audience believed even less in ghosts than he did and because it was impossible to believe in a ghost on the French stage with one third of the audience sitting around the stage in the wings. He tried it again in *Sémiramis* (1748), after getting rid of some of the difficulty by clearing the stage of the spectators.

Othello attracted him because it had a theme which, as a Frenchman, he was very familiar with: love as jealousy. One would think that, not approving of love as madrigal, he would have been skeptical of all kinds of love, but such was not the case. What is more, Racine had handled this theme superbly in *Bajazet*, as well as in *Phèdre*, though he had had no strangling of people with handkerchiefs. Voltaire, too, hesitated before the impropriety of this barbarous act, but he hoped he could get the effect without the kerchief. As Baldensperger put it, Voltaire "tient à couvrir de toute la bienséance possible cette passion de la jalousie."

Lastly, Voltaire was also attracted by the historical foundation of Shakespeare's plays. Having some interest in history himself, he attempted to set before his audience a dramatic clash between civilizations, which does not seem to have been Shakespeare's intention, at least not in the plays discussed here. In truth, *Zaïre* does not appear to be modeled to any great extent upon Shakespeare's historical plays, but *Le Duc de Foix* does. Even here, Voltaire is more interested in the effect of a cannon shot offstage than he is in France's history.

To say all this is not to diminish the value of Voltaire's dramatic production. But it does point up that the French author was attracted by particular details in the English author rather than by his plays, that he played up Shakespeare's beauties and defects with true Voltairean criticism, and that he attempted to imitate some of the beauties, with results that seem neither particularly successful nor even beautiful. This fact has given rise to a shift in critical approach on the part of Voltaire critics. Sonet provides what appears to be the most judicious conclusion to this problem of influence: "Si les résultats de l'influence de Shakespeare sur Voltaire devaient être jugés seulement par les tragédies que ce dernier nous a données, ces résultats n'auraient, somme toute, qu'une importance secondaire et l'étude des rapports des deux écrivains dramatiques n'aurait plus qu'un intérêt historique" (*Voltaire et l'influence anglaise*, p. 64). This judgment seems to be supported by the facts. It is not generally the conclusion proffered, however. Fontaine's critical edition of *Zaïre* (Lyons, 1889) tends to make that play totally un-Shakespearean, while Baldensperger, usually so excellent in his critical literary judgment, talks of "Voltaire, homme supérieur," being "saisi par la profondeur et le pathétique de l'inspiration shakespérienne."

The truth of the matter is that, having discovered a Shakespeare said by Voltaire's contemporaries to have been the great dramatist of England, he could find no one among his contemporary English friends who could show him in what that greatness consisted. Dryden, in his *Essay on Dramatic Poesy*, offered this as a well-considered opinion: "Let us therefore admire the beauties and the heights of Shakespeare, without falling after him, into a carelessness, and, I may call it, a lethargy of thought, for whole scenes together." Pope, in 1725, writing in his preface to an edition of Shakespeare, did not differ materially from Dryden in his remarks: "For of all English poets, Shakespeare must be confessed to be the fairest and fullest subject for criticism, and to afford the most numerous as well as the most conspicuous instances both of beauties and faults of all sorts." Lanson, in his edition of the *Lettres philosophiques*, cites (II, 89) a similar opinion from Thomas Rymer, *A Short View of Tragedy*, 1693. With this sort of introduction to Shakespeare, it is no wonder that Voltaire came rapidly to the conclusion that Shakespeare's greatness had ruined the English stage. Since the English stage was notoriously barbarous, there was to be gained here, in his opinion, only the snatches of scenes which had achieved dramatic success and which could perhaps lead to revitalizing the French stage. Thus, for Voltaire, Shakespeare's name was worth more than his plays, at least in the beginning.

It would seem that, before making of Shakespeare the fountainhead of drama for Voltaire, one would do right to seek the answers to certain preliminary questions. For instance, how many plays of Shakespeare did Voltaire know? Here we are in the land of surmise. Lounsbury thinks Voltaire knew only *Julius Caesar, Hamlet, Othello*, and *Macbeth*. Sonet (*Voltaire et l'influence anglaise*, p. 52), on the other hand, believes that Voltaire must have read or seen the majority of Shakespeare's tragedies. Lanson (*Lettres philosophiques*, II, 92-95) shows, by reference to the handbills of the time, that Voltaire could have seen a good many of the English author's plays. We should like to know whether, in view of the scant reference he makes to the English playwright during his stay in England (no reference to him in the first *English Notebook*, a mistaken reference to him in the *Cambridge Notebook*, and no reference whatsoever in the *Sottisier*), his interest extended beyond mere curiosity. Lastly, it has been pointed out by T. S. Russell, in *Voltaire, Dryden, and Heroic Tragedy*, that Voltaire's references to Dryden are far more numerous in his *Notebooks* than his references to other English dramatists, that his conception of tragedy as expressed in his theoretical works is far closer to Dryden's than to Shakespeare's, and that there are clearer cases of his imitation of Dryden than of his imitation of Shakespeare. Could it be, as Russell has suggested, that what we have become accustomed to attribute to Shakespeare regarding the important impact English tragedy had upon Voltaire belongs, in reality, to Dryden?

At all events, whether his infatuation with Shakespeare had produced only the imitation of some notable scenes, like the theme of liberty, and the imitation of some startling techniques, like the introduction of a ghost or the increase of action on the stage, or whether, after all, these were novelties engendered more by Dryden and the contemporary stage, it is certain that Voltaire returned from England to address himself to the theatre as at least one of his two major preoccupations. While occupying himself with the principles of the analysis of a foreign civilization, he was busily engaged not only in marking out the differences between the English and French theatres but in actually producing plays, as his *Brutus, La Mort de César, Eryphile*, and *Zaïre* attest. There is no gainsaying that the theatre had been also his preoccupation when he went to England.

There are even better indications that he was still the poet, the dramatist, the epic writer, the "littérateur," and the man of taste. No sooner had he returned than he resumed his association with his literary friends Cideville and Formont. Once again, he became the cynosure of the old Rouen literary circles, which he had haunted before his exile. He still assiduously attended Mme the Baroness de Fontaine-Martel's salon, where literature was deemed the reason for living. Voltaire even made some, though infrequent, visits to Fontainebleau, where he trailed along after the court. But, whether at Rouen, Paris, or Fontainebleau, Voltaire's interest, and the interest of his associates, was centered on poetry, not politics or philosophy. His business was to write poetry, to read poetry, to discuss the poetry of others, and to compare the great French classicists with contemporary authors, especially with himself. In this atmosphere of literature and criticism, Voltaire, thanks to his own production and thanks also to the broadening of experience that life in a foreign country had afforded him, became more and more the arbiter of taste, or at least claimed to be more and more its arbiter. It was this claim which turned him to the composition of *Le Temple du goût*.

Professor Carcassonne, in the introduction to his critical edition of Voltaire's sprightly poem and prose, has traced the origin of this little "bagatelle," and noted the important place it has in the production of Voltaire. Basically, the form was a conventional one, employed by writers from the Renaissance to Voltaire's time. Caporali, Cervantes, Sénécé, Guéret (*Le Parnasse réformé*), Pierre Charles Roy (*Le Goût*) in 1727, and Pope—to name only a few—had all composed works of this form. Voltaire was undoubtedly familiar with Sénécé and Roy, if not directly with the others. Sénécé he mentions in the catalogue of writers in the *Siècle de Louis XIV* as being singularly inventive, and Roy was a competitor whom he followed with great attention. It is even possible to find a number of similarities between Roy's poem and Voltaire's: both poets condemn preciosity, criticize Fontenelle and La Motte, and vaunt feeling for beauties in preference to rational demonstration; both also give to the Temple a solidly classical structure. But, as Carcassonne has so neatly pointed out, Voltaire's *Temple* is "aimable," while Roy's is only correct and judicious. The latter is lacking in both variety and gracefulness. It is, as Carcassonne says, the *Temple du goût* "moins le talent et la verve" (p. 24). What is praiseworthy in this lively, sprightly, dynamic style of Voltaire is the carefree way in which the allegory is conducted, the masterly manner in which the abstractions —Art, Nature, Mode and Merit, Gluttony, Sloth, and Pleasure— cease being abstractions and become charming little "lutins," as they would appear in an "avant-scène" of an eighteenth-century theatre. They have, as Carcassonne notes (p. 25), become moving silhouettes, which would later be used over and over in the *contes*. They are objects of the magic lantern which Voltaire shuts off from time to time in order to prolong the "boniment," heightened by a constant concern and a continual search for the expression which at the same time attains and clarifies the sensibility.

Although he passes lightly over authors and works, the "badinage" gives way to serious subjects; the tone is light and frivolous, the judgments are severe and often satirical, yet the subject matter is notwithstanding substantial and critical. The subjects proposed are no less than the respective rights of tradition and novelty, the genius of language (which had so preoccupied Voltaire in England), the value of rime in poetry, and, indeed, the nature of poetry. Voltaire undertakes in a light and airy way to treat critical problems which were already being discussed by the more formal prose critics of the day, particularly Dubos. Like his contemporary, whom he respected very much, Voltaire holds that each people has its own art, its own temperament, and its own language. The interest which lay at the basis of his discovery of the English now becomes a critical principle. But it is only one of several essential points of view: Voltaire is also a purist, and he seeks the solution of such problems as the nature of taste.

This taste is the apanage of the cultivated man and operates in the whole field of the arts. Voltaire does not scruple to mete out approbation or condemnation to architecture, painting, and music, as well as engravings and literature. He distributes some praise, but he is more inclined to censure. Although he had now learned to distinguish between satire, criticism, and libel, criticism still means for him the selection of details which contain either beauties or defects. To a twentieth-century critic, this kind of criticism is singularly limited, but it pretends to be good-natured and ingratiating, and it allows a lot of freedom for feeling. Not much importance is assigned to arbitrary judgment, no emphasis is placed upon the creation of a standard of criticism, and none whatever upon a way of judging. One is left with the impression that the best criticism is the result of an artistic intuition which is as selective and as rare as Jansenistic salvation. The "connaisseur" is the one who is blessed with an organism which can feel acute pain before the defects of a work of art or supreme enjoyment before its beauties. Light and unsubstantial, if not downright superficial, the *Temple* has the flavor of a critical Alexandrianism distinguished by finesse and delicacy. The joy of criticism consists, not in appreciating, but in judging, not in embracing a work of art, but in passing lightly over one of its aspects, not in understanding the sources of its vitality, but in picking out the reasons for its failure. Voltaire defends this way of criticizing by stating that only a fool likes everything in a work of art. But what he really wants to do is to give the impression of the superiority of criticism over artistic expression. This attitude had become very characteristic of Voltaire's time. Fundamentally, it is a manner of concealing artistic insufficiences with an appearance of critical, rational superiority. It is nothing more than a clandestine art, united with the art of conversation.

There are, to be sure, compensating views. Voltaire, no more than Boileau, can give valid reasons for becoming enthusiastic about a Racine play or a Molière play or a La Fontaine poem. Essentially, what this mundane criticism possesses to the fullest is superficiality, what it lacks is discrimination: it places Racine on the same literary plane as Leibniz and La Fontaine on the same level as Bayle. There are even those who have produced nothing and who still find a place in the Temple because they are, as Voltaire says, "aimables." What all this means is that, for Voltaire, after his sojourn in England, civilization forms an entity, and enjoyment is a luxury which embraces all the manifestations of life; "décent et mesuré," says Carcassonne, the *Temple du goût* "nous présente sous le jour le plus favorable cette philosophie qui veut tout accueillir . . . mais choisir." In its frank impertinence, it is an almost perfect example of post-Regency "insouciance"; in its importance for the author, it marks the curtailing of one career (creative poetry) and the beginning of another (creative criticism). But, above all, it offers opportunities for broadening the field of criticism to embrace all the activities of a civilization.

It is a matter of record that, having permitted, if not actually encouraged, the publication of the *Temple du goût*, Voltaire encountered in its wake an opposition to his work which causes some surprise. The general impression later critics have is that, the work being, as Voltaire himself called it, a "badinage," it would have been natural to expect the public to react by enjoying the lightness of its presentation and the gracefulness of its versification, without being in the least scandalized either by the malice of some sections or by the impertinent tone of the whole. Instead, the public received the work with decided hostility. Carcassonne has assembled some of these reactions from Rousseau, Brossette, Bouhier, and Marais: "libelle infâme," "temple du dégoût," "homme déshonoré," "homme à terre" (*Le Temple du goût*, p. 11, n. 1). Voltaire, as Carcassonne explains the situation, became disturbed by the violence of the storm and immediately set to work to revise his *Temple*. After reconstructing his "bagatelle," he attempted to get permission to print it in France. Crébillon, the official censor, did indeed grant his approval, but so strong had the opposition been that the authorities did not feel justified in giving the desired permission, and Voltaire, much against his will, was forced to bring out his revised edition with Ledet, in Amsterdam. Included in this edition by way of preface was a *Lettre de Mr. de V——à M. de C——*.

This letter to Cideville throws some light on the composition of the work. It was here that Voltaire called attention to the fact that the *Temple* was a "bagatelle," a "plaisanterie de société," and that he had scarcely had a larger role in its composition than that of being the secretary of the Rouen group where the book had originated. Some of the opinions herein recorded had actually been pronounced by members of the group. A. M. de—— had said that it was a pity that Bayle had given more than two hundred articles to Lutheran and Calvinist ministers and professors, and that, in looking for Caesar, he had found an article upon Jean Césarius, professor at Cologne, but not on Julius Caesar. Everybody had agreed that in the *Histoire de l'Académie Française* there had been discovered articles upon a long list of illustrious unknowns, such as Balesdens, de Porchères, de Bardin, Baudouin, Faret, Colletet, and Cottin. Someone had said that there was scarcely a "femme d'esprit" who did not write better letters than Voiture; someone else, that Saint-Evremond ought never to have written poetry; a third, that he should never have published all his prose. Voltaire contends that he has only set down in writing the verdict which others had pronounced.

In this same letter to Cideville, Voltaire assembles the charges which had been brought against his *Temple*. Those in the Administration resent the author's criticism of the architecture of Versailles and think it scandalous that he should dare to say that Le Brun lacks a feeling for coloring. Rigorists say it is a libel to have intermingled the "Filles de l'Opéra," Lucretius, and Doctors from the

Sorbonne. Authors not mentioned, or even thought of, complain that they are the victims of satire, that their faults are exposed and their merits passed over in silence. People are irritated that no one is praised without mention of some fault and that each caress is attended with a scratch. It is at this point that Voltaire draws his distinction between satire, criticism, and libel. He also attempts to make a distinction between a "pièce de société" which is his "plaisanterie," and a formal criticism: this "Temple du goût" is not at all a "Traité du goût." The latter, he says, would have to be written by critical experts; the former is composed by the "jeune noblesse" without attaching any importance whatever to it. In conclusion, Voltaire makes an observation which reveals his keen insight into the society of the day: this young nobility occupies itself in cultivating the arts and letters, in developing its talents, and in having "de l'esprit dans un âge où l'on ne connaissait que la débauche" (*Le Temple du goût*, ed. Carcassonne, p. 109).

Voltaire's apology for his *Temple du goût* was addressed to Cideville. Why? Apparently, the question did not occur to Carcassonne, who took it for granted that it was perfectly natural for Voltaire to address a preface-letter to his friend. He might have noted, though, that one reason for the choice of Cideville sprang from the fact that the Rouen society with which Voltaire had mingled since the early twenties had really given him the foundation for his *Temple*. He might even have added that Voltaire's taste at this time was strongly conditioned by the provincial taste of Rouen and particularly by the taste of his two friends Formont and Cideville. But there is more to this particular incident than that.

On 28 March 1733, Cideville wrote to Voltaire (B. 562): "Le dessein où vous me paroissés mon cher amy de faire une édition plus chastiée et plus modérée de Vostre temple du Goust m'engage à vous écrire très sincèrement ce que j'en pense et à vous dire avec ma candeur ordinaire les endroits qui m'ont blessé." Cideville goes on to say that he considers it "une des plus heureuses idées et des mieux exécutées en beaucoup d'endroits" that he knows. However, there are aspects which he does not approve. (1) The characterization of La Motte as a gentleman who writes unpleasant verses is excessive. La Motte does write bad verses, but he also writes good verses. At the very least, a smoother way of saying the same thing should be found. (2) Voltaire should delete from one of his notes the remark that La Motte "exhorte Rousseau, dans le reste de cette Ode à tâcher de devenir honnête homme." Voltaire's enemies are saying that these recriminations are the result of his jealousy of Rousseau. (3) The whole treatment of Rousseau is too one-sided. The *Temple* condemns all of Rousseau's work, whereas the public knows that much of it is very good. Besides, the poem blames Rousseau for having been condemned for felony, and that is indecent. It mentions that he was censured for having written some couplets, whereas there are lots of people who do not believe that he wrote them. Finally, the *Temple* gives four verses of Rousseau which are really bad, without compensating by citing some verses of his which are really good. (4) The verses on Fontenelle are charming, but why mention his *Lettres du Chevalier d'Her——* and *Aspar*? It is certain that he will be mortally offended. (5) Why mention the verses which Rousseau wrote criticizing Bignon? That only brings up an incident Bignon has probably forgotten or calls his attention to something he has perhaps never seen. (6) As for the seventeenth-century authors, what is said about Segrais is very solid. The condemnation of Pelisson, however, is questionable. It is true that Saint-Evremond wrote bad verses. But it is also true that Voiture has so much wit that he is esteemed by many in spite of his platitudes. (7) It is wrong to reduce Marot to five or six pages, or Bayle to a volume. (8) Corneille did have "l'esprit de discernement" united with a great genius. But (and this was Cideville's most important remark) "Je ne sais si en général dans toute cette tirade il ne faut pas plus louer Corneille, Racine, Despréaux, La Fontaine, Molière." (9) Finally, it was perhaps a mistake to mention M. de Surgère.

Cideville concludes his lengthy letter with a general evaluation of the effect of the *Temple*: "En général cet ouvrage a charmé les juges équitables par son heureux invention, par sa variété, et son stile, mais il a blessé par la critique amère que vous y faites de deux gens vivans tels que Mr. de Fontenelle et Mr. Rousseau, et par le jugement très solide mais peutestre un (peu) trop décisif que vous portés sur les illustres morts tels que Racine, Despréaux, La Fontaine, etc. Ce n'est dans ce dernier article que le ton que je crois qu'il faut adoucir." Thereupon, he ends with a piece of advice: "corrigés, effacés, mais surtout adoucissés, . . . il faut laisser cette ressource à ceux qui ne savent pas faire de bonnes choses. . . ."

Besterman has written a fairly lengthy and interesting note (B. 562) upon this letter, which, until his edition of the correspondence appeared, had gone unpublished. After pointing out that Cideville did not prepare his draft as carefully as he usually did, Besterman remarks: "Voltaire was fortunate to have so candid and conservative a friend as Cideville, for his *fougue* perhaps needed occasional restraint." This is undoubtedly a wise remark. He continues: "Yet it must be owned that Cideville's criticisms betray an almost total unawareness of his friend's purpose." This appears to me incorrect. On the contrary, Cideville seems to have known exactly what Voltaire was doing; indeed, he was in accord with Voltaire on every point except the lack of moderation, the unfairness, and the harsh tone. Besterman adds: "Did he really expect to convince Voltaire, even in 1733, that nothing was so gratifying as to be liked? He seems to have read the *Temple du goût* without seeing in it anything more than a literary exercise." This assertion is refuted by the letter itself. Cideville, in fact, attached a great importance to what Voltaire was doing. His great anxiety was that Voltaire was overdoing it, and, since he was in a position to gather the opinions of others between Rouen and Paris, he was urging Voltaire as tactfully as possible to take action to counter these opinions.

It is Besterman's conclusion, however, which is most obviously at variance with the facts: "Voltaire's response to these criticisms was to spare the feelings of his friend, for whom he had a real affection and regard. He writes briefly and in seeming haste [B. 565] to say that Cideville is right and that the temple will be rebuilt, and then gradually leaves it at that." It is clear that Voltaire did not *leave it at that*, since he brought out a revised edition. It is not only evident that he said Cideville was correct but that he meant exactly that Cideville had given him just the advice he needed. And, when he announced that the *Temple* would be rebuilt, he set to work to rebuild it.

It appears from Carcassonne's remarks that, when the first two versions of the *Temple* were merged into the definitive *Temple* of 1735, artistic preoccupations, rather than the search for favors or the desire for flattery, determined what form the new version would take. Many of the extraneous episodes were deleted: Colbert's speech, Ninon's sermon, Crozat's collection of engravings, the "Filles de l'Opéra" no longer mingle with the Doctors of the Sorbonne. Their place, says Carcassonne, was taken by the legitimate occupants: Corneille, Racine, Bossuet. "L'ouvrage revêtait son caractère littéraire, sérieux sous la fantaisie, et tendant à travers les digressions, à une fin bien déterminée: discerner, juger et classer les grands écrivains de la France" (*Le Temple du goût*, p. 15).

What Carcassonne could not state—because Cideville's letter was unknown at the time—was that Voltaire's Rouen friend had precisely turned him toward a literary temple of taste where the glory of the century of Louis XIV was celebrated, where the main contributors to that glory in the literary field were given their just reward ("Je ne sais si en général dans toute cette tirade il ne faut pas plus louer Corneille, Racine, Despréaux, La Fontaine, Molière. Ce n'est qu'à travers l'encens qu'il est permis de montrer aux peuples leurs défauts," wrote Cideville), and where the secondary contributors formed a chorus around the truly great. Already Voltaire was composing his list of those who made the century of Louis XIV, as he said in the opening of the *Siècle*, one of the four great epochs of humanity.

To accomplish that, he had to adopt Cideville's other general recommendation: "corrigés, effacés, mais surtout adoucissés." It is remarkable to what extent Voltaire listened to the exhortation of his friend. If the numbered suggestions from Cideville's letter we have analyzed are now reviewed in the light of the final revision, it can be seen how closely Voltaire followed these suggestions. The passage on La Motte has been revised. He is no longer a gentleman who writes displeasing verses. He still writes bad verses, but he writes good verses, too, and somehow the good seem more important than the bad. Voltaire has found a smoother way of saying the same thing. The passage in which La Motte exhorted Rousseau to try to be an "honnête homme" has been deleted. The whole passage upon Rousseau has been reworked, and the "indecent" passage about his condemnation has been removed. The four verses given as examples of Rousseau's bad poetry have been replaced by little snatches of expression which carry humor as well as satire, and he is now given credit for having been a good poet before his decline. The difference between the first version and subsequent ones is, indeed, so striking that even Carcassonne, who did not have Cideville's letter, noted that Voltaire finished by pardoning Rousseau in the *Temple du goût* (p. 16). This claim is perhaps excessive, for it is not clear that Voltaire ever really pardoned Rousseau; but it is certain that he did soften his criticism of him in the *Temple*. As for Cideville's other suggestions, the reference to Bignon has been deleted; the comments upon Segrais have been retained, but, for both Segrais and Pelisson, supporting material is offered for the adverse judgment. The criticism of Saint-Evremond has been rearranged so as to take the emphasis off the bad poetry, and the censure of Voiture has been softened to account for his popularity. Marot, who had been reduced to five or six pages, has been given a few more. The restriction of Bayle's *Dictionnaire* to one volume is justified by a quotation from Bayle himself. The "esprit de discernement" denied Corneille previously has been granted him, and all the great authors of French literature in the seventeenth century, including Corneille, are celebrated for their qualities. Mention of M. de Surgère has been removed. And, finally, the apostrophe to the young French nobility has been suppressed.

Thus, it is easy to see that Voltaire did not "let it go at that."[5] Recognizing the justice of Cideville's remarks, he rebuilt the *Temple* just as he had promised his Rouen friend he would.

The publication of the *Temple du goût* represents a milestone in the intellectual life of Voltaire. It is evident that he was slowly shifting some of his interest from poetry and drama to criticism. It is fairly clear also that, although literary criticism had assumed an increased importance for him and although the acquisition of taste was but an extension of his own poetic and artistic preoccupations, he had a tendency—seen with clarity in the correspondence—to branch out into history of thought and even to increase his preoccupation with history. In keeping with the English experience, he likewise had a desire to characterize a people. Indeed, the milieu into which Voltaire was moving seems to have absorbed his own varied

---

[5] Cideville even urged Voltaire, in a letter dated 11 August 1733, to merge the first two versions of the *Temple* into a definitive *Temple*: "Je vous exhorte fort à construire, comme vous le projettés, un édifice régulier des matériaux précieux qui composent ces deux bâtimens élévés à la haste" (B. 623).

activity. Formont writes about the double personality of the French, who are "légers" and "frivoles" and at the same time "plein de naturel et d'enjouement" (B. 541). The English, he adds, recognize no other king than liberty and law, and yet they can do nothing else than calculate, talk business, and sell votes. Voltaire, in the meantime, writes to Cideville that he has lost his good friend Mme de Fontaine-Martel, "c'est-à-dire que j'ay perdu une bonne maison dont j'étois le maître, et quarante mille livres de rente qu'on dépensoit à me divertir" (B. 544). To Formont, he relates how scrupulously his good friend had observed all the "bienséances" in her demise. His own attitude seems at the moment to have been one of complete indifference. *Zaïre* was still being enjoyed; every one more or less agreed with Bouhier that there were "de beaux endroits" and "des situations très intéressantes." It could be well appreciated by all those who judged by sentiment rather than by rules. It is true that Bouhier saw also in the tragedy an infinity of "constructions louches et vicieuses" (B. 546). Voltaire, writing to Thiériot (B. 550) and basking in his dramatic success, states that he has been spending the last two months being bored with Descartes and butting his head against Newton for the *Lettres philosophiques*. To Cideville (B. 551), he suggests that he would like to return to La Rivière Bourdet and discuss Horace and Locke. On 9 March, Linant wrote Cideville: "Mr. de Voltaire ne sait pas encore où il logera, *le Temple du Goust* est sous la presse, les vingt-quatre lettres sur les Anglais vont venir de Londres imprimées. Sa tragédie est au quatrième acte et la mienne est commencée" (B. 553).

In fact, it was for Voltaire the moment of indecision. The *Temple du goût*, with its diverse criticism, had driven its author to a refashioning of the work, which was rapidly becoming transformed, as he said, from a chapel into a cathedral. In these moments of indecision, Voltaire usually responded with increased activity. On 1 April 1733, he announces to Thiériot that he has just finished *Adélaïde*, is revising *Eriphile*, and is assembling the materials for the "grande histoire du siècle de Louis 14" (B. 564). The revision of the *Temple*, of course, proceeds apace: "J'ai tâché dans ce second aedifice d'ôter tout ce qui pouvait servir de prétexte à la fureur des sots, et à la malignité des mauvais plaisants, et d'embellir le tout par de nouveaux vers sur Lucrèce, sur Corneille, Racine, Molière, Despréaux,

La Fontaine, Quinaut . . ." (B. 564). Formont reports to Cideville
that Voltaire is preparing to write an opera. The poet himself confirms this bit of news on 21 April, in a letter to Cideville: "savez-
vous bien que j'ay en tête un opéra."

It is at this moment that the idea begins to appear in the correspondence that Voltaire must get out of Paris. To Cideville, he writes
that he intends to arrange matters so that he can come to Rouen
"philosopher et poétiser" during the summer, since his health is deplorable. By 6 May, however, the summer trip has been reduced to
only four days, since he now deems it necessary to prolong his stay
in Paris for some weeks, so that the public will get accustomed to
his absence without suspecting that he is up to any deviltry. He still
is in close contact with the poetic happenings in England: around
the tenth of May, he receives Pope's *Poem on the Use of Riches* and
the *Essays on Man*. He requests from Thiériot the poetry of Lady
Mary Wortley Montaigu. On 15 May, to Cideville, he sums up:
"Je suis malade, je me mets en ménage, je soufre comme un damné,
je brocante, j'achette des magots et des Titiens, je fais mon opéra, je
fais transcrire *Eriphile* et *Adélaïde*, je les corrige, j'efface, j'ajoute,
je barbouille" (B. 589). Mr. Richey, the "honnête et naïf hambourgeois" visits him, and he sends him to Rouen with a letter of introduction to Cideville (dated May 21), promising now to stretch out
his own visit to Rouen to eight or ten days. The "hambourgeois,"
with his quiet and serene disposition, seems to have aroused Voltaire's envy; once more, he dreams of spending his days in Rouen
"entre Formont et Cideville" (B. 594):

> Ah, qu'à cet honnête hambourgeois,
> Candide et gauchement courtois,
> Je porte une secrette envie!
> Que je voudrois passer ma vie
> Comme il a passé quelques jours,
> Ignoré dans un sûr azile
> Entre Formont et Cideville,
> C'est-à-dire avec mes amours.

Voltaire now seems to make a distinction between his two friends at
Rouen: Formont becomes more and more "le philosophe Formont,"
while Cideville remains the poet. Between the two, he dreams of de-

voting himself to his two activities: "philosopher et poétiser." But the plan still remains a bit nebulous.

By June 1 there is a slightly new note in a letter to the "philosophe Formont." Voltaire is still engaged with *Adélaïde*, and he is still composing *Tanis et Zélide*, his opera. But now he is busy also with Newton, presumably in connection with some final touches upon the *Lettres philosophiques*. He is of the opinion that the better section in these letters, "moitié frivoles, moitié scientifiques," is the part which concerns philosophy. He also fears that it will be the part less appreciated. And yet, he adds, "On a beau dire, le siècle est philosophe." He seems haunted with the idea that the *Lettres* will be either too philosophical or too literary. Maupertuis, he notes, who knows Newtonian science, has sold no more than two hundred copies of his little book. Voltaire asks himself how many copies he, being a frank scientific amateur, will sell, in spite of the fact that "j'ai tâché d'égayer la sécheresse de ces matières et de les assaisonner au goût de la nation." He is now considering adding some reflections on the *Pensées de Pascal*. "Il y a déjà longtemps que j'ai envie de combattre ce géant" (B. 596). Voltaire inquires of Formont what he thinks of the project. In the meantime, Linant gives a little account of the way he and Voltaire are living: "A propos de Latin nous voyons Ovide, Horace, Virgile et tous les honnêtes gens de l'antiquité [evidently, Voltaire was training the young man in the profession of poetry just as he had been trained at Louis-le-Grand]; nous allons aux spectacles, nous buvons frais, nous mangeons chaud et nous parlons fort souvent de vous et de Mr. Formont" (B. 598). A few days after this report, Voltaire announces to Cideville (B. 599) that he is revising the letter on Locke (10 June). In addition, Linant informs Cideville that Voltaire now judges *Mérope*, composed by Maffey, an "italien," an excellent subject for a tragedy "admirable par le pathétique et la noble simplicité" (B. 600).

The twenty-fifth letter on Pascal was sent to Jore by 1 July 1733. Voltaire now makes his apology for writing it. He acknowledges that the plan to attack Pascal is "hardi" but that this "misantrope chrétien, tout sublime qu'il est," is only a man like everybody else. He has no intention, he says, of attacking the *Provinciales*; what he has in mind, rather, is an attack upon Pascal's onslaught against humanity, which was more cruel than his quarrel with the Jesuits.

Pascal had rendered human nature odious. In a semi-humorous way, Voltaire declares war against the moralist for preventing him from completing his tragedy and his opera. He begins to wonder, however, whether it is not more important to write a good opera than to be right in his argument with Pascal. Since there is no way of answering this rhetorical question, Voltaire adds that he is writing an *Epître sur la calomnie,* dedicated to a lady who has been much maligned. It is the first reference we have to Mme du Châtelet (3 July 1733). On the fourteenth of July, Voltaire is still explaining why he is incorporating his attack upon Pascal in the *Lettres.* First of all, he has judged it more important to add the reflections on Pascal than to round out the volume with a preface on tragedy. He has rejected the idea of adding the *Temple du goût* because, he says, if the English publishers wish to bring out an edition of that work, they can do so without the assistance of Thiériot, whereas to publish the *Réflexions sur Pascal* they will need Thiériot's help. Voltaire adds that he cannot put off the twenty-fifth letter until the second edition of the *Lettres,* because that will only double the explosion against him later and he prefers that the opposition come out all at once. Moreover, he regards the work more and more as a philosophical one, rather than a literary one. What literature there is in it is treated only as an object of erudition (B. 609). Voltaire writes to Cideville, on the same day, that Formont does not approve adding the twenty-fifth letter but that the book is too short without it. Besides, he says, he is now counting on the support of the Jesuits. To Cideville, on 26 July, he states that there is some risk but that there are moments when one can avoid danger in an inexplicable way. He cites the *Lettres persanes* as an example of a book which, though very daring, only succeeded in pushing the author, Montesquieu, into the French Academy.

The above references for the year 1733 have been extracted from the correspondence not only to give an impression of the activities Voltaire was pursuing just before entering upon the Cirey experience but to highlight that, in this year 1733, there was a subtle change which had come over the poet. This change can perhaps best be characterized as a personal desire for solitude, to be divided between poetry and philosophy. The note is struck in a letter to M.

de Sade, dated 29 August 1733, where Voltaire sums up the change
in a few airy lines:

> Ovide autrefois fut mon maître,
> C'est à Loke aujourd'hui de l'être.
> L'art de penser est consolant
> Quand on renonce à l'art de plaire.
> Ce sont deux beaux métiers vraiment,
> Mais où je ne profitai guère.

Voltaire, as we have tried to show, had been preparing all during
1733 for this change. He had spent two months deciphering Descartes and Newton, evinced a desire to return to Horace and Lucretius, suddenly decided to incorporate the *Réflexions sur Pascal*
in the *Lettres,* undertaken a revision of Locke, and all the while been
reworking the *Temple du goût*, writing *Adélaïde*, revising *Eriphile*,
composing an *Epître sur la calomnie*, and planning for a work on
the great century of Louis XIV. No wonder that the philosopher
Formont and the poet Cideville were dazzled by their Parisian friend
and that even Linant was impressed! As the year reached its second
half, Voltaire became, as his *English Letters* show, more and more
philosophical.

On 26 July, he writes to Formont, asking him to review the whole
Lettres philosophiques. He is certain now that only a totally corrupted theological student could seriously object to Locke's philosophy. He cannot conceive that anyone would dare say that it is impossible for matter to think. In his opinion, this problem of thinking
matter had been misunderstood by Malebranche and Descartes. They
maintained that we can only know the existence of external bodies
by faith. Surely, the authorities would not persecute anyone who
maintained that we are sure of the existence of spiritual substances
only by faith. But the authorities are confused; since we are really
more certain of the verity of our feelings and our thoughts than of
the existence of external objects, we conclude that we are sure of our
thinking. But are we sure that we are anything but thinking matter?

Voltaire adds in his letter that philosophers will not reproach him
for his attack on Pascal. They will, he feels, certainly commend him
for handling Pascal with such care. He flatters himself that he has
been very circumspect in not bringing up the matter of miracles and

prophecies, two aspects of the problem which show to what extent the judgment of a great thinker can become clouded, when he is corrupted by superstition.

In the letter of 15 August, still to Formont, Voltaire announces that he has been rereading Clarke, Malebranche, and Locke. He is now convinced that Clarke was the best sophist that ever existed, that Malebranche was the most subtle novelist, and that Locke was the wisest man. Clarke, in the *Existence of God*, had endeavored to show that matter does not exist of necessity. Voltaire admits that he is not prepared to accept this idea. Malebranche was worse. He used half of the *Recherche de la vérité* to deduce the effects of original sin which he had already established at the beginning. The other half of the work he used to prove that our senses are always deceptive. Locke was more modest; he was content to say that God can accord thought to matter. He was, however, not the first to have had this idea. Hobbes had said so before him, and even Cicero, in the *De natura deorum*, had said something of the sort, too. Voltaire concludes that this is the doctrine which must be accepted (B. 625):

> Plus je tourne et retourne cette idée, plus elle me paraît vraie. Il serait absurde d'assurer que la matière pense, mais il serait également absurde d'assurer qu'il est impossible qu'elle pense. Car, pour soutenir l'une ou l'autre de ces assertions, il faudrait connaître l'essence de la matière, et nous sommes bien loin d'en imaginer les vraies propriétés. De plus, cette idée est aussi conforme que tout autre au système de christianisme, l'immortalité pouvant être attachée tout aussi bien à la matière que nous ne connaissons pas, qu'à l'esprit que nous connaissons encore moins.

Such was the intellectual situation of Voltaire when he and Mme du Châtelet planned their establishment at Cirey. For him, Newton, Locke, and Clarke were to be preferred to Descartes, Malebranche, and Pascal; English philosophy was superior to French philosophy and French theology. One had to know these things to pay court to the beautiful Emilie:

> J'avouerai qu'elle est tyrannique.
> Il faut pour lui faire sa cour,
> Lui parler de métaphysique,
> Quand on voudroit parler d'amour.

Voltaire congratulated himself that, as an amateur in metaphysics, he could qualify for the friendship of Emilie. He asked nothing more than to be permitted to retire to a retreat with M. de Sade and Mme du Châtelet. But de Sade was on his way to Avignon, and Emilie was at the court of Versailles. "Pour moi," Voltaire wrote, "je reste presque toujours dans ma solitude entre la poésie et la philosophie."

The crowning event of the six-year interlude between 1728 and 1734, that is, between the end of the English sojourn and the publication of the *Lettres philosophiques*, was, of course, the appearance of these *Lettres*. Voltaire, as we have seen, had undertaken the project before leaving England but had laid it aside upon his return to France. On 21 November 1731, he wrote to Formont that he now intended to complete the *Lettres*. From then until 24 April 1734, there is a long string of letters, addressed for the most part to Formont and Cideville, referring to his activities in putting the *Lettres* in shape, his intentions, his anxieties, and even his persecutions. Lanson has given us a list, with a little summary of the content of each (see *Lettres philosophiques*, I, xl-xliv). Many of them attest the fact that the *Lettres philosophiques* were practically ready and required only a final revision before publication. On 21 November, he wrote to Formont: "J'ai aussi à vous consulter sur la manière dont je dois finir mon *Essai sur le poème épique* et mes *Lettres sur les Anglais*." On 2 February 1732, he told Cideville: "Je ferais bien mieux de ne plus songer au théâtre. . . . Il vaudrait mieux cent fois revenir achever mes *Lettres anglaises* auprès de vous." On 9 July 1732, he informed Thiériot: "As to the *English Letters*, be sure I will put the last hand to them in a very short time." And, again to Formont, in September 1732, he wrote: "j'achèverai ces *Lettres anglaises* que vous connaissez, ce sera tout au plus le travail d'un mois." It is obvious that during this entire time they were, in his opinion, all but ready. Indeed, in November 1732, he started to put them in their final form for publication. He pursued his lessons in Newtonian philosophy with Maupertuis; he felt that he would have to devote one or more letters to Newton's philosophy, which he would attempt to enliven; he had to revise the letter on Locke. It is clear that he was trying to emend his work in accordance with the demands of the censor, but, to all intents and purposes, it was already complete.

He had long since decided upon the philosophical approach: a civilization, to be sure, is composed of manners and customs, but it is also a combination of institutions, arts, and letters. Voltaire elected to approach the analysis by way of institutions, arts, and letters. It is true that in Thiériot's preface to the English edition, which more or less expressed agreement with Voltaire, the editor pretended that the author had followed no other rule in the choice of his subjects than his particular taste, or perhaps the queries of his friend. Thiériot tried to give the impression that the value of the *Lettres* lay in "the variety of subjects, the graceful style of the diction, the solidity of the reflexions, the delicate turn of the criticism; in fine, the noble fire, which enlivens all the compositions of Mr. de Voltaire." And, indeed, these qualities are everywhere evident in the *Lettres philosophiques*. On the other hand, Thiériot also called attention to the serious letters, especially those which concerned Sir Isaac Newton's philosophy and the constitution of the English laws. These latter he praised not only for their pithiness but for Voltaire's general reflections, "the cast of which is entirely new." These reflections prove, said Thiériot, that Voltaire had made of British "polity" the particular object of his study.

The general framework of the *Lettres philosophiques* was carefully planned. Seven letters are devoted to a discussion of the religious situation, three to politics and economics, one to inoculation, six to philosophers, five to literature, and two to the condition of men of letters in England. In reviewing the religion of the Quakers, Presbyterians, Anglicans, and Lutherans, Voltaire passes lightly over their idiosyncrasies but praises the austerity of their morals and the simplicity of their faith. He notes that in England everyone has the right to go to Heaven by whatever route he chooses. He comments, with evident approval, upon the plurality of religions and remarks that, where there is one religion in a state, it is tyrannical, where there are two, they cut each other's throat, where there are thirty, they live in peace. In all this religious discussion, there is a strong, though not explicitly stated, undercurrent of deism. Even his presentation of the Quakers is made in such a way as to suggest that, fundamentally, what characterizes them in their simplicity of faith and purity of morals is a basic deism. Most outstanding in the religious situation in England, in his opinion, is this common belief in the existence of God and the simplicity of dogma, with an insistence upon the utility of morality and the necessity for tolerance. The letters upon the English government note enthusiastically the growth of political liberty and the corresponding restrictions placed upon the monarch who, "tout-puissant pour faire du bien, a les mains liées pour faire le mal." Voltaire explains the parliamentary system, commends the equalization in taxation and equality before the law, and speaks with approval of the custom which the nobility has of engaging in commerce. This dignifying of work was to become one of his cardinal points. In the letter upon inoculation, he celebrates the independence of mind of the Englishman. For him, it was evidence of a free-thinking, advanced people. In the following six letters upon philosophy, Voltaire extols Bacon's experimental method and remarks that it had become the characteristic way of British thought. He attempts to bring out its wider utility in contrast with the "a priori" rationalism which had prevailed on the continent. He stresses the importance of natural science and psychology in philosophy, giving Newton and Locke a position of supremacy in the realm of science and philosophy. And, although too much a classicist to admire without reserve English literature, he is nonetheless intelligent enough to recognize therein the expression of the English love of freedom and the antipathy which they showed to the literary rules of classicism. But there was another side to the picture: not only were the authors free from rules, they were also free from persecution and actually occupied positions of importance in the state.

The double purpose of Voltaire in composing his *Lettres* is immediately evident. He undertook first of all to analyze the spirit of a race, to reduce it, if possible, to a simple formula, and to apply this formula to every manifestation of its civilization. To do so, he had to study the expression of this spirit in the various aspects of English civilization. These aspects he deemed to be religion, politics and economics, philosophy (including science), morality, and literature. For him, they constituted an essential unity and together gave coherence to the British way of life. Further, this British way of life was characterized, as he saw things, by freedom. In religion, one was free to believe as one wished and free from persecution because of any particular belief. In politics, one's political liberty was guaranteed both by a parliamentary system and by constituted rights. In philosophy, this freedom was evident in the boldness with which the English analyzed and organized the thought of the time, scientific, moral, and metaphysical. In letters, freedom meant release from conventional rules, as well as freedom from government or religious persecution. Everywhere Voltaire looked, the greatest characteristic he seemed to find in England was the love of liberty—religious, political, philosophical, and literary. But liberty was precisely what was lacking in France. Consequently, Voltaire purposed to introduce to the French not only a foreign race but also the very spirit of that race. The *Lettres philosophiques*, which commented upon and, as we shall see, somewhat exaggerated the qualities of English freedom, continually called attention to its absence in France. They thus contained at one and the same time two novelties: they introduced a method for penetrating the civilization of a people which, properly understood, could be applied equally well to the understanding of any people, and they sketched out a whole program of reform for France. In this latter respect, they proposed the separation of reason and faith, the separation of religion and politics as two distinct realms, the establishment of equality before the law and of freedom in all aspects of life, the inauguration of the experimental method in science and philosophy, the equalization of taxation, and the encouragement of commerce. Lanson, in his compact little book, aptly characterizes the proposed reform as the first bomb dropped in the revolution against the "Ancien Régime." This was, so to speak, a negative effect; on the positive side, the *Lettres* introduced a whole new concept of civilization. A society is not something which is merely described on the surface; it is, as Voltaire intimated, something which has to be penetrated. The penetration should be carried out by analyzing the categories of living and by searching for their common characteristic. Once this common characteristic is found, the "genius" of the people, the "esprit" of the community, can be delineated. If the effects of this "esprit" are desirable, they can be introduced to another community; if they are undesirable, the conditions of living and thinking which have produced the undesirable "esprit" can be revised. Hence, re-form is possible, for tradition is made not only by the continuity of an "esprit" but by the merging of two or more "esprits." Cosmopoli-tanism was as much a discovery of the Enlightenment as attraction.

Professor Bonno (*La Culture et la civilisation britanniques*, p. 165) has already pointed out that the real significance of the *Lettres* does not lie either in the extent or in the novelty of the information they offer. Although they did inaugurate a new procedure for the penetration of a civilization, there were aspects of that civilization which Voltaire did not take up. Voltaire showed by his initial let-ter, which he eventually decided not to use, that he could be both informative and entertaining in dealing with the manners and customs of England. But he did not pursue this course, as we have already seen; it has usually been assumed that he judged the picture of English customs presented by Muralt and Prévost sufficient. More-over, although Voltaire devoted considerable space to letters and the position of men of letters in England, he neglected the other arts. More important, he neglected the new economic theories being de-veloped at this time. Bonno expresses surprise that he did not men-tion Milton, the *Spectator*, or *Robinson Crusoe*, and he notes with some astonishment that Voltaire did not attempt to give any full coverage to the scientific discoveries then being exploited. Bonno remarks, too, that it was a mistake to limit discussion of the scien-tific movement to the achievements of Newton and that philosophy was not at all adequately treated by referring only to Bacon and Locke. What causes the greatest surprise, though, is Voltaire's silence regarding the deist controversy. It was certainly not ignor-ance which motivated this silence, since we know that the French poet was familiar with Woolston even to the point of knowing that four of his treatises on miracles had appeared. Lanson attributes the omission to the danger Voltaire would have risked in taking up this subject. But this seems an unlikely explanation when one con-siders how Voltaire unreasonably added an attack against Pascal in the *Lettres*, when there was no logical justification for this sort of foolhardiness. Bonno suggests, rather, that Voltaire was more inter-ested in the Bayle type of skepticism at this time and did not con-cern himself with the English kind of deism until some years later, when he became acquainted with Collins and Chubb, and that, in any case, further insistence upon English deism at this time would not have accorded well with the aim of presenting a detached, skeptical country, since the battles waged over deism were very savage indeed.

When one passes from these omissions to the problem of Voltaire's originality in presenting England to the French, another difficulty arises. Bonno, who of all the Enlightenment scholars, has best covered the image which the French already had of the English before the *Lettres*, finds that there were really few innovations in them. If one examines the reports of Destouches, who was *chargé d'affaires* in England during the period 1717-1723, it will be seen that he, too, observed many of those things which attracted Voltaire's attention. Indeed, both commented upon the Protestant religions of England, the peculiar temperament of the English, and the growth of science, especially the progress made in medicine through inoculation. Both men observed the composition of the English government, the administration of English justice, and the liberty of the English people. Both were vitally interested in the difference between the English theatre and the French. It must be remarked, though, that, in spite of these striking analogies between the two writers, Destouches did no more than observe aspects of the English: he did not pretend to embrace the organic quality of English civilization, and that was precisely what Voltaire wanted to do.

Bonno describes very effectively the extent of the influence exercised by England upon France in the twenty years preceding the appearance of the *Lettres philosophiques*. He stresses especially that there were certain channels of communication, among them the French and Dutch journals, of which Leclerc's *Bibliothèque ancienne et moderne*, the *Journal littéraire de la Haye*, the *Bibliothèque anglaise*, the *Bibliothèque raisonnée*, and the *Mémoires littéraires de la Grande-Bretagne* were outstanding. These periodicals served, just as Bayle's *Nouvelles* had at an earlier moment, to introduce the theological, philosophical, and scientific preoccupations of the British to the Continent. There were the scientific societies: the Royal Society in London, into which a score of French scholars were accepted as members, and the Académie des Sciences, to which some thirteen British scholars, among them Newton and Halley, belonged as associate members. There was also the correspondence between scholars of the two countries: for instance, that between Hans Sloane, the Secretary of the Royal Society, and the Abbé Bignon, the Director of the Bibliothèque du Roi. And, finally, there were the two scientific publications: the *Philosophical Transactions*, which Hans Sloane endeavored to circulate in France, and the *Mémoires de l'Académie des Sciences*, which was the corresponding French scientific organ. One of these channels of communication was established by the Protestant refugees from France, who in and around the Rainbow Coffee House became translators, publishers, and disseminators of English works. The greatest of these was Coste, who had already in 1700 translated and published John Locke's *Essay concerning Human Understanding*. Desmaizeaux, who wrote biographies of Bayle and of Saint-Evremond and edited the two-volume *Recueil* on Leibniz, was also very important.

In a movement at the same time so diverse in its appeal and so widespread in its influence, it is difficult to measure the extent to which the civilization of England had penetrated the consciousness of the French. As in all problems of the interpenetration of ideas, the historian of ideas can only note the possibilities of understanding between the two countries involved. In the period between the Treaty of Utrecht (1713) and the *Lettres philosophiques*, the possibilities were potentially large. Politically, there had been a *rapprochement*: there was a community of interest between the two governments, and a larger ground of sympathy between the two peoples. One of the things which had separated the two countries was the almost total lack of knowledge of English on the part of the French. In the previous century this lack had not been too serious, because the scholars, at least, could always communicate in Latin. With the coming of the eighteenth century, however, Latin became less used as a means of exchanging ideas, and the French were faced with the necessity of either learning English or undertaking a rather large program of translation. The *Spectator, Cato*, and the works of Pope, Swift, and Defoe, for example, were all introduced to the French in translation.

In general, it is possible to mark out the various ways in which this penetration of England manifested itself. In regard to manners, the French no longer thought that the British character was unpleasant. Under the influence of the *Spectator*, the Englishman had become a milder, more moderate, more human, and much more likeable individual. To be sure, he retained some eccentricities, but there was a tendency to idealize them. Although the British government was noted for its parliamentary regime, the French did not yet show any very real enthusiasm for it, such as Montesquieu generated later. The undesirable traits of this regime, in the eyes of the French, were the widespread corruption and the savage fighting of the parties. Only after La Mottraye and Rapin de Thoyras presented the British constitution in its true light did French hostility toward the British system finally diminish.

In the field of literature, the French expressed a note of surprise at the variety and quality of English letters. They showed most curiosity over the *Paradise Lost* and the tragedies of Shakespeare. As for Milton, the general tendency was to point out the ways in which Milton's poem contravened the rules of the epic; his greatest sin as a writer, it was felt, was his disregard of "vraisemblance." Shakespeare was regarded as a "génie fécond," powerful in his conception and very original but likewise ignorant of the rules and lacking in taste. By and large, as we have already suggested, this French view was not too far removed from the contemporary English view.

In the field of theology, the French seemed unaware of the extraordinary richness of the deistic movement. Only a few of these deistic works were translated, and, although the periodicals often referred to the movement, the French public as a whole seemed to take little interest in it, probably because there was a French deism being developed clandestinely at the time and they could, if attracted to it, find their material in Bayle. English free-thinkers did not exercise any direct influence upon the thought of the libertines in this period; whatever resemblances they exhibited came from such common sources as Spinoza's *Tractatus* and Bayle's *Dictionnaire*.

If the impact of English deism upon French deism was small, the impact of English philosophy was very great. The most influential work was Locke's *Essay concerning Human Understanding*, which Coste had translated into French by 1700. Locke was not accepted wholeheartedly, however; Bayle and others questioned the doctrine of thinking matter, and there was some objection to the rationalism of the English philosopher in his pronouncements on the relationship between reason and faith. Still others resisted his attacks against innateism, notably the later Cartesians and Malebranche. On the other hand, Crousaz and Bouillier used Lockean psychology and Lockean empiricism to combat the Cartesian doctrine of the beast-machine, and Buffier adopted a fundamentally Lockean approach to philosophy.

In the area of science, British prestige was very high in France, especially among academicians. Exchanges were frequent, communications were continuous, and personal relations were developed in all branches of natural science. The mathematical discoveries of Cotes, Moivre, Stirling, and Maclaurin, the astronomical contributions of Flamsteed, Halley, and Bradley, the experiments in electricity of Hauksbee and Gray, the researches in botany and zoology by Sloane, Bradley, and Hales, and in geology by Woodward were all followed with eagerness by the corresponding scholars in France. The advance in medicine elicited a keen interest, too.

The outstanding representative of this English group was Newton. A real battle was waged against him by the French Cartesians, who saw in the theory of attraction a return to occult science. The theories of the vortices still supported by many of Descartes's successors were defended vigorously. Newton's studies in optics were at first keenly contested; there were those like Mairan, Castel, and the earlier Malebranche who still clung to the undulatory, as against the emission, theory. Newton's new chronology aroused active discussion. As for his mathematics, the French were more attracted by the mathematical notations of Leibniz than by the more complicated system of the Englishman. However, with the explanatory work of Keill and Gregory, and especially with Pemberton's lucid explanations, which Voltaire praised highly, Newton gained more and more acceptance in France, thanks not only to the support given him by his English colleagues but by the adoption of his principles among the Dutch scientists, especially Musschembrœck and S'Gravesande. Fontenelle still tended to the "tourbillon" theory; Cassini, Mairan, and Privat de Molières still sought justification for the impulsion theory in their own researches. In fact, it was not until 1732, with the publication of Maupertuis's *Discours sur les différentes figures des astres*, that a turning point was reached in favor of Newton over Descartes.

A summary would not be amiss here. During the twenty years from the Treaty of Utrecht to the publication of the *Lettres phi-*

losophiques, French intellectuals had ample means in the periodicals, in the exchanges of the scientific societies, and in their personal relationships with English scientists and intellectuals to get acquainted with their neighbors on the other side of the Channel. The information broadcast concerning England's activities was abundant and varied; its utilization by the French, though, depended to a large extent upon the interests and prejudices of those who received it and in some measure on the obstacles officials erected against its diffusion. By and large, in the area of psychology of a people, there had been more comprehension and an increase in sympathy. In the field of religion, the exchange does not seem to have led to much more than idle curiosity. In the field of philosophy, one name and one book stood out above all the others, that of John Locke and his *Essay concerning Human Understanding.* Similarly, in the field of natural science, one name, that of Newton, was preeminent, although Newton had a larger cast of supporters in his field than Locke did in his. In literature, there was some curiosity and a genuine interest in two or three writers, especially Pope, Swift, and Dryden, and some interest, but mostly of a negative sort, in Shakespeare and Milton.

After this analysis of the impact of England in the two decades preceding the *Lettres,* it ought to be possible to point out what was original in the *Lettres* themselves. Bonno (*La Culture et la civilisation britanniques,* p. 166) finds very little originality in the letters on religion. As far as contributing new information is concerned, they contain practically nothing upon which the French public was not already enlightened. Even the general conclusions on tolerance which Voltaire drew from his observations had been proposed by Bayle and Montesquieu, albeit from a more theoretical point of view. This method of observing the practice of tolerance before generalizing about it in theory, however, was very new. The tendency to see as much intolerance in the English political attitude toward religion as in the French was common to the previous observers, but Voltaire struck out boldly for tolerance after showing that it had been practiced in England. This plea for tolerance in religion was heightened by a plea in favor of English constitutional government. Here again, Voltaire made more comprehensible the meaning of the English civil wars: he played down the abuses of parliamentarism and brought out some real advantages in the system of limited monarchy. This he did with great discretion, and this approach, too, was new. Voltaire offered much more information on the state of English letters than was normally presented by his predecessors. He had a broader picture of literary activities, including comedy and light verse, in addition to Shakespeare. His attitude was more conciliatory, too, and in some respects genuinely sympathetic. In a critical way, it was fuller, and it was supplemented by an attempt to convey the flavor of English poetry, drama, and light lyrical verse through translation. This attitude, also, was to a considerable extent new. His innovation in philosophy was not entirely desirable. Harking back to a remark which Locke had made only incidentally, Voltaire made it the center of the Lockean credo. In science, he was more scrupulous, even to the point of consulting Maupertuis at great length so as to avoid errors. The letters on Newton really constituted the first attempt to explain in popular language the meaning of Newton's discovery. The presentation of Bacon as the exponent of a type of thinking was also novel. Indeed, the way in which Voltaire handled Bacon, Locke, and Newton brought out the fundamental difference between English thought and French thought (this pattern was destined to be continued thereafter) and the way in which, for the English, philosophy had a natural tendency to become scientific knowledge which led, not to the exclusion of metaphysics, but at least to a lessening of its importance. Voltaire descried this trait of English thinking and explicitly brought it to the attention of the French public. He was so successful in the case of Newton that Bonno states, with some exaggeration, that "la véritable contribution voltairienne est représentée par les quatre lettres sur Newton." The greatest novelty, however, is to be found in the compact way Voltaire tried to be accurate, selective, and complete, in the lively tone he employed, and in the constant appeal he made to wit, paradox and contrast in order to define what the inner spirit of a people is and how it differs from that of another people. There was, among his sources, no work which endeavored to be complete in introducing a new civilization, or which sought in the new civilization a way of bringing out the spirit of a people, or which, by a judicious comparison, contrasted so deftly the spirits of two peoples, or which, finally, achieved all these goals with the briefest possible expenditure of space and energy. In all these respects, the *Lettres philosophiques* were unique.

Voltaire therefore deserves much credit for his leadership in introducing England to the French. This question of primacy has been studied by Professor Dargan (*Mélanges Baldensperger*, pp. 187-198), who points out that there are about twenty passages in Voltaire's subsequent works in which the French poet lays claim to having started the vogue for English literature, having introduced particular English authors to the French public, and having performed a similar service for English philosophers. The two authors for whose introduction he claims particular credit are Milton and Shakespeare —Milton in the ninth chapter of the *Essai sur la poésie épique*, and Shakespeare in the *Lettres philosophiques*. In addition, he stresses that he was the first man of letters in France who learned the English language and who, by well-selected translations of poetry, made the French public acquainted not only with these two giants but also with Pope and Dryden. As for the philosophers, the two whom he claims to have introduced to the French public are Locke and Newton.

Voltaire's contemporary admirers were inclined to concede that his claim to have been the intermediary between these English notables and the French public was correct. It seems superfluous to quote over and over the same statement as it was made by Clément, Palissot, Marmontel, and, in general, by the Encyclopedists. Those who were hostile to Voltaire—Fréron, for instance—were also inclined to grant that Voltaire had been responsible for bringing English literature and philosophy to France; only, they queried whether the goods were worth importing.

Dargan concludes that Voltaire, in all probability, achieved what he claimed. "He really was the first to promote to any extent the vogue for English literature and philosophy in eighteenth-century France." It seems to me that, while this conclusion is justified, the problem is badly focused. It is not so much whether Voltaire was the first as whether he was the most effective; not whether he introduced several writers and thinkers but whether he introduced English civilization; and not whether he introduced English civilization to the French but how he contributed to bring about the merging of English and French civilization.

This latter problem appears to be the very crux of the matter. Lanson, in the *Revue de Paris* (1908, pp. 505-533), tries to explain how Voltaire composed his book. It is difficult for him to envisage this composition in any other than a historical way; for instance, he is much concerned with what Voltaire suppressed in one edition or added to another, how and why he changed an expression or modified, in a subsequent edition, an opinion. These observations are no doubt important, especially as a means of acquiring some insight into what Lanson calls Voltaire's "psychologie littéraire." For the moment, though, that part of the problem seems secondary to the question of how Voltaire became the intermediary in the merging of two different civilizations. It is assumed that in matters of influence the task is not so much to distinguish the movement as to mark out the merging of the two currents. Hence, one has to deal with sources and origins, with interpenetrations and with the union of the disparate elements. Lanson has done something about the sources. He insists that the *Lettres* owe most to journals, conversations, and daily impressions, which cannot often be grasped at a later period and which can be reconstituted only with the greatest difficulty. Some letters are derived from readings. Voltaire, for instance, like all travelers of the eighteenth century, informed himself about England from the guides of the time: Chamberlayne's *Etat présent de l'Angleterre*, Guy Miège's *Etat présent de l'Angleterre*, which appeared only in 1728, and, finally, Beverell's *Les Délices de l'Angleterre*. The book which seemed to synthesize the necessary information was Gregorio Leti's *Il Teatro Britannico*, published in 1684 in two quarto volumes or five twelvemo volumes. It was a book reviewed very favorably by Bayle in his *Nouvelles*. In addition, Voltaire certainly was familiar with and made use of the information in Muralt's *Lettres sur les Anglais et sur les Français*. These five general introductions to the manners and customs of the English were, so to speak, the foundation works. Lanson has meticulously compared the statements made by Voltaire in a descriptive way with corresponding statements drawn from these works.

Voltaire balanced his information from the general guides to English manners and customs against two English works which gave a composite view of British civilization seen through the eyes of an Englishman: these were the *Spectator* of Addison and the *Tatler* of Steele. It is thus evident that he was attempting to weigh foreign opinion against native opinion. For further control of his information, however, he depended greatly upon Rapin Thoyras's *Histoire d'Angleterre*, which he admired so much that he wrote in the *Siècle* (M. XIV, 120): "L'Angleterre lui fut longtemps redevable de la seule bonne histoire complète qu'on eût faite de ce royaume, et de la seule impartiale qu'on eût d'un pays où l'on n'écrivait que par esprit de parti; c'était même la seule histoire qu'on pût citer en Europe comme approchante de la perfection qu'on exige de ces ouvrages, jusqu'à ce qu'enfin on ait vu paraître celle du célèbre Hume, qui a su écrire l'histoire en philosophe." Voltaire supplemented the material of his Protestant historian, whose work deserved the praise he bestowed upon it, with what Bayle offered both in the *Dictionnaire* and in the *Œuvres diverses*. Finally, it is perfectly true that Voltaire, not content to gather his general information from the best source books which he could command, turned on innumerable occasions to everyday opinions as they were expressed in the newspapers of the time and also in common conversation. The latter source is difficult to reconstruct, but Lanson has done a magnificent job in ferreting out the newspaper opinion on the issues of the day and in laying it alongside the opinion expressed by Voltaire.

In addition to the recourse he had to the general books and newspaper articles on British manners and customs, Voltaire consulted special works which dealt with the larger subjects he treated. Thus, for the treatment of the Quakers, he at least scanned and, in some portions, read carefully Barclay's *Theologiae vere Christianae Apologia* (1676). He immersed himself in Sewel's *The History of the Rise, Increases and Progress of the Christian People called Quakers* (3rd edn., 1726) and perhaps in Croese's *Historia Quakeriana*, too. When he wanted to write about William Penn, he was careful to refer constantly to the *Vie de Penn*. For the government, besides Thoyras's history, he turned to Echard's *History of England* (1720) and, above all, to Bolingbroke's *Remarques sur l'histoire d'Angleterre* (1730-1731). For the chapter on inoculation, he sought his information in Jurin's work and perhaps in La Mottraye's *Voyages* . . . (1727). For Locke, he prepared himself by reading the *Essay* itself in Coste's translation, but he also gathered what he could from Bayle's *Dictionnaire*. For Descartes, he used Baillet's

Vie de Descartes (1691), which we still use. For Newton, he depended upon Fontenelle's *Eloges*, Pemberton's *A View of Sir I. Newton's Philosophy* (1728), which he seems to have seen in manuscript (B. 307), and, finally, Maupertuis's *Discours sur la figure des astres*. From all this enumeration, it can be seen that Voltaire spared no efforts in informing himself and exhibited an alert and well-informed acquaintance with the bibliography of British civilization in his day.

It would be a mistake to conclude, however, that Voltaire was preparing to become an "érudit" and that all this preparation was devoted to the development of a whole new endeavor. It is true that the "poet" Voltaire had suddenly taken upon himself an enterprise which could be more reasonably designated as that of a historian. But even that designation would hardly be correct, because, although history played a large role in his thinking now, philosophy played an even larger role, and religion continued to preoccupy his attention also. Once again, we must stress that this was a new kind of history, fundamentally a critique of civilization.

Above all, Voltaire did not show any inclination to abandon his interest in poetry or in literature. For the moment, indeed, he seemed intent upon deepening and enlarging his literary experience. Lanson, in his article in the *Revue de Paris*, has made a very important point in this respect. After demonstrating how Voltaire referred to these sources in order to indoctrinate himself detail by detail, Lanson shows how the English traveler modified each detail to suit his ideological or even aesthetic purposes—so much so that the conclusion we are compelled to make is that, although superbly well-informed and very desirous of preserving a reputation for accuracy and even impartiality, Voltaire deliberately subordinated historical accuracy to the pursuit of his own ends. Thus, to be entirely faithful to Voltaire's work, one should praise it not only for its documentation but also for the author's unfaithfulness to the documents. Lanson writes (p. 533):

D'un bout à l'autre des *Lettres sur les Anglais,* on peut suivre dans les infidélités de la rédaction, plus ou moins nettement selon qu'on aperçoit plus ou moins les sources, le jeu d'une activité qui réagit contre les textes. Il faut se garder de n'y voir que légèreté d'attention ou parti pris philosophique: pour une bonne part, les déformations des sources s'expliquent parce que Voltaire est encore plus artiste qu'historien.

The *Lettres*, then, offer an excellent example of the kind of writing in which verisimilitude is held to be of greater importance than truth itself. Such an attitude is not uncommon among poets.

It is nonetheless significant that the *Lettres* are *philosophiques*, not that they are primarily "systématiques," as Lanson says, but that they are grounded in thought content, or philosophy. It is extremely difficult to get at this foundation. Perhaps the best way of approaching the problem is through the table of principal matters which the 1734 London edition contains. The names of philosophers which appear in that table are Anaxagoras, Aristotle, Apollonius, and Archimedes among the ancients. The three philosophical sects of Epicureans, Stoics, and Platonists are referred to in connection with the problem of the nature of the soul, but they occur only in the addition to Letter XIII, inserted in 1748-1751. Among the modern philosophers mentioned are Bacon, Bayle, Descartes, Fontenelle, Gassendi, Hobbes, Leibniz, Locke, Malebranche, Newton, Montaigne, Spinoza, and Pascal. This is an impressive list; it contains every one of the major modern philosophers. However, many of these names are invoked for effect rather than for substance. Hobbes, Gassendi, Bayle, and Spinoza are named only once along with a group of others who are said never to have done anything to upset society. Otherwise, they do not enter at all into the picture. This seems very strange in the case of Bayle, particularly since he is supposed to be such an important source and since Voltaire is noted for repeating the names of his sources. A second group consisting of Malebranche and Leibniz is presented only very scantily. Leibniz is dealt with as the inventor of the infinitesimal calculus, and his dispute with Newton is recalled. The discussion of his optimism and the comparison of his point of view with Pope's dates only from 1756. Malebranche is spoken of in connection with the Quakers, who are said to regard him as one of the partisans of their sect. In the first draft of the chapter on the soul, Malebranche is classed with Descartes as being in error in his views on seeing all things in God. It is obvious from these references that either Voltaire's knowledge of these two philosophers, Leibniz and Malebranche, was at the time very limited or he was directing all his attention to others considered by him of more importance. The third one to receive scant attention is Fontenelle, who is only presented because of his *Eloge de Newton*, who is blamed for attacking the system of attraction, and who is condemned by the British for comparing Descartes with Newton. The philosophers who remain after these have been subtracted are Descartes, Newton, Locke, Bacon, and Pascal, to whom should be added, because of his relations with Newton, the theologian Samuel Clarke. In treating these philosophers, Voltaire tries to give some understanding of their philosophical position. The general pattern he follows is to identify the philosopher by a little thumbnail sketch of his biography, a word or so about his character, a judgment upon his talents and upon his works, a statement of his philosophical contribution, and sometimes a comment on his relationship with other philosophers. The pattern (except in the case of Clarke and Pascal) is repeated with some consistency, first with Bacon (XII), then Locke (XIII), then in a comparison of Descartes with Newton in which Dr. Clarke is involved (XIV). These letters are followed by the three on Newton (attraction, optics, the infinitesimal calculus and chronology).

One could easily get the impression that Letters XII, XIII, and XIV are a mere build-up for Letters XV, XVI, and XVII, that the philosophy of the *Lettres philosophiques* is really Newtonian science and nothing else. Bonno, it will be recalled, strongly urged that view. I think it is a mistaken one. It is highly probable that Voltaire was very preoccupied with Newton, because of the difficulties of grasping his scientific discoveries. But it is more likely still that Newton presented to Voltaire difficulties which he recognized he could settle only by devoting himself to a larger sphere of philosophy. He had by nature the type of mind that saw things in a perspective of time. Newton merely rendered more necessary an approach firmly grounded in the history of philosophy. It should be noted, moreover, that in two respects this new orientation was guided by two convictions: philosophers are not inspired, poets are inspired; philosophy is merely a kind of physical science. Voltaire seems to make no distinction between Newton, Descartes, and Galileo, Picart and Bernouilli, and, indeed, this was a characteristic of the time. But it must not be assumed that his new attraction to science had dulled his early preoccupation with ultimate philosophical problems of a more metaphysical nature. The table contains items on the nature of the soul, happiness ("bonheur"), the nature of man, thinking matter, and the existence of God. For all his lightness of touch, Voltaire did not avoid profound metaphysical subjects.

It would also be a misinterpretation of Voltaire to suggest that the acme of his philosophical interest was satisfied by Newton's philosophy. The Englishman's philosophy was seen in the same perspective that all the aspects of English civilization were seen in: the perspective of French civilization. Newton was placed in contrast with Descartes just as Bacon was placed in contrast with Descartes, because Newton represented the English approach to science and Descartes the French, just as Bacon typified the English approach to philosophical method and Descartes the French. The general purposes of the *Lettres philosophiques* were served by this kind of contrast and comparison. In effect, Voltaire's knowledge of Bacon and Newton did not extend much beyond Fontenelle's and nowhere near as far as Pemberton's, just as his knowledge of Descartes did not seem to extend beyond Baillet's. Maupertuis, with his *Discours sur les différentes figures des astres*, clarified the distinction between the two philosophers. The surprising thing, however, is that, for one pretending to write something philosophical, the author of the *Lettres* knew little about either science or philosophy. He pretended, nonetheless, to know at least what is the right kind of science and philosophy and what is the wrong kind.

The same might be said about the relationship of Voltaire to Locke and Pascal, though here he was less inclined to equate science and philosophy and more concerned with the distinction between "la morale" and philosophy. It is evident that he was anxious to contrast the empiricism and sensualism of Locke with what he thought was the rigorism of Pascal. The attack, however, was much more severe. Still, Voltaire did not show much more philosophical skill in handling these two philosophers than he had in presenting Descartes and Newton.

The clear-cut distinction which the *Lettres philosophiques* made between English science (Newton) and French science (Descartes) and between British philosophy (Locke) and French "morale" (Pascal) was made by these same *Lettres philosophiques* between poetry and philosophy. In this area, the priority which for twenty-three years had been accorded poetry and drama was shifted to science and philosophy. The shift had been going on since 1724, when Bolingbroke had awakened Voltaire to an interest in philosophical thought and history. How actively Voltaire took up this new interest we cannot measure, owing to lack of documentary evidence. It has always been assumed that, with the residence in England and as a result of his experience there, he transferred his interest from poetry to philosophy. We have seen, however, that the turn his interests took did not in any way exclude his liking for poetry and drama and his desire to be a poet and dramatist. On the contrary, the English experience confirmed him in these tendencies. It added, though, a new dimension. As a result of the extension it gave to the Dutch experience Voltaire had previously had, the English episode Europeanized Voltaire. It taught him that over and beyond French arts and letters there was a whole realm of thought represented by English science and philosophy. Voltaire understood—or, at least, thought he understood—that in a European context French arts and letters were as important as, but no more important than, English science and philosophy. He also learned that English science and philosophy were as fundamental to the English way of life as French arts and letters were to the French way of life. The logical conclusion was inescapable that the European way of life would necessarily have to comprise English science and philosophy as well as French arts and letters.

That was one manner of interpreting his experience. There was, however, a second method. The English way of life was preferable politically, economically, morally, and religiously to the French way of life. Liberty, equality, tolerance, and public spirit (for which he noted there was not even a French word) gave to the English approach to life a dynamism and charm which was all the more attractive to him since he came from a country where he thought, with some bitterness, he had been denied them. Hence, a second interpretation of the English experience consisted in analyzing the roots of English civilization and comparing it with the civilization of which he was an unwilling and dissident representative. This was certainly a fixed intention of Voltaire in the *Lettres philosophiques*. It must be added, however, that, although he succeeded magnificently in giving this interpretation to the English experience and clearly demonstrated that the categories of living which profoundly influence a way of life are religion, politics and economics, science and philosophy, arts and letters, and the norms of social action, he did not clearly demonstrate how these categories of living united to give an organic unity to the English way of life, nor did he see clearly how, on the part of the French, differing attitudes in these categories united to give a distinct organic unity to the French way of life. Hence, the *Lettres philosophiques* presented a clear and distinct analysis of the two civilizations, but it failed to bring out the necessary relationship between manners and customs, institutions, and art forms. In other words, Voltaire made clear the interactions of the categories of living, but he could not yet make distinct, owing to lack of knowledge, the differences between the two ways of life. His greatest contribution did not lie, then, in the framework of analysis he proposed for penetrating a civilization, important though that was. It came, rather, from an assumption that the two approaches were in reality one—that English science and philosophy, united with French arts and letters, would produce a real European civilization.

It can thus be seen that the violent opposition the *Lettres* met in France was something beyond the mere opposition of high functionaries (such as Cardinal Fleury, for instance) or dominant institutions (such as the Church) or important cliques (such as the Jansenists). All this hostility had its significance, to be sure, and Voltaire spent the greater part of 1734 in attempting to meet it, as we shall see. But over and above all this temporary antagonism was the opposition of a people brought, with the greatest reluctance, to revise its own way of living by merging with a foreign way of life in order to create in the interest of humanity a larger and more appropriate way of living. Voltaire's ultimate task, though complicated and sometimes difficult to elucidate, seems to have been very well performed.

8. FROM POET TO PHILOSOPHER

IT IS VERY DIFFICULT to state what constitutes a meaningful period in a man's biography. Normally, in Voltaire's case, it is customary for us to divide his life into his youth (1694-1725), the English period (1726-1729), Cirey (1734-1749), Potsdam (1750-1753), Geneva (1754-1759), and Ferney (1759-1778). Usually, the Geneva and Ferney periods are combined (1754-1778), thus leaving five periods—youth, England, Cirey, Potsdam, Ferney—each of which we regard as having a coherent effect upon Voltaire's total biography but not necessarily contributing to either the consistency or the continuity of that biography. These designations do represent realities in the biography of Voltaire, but they create difficulties, as we can see. There is some inconvenience in giving the impression that movement from one place to another was the occasion for a change of intellectual interest, when the important thing ought to be rather the continuity, the consistency, and the coherence of his intellectual life. Besides, there were times when movement from one place to another did not coincide with a new intellectual development, nor did a shift necessarily imply the abandonment of a previous interest. We have already noted that Voltaire had a tendency to superimpose a new direction to his thought upon a previous activity. And there were times, too, when a change of place did not give until later a new turn to his thought. The opposite also occurred: Voltaire often set out on some new path before he made a move from one place to another. We have already remarked upon the constant mobility that characterized Voltaire.

These problems are exemplified in the English period. The important part of that period was not at all the two or so years he spent in England. The five years or more he spent after his return to France culminating in the publication of the *Lettres philosophiques* were much more fruitful in bringing out the meaning of his English experience and its impact upon him. Indeed, the full effect did not reach its climax until 1738-1739 with the publication of the *Discours en vers sur l'homme* and the *Eléments de la philosophie de Newton* and with the writing of *Micromégas* and the third draft of the *Traité de métaphysique*. Consequently, to do perfect justice to the evidence, we would have to date the English experience as 1726-1739 rather than 1726-1729, as we usually do. There would thus be three stages in that episode. The first would be Voltaire's sojourn in England, where he became acquainted with the English language, with the people, and, in a rather superficial way, with a certain number of English writers, particularly with the literary figures but probably also, to a limited extent, with Locke and maybe Newton. The second, extending from 1729 to 1734, would be characterized by a more serious effort to consolidate in some meaningful way his knowledge of the English people, their writers, and their thinkers. Voltaire seems during this time to have given himself the dual task of adapting his experiences to his own literary productions and simultaneously devoting himself to an effort to share in a coherent way with his French public the divers aspects of his English adventure. This stage was certainly less superficial than the first, and the result eventually was an organic work on England, which was a landmark in Voltaire's production and one of the five or six outstanding works of the Enlightenment. However, although this second stage did what it set out to achieve in a perfectly superb way, it was still far from being profound. It was consequently followed by a third stage, from 1734 to 1739, in which Voltaire went deeply into certain aspects of English civilization (philosophy, science, history, economics, morality, and deism) and attempted definite imitations of English thought and letters in an effort to merge that thought with French arts and letters. This final stage would hence overlap the first part of the Cirey period, if not the whole of it. It was characterized, as we shall see, not only by a total reeducation of Voltaire but by a decided and definitive shift from poetry to philosophy as the foundation of a way of life.

We are thus faced with a rhythm which went beyond the geographical phenomenon of shifting from place to place (Paris, London, Cirey) and finally brought about the transformation, threatening to take place ever since the early days of Voltaire's career, of a poet into a philosopher.

We have seen that beyond any doubt Voltaire began his career as a Horatian poet, that he speedily turned his attention from Horatian poetry to drama, and more speedily still to epic poetry. Very early in his career, Horace, Virgil, Boileau, Corneille, and Racine were his masters. The focus of his interest was literature; it is obvious that he considered himself the poet of the time, but poet in the sense of master of all poetic form, whether light verse, epistle, ode, satire, drama, or epic. It was this interest which characterized the so-called period of his youth. It must not be forgotten, though, that what characterized the poetry was a certain deficiency of poetic values and a certain increase in thought content. It was as if Voltaire's poetic sensibility was inferior to his desire to be a poet and as if, lacking a genuine poetic talent, he was making every effort to conceal this defect beneath the mobility of a very alert intellect which found some difficulty in expressing itself poetically. As we have seen, Voltaire heroically opposed the "esprit de géométrie" and maintained, in a manner worthy of admiration, that the only way to be a man of letters was to be a poet, always a poet. He did so, however, at the risk of distorting his poetic talent. Others—La Motte, for instance—accepted the solution of turning to prose; this, likewise, distorted whatever poetic talent they had. To all intents and purposes, the poetic spirit was dead, a victim of geometry. This is, however, a narrow-minded way of looking at the situation. Voltaire had more choices than that between poetry and prose, between poetry and philosophy, or between poetry and metaphysics, physics, or morality. The ultimate problem was not how to conciliate one set of these alternatives but how to conciliate all of them. In its final form, the problem was the merging—that is, the coherence—of all of the factors of civilization. That was the challenge of Cirey.

Voltaire was loath, though, to accept the verdict of the death of poetry. He struggled to put new vitality into all the respectable genres of poetry as Horace and Boileau had designated them. He imitated first Jean-Baptiste Rousseau, then Chaulieu and La Fare, then Corneille and Racine, and, finally, Virgil, Le Moine, and Renneville. It was a heterogeneous group of worthy and mediocre poets, but it was a better one to follow than any composed of his contemporaries—Courtin, Roy, etc. Voltaire's persistence kept him in the forefront of a long line of inferior poets, and he was so superior to them that the contemporary public persuaded him that he was the greatest French poet of the time. Folkierski has pointed out that, in the first half of the eighteenth century in France, there was a general tendency among the men of letters to prefer decadence to change. This, indeed, seems to have been Voltaire's attitude also, but not entirely so, for he made many attempts to get away from the threatened sterility, practically all characterized by an earnest effort to increase the intellectual content of poetry. Voltaire, always adept at sensing what people were thinking, strove to inject into his verse the libertinism of that thought. The *Epître à Uranie* was especially distinguished for its boldness of thought, but everywhere Voltaire's verse attracted attention during this period, even though the attraction could be attributed to his unorthodox way of thinking rather than to any originality of poetic sensibility.

The usual explanation given is that poetry had dried up owing to the stultifying influence of geometry. There are even those who would have it that the magnificent poetic outburst of Louis XIV's age had been exhausted by the sheer vitality of its expression. It is conceivable that the intense philosophical and scientific preoccupation of the seventeenth century had a deleterious rather than a beneficial effect upon poetic sensibility. But it is more likely still that the rationalist spirit had difficulty integrating with the ancient aesthetic.

However that might be, it is certain that Voltaire aspired to the title of France's greatest contemporary poet and dramatist when he went to England in 1726 and that there were few who would have refused him the title. Once in England, Voltaire the poet and dramatist made perfectly reasonable efforts to get in touch with its poetic and dramatic production. His acquaintance with Pope, Gay, and Cibber, his investigation of Shakespeare and Milton, and his *Notebooks*, filled with extracts from British poets, all attest the continuation of his former interests. On his return to France, he resumed his writing of poetry and drama. To Horace and Boileau he now added Pope as the third of three great masters in literary criticism and poetry; to Corneille and Racine he added Shakespeare as the third of three great masters in dramatic art. Pope provided him with both the urge to enter more vigorously upon a type of philosophical poetry and the incentive to establish the principles of artistic taste: the *Discours en vers sur l'homme* derives from the *Essay on Man*, while the *Temple du goût* is a more positive *Dunciade*. Shakespeare, meanwhile, afforded him a new experience in the area of drama: he thought he understood better, after his acquaintance with Shakespearean drama, the value of scenic effect as well as the attraction of dramatic action, and, to some extent he was made aware of the possibility of powerful dramatic themes such as liberty.

Voltaire thus found in his English literary experience new ways of fostering his own devotion to literature, especially poetry. He discovered, as we have seen, other things which enlarged not only his literary but his philosophical experience. Something, not yet clarified, turned him to the writing of history as a literary genre. The *Histoire de Charles XII* represented for him a new departure or, at any rate, a more formal way of expressing an old preoccupation. The prose satire of Swift, with its philosophical and scientific overtones, appealed to him immensely. Some acquaintance with Locke and Newton opened up an immense new field for him. Philosophy and science became worthy rivals of poetry, all the more so since Voltaire had learned how poetry and fiction could be made more philosophical—thanks to Pope and Swift. Consequently, Voltaire returned to France having noted how useful philosophy and science could be to a man of letters and how interesting they could be as subjects of investigation. His greatest discovery in England was the way in which these things united to give a new vision of civilization, really a new vision of the world: England was a revelation solely because it contrasted in every respect—or, at least, in every respect which attracted the attention of Voltaire—with France. Voltaire's determination to introduce that new civilization to the French was, as we have seen, the culmination of his English trip.

It is, then, more accurate to characterize the period of Voltaire's youth as the age of poetry and that of England as the age of poetry and philosophy. To be both poet and philosopher seemed to Voltaire after the English experience the desirable way of achieving the full life. Just how poetry and philosophy appeared to him at his return we are not prepared to say, since we have no explicit statement of his to give us a clue. It is certain that he set to work to enlarge his theatrical productions: *Brutus*, *La Mort de César*, *Eryphile*, and *Zaïre* attest to that. It is also certain that he devoted much time to reworking the *Henriade*. He wrote both the *Temple du goût* and the *Histoire de Charles XII*. And, finally, after much hesitation, he brought to conclusion the *Lettres philosophiques*. It is evident that immediately after his return Voltaire was more interested in concentrating his efforts on poetry than on philosophy. This is understandable, for he needed time to initiate himself in philosophy. Hence, we are justified in saying that the philosophy and science which had attracted his attention in England offered new possibilities rather than actualities. Only after a few years of gestation did he feel capable of undertaking a merging of philosophy with poetry.

The introduction of philosophy and science nonetheless led to a complete reeducation of Voltaire, what might be called a modern education destined to be superimposed upon the classical education the Jesuits had given him. The five years between 1734 and 1739 were literally crammed with intellectual activity, ranging from history to metaphysics, to Newtonian science, to Lockean psychology, to Leibnizian optimism. One could say that Voltaire made every effort possible to unite the French intellectual and artistic achievements of the age of Louis XIV with the intellectual preoccupations of the English. He set out deliberately to temper the culture of the golden age of France with the present civilization of England. His one desire was to merge the taste which was the legacy of the previous age with the thought of his time. Seen in its true perspective, his undertaking was literally a *tour de force*, attempting to recreate the vitality of art through the expansion of thought, to retain the form of art while augmenting the content of thought.

Thus, the *Lettres philosophiques* played a very important role in the life of Voltaire and in the evolution of the thought of the time. For him, they marked the beginning of a distinct shift from poetry, which had held the dominant role, to philosophy, which was now destined to become paramount. They not only represented a transference of interest but posed a problem both of direction and of method. Since England was distinguished by its thought, that is, since it was the sort of country whose personality was created by the boldness of its thought, Voltaire was first of all forced to acquaint himself with the nature of that thought. To achieve this, he provisionally studied Locke, Newton, and Clarke as characteristic English thinkers. In them, he stressed not only what they thought but also their way of thinking. The achievement of the goal set by the *Lettres philosophiques* thus depended upon a new philosophical content and method. Briefly put, the content was scientific and moral, the method empiricist and commonsense. Voltaire recognized that the best way of bringing out the quality of English thought would be to contrast it with French thought. His method, therefore, consisted in weighing Descartes and Newton, Pascal and Locke in an effort to bring out the excellence of English philosophy and the errors of the French—or, at any rate, the superiority of natural science over metaphysics and of ethics over theology. The most important aim, however, was to show the superiority of empiricism over a priorism, of scientific observation over abstract rationalism. Voltaire suggested that these two methods were responsible for the different "spirits" of these two peoples: empiricism was what made the English "philosophical" and "public-spirited," abstract rationalism was what made the French "poetic" and "metaphysical." Consequently, by a simple inference Voltaire was persuaded that the English had a style of life permeated by this way of thinking, in which each category—religious, ethical, social, aesthetic, political, and economic—was given definite shape, in contrast to the amorphousness of these categories in the French way of thinking. This whole deduction, which took so much for granted, led from several really simple assumptions to enormous consequences. Voltaire, without any argument whatsoever, decided that what a people thinks and its way of thinking have a direct bearing on what it is and the way it acts. He concluded that the intellectual traits which seem so clearly apparent in one category of its life will in reality permeate all its categories of living. He assumes, finally, that any people that wishes to resemble this foreign group can do so by conscious imitation of this thinking and this way of thinking.

Voltaire's justification for these assumptions was drawn from the way he practiced the English method in his effort to know the English people. He was forced to observe them in all walks of life, in all classes, in all their institutions, from church to stock exchange. It was not enough to see them living and to discourse with them in their language. The products of their thought had to be studied. Since Voltaire was a "literary" person, he naturally addressed himself to their literary expression, broadly conceived. The language itself can tell us a lot about the nature of a people: "chaque langue a son génie déterminé par la nature de la construction de ses phrases . . ." (*Essai sur la poésie épique*). The literature can tell us much more. But getting acquainted with a foreign language or a foreign literature requires a long period of time and much study.

This period can only be abridged by a judicious selection of contemporary writers supplemented by a small number of outstanding writers of the past. From the contemporaries, Voltaire chose Pope, Swift, Young, Gay, and Cibber, to name a few. Of the immediate predecessors, he relied upon Addison and Steele. And, from the earlier predecessors, he selected Shakespeare, Milton, and Dryden.

Professor Dédéyan, in his published lectures on *Voltaire et la pensée anglaise*, has rigorously detailed the writers and thinkers with whose works Voltaire came in contact. He has sought carefully what opinion Voltaire held concerning each writer and thinker, and he has attempted some kind of estimate of how significant an influence each had upon the French traveler. It is a little confusing, however, to tell just what criterion to apply when we attempt to measure English influence upon Voltaire—whether we infer influence from some mention of a work, from some statement about a work, or from some imitation of a work. Usually, we mix up these various pieces of evidence, with the result that we exaggerate the influences. The case of Voltaire and the English poets will demonstrate the difficulty. There is no doubt that Voltaire knew Gay, Young, Rochester, Waller, Garth, and Butler. No one doubts either that he knew some of Rochester's poems, because he copied them in his *Notebook*; Garth's because he translated a few lines from the *Dispensary*; Butler's because he translated a whole section of *Hudibras*. He must have heard of the poems of Lady Montague, because he asked for them. His remarks show that he had some knowledge (between 1742-1745) of Prior's *History of the Soul*, and he probably was familiar with Young's *Night Thoughts* and Thompson's *Seasons*. To conclude that Voltaire developed his own satiric poetry in imitation of these poets, or that he modified his own light verse because of the imagination and grace of these English poets, is more than hazardous. I think that the most we can safely assert is that Voltaire, being a French poet of light verse, got acquainted with some English poets who had a similar reputation.

Two writers we always treat with much emphasis are Shakespeare and Milton. Voltaire is usually presented as having been much impressed by both, because of his remarks in the *Essay* on Milton and in the *Lettres philosophiques* on Shakespeare. In reality, these remarks hardly go beyond a press account. They are favorably disposed, but not eulogistic, and at times are highly critical of the works of both Shakespeare and Milton. There is no real evidence that Voltaire actually imitated Milton. Voltaire did make two or three attempts to imitate Shakespeare (particularly special scenes, or situations, or even a character), but the results of the imitation can hardly be considered to have been of great importance either to Voltaire or to his time. As the century progressed, Voltaire turned against Shakespeare because of the latter's barbarities and against Milton because of what he regarded as absurdities.

Two other writers—Dryden in drama and Pope in didactic poetry and criticism—were of much more consequence for Voltaire. In regard to both, it has been shown that Voltaire was not only acquainted with their overall production but interested in their specific work, also, to the point where he made extracts from this work, took part in translating interesting passages, or actually composed work of similar nature in imitation. Russell has shown clearly that Voltaire's understanding of the heroic play came by way of Dryden, that Voltaire cited not only the sources in Dryden, but accepted fully his concept of tragedy. The *Essay on Dramatic Poesy* (1668)—treating, as it does, the problem of the ancients and the moderns, the relationship between French and English drama, the importance of the unities, and the techniques of dramatic structure, such as rime and the liaison of the scenes—presents the same material Voltaire exploited in his *Discours à Milord Bolingbroke* and in the article "Art dramatique" of the *Dictionnaire philosophique*. As for Pope, Voltaire was in relatively close communication with him, giving evidence of knowing his works at first hand, from which he made and translated extracts. At one time, he claimed that he had written half the verses for Du Resnel's translation of the *Essay on Man*. Some of Voltaire's major didactic poems—the *Discours*, the *Mondain*, and *La Loi naturelle*—show a ready relationship with Pope and direct imitation of his ideas, as we shall see. As a matter of fact, Dryden and Pope were the two real English influences upon the French poet and dramatist; all the others merely gave him a taste of English letters and a certain feeling of grasping the English tone in literature. Only Dryden and Pope gave him material with which to work.

Among the fiction writers, we should perhaps make the same

distinctions. It is certain that Voltaire admired and appreciated Swift, whose *Tale of a Tub* made a deep impression upon him and whose *Gulliver* he thought sufficiently excellent to merit being translated by Thiériot. Voltaire coined the expression "Rabelais de bon ton" for Swift and imitated him in the *Micromégas* and, in a general way, in the *Voyages de Scarmentado, Candide*, and portions of the *Histoire de Jenni*. He repeated the incident of Partridge in the *Relation de la maladie, de la mort, et de l'apparition du jésuite Berthier*. In reality, his imitation of Swift never seemed to be pure. Usually, mingled with it were borrowings from Rabelais, from Cyrano de Bergerac, or from one of the other French utopian novelists. Still, the influence and the tone were genuine. As for the other English novelists mentioned by Voltaire—Sterne, Richardson, and Fielding —it can be noted that Voltaire was acquainted with their work, irritated and overwhelmed by their length, and a little dismayed by their tone. There is no indication that he was particularly interested in these novels, although it can be recalled that he once suggested writing a novel on the order of *Pamela*, a hint we have never been able to penetrate. Dédéyan tenders the opinion that, although they had no bearing upon his own fiction, Voltaire was sufficiently interested in their sentimental, realistic portrayal to find some expression in such comedies as *l'Ecossaise* and *Nanine*. It is really not too apparent, however.

We come now to a summary. In drama, Voltaire paid some attention to Shakespeare in the hope of renewing the French stage, and his judgment was on the whole more unfavorable than favorable. He did think that some of Shakespeare's scenes might lend animation and spectacle to the play, but he was for the most part unwilling or unable to adapt him to his needs and, eventually, fulminated against Shakespeare's monstrous taste. In the epic, he seems to have dealt in the same way with Milton, whom he judged ridiculous, paradoxical, and excessive.

The three writers who were of importance to him and whom he deemed of consequence to his time were Dryden, Pope, and Swift. Dryden he could understand better than Shakespeare because they were closer together in dramatic theory. Pope he could understand because they both were related to Horace and Boileau. Besides, Voltaire, as well as Pope and Boileau and Horace, was a devotee of the didactic épître which, owing to its moral tendencies, seemed to him philosophical. The other poets Voltaire perused because they were satirists like himself or were interesting for their light verse; but they did not differ materially from the libertine French poets from whom he had taken his origin. Swift, on the other hand, appealed to him greatly because of the energy of his imagination and the force of his satire, as well as his relative restraint in comparison with Rabelais. Dryden, Pope, and Swift represented the real impact of English letters upon Voltaire, but in each case the impact was united with a traditional French influence, from Rabelais, Cyrano, Boileau, or the utopian novelists and the libertine poets. Thus, the process was not a bit startling; it was, in fact, a merging, not a transformation. Voltaire simply selected those English writers who somewhat resembled traditional French classic writers, so that the merging became more or less natural.

PART III

CIREY: THE REEDUCATION OF VOLTAIRE

"Vous m'avez pris pour un poète, et les Allemands,
je ne sais sur quoi fondés, me prennent pour
un philosophe; peut-être ne suis-je ni l'un ni l'autre."
Voltaire to Mlle Quinault[a]

"Voltaire est le beau génie de la France, le plus
grand poète, le plus grand historien, et un des plus
grands philosophes, qu'ils aient jamais eu en
France."
Frederick to Wilhelmina[b]

"Il [Voltaire] s'adonne entièrement à la philosophie."
Wilhelmina to Frederick[c]

1. CIREY

BOUHIER ANNOUNCED to his friend Caumont on 6 August 1735: "Il est bien vrai, Mr., que Voltaire est à présent en Champagne. Il est à la suite de la Marquise du Châtelet qu'il ne quitte guère, et qui fait bâtir dans une de ses terres. Je n'ai pas ouï dire, qu'il ait enfanté de nouvelles *Lettres philosophiques*. S'il est sage, il se souviendra qu'il n'est pas né pour être philosophe." Bouhier's information was more accurate than his gift of prophecy. After the affair of the *Lettres philosophiques*, Voltaire had established himself at the Du Châtelet's château at Cirey-sur-Blaise, not too far from Troyes, Joinville, and Colombey-les-deux-Eglises. He had been contemplating getting out of Paris since 1733, as we have seen. We shall, in due time, examine the reasons for his retreat.

For the moment, we want to take a cursory look at the fifteen years which constitute the Cirey period (1735-1749). Biographers are wont to treat it as an unimportant episode. Lanson actually refers to it—or the last part of it (1740-1749)—as the most unproductive period of Voltaire's long life. Those who take an interest in it usually treat the whole fifteen years as a setting for the love affair between Voltaire and Mme du Châtelet. In reality, the years 1734-1738 were among the most crucial years of Voltaire's intellectual life. Only the span between 1719 and 1723, or between 1726 and 1729, or between 1758 and 1762 can be compared to them in importance. Curiously, each of these brief periods represents a time of intense activity: 1719-1723 is characterized by the choice of a career; 1726-1729 is marked by the opening up of the English experience; and 1758-1762 is the epoch when Voltaire passed from the formulation of a philosophy to the translation of that philosophy into action.

The period 1734-1738 can be characterized as the epoch of Voltaire's reeducation. The poet definitely became the philosopher, and everything he touched became philosophical. This epoch is thus of supreme importance to his intellectual development. It must not be thought, either, that the subsequent decade at Cirey (1739-1749) was fruitless and sterile. With the impetus engendered by the new

[a] B. 1156, quoted in H. Bellugou, *Voltaire et Frédéric*, Paris, 1962, p. 36.
[b] 23 December 1738.
[c] 25 May 1739.

education he had acquired, Voltaire needed a full decade to absorb the various fields of activity and organize them into a coherent intellectual position. What is more important, he experimented all during that decade with means of casting this new knowledge into an acceptable form, as well as with methods for creating a genre and a style of expression which would adequately support this new content. His excursions into Holland and Germany, moreover, were motivated by a search for ways of translating all this new knowledge into action. We are inclined to be deceived by the meagre results of Voltaire's initial endeavors with his new acquisitions. We stress that his entrance into science, metaphysics, and even history and morality was naïve and immature. We make sport of his entry into politics and diplomacy. And we cite the lack of published works between 1739 and 1749 to justify our belief in his sterility. In all of that, we are probably more naïve than our author, since we forget not only the intensity and diversity of all this activity but its clandestinity as well. To the untutored eye, Voltaire gives the impression, as always, of being in perpetual motion, scurrying about from Cirey to Paris, or to Amsterdam, or to Lille, or to Lunéville, or to Berlin, and constantly shifting from science to history, to morality, to drama, to philosophical poetry, or to the philosophical *conte*. He was the first to cover up all this diversity with an appearance of frivolity, and he did so primarily because he genuinely enjoyed mundane life and the pleasures of social intercourse. He wrote to Frederick that one must give oneself to all the muses, that man was not created to devote himself solely to study. And, in a letter to D'Argens, he counseled storing up when one is young material to use in later years. All of this excitement expresses his determination to play the role of the "mondain" to the fullest, but it had the added advantage of concealing from too inquisitive, official eyes the extent, and even the nature, of the activity. And what escaped the police can easily escape the critic.

That is the reason we insist so much upon the social life of Cirey and much less upon the intellectual activity. Naturally, we are fascinated by the casual accounts of those who visited Cirey. The coming and going continued at a dizzy pace, interspersed with Voltaire's and Mme du Châtelet's sorties. Each visitor—Maupertuis, Kœnig, Algarotti, Président Hénault, and many another—leaves us some little insight into the happenings at Cirey. Voltaire's and Mme du Châtelet's and Frederick's correspondence describe interminably the life led there, perhaps with more than a modest amount of exaggeration. Each wanted to add to the Cirey legend, until, with the aid of some nineteenth-century writers like the Goncourts and Sainte-Beuve, it became almost a myth. We do not wish to make too much of that myth, which has been overdone already, yet it would be particularly ungracious to pass it over in complete silence. In trying to describe that life, we shall appeal to the testimony of an individual who, so far as I know, has never been mentioned in this connection, a lawyer at Joinville named Valdruche, along with the testimony which all of Voltaire's biographers quote, the sprightly letters of Mme de Graffigny to her friend Panpan (Devaux). Valdruche, who was occasionally invited to the evening functions, saw the events from the outside, so to speak, while Mme de Graffigny, who spent several months at Cirey as a guest, saw them more closely from the inside.

Valdruche, being a totally unknown person, is perhaps the best sort of witness to balance the literary enthusiasms of Mme de Graffigny's letters. The Joinville lawyer entered upon a correspondence with Président Bouhier at Dijon and, like so many correspondents of the Dijon Président, undertook to acquaint him with the literary happenings of the time. The correspondence opened with an introductory letter in which the lawyer attempted to inform the Président of his career. He had studied law at Paris for five years, he said, after which time he had returned to Joinville where he had, over a period of twenty years, been an "avocat." Unmarried, aged forty-four, he lived with his eighty-four-year-old mother, in the same house with a married brother, a doctor, who had four children. Having received along with his law training a great respect for the culture of his time, Valdruche had assembled a library of some fifteen hundred volumes. His brother had one equally large. Valdruche had purchased a judgeship, which he renounced after ten months, finding that it interfered with his life of leisure and his cultivation of the muses. His one passion seems to have been literature, and especially poetry, which he confesses he wrote badly.

He does boast of having a sure poetic judgment, however, and he admits to having accumulated a body of 225 prose epigrams.

Valdruche is typical of the middle-class provincial of the time, content with his provincial life but determined to devote himself to culture and to pass his life in the company of men of taste. There were doubtless hundreds throughout France possessing fundamentally the same intellectual background as Valdruche: education in Paris, practice of a profession, brother also a professional, a clannish, family life; one brother married, with children, the other unmarried, directed by a matriarch, devoted to letters, to reading, to writing even poetry, meeting with friends to read his compositions, certain that he has retained from his experience in the capital the good taste of a cultivated Frenchman, a devotee, though at some distance, of Horace, and in constant correspondence with a circle of other *érudits* or other professionals, in other intellectual communities. Valdruche corresponded not only with Bouhier but with Dom Calmet; he had some intimacy besides with the Abbé de Rothelin, who carried on an exchange with the Marquis de Caumont, who, in turn, wrote consistently to Bouhier. And so the chain of intellectual communication went on continually. Each, in addition, had some special interest which turned out to be a life's work. For Valdruche, it was the assembling and publishing of a dictionary. His full ambition was not realized, unfortunately, but he did live to see his work taken over and incorporated in the *Dictionnaire de Trévoux*, together with his preface. Along with this private interest, he took a particular interest, as practically all these local *érudits* did, in the history of his native locality; thus, he sent to Bouhier (Bibliothèque Nationale, f. fr. 24420, f. 351^v) information about the town and the Seigneur de Joinville which is not without importance.

The correspondence of Valdruche and Bouhier naturally turned from lexicographical to literary subjects. A letter from Valdruche to Bouhier, dated 19 March 1728, contains a series of observations on "le style du temps." In due time, the Président at Dijon undertook to introduce his lawyer friend to the popular writers of the day, and thus Valdruche was led to make the literary acquaintance of Voltaire. In a letter of 4 January 1733 to Bouhier, he wrote (f. 357):

J'ai suivi votre conseil touchant les ouvrages du poète Regnier et de Mr. de Voltaire, en me contentant du texte du premier, sans commentaire et en achetant la petite édition in-8° de *la Henriade* que je crois avoir été imprimée chez Josse, de même que la tragédie de *Brutus,* et non pas à Londres, comme il est marqué au bas du titre.

His opinion of the epic poet was very favorable indeed: "versification aisée, noble, sublime. Beaucoup d'énergie dans les descriptions et les portraits." Like many of his contemporaries, he concluded that "*La Henriade* est dans son genre le plus beau poème français qui ait paru jusqu'à présent."

Acquaintance with the literary productions of Voltaire culminated in an acquaintance with the author himself. On the sixteenth of January 1737, the Joinville lawyer announced to the Président at Dijon that he had now come to know Voltaire: "J'ai fait en ce pays-ci connaissance avec Mr. de Voltaire qui n'étoit qu'à quatre lieues de Joinville." Needless to say, he was overwhelmed by the presence of the great man: "Je vous assure que la littérature même à part, c'est un très galant homme, et d'un agréable commerce." It seems that Valdruche had been invited the previous year to attend a presentation of one of Voltaire's plays: "Il y a un an qu'il m'invita à la représentation d'une comédie de sa façon, qui n'a pas été imprimée, où comme un autre Molière, il joua fort bien son personnage, et après la pièce, il se montra aussi bon danseur qu'auteur et acteur." The friendship ripened to the point where the Cirey playwright consented to show his lexicographical friend a production which was being jealously guarded in 1736-1737 (f. 360):

Je lus dans son cabinet une bonne partie de son Histoire de Louis XIV qui est écrite d'un stile à faire plaisir, et qui n'est rien moins que flatteuse. Malheur aux ministres et aux généraux qui font des fautes: elles y sont bien relevées. Son héros est M. Colbert, le protecteur des gens de lettres. Cette histoire regarde plutôt les arts et les sciences que les guerres et les traités de paix. L'historien ne s'attache qu'aux grands événements et traite le reste de minuties. Tous ses portraits sont de main de maître.

The judgment is important, since it is, to my knowledge, the first allusion to the content of the *Siècle de Louis XIV*. Although there is some resemblance between the intentions of the writer as seen by Valdruche and as they now appear in the *Siècle*, the divergences are more striking. It would seem that the work was not a glorification of Louis XIV, was not even in praise of the "siècle" of Louis

XIV, but stressed rather the faults, stupidities, and mistakes of the principal actors. It attempted at the same time to draw lifelike portraits of the principal actors, with decided emphasis upon Colbert and a great desire to celebrate the advance in the arts and sciences of the time. The moment of enthusiasm for the age of Louis XIV, it would seem, had not yet arrived. In fact, Valdruche's "qui n'est rien moins que flatteuse," along with the other characterizations of the work, would fit more properly the *Annales* of the Abbé de Saint-Pierre than the final text of the *Siècle de Louis XIV*.

The relationship between Valdruche and Voltaire continued throughout the year 1737. It had taken on the appearance of a friendship. On 15 January 1738, Valdruche described to Bouhier in a surprisingly full letter the closeness of that friendship (f. fr. 24420, f. 361):

La proximité de M. de Voltaire me donne de fréquentes occasions de le voir, il ne perd rien à être approfondi; plus on le pratique, plus on le goûte. Il y a eu plusieurs représentations de sa tragédie de *Zaïre* et d'autres pièces de sa façon et de celle de Regnard, à Cirey où il réside. Elles y ont attiré des environs un grand concours de noblesse et de gens d'esprit, parmi lesquels étoit M. l'abbé du Resnel, qui y a passé environ un mois, en y travaillant comme il aurait pu faire chez lui, à une nouvelle édition de Pope, qu'il publiera incessamment, et qui sera plus conforme que les premières à l'original anglais. Nous nous y sommes fort divertis, et tout cela a été parfaitement exécuté. Celui qui étoit chargé du rôle de Lusignan, s'en acquitta d'une manière à mériter les applaudissements des plus fins connoisseurs. M. de Voltaire et Mme la Marquise du Chastellet, qui jouoient les principaux rôles, furent aussi très applaudis. Les habits, les décorations, tout répondoit à la grandeur du sujet. Il vient d'achever une nouvelle tragédie intitulée *Mérope* dont il a fait huit cens vers en quatre jours. La veine de Scudéry ne fut jamais si fertile. S'il s'agissoit d'un poète médiocre, on seroit moins surpris d'une si grande fécondité; mais tant de vers bien frappés en si peu de tems font le sujet de mon étonnement.

Malgré ses diverses et continuelles occupations, il a eu la patience de lire mon *Nouveau dictionnaire français* d'un bout à l'autre, et m'a donné de bons avis dont j'ai tâché de profiter. Si j'avais pu prendre aussi facilement les vôtres, Monsieur, il me semble qu'après cela, je n'aurais rien eu à craindre de la critique, et à dire vrai je m'étois proposé de vous consulter, et au sortir de vos mains de faire passer l'ouvrage à l'imprimeur. Cependant comme le tems me presse à cause des Dictionnaires de la langue qui pourroient paroître avant le mien, et qui lui ôteroient une partie de la grâce de la nouveauté, j'ai résolu de ne pas différer davantage à le rendre public. Il ne s'agit que du choix du libraire. Mr. de Voltaire vouloit me tourner du côté de la Hollande, et avoit même déjà pris quelques mesures pour cela. J'y aurois trouvé le double avantage de la belle impression et de l'exemption de faire approuver mon livre et d'en obtenir le privilège; avec l'agrément d'envoyer mes cartes bien corrigées et beaucoup plus amples que le manuscrit que j'en avois fait d'abord, où je n'ai pu insérer mes additions postérieures. Mais la difficulté d'introduire en France les exemplaires, jointe à l'éloignement qui m'auroit mis hors de portée de corriger les épreuves, m'a fait changer de route et écouter favorablement les instances réitérées de Mr. Seneuze, fameux libraire de Châlons, qui m'a fait écrire à ce sujet. J'ai donc retiré la parole que j'avois donnée à Mr. de Voltaire, qui approuve ce nouveau dessein, sur lequel je voudrois bien avoir aussi votre avis, avant que de conclurre. . . .

Valdruche's references to Voltaire are at times very important. Here, for instance, he notes—by implication, at least—that the author of the *Henriade* had already turned to the printers of Holland and was well aware of the advantages of entrusting to them the publication of certain kinds of material. In addition, Valdruche mentioned in his correspondence from time to time Voltaire's comings and goings, as well as his varied activities. In a letter of 16 January 1737, for instance, he alleged—though incorrectly, since it was only a rumor—that Voltaire had departed for Germany: "Vous savez qu'il est parti pour la Prusse n'ayant pu se refuser aux pressantes solicitations du Prince Royal, qui lui marque que sans les affaires qui le retenoient, il seroit venu lui-même le voir." In a letter of 24 January 1740, he wrote (f. 363):

J'ai perdu de vue Mr. de Voltaire, qui l'année dernière a fait plusieurs voyages, et que je crois actuellement à Paris. Il ne convient point qu'il soit l'auteur de l'Epître contre Rousseau, qu'on attribue, dit-il, à Mr. de la Chaussée. Quoiqu'il en soit le vers qui vous manquoit il y a deux ans, et qui est peut-être remplacé à présent est: de ce grand homme osa quitter les pas.

In the same letter he recorded the quarrels of Voltaire with Desfontaines and registered his astonishment at the fierceness of these quarrels, which he deemed unseemly in cultivated men:

J'ai parcouru le *Préservatif*, qu'il nie aussi avoir composé, et la *Voltairomanie* ou *Réponse au Préservatif*. Je vous avoue, Monsieur, que j'ai été fort scandalisé de ces deux pièces et que je n'ai pû m'empêcher de gémir de l'aveuglement des écrivains de cette réputation qui se rabaissent ainsi à mille avanies réciproques, par lesquelles ils se rendent le jouet du Public, et se dégradent pour ainsi dire de ce haut point de gloire où ils sont parvenus. Ces sortes de disputes, quoique personnelles, feroient un tort irréparable à la République des lettres, si elle ne fournissoit en d'autres écrivains des exemples de sagesse et de modération, et de la manière dont les savants doivent s'y comporter.

Fortunately, not all writers conducted themselves thus. Valdruche seems to have had, for instance, a great respect for the other occupant of Cirey, Mme du Châtelet. On 27 September 1741, he noted (f. 366):

Il y a quelque temps que je n'ai reçu des nouvelles de Mme la Marquise du Chastellet, qui est peut-être présentement à Paris. Elle m'écrivit de Bruxelles sur la fin du mois de janvier dernier. Mr. de Voltaire y venoit pour lors d'arriver de Berlin. Elle m'a envoyé depuis par présent ses *Institutions de physique*, qui la font aller de pair avec les philosophes de la première volée. Elle fait assurément beaucoup d'honneur à son sèxe, où il seroit difficile de trouver des personnes d'un aussi grand mérite et d'un savoir aussi éminent. Sa conversation a des charmes infinis et je me rappelle toujours avec joie les moments que j'y ai passéz.

Valdruche's description of the Cirey atmosphere is far from complete, but it touches upon the essentials and at the same time humanizes the two principal characters. Not only does he show them attempting to integrate their activities with the provincial society in their midst; he also gives little glimpses into their activities and the diversity of their interests. His judgment of the events, social, scientific, and literary, are sound and remarkably sure. He even goes to the point of drawing distinctions between actions he finds commendable and others he considers questionable. His view of the Cirey scene is a normal, commonsense portrait which displays without fanfare his respect for the leading actors and his interest in their exploits. In the long run, it will be the Valdruches who will carry the inner meaning of Voltaire to its logical conclusion.

Mme de Graffigny, who was a guest at Cirey during several months of the latter part of 1738, also drew a comparison of the two illustrious occupants, much in favor of Voltaire. It is evident that she was intimidated by the Lady Newton, while she was completely conquered by the urbanity of the poet. No sooner had she arrived than he placed in her hands the very prosaic *Préservatif*, which he attributed to one of his friends and which he urged her to read. He also brought her a handsome edition of Newton, "relié en maroquin," which she began to peruse. The Lady Newton appeared shortly thereafter and then Mme de Champbonin, "gros chat," who adored Voltaire and who assured the new visitor that Voltaire distributed his profits from his writings among the young writers. After Mme de Champbonin, Voltaire appeared, followed by M. du Châtelet, who remained over two hours. No sooner had M. du Châtelet gone away than Voltaire sent for her to visit him.

This invitation gave Mme de Graffigny the opportunity to describe the poet's apartment, which was most sumptuous and naturally arranged for the writer: "Il y a peu de tapisserie, mais beaucoup de lambris, dans lesquels sont encadrés des tableaux charmants; des glaces, des encoignures de laque admirables; des porcelaines, des marabouts, une pendule soutenue par des marabouts d'une forme singulière, des choses infinies dans ce goût là, chères, recherchées, et surtout d'une propreté à baiser le parquet" (B. 1632). From his quarters, one passed to a gallery thirty or forty feet long furnished with two beautiful statues, the *Venus farnese* and *Hercules*, and with two chests, one full of books, the other crammed with laboratory equipment. A heater was set in the wall between them, hidden behind a statue of Cupid shooting an arrow. The gallery was paneled and varnished and was supplied with clocks, tables, and bureaux. At the end was a darkroom for the Newtonian experiments, but it, as well as the physical laboratory, was unfinished. The gallery thus served as a laboratory as well as a dining room. Screens of India paper and porcelains provided an added touch of charm to the décor: "tout est d'un goût extrêmement recherché." Finally, a door opened upon a garden, which led to a grotto. The meals were served in the gallery, along with "ces discours charmants, ces discours enchanteurs." Mme de Graffigny noted that she had before her "cinq sphères et toutes les machines de physique."

Mme du Châtelet's suite was more sumptuous still, with its wains-coting painted "en vernis petit jaune," its "cordons bleu pâle," its niche, and the charming India prints. Everything was matched in yellow and blue: chairs, bureaux, brackets, secretary, bed. The mirrors and the silver frames were wonderfully bright. A heavy door in the form of a large-sized mirror gave entry to the library, which was still unfinished. Mirrors were everywhere, and paintings by Paul Véronèse, as well as by Watteau, abounded. The ceiling was painted by one of Martin's students, who had spent the last three years at the château, and the whatnots were by Martin himself, "avec de jolies choses dessus," among them an inkstand in amber, gift of His Royal Highness, the Prince of Prussia, and a jewelry casket with fifteen or twenty golden snuffboxes, precious stones, admirable laquers in enameled gold, watches with diamonds, rings set with rare stones—"des breloques sans fin et de toutes espèces." All of this luxuriousness contrasted with Mme de Graffigny's apartment, which was draughty, cold, and apparently ill-furnished. Besides, the rest of the château she found "d'une saloperie à dégoûter."

Voltaire did everything he could to bring the visitor up-to-date on his activities, from the time of the reception accorded Frederick's ambassador, Keyserlingk, with theatre, fireworks, and "une illumination vraiment magique." He spoke of the Prince's letters and his poems and promised to show her the collection. He brought her his *Mérope* and the *Histoire de Louis XIV*, "que cette bégueule ne veut pas qu'il achève," and he offered to give her the biography of Molière, written as an introduction (finally rejected) to the deluxe edition then being printed, and an *Epître sur le bonheur*. At the present moment, he was revising *Charles XII*, having just composed an *Enfant prodigue*, written when he had a fever. According to Mme de Graffigny, he did not like to be in the public eye at this time; he was "furieusement auteur" at some periods and jealous of all the others.

Mme de Graffigny observed certain aspects of the Cirey life which are important for an understanding of the situation. She stated, for instance, that geometry and physics took up at least half of the time of the principal thinkers gathered there. She was determined herself to steer clear of these discussions, but in short order she was reading Algarotti and taking part in the discussions at the eleven o'clock coffee hour. She found Algarotti amusing but the *Siècle* infinitely more interesting: "Netteté, précision, réflexions courtes et pleines de sens, voilà ce qu'on y admire, en vérité, je n'ai rien vu de si beau." She, as well as Valdruche, had been informed of the underlying policy of Voltaire in his *Siècle*, to place more weight on the spirit of the century than on the activity of the King. She noted that Mme du Châtelet prevented Voltaire from completing the history, alleging that it could not be published anyway, and that Voltaire, who declared it the work which had brought him the greatest satisfaction, admitted that it would never be completed as long as he stayed at Cirey. Mme de Graffigny added that the Lady Newton had turned his head with all this geometry, while she was for her part totally ignorant of history. In addition, she often picked on Voltaire, for wearing a certain suit or for drinking a wine which usually upset him, and he, always fidgety and easily irritated, would abandon the party, announcing a colic. He would pout but would finally consent to read his *Mérope*: beautiful verses and fine thoughts, but badly organized scenes, declared the visitor.

Mme de Graffigny described the life at the château remarkably well, whether her subject was a projected carriage ride, or a walk with Mme de Champbonin, or a long conversation with "gros chat" about the neighboring gentry, or the visit of the Abbé Breteuil, or the evening entertainment when Voltaire manipulated the magic lantern, confusing the activities of Richelieu with the story of Desfontaines and all sorts of stories until finally the machine exploded, burning his hand, or the marionette performers who were invited to the château to give performances since there were excellent ones in the neighborhood. The greatest source of entertainment, Mme de Graffigny attested, was the theatre. The passion for drama was unbelievable: on one occasion, she confessed, she had rehearsed thirty-two acts in twenty-four hours. The arrival of the Abbé Breteuil was a signal for rehearsing the *Petit Boursoufle*, but Voltaire and the Marquise, she remarked, were just as likely to pass the time reading and examining a Latin passage from Christian Wolff in which that worthy discusses the size of Jupiter's inhabitants.

Cirey, as depicted by Valdruche and Mme de Graffigny, thus appears as a retreat where Voltaire could repair from the turmoil of Paris and the frivolous society of Rouen to devote himself to serious reflection and study. It undoubtedly entered into the plans of the two lovers to make of the charming château, with its mountain view and its gently sloping terrain, a trysting-place for their new-found love. We have to accept, of course, that Voltaire wanted it to be a place where he could find the peace and quiet and freedom he needed to address himself to his interests; possibly, he also gave some thought to the proximity of the frontier, to which he could hie himself if occasion demanded and across which he could send those works which would certainly be denied publication in Paris or Rouen. For her part, the lady perhaps had other ambitions. She was beyond a doubt as genuinely infatuated with her new friend as he was with her. But she, too, seems to have aspired to peace and quiet, though of another sort, and she accepted immediately the motherly task of protecting her lover from himself. One cannot avoid the feeling, however, that their mutual admiration was predicated upon a desire for tranquility, for a restricted social life, and for genuine intellectual pursuits. The lady perhaps understood those yearnings better than her hero, though it must be confessed that what seduced her was Voltaire's intelligence and what seduced Voltaire was ultimately, if not at the very first, Mme du Châtelet's intellectual interests.

But the château played its role, too. It really seemed at first to have engaged Voltaire's attention more than the lady. Before her arrival, he metamorphosed himself into architect and collector of art, busily engaged in remaking, refurbishing, and refurnishing his "temple de l'amitié." And when it was completed and the lady installed, he was already devoting himself to making of it a "Temple du goût," while she turned her efforts toward transforming it into a "Temple de la Gloire."

2. MME DU CHÂTELET AND VOLTAIRE

WE COME NOW to the most important aspect of Voltaire's Cirey experience: his association with Mme du Châtelet. We do not know too much about the beginnings of that association. Voltaire knew the Breteuil family in the early days of his career, and there is a legend that he had even once dandled the future Marquise upon his knee when she was a mere infant—as, indeed, he was in a position to do so, being twelve years her senior. We hear of his "affair," however, only in 1733 when there are hints of secret parties with the Duchess of Saint-Pierre and the Duke of Brancas completing the foursome. Mme du Châtelet was not totally inexperienced in these matters: by actual count, Voltaire was the third of her lovers, coming after the Duke of Guébriant and Duke of Richelieu, and there was, as everyone knows, a fourth, the Marquis de Saint-Lambert. One cannot be too sure about the statistics, of course; we may have missed a lover or two. At all events, the lady had a passionate temperament, and there was a story to the effect that, on learning of a lover's infidelity, she took a large dose of laudanum and notified the unfaithful lover of her intention of committing suicide. Fortunately, he was less skeptical than most disillusioned lovers and returned in time to have the lady saved. Some of her correspondence with Richelieu has been preserved, and it, at least, shows that her head was not the dupe of her heart.

It is in this correspondence that she explains her attitude toward Voltaire. He was, it seems, a guarantee against the solitude which threatened her peace of mind, and, in return, she offered him security and protection against himself. Their relationship started out as a distinctly second-class affair in which Richelieu, the ex-lover, became the confidant of the two. There is among the Marquise's papers at the Bibliothèque Nationale a fragment of a letter to the Duke, signed by Voltaire, in which the poet is pressing for a portrait of the lady. I can only surmise that the French Beau Brummell turned the request over to the lady, who kept it as a memento from 1733 to 1743 and then, conditions having changed (Saint-Lambert having displaced Voltaire as one poet often ousts another, and Mme Denis having displaced the lady), used the pitiful little note, blank on one side, to translate a corollary of Newton. Voltaire wrote (f. 54^v):

> Vous ne devez pas être surprise (*sic*) de mon empressement. Il est naturel de désirer passionnément les portraits des princesses auprès de qui on voudroit passer sa vie. Je vous prie de regarder . . .

Here the scissors have been applied, and a section which contained what Richelieu was to observe has been excised; another section, however, has been preserved. The poet continued:

> . . . plaisir de la curiosité feroit désirer aux personnes les plus indifférentes ce que demande mon attachement. Cette marque des bontés de mes dames deviendra ma consolation dans le temps que je serai privée (*sic*) de l'honneur detre aupres delles. la faveur que j'attends ne perdra point de prix en passant par vos mains et je me flatte de l'obtenir en m'adressant a un homme accoutumé à réussir dans tout ce qu'il entreprend.

It is to be presumed that the poet received the portrait; he even arranged to live with the original at Cirey over a period of fifteen years. We cannot record that they lived happily, since neither was blessed with this gift. But we can affirm that no association had ever promised so little in the beginning and yet produced so much in the end as this one. It is a pity that critics have always wanted to make of it one of the historical idylls of man. As an affair, it cannot compare with the world's great romances: Romeo and Juliet, Manon and her Chevalier, Tristan and Isolde. If it has to have an analogy with one, I would pick the love of Abelard and Heloise, without insisting too much upon the piety or the misfortunes of the medieval couple. When biographers get through with Voltaire and the Marquise, however, they usually resemble most closely Fénelon and Mme Guyon, which is probably just as well.

We do not intend to dwell upon this aspect of the life at Cirey, however. Nor do we wish to relate again the picturesque details which Mme de Graffigny furnished the world after her short stay. The point to stress is rather that the Cirey episode presented Voltaire with the opportunity to reeducate himself. Well aware that he was dissipating his intellectual energies without receiving satisfactory returns, he realized that what he needed was a retreat where he could remake his world. Voltaire, however, never wished to relinquish his many pursuits. Forever driven by the ambition to be superior in everything—to be an Enlightenment "uomo universale"—he had always found difficulty in channeling his energies. Hence, he was deeply conscious not only of lost energy but of insufficient background. He was unprepared in science, in philosophy, in history, and in the analysis of all social and political institutions. Some command of literature he had, of course, even some standing as a literary artist and especially as a literary critic. But literature now occupied a secondary position in the hierarchy of learning. The knowledge he had acquired at Louis-le-Grand appeared to him less important than what he had not yet learned. There is no doubt that, when he came to an understanding of his deficiencies, his desire for a more complete education was little else than a naïve desire to shine. It is certain, then, that this new intellectual curiosity was not altogether genuine. But the same statement would not apply to the lady.

It is difficult, though, to grasp the unity in Mme du Châtelet's complex personality. Professor Robert Mauzi, who has brought out a critical edition of her *Discours sur le bonheur*, attempts in a rather lengthy and certainly charming introduction to balance the various elements which entered into her character. It is his thesis that too much emphasis has been placed upon the legendary Mme du Châtelet, for which Mme de Graffigny, Mme du Deffand, Longchamp, and Desnoiresterres must accept the major responsibility, while not enough attention has been given to balancing the individuality of the Lady Newton against her real intellectual pretensions. Basing his initial approach to that personality upon some remarks made by Bachelard in his *Psychanalyse du feu* (Paris, 1938), he notes that the "Divine Emilie" had certain mysterious tendencies which could have originated only in the mind of an "exaltée en quête de son bonheur." Mauzi stresses, following Bachelard, that she made of fire not only the soul of the world—an opinion which grew out of the mysticism and Averroism of Paduanism—but the universal center of life. Indeed, for Mauzi, Mme du Châtelet's ideas upon fire, mystic as they were, and far removed from any scientific investigation she thought she was conducting, were in reality markedly similar to her reflections upon happiness. Her science, which he calls "piètre," was closely bound up with her philosophy, which she developed in a context resolutely deistic since she could not conceive of a nonfinalistic universe. In all of this, she did not differ appreciably from Voltaire, who proclaimed himself "déiste" and "cause finalier," along with the vast majority of his contemporaries.

Mauzi refuses, however, to see in the lady a "dry" pedant. Basing his judgment upon a study of her correspondence, he makes note of her numerous contradictions, among which he places her infatuation with Leibniz, her genuine humility before Maupertuis, and her unyielding haughtiness before Mairan. Above all, he points to her intense desire for freedom of thought, even a demand for independence of thought. For him, she was at the same time "une piètre savante, dont la pensée demeurait imprégnée d'éléments impurs, mais profonds, et une philosophe très éclairée, qui captivait ce que les mouvements d'idées contemporains offraient de plus hardi."

What is more impressive is the role of permanent protectress she assumed toward Voltaire. Her retirement to Cirey she presented to Richelieu as a desire to defend Voltaire against himself. Continually in her letters, especially to D'Argental, she described the almost impossible task which she had taken upon herself. When Voltaire went to visit Frederick, she warned him of the dangers of associating with a Prince just on the point of becoming a King; when he offered to entrust to that Prince his "rêveries métaphysiques," she violently opposed such indiscretion. When the Desfontaines quarrel burst into the open, she attempted to conceal the whole affair from Voltaire, to the point that he, who was more than aware of all that was going on, wrote that "Mme du Châtelet se moquait de moi." For her part, she complained that it took more ingenuity for her to guide him than it did for the Pope to defend Christianity.

Mauzi concedes that there is no common measure between the love affair of Emilie and Voltaire and the *Discours sur le bonheur*: in the affair itself, she displayed not the slightest bit of resignation or the least bit of wisdom. For these reasons, Mauzi rejects the generally accepted notion that the essay dates from 1743, when Voltaire was going through his diplomatic episodes with Frederick. In the *Discours* itself, Mme du Châtelet quotes two verses from *Sémiramis,* which appeared in 1746 (*Discours*, ed. Mauzi, p. 13). Moreover, he finds that in Mme du Châtelet's actions around 1743 there was neither, as we have just said, resignation nor wisdom. Egocentrism was the dominant trait of her character, for always she thought first of herself. She devoted herself entirely to her love affairs and to her work. In the former, she had a natural tendency to promiscuity. No sooner had she arranged her life with Voltaire than she began a series of passionate letters with her old lover Richelieu, demanding friendship with undue passion. Her letters to Maupertuis, though concerned with science, had a coquettishness which might easily be misinterpreted. With Voltaire, who indeed had fickle moments which seem to have escaped Mr. Mauzi's attention, except for a commentary on the *Discours*, she was swept away by a flood of passion, which she confided to D'Argental. Yet this conduct, irregular as it may seem, was nothing in comparison with the lack of restraint she displayed in her relations with Saint-Lambert, where she exceeded all sense of decorum. Indeed, as Mauzi indicates, her letters to Saint-Lambert were among the most passionate of the century. It is difficult, however, to draw sharp distinctions, as Mauzi does, between her relatively innocuous indiscretions in 1743 with Voltaire and her total abandonment of stability with Saint-Lambert. In the first place, we do not have her letters to Voltaire, and consequently we are forced to interpret her sensibility toward him through her correspondence with D'Argental. Although the tone is one of confidence (everyone had confidence in the "Anges," as Voltaire called them), it never exceeds the point of discretion. With Saint-Lambert, the letters are direct and immediate and convey much more intimate feelings.

Be that as it may, Mauzi is certainly correct when he tries to establish a difference between the solid happiness Mme du Châtelet enjoyed with Voltaire at Cirey and the utterly exasperated passion she experienced with Saint-Lambert. It was probably she who made every move to capture Voltaire, but, as we have seen, Voltaire was also at loose ends and was very willing to be captured. He seems, though, to have anticipated a relationship lasting a shorter length of time, one or two years at most, and then later on, four or five, while she always thought in longer terms. It was probably she, too, who instigated the excursions from Cirey and back, conscious as she was that the restless spirit of her lover would have to be appeased by a certain amount of relaxation abroad. Here again Voltaire seconded her move, since he was by nature the most social of men. If Maupertuis, Algarotti, Bernouilli, Kœnig, even the Président Hénault, and Mme de Graffigny made pilgrimages to the château, it was to add variety to a way of life which could not be all study or all love. If the solid citizens of the region, like Valdruche, were invited in to see a play, to attend a reading, or even to witness a discussion or take part in a dance, it was because they, too, served a purpose. Mme du Châtelet understood very well that, if her happiness was to be tied to Voltaire's, some attention had to be paid to his happiness as well. Even "gros chat" fitted into the picture according to a deeply laid plan.

That the scheme was highly successful there can be no doubt. The question is how long it lasted. At first, at any rate, Voltaire was charmed with his new existence: a life of love, of study, of social gatherings, dramatic presentations, readings from his works, discussions on history, biblical criticism, and laboratory experiments. We can see that he had a certain ideal of the good life from a remark he made to Thiériot on 3 November 1735, in speaking of Algarotti: "jeune homme qui sait les langues et les mœurs de tous les pays, qui fait des vers comme l'Arioste, et qui sait son Loke et son Newton: il nous lit des dialogues qu'il a faits sur les parties intéressantes de la philosophie." It is evident that Algarotti was the type of man he wanted to be. It is clear, too, that he had already identified himself with that type of man. In the same letter, Voltaire went on to say: "Moi aussi qui vous parle, j'ai fait aussi mon petit cours de métaphysique, car il faut bien se rendre compte à soi-même des choses de ce monde. Nous lisons quelques chants de *Jeanne la Pucelle*, ou une tragédie de ma façon, ou un chapitre du *Siècle de Louis XIV*. De là, nous revenons à Newton et à Loke, non sans vin de Champagne et sans excellente chère. . . ."

To the extent that all of this experience was a preparation for Voltaire's subsequent intellectual activities, one has to accept the demonstration Mauzi suggests. It is very true, as he says, that "Cirey, pour la sensibilité et l'imagination des deux amants, définit un style de bonheur." One may, without cavil, concede that the idyll of Cirey was something infinitely more complete, more rich, and less fragile than a love story. The retreat answered the needs of both Mme du Châtelet and Voltaire for happiness—study, love, social life, theatre. That it fulfilled these needs at least for Voltaire and at least for the moment can be seen in that gayest of all of Voltaire's works, *Le Mondain*.

Some rectification seems necessary, however, in some of the details. The sensibility of the lady may be very important to an understanding of the situation, but her intellectual preoccupations and her intelligent handling of the conditions are more important still. Voltaire's infatuation, only momentary, so to speak, may also have its importance, but that importance hardly goes beyond the contentment it produced, the stability it offered, and the social satisfaction he gained from it. In this connection, it would seem somewhat exaggerated to evoke "la vie de Clarens de la *Nouvelle Héloïse*, dans le domaine de l'imaginaire." On the other hand, as far as the lady is concerned, one could subscribe with some warmth to this final view of Mauzi's: "Sa première liaison [that is, with Voltaire], loin de l'obséder, de l'appauvrir, d'exclure tout autre sentiment ou tout autre plaisir, ne faisait que rassembler harmonieusement, en leur donnant un sens, les diverses composantes d'une existence large, pleine, et riche" (p. lxxii).

Her intellectual activity certainly paralleled Voltaire's. His acquaintance with England having opened up broad horizons, she set to work to learn English after having perfected herself in Latin. Voltaire having become interested in Du Resnel's translation of Pope, she undertook to master that poet. We cannot say very much about her translation of the *Aeneid* since we have no idea what has become of the manuscript. But Voltaire's interest in philosophical grammar found a ready response: she undertook to prepare one. Another of her early occupations at Cirey was the translation of a portion of Mandeville's *Fable of the Bees*. Although she had no talent for verses, she apparently did have a deep appreciation of poetry , for Voltaire consulted with her about his own. History she regarded as a very nebulous and uncertain subject—at least, that is the picture which Voltaire gives us of her antipathy toward history. Her interest in moral maxims was evident, but not greatly developed. The *Discours sur le bonheur*, which showed some analogy with the "Discourse on Pleasure" of the *Discours en vers sur l'homme*, was her one attempt in the field of moral philosophy. Incidentally, we should not forget that Voltaire at one time called these *Discours* essays on happiness.

Her greatest achievements, however, were in the areas of science and critical deism. She worked assiduously upon her *Institutions de physique* while Voltaire was engaged in his *Eléments de la philosophie de Newton*. Both prepared papers for the Académie des Sciences in the competition of 1738 on the nature of fire. She translated the whole of Newton's *Principia* (a translation which was published posthumously in 1759). To this was added some Clairaut material and a whole set of her mathematical analyses of Newton's third book on the system of the world. She likewise prepared a manuscript on optics, of which only the fourth section remains, although from the allusions of this fourth part the general arrangement of the whole work can be reconstructed. In the very different field of critical deism, she composed a manuscript of some 740 pages, a critical examination of the Bible, both Old and New Testaments. The work, which apparently circulated in manuscript (two full copies are extant), was never published. Its significance to Voltaire has been studied by Pomeau and myself.

There has been some difficulty in establishing her proficiency in science. Mauzi's opinion, formed in accordance with Bachelard's estimate that she was not "scientifique," is probably warranted, if her work is judged according to the standard which one scientist would apply to the work of another. In an age more interested in the interpretation of the effects of science and its expansion among the general public than in its development, however, her work of vulgarization stood better chance of being influential than any new discoveries which she might have made but which, in reality, both she and Voltaire were incapable of making. Still, her defense of Leibniz's ideas upon kinetic energy against Mairan was a worthy undertaking, and her presentation of Leibniz's ideas in her *Institutions de physique* was clear and concise. Her translation of Newton, moreover, received the approbation of an unquestioned scientist, Clairaut, and was closely scrutinized by another, the Abbé Jurin. On the other hand, when her *Institutions* appeared, the philosopher Kœnig, who had been her teacher at Cirey for a time, claimed that everything of merit in her work had been contributed by himself— a fairly good case of Germanic scholarship riding in on the petticoattails of a bluestocking. Later critics, too, have been inclined to judge her work negatively. But proof that she possessed some competence can be found in the fact that she was treated with professional respect by the Bernouilli, Mairan, Maupertuis, and especially

Clairaut. In the society of the time, she was regarded by other women with some suspicion and probably a good deal of envy. In her own surroundings, though, she was treated with more respect. Valdruche, who lived at Joinville, was invited to Cirey to see one of Voltaire's plays, or to read one of Voltaire's manuscripts, or to consult with the notables of the château about the publication of his own dictionary, and has left a concise account of the Lady Newton which testifies to the respect which she ordinarily received. Voltaire, of course, praised her excessively in his letters and in his verses, as it was perfectly proper for him to do under the circumstances. When he published his *Eléments*, he dedicated them to the lady and wrote a poem celebrating her own intellectual achievements. In a letter to Frederick, he came out with the famous remark: "Minerve dictait et j'écrivais."

In 1759, Mme du Châtelet's translation of the *Principes* appeared, with a "Préface historique" by Voltaire. A full decade had gone by since her death, in 1749. Between the end of the romance and this latter date, almost another decade had elapsed. For, now that we have Besterman's edition of Voltaire's letters to his niece, it would be naïve to give too much credence to the notion that what terminated the Cirey episode was the liaison between Mme du Châtelet and Saint-Lambert. It now seems that the Cirey episode had run its course by 1741, at least in its fullest sense. Mme du Châtelet's alarm in 1743 that everything was over was well-founded. The passionate way in which she responded to Saint-Lambert's advances was more hunger for love than wild debauchery. For these reasons, I am inclined to put the *Discours sur le bonheur* closer to 1741 than to 1747 in spite of the two verses from *Sémiramis*, which could easily have been added later. Or, rather, I am inclined to see in the essay a resignation to the circumstances which had been taking on more and more the air of finality since 1741 or 1742. It is of no great concern whether this version was a delayed first draft or a second draft of 1746, or even a first draft with later insertions. Delayed or revised, the essay took its roots in an episode already ended. It furnished the counterpart of *Le Mondain*, a "palinodie" of the first affair rather than a presage of the second. As a matter of fact, it is astonishing how quickly the Cirey atmosphere shifted from the love of love to the love of study. The rapidity of the shift can be seen in the poems of Helvétius which Voltaire corrected, and it can be sensed in the correspondence with Frederick. It was not, in fact, simple ingenuity and feminine jealousy which gave the lady all her clairvoyance about Frederick.

At all events, Voltaire in 1759 was sufficiently far removed from his emotional experience with Mme du Châtelet to see her real intellectual merit. He had always praised the mobility of her intelligence, the persistence of her intellectual interests, her capacity for uniting harmoniously her social life and her interest in "pompons" with her deep devotion to scientific study. Now, in the "Préface historique," he was able to view these achievements in fuller perspective still. He focuses attention on the diversity of her works, her study of her own language, her translation of the *Aeneid*, and most of all, her scientific work. Voltaire notes that she gave as her "coup d'essai" an explanation of Leibniz's philosophy. He had previously overstressed her attachment for Leibniz, giving the impression that, whereas he remained faithful to Newton, she had abandoned Newton for Leibniz. He now praises her *Institutions* (he had already written a long review of them in the *Journal des Savants*) in two respects: not only do they possess a clarity of expression which Leibniz never had, but they show a methodical approach to physics not apparent in any other work. Besides, Voltaire adds, having made the Leibnizian imagination intelligible, Mme du Châtelet understood that his metaphysics "si hardie, mais si peu fondée" was unworthy of her intellectual efforts. She thus abandoned Leibniz, feeling that monads and pre-established harmony deserved to rank with the three elements of Descartes and other systems as merely ingenious mental constructions. She then turned to Newton, who never had a system.

Voltaire takes this occasion to defend Newton and to attack Descartes, Cartesians, Platonists, Peripateticians, Epicureans, Zenonists, and all those who founded a sect upon their errors. He exonerates Newton from this failing on the ground that, not having a system, he did not need a sect. Fighting all over again the Newton-Descartes quarrel, when there was really no longer any need for it, he condemns the opinion prevalent in France that Newton had done nothing more than oppose Descartes, much as Gassendi had done. This struggle had long before been decided in the *Eléments* and in the subsequent discussion. Voltaire is merely engaging in a raking of old coals, a digression far removed from his present intention of eulogizing Mme du Châtelet.

Returning again to his central topic, Voltaire praises the Marquise for her intellectual modesty, her industry, her intelligence. What strikes him now as especially noteworthy is her style, remarkable for its "précision, justesse, et force." Voltaire observes that she wrote more like Pascal or Nicole than like Mme de Sévigné; hers was a vigorous, severe style. She was not without feeling for the beauties of poetry and eloquence, however. In conclusion, the erstwhile lover makes an objective summing-up of her merit, which was less objective than he thought, since he could apparently never discern a merit in another, not even a former mistress, which it was not his ambition to possess: "C'étoit un avantage qu'elle eut sur Newton, d'unir à la profondeur de la philosophie, le goût le plus vif et le plus délicat pour les belles-lettres."

Altogether, it was a rather modest eulogy, composed by one who was either too embarrassed to talk about the qualities of his mistress or too far away from Cirey to remember what she had given him. Anyway, he was not good at writing eulogies—of others. The striking thing about his remarks is the way he still, in 1759, connected philosophy with belles-lettres.

The contributions of Mme du Châtelet have been judged diversely, chiefly because no one has wanted to submit them to serious study.[1] Among those who have given some attention to the problem will be found critics who maintain that she was merely a follower of Voltaire in scientific matters. Those who take this stand are inclined to ignore as prejudiced Voltaire's praise of her in his correspondence. In their view, Voltaire did not need any assistance from the pedantic Lady Newton. At the present time, the consensus is that Voltaire was interested in Newton before he met Mme du Châtelet (see Mauzi) and that he refused to follow her when she turned her attention to Leibniz. It has been generally understood that in the Leibniz–Newton quarrel the two were poles apart. Voltaireans usually note with some satisfaction that Voltaire's judgment in selecting Newton was more justified than her persistence in adhering to Leibniz. Voltaire himself must bear some responsibility for present-day opinion in these matters, for he did everything he could to spread

[1] Professor I. Bernard Cohen, of Harvard, is the one exception.

the notion that she was a Leibnizian while he was a Newtonian. It must be added, though, that he did not deny her the right to be a Leibnizian; rather, he leaves the impression that, in his opinion, Leibniz was a metaphysician and therefore obscure and unworthy of the serious study which must be accorded Newton, who was an experimentalist rather than a metaphysician and who refused to entertain the thought of any system while the German naturally gloried in his. Voltaire was probably sincere when he asserted that there were many things in Leibniz he could not understand, particularly simple natures, that is, monads, and pre-established harmony. Probably, too, Mme du Châtelet did not understand their importance any more than he did, although she did make a genuine effort to understand what role they played in the history of thought. It is a fact, as I have shown elsewhere, that Voltaire held her exposition in great respect, while repeatedly expressing a niggling skepticism about each point. It is also a fact that, when one examines his commentary upon her work closely, one can see that he had accepted something barely less than three-fourths of it. But the two most important facts are these. Voltaire, as we shall see, could never have developed consistently without the aid of Leibniz's thought, whether he liked that thought or not. Moreover, he could never have hoped to give a unified interpretation of the Enlightenment without incorporating in that interpretation some very prominent aspects of Leibnizianism—not to mention that *Candide* would have had less chance to be the *Candide* it is had Mme du Châtelet not existed.

It should be stated, therefore, that Mme du Châtelet's contribution to the development of Voltaire's thought, in spite of some negative aspects, was substantial. Nor should it be forgotten that the quality of her contribution was worthy of some respect. At a moment when the classic textbook on physics was Rohault's, then over eighty years old, she undertook to write a comprehensive textbook embodying the problems considered by the great seventeenth-century physicists, the method employed in attacking problems of this sort, the results achieved, and other problems remaining to be solved. In large measure, she prepared herself diligently and intelligently. Like Voltaire, who consulted Maupertuis, the Bernouillis, S'Gravesande, and Musschembrœck, she, too, studied with outstanding scientists:

Maupertuis, Kœnig, Pitot, the Bernouillis, and Clairaut. Like Voltaire, she set up her "chambre obscure" and ran through the Newtonian experiments on light. She accepted fully the experimental method, but, unlike Voltaire, she remained open to any attempt to penetrate the secrets of nature. One of the peculiar traits of her writing is the way she repeats Voltaire's gibes at his predecessors; she was more careful, however, to distinguish the wheat from the chaff and more cognizant of what others had done. Hence, while Voltaire strove to discredit Descartes or Leibniz in favor of Newton, it being his tactic to reject what he could not understand and to propagandize rather than synthesize, she practically bludgeoned him into changing this tactic and made of him eventually, not a scientist (since he had no more talent as a scientist than she and had had no training at all in mathematical fundamentals), but a grand historian of science. His section on metaphysics in the *Eléments* in which he makes every effort to establish the metaphysical problems of science, deficient though it is, was forced upon his consideration by her insistence. Voltaire thereafter never forgot the method, and, when his book was published, he could truly say that he had tried to do more than Pemberton and could even boast that, more than any popularizer, he had put Newton "à la portée de tout le monde."

Failure to understand the differences between the *Eléments* and the *Institutions* have led to rather perfunctory judgments. Although Mme du Châtelet adopted early the fiction of an essay on physics written for her son, in reality what she was doing was producing a text on physics. When the book appeared in 1740, there was a published note to the effect that a text had been ready in September 1738 but that its publication had been suspended because the author desired to make some changes. These changes concerned the metaphysics of Leibniz, a summary of which, the editor stated, had now been inserted. In fact, the "approbation" dated 18 September 1738 was signed Pitot. It should be noted, however, that in the "approbation" Pitot spoke of a manuscript entitled *Institutions de physique*, "cet ouvrage dans lequel on a exposé les principes de la philosophie de M. Leibniz et ceux de Mr. Newton." It is evident from this statement that the suspension in publication was ordered for other reasons, since Mme du Châtelet was interested in Leibniz long before 18 September 1738. It is more reasonable, therefore, to accept the statement of the publishers at its face value. What prompted the suspension was the need felt for a discussion of the metaphysics of Leibniz which Mme du Châtelet deemed necessary to a full account of the *Institutions*. It is certain that Voltaire was conscious of a similar lack in his *Eléments*, since in 1740 he published a third part (not present in the 1738 edition) entitled "Métaphysique" in which he promised to present the philosophical principles of Leibniz and those of Newton. It would seem that both Mme du Châtelet and Voltaire recognized that no physics could be considered complete unless it was solidly grounded in metaphysics. But Newton's *Principia* supposedly was entirely divorced from metaphysics.[2] It is probable that Voltaire would have been willing to dispense with the whole subject. He viewed metaphysics with sardonic suspicion, as his statement to Frederick (echoed by Mme du Châtelet, incidentally) indicates. Nonetheless, in the section upon metaphysics, Voltaire outlined what the metaphysical subjects were that had to be treated if one wanted a solidly grounded physics and merely contented himself with stating how Descartes, Leibniz, and Newton would have solved each problem, leaving the impression that Newton's solution was certainly the best but giving no substantiation of this opinion. Mme du Châtelet was more serious. She realized that a physics without metaphysical guarantees would ultimately be useless, and she struggled hard to provide these guarantees. In this she was wiser than her lover. What Newton had in reality achieved was a physics without metaphysical guarantees, a physics which "calculates, weighs, measures" but which has no interest in purpose or in meaning. His "système du monde" was therefore concerned with the mathematical measurement of movement, Leibniz's with the origin of energy. Newton could claim no principles of reasoning, because his whole method depended upon what phenomena were observed. Logic consisted in observing carefully and measuring accurately. For Leibniz, on the contrary, a universe which was not built upon strict principles of logic (sufficient reason, contradiction, indiscernibles, etc.) could hold no interest for man. Mme du Châtelet understood these things better than Voltaire and exam-

---

[2] See, however, E. A. Burtt, *The Metaphysical Foundations of Modern Physical Science.*

ined them with more sincerity. Her book, which was designed to trace the activities of modern physics, did everything possible to incorporate the ideas of Descartes, Leibniz, and Newton and to describe the role each played in the establishment of modern physics. That does not at all mean that she abandoned Newton for Leibniz: she never forsook one for the other. Indeed, the most important chapter in her *Institutions* was the sixteenth, on Newtonian attraction.

In her "Avant-propos," she sets forth her intention clearly. She notes that the names of Descartes and Newton have become rallying points for present-day scholars. Her stand is that we should know the achievements of each. However, so many have tried to define and to rectify Descartes's system that she is, she says, determined to present the other side of the debate and to expound the system of Newton. Not that she does not have the greatest respect for the former. On the contrary, one may say, she writes, that the human mind owes him the most, because he has put it on the road to truth, a feat much more difficult than turning it from error. His geometry, his optics, and his method she calls "des chefs-d'œuvre de sagacité." Moreover, it was Descartes and Galileo who formed Huyghens and Leibniz, and it was in Huyghens and Kepler that Newton found the solution to the theorems which led him to discover that there is a universal force spread throughout nature. Mme du Châtelet looks at the development of modern physics in a much larger perspective than her lover, whose *Eléments* she refers to in her introduction as having "parus cette année." She criticizes Voltaire for having set himself such narrow limits and regrets "qu'il n'ait pas embrassé un plus grand terrain." The breadth of her vision is apparent here: although she intends to give the major part of the glory to Newton and although she considers his laws of attraction to be the climax of modern science, she understands modern science in a more comprehensive way. Thus, whereas Voltaire seems to have been content to couple Newton and Locke as the great men of science, she seems to envision a larger repertory. The science she is attempting to grasp is not adequately represented by just one discovery or so. It encompasses the efforts of the human mind not only in England but in Germany, in Holland, and in France. It comprises all kinds of scientists, each responsible for some contribution to method or for some definite discovery and, hence, for having helped to make the world better known. Did she convert Voltaire to this view? It is difficult to affirm categorically that she did. What is certain is that she gave him a broader outlook and made him a more tolerant, though an impossibly fidgety, historian of science.

For her, attraction and kinetic energy and Kepler's laws were all very important. But so were the principles underlying knowledge, the primary principle of metaphysics concerning the existence of God, and the proper philosophical definitions, which every physicist must know, of modes, attributes, essence, space, time, and the nature of matter. The desire to grasp these fundamentals drove her to consider both Descartes and Leibniz. In the analysis of knowledge, for instance, she adopts, not the Lockean, but the Cartesian criteria of clarity, coherence, evidence and the things which are derived therefrom "par des conséquences légitimes." She refuses, however, to adopt the Cartesian notion that we can always trust "un sentiment vif et interne de clarté et d'évidence." Just as she protested the Newtonians' condemnation of hypotheses, she opposed the Cartesians' idea of a "hunch," on the ground that it would always lead to interminable debate. The rules of logic—the principles of contradiction, sufficient reason, indiscernibles, and continuity—she drew from Leibniz. She explains carefully what she understands these principles to mean and expresses regret that Descartes did not have the benefit of them; if he had, she says, he would have given a different set of laws of movement (the first law excepted).

She asserts that the knowledge of God is more necessary for physics than for morality: "Elle doit être le fondement et la conclusion de toutes les recherches que nous faisons dans cette science." She protests against those who try to banish final causes from physics. She adopts the notion that the Creator of the universe is intelligent and infinitely good. Her proofs are, first, the ontological proofs proposed by Descartes. But she also gives the proof from Leibniz by the principle of sufficient reason. Voltaire also accepted these proofs and insisted likewise upon final causes. She accepts that intelligence can be added to matter, "puisque nous sommes matière et nous pensons." She adopts the Leibnizian theory of the best of possible worlds, which she explains as the result of an all-good, all-intelligent, and all-powerful God. This best of possible worlds was selected by God after He had given consideration to all other possible worlds. That means that this universe is not a chaos, not a disordered mass, without harmony and relationship between its parts. She believes, nonetheless, that it is impossible to know God. The Leibnizian notion of evil engaged her attention infinitely more in the second version of this chapter than in the first. It was to become the stumbling-block of all Leibnizianism. Here Mme du Châtelet is completely orthodox: we are finite creatures and in no way capable of understanding the whole which is infinite. Voltaire finally adopted this idea, too.

It must not be supposed, though, that Mme du Châtelet accepted indiscriminately the thought of these philosophers. She was far from accepting anything without discussion. Descartes, she finds, has gone too far in his doctrine of intuition. Locke has been foolish in his doctrine that God can communicate thought to matter. Descartes was wrong to maintain that essences are arbitrary. Locke's definition of substance, which she quotes, is "entièrement confuse," but she also rejects Descartes's definition, as well as Aristotle's. Newton has erred in condemning hypotheses. As a matter of fact, only false hypotheses should be censured: dangerous theses and monsters of the imagination, such as the primitive forces of the scholastics; attraction, if one would dare make it an inherent part of matter; and "la matière pensante du célèbre Loc."

Her rejections are less important than her evident desire to bring out the importance of different attitudes. Newton's condemnation of hypotheses, for instance, though exaggerated, must be understood as referring to the great intuitions of Descartes, which were also excessive. In fact, Descartes so little restricted their use, she says, that philosophy ended by becoming a "recueil de fables et de rêveries." What Mme du Châtelet brings into focus here is that great minds may err in their extremes. But, behind the opposition of these two philosophers, what she stresses is the method of thinking scientifically: hypotheses provide the justification for experiments. "Ce sont des hypothèses qu'on déduit des conséquences qui sont autant d'hypothèses qu'on tâche de vérifier." She is not content to affirm. She attempts also to demonstrate. Without hypotheses Huyghens, for instance, would never have solved the problem of Saturn's ring. There are, to be sure, rules which have to be followed; hypotheses are one way of following the rules. Newton himself formulated them.

Mme du Châtelet does not rest satisfied with having separated the wheat from the chaff of the great scientists of her time. She often endeavors as well to trace the history of a concept. The concept of space, for instance, has divided ancient as well as modern philosophers. Some identify space with bodies, others believe space to be a real being, separate from matter. Mme du Châtelet gives a veritable compendium of notions concerning space. Epicurus, Democritus, Leucippus thought space to be distinct from matter, a notion which Gassendi has renewed. Locke derived the notion from the two senses of sight and touch. Keill supports this opinion. Newton believed that space is the "immensity" of God, "son Sensorium," and Clarke defended this idea against Leibniz in the famous debate Desmaizeaux had published. Leibniz, Mme du Châtelet says, demolished this idea by his principle of sufficient reason and offered a new definition of space as the order of coexisting things, which Mme du Châtelet ends by adopting.

The *Institutions* lay as much emphasis on the concept of time as on that of space. Time is considered ordinarily "comme un être de parties continues, successives, qui coule continuellement, qui subsiste indépendamment des choses qui existent dans le temps." The author recalls that the same debate arose between Clarke and Leibniz over the concept of time. She observes that, in this case, too, Leibniz disposed of Clarke's argument by reference to the principle of sufficient reason. According to Leibniz, time is nothing but the order of successive beings, and the concept can be grasped by attempting to grasp the order of succession.

The chapter upon the nature of matter is very significant. Mme du Châtelet remarks that, in the philosophies of Descartes and Malebranche, the essence of matter is extension. Matter thus has four essential attributes: configuration, divisibility, impenetrability, and extent. She objects to this way of looking at things, though, the difficulty being that, with this view, it is impossible to conceive of force in thinking of matter. "Car quelques réflexions que l'on fasse sur l'étendue, qu'on la limite comme on voudra, qu'on arrange ses parties de toutes les manières possibles, on ne voit point comme il en peut naître une force, et un principe interne d'action." But, since the idea of energy is implied in matter, the Cartesians have been forced to have recourse to the Will of God. Thus, it is not the creature which moves but God who moves the creature according to certain laws of movement. This notion, too, is incompatible with the principle of sufficient reason. If extension were the essence of matter, all creatures would be alike. But the law of sufficient reason requires that no two things be exactly alike. Moreover, this force would have to come from some external principle. But we know by experience that this force is an internal energy which, working from within matter, gives it an infinite diversity. In adopting these views of Leibniz, Mme du Châtelet stresses more and more the idea of energy. She accepts that each body is subject to three forces: (1) extension, (2) *vis inertiae*, which she calls a passive force, and (3) active force.

Mme du Châtelet works out the theory that the elements of matter are the source of extension as well as active energy. Her conclusion is that "il n'y a de véritables substances que les êtres simples qui contiennent également un principe actif et un principe passif." She accepts the principle of conservation, that the same quantity of force remains in the universe since matter never perishes. However, neither matter, force, nor extension is a real substance; all of them are aggregates, composite beings. There are no substances except "êtres simples."

Mme du Châtelet, like Voltaire, was very impressed at the tiny dimensions of some insects. In connection with the divisibility of matter, she cites the enormous quantity of insects which can be seen on a grain of barley. Twenty-seven million animals are living there, she exclaims in astonishment, while a grain of sand can serve as the dwelling-place of 294 million! She concludes that "la subtilité des parties de la matière est inexprimable." And we are justified in concluding that an infinite number of things can come to pass in the smallest possible space as in the whole universe. Like Voltaire, she speaks often of the discoveries of Hartsœker in microbiology. She concedes, nevertheless, that there are minute particles of matter which nature does not divide.

Although she traces rapidly the history of those who have tried to reduce all matter to one substance, she remarks that "de nos jours, on ne fait pas de distinction entre l'élément de toute matière." This accepted notion is at the heart of Epicurus's old system, which has been renewed by Gassendi, she says. The indivisible and solid parts of matter differ only by size and shape. This leads her to return to the system of Leibniz and Wolff, who explain these "natures simples" under the name of monads. She gives a concise account of these "natures simples," which Voltaire continually refused to understand. They are without parts; they possess none of the properties which derive from the composition of particles; they are without configuration, and they have no extension. A simple being cannot be produced by a composite being, nor can it come from another simple being. They are all dissimilar from each other. Finally, there must be in each a principle of action called energy: "Ces êtres simples ont donc cette force qui consiste dans une tendance continuelle à l'action et cette tendance a toujours son effet quand il n'y a point de raison suffisante qui l'empêche d'agir." Thus, each little monad is, by virtue of its nature and through its inner force, in a movement which produces in it perpetual changes. They are veritable substances, that is, durable beings, susceptible of all the modifications which their internal energy produces. They are indestructible, and their essential function is to act. It is evident that, since the universe is full of these monads, the past, the present, and the future are produced by their constant action. Mme du Châtelet concludes this section with the remark that, in Leibniz's system, "c'est un problème métaphisico-géométrique." She confesses that there is one point for which she can see no solution: she does not understand how a "être simple," lacking extension, can unite with other "être simples" to form a composite being which has extension. Voltaire made much of the difficulty inherent in this point.

Up to this place (Chaper X: "De la figure et de la porosité des corps") of the printed copy of 1740, Mme du Châtelet has followed very closely the ideas of Leibniz. Her general scheme is to keep to the subject, to introduce those scientists who have contributed to the solution of each problem, and to stress the way in which Leibniz handled it. A statement can now be made about the general nature of this whole first half: it not only introduces physics as a general subject but attempts by definition to clarify particular points (for instance, what space, time, extension, etc., are). More important, it seeks to instill a particular way of looking at physical phenomena, and, most important of all, it establishes a whole set of metaphysical principles, such as the five principles of reasoning, the nature of knowledge, the existence of God, the nature of matter, etc. Contrary to what I have indicated in the past, I do not now believe that Mme du Châtelet made a perfunctory revision of the first part of her *Institutions* because of a sudden infatuation with Leibniz. All the evidence indicates, as does the remark of the first printer, that she had from the beginning wanted to write a textbook on physics using Leibniz and Newton as the "fond." The content of the work was planned carefully to assign Leibniz the metaphysical significance he deserved in the first half of the work and Newton the physical significance he deserved in the last half of the work. It cannot be denied, I think, that the last half of the work is as soundly Newtonian as the first half is solidly Leibnizian. There is thus every indication that the printing was suspended, not to provide time to introduce Leibniz into the work, but to allow for the incorporation of new knowledge about Leibniz she had assembled and for the necessary revisions thereof. Hence, the general framework is that of a modern textbook with introductions, definitions, historical development, and the development of a way of thinking. One can only conclude, then, that Mme du Châtelet did not deviate from her plan to unite the metaphysical aspects of Leibniz with the physical aspects of Newton. She wanted to do this on a historical background constituted by Descartes, Kepler, and Huyghens, and she bent every effort to keep the whole process up-to-date by introducing new material from Bradley, Keill, Hartsœker, Clarke, Wolff, and others. But her ambition exceeded even this complicated program: at times, particularly when talking of space, time, and the nature of matter, she attempted to bring in the Greeks, especially Epicurus, Democritus, and Leucippus, that is, the Greek atomists. As a result, she incorporated much of Gassendi in her work, or, rather, gave the impression that she was using Gassendi. Did she take this material directly from the seventeenth-century opponent of Descartes or from Bayle where all of it had been stored? The latter was probably her source. Since we know that she was an inveterate reader of Bayle, it is likely that she found this material ready-made in the *Dictionnaire historique et critique*.

One thing, however, is certain: the manuscript of the *Institutions de physique* she had deposited with the Abbé Sallier at the Bibliothèque du Roi at the time of her demise was not the manuscript from which the edition of 1740 had been made. To understand what had taken place, the layout of the manuscript must be compared with the printed text of 1740. The final arrangement of chapters in the printed text is as follows:

Avant-propos
  I. Des principes de nos connaissances
  II. De l'existence de Dieu
  III. De l'essence, des attributs et des modes
  IV. Des hypothèses
  V. De l'espace
  VI. Du temps
  VII. Des éléments de la matière
  VIII. De la nature des corps
  IX. De la divisibilité et subtilité de la matière
  X. De la figure et de la porosité des corps
  XI. Du mouvement et du repos en générale, et du mouvement simple
  XII. Du mouvement composé
  XIII. De la pesanteur
  XIV. Suite des phénomènes de la pesanteur
  XV. Des Découvertes de Mr. Newton sur la pesanteur
  XVI. De l'attraction Newtonienne
  XVII. Du repos, et de la chute des corps sur un plan incliné
  XVIII. De l'Oscillation des pendules
  XIX. Du mouvement des projectiles
  XX. Des forces mortes, ou forces pressantes, et de l'équilibre de puissances
  XXI. De la force des corps

The manuscript does not follow this pattern. There are, for instance, in the manuscript two versions of the "Avant-propos," of Chapter I, "Des principes de nos connaissances" (which in the second version is entitled "Des principes de nos raisonnements"), and of Chapter II, "De l'existence de Dieu." The natural assumption to make, in view of Mme du Châtelet's intellectual history, is that the first version of these chapters is Cartesian and the second Leibnizian. But this is not the case: both versions are, in fact, Leibnizian in their tendencies. In short, what distinguishes the two versions is the length and the amount of content in each version, not the nature of the content. The first version is shorter in the number of subjects treated and is, therefore, less complete. In the first version of Chapter I, for example, Mme du Châtelet does not deal with the principle of continuity. In the second chapter, these differences are even more apparent in the two versions. The proofs of the existence of God (19-24) are the same in the second as in the first, but they have been solidly rewritten. Section 24 is lacking in the first version, except for the last eight lines, which are placed at the end of the first version. Sections 25 and 26 appear in the first version, but very much abridged, especially Section 26. The first fifteen lines of Section 27 are lacking in the first version; so are Sections 28-31. Sections 26-31 of the text set forth the qualities of God—God is free (25), infinitely wise (26-27), infinitely good (29), and infinitely powerful (31)—and deduce from these qualities that this is the best of possible worlds (28) and that the imperfections of its parts contribute to the perfections of the whole (28). It is in this portion of the work that Mme du Châtelet makes her greatest efforts to establish philosophical optimism and to combat "toutes les objections tirées des maux qu'on voit régner dans ce monde."

Another set of changes which should be noted is the arrangement of the chapters in the central portion of the manuscript. Chapter X, "Des éléments de la matière," of the manuscript has become, in the edition of 1740, Chapter VII. Chapter VII, "De la nature des corps," has then been moved up to become Chapter VIII. Chapter VIII, "De la divisibilité et subtilité de la matière," has become Chapter IX. And Chapter IX, "De la figure et de la porosité des corps," has become Chapter X. There are in reality, three Chapter X's in the manuscript. One is entitled "Des éléments de la matière"; it became Chapter VII of the printed version in 1740. Another, entitled "Les lois du mouvement en général et du mouvement simple," was printed and apparently corrected on the proofs. I take it that this Chapter X came from the text as it was set up for publication in 1738 and suspended. Its presence indicates that at least half the book was set up before it was suspended. This fact, in turn, indicates that the Leibnizian half of the book and the need to revise it really did cause the suspension. The third Chapter X, entitled "Du mouvement et de ses lois," is in a hand different from Mme du Châtelet's. It contains the version of the printed Chapter X in 1738 and became Chapter XI of the edition of 1740. As a consequence, Chapter XI, "Du mouvement composé," became Chapter XII of the edition of 1740. On the other hand, Chapter XII of the manuscript, "Des forces pressantes ou des forces mortes," has become, in the edition of 1740, Chapter XX. Chapter XIII, or rather the chapter which became XIII in the edition of 1740, was originally marked 14, but the 4 was changed into 3. Chapters, X, XI, XII, and XIII are all written in the same hand, but not Mme du Châtelet's. The remainder of the chapters—XIV, XV, XVI, XVII, XVIII, XIX, and XXI—follow the same order in the manuscript as in the edition of 1740. Chapters XIV and XV are in a hand different from Mme du Châtelet's, as well as from the hand of Chapters X, XI, XII, and XIII. There are two versions to Chapter XXI, "De la force des corps," or, rather, there is a marked Chapter XXI in the hand of Mme du Châtelet and a second marked Chapter XXI in the hand of the one who wrote Chapters X, XI, XII, and XIII. But Mme du Châtelet has merged the material of the two versions. Finally, all the chapters from XII to XIX have occupied at one time or another different positions in the manuscript—some of them four or five different places—before becoming settled in their final arrangement. Chapter XV of both the manuscript and the edition of 1740, for instance, was marked first 18, then effaced, then marked 18 again, then effaced, and then marked 16, finally, the 6 was changed to 5.

From these observations some conclusions can be drawn. It is obvious that the manuscript we now have is not homogeneous in the sense that its text represents the final text of the edition of 1740. It is also evident that the various parts of the manuscript, written in divers hands, represent various stages of preparation. There were at least three of these stages, not counting the printed text of 1738, which may not have been complete. In addition, at least four chapters had two versions: "Avant-propos," I, II, and XXI. It is obvious that the first half caused Mme du Châtelet the most trouble. Every time she attempted to give the chapters on the metaphysics of Leibniz a more satisfactory content and a more logical sequence, she threw out of position the chapters designed in the second half of the work to present Newton. As a consequence, her work does not give the appearance of being very organic, but it does achieve what she wanted it to do. Above all, it discloses by its very structure the problems encountered by anyone attempting to coordinate the aspects of modern science.

This interpretation also gives more consistency to her intellectual activity than the view that she abandoned Newton for Leibniz and later Leibniz for Newton, which is the way Voltaire presented her actions. Her so-called return to Newton by translating the *Principia* was no return at all; it represented a perfectly logical continuation. It is likely, in light of her final action, that she regarded all this labor in physics and metaphysics as entirely coherent. Otherwise, it becomes a bit difficult to explain her final decision to store all her mathematical and physical manuscripts in the Bibliothèque du Roy. The letter accompanying the manuscripts reads as follows:

> J'use de la liberté que vous m'avez donnée, Monsieur, de remettre entre vos mains des manuscrits que j'ay grand interet qui restent après moi, iespere bien que je vous remercierai encore de ce service, et que mes couches, dont ie n'attens que le moment, ne seront pas aussi funestes que ie le crains. Ie vous suplierai de bien mettre un numero à ces manuscrits et les faire enregistrer afin qu'ils ne soient pas perdus. Mr. de Voltaire qui est ici avec moi vous fait les plus tendres complimens, et moi, ie vous réitère monsieur les assurances des sentimens avec lesquels ie ne cesserai jamais d'être votre très humble et très obéissante servante.
>
> breteüil du chastellet.

In all probability, she did not have the printer's copy of her *Institutions*. All that remained was the draft which had preceded the printer's copy, a draft made up of remnants corrected and brought up to date from three or four preceding drafts. Why she wished it preserved we can only surmise. Probably, she did so with the intention of bringing out a revised edition. With the translation of the *Principia*, the explanation is easier, since it had presumably just been completed and she would naturally have wished to have it published. But, besides the fact that Voltaire was with her and would have been the natural person to take charge of the publication of her manuscript, there are other intriguing details which make Mme du Châtelet's action rather incomprehensible. In f. fr. 12267, which is Volume II of the *Principes*, there is a curious note written by some unknown bibliographer. After listing that there is in this volume a batch of "quinze cahiers, contenant la traduction entière du *Second* livre (of the *Principia*)," the bibliographer adds the following explanation:

> ce second livre manquoit dans le ms. déposé d'abord par Mme la Mar. du Châtelet et annoncé par elle a Mr. l'abbé Sévin, dans la lettre rapportée ci en tête, ms. qui fut de suite enregistré sous le numéro 2116. Mme la Mar. du Châtellet avoit marqué que ce second livre étoit resté à Livry, ou avoit été égaré quelque part. Apparemment il fut ensuite retrouvé, et remis à la Bibliothèque du Roi. Mais la date de cette remise n'est point marquée.

There was, so far as I know, no Abbé Sévin involved in this affair, the letter being clearly addressed to the Abbé Sallier. It would seem that, if Book II of the *Principia* of this manuscript was lost over a period of time, this particular manuscript could hardly have been the printer's copy. This is all the more likely considering that there was in the second volume of the printed 1759 edition of the *Principia* an "Exposition abrégée du système du Monde, et explication des principaux phénomènes astronomiques tirée des principes de Mr. Newton." This item, for which I can find no counterpart in the manuscript, is a 116-page article, paginated separately, containing an abridged history of ideas concerning science in the seventeenth century, with Newton's solutions to the problems. This section in the printed text was supplied by Clairaut. Another peculiarity is that the table of contents at the end of the second volume does not refer to this manuscript, first, because the sections are marked by pages while this manuscript is marked by "feuillets" and, second, because the second book is not paginated as a continuation of the first book but, on the contrary, begins a new pagination of its own. Moreover, the alphabetical table of contents refers either to another manuscript or to a published edition, since the system of notation by pages cannot refer to this manuscript marked in "feuillets." Since both of these tables were made in the hand of Mme du Châtelet, one wonders whether the so-called edition of 1759 was the first. This question is all the more pertinent when one recalls that the "approbation" signed by Clairaut was dated "20 décembre, 1745," and the "privilège" was registered "7 mars, 1746."

At all events, the importance of the *Institutions de physique* and the translation of the *Principia* upon the intellectual development of Voltaire cannot be exaggerated. In the *Lettres philosophiques*, he had placed Newton, Locke, and Bacon in juxtaposition with Descartes and Pascal, as we have seen. Essentially, he envisioned the contrast as a Newton-Descartes quarrel in science and a Locke-Pascal quarrel in philosophy. He had already made his choice: following the counsel of Bolingbroke given to him many years before (1724), he was prepared to exalt Newton and Locke and to reject Descartes, Malebranche and Pascal. Mme du Châtelet, taking a much broader view, would not tolerate these exclusions. Her understanding of the history of science of her time included not only these philosophers but such others as Gassendi, Huyghens, Musschembroeck, Hartsœker, and, above all, Leibniz. Not content with a survey of the philosopher-scientists of her time, she even incorporated in her discussion the Greek atomists. Thus, not only did the *Institutions de physique* add to the Newton-Descartes quarrel and the Locke-Pascal quarrel; they extended these contrasting philosophical points of view to include Gassendi, Huyghens, and the Greek atomists and climaxed all this novelty with a Newton-Leibniz or, rather, a Clarke-Leibniz quarrel. Looked at superficially, the *Institutions de physique* seems a perfectly harmless textbook of seventeenth-century science; looked at a bit more carefully, it seems to mark the merging of Newtonian physics with Leibnizian metaphysics; examined with greater precaution still, it appears to summarize the whole movement in science and philosophy during the seventeenth century in a way that recalls the philosophy embodied in Bayle's *Dictionnaire historique et critique*, even to the point of giving some priority to Gassendi as the rediscoverer of the Greek atomists. Thus Mme du Châtelet not only provided Voltaire initially with material drawn from Gassendi, Leibniz, and Huyghens but actually seems to have called Voltaire's attention to the fact that all this material could be found in abundance in Bayle's *Dictionnaire*. Finally, she assembled and studied with unbelievable assiduity the works of contemporary scientists, English, French, Swiss, and Dutch alike—not to mention the very superficial work by Algarotti, *Il Newtonianismo per le dame*, which has always been credited with having inaugurated the scientific movement at Cirey.

3. VOLTAIRE AND FREDERICK

"Il me semble, Monseigneur, que ce petit *commercium episto-licum* embrasse tous les arts. J'ai eu l'honneur de vous parler de morale, de métaphysique, d'histoire, de physique: je serais bien ingrat si j'oubliais les vers."

Voltaire to Frederick, 20 May 1738 (B. 1443)

O N 8 AUGUST 1736, the Prince of Prussia sent Voltaire a letter the youthful enthusiasm of which, united with flattery, must have overwhelmed one so egotistic as the author of the *Henriade*. Frederick confessed that he was fully acquainted with the French author's works. He admired the taste, delicacy, and art displayed therein. He acclaimed the "ingénieux" author as a tribute to his time and an honor to the human spirit. Frederick saw in the Frenchman not only a superior poet but also a writer who combined with his poetic talents a broad conspectus of knowledge never before joined to poetry. Foremost among these talents was the ability to set to poetry metaphysical thoughts. Frederick admitted that he found infinite beauties in Voltaire's works. He adjured the author to send him the works as they appeared, as well as the manuscripts which remained for various reasons unpublished, promising to treat them with the greatest care. He invited Voltaire to enter upon a correspondence with him, from which he anticipated much intellectual and moral profit. He added that he saw in Voltaire's poetry qualities which surpassed the poetry of the ancients, especially "un cours de morale où l'on apprend à penser et à agir" and a taste for the sciences. Even in this first letter, the Prince disclosed a desire to "possess" the poet.

The fortunes of these two outstanding men of the Enlightenment became so intertwined over the subsequent forty years that critics have never been able to resist a tendency to romance the story of their relationship. Nor have they found it easy to follow this story without taking sides or, what is infinitely worse, emphasizing in the actions of both of these strange creatures a pattern of conduct altogether unworthy of men so highly placed in the esteem of the time. In some curious way, Frederick is often presented as that other character who exercised a powerful, though mysterious, influence upon the emotions of the poet, while the poet is thought to have asserted some sort of ascendancy over the sensibilities of the King. One could, if one wished, undoubtedly reduce their relationship to some sort of unnatural mutual admiration. Indeed, Voltaire's *Mémoires*, written after his break with the "Roi-philosophe," spread every possible innuendo about their relationship, which could lead only to the conclusion that the King's morals were anything but healthy and normal. The King, for his part, disclosed that he was dumbfounded by the poet's pettiness, immorality, and his total lack of dignity. The contempt which the King ultimately expressed for the poet could only be exceeded by the passionate and hypocritical hatred which the poet harbored against the King. Curiously enough, it was a contempt almost completely balanced by a feeling of admiration and a hatred only slightly greater than a feeling of deep affection. Besterman remarks that the two lived their lives in a neatly balanced "liebeshass." Beyond any doubt, the regard which each held for the other was so complicated that neither could have explained his "real" sentiments, or, if he could, ever did so publicly.

It is not this aspect of the relationship which I intend to treat, since it seems to me quite subordinate to the intellectual relationship. Critics have almost always fallen into the opposite vein, much like those who, in discussing Voltaire and Mme du Châtelet, have never failed to stress their amorous affairs to the detriment of their intellectual relations. It should be remarked right away that Frederick's importance for Voltaire lay precisely in the intellectual sphere: it was the Prince, rather than the King, who brought this intellectual influence to bear upon him. Frederick became acquainted with the French poet at a moment when the former, who had a great deal of talent and an overpowering ambition to become known as a "uomo universale," also wanted particularly to attain distinction in French poetry and European philosophy. It is rarely observed that Voltaire and Frederick met at a moment when both were sincerely interested in attaining an encyclopedic education. Both were confirmed poets whose respect for poetry exceeded their poetic talents, and both were eager to reach heights of glory in a world which showed every possible sign of decay. What stands out most in their "friendship" is the similarity of their "intellectual" condition. Frederick was trying to broaden his education in order to attain a culture which was French, though ultimately cosmopolitan; Voltaire, as we have been seeing, wanted in his reeducation to attain a culture which was English, but above all European. Both wanted this education to serve the purposes of creative art, by freeing the recipient from the menace of sterility. There was, however, a slight difference. The Prince readily admitted that he was the student of the poet, and, in fact, he did display an immaturity and a decided youthfulness which were not apparent in the poet. On the whole, though, their intellectual activities were so similar that it is difficult at times to tell which one was aping the other.

Voltaire was properly flattered by Frederick's proposal to enter upon a correspondence, especially since he had run upon one of those moments in his career when his opposition was again building up to the explosion point. He furthermore saw in Frederick's overture to him a golden opportunity to form a "Roi-philosophe." That the Prince was young and still acquiring his education and would be, as Voltaire doubtless thought, malleable, that he exhibited a tremendous enthusiasm, which seemed genuine enough, for study, and that all this study was to be centered upon poetry (French poetry at that) and philosophy all added up to a situation which must have appeared perfect to the Frenchman. He was, moreover, aware of all the possibilities of the situation, as his first letter to the Prince shows.

Voltaire freely confesses that he was highly flattered by his royal correspondent's opening letter. He quickly directs his remarks to the Prince's efforts to cultivate "la saine philosophie" in a soul "née pour commander." The whole tone of the letter is predicated upon the assumption that Frederick's devotion to science and philosophy will make of him a ruler fired by "l'amour du genre humain," which Voltaire is careful to affirm "fait mon caractère." The French poet whom Frederick celebrated as a "poète-philosophe" in the first letter responds by identifying his position with the aims of a "Prince-poète-philosophe."

Voltaire's highly vocal commendation of Frederick's intellectual ambitions sounds like a discarded section of *Télémaque*. The "sage" points out to his would-be student that all princely instruction is devised to insure that the student will become acquainted with the nature of man, will love truth, and will loathe persecution and "superstition." He warns the young man that there will always be "le tumulte des affaires" and "la méchanceté des hommes," that he must not ever be discouraged by the "querelle des savants" who, like courtiers, are "avides, intrigants, faux, et cruels," and that the greatest troublemakers are those who pretend to dispatch heavenly orders and to speak for Divinity—in short, the theologians. They sometimes are the most dangerous of all, because they are pernicious to the social order and obscure in their thought. Voltaire could hardly have been more explicit in his instruction to the Prince.

Voltaire's second letter was designed to instruct through the medium of poetry. Quickly recognizing Frederick's passion for French poetry, the French poet sent him an epistle in verse full of instructions to a young man preparing to be a ruler. In it he remarks that only a very few kings have ever prepared to enlighten the people whom they lead, that few have ever designed to make science adored and virtue respected, and that very few have ever dared drink of the fountain of truth. Indeed, throughout all history, only two or three have deserved the name of "philosophe." Voltaire mentions only the Antonins, especially Marcus Aurelius. He dares trace the meritorious activities of these "good" kings: "aimer la vérité," "fouler au pied la coupe de l'erreur," "confondre l'artifice des prélats courtisans," "enseigner la justice," "eclairer le savant et soutenir le sage." These are the lessons which "un roi sage" should follow. Voltaire simplifies, however, by stating that knowledge is nothing more than the art of living and that everything should lead to happiness.

The strange thing about this correspondence, now well begun under the most auspicious of circumstances, is that Frederick understood perfectly—and accepted cheerfully—the role of tutor which the Frenchman had assumed. In his second letter (B. 1139), the young man presents himself as an "écolier en philosophie" and pays homage to the "maître qui sait si divinement enseigner." He, naturally as a docile student, expresses the desire to be worthy of such a teacher. And he praises the lesson which the teacher has sent him, couched, as he said, in a most ingenious and obliging manner, a "tour artificieux" designed to lay before a prince the timid truth. Once again, one marvels at the young man's perspicacity, and one wonders whether the Prince was as naïve as he sounds or whether he was simply being ironical. At all events, he adopts immediately the note of love of humanity expressed by the master. He declares he will never permit the quarrels of scholars to turn him away from knowledge, since he hopes to be always able to distinguish between the idle ambitions of pedants and the truth, and he affirms his opposition to theologians, who are, he maintains, all alike: "leur dessein est toujours de s'arroger une autorité despotique sur les consciences; cela suffit pour les rendre persécuteurs zélés de tous ceux dont la noble hardiesse ose dévoiler la vérité." Finally, in a later letter (B. 1144), Frederick recalls the analogy between his relationship to Voltaire and Alcibiades's relationship to Socrates. In his reply Voltaire continues to exhort Frederick to protect the enlightened philosopher (Frederick had just extended his protection to Christian Wolff) against the absurd and intriguing theologian. He urges the Prince to crush "le monstre de la superstition et du fanatisme," this veritable enemy of Divinity and of reason. He proclaims his Prince the "Roi des philosophes," in contrast to those who are only kings of men.

The aim of the French poet, then, was to direct the German Prince through poetry and philosophy until he became a model king. And, apparently, the German Prince was more than willing to be directed. It comes as something of a surprise, however, that the French poet responded with such alacrity and with such well-laid plans. One cannot help being overawed by the deeper intentions of Voltaire in proceeding immediately to inculcate in the Prince a full quota of Voltairean propaganda. The response of Frederick was so enthusiastic that we are never quite sure that it was genuine. Later, long after the Prince had become King and his relations with the poet had been suspended, Voltaire acknowledged that the dispensing of flattery on the part of both had been rather lavish and carefree. He forgot to note, however, how painstakingly he had attempted with the aid of flattery to inculcate in his new ward his own basic Voltaireanism. Indeed, it is a little startling to see how well organized Voltaire's basic Voltaireanism had become and with what subtlety he insinuated it into the mind of his pupil.

We must not conclude, though, that the pupil was free from motive and that, consequently, his response was altogether spontaneous and naïve. It is quite apparent that he desired above all to enlist the assistance of Voltaire in the composition of his own poetry. Since he conceived of the poetic act as a combination of poetic structure and philosophic thought, he was prepared to engage in both an exchange of poetry and an exchange of philosophic ideas. His docility undoubtedly concealed a deep passion for poetry as well as a more than ordinary ambition to become a philosopher. It is obvious that he had made some effort to assimilate the philosophy of Wolff and Leibniz and that he was fully as eager to spread the gospel of Leibnizianism in France as Voltaire was to introduce Voltaireanism into Germany. Frederick's one desire in following these devious ways was to procure as his master of French verse the outstanding poet of France. It is rather amusing to see how quickly he had Voltaire correcting his poetic efforts, in return for doing what he could to make the French poet a Wolffian. And since, as often happens, we assume the posture of what our interlocutor wants to see in us, Frederick tried hard to be the "Prince-philosophe," while Voltaire made every effort to appear the "Poète-philosophe," although he did resist the "être simple" of Christian Wolff.

There ensued a real intellectual exchange between the two, which was anything but one-sided. Frederick did not make Voltaire a Wolffian, but it was Frederick who played the largest role in Voltaire's metaphysical thought. In his first letter to the poet, the Prince recognized that, although he was drawn to Voltaire principally because of the poet's taste, delicacy, and art, he did not fail to appreciate the addition to his poetry of "une infinité d'autres connaissances qui à la vérité ont quelque affinité avec la poésie." Frederick ventured to remark that never had a poet dared "cadencer des pensées métaphysiques." He spoke with admiration of Voltaire's liking for philosophy and offered to send him the writings of Wolff which were then being translated. We are inclined to forget that the friendship was built not only upon the two men's interest in poetry but also upon their mutual interest in philosophy (see letter of 8 August 1736). Indeed, what Frederick saw in the Frenchman's poetry was a course in ethics from which he could learn how to think and act. For his part, what Voltaire praised in the Prince was the "Prince-philosophe": "Je vois que les Newton, les Leibniz, les Bayle, les Locke ... sont ceux qui nourrissent votre esprit ..." (B. 1094). On the other hand, it is rather remarkable that Frederick saw in

Voltaire "l'amour du genre humain" and stated that, "si l'Europe entière ne reconnaît pas cette vérité, elle n'en est pas moins vraie." He announced that he was delighted to witness the homage Voltaire paid the "quatre plus grands philosophes que l'Europe ait jamais portés" (B. 1139). One could, having made due allowance for the youthful enthusiasm of the Prince, easily believe that he was more eloquent than sincere in these opening letters. When one reads, however, "Il n'y avait que vous, Mr., . . . qui fussiez capable de réunir dans la même personne la profondeur d'un philosophe, les talents d'un historien, et l'imagination brillante d'un poète," one begins to wonder whether the Prince was not endowed with an unusual perspicacity.

Having established their friendship upon this rather exaggerated esteem, the Prince and the poet entered upon a dialogue which often has all the earmarks of an echo. Frederick, after reading Voltaire's letter to Tournemine in defense of Locke, wrote Voltaire that we shall never attain first principles. It was a point Voltaire had made in his reply to Frederick's first letter. Similarly, the Prince did not question the position of Voltaire that God can unite thought and matter.

Encouraged by Voltaire's diversity, Frederick undertook also to pursue the broad interests of the poet. In his letter of 6 March 1737, he stated that he was devoting himself to the study of history, philosophy, poetry, and music. Indeed, Frederick's correspondence began more and more to take on a philosophical tone. On 1 January 1737, in fact, Voltaire promised to send a manuscript of his *Traité* to the Prince, whom he still praised for the diversity of his interests. Voltaire himself modestly regretted that he had only been able "de saluer de loin les limites de chaque science"—metaphysics, history, physics, and poetry.

From the very beginning of his correspondence, Frederick had promised Voltaire some of Christian Wolff's work. He finally did send a batch on 5 January 1737, explaining succinctly Wolff's treatment of "l'être simple" and affirming that "le grand ordre" (Wolff's geometrical order was notorious) is what he finds most admirable. In a letter of 8 February, he urges Voltaire to communicate his opinions of the part of Wolff's *Métaphysique* which he has received. Frederick promises to forward in due time the second part of Jordan's translation and adds that Wolff's *Morale* is "incomparable." He informs Voltaire that Wolff believed that the soul, being created instantaneously, cannot be destroyed except by an act of God's will and that apparently the world is eternal. Frederick asserts that, in his opinion, the world is eternal in time, or in the succession of actions, but that God, who transcends all time, must have existed before everything else. At all events, the world is much older than is believed. He confesses, in conclusion, that he does not know what is meant by the term "eternal." "Les questions métaphysiques sont au-dessus de notre portée"—a belief also firmly held by the poet. In these circumstances, it is best to adopt what is most reasonable. Frederick states what to him seems most reasonable: the adoration of a Supreme Being, all-good, all-merciful; relieving, as much as possible, the wretchedness of human beings; submitting, as far as the rest is concerned, to the will of the Creator, who will arrange things as He sees fit. Frederick adds that he suspects this is "à peu près" Voltaire's profession of faith also.

The translation of Wolff's *Métaphysique* which Frederick sent to Voltaire aroused in the latter some reservations, which he discussed in his letter to Frederick *circa* 25 April 1737. Voltaire rejects out of hand the concept of "être simple" proposed by Wolff. He fails to understand, he says, how the smallest substances of matter can be divisible. What is their "raison suffisante"? Either they exist by their nature necessarily, or they exist by the will of a Superior Being. For either view there are difficulties. But there are many more difficulties in the doctrine of the necessary existence of matter than in the doctrine of the existence of a Superior Being. The existence of a Superior Being, however, cannot be demonstrated. All one can say is that he believes this doctrine to be true because it is the more likely. "C'est une lumière qui me frappe à travers mille ténèbres." Voltaire states that metaphysics consists of two things: first, what all men of common sense know and, second, what no one will ever know. He gives as an example Locke's concept of simple and complex ideas: although everyone has ideas, no one will ever know what this being which has ideas is. We can measure bodies, but we will never know what matter is. We know that animals have ideas as we do and feeling as we do; we therefore assume by analogy that they are as we are. We know that matter is either eternal or created in time, that our souls either perish with us or enjoy immortality, but we are embarrassed when we attempt to divine which is the more likely. Voltaire concludes that the reasonable thing to do is to give one's soul all the virtues, all the pleasures, and all the enlightenment one can, to be happy and to make others happy. "Nous ne sommes point nez uniquement pour lire Platon et Leibnits, pour mesurer des courbes, et pour arranger des faits dans notre tête. Nous sommes nez avec un cœur qu'il faut remplir avec des passions qu'il faut satisfaire sans en être maîtrisé." The erstwhile metaphysician, who is already a "philosophe ignorant," assures his royal correspondent that the greatest good the Prince can do for humanity is to crush superstition and fanaticism and prevent judges from persecuting others who think differently.

In the subsequent letter on 14 May 1737, Frederick makes another effort to explain the "être simple," using the analogy of a geometrical line, but he concedes that, since one cannot perceive an "être simple," one cannot have a clear and distinct idea of its existence, seeing that all our clear ideas come to us from the operation of the senses. Frederick insists that Wolff has taken great precaution to separate the notion of "être simple" from geometrical reasoning (space, length, width), since it has no relationship with matter. He notes further that, although Wolff cannot define the "être simple," every composite object must be composed of parts, and these parts must ultimately be units; that we have no way of perceiving them should not prejudice their existence. Frederick concludes by adopting Voltaire's definition of metaphysics, but he adds that he cannot prevent his natural curiosity from trying to solve problems presented to his mind. Frederick insists upon Wolff's definitions, particularly of space and extent. He points out that the definitions are so carefully given that matter which is subject to space and possesses extent is infinitely divisible because it is a composite, whereas the "être simple," which is not a composite and is not divisible, is not subject to space and does not possess extent. He still insists that one cannot perceive the "être simple," since it does not fall under the domain of our senses (B. 1302).

Voltaire acknowledged receipt of the third batch of Wolff's material, *circa* 12 October 1737, along with the explanations of Frederick. He says he finds the philosophy of Wolff well-organized and profound, but tiresomely long and full of commonplaces. He persists in finding "êtres simples" unintelligible. He rejects Wolff's definition of extent and maintains that pure space is extent. But he grants that everyone has the right to hold these unintelligible views if he so wishes. He concludes that Wolff seems to be entirely of the opinion of Leibniz and confesses that he regards both as very great philosophers, "mais ils étoient des hommes."

Frederick accepted Voltaire's criticism of Wolff in good part: "On ne saurait réfuter M. Wolff plus poliment. . . ." He concedes that there are weak spots in his system, but he adds that this is true of all systems. He suggests adopting as the best that system which contains the least contradiction, the least impertinence, and the smallest number of absurdities. He professes that he understands that metaphysicians cannot speak with authority about their philosophical problems because they involve realms which are inaccessible to the human mind.

All that, however, did not prevent the French philosopher from concentrating upon metaphysics. Having composed his *Traité,* which on an earlier occasion he had offered to send to Frederick, and having had his offer vetoed by Mme du Châtelet, he now undertook, in a letter *circa* 15 October 1737, to explain to Frederick the substance of his metaphysical meditations. The fundamental principle of the whole work, as he describes it, is his love of humanity. But his fundamental idea is that, if man did not have full and absolute freedom, then there would be no vice and virtue, no rewards or punishments, and all social engagements would be nothing, especially among philosophers, but an association of wickedness and hypocrisy. All metaphysics, as he sees it, should lead to morality.

Foremost among the problems Voltaire examines in this work is the notion of the human soul. This thinking, free, active principle is much like the existence of God: reason tells us that God exists, but it also makes clear that we can have no notion of what He is. But, if we cannot know what our soul is, we can at least know something about man. The question of greatest importance is that of the existence of good and evil. Locke has taken the stand that in man there is no universal principle of morality. Voltaire disagrees. Although, he willingly concedes, there are no innate ideas and, therefore, no proposition of innate morality, it is false to assume that, because no one is born with the idea of justice, it does not come to all of us in time. It is perfectly evident that God has wished that we live in society. No one, however, could subsist in society without the ideas of just and unjust. God must therefore have given us the where-withal to acquire them. It is true that there is no common agree-ment among the peoples of this world about what is just or unjust. Each society has its own laws, its own customs, its own concepts of good and evil. But societies do always consider good that which is useful to them. "Voilà, Monseigneur," Voltaire concludes, "à peu près le plan sur lequel j'ai écrit cette métaphysique morale."

"MÉTAPHYSIQUE MORALE"

The significant part of Voltaire's plan in the *Traité* is the determi-nation of the author to reduce metaphysics to "la morale." This development was not present in the first draft. Only after Voltaire and Mme du Châtelet had been led to Mandeville did the former make the shift. The subject of "métaphysique morale" was ex-tremely attractive to the Prince also. Early in the dialogue in which he and the poet were engaged he had expressed the thought that, in spite of the uncertainties of metaphysics, one should always devote oneself to aiding one's fellowman and to seeking happiness. Fred-erick insisted (*circa* 15 December 1738) that every reasonable man must practice virtue, both because virtue is very attractive to a well-born soul and because it is in the interest of everybody to be virtuous. The virtue which he envisaged is that which springs from goodness of heart and which leads to doing good to another. Frederick invited the poet to communicate his ideas on the subject. The Prince ex-pressed the conviction that Voltaire was as sublime in the practice of virtue as he was in its theory.

Frederick, having composed an *Epître sur l'humanité*, sent it to Voltaire for his comments and grammatical corrections (B. 1672). Frederick claims that his poem was the predecessor of the sixth *Epître sur l'homme*. He modestly denies that he has fully developed his ideas upon humanity, which is an inexhaustible subject. He in-sists, however, that a king, great or small, must seek to remedy hu-man miseries and must endeavor to cure the ills of his subjects. He must furnish them abundance, prosperity, tranquility, and "tout ce qui peut contribuer au bien et à l'accroissement de la société."

Frederick develops this idea further. He states, for instance, that compassion and the desire to aid a person in distress are innate in the majority of men—an idea which both Voltaire and Mme du Châtelet stressed, too, in spite of their opposition to the concept of innateness. Perhaps the reason is that we foresee our own infirmities in the suffering of others. Indeed, the resemblance between all men, their equality of condition, the indispensable need which every man has of others, the miseries which bind them closer together, the natural sympathy which every man feels for his fellowman, our own self-preservation which demands humanity of us—all these things seem to unite to impose upon us a duty which augments our happiness.

HISTORY

Of particular importance in all this discussion of "la morale" was the bearing it had on history. Voltaire, having been so successful in his *Charles XII*, began to manifest some interest in Charles's antagonist, Peter the Great. Already in the biography of the King of Sweden, he had made a comparison between Charles, who had ruined his country, and Peter, who had planned for the new civilization of Russia. The historian, however, recognized that he had very scant materials upon which to base that opinion. Frederick, with whom he discussed his deficiency, undertook to supply them. As a consequence, much of the dialogue between the Prince and the historian turns upon the question of what interpretation should be given to Peter's activity. This aspect of the discussion was important in itself, all the more since Voltaire eventually wrote a history of Russia in two volumes (1759-1763) at the request of Catherine, in which he undoubtedly made profitable use of all this material. The broader implications of the subject, however, were more important still. From Frederick's personal vantage point—that of a Prince about to ascend the throne—Peter offered a model to be approved or condemned. And a history of Peter also presented an opportunity for a deeper discussion of the aims of history.

For his part, Frederick subscribed to Bayle's, as well as Voltaire's, belief that history is the archive of man's wickedness, which, in presenting the poison, at the same time supplies the antidote. In history, Frederick declares (B. 1378), there can be found an infinite number of wicked rulers, tyrants, monsters, hated by their people and held in abomination by the universe, who, in spite of their evil conduct, nevertheless wish to be considered models of virtue, men of probity, heroes. He concludes that, in view of the desire of these rulers to be judged a model of virtue, the portrait of the wicked kings and their opprobrium in the public eye can only serve as a warning to others who follow. He states naïvely that humanitarianism should be the foremost quality of a reasonable man and that, therefore, the pleasure of doing good ought to be uppermost in the mind of the king. Frederick, like Voltaire and Bolingbroke, indeed, like all contemporary historians, believed that history instructs and can only produce a desire for goodness in those who read it. He was, however, far from committed to the theory of the goodness of man. In fact, he viewed kings as ambitious monsters and all men as evil who conceal the wickedness and the blackness of their hearts. Each man, Frederick asserted, even when he sees the results of evil action, acts to gratify his unruly passions and does not scruple to justify his crimes by the example of some predecessor. The Prince had no illusions about the goodness of human nature, even while personally convinced of the necessity of being virtuous and desirous of performing his kingly task as a man of virtue.

With these opinions, Frederick and Voltaire entered upon a lengthy discussion extending over a considerable period of time.

Frederick had Von Suhm assemble the material upon the Czar which Voltaire had requested. He forwarded it to the poet on 13 November 1737, with the statement that he must revise his opinion of Peter. The Czar, Frederick admits, has the reputation of having been "un fantôme héroïque," which can be traced to some fortunate circumstances, a few favorable events, and the ignorance of foreigners. But, in reality, he had all the defects of men and few virtues. He was cowardly, cruel, brutal, feeble, a ruler hated by his subjects who, in fact, "a poussé le despotisme aussi loin qu'un souverain puisse le pousser." Frederick grants that he was industrious, mechanically minded, and ready to sacrifice everything to his curiosity. The Prince urges Voltaire to use this material prudently (B. 1329). Voltaire, in reply, promises to use it only in accordance with the wishes of his Prince (B. 1346).

Around 15 January 1738, the poet acknowledged the receipt of a shipment of two big packages of documents, containing papers on Russia. After having studied them, Voltaire expressed the conviction that there really was a violent contrast between Peter's crudeness and barbarity, on the one hand, and his desire to bring out the best in his subjects, on the other. Conceding the Czar's savagery, Voltaire insists also upon a "barbare qui a créé des hommes." He stresses that the Czar undertook a journey through Europe with the aim of learning how to reign and that he struggled to dominate his own defects, but he emphasizes as well that the Czar founded new towns, united the two ends of Russia with canals, built a navy, and tried to form a new society with the most unsociable of men. The author of *Charles XII* tried hard to balance the serious defects with the "esprit créateur" of the monarch. True to his directing idea, he proclaims his intention to celebrate in Peter's biography the progress of the human mind, the creation of the arts and sciences, and the fostering of the processes of civilization. The French historian promises that he will not conceal Peter's faults; he intends to display, as best he can, not only the things Peter did which were great and magnificent but the things he wanted to do. He protests against those historians who limit themselves to the presentation of crimes in history. He worries lest this history, by stressing the crimes, will teach rulers how to be criminals. "A quoi servent ces registres de crimes et d'horreurs, qu'à encourager quelquefois un prince faible à des excès dont il aurait honte . . . ?"

Frederick, however, was not convinced. He was willing enough to have the material prepared, and, when Voltaire solicited further documents upon the Czarina and Czarevitch, he undertook to secure them. He nevertheless opposed Voltaire's conclusion that Peter was more glorious in what he accomplished for his people than contemptible for his barbarities (B. 1378):

Si l'on voulait se donner la peine d'examiner à tête reposée le bien et le mal que le czar a faits dans son pays, de mettre ses bonnes et ses mauvaises qualités dans la balance, de les peser, et de juger ensuite de lui sur celles de ses qualités qui feraient le meilleur poids, on trouverait peut-être que ce prince a fait beaucoup de mauvaises actions brillantes, qu'il a eu des vices héroïques, et que ses vertus ont été obscurcies et éclipsées par un nombre innombrable de vices.

Later, on 28 March 1738, he announced that the papers he was now sending gave evidence of barbaric deeds and cruelties matching those of the first Caesars. Russia, in his opinion, was a land where the arts and sciences had not penetrated. The Czar had not the slightest bit of humanity; he was raised in the greatest ignorance, subject to the most unbridled passion. Finally, he had had his own son murdered. Frederick cited the Ambassador Printzen to substantiate his opinion. Frederick's portrait of Peter and Russia markedly changed Voltaire's attitude. Around 25 April 1738, he wrote the Prince: "Ce que V. A. R. m'a daigné mandé du Czar Pierre change bien mes idées. Est-il possible que tant d'horreurs aient pu se joindre à des desseins qui auraient honoré Alexandre?" Voltaire renounced for the moment his plan to write the history of Peter. But around the twelfth of July, he wrote Berger (B. 1484):

> J'ai de meilleurs mémoires sur le czar Pierre, que n'en a l'auteur de sa vie. On ne peut être plus au fait que je le suis de ce pays-là, et quelque jour je pourrai faire usage de ces matériaux; mais on n'aime ici que la philosophie et l'histoire n'y est regardée que comme des caquets. Pour moi, je ne méprise rien. Tout ce qui est du ressort de l'esprit, a mes hommages.

SIÈCLE DE LOUIS XIV

Voltaire's dialogue with the Prince on the importance of Peter's reforms in Russia naturally led the French historian to consult his Prince about the *Siècle de Louis XIV*. It is significant that, as soon as he felt he had a draft of this work ready, he sent it to Frederick by way of Keyserlingk. *Circa* 15 October 1737, he wrote the Prince that he was awaiting his verdict upon the *Siècle* and the *Eléments* and instructions about how they might be continued. He repeated *circa* 15 February 1738 that he was still awaiting the Prince's opinion of the *Siècle*. Finally, on 31 March 1738, Frederick wrote that he was enchanted by the *Siècle*. He took exception only to Voltaire's treatment of Machiavelli: it was the Prince's opinion that the Florentine politician was a wicked creature and that anyone who taught that one may go back on his word, or oppress, or do injustice with impunity should never be given a place of distinction in a history. Otherwise, Frederick found the *Siècle* to his liking: he praised the emphasis placed on manners, the "beau style," the intelligent reflections, the perfect impartiality. Voltaire (B. 1443) took pains to explain to his Prince that in the *Siècle* he had not wished to penetrate into the secret archives or to attain the first principles of historical phenomena. He was still sticking to his program of depicting the manners and customs of men, of writing the history of the human mind and especially the history of the arts. Frederick, on 17 June 1738, urged Voltaire to continue work on his *Siècle*, affirming that Europe had never seen such a history and did not even have a conception of a history as perfect as his. Not until 9 November 1738 did Frederick return to the *Siècle* in the correspondence. He had now reread it, and he pronounced it an excellent work which had no equal in this world. Frederick encouraged Voltaire to continue its composition but advised him against publishing it, since its author would be persecuted by all those he mentioned and by their posterity, too. Frederick judged that, since it was philosophical history, it should not be read by any but philosophers. Voltaire did not reply to this part of Frederick's letter until 18 January 1739, when he promised to complete the *Siècle* as Frederick had urged him to do. Once again, he asserted that his aim was to give, not a political and military history, but a history of the arts, of commerce, of internal and foreign policy—in a word, of the human mind—adding that there could be no controversy in this kind of history.

FREDERICK'S *CONSIDÉRATIONS*

On 17 June 1738, Frederick sent Voltaire a copy of his *Considérations sur l'état présent du corps politique de l'Europe*, with the request that the latter tell him his opinion of it. Voltaire received the pamphlet with enthusiasm. In his reply of 5 August 1738 (B. 1506), he compliments the Prince on his work, noting that he is not surprised that one who excels in the arts and who is so sublime and so wise a metaphysician should also be paramount in the art of reigning. Voltaire compares the ideas expressed with those of a member of the British Parliament. He finds that the author is not only better instructed in German freedom but also more closely allied with the political thinking of Leibniz. He concludes that the treatise is most worthy of the Prince. He inquires if it is true that there is a plan afoot to unite the Empire and France, which he thought would certainly upset the balance in Europe. In discussing with great clarity the present state of Europe, Voltaire makes an observation which seems extraordinarily important in one who was soon to try his hand in international affairs:

En réfléchissant sur tous les événements qui se sont passés de nos jours, je commence à croire que tout s'est fait entre les couronnes à peu près comme je vois se traiter toutes les affaires entre les particuliers. Chacun a reçu de la nature l'envie de s'agrandir, une occasion paraît s'ofrir, un intrigant la fait valoir, une femme gagnée par de l'argent, ou par quelque chose qui doit être plus fort, s'opose à la négociation, une autre la renoue, les circonstances, l'humeur, un caprice, une méprise, un rien décide.

Voltaire cites the case of Lady Masham, but much more important is the testament of Charles II of Spain. The French historian concludes that some evil genius mocks the efforts of man, but not entirely: wars, royal marriages, and other events which are the source of injustice, horror, and oppression upset plans and ruin countries, too. Voltaire praises his Prince for condemning these injustices. Still, he suggests that it would be wise to undertake a Protestant alliance in Europe under a strong king.

The importance of this discussion does not lie in the few general remarks Voltaire made. In this particular area, in spite of his observations, it is really Frederick who was informed. In his reply of 11 September 1738 (B. 1544), Frederick states that the Maréchal de Villars's project of uniting France and the Empire in an alliance has been adopted by the French ministry as its policy, and he predicts that this policy will prepare events which will overthrow empires and change the face of Europe. He adds that France, as Voltaire stated, could be likened to a prudent, rich person surrounded by wasteful and unhappy neighbors. It is to be expected that under a despotic ruler France will swallow up all its neighbors one of these days, a process which has already begun with the incorporation of Lorraine.

Frederick approves Voltaire's remark that those men who govern kingdoms and whose word often decides the happiness of a state are sometimes those who leave the most to chance. That is because they are, after all, only men and because, although they are driven to a position by circumstances, they are also determined by conditions. Frederick states that the word of a minister is worth no more than the oath of a lover. There is always a feeling on the minister's part that there is no difference between what he has said and what he meant to say. A minister who speaks for his king, that is, who makes his king say this or that, is, after all, like a good playwright who makes his characters say what he thinks is appropriate for them to say. Frederick concludes that it is humanity, "cette vertu si recommendable" which embraces all the other virtues, that should be the goal of every reasonable man. He assures Voltaire that, in spite of the latter's suggestion that he seek the imperial crown, he will not do so.

This little dialogue occurring at the climactic moment of 1738 was important to the Prince because it gave him an opportunity to ponder the situation in European politics at a time just prior to his accession to the Prussian throne. It displays a Frederick who, as Voltaire remarked, was no longer the poet but the ruler already trained in the art of ruling. The effect upon Voltaire was even greater, for it opened up to him possibilities of serving this European situation, through his Prince, by versing himself in the minister's art. The poet-philosopher could not fail to glimpse a future where he, too, might play a role in the making of Europe. If he had set out to make of Prince Frederick a poet-philosopher-king, he was surely not blind to the possibility of becoming, by virtue of being a poet-philosopher, consultant to the King. Voltaire must have felt an additional thrill when, in the letter of 14 September 1738, Frederick added: "Je vous estimerai toujours également, mon cher Protée, soit que vous paraissiez en philosophe, en politique, en historien, en poète, ou sous quelle forme il vous plaira de vous produire" (B. 1545).

That Voltaire was not blind to these possibilities can be seen by casting a look not only at his library but also at his borrowings at the Royal Library during the later part of the Cirey period, a number of which were works in the area of public affairs and diplomacy. Moreover, his intellectual interest was oriented to this study throughout the whole period. I think that we have never attributed to this fact the significance it deserves, in spite of the two excellent studies by Charbonnaud and Morize.[3] In general, we are more or less ac-

---

[3] See R. Charbonnaud, *Les Idées économiques de Voltaire*, and A. Morize, *L'Apologie du luxe au XVIIIᵉ siècle et Le Mondain de Voltaire*. See also I. Wade, *Studies on Voltaire*.

quainted with the main outlines of Voltaire's activity in entering upon this new field, but we are less informed about the way it was integrated with other preoccupations to give a definite direction to Voltaire's thought and action. Specifically, it involved not only the development of a modern economic theory but relation of this theory to a new morality and the further relation of this new morality to political and social responsibility. It was a perfectly logical extension of the "métaphysique morale" discussed above. The problem for Voltaire and Frederick became acute precisely in the 1736-1740 period and was at first fostered by the ambitions of both to play an important role in the making of the new European spirit. To recognize its true importance, it must be seen in that perspective. We must believe Frederick to have been perfectly sincere when he stated that, as Prince (and later King), he was obligated to work for the good of humanity; indeed, even though his ode upon that subject, written just at this time, may not be a particularly good poem, it does express a genuine and important ambition. We must believe, further, that Frederick divined that this position truly reflected Voltaire's and, finally, that Voltaire had constantly reminded his Prince that this devotion to the good of humanity did represent what he called "le fond" of his character. We do not have to believe, however, that this social idealism on the part of both led to a project to work for humanity's progress. Voltaire was certainly very willing to enter upon that project with the Prince. As things turned out, though, the Prince, once having become King, was either unable or unwilling to do so, and the poet, too, encountered difficulties and frustrations, as we shall see. Nevertheless, the ambition on the part of both was genuine, and the activity pursued in realizing it was thereafter continuous, consistent, and, for the most part, organic.

It must be noted, though, that, in Voltaire's case, the intellectual process had already begun before Frederick interceded with his humanitarian doctrines. And, in all probability, Voltaire also had his humanitarianism before Frederick began to talk about it. This matter of priority, however, is beside the point. What is important is that the doctrine already had a substance upon which it could be founded. This base was the theory of luxury as it was developed by Mandeville in the *Fable of the Bees* (1706), by Melon in the

Essai politique sur le commerce (1734), and by Dutot in *Réflexions politiques sur les finances et le commerce* (2 vols., 1738).

Voltaire's involvement started really as a poetic enterprise, a common procedure at the time, especially with him. In 1735, while he was enjoying the mundane life at Cirey with all its luxuries, he was led to sing spontaneously of this good life in the *Mondain* (1736). It was not altogether a personal expression, however. The luxuries Voltaire indulged in at Cirey were more than matched by those which the society of Paris and the easygoing merchants of London and Amsterdam enjoyed. They were amply illustrated by the age of Louis XIV, about which he was now writing, since that age represented for him the very acme of culture and civilization. Morize has brought together magnificently all the forces which vitalized Voltaire's "badinage," which was composed of ideas from Melon and Mandeville and the poet's wide social experience.

The *Mondain* was a genuine outburst of spontaneous poetry, but it was not too far removed from Voltaire's contemporary intellectual interests. Mme du Châtelet was busy with the translation of the *Fable,* and Voltaire was busy incorporating it into his *Traité de métaphysique.* He had only recently completed, in the twenty-fifth of the *Lettres philosophiques,* his attack against rigorism in morality. His little poem now united both moral libertinism and his personal happiness in a sprightly, impertinent defense of the mundane life against such moralists as Pascal, La Bruyère, and Fénelon. In a strict sense, it was a satire of moral rigorism written by a poet who, for once, was supremely happy. We all know how violently it was condemned and how Voltaire vindicated his poem in a *Défense du Mondain,* an apology of luxury in which he fell back upon the economic theories of Mandeville and Melon. Thus, in the two poems, Voltaire moved from a moral defense to an economic defense. The first poem was, in reality, a "défense du Mondain" against those who felt that it was sinful to enjoy the luxuries of a civilization, while the second was an "apologie du luxe" against those who felt that luxuries constituted a threat to the welfare of the state.

Voltaire, in 1738, wrote a little brochure entitled *Observations sur MM. Jean Lass, Melon, et Dutot sur le commerce, le luxe, les monnaies, et les impôts,* which was published in the following year in the *Bibliothèque française.* It consisted in a general commendation of both Melon and Dutot—a relatively difficult task, since the two have contradictory economic theories—with a certain number of mildly expressed doubts: whether the most uncultivated countries have the largest number of beggars; whether Spain became impoverished by its colonies; whether in a war the loss of troops is less dangerous for a country than the increase in taxes, as Melon had stated; or whether the change in value of a currency is always deleterious, as Dutot had affirmed. Voltaire does not seem to get anywhere in these discussions. He was apparently impressed by both works and even expressed the wish to become acquainted with the Abbé de Saint-Pierre's works also. This he did beyond a doubt, beginning with the published ones by 1738. After he had brought out the trial chapter of his *Siècle de Louis XIV*, he received a copy of Saint-Pierre's *Annales* in manuscript along with a letter from the Abbé which was severe but friendly. (A copy of this letter, apparently never published, is in MS 7929 at the public library of Neuchâtel.) Voltaire also read, and at a later time had published, D'Argenson's *Considérations sur le gouvernement de la France*.

The important thing to note here is how Voltaire entered into the field of politics and economics. It should be stressed that Melon's *Essai*, which proved quite valuable to Voltaire, is a nearly complete introduction to the study of economics. In the opening chapters, the author poses the problem of the duties of a legislator. He has, Melon says, three tasks: he must see that the country produces something which is needed by another country; he must look for means to increase the population; and he must find ways to regulate the flow of necessary funds. From these primary duties Melon deduces three important corollaries: wheat is the basis of commerce; along with an increasing population, a fertile land, and a broad domain must go an *esprit de corps*; and whatever measures are taken for one sector of society will necessarily have repercussions on other sectors. Melon concludes that commerce is the exchange of what is superfluous for what is necessary. The more prosperous a country, the more advantage it will find in trading with other countries. The more this trade is free and natural, rather than arbitrary, the more successful it will be. Melon already is making way for the *laissez-faire* doctrine; commerce, he adds significantly, requires only freedom and protection. This trade raises countries out of their "mœurs sauvages" to a more civilized state. Moreover, he judges that conquest and commerce are antithetical. It is commerce which leads to enlightenment. No European country can now expect to dominate Europe by conquest, since there will always be a coalition formed against the aggressor, but a nation can still rise to power by the wisdom of its internal government. Clearly implied in Melon's doctrine is the belief that economics, which had previously been a study in morality, has now progressed to a study in internal politics, as a means of enlightening the people and increasing their well-being with a consequent increase in the bounties of civilization.

The instrument which serves this purpose is luxury, which Melon defines as a "somptuosité extraordinaire que donnent les richesses et la sécurité d'un gouvernement." Melon affirms that it is the necessary effect of a well-policed society. There is a constant progression from necessities to more luxury, as things which once were luxuries become more necessary. He denies that this progression endangers the moral fibre of the nation; it can, he concedes, be dangerous for a small society, but never for a larger one. Always it contributes to further happiness. Therefore, in fostering luxury, the wise legislator is really working for the happiness of the largest number of citizens. By improving the internal affairs of the country, he can rest assured that he is defending the people against famine, contributing to the welfare of an increasing population, and improving the financial status of the nation in the way most in accord with its "genius."

If Voltaire found Melon instructive, he must have found the ideas of the Abbé de Saint-Pierre indispensable. The idea of service rendered to the public by increasing the means of their welfare and their enlightenment was stressed more strongly still by the Abbé, who, as Voltaire noted approvingly, coined the term "bienfaisance" and the phrase "Paradis aux bienfaisants," which he used as a kind of signature to his treatises. Voltaire alternately mocked and praised the Abbé. In general, he was well aware of the Abbé's proposals, which he called the "rêveries d'un homme de bien." He would certainly have heartily subscribed to the priest's definition of politics had he known it, as it can now be found among the Abbé's papers at Neuchâtel, MS 7929: "La politique complète est une science, un art qui embrasse toutes les autres sciences et tous les autres arts et les met en œuvre, pour la plus grande utilité publique; ainsi, c'est la science et l'art le plus important pour augmenter et multiplier les biens et pour diminuer les maux."

There can be no doubt that Voltaire was well acquainted with the Abbé and his ideas. It is clear that what had happened in 1739 is that Voltaire, who wanted to see the *Annales*, had approached Saint-Pierre by sending him a printed copy of the trial chapters from the *Siècle de Louis XIV*. Saint-Pierre had responded by sending a copy of his manuscript, as can be seen in the opening statements of the letter:

2 octobre 1739, au Palais Royal.

Je vous remercie monsieur de l'ouvrage que vous m'avez envoyé. En revanche en voilà un autre en manuscrit un peu plus ample que l'imprimé.

Je ne l'ai fait qu'en faveur des excellans auteurs pour les inviter a mieux choizir qu'ils ne font pour l'utilité publique le sujet de leurs ouvrages.

Je vous dirai même que lors que je l'ai revu l'année passée, j'ai pluzieurs fois pensé à vous en dizant c'est dommage qu'un tel génie n'ait pas vizé plus haut en sortant du collège et n'ait pas de bonne heure examiné quels sont les sujets les plus importans au bonheur de chaque homme en particulier et de la société en général morale et politique.

Mais comme il est encore dans la vigueur de l'esprit ne pouvoit-il pas se mettre bientôt à niveau de nos meilleurs moralistes et de nos meilleurs politiques et ne plus donner que des histoires des vies des plus grans hommes et des histoires des règnes des rois illustres.

Voilà ce que j'ai pansé aprez avoir lu votre ouvrage sur Charles Douze seulement de la première édition. J'ai pansé un peu plus profondément que d'autres sur la morale et sur la politique mais je n'ai pas animé mes pensées en comparaison de ce que vous savez animer les vôtres, or quelle déference pour l'agrément et pour l'utilité des lecteurs.

Destinez le reste de votre vie non plus à divertir les dames d'esprit et d'autres enfans, songez à gouverner ceux qui nous gouvernent. Enfin donnez nous des modèles d'histoire. Il est vrai qu'il faut pour cela une grande ambition et une grande pasience et je ne sais encore, si vous en avez assez. Essayez et laissez là vos ouvrages de *gloriole* pour marcher ainsi vers le sublime de la gloire. Paradis aux bienfaizans.

Saint-Pierre's letter to Voltaire opens up possibilities of relationship between the two which have never been adequately explored.

Coming at a moment when the ambition of the poet was already being fired by the enthusiasm of the Prince and containing direct instructions about how to devote oneself to the welfare of a country, it could not easily have been overlooked by Voltaire. Saint-Pierre was certainly one of the founders of the science of government, in both its theoretical and its practical aspects. History has recorded that he was the originator of innumerable projects, which he distributed very carefully among men of influence. He was, in his way, one of the most clandestine writers of the time. He wandered in circles—the French Academy, the Club de l'Entresol, the salons, not to mention his intimacy with Dubois, D'Argenson, and Fleury—where influence could best be exerted. His views were, therefore, of some consequence to the poet. That they were usually incorporated in articles resembling brochures, ranging from two to twenty pages, added to this influence.

Some of these views were surprisingly like those the poet himself entertained at the time. The Abbé held, for instance, that he who poses as a political scientist has the duty to counsel those who are in authority. He insisted in his proposals that all observations should be made with the stated intention of increasing the happiness of the nation and rendering it more durable. He counseled a total renunciation of all conquest in war and maintenance of the status quo. This policy would avoid war and the tremendous public debts which war entails. These ideas—avoidance of war, attempt to arbitrate important issues, avoidance of any balance of power theory in favor of a congress of nations, economy in government, development of colonies, and emphasis on increasing the happiness and prosperity of the people and continuing that happiness—were not foolish ideas at all and were very much in accord with Voltaire's.

The Abbé also held Voltaire's "great man" theory: he believed that the historian can always draw moral conclusions from the study of leaders for the edification of the public. He had, moreover, a full program for the education of the statesman. It consisted in defining the duties of the great man and in commending his determination to contribute to the happiness of the citizens. This required distinguishing between the evils of the state, its civil and foreign wars, and its real achievements, between internal tranquility over long periods of time and years of peace outside, between useful regulations and profitable establishments. External prosperity could be obtained in foreign relations by subscribing to the "Diète Européenne," the system of arbitration promulgated by Henry IV, also Voltaire's great hero. As a means of procuring this good internal government, it was necessary to create and pursue with intensity the science of government. The good Abbé wrote: "Il est très important de favoriser, et d'encourager par tous les moyens les plus eficaces les progrès de la science du gouvernement parmi les sujets, à proportion qu'ils sont plus importants au bonheur de la société que les progrès des autres sciences." The core of his educational program lay in the combining of the human sciences—history, politics, and "la morale"—to foster organic civilization.

Voltaire learned much also from D'Argenson's *Considérations sur le gouvernement de la France*, which he had Cramer publish at a later date. He now read the treatise in manuscript. It was an uncommonly advanced essay, the author having actually entitled it in the original manuscript (now deposited at the Affaires Etrangères) "jusqu'à quel point la démocratie est possible en France." The author explained this title in an opening statement revealing the plan of the work: "on examinera à cette effet les différents gouvernements des souverainetés de l'Europe, et on montrera par cet examen que l'administration populaire sous l'autorité du souverain, ne diminue point la puissance publique, qu'elle l'augmente même, et qu'elle seroit la source du bonheur des peuples." It was D'Argenson's theory that the governments of Europe were practically all mixed governments, although they conformed to three types: monarchy, aristocracy, democracy. He noted that the pure type of monarchy could lead to tyranny, while aristocracy and democracy could easily lead to anarchy. He asserted that the best kind of mixed government would be a royalty with some aristocracy and democracy, such as England had. He felt, nonetheless, that a democracy on the order of that found in Holland, which acted through elected deputies whose duty it was to provide means for achieving the desires of the largest number of citizens, had some merit, although he noted that in critical moments it inclined to slowness of decision. Switzerland he called a "pure" democracy. This way of distinguishing between a democracy, an aristocracy, and a "pure" democracy became very common in the eighteenth century. Practically always, it was applied to Switzerland, to Holland, or to an ideal democratic state which Switzerland and Holland were thought to approach. D'Argenson had no desire to transform France into a "pure" democracy. What he had in mind was a democratic local government which would be affiliated with a central monarchy; it was his theory that those who are granted the greatest freedom possible at the local level to manage their affairs will act more intelligently through their assemblies than upon the order of the central government. It was what had been called the "droit de commune," which was, he stated, a "véritable démocratie qui réside au milieu de la monarchie." As he read political history, the tendency was more and more toward increasing the rights of the people in contrast to the rights of the nobility. He approved this tendency, feeling that justice would eventually win out anyway and that reason would move mankind more and more toward equality. He noted that democracy is friendly to monarchy, whereas aristocracy is inimical. The statesman, after an analysis of all the principal European states, concluded that the land should belong after all to those who cultivate it and that all democratic states would undoubtedly insist upon this distribution if there were a reform in the law. This freedom, he suspected, would doubtless bring about other liberties.

Voltaire's ideas, even his later ideas on politics, can be considerably clarified if they are examined in the light of D'Argenson's work. In the meantime, the *Considérations*, as well as Frederick's treatise, offered to the poet a kind of textbook for study.

Very soon thereafter, Voltaire himself was entrusted by D'Argenson with a mission in the War of the Austrian Succession. Frederick was now King. The poet apparently felt that, if he was to play his role as statesman, it was not enough to be acquainted with some popular economic and political treatises. Recalling that Lenglet had stated that the best historian was one who was well versed in the practical aspects of political and economic affairs, the poet now plunged into a whole bibliography on foreign affairs. For acquiring diplomatic facility, he studied the Wicquefort, a guide for the making of ambassadors, and the Silhon. For a deeper knowledge of the situation in Europe, he borrowed from the Royal Library a whole array of works dedicated to bringing together this information (see my *In Search of a New Voltaire*, pp. 64-70). Among these works were:

Du-F. de Francheville, *Histoire générale et particulière des finances*, 3 vols., in-4°, Paris, 1738, and his *Annals of Europe ... for 1739*, 2 vols., in-8°, London, 1740-1741; Dupuy, *Traités touchants les droits du roi*, in-fol., Paris, 1655; Mably, *Le Droit public de l'Europe fondé sur les traitez conclus jusqu'en l'année 1740*, 2 vols., in-12°, La Haye, 1746; Rousset de Missy, *Recueil historique d'actes, négociations, Mémoires et traitez, depuis la paix d'Utrecht, jusqu'au second congrès de Cambray inclusivement*, 21 vols. in 23, in-8°, La Haye, 1728-1754, his *Le Procès entre la Grande-Bretagne et l'Espagne, ou Recueil des traités, conventions, mémoires et autres pièces touchant les démêléz entre ces deux couronnes*, in-8°, La Haye, 1740, and, finally, his *Etat politique de l'Europe*, 12 vols., in-8°, La Haye, 1739-1746.

PHYSICS

The Prince was relatively slow in taking up the study of physics. He was interested to the point of commending the *Eléments*, or rather that part of the *Eléments* concerning attraction which Voltaire sent him through Keyserlingk. He procured copies of the Amsterdam edition and promised at intervals to study it. His rare references to it, however, add little to the dialogue. He confessed freely that he found mathematics difficult and unattractive. Eventually, though, he ordered the *Mémoires* of the Académie des Sciences and promised, on his return to Remusberg from the army maneuvers, to devote himself to the study of physics. He seemed always in 1738 and the early part of 1739 to be engaged in something more interesting to him. In a letter to Voltaire, he dropped the remark that he was too young and too inexperienced to take sides in scientific discussions. Besides, he confessed, there were fully as many uncertainties in physics as in metaphysics.

However, his correspondence with the Lady Newton seems to have given him the necessary encouragement to enter upon a serious investigation of physics. Although he wrote to Mme du Châtelet on 23 January 1739 that, as soon as he returned to Remusberg, "j'entrerai dans la carrière de la physique," he still remained in the region of scientific generalities: "Les sciences doivent être considérées comme des moyens qui nous donnent plus de capacité pour remplir nos devoirs" (B. 1743). However, on 3 February 1739, he declared that he was now making some progress in physics. He had reviewed all the experiments with the pneumatic pump and devised others. He proposed a new theory on the cause of the winds, which he suggested should be attributed to the pressure of the sun upon our atmosphere. Frederick's scientific activity led Voltaire to predict that Remusberg was on the point of becoming an Academy of Sciences. He approved Frederick's notion that Mme du Châtelet erred in assigning forest fires to the friction of the trees and added that the memoirs of Frederick were full of interesting, bold research, as well as philosophical ideas. Mme du Châtelet, for her part, while complimenting the Prince for having thought of the watch experiment, informed him that it had already been performed and described in the *Philosophical Transactions*. She asserted that the great unsolved problem in physics was elasticity, which some attributed to attraction but which she was inclined to believe was another quality of matter. Voltaire repeated the watch experiment (B. 1823) without any positive result. Moreover, he failed to find any reasoning which would justify Frederick's theory about the cause of the winds.

The inference one must draw from Frederick's letter of 22 March 1739 is that the Prince had now taken up the study of physics energetically. The results of his study appear, however, to have been very meagre, and he admitted himself that he was persuaded we would never discover the secrets of nature. At the same time, he agreed with Voltaire that the most essential part of philosophy is "la morale," not "la physique," because it contributes to the happiness of man. He asserted repeatedly around this time that the ruler must accept as his duty to provide for the happiness of his subjects, even insisting that a king is a king of humanity. His ode on tolerance is an extreme statement of the ruler's duties.

L'ANTI-MACHIAVEL

Suddenly, Frederick announced that he was contemplating a work on Machiavelli's *Prince*. The situation brought about by Frederick's new preoccupation could not, from Voltaire's point of view, have been more propitious. The whole dialogue, which had started with poetry and which had embraced metaphysics, "métaphysique morale," history, physics, and, finally, politics, had now come full circle and brought up the very topic which Voltaire had envisaged from the very first letter. Frederick, in the poet's plans, was to learn the art of ruling from a broad humanistic training centering on the art of poetry. He was to be a molder of humanity, after having learned the art of poetry and the humanistic arts. Voltaire must have congratulated himself that the education of the Prince was finished, since he was now prepared to defend the "Prince-philosophe" against the onslaughts of Machiavellianism. No wonder the poet replied to the Prince that the desire to refute Machiavelli was "bien plus digne d'un prince tel que vous que de réfuter de simples philosophes" (B. 1886). He added that a prince must naturally be preoccupied with the knowledge of man and with his duties as prince. And he concluded that the Prince's work would surely be an instruction to other princes.

During the rest of 1739, Voltaire exhorted Frederick time and again to carry out his intention. In a letter of 25 April 1739, he urged his young friend to write his attack against the "infâme politique qui érige le crime en vertu." It is evident, however, that, once started, Frederick needed very little encouragement from his mentor. On 16 May 1739, he announced that he was busy composing notes to Machiavelli's *Prince* and that he had begun a work which would entirely refute the Italian's maxims. He promised a manuscript in three months, and, indeed, he must have been making considerable progress, since one month later he spoke of advancing steadily. His inquiry, though, slowed his speed, and soon he was complaining that he was forced to read many works in preparation for his attack upon Machiavelli. Voltaire, who knew well some of the difficulties attendant upon a study of this kind, answered that he felt sure the preparation would produce good results and advised Frederick to add to his reading list the *Discours politiques* of Gordon (B. 1955). For her part, Mme du Châtelet, while expressing regret that this new interest would prevent Frederick from entering seriously upon a study of physics, added her encouragement (B. 1956). Frederick replied to the Cirey couple that he had already been advised to seek refutation of Machiavelli in the "notes politiques" of Amelot de la Houssaye and in Gordon's translation of Tacitus, but that his plan of attack was entirely different from the approach of these two authors (B. 1962). He reassured Mme du Châtelet in the meantime that, although he was busy with his rebuttal, he would procure relaxation from this task in poetry and physics. He was finding his schedule a little complicated, though, he said, since he did not have the ability to be universal in outlook. Voltaire was now more enthusiastic than the Prince. In September 1739, he announced to Frederick that he had just bought a copy of Machiavelli's works, so as to be better informed. About a month later, on 10 October 1739, the Prince disclosed that he was now refuting the author of the *Prince* chapter by chapter. In the meantime, Voltaire continued his reading of Machiavelli and confessed (B. 1990) that the sections of the work he found most repugnant were the chapter on cruelty and the chapter on keeping one's word (Chapter XVIII). Voltaire now saw more clearly than ever that his Prince was destined to refute this work and thereby bring about the return of human happiness. On 27 October 1739, Frederick wrote Emilie that he expected to complete the refutation in two weeks. He now began to have some uneasiness about the composition, after having surmounted the difficulties of assembling the material. He felt that the outline he had made was inadequate and, as a result, badly organized and digested. Still, with his letter, he sent the "Avant-propos," noting that some of the material required severe condemnation, while other parts permitted a lighter touch. He now promised to send to Cirey the rebuttal chapter by chapter.

On 6 November 1739, Frederick wrote Voltaire that the *Anti-Machiavel* was finished and that he was now making a smoother draft in the hope of composing a work worthy of posterity. It was at this moment that he sent his mentor five chapters which he had already revised, with the request that Voltaire aid him in correcting the manuscript. He promised that other chapters would follow in short order. On 4 December 1739, he sent his tutor the first twelve chapters, with an urgent request that Voltaire correct the French. Voltaire replied, on 28 December 1739, that he had received the twelve chapters at Brussels. He reported to his student that he had devoured them at once and that he was certain that, for the good of the world, the work would have to be published, so that the public might see for itself the antidote to Machiavelli's pernicious doctrine written by a royal hand. In this letter (B. 2012), Voltaire requested of his Prince that he be permitted to write the preface and serve as editor. In the meantime, Mme du Châtelet, who had also read the twelve chapters, complimented the Prince for having written a work which would be the true source of human happiness (B. 2014). On 6 January 1740, Frederick sent five more chapters and promised in due time the last four. He added that it was his intention now to publish the work anonymously, chiefly because he had written it "librement" and only "pour la vérité." He disclaimed any other ambition than to serve the public "sans attendre de lui ni récompense ni louange." By the tenth of the month, however, he had not yet completed the last four chapters. On 26 January 1740, Voltaire acknowledged having received Chapter XXIII but said he still lacked Chapters XXII and XXIV. It was not until 3 February 1740, that Frederick completed the revised draft of the *Anti-Machiavel* and begged his mentor to send him his judgment upon it. He promised to correct any part not approved by Voltaire and reiterated his desire to have the work appear anonymously, since he had spoken about the princes of Europe. On 23 February 1740, Voltaire acknowledged receipt of the remainder of the work. He expressed his admiration for it but confessed that he found some of the chapters, especially those where Frederick had begun by quoting Machiavelli, a bit long. These quotes seemed all the more superfluous since the Prince intended to print the full text alongside the commentary. Further, Voltaire noted some places where Frederick opposed Machiavelli when the latter's argument had been twisted. In the meantime, Voltaire set to work sketching the preface which he had promised to provide. Mme du Châtelet, for her part, insisted that the work would have to be published—anonymously, if the Prince so wished—for the happiness of the world. Voltaire asked, on 10 March 1740, instructions for printing the *Anti-Machiavel*, especially whether Frederick wished the Amelot de la Houssaye translation alongside the commentary. The more confident he was that Frederick would sooner or later refute the Italian by his conduct, the more certain he was that the refutation should be published.

On 1 June 1740, Voltaire, after having notified Frederick that the correcting had been completed, wrote to Van Duren that he had a manuscript, "une espèce de réfutation du *Prince*," and stated the conditions under which it could be published. Obviously, Van Duren was slow in replying, because, on 5 June 1740, Voltaire wrote him a letter urging him to answer at once. The same day, he reminded Frederick that he had already notified him that the *Anti-Machiavel* was ready to be published. He had equalized the length of the chapters and the commentaries, had added a few paragraphs and some sentences, and now sought permission to suppress a section in Chapter XXI on the religious disputes. The following day, a week after the event, the Prince, now King Frederick II, broke the news of his father's death to Voltaire.

Biographers of Voltaire have not forgotten to detail at some length his eagerness to get the volume of the *Anti-Machiavel* printed and Frederick's desire to have the edition suspended. It is evident from Voltaire's letters to Van Duren that he anticipated some reluctance on the part of the King. One has to grant that he used the art of persuasion to an extreme in an effort to prolong in the King the qualities he had worked so hard to inculcate in the Prince. Besterman 2110 is a model of diplomacy, and so is Besterman 2128 (5 July 1740):

L'ouvrage digne de Marc-Aurèle est bientôt tout imprimé. J'en ay parlé à votre majesté dans cinq lettres. Je l'ay envoyé selon la permission expresse de votre majesté, et voylà Mr. de Camas qui me dit qu'il y a un ou deux endroits qui déplairoient à certaines puissances. Mais moy j'ai pris la liberté d'adoucir les deux endroits, et j'oserais bien répondre que le livre fera autant d'honneur à son auteur quelqu'il soit, qu'il sera utile au genre humain. Cependant s'il avoit pris un remords à votre majesté, il faudroit qu'elle eût la bonté de se hâter de me donner ses ordres, car dans un pays comme la Hollande, on ne peut arrêter l'empressement avide d'un libraire qui sent qu'il a sa fortune sous presse.

To tell the truth, Voltaire's activity and his affirmations concerning the King began now to show some inconsistency. His every move in regard to Frederick was amazingly courteous and persuasive, whereas his dealings with Van Duren gave every sign that he was expecting a change in the King. One senses Voltaire had a deep-laid plan to arrange things in such a way that the change would not be easy. It is true that he did not exhibit any uneasiness to D'Argental, to whom he wrote that, although he was not certain the King would add a royal magnificence to his other qualities, he could venture to predict that he would continue to possess philosophy, simplicity, an unfailing devotion to his friends, a stoic firmness, and a charming gentleness, unfailing justice, a constant application to his work, love of the arts, and extraordinary talents (B. 2135). The judgment was a bit premature. Two days later, Frederick started proceedings to stop the edition of the *Anti-Machiavel* in Holland. The difficulties involved in carrying out this desire were so great, though, that, at the beginning of August, the King left Voltaire free to continue the publication if he thought it best to do so (B. 2148). This permission Voltaire used not only to continue the first edition but to prepare a second. Even in October 1740, he wrote optimistically to Camas: "J'ai tout lieu d'espérer que la conduite du roi justifiera en tout l'*Anti-Machiavel* du Prince."

However, events marched swiftly thereafter. Frederick wrote Voltaire on 26 October 1740 that the Emperor had died and that his death was upsetting all his pacifist ideas. At the end of his letter he added that he was very obliged to him for printing the Machiavelli and that he was unable to work upon it since he was swamped with other matters. On 31 October 1740 (B. 2217), Voltaire must have begun to ask himself some very pertinent questions about the King's intentions. In a letter to Hénault, he declared that, to the extent he detested "l'infâme superstition" which dishonors states, to the same extent he adored real virtue, which he claimed he had discovered in the Prince and in his book. But he added immediately that, if ever the King should betray this trust, if ever the King was unworthy of himself, he would weep and would no longer love him. It is quite apparent that Voltaire's mind was not at rest. Almost every letter to the King in October and early November urged him to permit another edition of the *Anti-Machiavel*. Voltaire naïvely gave as excuse the faulty editions, a few passages some diplomats had taken amiss; but way down in his heart was the desire to see the King reaffirm the ideas of the Prince. It was a desperate attempt to defend the model prince he had worked so hard to form, but it all came to naught. On 7 November 1740, the King wrote him (B. 2223):

J'ai lu le *Machiavel* d'un bout à l'autre; mais à vous dire le vrai je n'en suis pas tout à fait content, et j'ai résolu de changer ce qui ne m'y plaisait point, et d'en faire une nouvelle édition, sous mes yeux, à Berlin. J'ai pour cet effet donné un article pour les gazettes, par lequel l'auteur de l'*Essai* désavoue les deux impressions. Je vous demande pardon; mais je n'ai pu faire autrement, car il y a tant d'étranger dans votre édition, que ce n'est plus mon ouvrage. J'ai trouvé les chapitres XV et XVI tout différents de ce que je voulais qu'ils fussent: ce sera l'occupation de cet hiver que de refondre cet ouvrage.

Suddenly, Titus metamorphosed himself into Nero.

There are several observations which should be made here. The general conclusion which is always made is that Frederick, who in the *Anti-Machiavel* had condemned the *Prince*, once having become King, repudiated his condemnation and followed political principles which Machiavelli would readily have approved. The obvious implication of Frederick's march into Silesia is that it was just the kind of move which Machiavelli had discussed in his *Prince* and that Frederick's own Machiavellianism in practice invalidated immediately his anti-Machiavellianism in theory. The old problem of wanting to be what our friends see in us reappeared. Since Voltaire tried so hard to instill a sense of political virtue in the Prince, it could be expected that the Prince would have tried to establish his sincere regard for political virtue. This is precisely what the Prince did: everywhere in the correspondence with Voltaire he tried to assume an attitude of moral responsibility, everywhere he admitted that a good prince must work for the happiness, the prosperity, and the welfare of his people. Frederick even agreed with Voltaire that a prince must do the same thing for humanity.

In reality, Frederick had modeled his attitude as well as he could upon the political literature and upon the behavior of contemporary or near-contemporary princes. The whole dialogue concerning the actions of Charles XII, Peter the Great, Louis XIV, and the moral rightness or wrongness of their actions offered the young Prince specific cases upon which he could build moral judgments. It was another instance of "history teaching by example." Frederick provided analyses of these cases to achieve a political philosophy in the same way that Machiavelli had produced in the *Prince* analyses of the Sforza, Alexander VI, and César Borgia. Frederick undoubtedly drew more idealistic conclusions than Machiavelli. He was perfectly sincere when he wrote, "Ce que je médite contre le Machiavellisme, est proprement une suite de *la Henriade*." His source was not only Voltaire's epic, though. Professor Fleischauer has shown that the young Prince drew much of his material from the *Lettres philosophiques,* the *Mondain,* the *Eléments,* and even *Micromégas.* But he also had recourse to Fénelon, Bayle, Montesquieu, and his own *Considérations sur l'état présent du corps politique de l'Europe*. Indeed, it has been noted that the positive aspects of the *Anti-Machiavel* are merely extensions of Frederick's *Considérations*.

It is undoubtedly true that the *Anti-Machiavel* was begun as a refutation of Machiavelli's *Prince*. Both Voltaire's preface and Frederick's "Avant-propos" make this intention abundantly clear. What these two introductions do not make so clear is what specifically is wrong with Machiavelli's maxims. Voltaire, in his preface, extols Frederick's desire to bring mankind back to virtue. He speaks highly of his student's thoughts, but without stating what they are or attempting to show what their worth is. He affirms very glibly that these thoughts will serve to give Frederick lessons in his chosen field and that they may be the source of man's happiness; but he does not indicate, insofar as can be seen, how this desirable effect may be obtained. He declares Frederick's book better written than Machiavelli's and assures that it will be an antidote to the Italian's poisons, but we never know what the poisons are nor how their effect will be nullified. As a matter of fact, Voltaire concedes that the book is only partially an attack against the Italian, since the latter preaches crime only in a part of the *Prince*. The result, Voltaire adds, is that Frederick's work contains reflections upon, rather than a refutation of, the *Prince*. Voltaire uses much of his preface to condemn Amelot de la Houssaye for defending Machiavelli by using Juste Lipse. Most of this condemnation is carried out by attacking the integrity of Juste Lipse. Even here, Voltaire's argument is difficult to follow. He declares that Juste Lipse has spoken in favor of a doctrine which is "funeste au genre humain." He asserts that both piety and religion are opposed to such a doctrine. He affirms that Juste Lipse changed his religion too frequently to be a good Christian, calls his book contemptible, and attacks Amelot for quoting imperfectly from it. All this, needless to say, is quite beside the point. Voltaire does conclude, however, that Machiavelli taught sovereigns how to be wicked, approved tyranny, and offered, as model princes, bad characters.

Frederick's diatribe against the Italian is fully as vague as Voltaire's. Machiavelli has corrupted politics. He has tried to destroy the precepts of true morality. His morality is pernicious, and he seeks the destruction of humanity. He incites to iniquity and to crime. The *Prince* is one of the most dangerous books in the world. It naturally attracts princes and those interested in politics. It flatters the passions of those who want to rule. It perverts princes who should govern, administer justice, and be an example to their subjects and an image of the Divinity. Frederick admits that kings often, without Machiavelli, are "dangerous" and "funestes"; he deplores that their crimes make the whole nation suffer; and he maintains that a king who followed the precepts of Machiavelli, his "affreuse politique," would be a monster. Forgetting this argument, he launches into a defense of good kings (the Tituses, the Trajans, the Antonins), while admitting the presence of bad kings (the Neros, the Caligulas, and the Tiberiuses). He concludes by asserting that only a good king should find a place in history. Thus, Machiavelli's *Prince* would cease to infect the schools of politics, and justice, goodness, and prudence would become preferable to cruelty, horror, and treachery. It is useless to insist upon the puerility of this diatribe.

CONCLUSION TO THE FREDERICK-VOLTAIRE DIALOGUE

The dialogue which Frederick and Voltaire entered upon in 1736 and which continued until the moment the Prince mounted the throne in 1740 thus turned upon the major subjects which interested Voltaire in his reeducation: metaphysics, morality, history, physics and, above all, poetry. The Prince undertook to equip himself in each subject at the moment Voltaire was developing it. He was beyond a doubt less competent in each subject than his tutor, as Mme du Châtelet pointed out. It was she who designated the Prince an "assez grand métaphysicien" in contrast to Voltaire, who had now become in her eyes a "grand métaphysicien." There was always about the same degree of difference in the other subjects as well.

Assessing the intellectual merit of each is not precisely the frame of reference in which to put the problem. For Frederick, whose occupation was that of ruler, all these discussions were so much cultural relaxation, but he was sufficiently serious not to accept a superficial approach. What he wanted above everything was to learn the art of writing French verse. For him, Voltaire's great service consisted in giving him instruction in that art. Voltaire, on the other hand, wanted to give him that instruction which would make of him a model ruler.

Frederick wanted to be the poet; Voltaire preferred to think of him as the "poète-philosophe" and of himself as the "philosophe-poète." He saw in his Prince, above all else, a future King to be instructed, and he judged himself quite competent to carry on the lesson.

This was doubtless their way of conceiving of the situation. What actually occurred was somewhat different. The Prince's alert mind encouraged the poet to pursue further and further the reeducation which he had undertaken. Voltaire worked hard to correct his deficiencies and to give himself the appearance of excellence which Frederick was prepared to grant that he had. Altogether, it was a good arrangement from which both parties profited. Frederick got the satisfaction he wanted from the verses he learned to write. He probably obtained from his tutor as well a more generally intellectual approach. And, if he did not eventually turn into the "Roi-philosophe" Voltaire would have liked to see, he did absorb some of the lessons Voltaire thought a philosopher-king should have. On the other hand, Frederick was so successful in persuading Voltaire that he was the "Uomo universale," as well as the greatest poet, that the latter actually felt encouraged to transform himself into an encyclopedic man. One should not give too much credence to the story of the origin of the *Dictionnaire philosophique,* but, still, it could be that Frederick was the one who first had the idea of its inception. At all events, even though the intellectual impact of Frederick upon his tutor was less important and perhaps less precise than Mme du Châtelet's, it was hardly less intense or less effective.

4. THE DIVERSITY OF ACTIVITY AT CIREY

THE TWO OUTSTANDING FEATURES of the Cirey episode were the intensity and diversity of its activity. To move from poetry to philosophy would have been sufficient to tax all the energies of a normal human being, even if he consented to drop poetry entirely and devote himself to the establishment of a philosophical position. This, of course, Voltaire was unwilling to do; consequently, one of his tasks consisted in making poetry and drama more philosophical still, even to the point of first presenting his understanding of a philosophical problem in prose and then presenting the same problem in poetry. For instance, after a discussion of free will in the *Traité*, he repeated the same discussion all over again in the *Discours en vers sur l'homme*. This procedure could be carried on very effectively, since the kind of poetry he espoused lent itself already to a rather wide intellectual content. Indeed, one of his earliest epistles, the *Epître à Uranie* (1722), was a philosophical poem. All that was required, from Voltaire's point of view, to turn a poem into a philosophical discourse was to increase its thought content.

It was more difficult to make the drama philosophical. Voltaire, however, tried the same technique, increasing the thought content to such an extent that we now often regard it as propaganda. Here he seized upon a characteristic of French drama: its tendency, as he said, to be a series of conversations. What he did was select the subject of conversation and produce a dialogue which was an amplification of the subject. But he did not have to pursue that method, since he could profit equally from a second characteristic of French drama: its practice of introducing at dramatic moments in the play "sentences," or what he called "maximes" in speaking of Boileau's epistles. Voltaire could reinforce the thought content of these maxims and obtain a similar effect. Indeed, he carried out both of these procedures to the point where his plays took on the air of a religious, social, or political problem and his conversations (that is, a scene) took on an increased number of maxims. The net effect was a shift from the importance of situation and character to what is said. By this means Voltaire frequently expressed his own opinions, which he literally put into the mouth of the protagonists. We are inclined to regard these moves as mistakes, since we believe in the inner autonomy of the work of art. In Voltaire's time, this was apparently not the accepted way of looking at things.

There resulted a phenomenon which we should keep in mind: around 1738, practically everything which Voltaire published had the trait of turning philosophical. The *Lettres philosophiques* (1734) set the pattern, but the poem, the drama, and, finally, the *conte* assumed as its greatest asset a philosophical tone. Even Voltaire's correspondence, as Lanson has shown, became philosophical. The elements were already clearly discernible: conversation, wit, a subject of some seriousness, an intellectual approach stressing precision, clarity, and order, a body of maxims, and often a dialogue form. These were the ingredients of the essay, the *épître*, the satire, the play, and even the letter. Looked at from the other side, the conversation of the dramatic scene became the dialogue, the prose letter took the place of the Horatian poem, history adopted the tone and structure of drama, and the maxim took on explosive thought content, particularly when presented in the style of wit, a device used to bring out the contradictions, paradoxes, tensions, and ambiguities of thought.

Voltaire, however, had to cope with more difficult problems than this shift from poetic genres to prose genres. He was forced, by the increase in thought content, to struggle with the problem of what constitutes philosophy. Hitherto, a poet had been a philosopher because he was a free-thinker. The poet's philosophy, as Descartes had explained, consisted in presenting "by means of enthusiasm" and "the force of the imagination" a way of life. Horace long ago had set the model. Now, however, it was not sufficient to present a way of life: poetry was no longer free-thinking. It was reflection upon the experience of living, all right, but the reflection was based upon knowledge. It was not free but, instead, conditioned by the facts of life. These facts took their source in the external world, or in the inner world of man, or in the succession of worlds which man had lived. Science of nature, human sciences, and history—these were the ultimate sources of knowledge. The eighteenth century, and Voltaire foremost among his contemporaries, did not accept philosophy as merely the knowledge of first principles. They believed in a metaphysics as many of us do, but they felt that the goal of metaphysics lay in the sciences of nature ("la physique") and in the sciences of man ("la morale"). Astronomy, biology, chemistry, physics; Biblical criticism, history, politics, economics, ethics, psychology—these were the materials of philosophy. Voltaire had caught a glimpse of this attitude in England. He was now threatened with being swamped beneath the breadth and variety of philosophy, understood in these terms. His statement that all knowledge leads eventually to "la morale" was just a device for putting some order into a terribly diverse situation.

These two qualities of Voltaire, intensity and diversity, are clearly visible to one who scans the correspondence of the Cirey period (1734-1749), particularly to one who studies carefully the first four years (1734-1738) of that period. It is as if the poet turning philosopher had suddenly decided to give himself a totally modern, liberal education.

Voltaire's activities during 1734, for instance, disclose that he was fully cognizant that he was unprepared intellectually to pursue to the fullest the merging of French and English culture into a European way of life. His interest in Charles XII and Peter the Great, however much it consisted of a genuine curiosity in contemporary events and a certain attraction to their dramatic qualities, and even a philosophical approach to the lessons to be learned from them, was motivated primarily by his desire to test out the limits of this European civilization which he was surprised to have discovered. His geographical horizons, which, until then, had been limited to Holland, France, and England, were extended to the Scandinavian countries, Germany, Russia, and Turkey. The establishment of the limits of European civilization was roughly accomplished by this move, but Voltaire was keenly aware that this represented only in a very perfunctory way what constituted the unity of Europe. Of more importance were the historical forces which, since the Renaissance, had been forming it. Thus, the subjects which had to be explored if one was to pursue this concept of the making of a unified European civilization were quite apparent: science and philosophy, arts and letters, geography and history, manners and customs, and, over and above them all, an ultimate philosophy of civilization embracing simultaneously science, an aesthetic, history, and an organic morality.

Voltaire's career was certainly cut out for him eventually by the English experience, and the general perspective of that career, as well as the deficiencies which he would have to overcome, should have been clear to him from the start. It is not at all certain, however, how fully he grasped, in 1734, the extent of the undertaking. From the evidence we have, we may infer that he understood the frame of reference in which he had cast the *Lettres philosophiques*. It is possible that he understood also what was philosophical about the *Lettres*, although I am by no means sure he did. It is certain that he understood the cultural mission of France in arts and letters and its role in the making of the new Europe. He understood less well the role of England, but he recognized that this lack of understanding came from his own limited experience in science and philosophy. In general, the whole organic set-up of his concept of a European civilization undoubtedly appeared to him to be a problem in the merging of philosophy and poetry. But one has to be adept in both areas before assuming that they can be merged, and this Voltaire was not. It was for this reason that he made a definite attempt to correct his deficiency in philosophy. He had already, to be sure, taken a step in this direction by undertaking, with the cooperation of Maupertuis, the composition of the letters on Newton, Bacon, and Locke in the *Lettres philosophiques*.

The writing and publication of the *Lettres* made more imperative the continuation of philosophical study. At the beginning of 1734, even before its publication, Voltaire thought of putting in writing his "songes métaphysiques" but complained that the persecutions attendant upon the too philosophical English letters prevented his acceding to this desire. He also felt incompetent to pursue this study. To Maupertuis, whose manuscript he had been perusing, he wrote (B. 675) that the more he reasoned, the more uncertain he became, but that he was certain he would like to live in freedom and converse with those who were wise. He concluded that he did not know what matter was, and was not at all sure that there were substances, but that he did know that he was a thinking being. On 29 April, he again wrote to Maupertuis (B. 708), this time to tell him that the persecution for the *Lettres philosophiques* was coming from the partisans of vortices and innate ideas. Cartesians, Malebranchists, and Jansenists were all jumping on him, he reported. Evidently, he was fully aware of the situation, which was, to be sure, of his own making. Having sided with Locke and Newton against Descartes and Pascal, he was hard put to defend himself and was thereby forced into a deeper study of these philosophers.

Voltaire's defense of the *Lettres* was characterized by an attack on the opposition. On 22 June, he wrote a letter to La Condamine (B. 737), justifying himself against the condemnation of Parlement and accusing its members of being incapable of judging the articles on Newton and Locke. All the difficulty had occurred because of the use of words, he explained, particularly Newton's word "attraction," which was taboo in Paris. "Ce sont les termes et non les choses qui révoltent l'esprit humain." Voltaire was convinced, in addition, that he had been condemned because of the flippant way he had treated the subject; but, had he not done so, he argued, nobody would have read the work. The charge of atheism brought against him had been occasioned by his attack upon Pascal and his espousal of Locke's ideas. For having asserted that the human mind could not prove that it was impossible for God to unite thought with matter, as Locke had maintained, and for having declared further that the human mind was incapable of proving two natures in man, contrary to what Pascal had said, Voltaire had been pronounced an atheist. He now maintained that there was no proof of original sin either, except through revelation. Philosophically speaking, there was no more chance of proving original sin by the miseries of men than of proving that horses have to draw carriages because at times in the past they ate too many oats.

These quibblings seem totally unimportant, but they do indicate that Voltaire was attempting to prove to himself that there was such a thing as philosophy. Shortly after sending the letter of defense to La Condamine, he wrote to Formont (Formont the philosopher) that he had reread Locke and that he was convinced that Locke could never have produced his work in France. He regretted that the English philosopher had not taken more liberties and had not exposed other truths which he suppressed because of his moderation. Voltaire now announced that he was continuing Locke's work: "J'ai voulu me rendre compte à moi-même de mon existence, et voir si je pouvais me faire quelques principes certains" (B. 741). He wrote to Cideville (B. 776), requesting him to tell Formont that he had completed a little *Traité de métaphysique*, while he informed Berger (B. 778) that, had he been writing poetry, he would have been glad to send it to him but that the things which now occupied his attention were of an entirely different sort.

In the meantime, he set to work to make his peace with the authorities in a letter to Chauvelin (B. 801):

Je déclare que je désavoue sans aucune réserve tout ce qui dans les *Lettres philosophiques* se trouve contraire à la pureté des mœurs, aux principes du christianisme, et à ce que je dois au Roy et au gouvernement; je regarde avec horreur et indignation tout principe qui peut aller contre la pureté des mœurs, et tous portraits qui peuvent les blesser. Je proteste de ma soumission entière, de mon respect profond et de mon attachement inviolable pour la Religion de mes pères, de la mesme soumission, du mesme respect et du mesme attachement pour le Roy, pour ceux à qui il confie son autorité et pour tout ce qui émane de cette autorité supreme à laquelle tout sujet doit obéir, et que tout sujet doit respecter. C'est un devoir que la naissance, les loix et la Religion m'impose et dont je ne m'écarteray jamais. Je me repends avec toute la vertu de mon cœur de tout ce qui m'est échappé de contraire. Ce sont là mes véritables sentimens, et je proteste que mes ouvrages, mes discours et ma conduitte prouveront à l'avenir la sincérité et la pureté de ces sentiments, qui sont et seroient toujours profondément gravés au fonds de mon cœur.

Voltaire, however, did not make his peace with any intention of returning to Paris. What he had in mind was a retreat to which he could retire and devote himself in peace to all his varied activities. He wrote to Thiériot that he proposed to stay a year or two in the country and requested his friend to bring him the fables of Dryden, two or three volumes of the *Lettres*, and a few of the best books about priesthood. It is evident that the exile into which he had been forced because of the *Lettres philosophiques* had made a deep impression upon him. Formont wrote Cideville that Voltaire had given up all idea of printing anything, that henceforth he intended to work only for his friends. It must be noted, however, that Formont did not have much confidence in these resolutions. On 25 January 1735, he had already written Cideville: "J'ai peur surtout de ses folies. Il se rétractera, il en sera honteux et fâché et sa mauvaise humeur luy fera faire quelque sortie violente contre les préjugés, en faveur de qui il aura fait la rétractation, et si cela arivoit il ne trouveroit pas un protecteur et seroit perdu à jamais" (B. 809).

In spite of this pessimistic prophecy, Voltaire started out to be orderly and quiet. To Formont, he wrote that he was beginning to take up again the work on the century of Louis XIV, and he added that he was reading the *Mémoires* of the Maréchal de Villars, the *Traité sur le commerce* of Melon, and *L'Ecumoire*, a novel by Crébillon. With characteristic excitement, he said he wanted to read La Bletterie's *Vie de L'Empereur Julien*, the *Préjugé à la mode*, and Linant's tragedy. To Desforges-Maillard, he wrote in February that "un peu de philosophie, l'histoire, la conversation partagent mes jours" (B. 820).

REASONS FOR THE RETREAT TO CIREY

It is practically always assumed by Voltaire's biographers that Cirey represented in the life of Voltaire another sort of interlude, devoted to the pleasures of love. The idyll has been presented over and over as if it were the central theme of the period. For the moment, what concerns us are the reasons motivating the retreat.

It is evident from what we have noted previously that one reason Voltaire withdrew from Paris was to escape the intense persecution to which he had been subjected. His act, in a way, was a repetition of his journey to England: he undoubtedly expected not only to escape the heavy hand of authority, which in the *Lettres philosophiques* affair had startled him by its severity, but also to counteract the unfortunate reputation he had gained with the public.

It might be added further that he was well aware that, if he had any intention of carrying out the program which the English experience had laid before him, he would need time to prepare himself in philosophy, science, and history, while enriching his philosophic poetry and drama. He seems at one point in 1733 to have hesitated just a little in undertaking that program. A letter to Maupertuis indicates that, having acquired a little insight into Newton, he would now have to drop the subject of physics and return to his native field of arts and letters. The hesitation was certainly only momentary; before the end of 1733, he was actively engaged in penetrating the philosophy of Locke, assembling material for the *Siècle*, and preparing to write his "songes métaphysiques." Even this part of the program must have seemed a large assignment. He soon learned that, if he was to retain his superiority as France's outstanding poet while adding these diverse interests, he would have to work even harder to meet the challenge.

He became very conscious that a change was taking place in the intellectual realm in France. On the one hand, there was a decided feeling that the century was entering upon an epoch of sterility. Formont, indeed, wrote an epistle on the decline of the arts and sent it to Voltaire on 1 April 1735. On 20 September, the latter noted that literature was flooded with brochures. "Nous sommes dans l'automne du bon goût, et au temps de la chute des feuilles" (B. 885). He added that he consoled himself for all the foolishness of the present with his *Siècle*. On 24 September, he reported to Thiériot that he had read a whole load of comedies, operas, and penny-sheets. "Ah, mon ami, quelle barbarie et quelle misère," he concluded. One of the causes of this sterility was the rise of academies, which stifled genius instead of fostering it; France, he noted, had had no great painter since the founding of the Académie de Peinture and no great philosopher since the establishment of the Académie des Sciences.

This attitude was rather common with Voltaire throughout the Cirey period. He elaborated upon this condition of sterility in a letter to Frederick (B. 1272). There he explains that the reason he speaks very little of the literary production of the time is that, living as he does in seclusion with Mme du Châtelet and with the works of the past century, he has become acquainted with very few works of the present which deserve to be sent to Frederick. He finds that, in general, French letters are beginning to degenerate either because, in an effort to outdo the previous century, contemporary writers have exceeded their ability or because nature, after having made such gigantic efforts in the seventeenth century, is now resting. Voltaire, though, gives as the main reason for this state of affairs the censorship prevailing in France. If Cicero were alive and wished to write the *De natura deorum* in France, or Virgil wished to write the *Georgics*, both would run a grave risk. To write history as it should be written, one would have to live in a free country. But there is an added difficulty: if a Frenchman, desiring to live in a free land, goes to Holland or to England, he loses the purity of his language.

Universities are stagnant in France; they have no Wolff, Maclaurin, S'Gravesande, or Musschembrœck. French professors are not even worthy to study under such men. The Académie des Sciences upholds the honor of the nation, but its influence is not widespread, and each academician has particular views on physics. There is no good physics text, nor are there any sound principles of astronomy. The opera seems to flourish, but French music has no appeal to other nations. The comedy is on the decline. In short, "Les Français vivent un peu dans l'Europe sur leur crédit, comme un homme riche qui se ruine insensiblement."

Frederick was not too inclined to agree with Voltaire's complaint. He stoutly maintained that the decline in taste was not so prevalent in France as Voltaire thought. The list of leading authors—Voltaire, Fontenelle, the elder Crébillon, Rollin, Olivet, Bernard, Gresset, Réaumur—was not without distinguished people. Frederick conceded that Louis XIV had done more to encourage the arts than was now being done. He suggested that metaphysics would never thrive anywhere except in England. And he thought it deplorable that conditions in Germany were much worse because of fanatics and superstition. "Nos universités et notre Académie des sciences se trouvent dans un triste état, il paraît que les muses veulent déserter ces climats." Frederick also stressed the low estate of letters in Germany (B. 1290).

On the other hand, Voltaire was conscious of another phenomenon which was taking place. From time to time, he would abandon Cirey for a rapid trip to Paris. He would then complain: "Je vis de dissipation depuis que je suis à Paris . . . mes idées poétiques s'enfuyent de moi" (B. 838). It was on one of these occasions that he noted the great change which had come over the cultivated world of Paris, in a letter of 16 April 1735:

Les vers ne sont plus guère à la mode à Paris. Tout le monde commence à faire le géomètre et le physicien. On se mêle de raisonner. Le sentiment, l'imagination, et les grâces sont bannies. Un homme qui auroit vécu sous Louis XIV et qui reviendroit au monde ne reconnaîtroit plus les français. Il croiroit que les Allemans ont conquis ce pays-ci. Les belles-lettres périssent à vue d'œil. Ce n'est pas que je sois fâché que la philosophie soit cultivée, mais je ne voudrais pas qu'elle devint un tiran qui exclût tout le reste.

He must have been startled to find that France was going through the same change which he himself had been undergoing. He, however, had been taking up these interests one by one, while the public had approached the problem differently. What he had been resisting all along had now taken place: the century had ceased being poetic and had become clearly philosophical. The civilization he admired as a Frenchman was giving way to the civilization he had just experienced. In spite of some inconsistency, Voltaire was firmly resolved to oppose this shift, or rather to oppose any attempt to put philosophy and science in the place of arts and letters. "Mais aucun art, aucune science ne doit être de mode." His solution was to pass from an experiment in physics to the writing of a comedy, from study to the cultivation of taste. He reiterated the same observation to Caumont: "J'ai trouvé, en arrivant à Paris, que la philosophie de Newton gagnait un peu parmi les vrais philosophes" (B. 840).

There was thus an additional reason for his retreat. If he intended to pursue both of these interests, he naturally had to have free time to practice one while preparing himself to be the leader in the other. He had no difficulty in adding his literary activities to his social life, but to add scientific and philosophical activities to the literary was something else. The challenge which he had already seen in these preoccupations was complicated by the realization that, to be superior in both areas, he would have to devote himself to serious study. It was here that he discovered the necessity for his reeducation.

It is therefore perfectly reasonable that Voltaire should have made plans to withdraw to Cirey, given the circumstances of the official persecution, the movement in Paris from poetry to philosophy, the necessity of concentrated work if he intended to write intelligently about the age of Louis XIV, and, above all, the need for serious application to philosophy and science if he expected to keep abreast of his time. At first, the plans seemed rather vague: a confession to Cideville and Formont that he had to get away from Paris (1733), a remark to Thiériot that he expected to spend a year or two in the country, another to the Abbé Asselin (B. 848) asking for an assistant and stating that he intended to spend a year away from Paris. Little by little, though, he began to understand the necessity of prolonging his stay.

Mme du Châtelet saw the situation differently and gave other reasons for the move. On 30 May, she announced to Richelieu that she was leaving the desert of Paris on the twentieth of June and that she was abandoning it for Cirey with the greatest of pleasure. She explained to her former lover that the more she reflected upon Voltaire's and her situation, the more she was convinced that all those who love passionately should, if possible, live in the country. But, what is more important, she could never restrain the imagination of Voltaire in Paris: "Je le perdrais tôt ou tard à Paris, ou du moins je passerais ma vie à craindre de le perdre, et d'avoir des sujets de me plaindre de lui. . . . Je ne puis allier dans ma tête tant d'esprit, tant de raison dans tout le reste, et tant d'aveuglement dans ce qui peut le perdre sans retour" (B. 849).

Thus, the underlying motives of the two principal actors in the Cirey episode become clear. Mme du Châtelet wanted, above all, to protect Voltaire from himself, to give him the opportunity to be himself and to develop, but to restrain him from his impudences and his sudden rebellions. It is somehow startling to find that Mme du Châtelet the lover accepted as her task to exercise a restraining influence on his intellectual activities. So much calm judgment is not to be expected from a beautiful young lady of twenty-seven, although it is true that she had had several amorous experiences before and probably had learned to appreciate the value of true friendship. For his part, although there can be no doubt that he was deeply infatuated with his Lady Newton, he was now forty, and he probably valued more than the amorous life he led the chance for study, for meditation, and the opportunity to catch up with himself and his time.

It is consequently not too surprising to read in a letter Voltaire wrote to Cideville on 26 June 1735, six days after Mme du Châtelet had left Paris, that *Jeanne la Pucelle* now had nine cantos and had become the amusement for the entr'actes of more serious occupations. He then went on to explain that metaphysics, a little geometry, and physics occupied an apportioned part of his day but that his principal occupation was the *Siècle de Louis XIV*: "J'ai aporté avec moy beaucoup de matériaux, et j'ay déjà commencé l'édifice, mais il ne sera achevé de longtemps" (B. 858). And he added: "Je suis tranquille, heureux et occupé. . . ." This was just what he wanted.

When Voltaire withdrew to Cirey, he made clear to Cideville and Caumont, as we have noted, that he was going to occupy himself with things which interested him, with no idea of writing henceforth for the public. There is no reason to suppose that he was insincere in this announcement, although it required very little, given his rather ebullient temperament, to make him change his mind. Still, there is visible in the correspondence in the early years of Cirey a perceptible change in tactics. Instead of talking indiscriminately about the work he was currently engaged in, as he did at first, he began more and more to talk about the areas of learning which attracted his attention. The occasions were now frequent when he would state that he was busy with poetry, mathematics, and philosophy, or philosophy, geometry, and poetry, or some other combination of studies. A partial explanation of this tendency lies in the decision he had made to pass from one area of learning to another; it was all a part of his desire to be the "uomo universale," or rather the "encyclopedic man." It should be noted also that this attitude created in the correspondence an impression of clandestinity, which was less apparent before.

It was very characteristic of Voltaire in this period to announce an interest and pursue it without all the publicity he had been accustomed to giving his activities in the past. Many times, in fact, he did not display the interest until he had a work already organized in the subject. And, although he seemed to be working on two or three things at any given time, he was always very careful to complete one before entering intensively upon another. The only exceptions to the rule were the theatre and poetry: in these areas he was likely at any moment, when his demon urged him, to lay everything aside and embark upon his dramatic or poetic enterprise. In general, though, the rule held. It was only when he had a finished *Traité de métaphysique* that he began talking seriously about his *Siècle de Louis XIV*, only when he had a finished *Siècle* that he referred consistently to the *Eléments de la philosophie de Newton*, and only when he had a finished *Eléments* that he mentioned his deep involvement in a *Discours en vers sur l'homme*. Consequently, it becomes rather difficult for the intellectual biographer to trace the

early stages of any of the Cirey works with the exception of the theatre, and it is practically impossible, because of this tendency toward
clandestinity, to talk intelligently about the first state of the finished
work. Voltaire, no longer feeling committed to the public, made no
effort, beyond general statements, to inform even his close friends of
his intellectual activities. He applied himself, however, no less strenuously to the preparation of his work over a relatively long period of
time. Then, in a sudden burst of activity, he composed his work with
a good deal of energy. This procedure enhanced the impression that
he was always passing from one work to another. Frederick remarked upon this rapidity in his letter of 16 August 1737: "D'où
prenez-vous, Mr., tout le temps pour travailler? Ou vos moments
valent le triple de ceux des autres, ou votre génie heureux et fécond
surpasse celui de l'ordinaire des grands hommes. A peine avez-vous
achevé d'éclaircir la philosophie de Newton que vous travaillez à
enrichir le Théâtre français d'une tragédie nouvelle . . ." (B. 1302).
In reality, though, once Voltaire had completed a manuscript and
was ready to pass on to another subject, he laid it aside for the future.
This view is deceptive, however, because, although he apparently
did store some of these manuscripts for future use, as we shall see,
and even put together dossiers of notebooks, for the same purpose,
he also had a habit in the early years at Cirey of revising his first
draft of a work into a second and sometimes into a third before
thinking of publishing it.

There were thus two rhythms underlying Voltaire's production
at Cirey: a rhythm which consisted in his passing from field to field
(metaphysics, morality, history, mathematics, Newtonian science,
drama, and poetry), usually at three-month intervals, and a second
movement which ran from work to work, more or less on an annual
basis (1734, *Traité de métaphysique*; 1735, *Siècle de Louis XIV*;
1736, *Eléments de la philosophie de Newton* and *Le Mondain*). In
a way, these undertakings began to converge in 1737, along with the
Discours en vers sur l'homme, so that the year 1738 is usually given
as the date for the unified organization of this material and the building of an organic point of view. It is as if Voltaire, in his four years
of reeducation, had devoted in succession one year each to specializ-
ing in philosophy, history, and science and one final year to join-
ing these special studies together in the study of man, "la morale."

However, before he could reach a satisfactory synthesis for the future, he had to decide what to do with two of his deepest preoccupations: poetry and religion. These problems of intellectual coordination and reorganization made the period of 1738-1739 rather crucial for him. We shall therefore attempt to follow the genesis of these major Cirey works as they appear in the correspondence.

TRAITÉ DE MÉTAPHYSIQUE

It has generally been thought that Voltaire composed his *Traité de métaphysique* at the instigation of Mme du Châtelet. The source of that supposition was the Kehl edition of the *Traité*. Ordinarily, we judge that it was written hastily. Mrs. Patterson actually stated that "it was probably written in the few days between June 22nd and 27th." (See H. T. Patterson, ed., *Traité de métaphysique* [1734], reproduced from the Kehl text with preface, notes, and variants.) I have shown (*Studies on Voltaire*, pp. 58-60), on the contrary, that it was the reading of Locke which led Voltaire to undertake to sketch out his own philosophical principles, or rather that it was the reading of Locke which induced him to reread Clarke's *Discourse concerning the Being and Attributes of God* and Malebranche's *Recherche de la vérité*, which, in turn, suggested a third rereading of Locke, which then prompted his enterprise.

These preparations reached back apparently even further into the past. A letter to Formont (26 July 1731) reveals that for some time Voltaire had been accustomed to discuss with him his views on philosophy. Writing to Mlle de Launai in December 1732, Voltaire compliments her on "les raisonnements les plus solides sur le libre arbitre," which she had incorporated in a letter to his Rouen friend. On 26 July 1733, in a letter to Formont, he calls him "mon cher métaphysicien" and rehashes with him the problem of thinking matter. In another letter to his "philosophe aimable," on 15 August 1733, he returns to the same problem. It is in this letter (B. 625) that he announces that he has already reread Locke, Clarke, and Malebranche and has become convinced that Clarke is "le meilleur sophiste," Malebranche "le romancier le plus subtil," and Locke "l'homme le plus sage." He refuses to follow Malebranche because he cannot accept the doctrine of original sin or that of the error of the senses. He rejects Clarke's view that matter does not exist of necessity. But he agrees wholeheartedly with Locke that God can communicate thought to matter. Finally, in a letter to Maupertuis, in December 1733 or January 1734, he complains that the persecutions visited upon him because of the *Lettres philosophiques* leave him but little time to devote to his "songes métaphysiques." Evidently, around the end of 1733, he had seriously begun to compose his *Traité*.

It is thus evident that the *Traité* was a perfectly logical development of the thirteenth *Lettre philosophique* and that Voltaire was induced to inaugurate its composition, not because of any urging from Mme du Châtelet, but because he felt, as he said in a letter to Formont (B. 741), that Locke had been too timid in his assertions and he wanted to complete his thought. Besides, he wanted to speculate upon his own existence and see if he could establish some incontrovertible principles. In all probability, the actual time spent in the preparation of the *Traité* extended from the letter to Maupertuis (December 1733 or January 1734) to the beginning of November or December 1734, when Voltaire wrote to Cideville: "Dites à l'autre [Formont] que j'ay un petit Traité de métaphysique tout prest. Tout cela est vray à la lettre" (B. 776).

On second thought, however, Voltaire became convinced that the *Traité* was less complete than he had supposed. What must have led to that conviction were Tournemine's articles in January and February 1735 in the *Journal de Trévoux*, the second of these letters being directed at the thirteenth *Lettre philosophique*, and a letter to Voltaire, published in the *Journal de Trévoux* for October 1735. We shall return to Voltaire's controversy with Tournemine. For the moment, it suffices to note that throughout 1735, Voltaire still struggled with his metaphysical preoccupations.

Constantly during the year, he announced to his friends that he was occupied with philosophy or metaphysics. To Desforges-Maillard, in February 1735, he stated: "Un peu de philosophie, l'histoire, la conversation, partagent mes jours." On 26 June 1735, he wrote to Cideville: "La métaphysique, un peu de géométrie et de physique ont aussi leurs temps marquez chez moi, mais je les cultive sans aucune vue marquée et par conséquent, avec assez d'indifférence." Already, on 19 April 1735, he had written to Caumont, stating that he was busy with more than one sort of literature but that he did not expect to publish any of it. To Thiériot, later on in the year, he still asserted (*circa* 15 August 1735): "La poésie et la philosophie m'amusent dans les intervalles." Throughout the whole year 1735, he pretended the greatest indifference to the publication of his new compositions. A letter from Voltaire to Thiériot, in January 1735, stated with very little enthusiasm: "We must read together your friend's plays, his operas, his epic poems, his philosophical follies, all that he has scribbled in your absence." This seeming indifference is deceptive; in reality, Voltaire was expending the greater part of his energy in combating Tournemine's articles, as we shall see, while revising the *Traité* in the light of that controversy. And, although between the announcements of the composition of the *Traité*, in December 1734 to Formont and to Cideville at the beginning of November 1735, there was no direct mention of the work, in all likelihood it elicited a great part of his attention during that time. On 3 November 1735, he confessed to Thiériot: "moi, qui vous parle, j'ai fait aussi mon petit cours de métaphysique, car il faut bien se rendre compte à soi-même des choses de ce monde." By the end of the month, he offered to send his friend portions of the *Traité*, provided he could find someone to make a copy of the passages. It is clear, however, that Voltaire did not do so, for, on 10 March 1736, he stated to Thiériot: "Pour ma métaphysique, il n'y a pas moyen de la faire voyager; j'y ai trop cherché la vérité" (B. 996). In the meantime, he recapitulated his arguments with Tournemine in two letters to his confidant Formont (B. 929 and 954) in the opening days of 1736.

It was at this time, at the beginning of 1736, that Voltaire offered his presentation copy of the *Traité* to Mme du Châtelet. There are two indications that he did, but there are still some assumptions which lack definite proof, the most important one being the statement that the text of the *Traité* which was first produced in the Kehl edition of Voltaire's works was printed from the manuscript copy presented to Mme du Châtelet. This text, as I have shown elsewhere (*Studies*, pp. 68-79), contained an insertion in Chapter V which could only have been made after the controversy with Tournemine. Further, it contained two additional chapters (VIII and IX) which could not have existed until 1735, because these two chapters were patterned upon Mme du Châtelet's translation of and commentary upon

Mandeville's *Fable of the Bees,* the introduction to which was dated 1735.

It would be well here to summarize certain conclusions concerning not only the origin of the *Traité de métaphysique* but also its development and the factors which contributed to that development. Begun at the end of 1733 or in the early weeks of 1734, under the inspiration of Clarke, Malebranche, and particularly Locke, it was brought to what was deemed a state of completion by December of that year. In that state, it consisted of not more than seven of the nine chapters which were published in the Kehl edition. It is even conceivable that the work contained at that time less than seven chapters, although it undoubtedly had a section on the existence and nature of God, one on the nature of the soul and thinking matter, and probably a section on free will. Voltaire leaned heavily upon Locke and Clarke for his material, and Formont was the confidant with whom he discussed his ideas.

However, Voltaire became convinced that the work was far from complete, and, although he had announced to Cideville that it was "tout prest," he set to work to revise it. It is fairly certain that, if he had not already reached that opinion, his argument with Tournemine throughout the year 1735 sufficed to bring him to an awareness of his philosophical immaturity and the unfinished state of his work. It is certain, too, that, as a result of this controversy, he revised his chapter on thinking matter (Chapter V) and that, sometime before the end of the year, he added two chapters upon "la morale" (Chapters VIII and IX). These chapters drew heavily from Mandeville's *Essay on the Origin of Moral Virtue,* rather than from Locke.

Just why Voltaire entered upon a discussion of vice and virtue in a treatise dealing with metaphysics requires a word of explanation. As we shall see, there had been in the general field of philosophy a considerable shift in philosophical materials. Science had become so closely identified with philosophy that the Cartesian tree of knowledge threatened to become all body and no roots with but few healthy branches. The Cartesian arrangement of knowledge, consisting of metaphysical roots, a body dealing with mathematics and physics, and branches treating of medicine, mechanics, and morality, no longer possessed the same integrity it had had in the early part of the seventeenth century. Spinoza, for one, had distorted the arrangement with both his *Tractatus* and his *Ethica,* but so had Leibniz, Malebranche, Locke, and Newton. It is true that Voltaire and Mme du Châtelet accepted in principle that all physics derived from meta-physics, which seemed to mean that, unless one held firmly to certain metaphysical principles, such as the existence of God, one could not have any assurance of the validity of the discoveries of science. Voltaire adopted without equivocation the metaphysical principle of the existence of God. But he also expressed a second philosophical conviction: all knowledge must be brought back to man. Over and over, he stated: "Je ramène tout à l'homme." It was this humanistic tendency which guided him to all the other subjects he treated: the immortality of the soul, thinking matter, free will, and moral action. God, he asserted, must accept responsibility for holding this structure together. His existence guarantees the rightness and wrongness of man's actions. For Voltaire, there is a grave danger in moving from ideas to action in an uncontrolled world.

It was to be expected that Locke would have furnished Voltaire with his principles of moral action, since he played so important a role in the chapter upon thinking matter. However, as Mrs. Patterson has pointed out, Voltaire rejected both Locke and Clarke as models for his thinking upon moral problems and adopted, instead, Bayle and Mandeville. Of the two, he relied chiefly upon Mandeville.

It has been difficult to establish an intellectual relationship between Mandeville and Voltaire because the latter made no reference to the English moralist until the Ferney period. Nonetheless, Morize has noted in Remark O of Mandeville's *Fable* a passage which was full of suggestions for Voltaire's *Mondain,* had he wished to avail himself of them. Mrs. Patterson, for her part, has turned our attention to numerous passages in Chapters VIII and IX of the *Traité* which seem reminiscences of the Mandeville *Essay* (see Wade, *Studies,* pp. 30-34; Patterson, ed., *Traité,* notes to Chapters VIII and IX). There is no longer any doubt that Voltaire was intimately acquainted with Mandeville's work in the Cirey period, since Mme du Châtelet made a translation and adaptation of it, to which she added an introduction dated 1735. I have noted some sixteen passages in Mme du Châtelet's translation which have been taken over more or less verbatim in Chapters VIII and IX of the *Traité* (see *Studies,* pp. 70-78). It is true that Mme du Châtelet first referred to her translation in a letter of 20 May 1736 to Algarotti. But she must have been interested in Mandeville's work before the end of the year 1735, or there would have been no sense in affixing that date to the preface to her translation.

There is thus every indication that Voltaire and Mme du Châtelet were working simultaneously with Mandeville and that, while her work resulted in the translation of nine chapters of the *Fable*, his work resulted in the writing of two additional chapters of the *Traité*, very strongly conditioned by the English moralist's work. Thus, the *Traité* now had a modified chapter upon thinking matter after the debate with Tournemine and two chapters on vice and virtue as a result of Voltaire's collaboration with Mme du Châtelet on Mandeville. It was in this form that Voltaire presented the *Traité* to his Lady Newton at the end of 1735, along with the famous quatrain. Just how much the other portions of the "petit Traité de métaphysique tout prest" of 1734 were revised, we do not know. We do know, though, that it was this second version presented to Mme du Châtelet at the end of 1735 which was eventually published in the Kehl edition. In all probability, it was this collaboration which gave rise to the Kehl story that the work was begun at the instigation of Mme du Châtelet. I think it is this collaboration which explains the presentation copy.

There are signs that Voltaire was still dissatisfied with his *Traité de métaphysique*, although the source of that dissatisfaction is still obscure. Most likely, it was either fostered or encouraged by the correspondence with Frederick which began in August 1736. Frederick in his opening letter had clearly demonstrated that what he admired in Voltaire was not only the poet but the philosopher, and especially the metaphysician. Frederick had likewise shown by his interest in Wolff that he, too, was drawn to metaphysics. What is certain is that Voltaire set to work during 1736 to revise the *Traité* a second time, but we can only surmise what the third redaction amounted to. From a note we can deduce that there was to be a new chapter on kinetic energy. In general, the work seems to have followed the arrangement of the second redaction, but, to judge by the section upon free will, which is the only one now remaining, it was fuller and more logically arranged. It was certainly influenced by Frederick's interests in German metaphysics. Indeed, Frederick quickly became

Voltaire's confidant in these matters, to the point that, at the beginning of 1737, Voltaire promised to send him the *Traité de métaphysique*, and actually did send him the chapter, much enlarged, on free will.

SIÈCLE DE LOUIS XIV

The idea of writing a history of the age of Louis XIV had occurred to Voltaire before 13 May 1732, at which time he mentioned to Thiériot his determination to employ his studious leisure in the writing of *Eriphile*, the *Lettres philosophiques*, and a work on the age of Louis XIV. Some months later, in a letter to Formont, *circa* 12 September 1732, he informed his Rouen friend that, once he had gotten the *Lettres philosophiques* out of the way, he would finish the history of the age of Louis XIV. To Thiériot, on 1 April 1733, he confessed that he was now gathering material for his great history on the *Siècle de Louis XIV*. To all appearances, he had not made any particular headway in the organization of the material, since, on 25 October 1733, he told Caumont that the history of Louis XIV's reign would become the occupation of his old age. Voltaire now calculated that it would take a decade to put it together. It is certain, though, that, however slow his progress, he continued his task. On 2 April 1734, he wrote Caumont that he was still assembling his documents for the *Siècle de Louis XIV*, which he intended to write at some future date. He nonetheless expressed the fear that he would have neither the leisure, the health, nor the talent to do so.

It is thus evident that, although Voltaire persisted in looking forward to a time when he would undertake a history of Louis's reign, he was rather inactive throughout the whole of 1734. Only on 26 January 1735 did he show signs of resuming his work on the subject. To Formont, he wrote that he had taken up again the idea he had formerly entertained of composing an essay on the age of Louis XIV. He added that, if it were only a matter of writing the history of the King, he would not bother with it but that the age was worthy of a work. He promised that, if he could ever get hold of the necessary materials, he would complete the enterprise. By the middle of 1735, he seems to have been seriously engaged in the task. To Cideville, on 26 June 1735, he confided that his principal preoccupation was the *Siècle de Louis XIV*, "dont je vous ai parlé il y a quelques années."

Voltaire now declared that it was the "sultane favorite," all the other studies being merely "passades." He added that he had collected at Cirey a lot of documents and had actually begun the composition, although he did not expect to have it completed for a long time. On 3 August 1735, he repeated to Cideville that "Le Siècle de Louis XIV est entamé." He now informed his friend that he did not know what to call his work. It was certainly not a history; it was more a painting of an admirable period. Voltaire constantly used this metaphor in treating his *Siècle*. He must have been deeply occupied with it by this time. To Thiériot, he wrote, *circa* 15 August 1735, that he gave every day "quelques coups de pinceau à ce bau siècle de Louis 14." He reaffirmed that he wished to depict the age rather than be its historian. The following month, he wrote to both Cideville and Formont (B. 885 and 886) that the work upon the *Siècle* consoled him for all the foolishness of the present. To Formont, he added: "Je ne laisse pas d'avancer chemin." In the middle of November 1735, he announced, again to Formont: "Je vais grand train dans le Siècle de Louis XIV" (B. 911). He boasted that he was leaping over the details "à pieds joints" and opening up broad vistas in the thickets he had assembled. Finally, on 1 January 1736, Mme du Châtelet informed a friend that "Voltaire fait l'histoire de Louis XIV et je neutonise tant bien que mal." It is apparent that Voltaire had worked strenuously upon his history during the last half of 1735.

Apparently, his enthusiasm for the subject really had become a passion. As early as 19 June 1735, he reiterated the extent of his interest in the age of Louis XIV to his friend Caumont. He confessed that he did not know whether Louis deserved the name of great, but he was sure the age deserved it, and he wanted to talk about "ce bel âge des arts et des lettres." He added that his respect for physics and astronomy did not diminish in any way his liking for history. He found, indeed, that there were close analogies between the two fields of study: "Il y a dans l'histoire comme dans la physique certains faits généraux très certains, et pour les petits détails, les motifs secrets . . . ils sont aussi difficiles à deviner que les ressorts cachez de la nature" (B. 859). He regretted that Mme du Châtelet did not have a high opinion of it. Of the Abbé d'Olivet, he inquired *circa* June 1735 whether he was busy with ancient and modern philosophy or whether he was focusing on the history of belles-lettres. Voltaire dis-

closed to Olivet just what he understood by history: "Si vous déter-
riez jamais dans votre chemin quelque chose qui pût servir à faire
connaître le progrès des arts dans le siècle de Louis XIV, vous me
feriez la plus grande faveur du monde de m'en faire part; tout me
sera bon; anecdotes sur la littérature, sur la philosophie, histoire de
l'esprit humain. . . , poésie, peinture, musique." In a letter to Desforges-Maillard, he counseled a mixture of amusements and useful
occupations, poetry and serious study, or rather an honorable position in which poetry, eloquence, history, and philosophy could be
used as recreation. He concluded that poetry should never be more
than the ornament of reason.

Little by little, his interest in writing the history of Louis XIV's
century led him to reflect upon his new "art." He very quickly
distinguished between the great man and the great epoch, as we
have seen. He differentiated almost immediately, too, between political and military history and cultural history. Great men, he held,
are those who have excelled in the realm of the useful or the agreeable, whereas those who lay waste a whole province are merely
heroes. A canal which unites two oceans, a painting by Poussin, a
beautiful tragedy, a new truth are far more precious than all the
annals of the court and all the accounts of military campaigns
(B. 864). Voltaire's remarks to Cideville that he did not know what
he should call this work, since it was not so much history as a painting of an admirable century, was repeated to Caumont on 24 August
1735: "C'est moins une histoire des faits qu'un tableau du siècle que
j'ai en vue." This time he gave examples of what he meant by a
painting: a battle is not important, because there have always been
battles, but a government order which releases from prison all those
held for sorcery is quite significant. What one wants to grasp is "le
génie des peuples, leurs goûts, leurs sottises," those things which
have always differed from people to people and which result in the
destruction of an error or the invention or perfecting of an art. To
Olivet, on 24 August 1735, he explained that he liked what was
healthy in the ancients, that he devoured what was good in the
moderns, but that he placed above everything "les douceurs de la
société." He even went so far as to say that, if the arts and the progress of the human mind were withdrawn, there would remain
nothing of any consequence. He returned to the metaphor of the

painter who sees objects in a different manner from other men and who notes the effects of light and shade that escape the sight of normal men. "Voilà comme je suis; je me suis établi le peintre du siècle de Louis 14." On 1 September 1735, he announced that he had done thirty years of the century. On 24 September 1735, he requested from Thiériot some memoirs on trade and all books on the history of the seventeenth century and the progress of the fine arts.

Thereafter, during the year 1736, we have but little in the correspondence which throws any light upon the development of the *Siècle*. It must be noted that the rhythm with which it progressed cannot be easily discerned. Lanson has remarked that, by 1735, one third of the work had been composed. In a letter to Cideville, on 23 December 1737 (B. 1348), Voltaire remarked that he had gotten up to the battle of Turin. Besterman notes that the battle of Turin occurred in 1706 and that Voltaire must have been at the time about halfway through the work. These estimates are not very satisfactory, because, in making them, one assumes that the arrangement of the material in 1736 and 1737 corresponded with the layout which we now have in the text. This assumption is most certainly unjustified. There are two indications that Voltaire must have deemed his manuscript relatively complete in the first part of 1737. As early as 16 January 1737, Valdruche, who was an acquaintance of the Cirey group of several years' standing and who had frequently been invited from Joinville to the soirées at Cirey, wrote to Bouhier: "Je lus dans son cabinet une bonne partie de son *Histoire de Louis XIV*."

Around 30 June 1737, Voltaire informed Frederick: "J'ai donc mis dans un petit paquet tout ce que j'ai fait de *l'Histoire de Louis XIV*." There is a strong presumption that Voltaire now felt he had a satisfactory first draft of his work. It is certain, however, that he did not at all entertain the notion that the work was completed. True to his procedures, once he had acquired this preliminary first draft, he wanted some confidant to whom he could show it. He apparently required some sort of encouragement from this confidant in order to continue the task. In this case, it is certain that he turned to Frederick, to whom he had sent his draft, because it was precisely Frederick who had already shown interest in the general problems of writing history. Voltaire must have felt the need of advice and counsel. Throughout the latter part of 1737 and the early part of 1738, he sought from the Prince his thoughts upon the *Siècle*. In a letter to Frederick around 15 October 1737, he stated that he was anxiously awaiting the Prince's opinion. Again, around 15 February 1738, he wrote Frederick that he was awaiting his verdict in order to know whether he should continue or suspend his efforts on the history. In a letter around 25 April 1738, still to his Prince, he declared that he would not proceed with the *Siècle* until he had received the order to go ahead.

Frederick finally responded to Voltaire's exhortations on 31 March 1738. "Votre histoire du siècle de Louis m'enchante," he told Voltaire. Frederick's long-awaited letter is very important, because it not only pronounced the verdict upon the *Siècle* but contained a reference to the *Essai sur les mœurs*, or rather an allusion to some preoccupation which Voltaire was now showing for universal history. In his letter, he added: "Si les histoires de l'univers avaient été écrites comme celle que vous m'avez confiée, nous serions plus instruits des mœurs de tous les siècles, et moins trompés par les historiens." He took some exception to the inclusion of Machiavelli among the other great men of his time, since he considered him a very dishonest man. Turning his thought again to the *Siècle*, he commended it for its "beau style": "Toutes les lignes portent coup; tout est nourri de réflexions excellentes; aucune fausse pensée, rien de puéril, et, avec cela, une impartialité parfaite."

Having received the endorsement of his Prince, Voltaire took up once again the redaction of his *Siècle*. In a letter written by Mme du Châtelet to D'Argental around July 1738 (B. 1470), she stated that Voltaire seemed on the point of resuming his history of Louis XIV. She added that it was the work which best agreed with his health. And she expressed the opinion that, if D'Argental could visit Cirey, he would derive great pleasure from reading the manuscript.

It was around this time that Voltaire reconstructed his conception of the *Siècle de Louis XIV* and, to a certain extent, coordinated his views on history. To Frederick, he explained that history had its pyrrhonism exactly as metaphysics did; one did not dare penetrate it too deeply. Voltaire admitted that in the *Siècle* he had attempted to describe the great events of the reign, but without any desire to arrive at the first principles of these events. "La cause première n'est guère faite pour le physicien, et les premiers ressorts des intrigues ne sont guère faits pour l'historien." He avowed that his sole ambition was to paint the manners of the time and to write the history of the human mind, and especially the history of the arts. He entered upon this task, however, with true historical curiosity. When he heard that some very interesting letters written to Louvois had turned up, he first rather arrogantly wrote Berger that he intended to ask no favors of administrators in authority but then urged him in a subsequent letter to try to get one or two dozen of those letters: "Si vous pouviez me faire transcrire une douzaine ou deux des lettres les plus intéressantes écrites à Mr. de Louvois et de ses réponses les plus propres à caractériser ces temps-là, vous rendriez un grand service à l'auteur du siècle de Louis XIV" (B. 1484).

The most explicit statement of the year 1738 concerning the *Siècle de Louis XIV* was made to Lévesque de Burigny on 19 October 1738. Voltaire related to his old friend that some years back he had undertaken a kind of "philosophical" history of the age of Louis XIV, intending to embrace everything which would be of interest to posterity. Everything of temporary importance would be omitted. The progress of the human mind and of the arts was to occupy the place of honor in the work. Religion would be treated with respect, and what public law had of greatest interest to society would be included. A law which had rendered service was to be given priority over towns surrendered or captured and battles which had never led to anything of consequence. Throughout the work would be seen the character of a man who attributed more value to a minister who doubles the production of grain than to a king who purchases or sacks a province.

If it was to Burigny that Voltaire explained his convictions on the methods of historical writing, it was to the Abbé Du Bos that he gave the fullest outline of the work. Voltaire insisted that it was designed to set forth the history of the human mind, selected from the most glorious century of the human mind. It would be divided into twenty chapters, which would present twenty outstanding tableaux of the events. The principal actors would stand in the foreground, the populace in the background: "Ce qui caractérise le siècle, ce qui a causé des révolutions, ce qui sera important dans cent années: c'est là ce que je veux écrire aujourd'hui." There would be a chapter devoted to the private life of Louis, two to the policing of the kingdom, in finance and in commerce, two for the ecclesiastic government, and five or six for the history of the arts, beginning with Descartes and ending with Rameau. In other words, the work had been more or less patterned after the *Lettres philosophiques*: politics, economics, religion, arts, and sciences. Voltaire detailed his sources: Dangeau, Larrey, Limiers, Lamberti, Roussel, for political history; Jurieu, Quesnel, and Doucin for Church affairs. He confesses that he would like very much to see the "journal politique" of the Abbé de Saint-Pierre. It was, however, in the fields of arts and sciences that he had broadened his formula since the publication of the *Lettres philosophiques*:

A l'égard des arts et des sciences, il n'est question, je crois, que de tracer la marche de l'esprit humain en philosophie; en éloquence, en poésie, en critique; de marquer les progrès de la peinture, de la sculpture, de la musique, de l'orfèvrerie, des manufactures de tapisserie, de glaces, d'étoffes d'or, de l'horlogerie. Je ne veux que peindre, chemin faisant, les génies qui ont excellé dans ces parties. Dieu me préserve d'employer 300 pages à l'histoire de Gassendi!

LE MONDAIN

Voltaire's intensive preoccupation with metaphysics, physics, and history during 1734-1738 did not prevent him from continuing his interest in poetry and drama. In both of these literary areas, though, he displayed a tendency to make his poetry more philosophical. There is some evidence that, even with its new thought content, he still found in it some consolation for the arduous labors in the three new intellectual fields he had adopted. For some reason, he felt relaxed if he could compose a poem to share with his friends. It is noteworthy, though, that even these philosophical poems he regarded now as a "badinage," a "plaisanterie." Still, being at heart an incorrigible, although immature, poet, he felt the need to apologize to Cideville, his poetic friend, for his desertion. On 18 February 1737, he wrote to him:

Je vais bien haïr la philosophie qui m'a ôté l'exactitude que m'avoit donnée l'amitié. Que gagnerai-je à connaître le chemin de la lumière? et la gravitation de Saturne? Ce sont des vérités stériles. Un sentiment est mille fois au-dessus. Comptez que cette étude en m'absorbant pour quelque temps n'a point pourtant desséché mon cœur. Comptez que le compas ne m'a point fait abandonner nos musettes. Il me seroit bien plus doux de chanter avec vous *lentus in umbra, formosam resonare docens Amarillida silvas,* que de voiager dans le pays des démonstrations. Mais mon cher amy il faut donner à son âme toutes les formes possibles. C'est un feu que Dieu nous a confié, nous devons la nourir de ce que nous trouvons de plus précieux. Il faut faire entrer dans notre être, tous les modes imaginables, ouvrir toutes les portes de son âme à toutes les sciences et à tous les sentiments.

It is remarkable how tenaciously he clung to his past interests and at the same time broadened his intellectual pursuits: lyric poetry, philosophical poetry, history, science, metaphysics, and now a kind of morality based on economic theory and an enthusiasm for the pleasures of civilization. The demonstration of this diversity can be seen in the publication in 1736 of the *Mondain* and, the following year, the *Défense du Mondain.* The first poem grew out of the twenty-fifth *Lettre philosophique* and the attack against Pascal, but it was also a product of the spontaneous gaiety of a man who enjoyed the refinements of an advanced culture. The natural context in which he placed his delight in these worldly pleasures contrasted with the severity of Pascal and the Jansenists; he celebrated not only the triumph of the worldly over otherworldliness but also the superiority of civilization over all arbitrary morality. In the last analysis, the poem was a frank expression of human happiness in this world by the "happy few." I doubt that Voltaire gave much thought to substantiating that happiness by economic and political theory; I would be inclined to see first of all in the poem some relaxation from the arduous toil of science and philosophy. We must record, nonetheless, that he was already cognizant of the importance of Melon and his *Essai sur le commerce* (1734). Since Mme du Châtelet was in 1735 translating Mandeville's *Fable of the Bees,* and since she did translate the chapter upon luxury, whether she made a full translation of the work or no, Voltaire was fully aware of Mandeville's theories about luxury. Moreover, his interest in these problems of political economy extended to a treatise in which he compared the economic ideas of Melon and those of Dutot, and his recognition of the relationship between these new economic ideas and the foundations of morality—particularly insofar as Mandeville and Shaftesbury were concerned—can be seen in the final chapters of the

Traité de métaphysique. Voltaire's poem was thus a spontaneous expression of the joy of living and a poetic expression in which the new theories of ethics were derived from an embryo social science. At the same time, the poem served as a relaxation from the Newtonian studies.

The history of its genesis is difficult to follow in the correspondence because, in spite of the lavish way in which the *Mondain* was distributed, Voltaire was very reticent in talking about his poem. By 7 October 1736, Cideville had received a copy. In a letter to Thiériot, the poet referred to the *Epître en vers* which he had sent to Frederick and explained that he had no time to lose "dans le travail misérable de compasser des mots" (B. 1121). On 18 October 1736, he offered to send the *Mondain* to Berger (B. 1125). That he was an incorrigible poet he confessed to Olivet: "Je m'égaye encore à faire des vers même en étudiant Newton. Je suis occupé actuellement à savoir ce que pèse le soleil" (B. 1126). On 21 October 1736, he asked Thiériot if he had a copy. On the same day, he told the Comte de Tressan that he was sending him the poem: "Je vous envoye le *Mondain*. C'était à vous à le faire. J'y décris une petite vie assez jolie; mais que celle qu'on mène avec vous est au-dessus." Voltaire related that Depuy had had distributed some two hundred copies which he had made. The scandal burst around Christmas, 1736, and Voltaire took off for Holland. On 10 January 1737, he wrote to Frederick announcing that he was prepared to send him a *Défense du Mondain*: "C'est un petit essai de morale où je tâche de prouver avec quelque guaité, que le luxe, la magnificence, les galas, tous les beaux-arts, tout ce qui fait la splendeur d'un état en fait la richesse, et que ceux qui crient contre ce qu'on appelle le luxe ne sont guères que des pauvres de mauvaise humeur."

There were those, especially the police authorities and the hierarchy of the Church, who strongly condemned Voltaire's "badinage." The description of life in the Garden of Eden in particular was severely denounced, but, to be precise, the whole poem glorified the kind of mundane morality which had become widespread since the Regency. Voltaire had quickly sensed how prevalent this way of life had become, and he had had the astuteness to perceive that it expressed a new morality of happiness, justified pleasures as natural to man, and showed at the same time its conformity with the new economy. What the *Mondain* lacked, however, was a tie-in with the new economic theories of Dutot, Melon, and the modern English economists—moralists like Mandeville and Shaftesbury. It was not that Voltaire was unfamiliar with the English and French developments of these ideas; he merely judged the moral problem more interesting than the economic problem and, true to his principle of reducing everything to "la morale," based it upon man's way of life. The poem thus became significant for espousing a new morality oriented more to the pleasures of this life than to the more permanent pleasure of virtue. There are reasons to believe that Voltaire wrote it, not to defend those enjoyments in any philosophical way, but to relate them for the delectation of the "happy few." When, as so often happened, the manuscript copies of the poem became so numerous that a printed edition appeared, Voltaire was genuinely and disagreeably surprised by its unfavorable reception from the authorities. He then set out to justify this joy in life by appealing to economic, rather than to moralistic, arguments. Things became a bit confused, and it was with difficulty that one could distinguish between the *Mondain* as a defense of the worldly man and as a defense of a new economic theory. The result was that copies appeared as the *Mondain* which were in reality the *Défense du Mondain,* and vice versa.

DISCOURS EN VERS SUR L'HOMME

In the meantime, Pope had sent to Voltaire the *Essay on Man.* On 22 January 1736, the latter wrote to Thiériot: "J'ay lu les lettres de Pope." On 9 February, he related to Thiériot that, during his indisposition, Mme du Châtelet had read to him the *Tusculanes* of Cicero in Latin and the *Fourth Epistle* of Pope *On Happiness.* This latter work did not altogether please him, and, to some of his close friends, he complained that the English poet had strange ideas upon the subject, although he did not specify clearly what constituted their strangeness.

It is quite evident that at this time his interest in Pope was increasing. He took more than a casual interest in Du Resnel's translation, in which he claimed an active role. He was also very intrigued by the content. To Mme du Deffand, on 18 March 1736, he undertook to explain what Pope understood by "amour social." Mme du Deffand had assumed that the "amour social" which Pope mentioned was a proof of the "tout est bien" theory. Voltaire informed her that the "tout est bien" theory was supported by the doctrine of a Being infinitely wise who is the Maker. "Amour social," on this view, was the providential goodness which causes animals to serve as subsistence for each other. Lord Shaftesbury, on the other hand, established that God had given to man the love of himself as a means of self-preservation and "amour social," an instinct of benevolence towards one's fellowman, as the foundation stone of society. Voltaire concluded that it was strange that Pope should have attached to the concept of "amour social" the fury which animals exhibit when they attack other animals. He conceded that this phenomenon reveals a divine plan but insisted that it cannot in any way be called "amour."

The two big events of the year 1738 for Voltaire were the publication of the *Discours en vers sur l'homme* and the publication of the *Eléments de la philosophie de Newton*. Voltaire gave a little sketch of the origin of the first item in a letter to Frederick on 23 January 1738. He offered to send the Prince two *épîtres* which "sont le commencement d'une espèce de système de morale que j'avais commencé il y a un an." He announced that he had already written four *épîtres*. The two which he transmitted with this letter were the *Epître sur l'égalité des conditions* and *De la liberté*. He excused himself for sending the first one to a crowned, or almost crowned, head and the second to a partisan of the system of absolute necessity. He still saw that there were two ways of interpreting free will: the system of Newton, Locke, and Clarke, and the system of Leibniz, Wolff, and Frederick. On 2 February, Mme du Châtelet wrote Algarotti that she had sent two *épîtres* entitled *Sur le bonheur* to M. de Froullay, but only for him and for Algarotti. Already the plan to unite them in a series of *épîtres* under a general title had been adopted. It had, indeed, been suggested by Voltaire in his letter to Frederick. The latter replied to Voltaire on 19 February that he regarded the poems, not as a "thème philosophique," but as "des ouvrages tissus par les mains des grâces." On 8 March, Voltaire announced to Frederick that he was sending the third of these *épîtres,* this time *Sur l'envie*, "passion que je voudrois bien que votre altesse royale inspirâst à tous les rois." He added that his fourth would be *Sur l'amitié:* "Sans elle il n'y a point de bonheur sur la terre." On 3 April, he wrote to Duclos that people were talking about an *Epître sur le bonheur* which was being attributed to him and which he had not read. This was the famous dodge he often used in order to feel the pulse of his audience. Voltaire repeated the same denial in his letter of 10 April to Berger: "Je puis vous dire, mon cher monsieur, que ces épîtres dont vous me parlez, ne sont pas de moi, et vous me feriez une vraie peine, si vous ne faisiez pas tous vos efforts pour désabuser le public" (B. 1418). To Frederick, on 25 April, he wrote that he was sending him the fourth *épître* and that he was busy correcting the third. Mme du Châtelet, around 1 May, inquired of D'Argental if he had had the time to read the *épîtres* which were being attributed to Voltaire. At the same moment, Voltaire wrote to Thiériot that he had not seen the *Epître sur la liberté* but that he would send for it. Frederick acknowledged receipt of the fourth *épître* on 10 June and called it a "chef-d'œuvre." He also added that he had already received the fifth (which finally became the seventh), but here he objected to the reference to the *Homme-Dieu*, which he found out of place. On 1 July, Mme du Châtelet wrote D'Argental that the second *épître* was *Sur la liberté* and the fourth *Sur la modération*, that Voltaire would correct the first three until they met with D'Argental's approval, and that he would withhold the fifth until D'Argental gave the word to go ahead with its publication. On 6 August, Frederick wrote that he had now received the sixth *épître* entitled *Sur l'homme*. He found in it, as he said, "de grandes vérités," and he added: "Vous n'êtes jamais plus grand ni plus sublime que lorsque vous restez bien ce que vous êtes." On 27 August, Mme du Châtelet wrote Algarotti that the fourth *épître* had been printed and was now on sale in Paris. On 11 September, Césarion and Jordan added to a letter of Frederick their enthusiastic approval of the *Epître sur l'homme*. On 30 September, Frederick acknowledged the arrival of the *Epître sur la modération* from Paris, this time a corrected *épître* which he found much better, especially in regard to the description of Cirey. On 13 November, Voltaire was still correcting the first *épître*, as his letter of that date to Thiériot reveals. On 1 December, Voltaire was making corrections, suggested by Thiériot, of the *Epître sur la nature des plaisirs*. Mme de Graffigny, then at Cirey, announced to her correspondent on 5 December that

Voltaire had promised to show her an *Epître sur le bonheur*. On the next day, 6 December, Voltaire announced to D'Argental: "Voici une autre sorte d'hommage. C'est une cinquième épître en attendant que les autres soient dûment corrigées. Lisez là, ne la donnez point; dites ce qu'il faut réformer. Je voudrais qu'elle fût catholique et raisonnable; c'est un carré rond, mais en égrugeant les angles, on peut l'arrondir." The same day, Voltaire wrote to Thiériot that four of the *épîtres* had been published in Holland and that he had now sent them to the printer "corrigées et très corrigées." He urged his friend to hurry the *Epître sur la nature des plaisirs* to D'Argental and to return to Voltaire a copy of the eight or ten verses which the poet had misplaced. On 12 December, they were evidently still not completed, for Mme du Châtelet wrote D'Argental: "Je voudrais que ces six Epîtres fussent finies, pour n'en plus rien craindre." The following day, Mme de Graffigny wrote Panpan that the *épîtres* "au nombre de six, sont en Hollande pour être imprimées." On that same day, Voltaire wrote to Thiériot: "Enfin, je corrige tout avec soin. L'objet de ces six discours en vers, est peutêtre plus grand que celuy des satires et des épîtres de Boylau."

It was at this point that Mme du Châtelet, not having been able to restrain Voltaire and his *épîtres*, appealed to D'Argental to withhold his approval and refrain from sending them to Prault until he felt sure that they would not offend the authorities (B. 1613). On 20 December, Voltaire was still denying the authorship, this time to Formont (B. 1621):

Il a couru quelques épîtres très informes sous mon mon. Quand je les trouverai plus dignes de vous être présentées, je vous les enverrai. En attendant, voici un de mes sermons que je vous envoye avant qu'il soit prêché publiquement. Je vous prie comme théologien du monde et comme connaisseur et comme poète de m'en dire votre avis. Vous y verrez un peu le système de Pope, mais vous verrez aussi que c'est aux Anglais plutôt qu'à nous qu'il faut reprocher le ton éternellement didactique et les raisonnements abstraits soutenus de comparaisons forcées.

Je vous supplie que l'ouvrage ne sorte point de vos mains. Je compte sur votre critique autant que sur votre discrétion, j'ai également besoin de l'une et de l'autre. Le fond du sujet est délicat et pourrait être pris de travers; je voudrais ne déplaire ni aux honnêtes gens ni aux superstitieux; enseignez-moi ce secret-là.

On 25 December, Mme du Châtelet wrote D'Argental that Voltaire had severely corrected the first four *épîtres* and that he intended to send them to Prault, his printer, with instructions to show them to D'Argental. Mme du Châtelet was obviously still uneasy about the *Epître sur l'homme*. Recognizing that it had already been distributed rather widely, she suggested that perhaps the safe thing to do would be to request permission for publication, promising that she would undertake to have Voltaire make whatever revisions were necessary. The *Epître sur la nature du plaisir*, she stated, had been sent only to D'Argental. Voltaire finally subscribed to Mme du Châtelet's idea about the *Epître sur l'homme*. On 29 December, he wrote to D'Argental to have Prault seek a review of the *Epître sur l'homme*. He added: "Pourquoi ne sera-t-il pas permis à un français de dire d'une manière gaie, et sous l'enveloppe d'une fable, ce qu'un Anglais a dit tristement et sèchement dans des vers métaphysiques traduits lâchement?" That Voltaire was still undecided about how he intended to have Prault publish the *épîtres* can be seen from the following remark in the same letter: "Je ne sais s'il ne faudrait pas que Praut imprimât à la fois les 5 épîtres corrigées. En tout cas ou qu'il vous plaise lui confier votre exemplaire ou qu'il vous plaise me le renvoyer. Je n'ai aucune copie des corrections que j'ai faites à cette épître sur l'homme."

Thus ends the history of the composition of the *Discours en vers sur l'homme*. It is a very unsatisfactory story. All it tells us is that six of the *épîtres* were composed in 1738. I do not find any record of the seventh, *Sur la vraie vertu*. The first two, *Sur l'égalité des conditions* and *De la liberté*, were published together by Prault and entitled *Epîtres sur le bonheur*. The first three—those named above plus the *Epître sur l'envie*—were published in Holland with Voltaire's name on the title page. These three plus the *Epître sur la modération* were ready for publication by Prault by the end of the year. I do not know whether they were brought out or not. The fifth, *Sur l'homme*, and sixth, *Sur la nature du plaisir*, were completed but held back because of fear of the censor. The seventh, *Sur la vraie vertu*, does not seem to have been written at this time. This fragmentary way of composing the *Discours* must be attributed to the desire to escape the persecution which the other publications of the time had encountered. It is evident that Voltaire had a general plan of uniting some *épîtres* in a poem on morality before he set to work. At least, he indicated his intention of uniting them into such a work in his first mention of them to Frederick. It is not clear, however, that he intended at that time to unite more than two of them, or perhaps four. Only later did he decide to combine the seven. There is every indication that, when he joined the first two or three, Voltaire regarded the work as a sequel to Boileau's *Epîtres*. However, with the addition of the fourth and the fifth, he came more and more to regard the full work as more closely allied with the poem of Pope. The title of the fifth and the general title of the whole series of seven indicate this shift in conception. Thus, the full poem becomes a good example of the way in which Voltaire merged the moral poetry of Pope with the moral poetry of Boileau. It is a clear example of the traditional moral poetry derived from Horace via Boileau and expressed in the French fashion (for the first four poems) and of the same traditional moral poetry derived similarly from Horace via Pope and expressed in the English fashion (for the last three poems). But there is another filiation in the poems. The *Discours* is clearly united with the *Traité de métaphysique*. The second *épître*, *De la liberté*, bears perhaps the closest liaison with that work. It is, moreover, as Voltaire explained to Frederick, the key to the poet's whole system of morality. Voltaire saw that what he was presenting was a new approach to morality, granted some incontrovertible metaphysical principles. Seen in this perspective, the *Discours* is at the same time an extension of the twenty-fifth *Lettre philosophique* and the *Mondain* poems, an extension of Horatian poetry, as it had developed via Boileau and via Pope, and, finally, a development of a new science of man paralleling the elements of Newton as the science of nature. As an integrating factor in Voltaire's intellectual evolution, it is as important as the *Eléments*.

ELÉMENTS DE LA PHILOSOPHIE DE NEWTON

The *Eléments* is very difficult to locate in the chronological scheme of Voltaire's production. One would think that, having succeeded so well in the Newton letters in the *Lettres philosophiques*, he would have been encouraged to undertake a more thorough study of Newton. But we have seen already that he considered abandoning his interest in Newton and returning to poetry; at any rate, he indicated to Maupertuis that such was his intention. And, in fact, there is no item in the correspondence during 1734 and all of 1735 which gives any hint that he was preparing a further work on Newton's philosophy.

In the fall of 1735, Algarotti visited Cirey. Voltaire announced his visit to Thiériot and commended the Italian Count for his lively interest in languages, poetry, and Newton's philosophy. It was at that time that the young Venetian traveler read to the two inhabitants of Cirey some passages from his *Neutonianismo*. Mme du Châtelet said at a later date that it was the Count's visit which fired in Voltaire a desire to compose a work on Newton also. Although that may well be true, I suspect rather that the interest must have been already present, even though there is no documentary way of proving this suspicion.

At all events, on 5 August 1736, Voltaire announced to Caumont: "Je pourrais bien aussi avoir l'honneur de vous envoyer un *Essai sur la Philosophie de Newton*." It was the first reference he made to this work. The same day, he wrote to Cideville that he is "entre Newton et Emilie" (B. 1077). On 1 September 1736, he informed Berger that he was studying Newton under Mme du Châtelet's instruction and that he expected to print a little work which would permit everybody to understand this philosophy. He imparted to Thiériot, on 5 September 1736, that "nous étudions le divin Newton à force" and quoted some ten verses of the *Epître à Mme du Châtelet sur la philosophie de Newton*, which appeared (1738) in the first edition of the *Eléments*. He added that precisely at that moment he was writing against the vortices, the plenum, the instantaneous transmission of light, the so-called swirling of imaginary "globules" which, according to Descartes, was the source of colors, and Descartes's definition of matter. Obviously, he was making much headway toward the completion of his treatise, as this remark at the end of his letter makes plain: "si vous étiez homme à lire un petit traité du newtonisme de ma façon, vous l'entendriez plus aisément que Pemberton." He apparently still needed to study the original text, however, for, on 18 September 1736, he requested the Coste translation of Newton's *Optics* and, on 25 September 1736, spoke of a package which had just arrived containing a work by Newton. On 30 September 1736, he again promised Thiériot the full treatise: "Vous aurez la pièce entière de la philosophie Emilienne dont vous avez eü l'échantillon." It was, however, only on 25 December 1736 that Mme du Châtelet wrote D'Argental that the *Eléments* were done and ready to be printed. Voltaire himself, in a letter to Olivet some two years later (20 October 1738), mentioned that the *"Eléments* m'ont coûté six mois." I take it he meant that the actual composition required six months. The preparation took longer. It is plausible, though, that he had been working quietly since 1735, assembling further material for a popular work on Newton's philosophy along the lines of Pemberton's, which he admired, and that he came to a firm decision to compose that work around the time of Algarotti's visit. I would guess, however, that that decision had already been made when he observed the change from poetry to physics which had taken place in Paris. The letter to Cideville of 16 April 1735 seems to be the crucial document marking his turn toward Newtonian physics. Once his decision had been made, it is likely that the visit of Algarotti and the reading of the *Neutonianismo* worked to strengthen it. But the most important factor in encouraging that determination was undoubtedly Mme du Châtelet herself. Voltaire wrote to Mlle Quinault on 29 October 1736: "Je suis toujours le très humble serviteur des goûts des personnes avec qui je vis. On aime ici la philosophie de Newton, et je me suis mis à l'aimer. Je calcule, je combine, je cherche à comprendre ce que les autres ont découvert. . . ."

Having considered the possibility of a work of this nature in 1728, having carried out in a preliminary way the research in composing the letters on Newton in the *Lettres*, having reconsidered the possibility of composing a work on the subject, and having been led actually to undertake that work by his observations of the interest then shown in Paris for physics, by Algarotti's visit, and by Mme du Châtelet's deep interest in the subject, Voltaire must have set to work in earnest in 1736, just after he was convinced that he had a competent manuscript of the *Siècle de Louis XIV*, and, from June 1736 until the end of the year, composed his *Eléments de la philosophie de Newton*. There is no reason to believe that it was not in shape to be printed, as Mme du Châtelet said, by the end of the year. The condemnation of the *Mondain* made necessary his departure from Cirey, and he took advantage of a disagreeable experience to consult S'Gravesande about his *Eléments* at Leyden and possibly, also, Boerhaave. These two scholars, along with Musschembrœck, were serious followers of Newton and had contributed to the shift from Cartesianism to Newtonianism which had taken place in the universities of Holland. Both of them, in fact, had studied under Newton in England. Voltaire thus had a chance to receive careful criticism of his work. He undertook to profit from it in two ways: he seems both to have attended some of the classes at Leyden and to have consulted S'Gravesande upon particular points. To Frederick, he wrote, on 1 January 1737, that in Leyden there were two simple citizens, Boerhaave and S'Gravesande, who were attracting five hundred foreigners to their classes. There is no doubt that Voltaire was in the audience and that the experience was a sobering one, because he added that he regretted very much that he had been unable to achieve more than a modest amount of progress in his several intellectual fields: "Je n'ay pu dans ma petite sphère que saluer de loin les limites de chaque science, un peu de métaphysique, un peu d'histoire, quelque peu de physique, quelques vers ont partagé mon temps."

Voltaire left a manuscript of the *Eléments* with the printer Ledet in Leyden, apparently with the understanding that he would write several additional chapters for the second part. He was, as usual, dissatisfied with his draft. That he continued his study during the remainder of his stay in Holland can be seen from this remark in a letter he wrote to D'Argental on 27 January 1737 (B. 1212): "Je vis assez en philosophe, j'étudie beaucoup, je vois peu de monde, je tâche d'entendre Newton et de le faire entendre" (B. 1212). He had apparently, in a moment of indiscretion, let slip mention of his intentions, because the *Gazette d'Utrecht* announced on 13 December 1736 that he was translating from English to French one of Newton's works and added that he had abandoned literature "pour ne plus s'adonner qu'à la physique, et en faire désormais ses délices."

Voltaire nonetheless felt the need for further advice from a Newtonian scholar, as he had earlier in composing the Newton letters for the *Lettres philosophiques*, when he had profited from the advice of Maupertuis. This time he turned to Henri Pitot, and, when the latter consented to review the manuscript, around 20 June 1737, Voltaire sent it to him, along with the explanation that he had tried to scatter some anecdotes among the thorny passages of physics. He claimed to be writing the history of science, rather than science, and he expressed the hope that this part would be read with some pleasure. He confessed, though, that the details of the calculations wearied and embarrassed him even more than they would the ordinary reader. "C'est pour ces cruels détails surtout que j'ai recours à votre tête algébrique et infatigable; la mienne, poétique et malade, est fort empêchée à peser le soleil."

Voltaire explained further to Pitot his intention in preparing the *Eléments*. He meant it to be a review of the Newtonian mysteries, which had been concealed up to the present from the majority of people, especially the theory of attraction, which appeared to him a new property of matter. He insisted that the effects of this attraction had been calculated, and he was convinced that it dispensed with all theories of impulsion. He had observed the experiments of S'Gravesande, however, and found that he now had to abandon Mairan's idea that the quantity of movement in a falling body is MV and accept instead the idea that it is MV^2. He felt that he now had to accept Berkeley's ideas on optics which explain why we see objects in a concave mirror placed otherwise than they should be according to the ordinary laws of vision. He recognized, also, that Berkeley had solved the problem concerning the size of the disks of the sun and the moon on the horizon, which Malebranche and Régis had discussed, and other physical problems of equal importance.

5. 1738-1739: THE REVOLUTION OF
A HUMAN MIND

VOLTAIRE IS CONSTANTLY after 1738 talking about the revolution of the human mind, which, as we shall see, he identifies with "mœurs," manners and customs, and which he thinks leads to "génie" and to "esprit." This revolution is the subject of history, since it marks not only the moment of crisis but the role assigned the mind in the structuring and creation of man's spirit. Since Voltaire's reeducation brought about one of those moments of crisis, we must now stop to make a summary of the nature of his reeducation and to examine the consequences. We shall try to show that the end of 1738 and the beginning of 1739 represent a turning point in the development of Voltaire, the point at which the poet became a philosopher. The two aspects of this change which concern us are, first, the way in which the new education formed a coherent pattern of thought and, second, the relationship it bears to the old education which Voltaire had received from the Jesuits. We shall then have to consider the problems which had to be resolved when Voltaire attempted to integrate the old education with the new.

The basic problem is what kind of coherent pattern of thought occurs when to an epic poem, a dozen or so plays, and a raft of circumstantial poetry a writer adds a book describing the civilization of a foreign country, a treatise on metaphysics in which religious problems are discussed along with philosophical and moral ones, a history of the decline of one foreign country (Sweden) alongside the rise of another (Russia), a work discussing the elements of Newton's philosophy, a history which endeavors to explain what makes a century in one country one of the greatest manifestations of the human mind that has ever existed, and, finally, some didactic verses which attempt to explain what the nature of man is, what brings out his happiness, what creates difficulties, what constitutes the good life of a man of society, and what are the economic requirements of a society which will guarantee this good life.

The character of the problems presented and discussed is, to say the least, quite varied. The analysis of English civilization entails a study of each of the elements of a civilization—religion, politics, economics, science, philosophy, literature—the result being a sort of combination, vicariously sketched, of manners and customs, political and social institutions, arts and letters. The aim is to reduce all these manifestations to the spirit of the society and to see therein the manifestations of its "mœurs." The history of Charles XII and Peter the Great is a study of the undertakings which ruin a country (wars, for instance) contrasted with those (arts, trades, industry, social reform) which enhance a country's power. It is a true history, which teaches by example. The *Siècle de Louis XIV* is a more specific case where an analysis is made of all the activities which raise a country at a given period of time to the acme of its glory and some attention is given to those incidents which contribute to its decline. All of these studies in one way or another assume that the purpose of life is material and spiritual progress and that each individual is engaged in the search for personal happiness. The directing organ is the human mind. Success is achieved by the intelligent application of thought by each to the possibilities of his life. But the application requires certain basic concepts: not much can be achieved unless one understands a good deal about the nature of the forces which rule, the nature of the external world, and the nature of man. The basic metaphysical questions (the existence of God, the nature of God, the immortality of the soul), the fundamental physical inquiries (the nature of matter, the difference between matter and spirit, the origin of ideas), the principal moral topics (the nature of free will, good and evil, vice and virtue), the primary social issues (the rapport between the individual and the group, the organization of the state, the nature of institutions, religious, political, and economic policies), and, finally, the essential aesthetic problems (the origins of taste, the nature of taste) have to be discovered and assembled before some coherent picture of civilization can be obtained. But, even before that, some choice has to be made between a heavenly city and an earthly city. And, above all, some sort of hierarchy has to be established in regard to the relative importance of religion, science, politics, economics, morality, aesthetics, and the other categories of living.

Each of Voltaire's works composed or published between 1734 and 1738 fits into this jigsaw puzzle of civilization in one way or another. Together they give a coherent picture of a man who wants to know what the foundations of society are and what will best guarantee enjoyment of the good life. Each work considers a particular item essential to a well-rounded picture, but each also throws out tentacles to the other works. In a curious way, each is performing three services at one time: contributing to a fund of knowledge and making the author more and more an encyclopedic man; adding a new dimension, that of science and philosophy, to poetry; and combining with another to lay the foundations of a new civilization.

There is thus no gainsaying that Voltaire had stuffed an immense amount of "new," "modern" material into his intellectual baggage between 1734 and 1738. It is hardly accurate to characterize it only as arts and letters on the one hand, science and philosophy on the other. When one attempts to break down what is meant by letters, one finds that, for Voltaire, it involved at least lyric poetry, didactic poetry, drama, and the epic. Similarly, when one attempts to analyze the scope of science and philosophy, one finds that it encompassed at least metaphysics, natural science, "métaphysique morale," morality, history, politics, and economics. If Voltaire's old training was exceedingly broad, his new training was broader still. The acquisition of each body of knowledge was an enormous task in itself; the integration of the two bodies of knowledge was nothing short of stupendous. Fortunately, Voltaire's English experience and the necessity of giving some coherent organization to it in the *Lettres philosophiques* offered the poet the framework into which all this diversity could be cast: the core of all these intellectual and aesthetic interests was certainly the concept of civilization, that concept which we have learned to define (mainly from Voltaire and his contemporaries, in fact) as the coordination of manners and customs, political and social institutions, arts and letters.

It is important that we understand clearly the relationship between the old and the new education. The poet undertook his reeducation with the firm intention of putting his new learning into proper perspective with his old learning. Nowhere in the correspondence between 1734 and 1738 do I perceive any desire on Voltaire's part to discard the activities which were the result of his Jesuit training at Louis-le-Grand. He states very plainly, in fact, that he intends to devote himself at intervals to both kinds of learning: literature and the arts on the one hand, science and philosophy on the other. There is visible in his statements, however, a tendency to alter the relative positions of importance of the two types: more and more, science and philosophy engaged his attention to the detriment of arts and letters. And there is also evidence of the general tendency to make arts and letters more philosophical. Voltaire's genuine enthusiasm for things modern naturally led him to give an added emphasis to the new subjects he was investigating, with the result that less attention was paid to the older subjects. There were thus shifts in emphasis which would eventually require readjustments, but there was not yet any radical change which would render necessary the abandonment of one career and the adoption of a new one.

We later critics will have to accept some responsibility for exaggerating the predicament of Voltaire at this juncture. Usually, we incline to the conclusion that Voltaire's poetry was not at all of the first order, that he was very conscious of this fact, and that he switched from poetry to thought because he recognized clearly his inability to be a world poet. We then seek the justification of this action in the circumstance that he was living in an age which was doing precisely the same thing. Once having accepted these facts as basic, we are led either to look upon the move as logical and, therefore, intelligent or to argue that, although Voltaire's literary production cannot compare in quality with that of Shakespeare or Racine, much of it deserves consideration and respect or, finally, to maintain, as Professor Topazio has done in his very recent critical study of Voltaire's works, that this literary production has been ill-appreciated even though it really is excellent. It is clear that we cannot have it all three ways. And yet we feel, very reasonably it seems to me, that, since Voltaire spent forty-five years of his life as a literary figure, twenty-five of them given over to active literary production, and was regarded by his contemporaries as the foremost literary personage, as *the* Poet, of his day, and since the remaining forty years of his long life were not at all divorced from further literary production, there can be nothing incongruous in attempting to discover his worth as a poet. Knowing his immense popularity in the society of his time as an outstanding lyric poet of the Horatian order, as an outstanding didactic poet, also of the Horatian order, as France's great dramatist of the century, greater than Corneille and equal to Racine, and as the only epic poet of consequence that France had ever had, we naturally feel that something is wrong if we cannot explain the nature of that excellence, the causes of his decline in reputation, or at least the conditions under which, around 1738-1739, he concluded that there were things much more important, much more serious, than being a poet.

The contemporary evidence, which has been assembled from the critics and the public at large, has always indicated that Voltaire's poetic production was superior in quality to that of any contemporary poet. Often it was declared excellent and placed above that of the great writers of the age of Louis XIV. Notwithstanding this evidence, the curious fact remains that, despite Voltaire's pretensions to lyrical, epic, dramatic, and mock-epic poetry, despite his declared intention to become France's foremost poet and the greatest epic poet and dramatic poet of the eighteenth century, despite a production which can only be qualified as enormous in those areas, subsequent biographers and critics have been loath to touch upon his accomplishments in those fields.

Several reasons are given to justify this avoidance, not all of them very explicit. Some critics, like Faguet, feel that Voltaire had no talent for poetry. Of the three indispensable qualities demanded of a great poet—poetic imagination, poetic sensibility, and eloquence—Voltaire, says Faguet, lacked the first two elements and distrusted the third, believing it to be a sign of inferiority. According to this view, poetic imagination and poetic sensibility had been stifled by Voltaire's abundance of wit, by his destructive critical spirit, or by his excessive intellectualism. On the other hand, Faguet concedes that Voltaire is charming in light verse—the *conte*, the epigram, the *stances*—where gracefulness, wit, and elegance are required, qualities which Voltaire possessed in ample quantity. But, he adds, this light verse is frivolous and transient, based upon day-to-day experience and divorced from deep, poetic meaning.

Lanson more or less echoes Faguet's opinion, although he is more generous. The Voltairean odes he finds distinctly inferior to those of J.-B. Rousseau. They suffer particularly from too many poetic trappings and are patently artificial. His epic, on the other hand, is an example of the great classic art, noble in taste, pompous but humanized, interpreted in the Louis XV style. It has "détails ingénieux," "des échappées d'humeur spirituelle," and a "tour de philosophie hardie et provocante," but it is dated by the Louis XV style. Lanson judges the *épîtres* to be superior. They are far more natural and far more lively, full of satire, malice, some sentiment, and much gaiety. Lanson considers them less heavy than those of Boileau and more philosophical than those of La Fontaine. The free *stances*, which in a way are minor *épîtres*, and the satires, epigrams, *contes*, and madrigals—"poésie légère," as they are often collectively called— are the most attractive of all his poetic work. Here all the qualities Voltaire saw in Horace reappear: the gentle satire, malicious but restrained, witty and lighthearted, full of fancy and gaiety. Into them is infused the temperament of the author, sometimes irascible, at other times sentimental and even affectionate, indifferent yet serious, contradictory and mobile. They carry the moods of the poet into the events of everyday living and withal express a moderate, though impertinent, epicureanism. "Une pointe de regret de l'amour perdu ou de la vie qui s'en va, un accent de volupté ou de mélancolie épicuriennes, un élan de haine ou de colère terminé en moquerie amusée, une image de la nature gracieuse"—these are the subjects of the light verses. They are cast in the clear, almost colorless expression of the time, with facile tones, monotonous phrasings, poor rimes, some slight archaisms from Marot, and even some of the trappings of neoclassic ornament. Yet they possess good taste, a neat, though risky, vocabulary, and a careful workmanship, which equally characterizes Voltaire's prose.

Faguet and Lanson, for all their reservations and apologies, certainly leave the impression that, despite a general apathy toward Voltaire's poetry, poetic qualities are discernible in it and even, on occasion, that some of it has genuine poetic flavor. But they also leave the impression that, for all kinds of reasons, Voltaire's poetry lacks depth, those universal traits which give lasting merit to a poem, and that perfection of poetic expression which assures its everlasting durability. It is poetry written for the poet's contemporaries, not for posterity. Finally, it has an air of modernity, but a modernity which is trite, superficial, and often contrived.

We have to be very careful in discussing Voltaire's poetry that we are seeing it in the right perspective. Two things which militate against our success are our own preconceptions about what constitutes excellent poetry and a lack of a critical standard whereby to judge poetic excellence. Ascoli has made the remark that, having learned to love and admire the extraordinary poetry the symbolists created, it is difficult for us to appreciate at its fullest preceding poetry which has none of the excellence of symbolism. And it is undoubtedly true that, in poetic values, we would make some very serious distinctions between Voltaire and Baudelaire, although I doubt that we would go as far in distinguishing between Racine and Baudelaire.

We suffer, particularly, from a kind of myth which consists in believing that what is philosophical cannot be poetry. Hence, the more poetry tends to be philosophical, the more we are inclined to condemn it. That is surely an error; there is no reason whatever to conclude that making art more philosophical is tantamount to ruining its artistic qualities. We repeat: the didactic poetry of the Horatian order which Voltaire composed between 1736 and 1756 is as good as any produced elsewhere (in France or in Europe) at that time. The *Mondain*, the *Défense du Mondain*, the *Discours en vers sur l'homme, La Loi naturelle,* and the *Poème sur le désastre de Lisbonne* are more than worthy poems. We should also remember that the lighter verse, that is, the lyric, satirical Horatian verse (the *épîtres*, the *stances*, the epigrams, the "Poésies mêlées") which Voltaire wrote from 1715 to 1738, is composed with gracefulness and ease and does not show any signs of deterioration as Voltaire gives himself more and more to the study of science and philosophy. It is certainly not of the quality of Horace, yet it compares favorably with other Horatian poetry in eighteenth-century Europe. Moreover, compared with the production of the long line of seventeenth-century French imitators of Horace extending from Théophile de Viau to Chaulieu who preceded him, Voltaire's Horatian poetry does not appear strikingly inferior. His poems, like Théophile's, often express sadness at the passing of time, stress man's inability to find within himself a source of human satisfaction, and reflect the fears and uneasiness of life. Voltaire often matches the bravado, the unorthodoxy, the contempt of Des Barreaux for the hypocrisy of his time. He echoes constantly Blot's impertinence and lack of reverence. Like Dehénault and Mme Deshoulières, he celebrates the passing of glory, the nothingness of death, and the cares, suffering, and sorrows of life. Like Chaulieu and La Fare, he talks much of the pleasures of love, the joys of society, the life of volupty. His poetry is probably not as good technically as Théophile's and Des Barreaux's, certainly less good than that of the early La Fontaine. Professor Grubbs, who has studied his verse from this point of view, finds him inferior to J.-B. Rousseau. But caution should be taken here, for to admit that the judgment of his contemporaries, which habitually placed him above all these poets, was certainly excessive is not to say that he should be placed below them; and, indeed, only La Fontaine and Boileau clearly deserve a higher ranking. In addition to the themes, the tone, and the poetic devices which Voltaire copies from his predecessors, he possesses by comparison a wider perspective, a deeper feeling, a lighter fancy, a more personal and constantly fluctuating response to life, and, above all, a saving wit. It would not be difficult to put together a modest anthology of Voltaire's lighter poetry which would compare favorably with that of any lyrical French poetry between Malherbe and André Chénier. Such a volume would certainly comprise *Les Tu et les Vous*, some of the shorter *épîtres* to Mme du Châtelet (M. 45, 46, 47, etc.), *Sur les poètes épiques* and the chanson "Si vous voulez que j'aime encore" (M. I and VIII) among the *stances*, and a fair number of epigrams. And, if one is prepared to accept didactic poetry as lyrical poetry, it would also surely include the *Discours en vers, La Loi naturelle,* and the *Poème sur le désastre de Lisbonne*. If one prefers satires, two of the best are the *Mondain* and the *Défense du Mondain*. If one enjoys *contes en vers* (and the eighteenth century greatly appreciated these *contes*), Voltaire's are hardly inferior to any save La Fontaine's. Voltaire himself even felt—and sincerely so—that in didactic poetry he was superior to the Boileau of the *Epîtres* and in the "art de raconter" at least the equal of La Fontaine.

It seems to me, though, that trying to defend Voltaire's poetry is an injudicious way of using our time, just as defending the work of any poet would be. What is important is not whether Voltaire's poetry is good or bad or indifferent. We do not have very accurate ways of making these mass evaluations in literature, anyway. The best we can do is maintain that a certain poem is noteworthy for particular features. *Les Tu et les Vous*, for instance, is as rigidly structured as the *Epître à Uranie*. Both poems use the classical structures of contrast, contradiction, tension, paradox, and superficial irony of the

Iliad. But that certainly does not mean that they are as good as the *Iliad* or as Horace's poems, many of which exhibit these same classical structures. It only means that, in this one respect, both poems possess real merit. That, too, could also be beside the point. What is important is that Voltaire began to think that, although his poetry had merit, there were other things more meritorious and, in 1738-1739, began to say so and to act upon that opinion.

VOLTAIRE'S DRAMA

Similar remarks apply to Voltaire's theatre. It was by common consent the outstanding drama of the Enlightenment. Judged in terms of the popular response, it was the greatest of the time. Judged in terms of the literary critics' reaction, it was superior to any French drama save Racine's, and to that it was at least equal. Incidentally, what Voltaire produced between 1732 and 1743 (*Zaïre, Alzire, Mérope, Mahomet*) was the best of his theatre. He was justly proud of it, and contemporary taste deemed it excellent. In the renunciation of 1738, Voltaire was willing to give up lyric poetry, but he clung tenaciously to the drama. However, he did subordinate its role in his production, and after *Tancrède*, though still an amusement, it was no longer at the center of his activity.

It is not easy to formulate an accurate judgment upon this theatre either. We have very full treatments of it. In fact, the bibliography of Voltaire's drama[4] is extraordinarily rich, richer than that of any other genre, even the *conte*. We are told how successful the plays were in their day, how they broke the tradition of French classical tragedy by introducing innovations drawn from Shakespeare and the English stage, how they push thought content to the point of propaganda and become philosophical rather than artistic, how they have ceased to attract any attention at the present time. Historically, we are told, Voltaire's dramatic theories have their importance in the evolution of eighteenth-century dramatic art. His production of

---

[4] See H. Lion, *Les Tragédies et les théories dramatiques de Voltaire*; E. Deschanel, *Le Romantisme des classiques: Le Théâtre de Voltaire*; G. Lanson, *Esquisse d'une histoire de la tragédie française*; R. Lowenstein, *Voltaire as an Historian of Seventeenth-century French Drama*; H. C. Lancaster, *French Tragedy in the Time of Louis XV and Voltaire, 1715-1774*; H. Fenger, *Voltaire et le théâtre anglais*; R. S. Ridgway, *La Propagande philosophique dans les tragédies de Voltaire*; J. Vrooman, "Voltaire's Theatre: A Study in Tragic Focus."

some fifty plays is undoubtedly essential to an understanding of the eighteenth-century French theatre. It is even possible to defend the literary worth of five or so of his plays: *Zaïre, Alzire, Mérope, Mahomet,* and *Tancrède,* for instance.

One would hardly want to establish Voltaire's literary reputation upon his theatre, however, any more than upon his epic poetry or his Horatian verse. Lanson (*Esquisse,* p. 123), for instance, asks the categorical question: "Why is the Voltaire tragedy so completely dead?" Naves (*Goût,* p. 465) protests against any attempt to approach Voltaire's theatre as one would study Racine's without taking into account the critical intention of the author. Naves insists that the great merit of Voltaire's dramatic art is to raise questions rather than to solve them. He concedes that whatever unity exists in the ensemble of this theatre is a "unité critique" rather than a "unité poétique," each tragedy representing a distinct experiment, while the test of its success depends basically upon taste, along with contemporary fashion and personal preference.

There is no denying Voltaire's passionate love of the theatre, which was all-embracing and genuine. He accepted it as the ultimate expression of civilization, as the highest form of social art, and as the literary genre which best expresses the manners and customs of a people, as well as their apprehension of a "morale." These qualities, which we have learned to attribute to the epic, Voltaire ascribed without question to the theatre. In that respect, his love of drama was in perfect accord with the sentiment of the society of his time. From repertories of the eighteenth-century French theatre assembled at the end of the century and during the first third of the succeeding century, it is possible to compile a list of some forty to forty-five thousand titles of eighteenth-century and early nineteenth-century French plays. Statistics, of course, mean little in literary matters, and these merely show that the drama of the period had a moral, social, and civilizing function, as Voltaire constantly asserted. They do not necessarily denote that it was an exceedingly vital or highly artistic literary genre. It had become, though, the expression of a society and served a function similar to that of the movie in early twentieth-century society or television at the present moment. There are, however, distinct differences. Drama had been during the whole of seventeenth-century Europe the one artistic literary genre which had dominated all others, so much so that, if only two periods of history could be designated ages of drama, one would have to be fifth-century B.C. Greece, the other seventeenth-century Europe. In the latter epoch, moreover, not only was drama the dominating genre, but dramatic art was the highest expression of art. In the subsequent epoch, when Voltaire entered upon the literary scene, the theatre was on the wane, a phenomenon which was apparent to everyone but which seemed attributable to no particularly recognizable set of conditions. Yet everyone still accepted dramatic art as the highest expression of civilization, even while deploring its loss of vitality.

Voltaire's attitude was not one whit different from that of his contemporaries. He was well aware of the decline in dramatic art after its period of predominance in Europe. He reflected, as everybody did, upon the reasons for its degeneration, which he attributed in part to Nature's resting after a magnificent display of energy and in part to altered social conditions, particularly the institution of censorship. The measures which he took to combat the deterioration were of three sorts. He first tried to rediscover in fifth-century Greece the source of French classical vitality. His first play, *Œdipe*, was a conscious effort to renew that vitality, so conscious, in fact, that his *Lettres sur Œdipe* were devised to discuss how the renewal could be brought about. Voltaire at that moment could think of no better way than to eliminate the errors of Greek and French classical drama, a move which he interpreted to mean modernizing the theatre. Fundamentally, his method was to imitate simultaneously Racine and Shakespeare. *Zaïre* thus owed its birth to both *Othello* and *Bajazet*. Eventually though, Voltaire was reduced to imitating certain dramatic effects—action, for instance, or incidents, or staging—or certain emotional responses—tears, for instance, or terror, or pity—rather than whole plays. All of this scurrying around in a search for new dramatic principles not only evidences the extent of Voltaire's commitment to the art of the drama and the high place he accorded his own dramatic production but also betrays a good deal of confusion.

We never can be sure, however, that we are looking at Voltaire's drama in the right perspective, and that uncertainty causes no end of embarrassment, not to mention some very trivial, if not erroneous, criticism of his theatre. Lanson (*Esquisse*, pp. 114ff.), for instance, insists that Voltaire's dramatic theories preceded his dramatic creations. This assertion, however, is only partially true, since in many instances Voltaire's practice gave rise subsequently to long discussions. In reality, more than three-fourths of his dramatic theories came from prefaces or similarly fragmentary items, such as letters or "rogatons." That is why they are rather unsystematized and unstable. It is true that Voltaire seemed to be subject to all kinds of currents and even personal influences, such as that of the D'Argentals, whom he consulted endlessly. He was conscious of all sorts of efforts being made elsewhere, by Destouches in comedy, by Nivelle de la Chaussée, by Diderot, even by the elder Crébillon. And he was hard put to decide whether he approved or opposed these efforts. In general, he ended by denouncing them, chiefly on the score that the change introduced only another mediocre theatre, not a really vital one. Voltaire found difficult any attempt to be dramatic after the classical manner and resolutely modern at the same time, and, like his time, he accepted the decline as preferable to change. He did not, however, do so without interminable activity and discussion—long letters to the D'Argentals about specific details in a play, explanations of the way a character is conceived, lengthy expositions of the situation as he understood it, even discussions about the propriety of a verse. Naves has remarked that the theatre of Voltaire was just one everlasting workshop: in his opinion, Voltaire was continually experimenting, always demonstrating a new technique, presenting a new subject, inventing a new situation, or defending a new idea. A play was seldom judged capable of justifying itself; it had to be accompanied by commentaries, as *Le Triumvirat* was, for instance. Indeed, often a play was an excuse for the commentaries. For the author of *Le Goût de Voltaire*, this attitude of Voltaire is a real merit. But, for those of us who think that the role of an author is to produce literary works, the whole procedure reveals a real deficiency in drama. It is perhaps amusing and sometimes instructive to listen to Voltaire discuss his problems of creation. Yet we would prefer some really superior plays to all this detailed discussion. Naves concludes, quite rightly, that Voltaire had no confidence in his plays, although he did have great devotion to the art of tragedy. There is no doubt that some of his embarrassment arose from his inability to conceive of a work of art as an organic living thing. It should be noted also that he had some difficulty in writing for posterity: he was far too interested in the immediate effect, and he actually wanted to be present to witness the effect. Indeed, he could never separate himself from the effect produced, with the result that he wanted to be not only playwright and critic but actor, too. It was all a part of his dramatic workshop.

There must have been conditions, though, which more adequately explain the phenomenon of his drama. We have a way of posing the problem so that one half of it is always lost. When we consider the reasons for the eclipse of his theatre after his time, we are inclined to forget to balance them against the reasons for his immense success among his contemporaries. Moreover, it is easy to condemn Voltaire for not writing ritual plays as Sophocles did, but we forget that Voltaire never intended to do so and that his public never expected it of him.

If one asks instead how Voltaire conceived of tragedy, perhaps some headway can be made. In general, we can ferret out his answers. The starting point should undoubtedly be Aristotle or, at any rate, Voltaire's understanding of Aristotle. A tragedy according to this conception, is the representation of an *action* offered for the entertainment of a highly sophisticated group, trained to recognize and appreciate beauties (of situation, of character, of response, and of expression). Its immediate effect is one of terror and pity: it is successful only insofar as it strikes terror into the beholder and arouses sympathy for the suffering of another human being. Its best chance of succeeding is to stay within the existing framework of a set of conventions accepted by the artists and the public as reasonable: the expression should be poetic, the tone rhetorical, the assertions general rather than specific, the thought noble, and the presentation dignified, uncomplicated, and intellectually acceptable. Decorum should be observed both in word and in deed. Fundamentally, a group of highly intelligent, sophisticated people assemble to witness the presentation of an action, an event, or a situation and to appreciate the way it has been constructed, the accuracy of the poetic expression, the quality of the action, and the lesson to be learned. The ultimate distribution of praise or blame lies in the taste of the beholder, who judges in the light of his sensibility and his spontaneous reaction. He defends that judgment by explicit details analyzed in conversation. Every French classical play, as Voltaire under-stands it, is an open-ended work of art which can always be con-tinued in conversation, in the same way that the *Ecole des femmes* can always be continued by a *Critique de l'Ecole des femmes*.

The strange thing about this concept of tragedy is that super-ficially it looks like Aristotle's. As a result, since his definition of tragedy has always been thought to have been derived from the *Œdipus*, we think of it immediately in terms of the great Greek tragedians. Voltaire encourages that approach on our part. Moreover, since we justify the excellence of French classical tragedy, and par-ticularly Racine, the supreme French artist of tragedy, in terms of the Greek ideal, we assume that we should apply the same criteria to Voltaire's plays. Voltaire is perfectly willing to encourage that as-sumption also. The truth of the matter, though, is that Voltaire's understanding of Greek tragedy and Racine's connection with it do not at all coincide. For, although Voltaire is fully prepared to defend the traditional concept as long as it gives him a talking point, he is thinking of something entirely different. Simple inspection of the way the normal key words of tragedy—tragic effect, tragic hero, tragic flaw, tragic irony, tragic purgation—are defined will show how far removed he is from tradition. In each case, the Aristotelian definitions make no sense when applied to Voltaire's tragedy. One need only lay the statement that tragedy is the representation of an *act* (that is, a cosmic act, of course) alongside Voltaire's statement that "it is the representation of an *action*" to see how far apart Voltaire and Aristotle are from the very beginning. Similarly, if one takes "To hold the Gods in awe" of Sophocles and tries to apply it to one of Voltaire's plays, one can see immediately how far apart they are.

We do not very often undertake these comparisons, however. Nor do we stop to inquire why Voltaire's understanding of Shakespeare is so different from Shakespeare's understanding of himself. Our regular way of proceeding is to recall that in Voltaire's day the French classical tragedy was declining and that Voltaire, very con-scious of this state of affairs, set to work to reinvigorate it. His pro-cedure consisted in a certain number of moves to modernize tragedy, one of the most important being the adaptation of Shakespeare's tragic art to French classical tragedy. We seldom get very far when we endeavor to explain the process, however. So we discourse upon Voltaire's determination to increase the action of French classical tragedy, arising from his conviction that a French tragedy is a conversation with little action, while an English tragedy is just the opposite. French tragedy, for its part, is very civilized and, consequently, more decorous, more refined, and better structured than English tragedy.

Voltaire's ideal was to combine English action with French art. In addition, he wanted to adopt certain English scenes, such as the rabble scene in *Julius Caesar* or the ghost scene in *Hamlet*, because they seemed to him so dynamic and so capable of instilling terror in the beholder. It was just another way of increasing the action, but, of course, it also gave an added importance to the spectacle. Voltaire also pretended to add the bold thought he deemed characteristic of the English theatre, but beyond embracing an expression of English freedom he did not accomplish very much.

In all this manipulation, Voltaire clung to certain convictions which belonged to his inheritance as a Frenchman. The aim of art is beauty; truth or, rather, the appearance of truth is merely a way of guaranteeing beauty. Art must be granted a certain freedom to achieve its end. This freedom is a license to make something not true appear true. Voltaire, like all the classicists, protested against the very constraints he imposed, but the protest was more a complaint than a revolt. The important thing was how many constraints the artist could dare eliminate. Finally, art is achieved only by keeping things in proportion, never by excesses. In classical drama, all things work together for those who love it. With these generally accepted notions, Voltaire could espouse the traditional classical doctrine: tragedy depicts the characters and passions of humanity by presenting a portrait of the suffering of humanity's heroes. Our interest lies in the depiction of those characters and in the analysis of these passions, but it lies also in the verisimilitude of the action and the reaction. We judge, admire, and appreciate the accurate human relationships between the passions, the characters, and the situation in which they are caught; but we judge more accurately and appreciate more deeply the expression which accompanies the passions and the action. Thus, the style, the poetic expression, and the technical apparatus come to be considered safer criteria of judgment than passions, action, and interest.

Voltaire, however, added or subtracted some special things. He made every effort, for instance, to suppress the theme of love, probably because after Racine not much room was left for experimenting with that theme. He, however, condemned it as gallantry, while reintroducing it into his plays as chivalry, to such an extent that Naves can hardly see anything else in them. He insisted more upon increasing such effects as emotional response. The test of tragedy became, for him, the extent to which it gives rise to tears. Voltaire desired a more visual representation and a more physical enactment, which he judged would be more capable of increasing this emotional response. Most of all, he wanted a closer relationship between manners and customs and characters and action. Indeed, Voltaire pushed this aspect of his modern tragedy to the point where it became a careful delineation of historical time and place. One of the tragic effects he sought to achieve arose from the clash between civilizations, with the resultant exoticism, which became so prevalent in the subsequent period. He had also a tendency to select material subjects, at least in theory.

Many of these things have been said over and over, with the intention either of justifying Voltaire's drama or of condemning it. In his time, his drama was completely justified: his glory as France's greatest playwright was not surpassed by any other, and, indeed, he was usually placed above Corneille and at least equal to Racine. When all this has been said and resaid, one can still legitimately ask whether tragedy was not a fruitless undertaking for Voltaire, simply because he was totally lacking in a tragic sense of life. Lion (*Tragédies*, pp. 431-433) attributes his weakness to a constant repetition of similar themes, that is, to a lack of inventiveness, and Naves has cited a fair number of places where Voltaire himself confessed to this deficiency. Lion also ascribes it to an excess of melodramatic action. Lanson feels that Voltaire's weakness sprang from his inability to understand the tragic workings of fate. Rather than impute an action to the inexorable working of destiny, Voltaire was more likely to assign it to the working of chance exemplified in some small incident or to some material object playing the role of chance. And just as he was normally incapable of hearing those deep in-sistent voices which drive men to want to know themselves better in that inner world which is to a large extent unknowable, so he found difficult any comprehension of the human condition in which was manifested a desire to surpass one's self. The distinction, for Voltaire, lay between surpassing one's self, which he could not understand, and achieving one's self, which, like all satirists, he understood perfectly. Unfortunately for Voltaire's renown, in our day tragedy seems to have something to do with surpassing one's self, rather than with achieving one's self.

It ought to be apparent by this time that this matter of perspective in judging Voltaire's theatre is not an empty problem. Since he started by throwing his conception of French classical tragedy out of perspective, he will have to accept some responsibility for this misunderstanding. He will have to answer also for his effort to revivify French classical tragedy with dramatic procedures borrowed from Shakespeare and the English theatre. His inability to understand Shakespeare may be pardonable, but his assumption that two different procedures may be merged to produce a desired result was undoubtedly an error. And his belief that a traditional form may be rendered modern by tinkering with a few details displayed real naïveté. He would have been better advised if he had really wanted to modernize the theatre to start from the ground up, as Diderot did. He would not have produced more dynamic theatre for us, but he would have at least set the stage for the future.

All of this attempted vindication misplaces the emphasis, though, because it is predicated upon Voltaire's paramount desire to be an outstanding playwright. He did, it is true, have a passion for the theatre. He did regard it as the supreme expression of his civilization and as the highest form of art. And he did write many plays and, naturally, being human, wanted them to be successful in the terms of his time. Still, we have no evidence that he regarded the theatre as the medium whereby his reputation would pass to posterity. He understood that *Zaïre* was a good, successful play in his day, but he judged it inferior to *La Mort de César*. He was always inordinately enthusiastic about the play he was producing, as uneasy as a child about its reception, and capable of the most puerile excitement, but he understood better than any of his contemporaries and all his successors what his audience wanted.

We, therefore, are reduced either to accepting some of his plays as good, but not superior, drama or to granting his production a historical importance in the evolution of the theatre or, finally, to straining in every direction in a search for a superiority which is rarely present. We may even want to lay some claim to his excellence in all three of these aspects. It is, as I have said, quite possible to select a half-dozen or so plays from his repertory—*Zaïre, Alzire, Mahomet, Mérope, Tancrède*, to name a few—and defend them, not as excellent, but as good theatre. Our defense would have to be couched in terms of the eighteenth-century audience, however. Any effort to give a superiority even to Voltaire's better plays as world literature seems a useless undertaking. One could, of course, attribute to them a historical importance and show how they initiated many of the characteristics of the so-called romantic drama. One might even insist that Voltaire's innovations displayed real merit. In all probability, though, Voltaire would not be elated to have become the predecessor of Victor Hugo and Scribe in drama.

Usually, we Voltaireans want to settle for nothing less than a bevy of exceptional masterpieces. Although Voltaire would be delighted, were we successful, it is evident, both from the way he talked and the way he worked, that he would be more than surprised by this result. He once made a remark about the difficulty of reaching posterity when encumbered by so much baggage. I imagine that, once he had enjoyed the renown of being an outstanding playwright of his time and the more enjoyable pleasure, for him, of having received on numerous occasions the acclamations of his audiences, he would be content to rest his reputation upon other achievements than the excellence of his drama.

It is obvious that, when a poet turns philosopher, a gigantic revolution takes place within him. We have seen that this threatened metamorphosis had been building up ever since the beginning of Voltaire's career. Always he had seemed to mingle his love of poetry with the love of ideas. It was not a mere quip of Lejay's when he described the youthful Arouet as anxious to weigh the destiny of Europe in his little head. Fortunately, the early Horatian poetry to which he and his times were committed allowed and even invited a satiric, ironic, and intellectual content. Moreover, this kind of

poetry had the characteristic of limiting the content to the possibilities of the form. When, however, the youthful poet extended
his interest from Horatian satire to the dramatic and epic arts, he, as
well as his time, found these genres less adaptable to the thought
content than the Horatian verse. It was still possible, though, within
limits, to adjust "philosophic" thought to "poetic" expression, provided the thought did not go beyond the confines of free-thinking.
The more thought tended to be systematic, and especially scientific,
the more difficult it became to make the adjustment.

Along with the cleavage which developed between thought and
expression in terms of the poetic art, there developed a tendency to
anti-poetry. Geometry became the habit of the time, and prose was
thought a more satisfactory expression of the modern age than
poetry. Voltaire, however, resisted this trend; he insisted upon the
value of poetry, although he wanted to be resolutely a "modern"
man. The English experience had taught him that, to be "modern,"
one had to be philosophical, scientific, and moral, that, above all,
one had to learn how to merge with arts and letters the benefits of
political, social, and moral institutions. The challenge of England
was clearly a challenge of civilization in which there had to be a
merging of the arts with the institutions, or the ways of expressing
life with the means of fostering life, or the "mœurs" of the individual
with the "esprit" of the society. The importance of the lesson he
learned lay in the organic way in which life had to be interpreted.
French art and English thought, poetry and philosophy, "mœurs"
and "esprit" all had to be integrated in favor of a European civilization. Voltaire eventually learned not only what were the necessary
ingredients of that civilization but what were the vital consequences
of their integration. That took time and much adjustment of detail. Hitherto, consequences had always been achieved by modifications, rather than by revolutions. Voltaire still made every effort to
preserve the privileges of the poet while attempting to acquire the
advantages of the philosopher. Now, however, he was all but forced
to give full attention to the new aspects of civilization: science and
the new organization of institutions.

This investigation led him to a totally new epistemology. Not
only was there a whole new body of learning, but the whole corpus
had to be organized differently. New subjects had to be integrated

with old ones; metaphysics, natural science, "métaphysique morale," morality, history, politics, economics had to be coordinated with religion, aesthetics, ethics. New institutions, political, social, educational, had to be set up alongside old ones. Reform had to be undertaken, priorities revised, norms established. The old hierarchy of religion, art, state, society, morality had to be recast. To a present-day critic of the Enlightenment, the whole process may appear simple: to Voltaire, it was anything but easy. The whole fundamental structure of life had to be reexamined. At first, the task did not seem so impossible. As long as it was carried out on a "préjugé-rapport" basis, in which reason and nature guaranteed the right answers in specific matters, it did not look to be too difficult. When all the underlying assumptions of reason and nature had also to be subjected to critical scrutiny, however, things became increasingly complicated. And the obstacles appeared insurmountable when things reached a point where life itself had to be summoned to justify itself, as an organic something. This justification had been carried out in the past in terms of religion or, more recently, in terms of art; now it seemed that it could only be set forth in terms of the social group.

These imperatives literally harassed Voltaire throughout the Cirey period and beyond, as they did all his contemporaries. Voltaire, however, had a way of rejecting things he could not understand and simplifying things which had become complicated. He also clung to things he had already developed, while reaching out for new things achieved by others. Fortunately, he was blessed with a very observant nature, a genuinely curious disposition, and a confidence in his ability to attain right solutions which bordered on impertinence. These qualities possessed real advantages, but they could also produce frustration. When things were developing hectically but nonetheless consistently, Voltaire was remarkably dynamic; when frustrations appeared, he was left totally defenseless.

In any case, he sought his solutions in thought, in energy, in art, and in the release of creative forces from within. His confidence in the ability of man to transform phenomena into thought and thought into action and action into the release of creative forces was almost limitless. He insisted, as we shall see, that all intellectual force leads inevitably to the release of creative energy.

In general, his dynamism, his intellectual mobility, his innate curiosity, and his sense of art helped him out of his difficulties. It nonetheless remains true that these difficulties increased immeasurably with time, and there arose situations in which there was lack of harmony between form and content, between poetry and prose, and between categories of living, such as science and religion, metaphysics and physics, physics and "morale," even history and religion, and especially art and philosophy. The point of danger was very apparent. It all seemed to center on the weakening of religion and art. The wide diversity of intellectual interests not only invited a dispersal of energy, with a consequent risk of diminution in quality, but presented problems of coordination and consistency and continuity which upset any effort to be vital and organic. The threat of decadence, of sterility, became very real. Specifically, Voltaire, as I have tried to show in my edition of *Micromégas*, was faced with the necessity of choosing the right art form for containing the new subject-matter and even of selecting the correct content to cast into the acceptable art form. He asked himself categorically whether the Horatian poem was capable of transmitting Newtonian physics and Lockean sensationalism, whether the drama could be modernized to convey the social and moral problems facing his contemporaries, whether the epic was now adequate to portray the "mœurs" and "esprit" of a people. He does not seem to have had any hesitation in assuming that these things must be presented to the French. He had no doubts about the "public spirit" of the English or about the sciences, both natural and human, they were developing. Their metaphysics, their physics, their histories, their morality appealed to him immensely. It was evident, though, that all this new content could not be expressed in classical forms. Lyric verse could be made philosophical within limits, but both it and the drama and the epic could not adequately appropriate the new science or the new philosophy. As a matter of fact, practically everyone agreed that poetry was ill-adjusted to mathematics, physics, metaphysics, history, and criticism. Prose was now thought much more effective.

Notwithstanding the establishment of the concept of civilization as a core, there is some evidence that the enterprise threatened to get out of hand and that the dangers of dispersal became very real indeed. Voltaire tried to explain all this activity in two different ways.

To D'Argens, on 22 June 1737, he presented in a roundabout way the plan which he proposed to follow and his justification for it:

Vous faites fort bien tandis que vous êtes encore jeune d'enrichir votre mémoire par la connaissance des langues, et, puisque vous faites aux belles-lettres l'honneur de les cultiver, il est bon que vous vous fassiez un fonds d'érudition qui donnera toujours plus de poids à votre gloire et à vos ouvrages. Tout est également frivole en ce monde; mais il y a des inutilités qui passent pour solides et ces inutilités là ne sont pas à négliger. Tôt ou tard vous en recueillerez le fruit, soit que vous restiez dans les pays étrangers, soit que vous rentriez dans votre patrie.

In this passage is the thought that the acquisition of knowledge leads to an enrichment of letters. To the Abbé d'Olivet, a former teacher at Louis-le-Grand, he wrote on 20 October 1738 to reiterate his conviction that there is no reason why the study of physics should crush the flowers of poetry; he refuses to believe that truth is so unfortunate as to reject the aid of art. He protests against those who would believe that the art of thinking, of speaking with eloquence, of feeling deeply, and of expressing these deep thoughts poetically runs counter to the interests of philosophy. He concedes that there are those who hate him just because, having begun with poetry, he had turned to history and finished with philosophy. That is precisely what he had learned at Louis-le-Grand: "Que me faisiez-vous lire et apprendre par cœur à moi et aux autres? Des poètes, des historiens, des philosophes." Voltaire repeats the remark of Frederick that, just because the spirit of man is very limited, he should make every effort to extend the frontiers of knowledge. He promises not to devote himself to physics and to the writing of a tragedy on the same day, since *omnia tempus habent,* but he acknowledges very cheerfully that, after three months spent with the "épines des mathématiques," he is very glad to return to poetry.

It is evident that he had given much attention to the problem of dispersal. In a letter to Formont of 11 November 1738, he somewhat repeats what he had written to Olivet: "Nous sommes bien loin d'abandonner ici la poésie pour les mathématiques." He recalls the statement of Virgil that one should give himself to all the Muses. It would be an act of barbarism to scorn any art, an "étrange rétrécissement d'esprit que d'aimer une science pour haïr les autres."

It should be noted that the threatened dispersal which assailed Voltaire was quite apparent to Frederick, who was trying to follow him in all his intellectual meanderings. The Prince was astounded by his tutor's intellectual gyrations. He confessed that he could only follow his master "de loin dans [mes] occupations comme une tortue qui rampe sur la piste d'un cerf." There is a striking difference he noticed between himself and his poet-philosopher-historian-publicist-friend. He was completely outdistanced, and he urged Voltaire not to make comparisons between his works and those of himself. "Vous marchez d'un pas ferme par des routes difficiles, et moi, je rampe par des sentiers faciles" (B. 1507). To Mme du Châtelet, Frederick confessed on 9 November 1738 that he flitted from metaphysics to physics, from "la morale" to logic to history, and from music to poetry. "Je ne fais qu'effleurer tout sans réussir en rien," he added (B. 1577).

Mme du Châtelet and D'Argental, as well as Frederick, were very aware of the dispersal of Voltaire's energies. On 5 October 1738, she wrote to D'Argental (B. 1552):

> Je pense absolument come vs. sur les petits ouvrages, d'autant plus que cela occupe le tems qu'il pouroit employer à de plus grands tableaux. J'en excepte cependant les Epîtres (the *Discours en vers*); je regarde cet ouvrage quand elles seront rassemblées come très digne de son auteur. Il est beau d'avoir encore le genre didactique, je crois qu'en les corrigeant avec soin elles pouront faire le pendant.

And Voltaire, even a year before, had lamented to Frederick that he was engaged in so many different activities that he could hardly do more than touch upon them.

It was this dilemma which brought about certain transformations in Voltaire's intellectual activities. From 1715 to 1738, he had taken part in the great debate between form and content, holding tenaciously to the traditional genres while proclaiming loudly his desire to be strictly modern. The result was clear: whatever of this modern spirit he wished to express was confined to the Horatian genres of lyric, satiric poetry, the epic, and the drama. As long as the thought content was of a moral nature, no great difficulties were encountered. But, when to the moral thought were added the scientific theories and the metaphysical ideas of Locke, the difficulties increased rapidly.

Voltaire still held tightly to his traditional poetic genres between 1734 and 1738, thereby giving to everything he wrote a philosophical appearance. Yet, in reality, he had already made the compromise. History with *Charles XII* retained some of its epic qualities but became prose; the drama also retained its epic traits, but Voltaire experienced more and more difficulty in maintaining its poetic beauties. The lyric Horatian verse was still possible as long as it restricted itself to moral subjects. But, even with moral subjects, Voltaire soon became aware that prose could achieve effects—such as clarity, for instance—not always accessible or desirable in poetry. The result was a tendency to discuss physics, metaphysics, and morality in prose and then to repeat the discussions of metaphysics and morality in poetry—the new physics requiring, beyond a doubt, prose. The year 1738 witnessed the last heroic stand of the poet, with the *Eléments de la philosophie de Newton* in prose and the *Discours en vers sur l'homme* in the traditional Horatian genre. What really had taken place, though, was that the *épître* had become a prose epistle, as in the *Lettres philosophiques*, the epic and the epic qualities of drama had become history, and the dramatic qualities of drama had become prose dialogue. The histories, the dialogues, and the correspondence adjusted perfectly to this change. Voltaire had no real difficulty in adjusting his style: clarity of expression, tension brought about by contrast, contradiction, and ambiguity, satire and wit all fitted in the new expression. Only the drama produced some trouble. Voltaire was so passionately devoted to it that he refused absolutely to yield, but he might as well have capitulated, since it ceased being—even for him—the dominant artistic form. From 1738 until the end of his life, he still continued to produce Horatian epistles, sometimes writing in his own correspondence a part in verse and a part in prose, and he often reverted to the epic and especially the mock-epic, as well as to drama. But, to all intents and purposes, with but few exceptions, Voltaire's poetry after the crisis of 1738-1739 was dead.

It is possible to trace the various steps of the poet as he transformed himself into a philosopher. We can mark out very clearly the period in which his major preoccupation was with literature, more specifically with poetry, and more specifically still with the satire, the ode, the *épître*, the epic, and tragedy. That period extended from 1715 to 1738. His devotion to his career as poet and dramatist can be followed in the correspondence. We can even begin to perceive his deviations from the life of a poet to that of a philosopher, beginning with his return from England and continuing until his definite declaration of the change. More important, we can trace his evolution from poetry to philosophy as it occurred between 1735 (just after the publication of the *Lettres philosophiques*) and the composition of the second draft of the *Traité de métaphysique*. Between that time and the end of 1738 and the beginning of 1739, there were many indications that Voltaire was reflecting carefully upon his problems as poet and philosopher and that he was now prepared to make important decisions to bring about a solution.

It all began in the letter which he indited to Cideville on 16 April 1735. Voltaire had just made a trip from Cirey to Paris, and he had become aware that poetry, no longer the fashion of the day, had yielded to mathematics and physics. He notes that everybody is now philosophizing. It is evident that he was disagreeably surprised by the discovery, for he protests to his friend that feeling, imagination, and gracefulness have now been excluded. One who has lived under Louis XIV would not be able to recognize the French any more; he is ready to believe that the Germans have taken over the country. Voltaire laments that belles-lettres are obviously on the wane. To tell the truth, this was not the first time he had been conscious of a decline in art. Now, however, he is a little more tolerant of the change. He confesses that he does not object to the cultivation of philosophy. What irritates him is rather the tendency to exclude the arts. His complaint is precisely that philosophy has become a fad, just as poetry was formerly a fad. He believes that both should exist, that they should both work together organically and be cultivated together. The poet still recognizes the importance of thought content to artistic form and expression.

Recognition that times had changed, that poetry had given way to mathematics, science, and philosophy, that there was a fundamental antagonism between the two manners of living, that abandoning arts and letters in the interest of science and philosophy was but a passing phase, and that eventually there would be a return to letters is clearly indicated in the letter to Cideville. Voltaire even states in the letter his refusal to pay tribute to the prevailing fashion, but in the remainder of his sentence it is evident that he was capitulating: "Je veux passer d'une expérience de physique à un opéra ou à une comédie, et que mon goût ne soit jamais émoussé par l'étude."[5]

He reiterated that a serious change had taken place in French society in his *Epître à Mme du Châtelet* (1736), which later was published at the beginning of the *Eléments*. Here he admits that philosophy is not a passing phase; it is rather a movement which has been going on in France since the end of the seventeenth century. Voltaire accords his approval to this development. He is especially pleased that women are now taking a leading role in it. If Boileau were still alive, he adds, he who did not hesitate to make fun of a noble lady because she saw Roberval and Sauveur clandestinely would have to respect and even imitate the women who profit openly from their association with people like Maupertuis, Réaumur, Mairan, Dufay, and Clairaut. These are true scientists who have no other aim than to make science useful and who, in making it likewise attractive, "la rendent insensiblement nécessaire à notre nation."

Once again, he draws the conclusion that in these changing times the poet will have to change, too: "Nous sommes au temps, j'ose le dire, où il faut qu'un poète soit philosophe, et où une femme peut l'être hardiment." There is still, however, the implication that the poet will profit as poet by addressing himself to science. There is not yet any suggestion that the poet is ready to abandon voluntarily his calling as poet in order to become a philosopher.

Nonetheless, Voltaire's ideas concerning the role of the poet were certainly evolving. To Frederick, he wrote on 26 August 1736: "Vous sentez qu'il n'y auroit rien de plus méprisable que de passer sa vie à renfermer dans des rimes des lieux communs usés, qui ne méritent pas le nom de pensées; s'il y a quelque chose de plus vil, c'est de n'être que poète satirique et de n'écrire que pour décrier les autres." Anyway, the Horatian satire was beginning to wear thin. Indeed, his determination to write verse, at least light verse, which had been so important to him at the beginning of his literary career, was obviously weakening. But he was still not prepared to abandon the writing of tragedy. About the same time, he made a comparison between lyric poetry and tragedy, which turned out to be all to the

[5] Voltaire noted the enthusiasm for Newton's philosophy in a letter to Caumont also (B. 840).

advantage of tragedy. He pronounced that there is no match between a poem and a good play: the latter requires more talent in composition and gives more pleasure upon being presented. Even if an epistle or a satire, which is very easy to compose, were as well-written as a play, there would still be infinitely more merit in writing the play, and much more pleasure in seeing it, than could be had in writing or reading "des lieux communs de morale." Voltaire added that a good moral *épître* teaches one nothing, a good ode still less, and that this frivolous light verse serves no other purpose than to amuse professional writers for a quarter of an hour.

However much his attitude toward poetry had changed, then, his deep devotion and his commitment to the theatre still continued. Whereas he was now prepared to express a certain indifference toward the Horatian genres, because they were too facile, devoid of serious content, and merely displayed a kind of technique, his enthusiasm for tragedy was apparently as strong as ever. One very revelatory passage at this time discloses not only in what way drama was a challenge for him but also what in drama accounted for its superior production:

> Mais créer un sujet, inventer un nœud et un dénouement; donner à chaque personnage son caractère, le soutenir, le rendre intéressant, et augmenter cet intérêt de scène en scène; faire en sorte qu'aucun d'eux ne paraisse et ne sorte sans une raison sentie de tous les spectateurs; ne laisser jamais le théâtre vide; faire dire à chacun ce qu'il doit dire, avec noblesse et sans enflure, . . . avec simplicité, sans bassesse; faire de beaux vers qui ne sentent point le poète, et tels que le personnage aurait dû en faire, s'il parlait en vers: c'est là une partie des devoirs que tout auteur d'une tragédie doit remplir, sous peine de ne point réussir parmi nous; et quand il s'est acquitté de tous ces devoirs, il n'a encore rien fait.

These lines not only confirm his continuing interest in the theatre but give an insight into his new conception of drama. Bellessort (*Essai sur Voltaire*, p. 82) has noted that the eighteenth-century dramatist conceived tragedy in his own special way; he regarded it as the most moving of sermons, as an exaltation of virtue, as a fearful display of the dangers of the passions, and, finally, as an appeal to mankind couched in the most harmonious language possible and shrouded in pomp which lends it something sublime. If we bear in mind also that the performance of it took place before the most enlightened, sophisticated, cultivated, and artistically sensitive audience in the world, we can begin to understand the reasons for Voltaire's enthusiasm.

There was, however, in Voltaire's artistic ambitions a deep desire to dominate. In the very passage from which we have just quoted, Voltaire stated: "Il faut tenir le cœur des hommes dans sa main; il faut arracher des larmes aux spectateurs les plus insensibles, il faut déchirer les âmes les plus dures. Sans la terreur et sans la pitié, point de tragédie." This desire to dominate his audience, this desire, often expressed, to draw tears from his spectators, was only one aspect of his dramatic art. He sincerely felt it his right to exercise similar domination over the characters of his plays: since he had created them, given them a chance to act, he should therefore have complete control over their lives. To the Président de Meynières, he wrote: "Quand il s'agit d'une tragédie ou d'un poème épique, je fais de mes personnages ce qu'il me plaît, je suis créateur et déstructeur à mon plaisir . . ." (from Fichier Charaway, Vol. 176, No. 39697). This attitude toward his creations and toward his audience was really similar to that of Brioché toward his marionettes.

This desire to dominate his characters and audience was complicated by his inability to dissociate himself from the drama. Critics have noted that Voltaire appealed to his actors to bring out the reality of the play in contradistinction to the reality outside the play. If the dramatic quality was not heightened tremendously, he felt the vitality had disappeared. This viewpoint explains his constant effort to summon forth more vitality from the actors. He even demanded the same heightened vitality of himself when he took an active role in one of his own plays. It was, indeed, because he was no more capable than his contemporaries of distinguishing creatively between art and life, between verisimilitude and reality, that he made such a tremendous effort to retain the drama. But there were difficulties. Even on 20 June 1738, Voltaire wrote to a M. R———: "Ce que Virgile et la Fontaine regrettaient, je l'étudie. La connaissance de la nature, l'étude de l'histoire, partagent mon temps. C'est assez d'avoir cultivé vingt-trois ans la poésie, et je conseillerais à tous ceux qui auront consacré leur printemps à cet art difficile et agréable de donner leur automne et leur hiver à des choses plus faciles, non moins séduisantes, et qu'il est honteux d'ignorer."

All of this seems a perfectly logical development. Always art has renewed itself with science, always science has attempted to achieve organicity in art, and always the human in man has profited from both activities. The operation, however, rarely develops smoothly, because, if there is a dependence of art upon science and science upon morality, if content and form and man possess some kind of organic affinity in which the true, the useful, and the beautiful are one and the same, there is notwithstanding a constant discrepancy, looked at from another angle, between them. Always conditions have arisen in which science is opposed to art and art is just as opposed to morality. This was precisely an aspect of Voltaire's situation. While he was busily engaged at Cirey in reducing thought to art and art to morality, he was very aware that a conflict was present between thought and art and morality. This was, of course, the basic conflict of the Enlightenment. What naturally should have existed as an organic whole had a tendency to fall apart. The problem of the cohesion of thought, art, and morality had to be faced by all the great philosophers: Diderot, Rousseau, Montesquieu, as well as Voltaire. Indeed, it is fairly certain that, fundamentally, every man of the Enlightenment could not avoid the necessity of transforming Enlightenment thought into creative action. But for the moment, during 1738-1739, Voltaire was preoccupied with that part of the problem which concerned the correct form in which to cast that creative action. Since he was by profession a writer, it was perfectly reasonable for him to look about for a literary form. Put concisely, he had to seek the genre best adapted to express artistically the thought content he was elaborating.

What was needed was a literary medium which could carry not only the thought content of science, history, civilization, and reform but also the meaning of this science, this history, this civilization, and this reform. It would have to have all the qualities of the Horatian poem—the satire, the irony, the epicurean joy of life, the deep seriousness of stoicism—and at the same time be capable of uniting the conversational quality of the *épître* with the light, airy, superficial quality of the chanson and with the terseness of the epigram and the eloquence of the odes. In other words, it would have to have all the variety of modes, all the variety of tones, and all the lightness of touch of Horace. Moreover, it would have to integrate qualities with their opposites: it would have to be both satirical and serious, reasonable and mad, verisimilar and true, true and false, ironic and committed, and it would have to express with wit all the contradictions, contrasts, ambiguities, tensions, and symbols which the life of the mind always brings to its interpretation of everyday life. It would have to have the power to cut away ruthlessly the "préjugés" of life and establish the "rapports," to shift the perspective whenever desirable from reality to the idea. In fact, it would always have to drive toward utopia, knowing full well that the drive is doomed to failure but realizing that success lies in the drive, the *élan*, the energy, the will-to-be, and that all this has nothing to do with our finiteness or our damnation. It had to be a conversational art. People would have to meet, and they would have to discuss— but not interminably—in a manner at once witty, ironic, and satirical. The subject of the conversation would be the ambiguities of life as it is really lived and its deviation from the ideal "good" life. The discussion would be controlled by the human mind, which derives its energy from thought. The formula (because in philosophy, everything eventually gets formulated, crystallized, systematized, or at least abstracted) would consist in proving the existence of being by thinking, saying, and doing. What one is is the sum of what he thinks, what he says, and what he does. Philosophy may be the love of wisdom, all right, but love of wisdom is cherishing that which we believe we have created through our intellectual response to the conditions of living. Life offers possible experience in infinite quantity, and the human mind feels sure that it can reduce that experience to meaning. The process is just another way of "history teaching by example," but it is best known to all of us nowadays as "penetrating reality with consciousness" or "turning criticism into creation." The *conte philosophique* was the Voltairean instrument for doing all these things simultaneously—and in the simplest way possible.

It should be stressed that, although it unites the qualities of all types of Horatian poetry and all its tones, it is not poetry. Basically, it is prose, but that does not mean at all that it is lacking in rhythm, balance, or music. Lanson has shown in his *Art de la prose* how extraordinarily musical it is, how phrases often return as refrains, and how ideas even sing themselves into existence, and I have tried to show how with two colorless words, "great" and "small," one may build a universe. Voltaire's poetry may have died in 1738, but the poet lived on. Usually, it is the reverse which happens.

It should be stressed, also, that the very characteristics which prevented Voltaire from being preeminent in the conventional genres of literature—namely, his desire to dominate both his creation and the audience—contributed here to his success. Whereas it is questionable whether in the drama and the epic the author can ever assume responsibility for the characters, whether he really can move them around like puppets, make them say what he wants them to say, make them act as he wants them to act, put into their mouths what he wants said, bring them on stage when he wants them there, and withdraw them when he has decided that it is time for them to leave, it is necessary in the *conte philosophique* that the characters, their sayings, and their actions be completely controlled by the creator. I suspect that it is the ideas, not the characters, that get beyond the control of the author in this type of work. And, whereas it is undoubtedly an error to dominate the audience in both the drama and the epic and, indeed, in all forms of Horatian verse, in the *conte* this domination is essential, for it is the author's ego which guarantees both the organic unity of the work and its total effect.

This necessity can be seen if some attention is given to the difference between characters as characters and thoughts as characters. If thoughts are given autonomy in the *conte*, it is done with the assumption that ideas possess existence just as human beings do. Montaigne's ideas, or Diderot's, or Voltaire's may run around, clash, and produce eloquent results as readily as Boccaccio's characters. The *conte*'s task is not to relate incidents and develop characters—a task the author must perform—but to set forth ideas and put them in proper perspective with incidents, characters, and opposite ideas. It is, therefore, not surprising that the *conte* was peculiarly adapted to the purposes of Voltaire, willing and anxious as he was to assume full responsibility for the creation of all the elements of his work and determined to allow no autonomy to any.

What I have attempted to deduce in terms of continuity is very clearly presented in three excellent definitions given by Professor Bottiglia in his *Analysis of a Classic*. Naves calls the *contes* "promenades philosophiques sous la forme d'enquête romancée" with well-defined stops at intervals for purposes of discussing the meaning. In general, the situation is everywhere man finds himself at grips with life and its natural and social conditions. Naves notes that often the situation corresponds to a scene in drama. In reality, it corresponds rather to a dumb show. Lanson, more briefly, defines the genre as designed to "réaliser la pensée philosophique." There are, in his opinion, two types, the loosely constructed *conte*, which comprises several themes treated satirically, and the tightly constructed *conte*, which contains one central theme treated as a philosophical demonstration. Both types fluctuate between symbolism and reality, but both express a strict unity in variety—variety of themes in the first type, of demonstrations in the second. Bottiglia endeavors to give some overall definition combining the elements of these two types: the *conte* is a "fictitious prose narrative wherein theme moulds all the other component elements (action, character, setting, diction, etc.) into a stylized, two-dimensional, emotionally sublimated demonstration." Its greatest quality, he says, is its fluidity. He might want to add that it flows with the rhythm of consciousness trying to catch up with reality.

Voltaire developed the *conte* in such a way that it contained all the variety of moods and tones of the Horatian poem. It is hardly fair to claim, however, that it was taken entirely from that genre. As a matter of fact, it owed as much to the utopian novel as it did to the libertine Horatian poetry. Starting with Rabelais, there had been a long line of these utopian novels, which ran parallel with the travel literature of the sixteenth and seventeenth centuries, as well as with the libertine Horatian poetry. The outstanding novels of this group are Rabelais's *Gargantua et Pantagruel*, Cyrano de Bergerac's *Voyage à la lune* (1657) and his *Histoire de l'Empire du Soleil* (1662), and a group of imaginary voyages beginning with Gabriel de Foigny's *La Terre australe connue* (1676) and including Vairasse's *Histoire des Sévarambes* (1677-1679), Fénelon's *Télémaque* (1699), Gilbert's *Histoire de Caléjava* (1700), Lahontan's *Mémoires sur l'Amérique septentrionale* (1703) and his *Dialogues* (1703), Tyssot de Patot's *Voyages et avantures de Jacques Massé* (1710), and Swift's *Gulliver's Travels* (1726). These works, many of them written between 1675 and 1710, along with the travel literature, particularly the literature on China and the Orient, constituted one of the four major sources of Enlightenment thought (the other three being the libertine Horatian poetry, the free-thinking essay, and the formal philosophical treatise). All of these sources were well known to Bayle, who collected articles upon the principal exponents of each of these groups in his *Dictionnaire historique et critique*. They were known to Voltaire also, although not many of the utopian novels can now be found in his library. We know, however, that he had definite ideas about Rabelais and Swift, even from the days of the English trip, that he was literally raised on the *Télémaque*, from which he extracted phrases verbatim, and that he owned copies of Foigny's work and the two volumes by Lahontan. There is, besides, a strong parallelism of ideas between Voltaire and Tyssot de Patot, as has been shown in McKee's thesis, and between Voltaire and Vairasse, as has been shown in Von der Mühll's study.[6] The genre carried with it the "philosophical" examination of life in all of its aspects: religious, social, political, economic, moral, aesthetic. It usually embraced in one way or another all of these aspects. One of the techniques employed was to compare the manifestations of these aspects in Europe with their description in the imaginary land. The effect of this comparison was practically always satirical and ironic, and the conclusion quite frequently idealistic. Sometimes, as with Cyrano and Swift, discussions of contemporary ideas were mingled with rather severe satire of a moral nature. More often than not, the religious and political satire was very biting. The conclusion was rarely favorable to the civilizations of Europe, which were usually displayed as being religiously false and weak, politically absurd, and morally corrupt. In a way, all these utopian works performed the same function as Horatian satire, for their conclusions were critical of all the European manifestations of life, as one would expect from authors who were self-declared opponents of civilization, avowed free-thinkers, and idealistic satirists. The one thing which they sometimes lacked—the writings of Rabelais, Cyrano, and Swift excepted—is wit.

Although the Voltairean *conte* derived from the Horatian poem and the utopian novel, we should not forget that it appeared at a period when the Orient and Oriental tales were very popular in France. The *Lettres persanes* (1721) undoubtedly is the masterpiece of the genre, but there were a large number of these short stories, which took their origin in the *Arabian Nights* of Galland. We should not insist, therefore, too exclusively upon the intellectual content to the detriment of the fairy-tale effect and the fantasy and the pure

[6] See D. R. McKee, *Tyssot de Patot*, and E. Von der Mühll, *Denis Veiras et son Histoire des Sévarambes, 1677-1679.*

joy of relating a story, since, after all, the important thing about a *conte* is that it is fundamentally a story.

We have certain pieces of evidence that lead to the conclusion that Voltaire was a master showman as story-teller. We know from Mme de Graffigny that, at precisely this time, he was very happy when he was giving the magic-lantern performances or when he could bring marionettes to Cirey. The art of conversation, as well as the techniques of amusing a social gathering with a performance, were two pastimes which he could apparently never resist. If he had not needed the new genre to carry the meaning of the new content, it is perfectly plausible that he would have invented it anyway, just because it was so well adapted to the social organization of this time. Indeed, there are *contes* in his repertory which do not much trouble about communicating a message or even a theme; they are related for the sheer joy of putting into an art form a package of human phenomena. They attract attention, not because they are particularly philosophical, but because they are simply charming. *Le Taureau blanc, Cosi Sancta,* or *La Princesse de Babylone* are bristling with malice, but not overly weighty with ideas. On the other hand, *L'Homme aux quarante écus* is bursting with ideas, but not particularly charming. The four greatest—*Micromégas, Zadig, Candide,* and *L'Ingénu*—have balanced beautifully the art form with the philosophical content. Curiously enough, if we take Voltaire's intellectual preoccupations at Cirey to be science, metaphysics, history, and the virtues of civilization, then each of these *contes* represents an attempt to give the inner meaning of one of these Cirey preoccupations. Of these four, the first one in point of time was undoubtedly *Micromégas* (1739). I am not sure, however, that it was the first of all the *contes*. Voltaire experimented with *Le Petit Boursoufle*, of which we have only a fragment. That one did not work precisely because it was divorced from all of his major preoccupations. But it is quite possible that directly after *Boursoufle* came *Le Crocheteur borgne*, which is closely, though discreetly, identified with Newtonian optics, and only then *Micromégas*. At all events, it is quite certain that the poet found a way to become a "philosophe" and yet remain a poet, thanks to that curious thing which Voltaire called "la révolution de l'esprit humain."

6. CONTROVERSY

I T WAS CHARACTERISTIC of everything Voltaire did that it always gave rise to controversy. His thirteenth letter of the *Lettres philosophiques* was no exception. In the review which the *Journal de Trévoux* gave of the *Lettres*, Voltaire was taken to task for having asserted that God could give to matter the attribute of thought. Voltaire did not reply immediately to this criticism. However, in a letter to Tournemine *circa* June 1735 (B. 852), he argues that, if it is possible for God to give matter a principle of attraction, as Newton has shown, it is equally possible for Him to give matter a principle of thought. He does not assume that in either case we can understand what is the nature of this principle, any more than we can understand the nature of any first principle. Voltaire concludes that Newton only maintains that we can calculate, measure, compare with some certainty. Nevertheless, the elements do move in such a way that we can prove that matter gravitates according to certain laws. Voltaire denies that he is prepared to assert that thought is matter. Nor can he affirm that he has the slightest idea what "esprit" is. He is merely convinced that animals have the same feelings and the same passions as men. They have memory, and they can combine ideas. Voltaire rebels against the Cartesian notion that they are pure machines whereas humans are something else. His notion is that God has given feelings to animals as He has given them to man.

Voltaire, it should be noted, uses a very minor point in Lockean philosophy to disprove Descartes's thesis. At the same time, he continues his attack on Pascal. After professing his admiration for the *Pensées*, he focuses his attack on the foundation of the work, the belief that a religion cannot be true unless it knows human nature thoroughly and explains everything that happens in our heart. Voltaire protests that this test is inapplicable, since it treats religion as if it were a system of philosophy. The test of a religion's authenticity is whether it is revealed or not. It is a mistake to argue that men are fickle, inconstant, full of desires and weaknesses, and that, therefore, the Christian religion must be true. One must prove first that the Christian religion has been revealed, and then we will know why men are fickle, inconstant, etc. Voltaire concludes that original sin cannot be proved by reason but must be accepted on faith.

In his reply, Tournemine maintains that "la répugnance de la pensée à la matière est manifeste." He adopts the opinion that thought is an "être sans parties," whereas matter is divisible, and that an "être divisible composé de parties ne peut penser, ne peut juger d'aucun objet." This position is wholly Cartesian, of course. He adds that there is an incongruity in having a divisible, multiple being become indivisible and one.

Voltaire resumed his argument in another letter, *circa* August 1735 (B. 871), to his old teacher. He now takes it for granted that there is a principle of attraction in matter, and he seeks what reasonable objections the Jesuits have to it. He complains that Tournemine has evaded this question by talking about one object which pushes another when it impinges upon it. This is an indication to Voltaire that Tournemine has not read Newton. He further notes that, although half of the members of the French Académie des Sciences now recognize this truth and although all of England, "le pays des Philosophes," acknowledges it, there is no acquaintance with these ideas in the French universities. Voltaire naturally deplores this state of affairs. He suggests that the Jesuits, who introduced the teaching of mathematics in French education, undertake the teaching of Newtonian physics.

He thereupon enters into an explanation of the Newtonian theory of attraction. He does not claim that attraction is essential to matter; he merely asserts that it is a property given by God to all matter which can be defined and actually measured. Voltaire denies that this theory has anything to do with the notion proposed by Tournemine that movement proves the existence of God. He disclaims altogether that Newton has any atheistic tendencies. However, once one has recognized that God can give a particular attribute to matter, one is forced to concede that God can give to matter other attributes unknown to us. Voltaire objects to Tournemine's argument that, thought being indivisible and matter being divisible, it is impossible for God to give thought to matter. For Voltaire, the power of the Deity to give some attribute to, or withhold it from, matter has nothing to do with the indivisibility of matter. Furthermore, to the argument that the attribution of thought to matter may ruin the doctrine of the immateriality of the soul, Voltaire replies that the notion of immateriality is no more foreign to material things than the idea of infinity to finite beings. His final conclusion is that we have no thorough knowledge of matter, any more than we do of spirit, but that we do know some of its properties. It is obvious to Voltaire that Tournemine's arguments are motivated by the fear that admission of the doctrine of attraction or the notion of thinking matter would jeopardize the explanation of vice and virtue and endanger the doctrine of the immortality of the soul. Voltaire denies that these results necessarily follow.

He does incline, however, to the thought that there is no reasonable proof of the immortality of the soul. He states that it is very likely that animals have feelings, although not a spiritual soul, such as man possesses. But there are also many things which man has in common with animals. In fact, the only difference seems to be, Voltaire suggests, that man has developed the faculty of combining ideas more powerfully than animals. Most important, he possesses an immortal soul, which God apparently has not given to animals. In substantiation of this attitude, Voltaire refers to the chapter on the extent of human knowledge in Locke's *Essay*. He counsels, however, an open mind. He confesses that hitherto he had taken the position that one cannot prove the existence of God except by a posteriori reasons but that, having read the work of Dr. Clarke, he has been entirely undeceived. Indeed, he remarks that Clarke's explanation of free will is the best he has ever seen. "Tous les autres écrivains n'ont fait qu'embrouiller cette matière."

It is evident that in his discussion with Tournemine Voltaire found himself under the obligation to take a stand upon certain theological problems which he deemed secondary to the truths of philosophy and science. He was, of course, not the first to feel embarrassment before the necessity of making such a decision. For him, there were no rational proofs of the doctrine of original sin, or of the immortality of the soul, or of the union of body and spirit, and, finally, no rational proofs that men and animals are not endowed with the same organs, the same functions, and the same operations. He was apparently, however, not yet prepared to exclude these possibilities because of their lack of positive proofs. They seemed to him to be more in the category of the doubtful, to be believed, if one wishes, on grounds of faith. In reality, though, Voltaire no longer saw any advantage in believing these things on grounds of faith. Faith, for him, had become faith in the power of God, especially the power to do those things which have been observed in the workings of nature. If man has the capacity of thought, then God has given it to him. If animals have the same capacity, then God has given it to them. If man has free will, it, too, is a gift of God. If objects attract one another, this attraction derives from the creative activity of God. Voltaire willingly admitted that, in spite of the discoveries of science, man knows nothing about the nature of matter or of spirit—a view which, incidentally, was shared by Pascal, who, however, drew very different conclusions from this fact. Voltaire was prepared now to accept unqualifiedly only the existence of God as the one indispensable foundation of scientific discoveries and rational speculations. This type of deism was perfectly logical; it was already implied in the thought of Locke and Newton. Indeed, it was implied in English thought in general, where Christian dogma was likely to be regarded as a type of theological ideology.

Just how much these problems were clearly perceived by Voltaire will never be determined. Seen from an orthodox point of view, he will always appear quibbling; seen from a philosophical point of view, he will seem pedestrian; cast in a more objective light than in these two views, he will be seen as shifting from orthodox theology to philosophy and from philosophy to science, but with a sincere desire not to abandon completely certain dictates of each realm. This, of course, is precisely the position of the libertine.

Tournemine understood this to be Voltaire's position. Consequently, the one letter which we have in reply from Tournemine is constructed from the point of view of a theologian using the art of persuasion upon a wayward pupil who has become a libertine. The Jesuit priest loses no time in distinguishing between what is important and what is not. A scientific discovery is not of any supreme importance; on the other hand, the defense of the orthodox way of thinking is. Any belief that God is capable of endowing matter with thought is condemned, because not only does such a notion imply contradiction on the part of God, but it runs counter to the orthodox view that God has produced the union of body and soul. Tournemine rejects the idea on the grounds that body is divisible and soul indivisible: matter endowed with thought would have to be both divisible and indivisible. For the Jesuit, the *je*, the *moi*, which is the unity of "esprit," is something superior to the body, not a part of it. He rebels against the idea that one knows not what matter and spirit are. This, he finds, is the way of the free-thinkers, who deny any conception of matter, spirit, vice or virtue, perfection, justice, and goodness. As for the analogy between man and beasts, the Jesuit grants that there are several ways in which animals can be regarded: they may be pure machines, or they may have a spiritual soul, or even something which lies between body and soul called an animal soul. Tournemine confesses that he is ignorant about these things, but asserts that he does know that he possesses a body and a soul. Finally, he says, Newton should be praised for his specific measurements of the weight of bodies, but his calculations have nothing to do with the subject under discussion. He has not attempted to prove that there is in matter an inherent principle of attraction. Indeed, the force of movement comes from elsewhere. Tournemine insists upon this point, as well as upon the argument that acknowledging any such force to be inherent in matter would bring back belief in the occult qualities of Aristotle. But the center of the controversy is not there. The controversy arises from the libertinage of the time, the desire to gain pleasures at the expense of doubts, to renounce a religion which condemns vices. Tournemine has no illusions about the positions in the debate; for him, Voltaire has clearly espoused the anti-orthodox attitude of the libertine.

Voltaire made reply in a third letter to Tournemine in December 1735 (B. 932). In this letter, he does exclude the question of religion ("sans aucun rapport à la foi") and places the problem firmly on the principle of the limits of human intelligence. He specifically states that the question is, not whether matter thinks by itself or whether our soul is spiritual or not, but simply whether in the present state of our knowledge we can assert that God cannot communicate thought to matter. Tournemine had answered no, alleging the indivisibility of the soul and the divisibility of matter. Voltaire counters that he cannot accept this demonstration, since, in spite of his efforts, he is unable to penetrate the meaning of the axiom "pour apercevoir un objet, il faut le voir indivisiblement." He can neither perceive its truth nor divine its sense. Moreover, he notes that the problem is not what the mechanics of perception is. He admits that, to the question how one proceeds to perceive an object, he has no answer whatever. "C'est le secret du créateur." We do not know how we think, or how we live, or how we feel, or how we exist. He confesses that he does understand that a perception cannot be divisible, that a thought cannot be measured, that there is a manifest contradiction in the statement that a thought is material. He concedes that God cannot create thought from matter. But he points out that these statements have nothing to do with the problem at hand. Granted that God cannot contradict himself, wherein lies the contradiction in asserting that matter can receive from God the faculty of thought? To know whether a thing is capable or incapable of an act, it is necessary to know it thoroughly. But we do not know anything about matter. We know that we have certain sensations, certain ideas, but we are entirely ignorant of the substance to which these mental entities are attached.

Voltaire admits that he does not understand how matter thinks and that he is equally ignorant about how spirit thinks. It is evident that the trend of all this argument is that one can no more prove the immortality of the soul by alleging its immateriality than one can prove the immateriality of matter by alleging its spirituality. There is, however, a difficulty: if matter is constantly changing, dividing itself in infinite ways, to what part could God attribute thought, and how can this portion of matter conserve the thought? Voltaire accepts that the portion receiving thought can easily remain a personality, a unity, like our body. Then, too, matter is not really divisible infinitely; there must be small, unchanging portions of solid matter, for otherwise there would be no matter at all. We approach closely here to the Leibnizian monad. Voltaire, however, without specifying that there is any analogy between this notion and Leibniz's theory, states only that it is necessary that there be solid portions of matter to which God may, if he wishes, attribute thought and feeling. The whole philosophical position of Diderot will evolve from this premise.

To Tournemine's question of how a material thing can have an idea of an immaterial thing, Voltaire answers that we, who are material beings, conceive of immaterial things in the same way in which we, who are finite creatures, have the power to conceive of infinite things. To Tournemine's remark that we can easily conceive of spirit through the idea of *je* and *moi*, which constitute a unity, Voltaire opposes the thought that *je* and *moi* carry as much the idea of unity of matter as of substance. He rejects entirely Tournemine's assertion that the free-thinkers profess the same ignorance of vice and virtue as they do of matter and spirit. Locke, "le plus vertueux de tous les hommes, était bien loin d'avancer une impiété aussi absurde et aussi horrible." He reproaches his Jesuit opponent for taking so lightly the analogy between man and the animal world. He concludes this section by laying down the principle that, when a problem is not susceptible of demonstration, one must seek what is the more probable solution, not to adopt it as a belief, but to accept at least that it is possible. Applied to the animal world, the principle leads to the probability that they have feelings, ideas, memory, etc. They have the same organs of feeling as we do, and, since nature does nothing in vain, it is very likely that, with the organs of feeling, they feel. Consequently, one must argue either that animals are portions of matter which have received feeling from God or that they have a spiritual and immortal soul just as we do. And, if we conclude that God has given animals feeling why can He not have also given them thought?

Fundamentally, however, Voltaire bases his argument upon the great discovery of Newton. His argument consists in maintaining that, if matter can be shown to have a property hitherto unknown called attraction and if this attraction is universally present in matter, then it explains the centripetal forces which operate around the sun and the planets. To Tournemine's assertion that Newton did not regard this attraction as inherent in matter, Voltaire concedes that he did not use this term but fails to see how the concept of inherence could have been rejected by philosophers. However, that is not the point. Tournemine had conceded that Newton's measurements of movements were more accurate than those of any other philosopher. Voltaire rejects this concession as praising only the trivial aspects of Newton's observations. What Newton has actually done, Voltaire says, is to discover a new law of nature as certain and hitherto as unknown as the life of animals, the vegetation of plants, movement and electricity. The implication is that if new laws of nature can be discovered in the physical world, it should be possible to discover equally important laws in the spiritual, moral world of man. Voltaire stresses that those who search for these laws are not necessarily atheists. He maintains that both Locke and Newton suppose the existence of a first Cause; they are among those who have demonstrated God's existence with the most energy. Moreover, Voltaire objects to Tournemine's tendency to bring up moral problems, such as free-thinking, passions, and disorders, when the problem under discussion is purely philosophical. Voltaire's conclusion sings the praise of Locke, Newton, Clarke, Tillotson, Galileo, Descartes, and especially Bayle, "cet esprit si étendu, si sage et si pénétrant, dont les livres tout diffus qu'ils peuvent être, seront à jamais la bibliothèque des nations."

The discussion with Tournemine illustrates the way in which Voltaire began with a simple statement made by Locke and turned it into a focus around which could be gathered the main tendencies of seventeenth-century free-thinking. The nature of matter, the nature of spirit, the union of matter and spirit, the mechanism of animals with all the accompanying circumstances of animal soul, the analogy between the animal soul and the human soul or between animal mechanism and human mechanism all entered into the discussion. The arguments presented depended for their support upon two fundamental ideas, one drawn from deism, the other from Newtonian science: Voltaire based all his arguments upon the existence and power of God and upon analogy with the Newtonian law of attraction. It is as if the heavens declared the glory of God, and Newton and Locke disclosed His handiwork. This simple exposition in the *Lettres philosophiques*, which started the debate between Voltaire and his former Jesuit teacher, brought out how necessary it was for him to penetrate beneath the surface of philosophy. He must have learned how much he needed to acquaint himself with philosophical thinking: Malebranche, Descartes, Leibniz, Spinoza, Pascal, and, above all, Bayle had their importance. Voltaire must have understood that his erstwhile professor reasoned philosophically with much more ease than he did. The account he was drawing up of his thoughts and beliefs, which had seemed complete at the end of 1734, could now only appear terribly inadequate. It had to be revised.

The revision certainly was carried out along the lines of the

Voltaire-Tournemine controversy. The full details cannot be traced, though, because we now possess the second, not the first, draft of the *Traité*. But the impact of the controversy can be clearly seen in the following passage from Chapter V of the *Traité*:

> Des philosophes me disent: Ne vous y trompez pas, l'homme est en-tièrement différent des autres animaux; il a une ame spirituelle et im-mortelle: car (remarquez bien ceci) si la pensée est un composé de la matière, elle doit être nécessairement cela même dont elle est composée; elle doit être divisible, capable de mouvement, etc.; or la pensée ne peut point se diviser, donc elle n'est point un composé de la matière; elle n'a point de parties, elle est simple, elle est immortelle, elle est l'ouvrage et l'image d'un Dieu. J'écoute ces maîtres, et je leur réponds toujours avec défiance de moi-même, mais non avec confiance en eux....

It is for this reason that there is a progression from the thirteenth letter on Locke in the *Lettres philosophiques*, to the letters exchanged with Tournemine to Chapter V of the *Traité*. Thus, one result of the quarrel was to convince Voltaire of the necessity of clarifying his ideas on matter. A second effect was to show him the desirability of enlarging his philosophical background. It was not enough to be content with Locke and Newton. Important as they were, he would have to argue with those who knew profoundly Pascal, Descartes, and Malebranche. Lastly, he must have realized that it was not enough to have a superficial acquaintance with these English phi-losophers; he would have to dig more deeply into their meaning. Among the reprimands which Tournemine had given him as teach-er to student was the accusation of talking about philosophical mat-ters without a sufficient knowledge of philosophy.

For the moment, however, Voltaire attempted a summary of his metaphysical ideas in a series of letters to his friend Formont (see especially B. 911 and 929, but also 933). Since they merely summar-ize the points already made to Tournemine, nothing is to be gained from discussing them here.

The debate with Tournemine on the occasion of the thirteenth *Lettre philosophique*, concerned with thinking matter, was extended to attraction after the publication of the *Eléments*. There is every indication that Voltaire had been working or, at least, meditating upon this work since the preparation of the letters on Newton in the

Lettres philosophiques, that is, at least since 1732. I doubt, though, that he had a chance to do any very serious work on the *Eléments* until 1735. During that whole year and the year following, he must have devoted himself to study and then composed, with extraordinary energy, the *Eléments*, which he took with him to Holland on the occasion of his departure from Cirey following the scandal over the *Mondain*. It seems perfectly true that, while in Holland, he did profit from his exile by studying under S'Gravesande and Musschembrœck. However, this additional study does not seem to have equipped him with the proper material to complete his book. By the time of his return from Holland, he (or, at least, Mme du Châtelet) was dissatisfied with his chapter or section dealing with metaphysics. There were other chapters which he proposed to write, too, but which he did not yet feel sufficiently informed to complete. This situation explains in part the rather large number of commentaries which he deemed necessary to his work in 1738, and it also offers some explanation of why many of them were commentaries on Newton by English mathematicians and physicists.

Controversy arose around the *Eléments* even before its publication. It is certain that, on his return from Holland, Voltaire gave much consideration to having his *Eléments* published in France. As he had conceived them for a French audience, he had not neglected a continual comparison of Newton's ideas with Descartes's. It became more and more evident, however, from the early months of 1738, that there would be no opportunity of bringing them out in France. Mme du Châtelet wrote to Maupertuis, *circa* 10 February 1738:

> Mr. de V. a perdu, non sans regret, l'espérance de faire imprimer son livre en France, il n'est fait que pour des François, il y perd beaucoup de tems à réfuter le sistème de Descartes, et cette peine, très nécessaire quand on parle à des françois, est inutile dans les pays étrangers, où c'est se battre contre des moulins à vent, que de réfuter une philosophie abandonnée entièrement et unanimement reconnuë pour fausse.

On 28 March, Voltaire complained to Thiériot that he was having all sorts of unpleasant experiences because of his *Eléments* and that he was resolved to abandon the whole matter. "Je ne veux pas perdre mon repos pour Newton même. Je me contente d'avoir raison pour moy. Je n'aurai pas l'honneur d'être apôtre, je ne seray que croyant."

On 10 April, he wrote again to Thiériot that he would be surprised if his *Eléments* appeared. He stated that he had left a fairly disordered manuscript with the publishers in Holland and that he was urging them to send him the proofs but not to hurry. He added that the manuscript had been read by two members of the Académie des Sciences and that he was certain to be supported in his scientific presentation. By 1 May, there seemed to be reason for alarm. Mme du Châtelet expressed some anxiety that D'Aguesseau, the Chancellor, would become angry if the work were published in Holland after he had indicated that he did not wish to have it appear in France. She urged D'Argental to have the younger D'Aguesseau point out to his father that half of the work was already in print at the time Voltaire had submitted the manuscript, that Voltaire had understood, by D'Aguesseau's refusal to allow the book to appear in France, that he would not like to see it appear in Holland, and that, in accordance with that feeling, Voltaire had refrained from sending the last part of the manuscript. Mme du Châtelet insisted that, since five chapters were still lacking in the Holland edition and since the chapter on metaphysics of which the Chancellor expressly disapproved had been suppressed, no further proof was needed to demonstrate that Voltaire was not directly implicated in the publication.

Mme du Châtelet's fright was not particularly shared by Voltaire. To D'Argental on the same date (1 May), he expressed only a mild concern that he might be separated from her and forced to live away from D'Argental. In reality, he was more preoccupied with the situation than he wished to confess. To Thiériot, he admitted that the indiscretion of the Dutch printers in bringing out the work "m'occupe très désagréablement." He objected, first of all, to the ridiculousness of the title. But his major worry was the reaction of the Chancellor. In a letter on 5 May, he wondered if he ought not to present a *Mémoire* to the Chancellor, dissociating himself from the whole enterprise. He suggested submitting the *Mémoire* through Pitot and Moncarville, hoping perhaps to secure after all permission to print his revised work in France.

Mme du Châtelet, in a letter to Maupertuis on 9 May, mentioned another difficulty. The reference to the "marquise imaginaire," which had been a sly shot at Fontenelle's *Mondes*, inserted, in all probability, in a moment of pique when Algarotti had changed his previous intention of dedicating his *Neutonianismo per le dame* to Mme du Châtelet and had dedicated it instead to Fontenelle, had been retained by the Dutch printers. Mme du Châtelet felt certain that it would not be welcome either to Fontenelle or to Algarotti. As a matter of fact, it did cause embarrassment to Voltaire. In a post-script which he added to Mme du Châtelet's letter to Algarotti of 12 May, Voltaire wrote: "J'ai une bonne tracasserie avec luy pour avoir commencé mon petit essay de catéchisme neutonien par ces mots: Ce n'est point icy une marquise ny une philosophie imaginaire." Voltaire explained that he had attempted to justify his indiscretion by attributing it to the conversations he and Algarotti had had at Cirey.

Voltaire, in the meantime, did not renounce his desire to have his work printed in France. He wrote to Thiériot on 11 May that he still hoped to get permission and again, on 13 May, wrote him to say: "Sans doute je vais travailler à une édition correcte des éléments de Neuton, qui ne seront ny pour les *dames* ny pour *tout le monde,* mais où l'on trouvera de la vérité et de la méthode." Voltaire was particularly sensitive to Algarotti's *Neutonianismo.* To Thiériot on 18 May, he expressed the conviction that there are more truths in ten pages of the *Eléments* than in Algarotti's whole book. Similarly, in his letter to Maupertuis on 22 May, he stated that there are, in the *Neutonianismo,* "plus de tours et de pensées que de vérités."

As a matter of fact, there was not only rivalry between Voltaire and his predecessor Fontenelle and between himself and Algarotti but also a self-assurance on Voltaire's part which amounted to boastfulness. Voltaire became with the success of the *Eléments* more and more proud of his presentation. In a letter to Thiériot on 23 June, in which he announced the establishment of a physics laboratory, he laid down certain claims to fame for his book:

Je croi bien que les gens aimables ne parlent plus des *Elémens de Newton*. On ne s'entretient point à souper deux fois de suitte de la même chose, et on a raison quand le sujet de la conversation est un peu abstrait. Cela n'empêche pas qu'à la sourdine les gens qui veulent s'instruire ne lisent des ouvrages qu'il faut méditer, et il faut bien qu'il y ait un peu de ces gens là puisqu'on réimprime les *Elémens de Neuton* en deux endroits. Mr. de Maupertuis qui est sans contredit l'homme de France qui entend le mieux ces matières en est content, et vous m'avouerez que son suffrage est quelque chose. Je sçai bien que malgré la foule de démonstrations que j'ay rassemblée contre les chimères des tourbillons, ce roman philosofique subsistera encor quelque temps dans de vieilles têtes.

Voltaire concluded that, after all, he was the first in France who had clarified these things, and even the first in Europe—"car S'Gravesande n'a parlé qu'aux matématiciens et Pemberton a obscurcy souvent Neuton."

Though quite confident that the work was a success, he nevertheless felt obliged to defend it against the attack of his opponents. He therefore sent, on 3 August, a fairly long notice to the *Pour et contre* not only to call attention to the *Eclaircissements* which had been published in the *Journal de Trévoux* but to take exception to the negligent way in which the editors of the second edition had produced his work. He also used the occasion to respond to the *Lettre d'un physicien sur la Philosophie de Newton*. In his reply, Voltaire protests against the banality of the objections made against his work. He concludes by promising to answer all reasonable objections: "Si on me fait des objections plus raisonnables, j'y répondrai, soit en me corrigeant, soit en demandant de nouveaux éclaircissements; car je n'ai et ne puis avoir d'autre but que la vérité." He then discloses the procedures of his work. The names of Galileo, Kepler, Descartes, Newton, and Huyghens are of no importance; it is their ideas that Voltaire claims to have analyzed and to have presented in accordance with his own way of thinking. As for the charges brought against his presentation, he affirms that by far most of the things criticized can be found explicitly in Newton or in Keill, Gregory, Pemberton, S'Gravesande, and Musschembrœck. This is equivalent to saying that Voltaire has arranged his work to express the best thought in Newtonian philosophy since Newton's own day, and, indeed, these were his principal sources.

He grants that what causes the most difficulty is the concept of gravitation, or attraction. To the objection of his detractors, he replies that Maupertuis has already shown in his *Figures des astres* that it is as difficult to justify the concept of impulsion as that of attraction. Voltaire invites his critics, after they have perused Maupertuis's demonstration, to read Chapters XV, XVI, and XVII of the *Eléments* and judge whether the arguments alleged against the plenum and against the "tourbillons" are sufficiently strong. He insists that, when the impossibilities in explaining mathematically the "tourbillons" are balanced against the way in which they confirm the hypothesis of attraction, the way will be clearer to choose.

Voltaire understood, or claimed to understand at any rate, the reluctance of those who clung to the theories of Descartes in order to preserve the "mécanique" which he established against Aristotle. Their argument was simple: any attempt to explain the workings of the universe by some mysterious force was tantamount to the reintroduction into physics of occult powers. Voltaire here insists that he respects both Descartes and this point of view. He wants to keep Cartesian mechanism, the universe being, as he conceives it, like a clock. But, when it comes to seeking the springs which make it work, when the assumed mechanism fails to operate, when all nature conspires to reveal to us a new property of matter which functions perfectly, should we reject it on the grounds that we do not understand its nature? Voltaire comes back to his one defense for what he cannot explain (which he had taken, of course, from Locke): how can we dare say that God has not given attraction as a quality to matter when we admit that He has given it movement and inertia and impenetrability. Since it is possible for God to do so, Voltaire concludes that He did do so. "Pour moi, je ne reconnais, dans cette propriété des corps, d'autre cause que la main toute-puissante de l'être suprême." He asserts that, even if "tourbillons" did exist, they, too, would be subject to the Newtonian law of attraction. His final remark is a boast that he has surpassed Newton, since he dares assert that light is also subject to the same law of attraction.

Voltaire's article in the *Pour et contre* indicates the extent of the opposition which his *Eléments* provoked. He himself complained that he was being subjected to persecution by those who accused him of lack of patriotism in supporting an Englishman against a Frenchman. There was something of the missionary in his attitude. He wrote to Thiériot on 7 August that the French were very petty in their approach to physics. He added that it was perfectly true that there were no new opinions in Newton, but that there were experiments, calculations, and that with time everyone would have to yield to their accuracy. "Les Renauds et les Castels n'empêcheront pas à la longue le triomphe de la raison." Mme du Châtelet accorded Voltaire's performance a higher rating than even Voltaire wanted to give it. In a letter to Richelieu, on 17 August, she announced that she was sending him the second edition of the *Eléments*. With all her openness and frankness, she commended it thus: "Je sais qu'on peut faire beaucoup de critiques de ce livre, mais avec tout cela il n'y en a point de meilleur en français sur ces matières, car hors les mémoires de l'académie des sciences il n'y a que des livres de physique pitoyables." Evidently, in the opinion of the two workers at Cirey, the cause of this sterility was to be found in the insistence of French scientists on defending Cartesianism against the new discoveries following Newton.

That this situation was not at all a fiction or a creation for propaganda purposes can be seen in Tournemine's letter to Voltaire on 28 August 1738. Voltaire's former teacher at Louis-le-Grand compliments his student on the brilliant success he has achieved in the field of poetry and history. He notices now that Voltaire is attempting to achieve glory in the field of physics. "Vous vous efforcez de déthrôner l'illustre Descartes; vous tentés de porter la lumière dans les ténèbres du savant et proscrit Newton." Voltaire, the wily Jesuit acknowledges, has succeeded in the second enterprise: Newton is only intelligible in the *Eléments*. As for the first enterprise, Tournemine as a "compatriote," as an "ancien admirateur de Descartes," undertakes his defense, although he asserts that the French philosopher does not need his feeble assistance.

His defense of Descartes is based on the state of science and philosophy when Descartes brought out his work. It required a keen intellect to bring out at that time the true idea of God, supported by a thousand other verities, to mark out the boundaries between the properties of the soul and matter, to reinstate physics, which had been lost in the vain subtleties of Aristotle, and to encourage idle minds, nurtured in meaningless words, to return to the search for reality. In this reality, as far as the corporeal world is concerned, everything is effected by movement alone, "que la masse, la figure, l'impulsion, le choc, définissent le mouvement." That is all there is to the secret of nature. Tournemine concedes that Descartes may have been mistaken about the laws of movement, and he even grants that his system is more subtle than solid. Still, these shortcomings do not prevent contemporary physicists from being heavily in his debt. Although not infallible, Descartes nonetheless taught Newton how to philosophize. "La méthode de Descartes ne trompe que les esprits peu attentifs; elle arrive à la vérité par l'évidence, elle s'en aproche par l'expérience." Although it is true that he sometimes deviated from his principles, we draw heavily upon his precepts and his example, and the excellent geometry he invented aids in correcting his physics.

The eloquent Jesuit even pushes his argument to the point where he is prepared to maintain that "le système de Newton est presque le système de Descartes" concealed by a whole new set of terms. But, he adds, in changing the terms, Newton has substituted conjecture for certainty, embarrassment for clarity, and ignorance for evidence. It is true that Newton has breadth, profundity of mind, infinite concern for details, and exactness in computation. Nonetheless, his final conclusion brings back the occult qualities of medieval philosophy.

The Jesuit's final argument, is addressed to the patriotism of Voltaire. How can he, Voltaire, attribute superiority to an English philosopher when he is a Frenchman and fully as respected in France as in England? The old teacher closes with the expression of an earnest desire that his pupil, now that he has become famous as "poète, historien, philosophe, architecte, politique," will undertake the study of religion "sans prévention, sans préjugés." Descartes, who made every conceivable effort, though to no avail, to enlist the support of the Jesuits for his philosophy, would perhaps have been astounded and certainly delighted had he been permitted to hear the eloquent plea of Voltaire's former Jesuit teacher. Times do change.

Voltaire made answer to all these defenses of Descartes in a letter to Maupertuis (B. 1551) around the beginning of October 1738, which he published openly in the *Bibliothèque française*, Amsterdam, 1738. After noting that there is "une assez grande fermentation en France" and that the names of Descartes and Newton have become rallying points for two parties, he asserts that these civil wars are not made for philosophers. All of this defense of one's countryman against the scholar of another country is foolish. In the eighteenth century the only founder of a sect is a true demonstration. Those who proclaim that they oppose the new discoveries and draw con-

clusions in favor of the "tourbillons" are really not true disciples of
Descartes. Scientists long ago rejected his theory of light, his laws
of movement, which were proved false just after their formulation,
his "tourbillons," which overthrow, as he presented them, the rules
of mechanics, his explanation of the loadstone, his "matière cannelée," his imaginary formation of the universe, and his anatomical
description of man. Every explanation which Descartes gave of the
physical universe has long since been discarded, and yet there are
still those who call themselves Cartesians. Voltaire insists that there
is no point in trying to prove that Descartes was a greater man in
his century than Newton was in his. Nor, he adds, is it very illumi-
nating to discuss which of the two is the greater physicist. It is true
that Descartes made practically no experiments. If he had, he would
not have given false laws of movement. It is also true that he was not
well-read in the scientific literature of his time. Had he been, he
would not have given an erroneous explanation of the circulation
of the blood. And, finally, it is true that Descartes made no observation of falling bodies as Galileo did, nor did he reveal a new heaven
as Galileo did, nor did he guess the rules for the movements of the
stars as Kepler did, nor did he discover the weight of air as Torricelli
did, nor did he calculate the centrifugal forces or the laws of the
pendulum as Huyghens did. Newton, on the other hand, with his
knowledge of geometry and experiments, brought to light the laws
of gravitation between all bodies, the origins of colors, the properties of light, and the law of the resistance of fluids. All of Descartes's physics stems from a series of hypotheses, all of them wrong.
His universe is an imaginary one, created by him; it is not the universe created by God. Quoting Boerhaave, Voltaire willingly concedes that Descartes was a great geometrician but insists that in physics he was totally in error and that all his principles fail to explain a
single phenomenon in nature.

Voltaire stresses that this is the general European view of Descartes everywhere except in France. He protests that it is unfair to
consider him a criminal because he shares that view. Even in France
in Descartes's time, Gassendi held many of these opinions he is now
expressing. There is not any sense whatever in appealing to one's
province or country. One has to seek truth wherever it is.

The point under discussion is uniquely whether, granted that

Newton has discovered a tendency, a gravitation, an attraction, which exists between celestial and all other bodies, and has calculated the force of this gravitation between the celestial bodies, this attraction should be regarded as a primary quality necessary to the formation of the universe and given to matter by God, or whether this property of matter is the mechanical effect of some other principle. In either case, it will have to be admitted that the origin of the phenomenon derives from the will of the Creator of the world, whether He filled all space with matter or whether He created matter in space; whether He gave gravitation to bodies or whether He formed "tourbillons" upon which gravitation depends. Thus, ultimately, all explanations lead to God. The only difference between Newtonians and anti-Newtonians is that the latter, thinking that they have found the simplest explanation by advancing impulsion as the cause of movement are in fact complicating the issue infinitely by having to invent all sorts of other movements. In reality, Newton has invented the simplest of all explanations.

Voltaire almost reaches poetic heights when he speaks of Newton's law of attraction. His insistence that nobody can deny that God has the power to give attraction to matter is presented with such energy that the purpose of the eloquence is lost:

Je demande d'abord s'il y a quelqu'un qui ose nier, que Dieu ait pu donner aux corps ce principe de la gravitation? Je demande s'il est plus difficile à l'être suprême de faire tendre les corps les uns vers les autres, que d'ordonner qu'un corps en pourra déranger un autre de sa place; que celui-ci végète, que cet autre ait la vie, que celui-ci sente sans penser, que celui-là pense, que tous aient la mobilité....

He approves the modest way Maupertuis explained attraction in order not to upset those who believe that everything in nature should be effected by mechanical means. "Mais enfin personne n'ayant pu expliquer cette nouvelle propriété de la matière par aucun mécanisme, il faut bien qu'on s'accoutume insensiblement, à regarder la gravitation comme un mécanisme d'un nouveau genre, comme une qualité de la matière inconnue jusqu'à nous." Voltaire pushes things even further. Since no cause—mechanical cause, that is—can be found for attraction, we must admit that the cause resides in the effect and is due to a principle which is not at all mechanical.

In fact, Newton, says Voltaire, did not think that ordinary mechanism could ever explain the gravitation of matter.

Voltaire takes up also Newton's attitude toward hypotheses, which was one of the points being actively discussed at Cirey. Mme du Châtelet, for instance, tried to make the distinction between the working hypothesis, which is characteristic of all scientific thinking, and the predictive hypothesis, which was thought to be Descartes's way of thinking about scientific problems. Voltaire aptly defines this kind of hypothesis as "ce qui ne se déduit point des phénomènes" and goes on to state that the hypotheses, whether metaphysical or physical, or whether the source of occult qualities or of mechanical actions, have no place in experimental philosophy. It is his contention that the notion "hypothèse de mécanique," supposedly invented by the Cartesians, is as unscientific as the occult qualities which they attribute to Newton's attraction. Voltaire is obviously anxious to exculpate Newton of this charge. He takes great pains to explain how the anti-Newtonians have fallen into this error because of their failure to distinguish between what Newton said in the first two books of the *Principia* as mathematician and what he said in the third as physicist. The geometer examines the point where the forces converge, whereas the physicist studies these forces as a composite distributed throughout matter. The distinction can be seen in the way the geometer and the physicist regard a pair of scales: the geometer is interested in the mathematical center of gravity, the physicist in the fact that the two masses in the two basins of the scales are equal.

Voltaire cites Newton's demonstrations which disprove the whole theory of the "tourbillons." He was particularly impressed, it seems, with Newton's ability to determine where in the sky the comet of 1681 ought to be at a fixed hour according to his theory. He was equally impressed with Newton's determination of the derangement which Jupiter and Saturn would experience in their conjunction. These two achievements he contrasts with the theory of "tourbillons," which cannot explain these phenomena. At the same time, he opposes all explanations which suggest that there is matter which is dense without being heavy. It is evident, he maintains, that all matter has weight and that gravitation operates in direct proportion to the quantity of matter.

Voltaire concedes that it is reasonable that an effort be made to conciliate Descartes's "tourbillons" with Newton's discoveries and grants that both theories should be in accord, if possible, with the laws of Kepler and, in general, with the laws of nature. He welcomes that physicists of repute should have attempted to conceive of "tourbillons" in other terms: Huyghens with his "tourbillons" darting off in all directions, Perrault with his notion of northernly-southernly "tourbillons" meeting with easterly-westerly ones, Bull-finger with his suggestion of four "tourbillons" opposed to each other two by two, Leibniz with his "circulation harmonique," and, finally, Malebranche with his "tourbillons mous." He ventures to predict, however, that they will never succeed in finding the solution this way: "Non seulement le soleil gravite vers Saturne, mais Sirius gravite vers le soleil, mais chaque partie de l'univers gravite, et c'est bien en vain que les plus savants hommes veulent expliquer cette gravitation universelle par de petits tourbillons qu'ils supposent n'être pas pesants; toute matière a cette propriété."

Voltaire reverts to his position of the *Traité de métaphysique*. Animals have what we call instinct, humans have what we call thought. How do they come to possess these faculties? Only God who has bestowed them knows. The great principle of Leibniz that nothing exists without a cause is very true, but it is also very true that the first springs of nature have as their sufficient reason only the infinite will of the infinitely powerful Being. Gravitation is in the same situation, and all nature shouts, as S'Gravesande and Mus-schembroeck have affirmed, that this gravitation does not depend upon mechanical causes. All we can do is to calculate the effects and examine the properties.

Voltaire claims that he has done nothing to add a system to Newton's system. All he has done is to present to a public little versed in these matters the effects of gravitation. Some maintain that there is no need to make such a fuss over these discoveries of Newton, because every philosophical system has given way eventually to a subsequent one—Aristotle's system having replaced Plato's, Bacon, Galileo, Descartes, and Boyle, in turn, having destroyed Aristotle's system, and Descartes's having finally succumbed, too—and it is likely that Newton's system will be supplanted by another in time. Voltaire insists, though, that Newton has no system, that he has merely given the results of his experiments. But this information is very useful. We can now weigh the moon and explain a limitless number of astronomical phenomena. Voltaire concludes his vindication of Newton with four or so pages in defense of his *Eléments* and in protest against the changes which the Dutch scholar inserted in his manuscript.

Voltaire wrote to Lefranc de Pompignan, with whom he was on fairly good terms at the time, that he had dared point out the mistakes in Descartes. France, he adds, is the only country where the theories of Newton in physics and of Boerhaave in medicine are rejected. There is, in fact, no elementary, introductory book in physics and no text in astronomy except Bion's, which is a collection of articles from the Académie. To find out about these fields, a Frenchman has to turn to foreigners: Keill, Wolff, S'Gravesande. Soon, the *Institutions de physique* of Mme du Châtelet will be available. In the meantime, he claims that his *Eléments* has at least the merit to stammer the truth.

The composition and the defense of the *Eléments de la philosophie de Newton* display a good acquaintance with the scientific and philosophical world of the preceding hundred years, which is confirmed in part by the correspondence for the year 1738. We have seen that Voltaire had become competent to handle the representatives of that scientific and philosophical movement who stood at the two ends of that century—Descartes at the beginning and Newton at the end. To the reproach of Dortous de Mairan that he had treated both Descartes and Malebranche rather cavalierly and that he would have done better to speak more modestly and lead his readers along, he replied that he was only too aware of this defect. He even conceded that, if he had used less forceful tactics, his readers would have been more willing to consider the theory of attraction. He offered as his excuse that he had scarcely studied philosophy except in those countries where these two philosophers were treated with scant respect and where Descartes's ten volumes were sold for only three florins. In the same letter, he indicated that he not only had been led by the Dutch physicists, particularly S'Gravesande and Musschembrœck, to denigrate the philosophy of Descartes and Malebranche, but had followed with more than casual attention the discussion between Clarke and Leibniz and was convinced by the arguments of Clarke that impulsion could never elucidate the phenomena explained by attraction. He had been convinced, too, by the strong opposition of Désaguliers, Pemberton, Saunderson, Stone, and, above all, Bradley, who burst out laughing whenever "tourbillons" were mentioned.

VOLTAIRE AND FREDERICK

The second of the great debates Voltaire engaged in during the Cirey period was with Frederick. It was occasioned by Voltaire's promise to send the Prince the *Traité de métaphysique*. Voltaire was then in Amsterdam, where he sought refuge from the police because of the *Mondain*, and presumably had a copy of the *Traité* with him. Mme du Châtelet, hearing of this projected indiscretion, complained bitterly to D'Argental, tacitly admitting that she was in no position to prevent it. Yet she did prevent it after all. Voltaire, on second thought, decided to heed her warnings. He wrote to Frederick not to expect the *Traité*, and the latter suggested that, if Voltaire did not dare send him the whole *Traité*, he might excerpt parts of it from time to time in the correspondence. Voltaire acceded to this suggestion. In a letter which we have already analyzed, he described the main lines of the *Traité*, including therewith a section on free will. This section, though marked "Chapitre V. *De la liberté*," was in reality a portion of a treatise constructed in numbered sections, this particular portion being the last part of Section 83 and the whole of Sections 84, 85, 86, and 87. Evidently, though, it was now being put into chapters, because a note states that the relationship between kinetic energy and free will is treated in a "Chapitre 8." Another note in the handwriting of Mme du Châtelet says that the "preceding chapter" dealt with the nature and existence of matter. It seems impossible to deny that this was a longer third draft of a portion of the earlier *Traité* and that it had been composed originally in sections but was now being turned into chapters. It is also possible to follow to some extent the subjects treated. A reference to a Section 15 discloses that it concerned the nature and existence of God, and Mme du Châtelet's remark indicates that there was to be a chapter on the nature and existence of matter. That there was a chapter on free will is evident; Voltaire himself stated that the whole problem of free will conditioned entirely the problem of morality. Thus, to a considerable extent, this full treatise was a recapitulation of the matters discussed in the earlier *Traité de métaphysique*. However, one should add that this chapter on free will was not only fuller but more solidly constructed. It is likely that this draft represented the "rêveries métaphysiques" which he sent to Formont, at least a part of them, the "morceaux de philosophie" which he forwarded to Frederick, and the work to which he referred when he wrote to Thiériot that he had spent the whole day "à éplucher de la métaphysique."

Voltaire's discussion with Frederick played a significant role in his intellectual development. Voltaire had begun the *Traité* with Locke, Newton, and Clarke as the sources of his metaphysics. He had continued it with Mandeville as the reference for the section on morality. Frederick now brought into the discussion considerations drawn from Leibniz and Wolff. When the Prince received the section on free will, he wrote his correspondent that he was mortified not to be of his opinion. Voltaire had made two positive points in the article: man has a feeling of being free, and it would have been a deception on the part of God to have given him this feeling without actually having made him free; man's freedom does not run counter to God's prescience, any more than God's own free will does. In his reply, Frederick takes the position that God, being all-wise and all-powerful, must have had an ultimate objective in creating this universe. All events should therefore work toward this end, including man's actions. For Frederick, it is more reasonable to conceive of a God who does everything than of a deity who creates the universe and then withdraws from it, leaving it to work out its destiny without any fixed plan. The idea of God's active participation in His universe is the core of Frederick's argument. Everything is determined in a precise way: man's character, ideas, and actions. Frederick thus firmly supports the doctrine of absolute necessity.

Voltaire, who had already, thanks to Frederick, some acquaintance with Leibniz through Wolff, saw at once that Frederick was basing his argument upon Leibniz's doctrine of sufficient reason. He, too, subscribes to the doctrine, but in another way. Man's freedom, for him, consists in the power to think and to act in consequence of that thought. If man possesses that power, he is free; but, if God alone possesses it, the individual is deceived into believing himself free. Voltaire, declaring that this deception can come only from God or from the nature of matter, excludes both possibilities, on the grounds that it is contrary to our conception of God to believe that He would deceive, and matter, being devoid of intelligence, certainly could not do so. Voltaire's one decisive proof for freedom lies in his "sentiment intérieur" of freedom. He asserts that, in the presence of this strong, inner feeling, the only way of disproving freedom is to prove its impossibility. There are only two ways in which this can be done: one must prove either that the idea of free will contains a contradiction or that there is no power capable of granting freedom. Voltaire affirms that God, being free, can grant a portion of His freedom to man. He concedes, though, that just because He may do so does not mean that He necessarily has done so. Some argue that, were man to possess some freedom, he would be to that extent independent of the Deity. Voltaire replies that the attribution of some freedom to man would, on the contrary, be an expression of His infinite power. Others offer as proof of man's lack of freedom that he is often carried away by his emotions. Voltaire admits the fact but retorts that sickness is proof of the existence of health. Still others claim that action arises from desire, which, in turn, is served by will and that, therefore, action is determined. To this point, Voltaire replies that will and desire are two different things, one of which often successfully combats the other. To a final group which maintains that, if man is free, there can be no God, Voltaire makes answer that it is precisely the gift of freedom that proves the existence of God. He does grant that free will is incompatible with divine foresight but offers in rebuttal Clarke's definition of God's foreknowledge: that God has the power to predict, just as a well-informed man may predict, but that God, being all-wise, predicts unerringly. Voltaire concludes that man must believe that he is free.

Frederick's reply consists in a point-by-point analysis of Voltaire's arguments. In effect, he concludes that God, being all-wise, could not grant freedom to man, since it is a contradiction to say that God can dispose of His essence to man. Such free will would thus not have a sufficient reason. Frederick concedes that man has the capacity to think and to act, but always within the inviolable laws of fate. All his actions tend to carry out the decrees of Providence, though, of course, he is unaware that they do. One cannot assert that God has deceived man; He has merely concealed "les ressorts qui le font agir." Man's actions are guided by self-interest, what he seeks is happiness; but this tendency is no proof of freedom. The best proof of necessity lies in the immutable laws of the physical world. Man is subject to similar immutable laws. And let no one say that God could not care for these small details of existence. Such a stand neglects God's immensity.

Frederick rejects Voltaire's claim that the presence of sickness proves the existence of health. The passions do not prove freedom. Nor can one allege the triumph of will over desire as a proof of free will. This triumph merely proves man's egotism. The conclusion of this argument is that, since God created the world and since man cannot be free, there exists an absolute necessity to which man must submit. Frederick admits that Divinity is the source of evil, no matter what system one adopts, but he insists that this fact does not excuse man's departure from virtue.

Voltaire was forced to acknowledge the strength of Frederick's position. "J'avais déjà beaucoup de respect pour l'opinion de la fatalité, quoique ce ne soit pas la mienne," he wrote in his letter of 8 March 1738. But he still rests his conviction on the belief that man is free. Even those who accept the system of fatality, he points out, act as if they were free. Voltaire argues that, since our feelings are ordinarily real, our feeling of liberty must be real also. Moreover, if free will in man were impossible, then God, possessing foresight, would foresee not only man's action but His own as well and, therefore, would not be free either. But that is impossible, because then He would no longer be God. Voltaire concludes that, since even fatalists must grant freedom to the Deity, then there seems no reason why He cannot bestow some of His freedom upon man as He has granted him a portion of existence, thought, movement, and will. Finally, we are either automata or free beings. The only proof of our automatism lies in God's prescience, but we know nothing about that foresight. Voltaire concludes that we cannot reason a priori upon these matters, for the principles of metaphysics are concealed from us.

Frederick, in his reply of 19 April 1738, grants that there are valid objections which can be made to the system of absolute fatality. He admits, too, that man has a feeling of being free and possesses the power to will and to act. But he continues to insist that the principle of sufficient reason requires that every effect have a determining, not a chance, cause. Thus, although man is free to direct his will and to act, he is not free to govern the reasons which determine the will to act. These are fixed—the idea of happiness, for example, which is a mainspring of action bound up with man's temperament. Hence, though an action may appear free, it is nevertheless determined: "l'homme agit donc selon une loi, et en conséquence du ton que le Créateur lui a donné." All man's actions, indeed, may be traced back to God, who is the supreme sufficient reason. Frederick denies that this account makes God the source of evil. He argues rather, as Leibniz did, that we have no right to judge the whole by its parts and cannot judge the whole directly, since it is infinite whereas we are finite.

Voltaire attempts in his letter of 20 May 1738 to sum up the discussion. He grants that free will has not been fully demonstrated, since two attitudes are possible. Those who present God as the infinite master of all things seem committed to the idea of an inevitable fatality. On this view, God is the Creator of machines. Those, on the other hand, who attribute a far greater power to the Deity believe that He bestows upon man a portion of that power. They maintain that He is the God of thinking beings.

These debates, which seem to us now so sterile and uninteresting, were absolutely essential to Voltaire's development. To us, they turn about a point which we have always thought minor to Locke, thinking matter, and about a second point, attraction, which, though certainly not minor, is so established now that we take it for granted, and about a third point, free will, which, we have learned to believe, only has sense when it is connected with determinism. For Voltaire, however, precisely at the moment of his reeducation, it was not enough to know the opinion of Locke on thinking matter, that of Locke and Collins on freedom of the will, and that of Newton on attraction; it was necessary to know as well which of the discussions from the immediate past threw the most light on the problems these opinions raised. More important still, it was essential for Voltaire to know what it would mean for his time to adopt the opinions of Locke and Newton in opposition to those of Leibniz

and Descartes and, in addition, what it would mean for science, religion, and philosophy as an organic way of life if the three paramount issues in the realm of ideas were taken to be the origin of
thought, the orderly universe, and the freedom of man. Voltaire's
understanding of these issues may not have been profound, especially in 1738. It is very significant, though, that he not only
identified them as the crucial issues but selected those of his predecessors who offered the best solutions. His defense of these solutions
against Tournemine and Frederick and others does not reveal any
profundity either, but it does prove that he was attempting to organize a view of the universe and of man's place in it which would be
consistent and coherent. It is possible even to outline that view in
some systematic way. Indeed, Lanson has done so beautifully in his
biography of Voltaire. More important than any systematization
of the view, however, is the fact that the poet was now in search
of a philosophy.

7. VOLTAIRE AND THE SCIENCE OF 1738

IT WAS INEVITABLE, given Voltaire's wish to stand out as the leader of his time, that he should eventually come face to face with the problem of science. Indeed, it is surprising that he postponed the confrontation until 1735. Nothing bespeaks the strength of his determination to be the outstanding poet, dramatist, literary figure, and critic so eloquently as the long period in which he resolutely resisted all contacts with scientists and philosophers. Long after Fontenelle had traded upon his reputation as a popularizer of science, Voltaire, who had encountered the same literary difficulties, remained adamant in his loyalty to the art of poetry. In fact, we have no evidence that the training he had received at Louis-le-Grand in scientific studies had any effect upon him whatsoever, in marked contrast with the program in the arts, which proved for him a source of enthusiastic inspiration. There is in the early correspondence just one letter to Fontenelle, written around 1719, just at the moment when Voltaire was preparing to launch his career as a poet, which shows that he had just become acquainted with the *Entretiens sur la pluralité des mondes* and that, in the provincial château society he was frequenting, Fontenelle was a scientific celebrity of sorts.

In retrospect, it seems to us that the intellectual movement from 1543 to 1730 had been preeminently in the realm of science. The last half of the sixteenth century and the whole of the seventeenth had been distinguished, above all, by the dynamic development of scientific theory. Extending from Copernicus (1543) to Newton's death (1728), a complete scientific revolution had taken place and brought to the fore a whole line of intellectual giants—Galileo, Kepler, Descartes, Pascal, Kircher, Huyghens, Locke, Newton, Leibniz, and Malebranche—a line which has never been surpassed or even equalled in any other era. We cannot tarry over the scientific contributions of these men, whom Voltaire was eventually forced to consider at least in a serious, elementary way. But it is worth noting that they were scattered throughout Europe, in Poland, Germany, the Netherlands, Italy, France, and England. Science was now the means of forming a true European spirit, since its rebirth had become a truly European manifestation. Indeed, Jaspers considers science and technocracy the two outstanding characteristics of Western civilization. These scientists were aided in their pursuits by the private centers of scientific activity, such as those around Mersenne and Montmor, and eventually, after the middle of the seventeenth century, by the various academies, of which the Royal Society and the Académie des Sciences were certainly the most eminent. Ultimately, of course, urban scientific societies were to become widespread throughout Europe.

There are two historical currents which should be mentioned here. In the first half of the seventeenth century (1637-1650), Descartes dominated the scientific scene not only in France but in all of Europe. Even at that time, though, he was opposed in France by Gassendi, who revived the Greek atomists. Later, throughout the latter half of the century, Descartes was violently criticized by all philosophers, including such prominent thinkers as Spinoza, Pascal, Leibniz, Locke, and Newton. In the last quarter of the seventeenth century (1687-1738) and the first third of the eighteenth century, Newton dominated the scene in England and everywhere in Europe except France. The resistance his theories met with in that country led to a Newton-Descartes quarrel between English and French scientists in which the a priori, rational principles advanced by Descartes were contrasted with the experimental method promoted by Newton. The points stressed were, on the one side, that Descartes's system of the world was totally false and, on the other, that Newton's theory of attraction merely brought back in a different guise the occult explanation of the universe which had been so prevalent in the middle ages. There were, however, two circumstances that tipped the balance in favor of the English scientist. First, the Dutch scientists Boerhaave, S'Gravesande, and Musschembroeck supported Newton in the quarrel. These Dutch scientists set up centers at the universities of Leyden and Utrecht where they explained the theory of Newton and insisted upon a rigorous application of the experimental method. They greatly influenced the outcome of the quarrel, since they attracted, as Voltaire reported, hundreds of students from all corners of Europe. Second, La Mettrie, who played a key role in introducing Newton to the French, studied under Boerhaave, and Nollet, who took a very important part in instructing the French in the experimental method, studied under S'Gravesande. Voltaire also consulted with S'Gravesande at the time he was composing the *Eléments*.

The Newton-Descartes quarrel waxed strong during the first third of the eighteenth century (until 1738), chiefly along national lines. At the same time, in company with a general tendency toward the popularization of science, there developed in France, England, Italy, and Holland an expansion of scientific activity. It was evident in various ways. The Duke of Orleans, for instance, had a laboratory installed in the Palais Royal in 1715. All the outstanding philosophers of the time devoted some of their intellectual energy to the study of natural history, chemistry, or medicine. Montesquieu, in 1716, wrote essays on the renal glands and the causes of the winds; Rousseau, at the Charmettes, in 1738, read Pluche and conducted chemical experiments; Diderot, at about the same time, was following the Rouelle lectures on chemistry at the Jardin du Roi. Apparently, in England, the observation of nature, especially microscopic nature, became a veritable craze. Those who did not practice the art read about it in books. Two of the most attractive of these works were Nieuwentyt's *Les Merveilles de la nature* (1725) and Pluche's nine-volume *Spectacle de la nature* (1732-50), which had become Rousseau's textbook. There was, in addition, a quite diverse, popular scientific literature in England; among the leading works in this area were Whiston's *A New Theory of the Earth* (1708), *Astronomical Lectures* (1715), and *Astronomical principles of Religion* (1717) and Derham's *Astro-theology* (1715) and *Physico-theology* (1713). The general objective of all these works was to give some kind of religious interpretation to the marvelous discoveries and to offer them as proof of the magnificence of God. Practically all of them proclaimed the doctrine of final causes as the conclusion of the examination of nature. This tendency toward final causes, however, was not limited to the theologians who were studying nature. It was fully as strong, for instance, in Réaumur, who was a scrupulous scientist and whose *Mémoires pour servir à l'histoire des insectes* (6 vols., in-4°, 1734-1742) stressed the miraculous designs of his little creatures: "Il ne se trouve nulle part autant de merveilleux, et de merveilleux vrai que dans l'histoire des insectes" (p. 10). Réaumur, quite as much as the theologians, saw in them proof of the existence of God: "L'histoire naturelle est l'histoire de ses ouvrages, il n'est pas de démonstrations de son existence, plus à la portée de tout le monde que celles qu'elle nous fournit."

Pluche's work was by all odds the most popular of these general French works in science. By the use of dialogues, all of the problems in physics are introduced and discussed, as the subtitle indicates: *Entretiens sur les particularités de l'histoire naturelle qui ont paru les plus propres à rendre les jeunes gens curieux, et à leur former l'esprit.* The work not only was translated into English, Spanish, and other languages but went through eighteen French editions. The author confesses in the preface that, in writing the book, he had particularly in mind the young people "où l'esprit vuide de connaissances saisit avec avidité ce qu'on lui présente, se livre volontiers à l'attrait de la nouveauté, et contracte tout naturellement l'habitude de réfléchir et de s'occuper" (p. iii).

Pluche insists that every surrounding body, whether the smallest insect or the largest animal, teaches us some useful truth. Each discloses to us the intention of the Maker. All offer to us their services and are in that way of use to us. "Enfin l'on peut dire que la Nature est le plus savant et le plus parfait de tous les livres propres à cultiver notre raison, puisqu'il renferme à la fois les objets de toutes les sciences, et que l'intelligence n'en est bornée ni à aucune langue, ni a aucunes personnes" (p. v). The author confesses that he has in view only the beautiful, the useful, and the true. He celebrates with simplicity the joy of knowing, always acknowledging that "prétendre pénétrer le fond même de la nature, vouloir rappeller les effets à leurs causes spéciales, vouloir comprendre l'artifice et le jeu des ressorts, et les plus petits élémens dont ces ressorts sont composés, c'est une entreprise hardie et d'un succès trop incertain" (p. ix). The good Abbé is already convinced that many of the problems suggested by the spectacle of nature are beyond the powers of our reason. Consequently, he excuses himself for remaining on the surface of things with the remark that "c'est une démarche bien dangereuse que celle de faire parler Descartes, Malebranche, ou Newton, et de prêter à ces grands hommes nos pensées et nos vues." He notes that it is easy to announce that we are going to introduce Gassendi, Rohault, and others—"faire revivre leur esprit, leurs sentiments et leurs caractères" (p. xii). But it is difficult to carry out this promise, because not only is it impossible to seize their thought, but it is equally impossible to transmit it to others. Still, he has been careful throughout the discourse to note in the margins of the dialogues those who have discussed most competently the problems brought up. He acknowledges that he has used generously both the *Mémoires* of the Académie des Sciences and the *Transactions* of the Royal Society, as well as the treaties of Nieuwentyt, Leuwenhœk, and Derham, among others, and he praises highly the scholarly method of Réaumur's *Mémoires sur les insectes*, while affirming that he will not avail himself of this method: "L'anatomie des insectes, leurs changements, et leurs opérations y sont traités avec une sagacité, une netteté, et une étendue qui ne laissent rien à désirer. Mais les lecteurs que nous nous sommes proposé de servir ne demandent point de nous cette méthode" (p. xxi). What he aspires to accomplish is to interest the young, awaken their imagination, and, above all avoid treating scientifically the minutiæ of science.

It should be noted that halfway through the fourth volume the dialogues cease, although the *Entretiens* (which are, in reality, essays) continue. We forget often that the work not only treats the phenomena of nature (insects, animals, astronomy, etc.) but also the phenomena of man (the nature of man, governments, morality, and man's relations with God). In addition, with the aid of woodcuts which the work contains, Pluche discusses the occupations and technology in a way which makes his work a distinct predecessor of the *Encyclopédie*.

Pluche steadfastly refused to treat science in a scientific way. Maupertuis, one of the outstanding scientists of his time, member of the Académie des Sciences and eventually Président of Frederick's Berlin Academy, though of an entirely different stripe from Pluche, also formulated his ideas so that they could be popularly received. He treated scientifically a broad set of problems in works ranging from an *Essai de cosmologie*, in which he took up the proofs of the existence of God, to a treatise on moral philosophy, in which, contrary to Voltaire, he concluded that there are more ills in life than pleasures and justified, under certain conditions, suicide. He even wrote one of the numerous treatises on the origin of languages. For us, however, his importance lies in his defense of Newton and his close relationship with Voltaire and Mme du Châtelet. Indeed, this relationship was so close that he played the role of scientific father-confessor to them during the period 1732-1740. He had visited England in 1728 at the very time Voltaire was there (see Brunet, *Maupertuis*). He, too, knew Clarke and Pemberton and had become converted to Newtonianism. On his return to France, he and his friend Clairaut, both now members of the Académie des Sciences, upheld the Englishman and his new theory of attraction against a scientific society which was almost solidly Cartesian. In 1732, Maupertuis published the first defense of Newtonianism in France in the *Discours sur les différentes figures des astres*. It speaks well for the openmindedness of the Académie that it was published in Paris.

Maupertuis in the *Discours* gives a very succinct historical account of the Newton-Descartes quarrel, basing it upon Richer's discovery in his expedition to Cayenne that his pendulum clock slowed considerably. Maupertuis remarks that the oscillations of a pendulum depend upon two factors: the force with which bodies tend to fall perpendicularly to the earth, and the length of the pendulum. Since the length of the pendulum had not varied appreciably from Paris to Cayenne, the inevitable conclusion was that the force must have varied. Maupertuis explains that in astronomy there is some correlation between the force and the shape of the celestial bodies. Following Huyghens, he notes that the character of these celestial bodies depends upon weight and centrifugal force. Everyone agrees on the nature of centrifugal force; there is, however, a great divergence of opinion on the nature of weight. Some regard it as the effect of the centrifugal force of some matter which, circulating around bodies, sweeps them to the center of its circulation, whereas others regard it as if it were a property of bodies. That is, some explain the phenomenon by "tourbillons," others by attraction.

Maupertuis modestly declines to pronounce in a matter which has divided the outstanding philosophers of his time. He limits himself to a comparison of their ideas, showing that the core of the Cartesian explanation lies in the concept of impulsion, whereas the core of Newtonianism lies in attraction. Maupertuis remarks that the term "attraction" has upset many who fear the return in philosophy of the doctrine of occult qualities (*Œuvres*, Paris, 1752, I, 91). Newton, of course, never regarded attraction as the cause of weight but merely used it to designate a phenomenon which was everywhere present in bodies. Maupertuis, however, argues that it is just as much a property of matter as extent, solidity, or impenetrability. It would be silly, he concedes, to give to matter properties beyond the realm of experience, but it would be no less foolish to exclude dogmatically all other properties than the few primitive ones we know. By an intricate argument, he proves, not that attraction resides in nature, but that it is at least metaphysically possible. From there, he concludes that one has only to inquire whether it is really in nature and to what extent it is necessary for the explanation of phenomena. The remainder of the demonstration is relatively simple. Maupertuis declares that Kepler's laws are realities, that is, facts, and that Descartes's "tourbillons" run counter to either one or the other of these laws. He acknowledges that attempts have been made to square the vortex theory with Kepler's laws, particularly by Huyghens and Bullfinger, but emphasizes that the result has in some respects been to increase the difficulties. On the other hand, Newton's theory of attraction, since it was based on Kepler's laws, squares with them already. Maupertuis, in spite of his modesty, concludes (*Œuvres*, Paris, 1756, I, 130):

> C'est ainsi que l'attraction et sa loi ayant été une fois établies par le rapport entre les aires que les planètes décrivent autour du soleil et les temps, et par le rapport entre les temps périodiques des planètes et leurs distances; les autres phénomènes ne sont plus que des suites nécessaires de cette attraction. Les planètes doivent décrire les courbes qu'elles décrivent; les corps doivent tomber vers le centre de la terre, et leur chûte doit avoir la rapidité qu'elle a. Enfin les mouvements des planètes reçoivent jusqu'aux dérangements qui doivent résulter de cette attraction.

He adds that there is no great risk in accepting Newton's explanation. He notes, finally, that some French scientists had even suggested (though without proof) some such theory before Newton.

Voltaire, recognizing his incompetence in these matters, turned to Maupertuis for assistance. In a letter of 30 October 1732, enclosing his "petit mémoire," Voltaire urged Maupertuis to tell him whether he should accept or reject the theory of attraction. Voltaire's *Mémoire*, published by Besterman (B. 515), is a declaration of faith asserting that, if the same power which causes gravitation among the objects on the earth retains the celestial bodies in their orbits according to a fixed law, then attraction should be admitted and regarded as "le principal ressort dont dépend la mécanique de l'univers." Voltaire is perplexed, however, by the application of the fixed law. Is it true, he asks, that a body falling from the moon to the earth covers only fifteen feet in the first minute of its fall? In view of the speed with which the moon describes its orbit (151,600 feet, according to Voltaire), how could it fall only fifteen feet in the first minute? We do not have Maupertuis's reply, but we do know from Voltaire's letter of 3 November 1732 that it satisfied the doubts of the Newtonian "néophyte," who concludes: "On ne peut plus s'empêcher de croire à la gravitation newtonienne, et il faut proscrire les chimères des tourbillons." Voltaire states that he awaits Maupertuis's *Discours* with the greatest impatience and enthusiastically proclaims his admiration for Newton's philosophy: "Plus j'entrevois cette philosophie et plus je l'admire. On trouve à chaque pas que l'on fait, que tout cet univers est arrangé par des lois mathématiques qui sont éternelles et nécessaires." The "néophyte" still has questions. Why doesn't the theory of attraction explain the rotation of the planets on their axes? Why wasn't the comet of 1680 swallowed up by the sun? Why doesn't a heavy body increase its velocity in falling to the earth after a certain point? Voltaire laments that the small amount of time he can apportion to these "sublime" studies is totally insufficient.

In spite of this conversion, Voltaire was assailed by "un scrupule affreux," and, in a letter of 12 November 1732, he returned doggedly to the "fifteen feet" problem, now that this result did not seem to square with the law of movement for falling bodies. We again lack Maupertuis's reply, but we know from another of Voltaire's letters (B. 519) that the "scrupule affreux" was allayed. The "néophyte," promising to keep Maupertuis's letters forever, calls them a "lumen ad revelationem gentium." Voltaire now devoured the *Discours* with the pleasure of a young girl reading a novel and the faith of a Christian reading the Gospel (B. 520). One month later (*circa* 1 December 1732), the "néophyte" addressed a little essay to his "maître en physique," with the request that he scrutinize it. A fortnight later (*circa* 15 December 1732), he requested permission to submit to the teacher's judgment some letters "écrites autrefois d'Angleterre et qu'on veut imprimer à Londres." Voltaire explained that he had selected particularly those letters concerned with Newton and offered his opinion that they still needed "d'être revues par des yeux comme les vôtres." Five days later (*circa* 20 December 1732), the obedient "néophyte" assured his teacher that "il n'y a aucune de vos réflexions sur mes lettres à laquelle je ne me sois rendu dans l'instant." He was careful, nevertheless, to clear up a misunderstanding concerning Descartes, by explaining that he had lost a page of his manuscript. The student excused himself for confusing "aphélie" with "périhélie," announced that he now had Pemberton, regretted that the material about which he was writing in the letters would require a whole book of philosophy, and lamented that he was scarcely capable of understanding Maupertuis's *Discours*.[7]

The close companion of Maupertuis in the Académie des Sciences was Clairaut (1713-1765), who began his career in geometry but who quickly switched to celestial mechanics and to the theory of the figure of the earth, along with Maupertuis. Clairaut had distinguished himself as a child prodigy in mathematics at the age of sixteen; already, in 1728, he had read to the Académie des Sciences a treatise on the application of algebra to geometry. It was at this time that he joined a group of young, enthusiastic scientists composed of the Abbé de Gua, La Condamine, and the Abbé Nollet. The ages of the members of this group ranged from sixteen to twenty-six. Three years later, in 1731, though he still did not have the necessary age of twenty to be admitted to the Académie des Sciences, an exception was made and he was granted admission. He was thus able the following year to join forces with Maupertuis, whose *Discours sur les différentes figures des astres* had just been published, in an effort to introduce into the Académie a better understanding of Newton. His influence, however, extended beyond the Académie des Sciences. Both he and Maupertuis made a protracted sojourn in Basel, where the Bernouillis had a veritable scientific center—Mau-

[7] The years 1733 and 1734 passed without any active correspondence—in the field of physics, at any rate—between Voltaire and Maupertuis. On the other hand, there was a fairly brisk correspondence between Mme du Châtelet and Maupertuis. It is of no consequence for the scientific activities of Voltaire and Mme du Châtelet, however, for it consists mainly in reproaches to Maupertuis for having missed appointments.

But, beginning at the end of 1735 and continuing up to the publication of the *Eléments*, Voltaire consulted Maupertuis frequently on points in Newton's philosophy. See B. 1268, 1338, 1445, 1454, 1465, 1481, 1551, 2362.

pertuis in 1729-1730, and both Maupertuis and Clairaut at the end of 1734 (September-November). On their return, the two retired to the Mont Valérien, and it seems that Mme du Châtelet then became acquainted with Clairaut. It was an acquaintance which had a lasting effect upon the scientific work at Cirey. Clairaut visited Cirey on several occasions and was consulted numerous times by the occupants about scientific matters. Indeed, he is supposed to have stated: "J'avais là deux élèves de valeur très inégale, l'une tout à fait remarquable, tandis que je n'ai pu faire entendre à l'autre ce que sont les mathématiques." The observation was certainly well made: while Mme du Châtelet actually took lessons in mathematics under Maupertuis and progressed markedly in the science, Voltaire's knowledge of mathematics seems to have been always very paltry. Clairaut remained at the service of the two erstwhile Cirey scientists, but he also was active in the operations which were devised throughout France to further the theories of Newton. He had already questioned the accuracy of Cassini's measurements of a meridian. In 1733, La Condamine organized a scientific expedition to Peru to measure a meridian, and Maupertuis proposed another expedition to Lapland to perform the same experiment. Clairaut was invited to accompany Maupertuis. Though he seems to have more or less abandoned Cirey, he remained interested in the work of Mme du Châtelet and actually saw through the press in 1759 her translation of Newton's *Principia*. He added to the second volume of her translation a *Système du Monde dans les principes de la gravitation universelle.*

Réaumur, Maupertuis, and Clairaut were professional scientists. Pluche and Nieuwentyt were, if not amateurs themselves, writing for amateurs. The Abbé Nollet united both activities. He had been partially trained by Réaumur in France and by Désaguliers in England. Later, in 1736, he studied in Holland with Musschembrœck and S'Gravesande. He had already inaugurated, in 1734, a public course on experimental physics, out of which came his very popular *Leçons de physique expérimentale*, first published in 1743 and republished continually throughout the century.

In the preface of this work, Nollet remarks upon the role of Descartes, who first rescued the subject from the obscurity of the scholastic schools where it had grown old under the authority of Aristotle. Descartes's reform, Nollet points out, transformed the study of nature's phenomena. Instead of guessing, as had been done hitherto, scientists questioned nature with experiments, studied its secrets with carefully thought-out observations, and conformed to the general law of admitting nothing except that which is clearly and distinctly true. Since then, there had been a tremendous increase in the number of scientists, whose discoveries have excited the interest and curiosity of many amateurs from both sexes and from all classes of society. The Abbé adds that it is this widespread interest which has led him to put the principles of physics at the disposal of everybody. He notes with some satisfaction that this is being done in all the principal European languages: "Le goût de la physique devenu presque général, fit souhaiter qu'on en mît les principes à la portée de tout le monde" (1754 edn., p. x). He adds that he is much gratified to see that his course has been imitated in the provinces by the colleges, universities, and academies—among them, the Académie de Bordeaux, the Université de Reims, and the Oratorian schools throughout the country.

Although he is aware of a Descartes-Newton quarrel, he refuses to take sides, maintaining that it is neither Descartes's physics, nor Newton's, nor Leibniz's that he proposes to follow. He intends, rather, to present a body of scientific thought consisting in a set of facts and a general framework solidly established. Everything he presents will be confirmed by experiment and proved according to the rules. He proclaims that, in matters of science, one must not be the slave of authority or of one's prejudices. One should refuse, above all, to be a Cartesian in Paris and a Newtonian in London and, instead, recognize the truth wherever it appears. Curiously, he promises to restrict himself to a physics of facts which eliminates all questions of metaphysics, referring those who are interested in the metaphysical interpretation of these facts to Malebranche's *Recherche de la vérité*. He justifies his experiments by explaining that they increase the interest of his public, who would sometimes be bored by the abstract principles alone, and he defends them further on the ground that they interest to the point where their truth and their usefulness are recognized. This last point he stresses, asserting that, "grâce au bon goût qui règne dans notre siècle, je puis me dispenser de prouver que la physique est utile, et qu'il n'y a personne qui ne puisse prendre part aux découvertes dont elle s'enrichit tous les jours" (p. xxxvii). Nollet concludes, in accord with Réaumur and all the scientists of his time, that its greatest utility is to prove the existence of God: "Mais l'avantage le plus précieux, et que toute âme bien née ne manque pas de ressentir en étudiant la nature, c'est la nécessité où l'on est de reconnaître partout l'Etre Suprême qui a formé ce vaste univers, et qui préside sans cesse à ses propres œuvres" (p. xli).

One of the Newtonians who was connected with the Maupertuis group, as well as with the Cirey group, was the Count Francesco Algarotti, a young Venetian who had been trained in the scientific school of Bologna. He visited Rome in 1733 and became acquainted with the Vice-President of the Royal Society in Newton's day, Martin Folkes. He journeyed to Paris in 1734 and there met both Voltaire and Mme du Châtelet, as well as Maupertuis and Clairaut. He was invited by Maupertuis to join the expedition to Lapland but, after first accepting, finally declined. Eventually, he made his way to Berlin, where Frederick installed him in the Royal Academy with Maupertuis. Algarotti was a kind of international figure who in many respects resembled Voltaire. He was both a scientist and a poet and had become enthusiastic over Newton's discoveries in optics. By nature, he was drawn to the manner Fontenelle had employed in the *Entretiens sur la pluralité des mondes*. Having decided to compose a work upon Newton's discoveries, he adopted this manner and eventually brought out the *Neutonianismo per le dame*, which he dedicated to Fontenelle.

At the urging of the two Emiliens, Algarotti visited Cirey in 1735, where he read to Voltaire and Mme du Châtelet from his manuscript. Voltaire was delighted with the guest, who, he noted, was proficient in foreign languages and thoroughly acquainted with the manners and customs of other countries. Voltaire added that he was as distinguished a poet as Ariosto and well-versed in both Locke and Newton. Mme du Châtelet stated later that the reading of Algarotti's manuscript was what gave Voltaire the idea for his *Eléments* (Asse, *Lettres de la Marquis du Châtelet*, p. 330). That may well be true, but it is more likely that Voltaire had been turning over in his mind the possibility of a work upon Newton for some time. He had urged Thiériot to undertake the translation of Pemberton's work, and, when his friend showed no interest, he himself had attempted

a modest introduction to Newton in the *Lettres philosophiques.*
After this task had been completed, the tone of his letter to Maupertuis indicates that he contemplated devoting himself henceforth
to literature. It could well be that the arrival of the Count, with his
enthusiasm and his airiness, again suggested to Voltaire the idea of
popularizing Newton's philosophy. It is even very likely that, as
Professor Walters has proposed in his thesis ("Voltaire and the Newtonian Universe"), Algarotti's utilization of the theory of attraction in his exposition of the Newtonian theory of light stimulated
anew in Voltaire the desire to enter upon a work on Newtonian science. This could not have been the only source of inspiration,
though, for one of the criticisms which was directed at Newton's
theory of attraction at the time was that later Newtonians were applying the theory to all sorts of phenomena to which Newton had
never intended that it should be applied. However that may be, it is
perfectly correct that Voltaire was among those who saw an analogy
between the theory of attraction and the problems concerning refraction and reflection. Mme du Châtelet, for her part, denied the
analogy between the two phenomena and actually criticized the followers of Newton who were prone to attribute to attraction all kinds
of chemical and physical phenomena.

The attitude of Voltaire and Mme du Châtelet toward the *Neutonianismo per le dame,* at least as expressed in the correspondence,
is a little mixed. In general, both were enthusiastic about the work
while Algarotti was visiting Cirey, though some of this enthusiasm
may be attributed to courtesy. There was some dampening of this
zeal after Algarotti dedicated the work to Fontenelle. Mme du Châtelet had wanted (and probably expected) it to be dedicated to herself. However, when the work was finally published, Mme du
Châtelet and Voltaire made some effort to be fair in their judgment.
The Lady Newton declared the *Dialogues,* as she often called them,
at least equal in quality to Fontenelle's *Entretiens* (B. 945). She
noted that Algarotti extracted material from Maupertuis's *Discours
sur les différentes figures des astres* without acknowledgment.
She found his wit misplaced in a work of this kind and protested
against what she called "cette bigarure d'arlequinade et de vérités
sublimes" (B. 1541). Fundamentally, her final verdict was the
one she conveyed in a letter to Richelieu (B. 1521), where she

said that the *Dialogues* were "plein d'esprit et de connaissance," adding that she found the excessive wit disagreeable. Voltaire's opinion was not very different, but he shaded his remarks more subtly. To Thiériot, he wrote on 16 March 1736: "Apprenez que ce Vénitien là a fait des dialogues sur la lumière, où il y a malheureusement autant d'esprit que dans les mondes, et beaucoup plus de choses utiles et curieuses." Some two months later, he confided to the same correspondent that there were more truths in ten pages of his *Eléments* than in the whole of Algarotti's *Dialogues*.

As we have remarked already, the *Dialogues* could have given the initial impulse to Voltaire, in the sense that it could have confirmed Voltaire in his belief that a popular French work on Newton's philosophy was needed. There were, however, other important factors. It should not be overlooked that Voltaire had already, by 1728, come to know Pemberton's *View of Sir Isaac Newton's Philosophy* and had even proposed to Thiériot that he make a translation of it; that similarly, in 1732, impressed with Maupertuis's *Discours sur les différentes figures des astres*, he had succeeded in enlisting that Academician's aid in composing his letters on Newton in the *Lettres philosophiques*; and that both he and Mme du Châtelet had attempted to draw Maupertuis, Clairaut, and even Algarotti to Cirey as guests because of their continuing interest in Newton's thought. We might point out, too, that Voltaire's first exchange of letters with Tournemine in 1735 had convinced him that Newton was much misunderstood by French intellectuals and was practically unknown in French universities. Nor should we forget the enthusiasm for the study of science Nieuwentyt, Pluche, Réaumur, and Nollet had engendered, which Voltaire observed with mixed feeling in the famous letter to Cideville (16 April 1735) and again in a letter to Caumont (19 April 1735)—not to mention the excitement aroused in the intellectual public during 1735 by the announcement of Maupertuis's expedition to the North Pole. It was doubtless the combination of these circumstances which interested Voltaire more and more in his plan to bring out a popular work on Newton and which had prepared him for a ready, positive response to Algarotti's *Dialogues*. Voltaire would not have been himself if he were not aware of all these currents and cross-currents and if he did not plunge into them with his usual energy.

At all events, once the situation had been analyzed, Algarotti's *Dialogues* became the catalytic agent which turned Voltaire to active composition of the *Eléments*, and it served as something more than a model. Walters has clearly demonstrated in his thesis that Voltaire not only organized his material in the same way as Algarotti had done, beginning with optics in Part I and continuing in Part II with attraction, but that he actually made the focus of his work Algarotti's idea that the same attraction which operates in matter also operates in the phenomena of light. This notion, which Walters declares to be the central idea of all the remainder of Voltaire's scientific thought, united the two areas of Newtonian science, optics and mechanics. Since this notion occurred in none of Voltaire's other sources and had not been suggested in any of his previous scientific writings, and since Algarotti laid such stress upon it in his fifth and sixth dialogues, it is very likely that Voltaire was indebted to the Italian for this position. It does, however, show up as a query at the end of Newton's *Optics*.

The composition of the *Eléments* goes far beyond an imitation of the *Dialogues*, since it is evident that Voltaire knew, admired, and worked with both Pemberton and Maupertuis. One of the curious things about these relationships is that there is always scant evidence of direct imitation. Indeed, in the case of Algarotti, direct imitation seems well-nigh impossible, since, although he promised to send a copy of his manuscript to Cirey, he does not appear to have done so. (See, however, B. 1197, commentary No. 1.) Walters assumes that Voltaire retained by memory the ideas which struck him in the readings at Cirey. It is not surprising that the evidence of direct imitation is scant, for Voltaire had the curious faculty of being able to absorb other's ideas so completely that he often did not need to refer back to them. At times, when he wished, he could actually reproduce the expression, although he was not too accurate in his quotations.

The important thing about the composition of the *Eléments* is that Voltaire did not restrict himself to his three popular sources. He addressed himself as well to the original text and established a laboratory where both he and Mme du Châtelet prepared to conduct Newtonian experiments. In this respect, though, Mme du Châtelet was certainly more active than Voltaire, especially with regard to optics but with regard to mathematics also. Her correspondence gives much evidence of her efforts to attain a relative proficiency in conducting experiments and a solid mathematical background. Concerning Voltaire, the evidence is more spotty. It is certain, though, notwithstanding Mme du Châtelet's remark that she now had a good scientific library while Voltaire's library was filled mostly with "anecdotes" (meaning, I suppose, historical writings), that he gathered an immense amount of his material from books. Indeed, the most characteristic thing about all his scientific activity is that it was predominantly bookish. The most essential of these works were doubtless the Cotes edition of Newton's *Principia* and the Coste translation of the *Optics*. It was typical of Voltaire's erudition that he went straight to the texts. He also made a practice of gathering the best secondary materials available. The correspondence refers to the works of Dutch Newtonians: S'Gravesande's *Physices elementa . . . sive Introductio ad philosophiam newtonianam* (1719); Musschembrœck's *Phisicae experimentales et geometricae* (1729); Boerhaave's *Elements of Chemistry* (1738). In addition, Voltaire read widely in the literature produced by a whole group of English commentators on Newton, or collaborators with Newton: Flamsteed's *Historia cœlestis britannica* (3 vols., 1725); Berkeley's *New Theory of Vision* (1709); Gregory's *The Elements of Physical and Geometrical Astronomy* (1726); Hooke's *Micrographia* (1665); Keill's *Introductio ad veram astronomiam* (1721); Molyneux's *Dioptrica nova* (1692); Smith's *A Compleat System of Optics* (2 vols., 1738). He acquainted himself with the writings of other philosophers, too: works by Huyghens, Kepler, Leibniz; Locke's *Essay;* Malebranche's *Entretiens sur la métaphysique* and other of his works; above all, Wolff's solid, ponderous volumes on Leibnizian logic, physics, and metaphysics—not to mention the French translation of Wolff's thoughts and Desmaizeaux's publication of the controversy between Leibniz and Clarke (2 vols., 1720). Voltaire assembled for his use the *Philosophical Transactions* of the Royal Society and the *Mémoires* of the Académie des Sciences, as well as the Dutch periodicals: *Histoire des ouvrages des savants,* Leclerc's *Biographie universelle et historique,* the *Bibliothèque choisie,* and the *Bibliothèque ancienne et moderne.* So many volumes perused in so short a time must have left an impression of extreme superficiality and scientific indigestion, and yet it is remarkable that he picked what we still consider the best books and the most pertinent scientific articles in the scholarly journals.

Because of Voltaire's tendency to absorb the ideas of others and present them as if they were his own original thoughts, it is difficult to gauge accurately the sources of his work. If he studied the original texts, it was naturally with the intention of collecting the material first-hand. If he consulted the three Newtonian popularizers—Pemberton, Maupertuis, and Algarotti—it was because he wished to familiarize himself with the problems a popular work should discuss and with the format into which they should be cast. I think he needed their advice also because he was a frank amateur in the field of Newtonian science. If, further, he assembled and studied the works of all the important descendants of Newton in England (Smith, Bradley, MacLaurin, Keill), in Holland (Musschembrœck, S'Gravesande, Boerhaave), and in Paris (Maupertuis, Clairaut, Mairan, Pitot), it was because he wanted to be up-to-date in knowing about the most recent discoveries of Newtonian science. If, finally, he scanned scrupulously the offerings of the two famous scientific academies (the Royal Society and the Académie des Sciences) as well as the scholarly journals (*Journal de Trévoux, Journal des savants*, and the Dutch periodicals), it was to keep abreast as well as he could of this scientific effervescence which was present everywhere in Europe. Voltaire's documentation of his work was remarkably thorough, his absorption of the "épines de la science"—as far as a layman can judge—unbelievably acute, and his presentation of material both intelligent and clear. Moreover, he carried out his research with the greatest diligence and dispatch. Active investigation in 1733 for the *Lettres philosophiques*, extraordinary activity in 1736 and the first half of 1737 in preparation for the *Eléments*, some time, but not much, given to the preparation of the *Métaphysique de Newton*—these were periods of intense feverish study. It was, indeed, during the years 1732-1738 that Voltaire's study of science reached its climax.

One wonders what he actually accomplished. Here, it is very difficult to be specific. It may be stated outright that Voltaire during this period gave himself enough of a scientific education to counter the literary education of his youth. We have to add, though, that there were certain aspects of this education which he was unable to develop. There is no evidence that he had any proficiency whatever in mathematics. Wherever Newtonian physics touched upon mathematics—and there were innumerable places it did—Voltaire had either to pass over the passage or to seek help from one of his scientific friends. He was immensely benefited by having Mme du Châtelet with him, because she did understand what mathematics was about and seems to have acquired a more than ordinary proficiency in its use. In this area she could, and did, provide assistance. It is fruitless, however, to suggest that Voltaire and Mme du Châtelet were scientists in the strict sense of the word. Nothing whatever is gained in pointing out that the two, as scientists, were "piètres" or that Voltaire or she misundertood Newton on many occasions. We have many discussions about which of the two was the better "scientist," but even now we do not know what the term means. Our only sound basis for an opinion is Clairaut's remark that she was an excellent pupil whereas Voltaire did not comprehend what mathematics was about. We do have to admit that she had a wider outlook on the science of her time and was more open to other, non-Newtonian scientists, more original in her investigations, and more imaginative (but not so very much more) in her approach. The fairest judgment would probably be that Voltaire did more to popularize Newton in France, while she did more to popularize science in general, Newtonian and Leibnizian alike. Her one great achievement, though, was encouraging Voltaire to enter upon, and pursue, scientific study. Indeed, she made science the center of her intellectual career, whereas Voltaire, once having achieved what he sought in this area, turned to other fields (though he never relinquished his interest in science and its discoveries). I doubt that he would have had the patience to complete even the *Eléments* had it not been for Mme du Châtelet's proficiency and her encouragement.

That, however, is posing the problem wrongly. Owing to the activities of these two, Cirey became a kind of institute of physics at a crucial moment in the development of European science. If there was one place where the efforts of Newtonians could be made to have an impact on the Académie des Sciences, Cirey was that place, for Voltaire and Mme du Châtelet were the foremost propagators of Newtonian science in France. The comings and goings of scientists—Maupertuis, Algarotti, Kœnig, Clairaut, the Bernouillis—were so frequent as to appear, after a while, comical. There was, besides, the correspondence with Frederick and with the Berlin Academy, not to mention contacts with the innumerable intellectual centers of Germany, with Mairan and Pitot in France, and, in time, with the academies of Russia and the Scandinavian countries. The two Emiliens served as liaisons in all this scientific hullabaloo.

This kind of activity seems at first glance of scant value. One should have a perfect right to assume that the duty of a scientist is to make scientific discoveries. Those who merely dabble in scientific thought and produce no new insights into the way this world of ours works should deserve no consideration from those who devote themselves to the goal of expanding the horizons of scientific knowledge. A historian of science should be at best a curious human phenomenon to a bona fide scientist. Still, someone is needed to draw conclusions for the general public, since scientists are usually inept in explaining their activities to laymen. If this general public has to be informed about the significance and the usefulness of these matters, somebody has to busy himself in gathering the material, sifting out what is important, learning how to express it clearly, keeping it up-to-date, and drawing some modest conclusions about its human value. It so happened that, at this particular moment in the history of Western Europe, science, which had been the apanage of a relatively small elite, became the property of the general public. That Voltaire, in his early correspondence with Maupertuis, used the vocabulary of the religious neophyte was more than just a joke. His understanding of the situation was perfectly plausible. If science was to be the faith of modern man, as the Christian religion had been the faith of medieval man, a scientific priesthood had to be developed to carry the gospel. Historians of science or, better still, critics of scientific thought and method were needed. Indeed, they were already learning their task in the scientific journals of Europe. Voltaire and Mme du Châtelet merely took time out to learn it better than any of their contemporaries. Thus, the real problem is what all this Cirey activity meant for Voltaire and Mme du Châtelet and for their contemporaries.

The answer to this problem, once we have put aside any thought of making either of them out to be prominent scientists, can be very specific. We shall begin with the impact of the new science upon the public. In general, it has always been thought that it impressed upon the public the value of facts, which Diderot eventually described as the real riches of the philosopher. These facts were established by a method which insisted upon experimentation and observation and which was inclined to proscribe unwarranted hypotheses and all preconceived theories. This insistence upon the validity of facts and the experimental method has often been cited as the origin of a more realistic approach to life and a more materialistic explanation of phenomena. We have become at the present time imbued with the notion that science is an enterprise completely divorced from religion. As a result, we readily assert that the development of Newtonianism not only discredited a priori rationalism as irrelevant in experimental science but also clashed with religion and metaphysics. The goal of science, we say, is not to seek first principles or to explore metaphysical problems; it can only occupy itself with physical phenomena. In many respects, this view we now hold of science carries over to our understanding of science in the Enlightenment. We are prone to forget, first of all, Newton's sincere theism, as well as the insistence of all the expounders of Newton's thought (including Voltaire) upon the existence of God. Only recently has the tendency appeared to recognize in the development of Newtonian thought in Voltaire's day a bulwark against atheism. Voltaire himself went so far as to assert—probably on the basis of Pascal's attack upon Descartes—that Cartesianism readily leads to atheism, whereas Newton's philosophy not only stresses the doctrine of final causes but supports this view with a strong theism. There is a decided move now (cf. Pomeau, *La Religion de Voltaire*) to see in Voltaire's espousal of Newton a sincere desire to adopt a way of life which would gratify his restless search for God. This view has been questioned, though, by J. Ehrard in his *L'Idée de nature en France dans la première moitié du XVIIIᵉ siècle*. Ehrard (I, 132) admits that the essential role in the diffusion of Newtonian theology in France belongs to Voltaire, who demanded that this philosophy be, in effect, a religion. But he maintains that Voltaire presented attraction rather as a mysterious phenomenon (especially in the *Lettres philosophiques*) than as a phenomenon of divine origin. Moreover, while recognizing that Voltaire tried to give a résumé of the Clarke-

Leibniz quarrel as a way of stressing Newton's piety in contrast with Descartes's arrogance, Ehrard questions whether Voltaire was not more interested in exploiting Newton's religious convictions for purposes of his own than in making a genuine effort to give a theistic justification of a new scientific approach. "Dire que Voltaire est newtonien ne suffit pas, il convient de s'interroger sur la portée et les limites de son newtonisme" (I, 136).

It is, therefore, very difficult to determine exactly what effect Newtonianism had on the public. It is certain that, ultimately, the "mécanique" of Newton's system was as much a menace to theology and metaphysics as Descartes's "mécanique." It was inevitable that a system primarily concerned with describing the physical laws that govern events in the universe should sooner or later come into conflict with a system that tries to describe events in supernatural terms. Pascal's defense of the God of the prophets against Descartes's God of the philosophers foreshadowed the fate of Newton's philosophy.

One consequence of the conflict was the growth of the conviction that truth is relative. Buffon, in a little essay, actually noted five kinds of truth. It is easy to see how the public might become confused in the midst of such complexity. The one truth which became more and more evident was that there was no special dispensation in science for the phenomenon of man. He was subject to the same forces as all other animals. Voltaire had placed great weight on this point in his one-sided debate with Pascal. Time and again, he returned to it. The impression was thus easily gained that man does not occupy any preeminent position in the world of nature. And from this notion it was but a short step to the conviction that man is subject to the same mechanical laws to which nature is subject. Man could no longer be regarded as the center of the universe: things do not happen for him, they merely happen to him. To understand the nature of these happenings, one must seek out in the human sciences, through observation and experience, the factors which disclose the significance of personal and social events. Natural science thus led to psychology, history, and social sciences.

We shall see in due time that the development of Newtonian science had these effects on Voltaire, also. He, too, became more positivistic, more pragmatic. His desire to abandon metaphysics as

useless and turn to "la morale" instead grew stronger and stronger
—at least, that was the impression he gave. In some respects, he was
the leader in the attempt to establish a theism which would justify
that "morale." His denunciation of a priori speculation, of hypotheses,
of philosophical systems, grew out of his scientific experience. One
could concede that, at first, his primary interest in Newtonianism
was motivated by a sincere desire to avoid the atheism fostered by
other scientific philosophies. He admits as much himself in the *Métaphysique de Newton*; the chapter on the existence of God in the
Traité de métaphysique likewise discloses a very genuine desire to
preserve theism. This desire continued throughout his life, although
the exigencies of day-to-day living constantly eroded his efforts to
practice a sincere theism.

Rather than attribute to his deism a superior importance in his
defense of Newton, it would perhaps be better at this point to see
just where Voltaire stood in regard to science. His acquaintance
with the movement, as well as with the principal exponents of scientific thought, was very great. The breadth of his interests down to
1741 cannot be doubted. The extent of his knowledge was, for a layman, wide. His interests, though expressed in only one work, the
Eléments, and in some feeble attempts at experimentation (*Essai
sur la nature du feu*) and description (*Les Changements arrivés
dans notre globe, Les Singularités de la nature*), reached from physics
into astronomy, geology, biology, psychology, and chemistry. It is
true, however, that, though these interests were always apparent, he
scarcely did anything further to develop them.

His attitude toward science was consistent. He insisted upon the
experimental method as a means to scientific truth. He stressed the
limits that human understanding encounters in achieving great
truths in physics. He repeated over and over that analysis is the only
means of approaching nature and that we can only calculate, weigh,
and measure, never being able to know either principles or ultimate
things. He decried any idea of synthesis: systems were anathema to
him, and he proclaimed that they were to be rigidly excluded. In
this respect, he already had the outlook of a modern scientist. Indeed,
everything in his attitude confirms the belief that he understood
the method of science. He insisted on the utility of science; even
when, in a moment of discouragement, he rejected scientific

study, he did so because he no longer found it useful. Hypotheses, foolish notions, everything which does not lead directly or indirectly to "la morale," he condemned. Thus, he really believed that natural science is but a component of metaphysics—especially the existence of God—and "la morale" and that its true function is to give man a view of his place in the universe. The best statement of this conviction is in the Introduction to Part II of the *Eléments*: "Mon principal but, dans la recherche que je vais faire, est de me donner à moi-même, et peut-être à quelques lecteurs, des idées nettes de ces lois primitives de la nature que Newton a trouvées. . . . La science de la nature est un bien qui appartient à tous les hommes."

His success was consequently a limited one. He never made a significant discovery. His actual theories, when he did venture to set them forth, were as erroneous as Descartes's, and probably for the same reason. But he became, nonetheless, the first important historian of science. What science taught him—a respect for law, insight into mechanical processes, a limited belief in determinism—he passed on to his public. His role was greater than that, however. He seems to have single-handedly eliminated Descartes and to have given a wide circulation to the discoveries of Newton. In doing so, he instilled in the public a respect for modern scientific method. The points of this method he applied to his own development of history and the social sciences.

8. VOLTAIRE AND HISTORY

IT IS CUSTOMARY for all who undertake to discuss Voltaire's interest in history to mark out the grave defects in the writing of history as it was practiced before he entered upon the scene. Thus, Lanson, in his *Voltaire*, has pointed out the extent to which writers of history stressed the role of Providence in the unfolding of events. Bossuet was most representative of this school of historical thought. Seen in this abstract way, Lanson's view is rather exaggerated. It is true that, as a fervent theologian, Bossuet naturally thought that the affairs of this universe are ultimately ruled by God's Providence, and he presented history as the unfolding of events which work for the greater glory of the Christian Church. The assumption that this attitude is both unscientific and wrong, which is often taken for granted by those who discuss these matters, is, however, unwarranted. In the first place, the theological interpretation of history is required of all theologians, as the word "theologian" itself implies. Consequently, not only Bossuet but all of his predecessors and practically all of his descendants (people like Dom Calmet, for instance) started with the conviction that "Diós sólo es vencedor." It would be an error on our part, though, to assume that, because of this conviction, theological historians were disinclined to recognize the play of historical forces which were more immediate and more subtly human than providential. To overemphasize the role of Providence would imply that the theological historians did not believe in free will. As far as Bossuet was concerned, he strongly adhered to the principle of free will in history but, of course, within limits. His attitude was that man has freedom of choice but that, after he has exercised his right to choose and has assumed his position in any given situation, there are always additional forces which enter into the situation and rectify the limitations of the choice. "On a beau," he said, "compasser dans son esprit tous ces discours, et tous ces desseins, l'occasion apporte toujours je ne sais quoi d'imprévu, en sorte qu'on dit et qu'on fait toujours plus ou moins qu'on ne pensait. Et cet endroit inconnu à l'homme dans ses propres actions et dans ses propres démarches, c'est l'endroit secret par où Dieu agit, et le ressort qu'il remue." It is evident that there was a difference between Bossuet and Voltaire as historians, but it consisted in a more careful weighing of these forces, not in a denial of their existence. I think, also, that there was a certain shifting of emphasis from one aspect to the other. Still, we must bear in mind that Voltaire and Bossuet seem often to have thought alike in dealing with historical phenomena.

One could also make reservations about other, more academic defects which are said to have beset the writing of history. It is true that it was subject to the authority of the state and that by tradition it encountered particular difficulty when it tried to illuminate the recent past. There was a real problem, too, in finding means of assembling facts and of controlling them once they had been assembled. The technical devices for presenting history—dialogues, monologues, speeches, and, above all, anecdotes—did not create an atmosphere of complete authenticity. And, although many efforts were made to give the impression of accuracy, there was a real difficulty in distinguishing between the *true* and the *seeming true* in a society which gave more importance to verisimilitude than to truth. The result of this particular attitude was far-reaching. The feeling is easily gained that the public actually preferred romanced history to history and personal memoirs to political history. Courtilz de Sandras and his fictional histories were undoubtedly very popular, and Dangeau and a long line of memoir-writers were much appreciated. I think, though, that these conditions, which would admittedly be a handicap to anyone wishing to write authentic history, obtained throughout the period in which Voltaire wrote, too.

All of this is by way of stating that it would be false to leave the impression that historical writing was at a low ebb in the final years of the seventeenth century and opening years of the Enlightenment. One would think that Descartes's disdain for history and the corresponding anti-historical attitude of Malebranche would have made the century more negative than positive toward history. Such, however, was hardly the case. There were, in addition to Bossuet, other outstanding historians during the closing years of the century, men like Mézeray and Daniel, not to mention Boulainvilliers and the Abbé de Saint-Pierre. History was, though, more a branch of arts and letters than a scientific discipline, and the writing of it was carried on by humanistic historians who stressed its literary values. There was, nonetheless, a whole literature on the nature of history

—its techniques, its methods, its purposes, and its uses—and on the qualifications one needs to be a historian and the rules one must use in judging historical phenomena.

One of the first and most important of the seventeenth-century writers who undertook the treatment of these matters was Fontenelle. He is practically always ignored when the development of history in the Enlightenment is discussed. This oversight is unfortunate, because he, more than any other of the early theorists, even Bayle, had a clear understanding of the beginnings of historical writing, of its inner meaning and its ultimate intellectual goal, and of its relationship to the science of man.

In the *De l'origine des fables*, Fontenelle attempts a history of the world in its early stages. In his opinion, all ancient histories are nothing but fables. We always have had the happy faculty of picturing to ourselves the unknown of the past by the known of the present. This error in analogy, however, is not particularly serious, because, fortunately, it is most likely that the unknown events cannot help resembling the known events of the present. What we call the philosophy of early times was entirely adapted to the contemporary historical facts. Fontenelle is prepared to accept these facts. They have, nevertheless, been merged with false imaginings, resulting in fables which have in time become false fables. For this reason, there are no peoples whose distant past is not shrouded in mysteries which have proven false, except, Fontenelle adds prudently, God's chosen people, who have been shielded from this defect by a special dispensation.

Fontenelle is ready to accept the mythical situation of early history as a reality. He would prefer, however, that a people preserve the memory of its historical facts as they occurred free from myth and false fables. He concedes that this is asking too much of early races. Centuries elapsed before the art of preserving the facts of history was learned. That is why practically all the early so-called facts are nothing but "visions" and "reveries."[8]

Still, in time, ignorance diminished bit by bit. There were fewer miracles, philosophical systems appeared in smaller numbers, and histories became less fabulous. The point of view also changed.

[8] This same idea is developed in the early part of Voltaire's *Philosophie de l'histoire*.

Until then, people wanted to preserve the memory of things past out of simple curiosity; now, they began to suspect that the record of these things could be useful in bringing honor to the race, either by deciding disputes between races or by producing examples of virtue. It now became necessary that the facts be correct, that history be "true." Some historians began to write of these events in a more reasonable way, or at least in a way which appeared more reasonable. The change was thus effected between the writing of fables, which were fundamentally catalogues of the errors of the human mind, to the writing of "true" history.

The utility of history is Fontenelle's basic assertion. Everyone agrees with this point, he adds, but, when it comes to considering the way in which history is useful, practically everyone fails to understand what it can do. Fontenelle here introduces his own ideas on the subject by talking of "making the history of history itself." What he stresses is the thought that, beneath the facts of history, there is a continuity of meaning which the historian must grasp. Fontenelle explains that, when historians abandoned the fabulous and concentrated upon facts "selon la vérité" or "selon la vraisemblance," they were forced by circumstances to record them confusedly, as well as very dryly. They refrained almost entirely from inquiring into the motives behind the incidents or from penetrating the character of those implicated in the events. In time, however, they remedied these defects and examined both the motives underlying the actions as well as the character of the actors. Fontenelle notes that this change in the method of studying history resembles natural science, which has introduced the notion of cause and effect. Upon the events of history for which the motives are now ascertainable, the historians have constructed as well as possible a system of history. Fontenelle warns that we should be wary of these systems, though, since they are much more uncertain even than systems of philosophy.[9]

Returning to the idea of utility, he explains: "J'appelle utile, quant à ce qui regarde l'esprit, tout ce qui nous conduit ou à nous connaître ou à connaître les autres." In spite of the risk involved, he urges the historian to form general notions from facts. Insofar as

[9] Voltaire expressed the same attitude in the *Philosophie de l'histoire*.

these general notions prove valid, we can omit details. Fontenelle deplores that most people preoccupied with history do nothing more than wander inconclusively among the details, eschewing any effort to uncover the general principles. History, for them, consists in piling facts upon facts, memorizing dates, filling the memory with wars, peace treaties, royal marriages, and genealogies. When it comes to reasoning upon these countless facts, to seeking out the general principles which account for them, they exhibit no skill whatever.

This search for principles is what Fontenelle understands by the morality of history: it is, or should be, the objective of every historian. It is not the chronicle of the revolutions in a state, its wars, or the marriages of its princes which we need to study; rather, we must probe behind these events to develop the history of the human errors and passions concealed there. The human mind, Fontenelle adds, is less inclined to err once it realizes how many are the ways in which it can err. Never can it study too profoundly the history of its useless meanderings. Moreover, from the teachings of the aberrations of the human mind and the passions of the heart is derived the greatest of all benefits: knowledge of the manners and customs of men, their peculiar usages, in short, their civilization (Fontenelle did not use this word, of course, since it did not yet exist.) From an understanding of manners and customs, in turn, is derived insight into the personality of a people, its "esprit" (a word Fontenelle did use).

If Fontenelle's remarks are studied with the care they deserve, it will be seen that he has already formed here a general concept of history which gives much consideration to the nature and purpose of the historical act, as well as close attention to the meaning to be derived from the accumulated facts. This part of the study and writing of history as he conceives it is, however, secondary to the making of history. Already Fontenelle, like Voltaire later, regards the inner reality of history as something which depends upon people's thinking, feeling, and acting. For him, an understanding of this inner reality can be gained only through an analysis of the motives and passions of the actors; motives and passions, in turn, can be accurately grasped only through an understanding of manners and customs; and this understanding is developed only by insights into their "esprit." This, however, is the process working backward. The critic of history, in reality, has to work in the opposite direction, at least ultimately. He has to start with "l'esprit" in order to attain "les coutumes" and "les mœurs," and then through them he grasps the motives and passions. Once the point is reached where all these aspects are comprehended, the utility of historical understanding becomes clear, since it teaches us to know ourselves in others. The terms employed by Fontenelle, as well as the arrangements whereby they unite to give a coherent meaning to history, were all to be taken over eventually by Voltaire.

Fontenelle's remarks upon history are fully confirmed by Bayle, who has always been thought the master craftsman of the subject for the eighteenth century. It was, one might say, his major preoccupation. Even before the appearance of the *Dictionnaire historique et critique*, in the *Critique générale de l'histoire du Calvinisme*, he had attended closely to the underlying principles of historical research. At first glance, as Delvolvé points out (*Religion, critique et philosophie positive chez P. Bayle*, pp. 94-96), the reader is inclined to suppose that this treatise is designed to bring out the basic uncertainty of history. Indeed, the three sections of the treatise could easily substantiate that view: "I. Qu'il est facile d'altérer la vérité de l'histoire"; "II. Incertitude de l'histoire"; "III. Jusqu'où on peut pousser la certitude de l'histoire." Bayle maintains that one can scarcely have faith in a historian who is so little committed to his subject that his anger and hatred are obvious to everyone. He affirms that he no longer reads histories with a view to finding out what actually took place. He is now content to learn what each group or nation says took place. He grants, though, that certainty in history can be achieved up to a certain point: "L'on peut quelquefois pousser la certitude de l'histoire jusques à quelque détail. Par exemple, l'on peut être persuadé d'un fait, ou d'un dessein, ou d'un motif particulier, lorsque tous les partis en conviennent . . ." (*Œuvres diverses*, II, 11). One can even make unsuspected progress in the achievement of historical awareness if one is careful to apply a rigid method to the facts assembled (II, 12):

J'avoue encore qu'en examinant l'enchaînure de plusieurs faits, en considérant le génie des acteurs, en pesant toutes les circonstances, en comparant ensemble ce qui a été dit par les uns et par les autres, on peut éclaircir bien des choses, découvrir bien des impostures, réfuter bien des calomnies. Mais en ces choses-là, Monsieur, soyez assuré que l'historien qui a le plus d'esprit, est ordinairement celui dont la cause paraît la meilleure, et qu'il est bien malaisé de parvenir jusqu'à l'évidence.

Bayle insists upon the proper method, certain as he is that the discovery of truth in history is more difficult than in philosophy even, because of the inherent malice within man. He is convinced that it is almost impossible to present the facts without coloring them: "chaque nation, chaque Religion, chaque secte, prend les mêmes faits tout crus où ils se peuvent trouver, les accommode et les assaisonne selon son goût" (I, 510). History, he says, is served up exactly like roasts in cooking, according to each man's taste. To avoid this tendency, only adherence to a strict method is efficacious.

The main outlines of Bayle's method are not easy to grasp. Throughout the four folio volumes of the *Dictionnaire historique et critique*, he scatters in his rambling and diffuse way the observations which he wishes to insinuate into the minds of his readers. Fundamental to him are the rules of Cicero: "ne quid falsi audeat" and "ne quid veri non audeat." Even while approving these injunctions, though, Bayle believes them almost beyond human capabilities. But, he adds, if they are rightly tempered, the historian can be trained to respect them. The writer of a history should avoid romanced stories, which are detrimental to historical accuracy. He should affirm nothing unless it is well substantiated. When public accounts differ from written ones, he should follow the latter and eschew the former. He should divest himself of prejudices and forget his injuries. He should avoid thinking of himself as a collector of anecdotes. He should not give excessive praise to the monarch. He should be particularly scrupulous when treating events which he believes untrue. When discussing miracles related in the works of other historians, he should consider the reputation of the author: if he is not a man of high standing, his account can be ignored; if he is of more importance, his account should be refuted. The historian should be skeptical of all oaths and declarations of condemned persons, and he should abolish harangues. His most essential trait is probity, but it should be allied with other qualities (IV, 46 b):

L'histoire généralement parlant est ou la plus difficile de toutes les compositions qu'un auteur puisse entreprendre, ou l'une des plus difficiles.

Elle demande un homme qui ait un grand jugement; un style noble, clair, et serré; une conscience droite, une probité achevée, beaucoup d'excellents matériaux, et l'art de les bien ranger et sur toutes choses la force de résister aux instincts du zèle de religion qui sollicitent à décrier ce qu'on juge faux, et à orner ce qu'on juge véritable.

Bayle seems never to tire in his injunction to the historian to raise himself above party, even country, and to devote himself with stoic fortitude to the search for truth. In the article "Usson," he gathers together, under a section entitled "Considérations sur le devoir d'un historien," his views on this subject (IV, 486 a):

Tous ceux qui savent les lois de l'histoire tomberont d'accord qu'un historien, qui veut remplir fidèlement ses fonctions, doit se dépouiller de l'esprit de flatterie, et de l'esprit de médisance, et se mettre le plus qu'il lui est possible dans l'état d'un stoicien qui n'est agité d'aucune passion. Insensible à tout le reste, il ne doit être attentif qu'aux intérêts de la vérité, et il doit sacrifier à cela le ressentiment d'une injure, le souvenir d'un bienfait, et l'amour même de la patrie. Il doit oublier qu'il est d'un certain pays, qu'il a été élevé dans une certaine communion, qu'il est redevable de sa fortune à tels ou à tels, et que tels et tels sont ses parents, ou ses amis. . . . Tout ce qu'il donne à l'amour de la patrie est autant de pris sur les attributs de l'histoire, et il devient un mauvais historien à proportion qu'il se montre un bon sujet.

Bayle offers some judicious rules also for the writing of history. In general, he finds that ancient historians have related incidents too succinctly without regard for substantiating details, whereas modern historians have fallen into the opposite defect by burdening their accounts with a plethora of details. He expresses an especial regard for Suetonius, in spite of the latter's habit of neglecting precise dates for events (IV, 299):

Il aima mieux s'attacher à faire connaître la vie des empereurs, et leurs personalités et rassembler pour cela dans un chapitre ce qui concernait leurs mariages, et dans d'autres chapitres ce qui concernait leur éducation, ou leurs amitiés, ou leurs bâtiments, etc. C'était choisir ce qu'il y a de plus pénible dans les fonctions de l'histoire; car il est bien plus aisé de recueillir les matériaux des guerres, ou des autres affaires publiques, que le détail du Palais, je veux dire les inclinations, et les actions particulières du Monarque, ce qu'il était en tant que mari, que père, que frère, que maître, qu'ami, qu'amant; quels étaient ses dégoûts, ses caprices, ses habits et ses repas, etc.

Here Bayle comes close to counseling cultural, social, and intellectual history, rather than political history. For him, as for Voltaire, manners and customs are more interesting than battles. Moreover, like Voltaire, he has a decided preference for the history of the present. He who would write the history of the Popes, the Emperors or the kings of France during the last one hundred and fifty years, as Suetonius did for the Emperors of Rome, says Bayle, would surely encounter many difficulties, but, if he succeeded anything like as well as Suetonius did, he would make himself admired and would be considered an excellent author of anecdotes. "Oh, qu'un tel ouvrage serait propre à enrichir le libraire!" he exclaims in a passage which could have attracted the enthusiastic attention of Voltaire. But Bayle's taste is not limited to "modern history," that is to say, the recent and the contemporary. In a passage of considerable consequence, since it might have served also as an exhortation to Voltaire, the Rotterdam recluse counsels a universal history, a compendium of manners and customs, a sort of essay on the spirit of nations: "Car enfin l'histoire de l'esprit humain, de ses sottises, et de ses extravagances et l'histoire des variétés infinies qui se trouvent dans les lois, et dans les usages des nations, ne sont pas des choses dont on doive frustrer les lecteurs, et dont on ne doive pas espérer des utilités" (I, 579 b). After all, Bayle is not far removed from Voltaire in his final opinion of history. In speaking of Orosius, the author of the *Dictionnaire* notes that the Church Father had given to his work the title *De miseria hominum*. It was, says Bayle, an exceedingly appropriate title, and one which might be attributed to history in general. "L'histoire," he continues, "est le miroir de la vie humaine, or la condition de la vie humaine est que le nombre des méchants et des impies, tout de même que celui des fols, soit infini, l'histoire n'est autre chose que le portrait de la misère de l'homme" (III, 548).

His ideal of history seems to have been exemplified in the book by Leti, *Il Teatro Britannico*, which he reviewed in the *Nouvelles de la république des lettres* for April 1684. It would be well, says Bayle, if all the histories which we have were as well substantiated as this one. Not only would we derive more pleasure from reading them, but we would be able to profit more by them. He continues:

On apprendrait non seulement les événements, mais aussi les causes secrètes, les intrigues, et les moyens qui ont contribué aux grandes révolutions, et c'est ce qui peut nous instruire utilement. Que sert-il de savoir en général qu'une certaine chose est arrivée dans une certaine année, si l'on ne sait comment et pourquoi? C'est la conduite des hommes qui nous sert d'exemple, et d'instruction, et non pas les simples événements, qui par eux-mêmes ne nous sont d'aucun usage. Mais où trouve-t-on des gens assez courageux, pour écrire sans flatterie l'histoire de leur temps? Où trouve-t-on des princes qui aient assez d'équité pour souffrir qu'on leur disent en face toutes leurs vérités? Où trouve-t-on même des ministres d'Etat qui veuillent permettre qu'on divulgue leurs défauts pendant leur vie? Ce n'est néanmoins qu'alors qu'on le peut bien faire; car si on laisse passer le temps où les choses sont récentes, on en oublie plus de la moitié et on prive par ce moyen les siècles suivants de la connaissance de mille faits particuliers qui ont produit les grandes affaires.

This is a far cry from the factual history which a superficial reading of the *Dictionnaire* suggests. Bayle, indeed, did everything he could to get away from the plethora of facts which he felt characterized contemporary historians. Did he not write that, in training historians, it is better to teach students to judge a small number of facts than to teach them in such a way that they fail to judge a large number of facts? But judgment itself is not enough. Since he believed that it is the duty of a historian to make known the character of his actors by the most detailed analysis of those of their traits which disclose the extent of their virtues or their vices (II, 203 a), he seems to have conceived of the historian in the final analysis as a sort of poet:

> ... généralement parlant, ce n'est point un fort bon préparatif à la profession d'historien que d'avoir employé plusieurs années à faire des vers, ou à prononcer des sermons et des harangues. . . . Mais pour des esprits supérieurs qui se rendent maîtres de leur sujet, et de leurs forces et qui entendent le réglement des limites, rien ne peut être plus avantageux quand ils écrivent une histoire, que de s'être bien nourris du suc de la poétique, et de l'éloquence des orateurs.

Bayle was not the only one who regarded the historian as a poet and history as an art. In general, all the historians of the Enlightenment from Bayle to Hume and Gibbon had much to say about the art of history. Their statements throw an interesting light not only upon the way history was viewed but also upon the more prosaic considerations of how it should be written and how the material for it should be assembled, sifted, and—in cases where contradictions appear owing to the effect of bias—judged. Bayle, as we have seen, had much to say upon this subject, and Montesquieu, Voltaire, Hume, Robertson, and Gibbon all were to add comments of great pertinence which reveal the extent to which all those who practiced the art of history reflected upon that art.[10]

The master theoretician in the field of history for the Enlightenment was undoubtedly Lenglet-Dufresnoy, who composed in a clear and consistent way the best work on historical methodology: *Méthode pour étudier l'histoire* (Paris, 1714).[11] Lenglet enters initially into the problem of how historians view history, since, as he says, only a few have a clear idea of the proper attitudes which can be taken to the subject. First, there are those who regard it as a respectable occupation which helps to pass the time. They are the dilettante historians. Others consider it a means of satisfying their curiosity. They think themselves very skillful when they come to know the outstanding men of all times and all places. They are the hero worshippers. Finally, there are those who "se piquent de littérature et d'érudition" and who feel that they have made much headway when they can discern the elements which constitute history and the various manners in which these elements are presented: the propriety of the language, the elegance and polish of speech, the manners and customs of the ancients, the geographical descriptions, the rise and the fall of empires, the origins of religions, the wealth and powers of nations, the miracles which have come to pass. These are the interests which history holds for this third group. It only remains for them to find the appropriate expression to deal with them.

Lenglet, in general, approves these ways of viewing history, but he notes that the goal of past historians in writing history was neither to instruct us in speaking nor to bring to light the customs of each nation. Rather, they held it to be their purpose to lay down the rules of conduct for humanity and to encourage the practice of virtue by

[10] See J. P. Black, *The Art of History*; C. Becker, *The Heavenly City of the Eighteenth-century Philosophers*, Chap. IV; J. H. Brumfitt, *Voltaire Historian*; F. Diaz, *Voltaire storico*. See also these works by Voltaire: *Essai sur les mœurs*, ed. Pomeau (which contains an excellent introduction); *Œuvres historiques*, ed. Pomeau; *Siècle de Louis XIV*, ed. Bourgeois.

[11] Quotations and analysis are from the edition of 1735.

depicting those who have eminently possessed that quality. Or, if they could not attain to so high an undertaking, they, at least, turned their readers away from vice, by inspiring in them a disgust for the impious actions of great men. This responsibility which Lenglet attributes to historians was really assumed by the historians of his day with considerable scrupulousness. One recalls that Voltaire's studies on Charles XII led him to Peter the Great but that, upon learning about the crimes of Peter, he was so revolted that he rejected the idea (at least for the time being) of writing Peter's biography.

Lenglet finds value in the portraits which historians give of great men. From these portraits, he judges, the public may gain a very useful advantage, since readers always seek to imitate the actions of those who are admired and to eschew any imitation of those whose conduct is condemned. Lenglet explains that this is the utility of history as we understand it: "faire une égale attention sur le bien et sur le mal, pour imiter l'un, et pour éviter l'autre." It is, as states the phrase so often quoted during the century, "history teaching by example," which represents a certain exteriorization of ourselves in history.

There is, however, a contrary aspect to this historical problem. While one reads history in order to distinguish between virtue and vice and in order to learn how to practice virtue and avoid vice, one studies history with other intentions. Lenglet does not approve, any more than Fontenelle, Bayle, and Voltaire, the practice of cramming into the mind a mass of historical data. Knowledge of history is not determined by the quantity of historical facts. To know anything, one must seek the principles which govern it, and to know history is to be acquainted with its underlying principles. They must be discerned in the deeds and words of the men who furnish the material of history; we must have a standard of judgment to weigh the material and evaluate the principles.

The study of history consequently differs from the reading of history. In study, the historian is preoccupied with the motives, opinions, and passions of men. The object here is to penetrate all the springs of action, all the tricks and subterfuges of life, by analyzing motives, opinions, and passions. We have to seek out all the ways in which these latter deceive the mind and take the heart by surprise. It is evident that Lenglet attributes to the historical act the same sort of analysis which Marivaux attributed to the aesthetic act. Knowledge of the illusory effects of history and the spontaneous repercussions of feeling teaches us how to know ourselves in others.

The coordinate sciences which supplement the study of history are geography, manners and customs, and chronology. Indeed, seen in their true perspective, these are properly speaking the three main branches of historical study. Geography should be studied in its principles rather than in its overabundant detail. Lenglet finds that geographical details pushed to exorbitant limits tend to obscure the principles rather than enlighten them. However, he concedes that details have their place in the formation of geographical principles: "On ne peut juger sainement des actions d'un peuple, qu'après avoir bien connu sa situation, son climat, la fertilité de son terroir, l'indigence ou la richesse du pays, les mœurs et le caractère de ses habitans" (I, 14).

The study of manners and customs is, in reality, a separate subject. It serves to give an exact knowledge of history, but it serves also to make known the inclinations of men. Lenglet's thought at this point, though not entirely clear, becomes more understandable when seen in connection with his views on chronology. Strictly speaking, he understands by chronology what we now understand as the sequence of historical events. He places no great stress himself upon these sequences, except in two respects. He assumes that there is a relationship between manners and customs and the sequence of historical events. This, he finds, is particularly true in the area of religion. For this reason, the study of manners becomes essential to the understanding of events. "Ainsi l'ignorance dans laquelle on seroit de ces mêmes coûtumes, soit par rapport à la religion, soit par rapport à l'usage ordinaire de la vie, ne manqueroit pas de couvrir d'obscurité beaucoup d'endroits qui se rencontrent dans l'histoire" (I, 29). Conversely, many obscurities in history can be illuminated by an understanding of manners and customs. But customs themselves are sometimes obscure and must be traced to their origins. However, this relationship does not exist only in the form of manners and customs producing historical phenomena; there is the opposite relationship where historical phenomena have a great impact upon manners and customs. Lenglet recommends the study of both sets of relationships, but particularly the latter. "C'est par l'étude exacte de l'extérieur des hommes que l'on peut connoître leur intérieur, qu'ils ne peuvent s'empêcher de faire paroître dans toutes leurs actions" (I, 30). Lenglet is convinced that every people forms the structure of its government upon its inclinations and its interests. Each people acts from its own set of principles, which differs from those of all others. The author ultimately concludes that what the historian is actually seeking is some way of getting at them. Facts, of course, lead to their establishment. Inclinations and interests, moreover, are the basis of manners and customs, and these, in turn, are the legitimate sources of action. There is a further relationship between principles and action which involve inclinations, interests, and manners. Fundamentally, all history is concerned with the interplay of "mœurs" and historical action, and all facts should throw light upon this interplay. Lenglet condemns historical curiosity to the extent that it represents only our ever-present search for new facts. It is true that what one seeks is facts, but only facts "pour servir à éclaircir ou prouver la religion . . . tirer quelque maxime pour les mœurs, pour le gouvernement, ou la conduite," or even facts, he adds, useful in literature.

Lenglet, like Bayle, attempts to define what makes a good historian. There are, he says, historians who are faithful to the body of history and to the facts they relate but who are defective in the portraits they provide of rulers and illustrious persons, or in their method of reporting facts, or in the malicious way they present them. It is consequently desirable, before taking up a work by a historian, to know his character, his interests, his passions, and the circumstances of his life. This type of investigation, however, can go too far and discourage historians who are most disinterested. To circumvent this difficulty, Lenglet proposes to divide historians into three groups: those who have literary talent and experience in public affairs which can be united with their natural talents in history, those who have much experience in public affairs but little preparation in the study of history, and those who have talent in the writing of history but no experience in public affairs.

Obviously, the best historians are those in the first class. One should always prefer a historian in whom there are all three perfections: natural facility in writing, erudition, and experience in public affairs. Lenglet offers Thucydides as a model. Naturally, those in the second and third groups are not useless in Lenglet's opinion; they merely are defective in complete historical experience. However, the three perfections are not easily divorced from personal passions and prejudices. It is consequently better for a good historian to be separated from any party, or any country, or even any religion he is treating. Total disinterestedness, Lenglet recognizes, is well-nigh impossible, yet a moderate amount of objectivity is desirable. The necessity that the historian be sincere often prevents an attitude of impersonality or objectivity, too. Where these problems arise, Lenglet recommends a reasonable approach. He ranks his good historian in two other ways: the approbation with which he is regarded by his contemporaries, and his scrupulousness in selecting the best material possible.

In contrast, a bad historian is not only deficient in these merits but is also distinguished by his lack of sincerity, his negative criticism, and his satiric nature.

Lenglet attempts, also, to define a rule for judging the authenticity of an event. In general, he offers the suggestion that the likelihood of an event is not a valid proof that it happened. It is useful, therefore, to examine the event in all its relationships, both internal (that is, attendant circumstances) and external (that is, the nature of the witnesses). If, after a thorough analysis, it is found that the event is contradicted by contemporaries, one can only present the occurrence as possible. Lenglet urges that these two rules be applied even to miraculous events, where one would have to distinguish between common and particular circumstances. However, these rules are also subject to caution: a contemporary witness is, says Lenglet, a very valuable witness, but he is valuable only in his personal merit as a historian, in which case he may be more valuable as a witness than a whole group of other contemporaries.

Lenglet tries to give his final thought in a chapter entitled "De la Manière d'écrire l'histoire" (Chapter 62, II, 435ff.). He, like Bayle, bases all his advice upon Cicero's remark in the *De Oratore* (Lib. II): "Quis nescit primam esse historiae legem, ne quid falsi dicere audeat, deinde ne quid veri non audeat. . . ." He further recommends the work of Père Rapin and especially J. de Silhon's *Conditions de l'histoire*. Since the latter work had become difficult to locate, the author extracts seven pages of advice. Silhon has divided his subject into narration, judgment, maxims, and harangues. He finds that narration, the basis of history, sustains the other parts. It consists in relating faithfully the most illustrious events. One must be prepared to find the narration defective: either it is too detailed and not sufficiently general or it is too general and not sufficiently detailed. Narration requires a historian "de bonne foi," a man of honor; otherwise, he becomes a traitor who takes advantage of the credulity of his public. It is undeniable that history can attain an infallible certainty, but, since it seeks to determine the motives of an event and the characters of those who participate in it, it can rarely clarify the truth of the happening completely. Silhon has but little confidence in rationalizing an event. When there is contradictory evidence, however, the historian is forced to weigh it and to present it impartially. One should not conclude that the historian must not pass judgment either upon the event related or upon his sources. He should remember to be judicious. As for maxims, they are the flowers strewn over the other parts of history. They must add beauty to the narration, but not overwhelm it. In general, harangues should be used very sparingly, and then only indirectly. Finally, the style must not be too uniform, or too even, or too colorless.[12]

[12] The works recommended by Lenglet for the preparation of a study in modern history are (I have included pertinent comment when it seemed desirable):

Joannis Barclaii, *Icon animorum*, 8°, Londini, 1614.
 "Ce petit ouvrage est utile pour connaître les caractères de chaque nation; chose nécessaire pour commencer l'étude de l'histoire moderne."
J. Bodin, *De la république*, fol., Paris, 1578.
 This work was highly recommended by Lenglet.
H. Grotius, *De iure belli et pacis*, tr. in 1687, Francfort edn., 1696.
 "Il ne s'est encore rien fait ni de plus sage, ni de mieux raisonné sur les principes du droit."
Justus Lipsius, *De Politicis*, in-4°, Antwerpiae, 1610.
G. Naudé, *Des coups d'état*, in-4°, Rome, 1639.
 "Son livre promet plus qu'il ne donne."
A. Sidney, *Discours sur le gouvernement*, tr. Samson, 3 vols., in-12°, La Haye, 1702.
 This work discusses opposition to absolute monarchy.
J. de Silhon, *Ministre d'état*, in-4°, Paris, 1631-1643.
 "Un des plus savans, des mieux raisonnez, et des mieux écrits en matière de politique."
Wicquefort, *L'Ambassadeur et ses fonctions*, 2 vols., in-4°, Amsterdam, 1690.
 "On y trouve une infinité de faits curieux et essentiels qui échappent ordinairement aux historiens et qui sont néanmoins nécessaires pour l'etude du droit public."

The important thing to note in Lenglet's presentation is the remarkable conformity of his views on history to those of Bayle. There is, of course, some difference. Whereas Bayle's remarks are for the most part scattered throughout his eight ponderous volumes, with only occasional attempts to bring the material together (as in particular articles, for instance, such as "Elizabeth," "Concini," "Usson," "Abimélech," "Suétone," and "Bellarmin") and then only in a rambling, desultory way, Lenglet leaves the impression in his work that he has not only studied Bayle's pronouncements carefully but has assembled and classified them and attempted to give them a coherent organization. It is, of course, only reasonable that this should be the case, since Bayle's intention was more general than Lenglet's. Delvolvé (*Religion, critique et philosophie positive chez P. Bayle*, p. 226) has noted that "le but du *Projet de Dictionnaire critique* est de donner au public l'idée d'exactitude historique, de sa possibilité, des moyens de l'atteindre, de son importance" and that, in the *Dictionnaire* itself, "le but que Bayle vise très consciemment, c'est de répandre dans le public lettré l'idée et la méthode d'une science historique dont il a longuement médité le caractère et la portée." Lenglet's book is naturally different in intent, since it is at the same time a bibliography and a manual for writers of history. Consequently, though the material is very much the same, the manner of presentation and the general intent offer a considerable contrast.

Bayle, with his general tendency to factualism and positivism, is more concerned with keeping the facts straight. In a way, he is anxious to know how to distinguish between the true and the false. Otherwise, he shows but little interest in establishing a hierarchy of facts: he seems to assume that all facts which are true are important, while those which are false are, naturally, unimportant. In other words, all true facts are equally interesting. He does give a moral interpretation to them, but it consists more in personal precepts and observations than in general conclusions. Bayle does not assign to history a philosophical or a teleological goal. He does assume that facts of history reveal something about man, and he, like Fontenelle, believes that they disclose particular manners and customs, as well as definite opinions. He does not pose the problem of the inner purpose of history, though. In this respect, he differs completely from Bossuet and those eighteenth-century historians who followed him. His attitude toward the doctrine of progress is characteristic of his indifference to the larger question concerning the meaning of history. He is confident that each generation acts in the same way as the generations which have preceded it.

He shows little interest in working out a synthesis in an effort to arrive at a general comprehension of history. It would therefore be useless to inquire into his philosophy of history, because he has none. On the other hand, he has a critical historical method. He is deeply interested in seeking the sources of historical facts, in weighing contradictions in the evidence, in examining the differing motives behind facts, and, most of all, in determining what can be known in history and what must always remain in doubt. In the criticism of evidence, he is superb. He even enlarges this historical criticism to the point where it resembles that of many twentieth-century historians. Finally, by the scrupulous application of this critical method, he arrives at the separation of history from the realm of faith. Although he has nothing to propose in place of Bossuet's doctrine of Providence, he does make it clear that a teleological interpretation of history is no longer acceptable to a historian.

As for Lenglet, although he has adopted the views of Bayle and practically all of his method, it is evident that what interests him is not an assemblage of facts but knowledge of things by the principles which govern them. That is why he insists upon an acquaintance with those who furnish the matter of history and upon a constant search for the opinions and passions of men. Fundamentally, what he demands is a judicious selection of facts and an effort to derive principles therefrom. This result can be achieved by continual study of customs, manners, religions, and their application to an analysis of the character of a people (*Méthode*, I, 29). It is essential to know the changes which have occurred externally in a social group in order to arrive at its underlying character. Lenglet even lays down the general principle that the best way to understand the manners and customs of a people is through an analysis of its personality—what was called in the Enlightenment by Voltaire and others "l'esprit des nations." Lenglet admits that ancient history is too far away to be known in great detail—hence, the great difficulty in discerning the customs, manners, and characters of ancient peoples. It is equally hard to separate the fabulous from the true, as

Fontenelle had pointed out in *De l'origine des fables*. Lenglet, nevertheless, persists in his view: what one seeks in this kind of study are facts which define clearly the religion of a country and which produce equally clear statements concerning the government, manners, and conduct of the people (I, 69). In the treatment of modern history, there is an additional obstacle: we do not know how to separate adequately the important facts from the immense mass of facts. All the same, we have to keep steadfastly in mind that we are seeking the general principles of an action, its causes, its motives, and its effects. A good rule to remember is that "chaque peuple a formé la nature de son gouvernement sur ses inclinations et sur ses intérêts" (I, 70). It is, however, not sufficient to address oneself to the history of a single people. The author notes with approval the general tendency to compose universal histories (I, 54). It is essential for the historian to trace the relationship of one country's history with the histories of other countries. For this enterprise, Lenglet recommends that Bossuet's *Histoire universelle* be taken as the model and, in conclusion, insists that these universal histories must always be abridgments of particular histories, that is, they should avoid the mass of unnecessary facts in the interest of presenting the very necessary principles. It is thus clear that, although Lenglet has absorbed well his Bayle and his Fontenelle, he has progressed far in his own right toward a theory which would eventually produce, with Voltaire, a philosophical history, if not a philosophy of history.

Professor Brumfitt, in his *Voltaire Historian* (Chapter II), has sketched the historical theories of Voltaire's predecessors and attempted to mark out his debt to them. He notes that Voltaire was not at all consistently opposed to the preceding humanist historians, particularly as regards their art and their style. Indeed, he was inclined to judge them, at least at first, on the basis of literary merit. Later, he examined more carefully their facts and their ability to organize these facts in a convincing "tableau." The two whom he discussed most frequently were Mézeray and Daniel, both of whom were writers, rather than historians, and whose writings were relatively free from historical theory. Daniel, in fact, while writing his *Histoire de France*, visited the Royal Library, where he was shown 1,100 manuscripts dealing with his subject, and returned to write in his "Préface" a glowing account of the impressions which they made upon him; but he confided later to a friend that he did not need all that junk to write his history. Voltaire actually came to praise this "Préface," but not for this attitude toward documentation. Two historians whom he praised more fully were Giannone and Rapin de Thoyras, the first for the scholarly accuracy of his *Istorie civile del regno di Napoli* and the second for the impartiality of his *Histoire d'Angleterre,* a work which Voltaire characterized as the best history of England in existence. Indeed, it has often been thought that Rapin de Thoyras was influential in a general way in turning Voltaire to the writing of history.

Among the preceding historians who were of greatest interest to Voltaire were Bossuet, Bayle, Fontenelle, Fénelon, Boulainvilliers, and Bolingbroke (see Brumfitt, *Voltaire Historian,* Chapter II). The important thing to note is that Voltaire seems exceedingly critical of each. Bossuet, for instance, he criticized severely for his uncritical acceptance of ancient legends, for lying, and for insincerity. Voltaire condemned him for limiting his universal history to only five or six peoples. His theory of Providence in the working of history, Voltaire felt, was too theologically oriented to be historically sound. Voltaire, however, was not inclined to attack it except in terms of a Jewish Providence. If it were viewed as an expression of deism, he asserted, he would look favorably upon it. Moreover, we must not forget that Voltaire inaugurated his own *Histoire universelle* as a continuation of Bossuet's and that he did appreciate the latter's literary qualities.

Bayle has always been presented as the one undoubted influence on Voltaire, and the *Dictionnaire historique* has passed as the one incontrovertible mine of material Voltaire referred to in composing the *Dictionnaire philosophique.* Brumfitt himself suggests that the general skepticism shown by Voltaire had its origin in Bayle. Voltaire did, of course, criticize his style, condemn him for sterility, and decry his puerility in treating history. But, for all that, he agreed with Bayle in regarding history as an endless series of crimes, in believing that the major causes of an event can be known even if the details always escape the historian, and, finally, in criticizing the intolerance of Christian civilization. This latter similarity is particularly striking, since Bayle's *Compelle intrare* was an important source for Voltaire's *Traité sur la tolérance*. In spite of these shared attitudes, Brumfitt concludes that Voltaire received no help from Bayle in all the positive aspects of his work. "Despite the many similarities, the gulf between the sceptic and the philosophe remains a wide one" (p. 34).

Voltaire likewise found fault with Fontenelle, whom he criticized for his precious style and for his lack of depth. Fontenelle's two works on history, *Sur l'histoire* and *De l'origine des fables*, received no attention in Voltaire's work, as Edsall ("The Ideas of History and Progress in Fontenelle and Voltaire") has shown. It should be noted also that, although he possessed a copy of the *De l'origine des fables* (1724) and although he agreed with Fontenelle's position that ancient history is inclined to be nonhistorical, he did not quote him. He also agreed that the interesting history is not the description of wars or of states, but rather the account of man's errors or his passions. He, like Fontenelle, was deeply interested in the problem of causation and was inclined to insist paradoxically upon minor causes for great events. And, finally, like his predecessor, Voltaire believed that history should mark out the progress achieved by a person, a period, or a race, in spite of the essentially static quality of man.

Brumfitt stresses that Voltaire probably adopted some of Fénelon's historical views also: the moral value of history, the importance of style and form, the similarities between history and the epic, the desire to suppress the superabundant details, and, above all, the insistence upon the study of the customs, social conditions, and institutions of a people. Brumfitt concludes that, since Voltaire was well-acquainted with Fénelon's work at an early date, he could have known these views. But he observes, also, that the difference between the prelate and the philosophe is all too great to expect too much influence.

The resemblances between Boulainvilliers and Voltaire are more striking. Boulainvilliers protested against the history of kings, wars, and treaties. He deplored that historians failed to seek the inner springs of action, of government, and that they neglected the genius of each epoch, the opinions, the manners, the dominant ideas, and the passions of men. Boulainvilliers affirmed unequivocally that he would bring to light the manners, opinions, and religions of the peoples of the earth. There are, to be sure, some differences, such as the opposition between their attitudes regarding miracles.

Finally, there remains the influence of Bolingbroke. This has been affirmed and denied with such regularity that it is only with difficulty that one can strike a reasonable balance. It is certain that Voltaire echoed many of Bolingbroke's views on history: the utility of history, the condemnation of excessive erudition, the espousal of "modern," rather than "ancient," history, the advice to doubt consistently the details of history, the insistence upon moral value, and, above all, the desire to foster a history of the sciences and the arts. A real difficulty has always been that Voltaire might have had access to them too late for them to have had any considerable influence, since the *Lettres* appeared publicly only in 1752. Recently, though, Professor Nagel has shown that Voltaire could have been exposed to these ideas earlier, since the *Lettres* had a private printing in 1735. Further, the publication of the Bolingbroke letter of October 1724 discloses a more consistent influence than had hitherto been considered possible.

What stands out in this way of posing the problem is not so much the influence which these predecessors of Voltaire had upon him as the fact that many of them entertained ideas concerning history which he himself held. It is likely that in our search for influences we cloud the issue by assuming that, where similar approaches to the subject occur, there must be some influence of the earlier upon the later writer. When dissimilarities also occur, we have a tendency to conclude that the similarities must be accidental and do not necessarily bespeak an influence. This type of on-again, off-again assertion of influence leads precisely nowhere. Even though it is probable that Voltaire, who was a rapid reader, could have read all those works represented here and actually did read many of them, it is not very helpful to dwell too long upon what he may have extracted from them. As a matter of fact, none of the ideas of these previous historians is absent from Lenglet's book, an edition of which appeared in 1735. And, since his work had as its subject the reading, writing, and studying of history and contained, besides, a bibliography of pertinent works upon the various aspects of the subject, and since Voltaire is known to have had a copy of it in his library, it seems perfectly reasonable to assume that whatever advice and method he needed he found in that work. This does not mean, however, that Voltaire did not know these other preceding historians: in all probability, he knew them all and found in them material confirming the points assembled in the *De la Méthode d'étudier l'histoire*. The most important role these historians fill is the way they demonstrate how closely Voltaire's ideas on history were, as in other areas, in accord with those of his contemporaries.

Although the Cirey period was undoubtedly the time when Voltaire addressed himself to the writing of history with great seriousness, he had long before held this subject as one of his intellectual interests. His biographers never fail to stress that, although *La Ligue* (1723) was not history, the events of that epic were surrounded by a plethora of historical notes, presumed, according to Haxo, to have been drawn in large part from Bayle's *Dictionnaire*. If this interpretation is exaggerated, it is nonetheless a fact that the *Essay sur les guerres civiles en France* (1727) was a historical document called forth by the exigencies of the *Henriade*. It is a fact also that Voltaire early admired Bolingbroke (1724) precisely for his competence in history, and it is highly probable that he was led toward Bolingbroke and toward history by Lévesque de Pouilly. There was a close relationship between Bayle's thought and the *Lettres philosophiques*. Professor Lanson has shown in his critical edition of that work that there are numerous specific references to Bayle. It should be noted also that Voltaire returned from England in 1729 convinced that he had a complete *Histoire de Charles XII* ready for the printer. He presumably had composed it in 1728 while staying at Falkener's home, and, although he published it only in 1731, preparation of it was undoubtedly well-advanced before his return to France. Finally, he appears to have been much impressed with the historical plays of Shakespeare and to have made plans to introduce the national history of France in his own drama. Although he did not make a very great success out of the genre, it was practiced to a great extent subsequently by his contemporaries.

Critics (see Brumfitt) often stress this historical interest as a novelty, while treating *Charles XII* as strictly a work of art. There is, of course, some justification for this point of view. It will be recalled that La Fontaine in his *Epître à Huet* mentions history as a new genre of literature. It was perfectly natural that Voltaire, fully aware of the difficulties of writing poetry in an age of prose and ever ready to launch forth into any new domain, should have explored actively the possibilities of history as an art form. It is significant that he often likened it in structure to drama, of which he was, as we have seen, passionately enamored.

Brumfitt notes that the *Histoire de Charles XII* is in the humanist tradition, of which it is one of the finest examples. By this he seems to mean that it is neither philosophical history nor social history. He nonetheless concedes that Voltaire attempts to give a detailed analysis of a society and even draws conclusions from Charles's rashness which, if not very profound, are philosophical. It is perfectly true, though, that Voltaire did not offer this work as a history of the human mind, although one could argue that the contrast between Charles and Peter—one king ruining his country by his rashness and the other creating a new civilization by his prudent calculation—is philosophical enough. At all events, once the work had appeared, a storm of protest arose from those who objected to its fictional style, from those (Nordberg and La Mottraye, for example) who attacked the inaccuracy of presentation, and, finally, from those who refused to grant it any historical authenticity whatever because of a faulty method.

All this controversy only served to render acute the necessity on Voltaire's part of establishing a more coherent view of history. This he attempted in a series of short introductions: the *Remarques sur l'histoire* (1742), the *Nouvelles Considérations sur l'histoire* (1744), not to mention the *Discours sur l'histoire de Charles XII*, which had already served as preface to the first edition. These general introductions were interspersed with the actual documents of the controversies over *Charles XII*: the *Notes sur les remarques de la Mottraye*, the *Lettre au Journal des savants*, the *Lettre à Mr. Nordberg*, etc.

In the meantime, Voltaire had decided almost immediately after the *Charles XII* appeared to compose a *Siècle de Louis XIV* (1732). For almost two decades, he devoted himself to that task, leaving to his correspondence (letters to Du Bos, Lord Hervey, etc.) the statement of the objective which he had set himself. Some time after 1736, he announced his interest in a universal history. On two occasions, he determined to try out the temper of the public and particularly the policy of the government: once in 1739, with a book of *Mélanges* in which he incorporated some small extracts from the *Siècle*, and again in 1745-1746, when he permitted several chapters from the *Abrégé*—on the early centuries and on the crusades—to be published in the *Mercure*.

Voltaire's first entry into the writing of history was conditioned severely by his love of letters. It is not known just how closely he followed Saint-Réal's *Conjuration des Espagnols contre la République de Venise*. There is evidence that he greatly admired the work, precisely because it presented history as proper material for a man of letters. The assumption was that what attracts the man of letters to the writing of history is its dramatic quality, its moral goal, and its psychological study of motivations, passions, and opinions. This definition of history was to be repeated over and over in the eighteenth century. The stress here should be placed upon the obvious understanding that history offers the literary man an occasion to bring out the dramatic quality of events, to arrange in some effective way the unfolding of phenomena, to study character, motives, passions, opinions, and to draw moral conclusions for the public from the "conditions" and "situations." In theory, it is probably true that what was involved in the "gestes" of Charles XII, Louis XIV, Peter the Great, etc., was the same "matter" which appeared in Racine's *Bajazet*—no more, no less. That explains why Voltaire, when he met Fabrice at Falkener's, was ready to undertake his *Histoire de Charles XII*. As a man of letters, he acknowledged that what art ultimately seeks is human and moral truth and that it achieves its end only through the means at its disposal for pleasing. Voltaire defined these means as "netteté, précision, réflexions courtes et pleines de sens." The working out of this ideal is easily perceived in *Charles XII*; it takes no great analysis of the work to see how Voltaire conceived his subject, how he worked out the action, and how he decided to contrast Charles with Peter in the interest of the character, the action, and the moral which he wished to draw eventually. There is no break between the character of Charles, "moitié Alexandre, moitié Don Quichotte," the action, and the moral, and the constant relationship between these parts is heightened by the contrast with Peter, who is entirely different in character, produces a totally different action, and creates another moral effect.

Discussion of the work led to a sharpening of Voltaire's thought on the writing of history. Such points as the authenticity of the action and the motives attributed to the protagonist had to be examined more closely. Voltaire had invited this close examination in the *Discours sur l'histoire de Charles XII*. There he notes that the only rulers who survive are those who are described by some excellent writer, that Charles and Peter deserve this honor because they are "les personnages les plus singuliers qui eussent paru depuis plus de vingt siècles" (*Œuvres historiques*, ed. Pomeau, p. 55). Voltaire adds that he hopes the work will prove useful to other princes. Charles XII's conquests, which appear so brilliant, really ruined Sweden and should stand as a warning to later monarchs. Voltaire declares that he has based his statements of the events upon the most scrupulous testimony and that, consequently, the facts are true. He insists that these facts must be seen in the light of the times. Indeed, although he lays no great emphasis upon the social milieu, he does require that the background be accurate.

In 1742, Voltaire published a manifesto entitled *Remarques sur l'histoire*, which contained additional reflections on history. The central attack of this little essay is launched against the writers of ancient history, particularly M. Rollin, who had published his *Histoire ancienne* in 1730 and his *Histoire romaine* eight years later. Voltaire protests with some vigor against the "fables" of ancient histories, as well as against the lack of proper documentation and the inaccuracies in the presentation. He waxes eloquent in his condemnation of the tendency to give false statistics and, even more, in his opposition to any attempt to attribute to Egypt the earliest antiquity. Finally, he rebels against those who find in this early antiquity all kinds of evidence of an advanced culture. The point was taken by Fontenelle in the *Essai sur les fables*. Voltaire objects to ancient history precisely because we do not have the proper documents to characterize the times and because what documents we do have present fables as true events and take false facts for truths. It is thus impossible under these circumstances to compile history, because of the lack of an "esprit philosophique." The greater number of historians, instead of discussing facts with men, tell stories for children.

Voltaire's negative attitude toward ancient history is countered by his very positive attitude toward "modern" history. "Il me semble," Voltaire writes, "que si l'on voulait mettre à profit le temps présent, on ne passerait point sa vie à s'infatuer des fables anciennes. Je conseillerais à un jeune homme d'avoir une légère teinture de ces temps reculés" (*Œuvres historiques*, pp. 43-44). Instead of these fables, Voltaire proposes that the study of history for modern man begin toward the end of the fifteenth century, when the fall of Constantinople occasioned the dispersal of belles-lettres throughout Italy, whence they spread to France, England, Germany, and the North; when printing, which had just been invented, made history more certain; when a new religion separated one half of Europe from its allegiance to the Pope; when new discoveries, like the compass, led to the expansion of commerce; when a New World was discovered. These events, writes Voltaire, completely changed Europe. "L'Europe Chrétienne devient une espèce de république immense." In spite of wars, especially religious wars, Europe became a more coherent whole; the arts, which are the glory of a state, were developed to a point unknown in Greece and Rome. This is the history we should know, a history free from chimerical predictions, lying oracles, false miracles, and foolish fables. "Tout y est vrai."

Voltaire returned to the same theme two years later, in 1744, in the *Nouvelles considérations sur l'histoire*. Still with Rollin in mind, he condemns the miraculous events, the picturesque accounts. He casts ridicule on the stories about King Nabis who permitted those who brought him money to embrace his wife and had those who refused him money placed in the arms of a doll armed with spikes, about the Archbishop of Mainz who was eaten by rats, about the rain of blood which inundated Gascony. He proscribes the miracles, the prophecies, and the trials by fire.

What one demands in modern history, he says, is entirely different. Accuracy is essential: the date of an event is important; so is the nature of a treaty; a political event (a coronation or even the arrival of an ambassador) must be correctly portrayed. Archives must be kept and consulted, but it is not enough to be informed about battles: one must know also how to select the significant details and how to arrange them coherently. We must be chary of anecdotes, particularly court gossip. The time wasted on these frivolous matters should be spent instead in the investigation of far more important questions: What are the collected forces of a nation before and after a war? Did Spain prosper from her conquest of America? Was her population larger or smaller at the time of Charles V than it is now? Why did Amsterdam grow so rapidly in two hundred years? Has the population of England grown? Demographic, geographic, and economic considerations, Voltaire now feels, must be taken into account in any attempt to comprehend the forces of a nation. He protests loudly against those who try to prove that everything is in decline. He demands a history which may be read "en philosophe" and "en citoyen," a history which is scientific, having proper statistics on commerce, accurate descriptions of the arts, and clear recording of the changes in "mœurs": "On saurait ainsi l'histoire des hommes, au lieu de savoir une faible partie de l'histoire des rois et des cours." Such a history is useful, because it is based in every respect upon the *Homo sum* of Terence. To be properly executed, however, it must be written by historians who have had experience in public affairs, as Lenglet had already advised.

The writing of *Charles XII* led Voltaire to reflect upon the possibility of a volume on Charles's great rival Peter. In a way which is still not entirely clear, he began to assemble material for his biography of Peter. He asked César de Missy for his work on Russia.[13] In 1737, he requested Frederick to get some information for him from Russia. This Frederick did, but, as we have seen, he expressed considerable distaste for the Russian Czar because of his cruelty. Voltaire was still inclined to defend him for having changed the Russians from savages into civilized men. When, however, Frederick convinced him that Peter had had his own son murdered, Voltaire renounced for the time being his projected biography. In 1748, he published the *Anecdotes sur le Czar Pierre-le-Grand* (see M. XXIII, 281). In 1757, at the invitation of Shouvaloff, he resumed his project, with the result that the first volume of the *Histoire de Russie sous Pierre-le-Grand* appeared in 1759, the second in 1763. As the final title reveals, Voltaire had shifted from a biography of Peter to a

---

[13] There is one of these documents on Russia in the Voltaire manuscript collection at the Bibliothèque Nationale (see the Collection De Cayrol).

study of the Russian people. The work, therefore, has as its goal a picture of Russian society and, in that respect, ultimately resembles more *Le Siècle de Louis XIV* than *Charles XII*. Voltaire, however, kept in mind his original intention of showing that Peter's reign was characterized by reform: the establishment of schools, the abolition of poverty, the standardization of weights and measures, the fostering of industries, the encouragement of foreign commerce, and a whole series of legal and religious reforms.

The year following the publication of *Charles XII*, Voltaire announced to Thiériot (13 May 1732) that he was engaged in composing a work on the age of Louis XIV. There is no hint given here of the way Voltaire conceived his new project, nor do we have any specific information about how he was led to consider the task. Brumfitt suggests that the author had two aims: to treat the ways the arts developed in an age when they had a European renown, and to compare the outstanding glory of Louis XIV's time with the relative stagnation of Louis XV's age. In all probability, Voltaire did want to bring out the magnificent artistic achievements of a period which he greatly admired. There is no doubt that he was still preoccupied with the notion that the great man is responsible for the great age. He was also deep in the final composition of the *Lettres philosophiques*, and it is very plausible that he was conceiving of his new interest as a counterpart of those letters. Having mastered the technique of characterizing a foreign civilization, he decided to apply that technique to an analysis of his own. It is not correct to say that we know Voltaire's original plan for the *Siècle*, as Brumfitt contends, citing the letter to Du Bos in 1738. The letter to Du Bos outlined the plan as Voltaire conceived it in 1738; we do not know how he regarded it in 1732. We do know that there was a practically completed version of the work in 1736, when the manuscript was shown to Valdruche. We have the latter's enthusiastic reaction to the work, but no definite indication of its structure. In fact, Valdruche's remarks, such as they are, indicate that the plan which had been executed in 1736 was modified in 1738.

The letter to Du Bos is, notwithstanding, very important. Du Bos had played a role of consequence in the genesis of the *Henriade*, and his essay on painting and poetry, of 1719, had attracted the attention of the young Voltaire. In a letter on 30 October 1738,

Voltaire outlined for Du Bos his manner of arranging the *Siècle*. Voltaire comments that the book is not designed to be a biography of the King or an account of his reign. Rather, it is meant to be a history of the human mind, seen at the moment when the human mind was at the peak of its achievement. This is, so far as I know, the first reference Voltaire ever made to the identification of history with the achievements of the human mind ("l'esprit humain"). The idea was not original with him, since Fontenelle and Bayle had used it long before 1738, as we have shown above. Voltaire, however, as we shall see, was to give the notion a central focus in the unfolding of history. Having established the point that what is most significant in the age of Louis XIV is not the record of the King's exploits—the wars, the battles, the treaties—but rather the way the spirit of man enhanced the glory of man at the moment when this spirit was at its height, Voltaire undertakes to sketch out his design for the work. There will be twenty chapters devoted to general history, representing twenty "tableaux" of the great events. Voltaire conceives of them in terms of drama. The main characters will be in the front of the scene, the mass of people in the background. On this stage, he intends to mark out "ce qui caractérise le siècle, ce qui a causé des révolutions, ce qui sera important dans cent ans." There will be a chapter on the private life of the King, two on the changes in the administration of the state, two on the ecclesiastical organization, and five or six on the history of the arts. Voltaire details the sources at his disposal: the historians of Louis XIV who have preceded him (Larrey, Limiers, Lamberti, Roussel); the two hundred printed volumes of memoirs written by those who lived at the time; Dangeau, for the private life of the King; the conversations and interviews with those who lived through the reign; the reports of the public officers, especially the intendants, and the unpublished *Annales* of the Abbé de Saint-Pierre, which he hopes to see; and all the "fatras des injures de parti de Jurieu, Quesnel, Doucin" for the ecclesiastical affairs. It is evident, though, that Voltaire's interest centers on the sciences and the arts: "A l'égard des arts et des sciences, il n'est question, je crois, que de tracer la marche de l'esprit humain en philosophie, en éloquence, en poésie, en critique; de marquer les progrès de la peinture, de la sculpture, de la musique, de l'orfèvrerie, des manufactures de tapisserie, de glaces, d'étoffes d'or, de l'horlogerie" (*Œuvres historiques*, p. 606). Voltaire adds that he merely wishes to give portraits of the geniuses in the artistic fields, and he concludes, with a sly remark which is a bit ambiguous: "Dieu me préserve d'employer trois cents pages à l'histoire de Gassendi."

When critics of Voltaire compare the actual *Siècle* with the plan sketched in the letter to Du Bos, they often note that there is a great disparity between what he gave as his intention and what he finally presented as the product of that intention. There are in the finished work thirty-nine chapters, rather than the thirty proposed by Voltaire. Twenty-four of them are devoted to what he called "histoire générale." Six of them concern the state of Europe and the state of France before Louis XIV's time. Two of the six are occupied with the Fronde. Chapters VII to XXIV deal with wars, battles, and treaties—just those things that Voltaire had said he did not want to treat. It is true that each chapter gives a different "tableau" and that the "tableau général" is practically always Europe, but it takes lots of patience to see the "age of Louis XIV" in the confusion of battles and treaties. The next four chapters (XXV-XXVIII) are given over to "particularités et anecdotes de Louis XIV," after a modest essay on anecdotes and a caution that they should be treated with prudence. Voltaire notes that Plutarch's anecdotes cannot be accepted, and he proceeds to criticize them as "plus agréables que certaines." Likewise, in the maxims Plutarch puts into the mouths of his heroes "plus d'utilité morale" que de "vérité historique." Voltaire defines these anecdotes as "petits détails longtemps cachés," observing that the public is avid for them when they are connected with famous people. He might have added that the French are particularly susceptible to these anecdotes about famous people, since they are undoubtedly the most gullible race in the world. Thus, Voltaire, who was going to eliminate insignificant details ("malheur aux détails"), was caught between French love for "potins" and the desire to paint the march of the human spirit, and he ended up writing four chapters of "potins." This is probably the reason his work was so much admired. In the remaining chapters (XXIX-XXXIX), Voltaire attempted to carry out his new design: in XXIX, "Gouvernement intérieur," he discusses "la police du royaume"; in XXX, "Finances et Réglements," the "commerces et finances"; in XXXI-

XXXIV, the sciences and the arts (four chapters, instead of the five or six he had promised); in XXXV-XXXVIII, the "gouvernement ecclésiastique" (four chapters, as opposed to the two he had said he would write). The last chapter (XXXIX) is an "hors-d'œuvre" on the Jesuits in China. From this analysis, it appears that Voltaire's letter stressed the novelty of none but the last ten chapters, and, even in them, he fulfilled his intentions only moderately well. Indeed, the chapters on the sciences and the arts are the weakest in the book. For one who had promised to make them the center of his history, the result would seem to be a glorious failure.

For these reasons, I disagree a little with Brumfitt's characterization of the *Siècle* as a pyramid at the base of which "came the ordinary narrative of political and military events" (*Voltaire Historian*, p. 48). It is certainly true that they come at the base, but I would hardly grant that they occupy only "the first part of the work." In reality, they occupy about the first two-thirds. It is an exaggeration, moreover, to call the chapters "analyzing social, economic, legal, and ecclesiastical affairs" the center of the work when they really come at the end. If there is any center to the pyramid, it must be the section comprising the four chapters of anecdotes. It is also very difficult to regard the four chapters on sciences and arts as the apex, since they are contained among the chapters which were, a moment ago, considered to be in the center. From the point of view of structure, given Voltaire's avowed intentions, the *Siècle* can only with difficulty justify itself.

These observations have often been suggested, at least in part. Indeed, hardly had the extracts from the *Siècle* appeared in 1739 when Lord Hervey took exception to the title. At any rate, one can assume that he did from the long letter which Voltaire wrote to him in reply (*circa* 1 June 1740) and which Voltaire took great pains to have distributed to the public—a letter, as he explained to Berger, of a good Frenchman. There he goes to extremes to prove that Louis XIV was a king who had rendered great service not only to France but to all humanity. Voltaire succinctly but very carefully describes what these services were, and the whole is done so effectively that the impression is given not only that seventeenth-century France deserves to be ranked with fifth-century Greece, first-century Rome, or sixteenth-century Florence but that the ruler was so superior that he deserves, at least as much as Pericles, Augustus, or the Medici, to have his name given to his age. Curiously, the letter to Hervey is more convincing than the letter to Du Bos or the *Essay* itself, because it is inspired by a totally different concept of history. Voltaire is certainly not uninterested in the glorious achievements of the classical age. He still rejoices in the institutions, in the sciences and the arts, he still revels in the anecdotes he condemns, and he even has difficulties in suppressing his pride at the wars which were fought, the battles which were won, the treaties which were imposed upon the enemy. But he has somewhat forgotten the adventures of the human mind. It is not the spirit of man's mind that he sees directing the history of Louis XIV's time, but rather the leadership of a great king and his great ministers who had wrought a nation which dominated Europe—but which no longer does. History is the result of a series of successes manipulated by a great man or great men. There is an important remark in the "Avertissement" to the Walther edition of 1753. After stating that the *Essai sur le siècle de Louis XIV* was the "suite d'une histoire universelle" in which the author was interested in depicting the principal events, Voltaire claims that "c'était plutôt l'histoire de l'esprit et des mœurs que des récits de batailles." To this tongue-in-cheek assertion, he adds: "Aussi il ne faut pas s'étonner si cette dernière partie de l'ouvrage et surtout le second volume, est conforme au reste de cette histoire universelle." We can now at least see that Voltaire was torn between two theories of history in the *Siècle*: history as the result of principal events shaped by great men, and history as the result of the action of the human mind and the manners and customs of the people.

There was, in fact, an incompatibility between the view that history should be written in the scientific way in which problems of natural sciences are treated, the view that it should be written to glorify the great man of the past, and the view that it should be written to bring out "l'esprit des nations" and "les mœurs." Voltaire was evidently trying to do too many things at once. To Mme du Châtelet, who thought that history was boring because it did not treat clearly, as natural science did, the phenomena of man, Voltaire was trying to prove that scientific history was entirely possible. To a group of historians, and the Abbé de Saint-Pierre in particular,

Voltaire was trying to prove the greatness of Louis XIV in shaping Europe through the domination of France. Since the Abbé de Saint-Pierre had also adopted a theory of the great man in history and had refused that title to Louis XIV, whom he finally called "un grand enfant," Voltaire was undertaking to present the opposite point of view. But not only to Saint-Pierre but to all those who, because of a decline in the power of France during the last half of Louis XIV's reign, had come, by reaction, to regard the King as responsible for the decline, Voltaire was trying to show that, in spite of the decline, the age itself was glorious. His real view of the age is given in the opening sentence of the *Précis du siècle de Louis XV:* "Nous avons donné avec quelque étendue une idée du siècle de Louis XIV, siècle des grands hommes, des beaux-arts et de la politesse; il fut marqué, il est vrai, comme tous les autres, par des calamités publiques et particulières, inséparables de la nature humaine" (édition encadrée, 1775, XIX, 345).

In his subsequent historical work, Voltaire broadened his concept of history. When he published in the *Mercure* in April 1745 the first selections from what was to become at a later date the *Essai sur les mœurs et l'esprit des nations,* he wrote: "Ma principale idée est de connaître autant que je pourrai les mœurs des hommes et les révolutions de l'esprit humain" (p. 5).

It would be helpful to know what is involved in these two expressions: "les mœurs des hommes" and "les révolutions de l'esprit humain." As for the first, one may ask how the historian can really determine the manners and customs of a people. Can he find any accurate way to analyze them? Some thought given to the *Lettres philosophiques* will provide at least one answer. In that work, Voltaire presumed that, if one understood the role played by a certain number of elements in the civilization of the time, one would better comprehend the reality of a people. These elements, in his mind, were merely the institutions which existed to serve a group of people—the religious, political, social, economic, philosophical, and artistic institutions. If one could penetrate, for instance, the nature of the religion practiced in a group, one could learn something about the people. This process of penetration is not easy to grasp, however. If it consists merely in a record of the idiosyncrasies and peculiarities of a people, or in a description of their reactions, or in a selection of their picturesque activities, not much progress will be made in the comprehension of their manners and customs. But, if one always tries to find in these private actions a more fundamental meaning, if one seeks behind the "mœurs" the "esprit" of the manners and customs, then, and only then, will one penetrate the living reality of a people.

The steps whereby this living, meaningful reality is reached are clearly delineated. First, the analysis of an activity in one category of living is made. This analysis leads to a description. The description itself, in turn, leads to a selection, and from the selection may be deduced qualities characteristic of the people. The qualities in one category should appear, under scrutiny, related to those in other categories. Then, the combination of the qualities of one category with those of all the other categories should give the "mœurs." And, finally, the "mœurs" should disclose the "esprit" of a people.

The "esprit" has another function besides. For Voltaire, it is at the same time agent and resultant. The "esprit" is not only what makes the characteristics of a people effective, it is also the force which leads a nation to its destiny. In the thinking of Voltaire, there is always a definite relationship between the "spirit of the race" and the "drive of man's intelligence." The "esprit" which marks a tendency is definitely connected with the "esprit" which is man's thinking faculty. This relationship leads to the inevitable changes of history. Hence, the "esprit des nations," once grasped in broad outline, is subject to change, to "revolutions." In fact, it brings about inevitably conditions which lead to change, to "revolutions."

The duty of the historian thus becomes twofold: he must derive the "esprit" from the study of manners and customs, but he must also trace the modifications of the human mind and the ways in which it brings about changes, "revolutions" in manners, customs, and characteristics. He is at the same time intellectual historian and analytic psychologist. For Voltaire, there is no doubt: intellectual history is the history of the modifications that have taken place in human thought, but it is also the changes in living, in being, in the reality of life, which have been the product of this modified human thinking. He subscribes without question to the opinion that history is right reason working in the affairs of men. There is a direct relationship between what one thinks and what one is, and between what one is and what one does. The same is true of nations.

History as the result of the interaction between great and illustrious men and events, which occurs in such a way as to offer opportunities to these leaders for shaping an epoch, is one conception that can be used to explain the *Siècle de Louis XIV*. The explanation runs a grave risk of explaining very little, however. Louis XIV had the genius to select assistants, such as Colbert, who knew how to mold events to shape a glorious epoch. Such a view of history presupposes that there must be conditions behind the genius of the great man which create that genius and corresponding causes behind the events of an epoch which render them malleable by great men. Those who live at the time naturally undergo some change from the impact of these geniuses and these events and, therefore, play some role in the unfolding of history. In short, there must be some way to grasp "une idée générale des nations qui habitent et désolent la terre."[14]

It was this problem which motivated the writing of the *Essai sur les mœurs*, of which the *Siècle* was only one part. Voltaire gives as his immediate excuse for undertaking the study Mme du Châtelet's disgust with "modern" history. She seeks, according to her lover, in the mass of historical phenomena only what is worth being known: "l'esprit, les mœurs, les usages des nations principales," supported by the facts absolutely necessary to bring out these things. Voltaire now hazards the remark, in the introduction to the *Essai*, that we must know the great exploits of rulers who have made their subjects better and happier. But there is a mass of material from which we have to make a selection. Voltaire notes that Bossuet "en a saisi le véritable esprit." Indeed, in the *Discours sur l'histoire universelle* (Part III, Chapter 2), Bossuet defines this "esprit des hommes":

Il ne suffit pas de regarder seulement devant ses yeux, c'est-à-dire de considérer ces grands événements qui décident tout à coup de la fortune des empires. Qui veut entendre à fond les choses humaines doit les reprendre de plus haut; et il lui faut observer les inclinations et les mœurs, où, pour dire tout en un mot, le caractère tant des peuples dominants en général que des princes en particuliers, et enfin de tous les hommes extraordinaires qui, par l'importance du personnage qu'ils ont eu à faire dans

[14] From the "Avant-propos" of the *Essai sur les mœurs*, ed. Pomeau, I, 195ff.

le monde, ont contribué, en bien et en mal, au changement des Etats et à la fortune publique.[15]

Voltaire comments that, in spite of this wise remark, Bossuet seems to bring everything in history back to the Jewish race. He subscribes unreservedly, though, to what Bossuet had written, adding, however, that there are other causes which Bossuet, in talking about the spirit of nations, has not neglected. Voltaire approves this attitude; he regrets only that Bossuet has not extended his interest to the Orient, "berceau de tous les arts, et qui a tout donné à l'occident."

In the *Nouveau plan d'une histoire de l'esprit humain* (*Essai*, ed. Pomeau, II, 815ff.), Voltaire confesses that his principal objective is to know as well as possible "les mœurs des hommes" and "les révolutions de l'esprit humain." He rebels here against the notion that the history of the earth has been created for some monarchs. While still retaining the belief that one must know the great deeds of those who have changed the face of the earth and especially those who have made their subjects better and happier, Voltaire now aims to seek out the "principaux citoyens qui représentent en quelque sorte l'esprit de la nation." And, while employing the approach by centuries, he promises to seek out the origins "d'un art, d'une coutume importante, d'une loi, d'une révolution."

In the *Lettre de M. de V., à l'auteur de la Bibliothèque impartiale* (*Essai*, ed. Pomeau, 11, 859), Voltaire notes that he adopted this new plan less to establish a chronology than to follow "l'esprit de chaque siècle" and to study "les mœurs des hommes." These concepts of "esprit," "mœurs," and "révolutions" reappear quite frequently. In speaking of the *Histoire universelle* in a *Lettre de M. de V. à M. de ——, Professeur en histoire* (*Essai*, ed. Pomeau, II, 865) at the beginning of the *Annales*, Voltaire affirms what he had said in several other places, that his chief aim had been "de suivre les révolutions de l'esprit humain dans celles des gouvernements." The change in statement here, however, is remarkable, since the author establishes a direct relationship between the "révolutions" which happen in "l'esprit humain" and the "révolutions" which happen in political societies. The conclusion which Voltaire draws from this relationship is more important still. In order to get at the "révolutions de l'esprit

[15] Quoted by Pomeau.

humain," he admits that he has been forced to seek "comment tant de méchants hommes, conduits par de plus méchants princes, ont pourtant à la longue établi des sociétés où les arts, les sciences, les vertus mêmes ont été cultivées." That is to say, king and citizen establish societies, and societies are made up of arts, sciences, morality. These three things are the substance of "mœurs," and an understanding of "mœurs" is necessary to arrive at a knowledge of "l'esprit humain." But other things are necessary also: "Je cherchais les routes du commerce. . . . Je m'étudiais à examiner, par le prix des denrées, les richesses ou la pauvreté d'un peuple." This information is essential, Voltaire indicates, because economic welfare is central to the revival of the arts, just as the arts and sciences are central to the rise of an "esprit." Eloquence and poetry, adds Voltaire, reveal the character of nations. To illustrate his point, he gives some translations from Dante, Petrarch, and Sadi. He still affirms that he has eliminated details, avoided all the minutiæ of war, and suppressed all the little facts in an effort to compose a "vaste tableau"—the same expression he had used for the *Siècle*, incidentally. Finally, in an "Avertissement" to an edition marked Colmar (Lambert, Paris, 1754), he declares his goal to be "moins de faire des narrations que de nous peindre la scène du monde telle que la voit l'œil philosophique."

In the preface to Volume III of the Walther edition of 1754 (*Essai*, ed. Pomeau, II, 883), Voltaire makes some effort to summarize his point of view as a whole. His starting point is still the attitude of Mme du Châtelet, who insists that, although she enjoys ancient historians, she cannot endure modern history. According to her, the difficulty arises from too much confusion—too many little events and facts, with no coherence or coordination among them. There are thousands of battles which lead nowhere. In answer to this criticism, Voltaire suggests a more intelligent selection of events and a ruthless suppression of the details of war, of all the little negotiations which are nothing but tricks, and of all the private adventures which submerge the important event. What one should select are the great happenings which exhibit the manners and customs of the country. They should unite to give a general tableau of a period, while in these events should be contained the history of the human mind.

Voltaire asserts that this method is the basis of his investigation;

he now endeavors to find histories which have this plan in view. In this search he meets with disappointment. In selecting Pufendorf as a possible model, he is confident that he will find the answers to a set of important questions: What were the forces of the country? What was its population? What was its ethnography? How were the arts developed? What were its laws, its economic status? The answers to these questions are what Voltaire seeks to establish in the analysis of any period of history for any country studied. They are, he maintains, essential to any historical study.

He next adopts the thought that a scientific approach to history similar to the method used in the study of nature is required. He writes in the *Nouvelles considérations*: "Peut-être arrivera-t-il bientôt dans la manière d'écrire l'histoire ce qui est arrivé dans la physique. Les nouvelles découvertes ont fait proscrire les anciens systèmes. On voudra connaître le genre humain dans ce détail intéressant qui fait aujourd'hui la base de la philosophie naturelle" (*Œuvres historiques*, p. 46). This approach, however, can be used only by posing to history a certain number of questions and exacting a definite reply. These questions are sketched in the *Nouvelles considérations:* "Quel a été le vice radical et la vertu dominante d'une nation; pourquoi elle a été puissante ou faible sur la mer; comment et jusqu'à quel point elle s'est enrichie depuis un siècle; . . . comment les arts, les manufactures se sont établies. . . . Les changements dans les mœurs et dans les lois seront enfin son grand objet" (*Œuvres historiques*, p. 48). The formula has at last been found. Voltaire, like Galileo, insists that history will not reveal her secret any more than nature unless the right questions are put to her. The questions, though, are not necessarily of a mathematical sort. Although some of them require statistical answers, in general they are of a demographic, economic, and geographic order. But answers to these questions must be supplemented both by cultural and technological successes. The arts and manufactures of a country are as important as its laws. All of these factors enter into its manners and reveal its spirit. Voltaire sees clearly that these are the major components of a civilization. In a letter to D'Argenson of 26 January 1740, he writes: "Il semble que, pendant 14 cents ans, il n'y ait eu dans les Gaules que des rois, des ministres et des généraux: mais nos mœurs, nos lois, nos coutumes, notre esprit ne sont-ils donc rien?"

In the preface to Volume III of the Walther edition of the *Histoire universelle*, Voltaire repeats in connection with Pufendorf the essential questions of history, but, as a literary man, he naturally is inclined to stress the importance of the sciences and the arts, especially poetry. This tendency he sums up laconically: "Je fis autant que je le pus des traductions exactes en vers des meilleurs endroits des poètes des nations savantes; je tâchai d'en conserver l'esprit. En un mot, l'histoire des arts eut la préférence sur l'histoire des faits."

Voltaire maintains that the application of these principles will transform history and affirms that that was his purpose in the *Siècle:* "Les lois, les arts, les mœurs ont été mon principal objet" (*Essai,* ed. Pomeau, II, 889). That is now, he proclaims, his purpose in approaching universal history, which requires the portrait, not just of one century, but of all centuries, not just the portrait of one country, but of all countries.

We come now to the main problem concerning Voltaire's treatment of history, that of his philosophy of history. The first thing critics are prone to do on entering upon this subject[16] is to warn that it is not wise to expect from Voltaire a philosophy of history in the sense in which we use the term today. Still, as Professor Dagens has pointed out, history for Voltaire being that of a philosophe, one might reasonably expect him to have established his principles upon firm philosophical ground. He did have a conception of history, and, although he was forced by circumstances and the limitations of his own knowledge to keep that conception open, it nevertheless became an essential part of the philosophy of the Enlightenment. Moreover, Voltaire himself was the first to use the term "philosophy of history." It is certainly true that he did not create a system explaining the historical process, as Hegel did. Yet he was not lacking in notions concerning the fundamental aspects of history, such as the purpose and nature of history, causation, determinism, progress, and decline. Moreover, as we have seen throughout our analysis of his works, he had very decided notions—though often he expressed them rather vaguely—about the factors which give history its reality. Indeed, for one so opposed to the idea of

[16] See J. Dagens, "La Marche de l'Histoire suivant Voltaire"; J. H. Brumfitt, *Voltaire Historian*; and J. H. Brumfitt, ed., *La Philosophie de l'histoire.*

a system, Voltaire in this case came close to conceiving of these factors as working organically and, to some extent, mechanically.

One would do well to ponder the formula suggested by Lanson in his *Voltaire*. For the historian Voltaire, history is an art, a science, and a philosophy. As an art, it resembles drama in structure: that is, it has an introduction, a development to a climax, and a denouement. It is like drama in tone also: that is, it is full of tension and produces a dramatic effect. As a science, it resembles the natural sciences, in that one can penetrate the phenomena only by observation, a judicious selection of the material, and a rigid method of analysis. As a philosophy, it is capable of passing from structure to form to meaning; in other words, the organization of the phenomena becomes organic, and, being organic, it becomes possible to bring out its inner reality and its total effect. Voltaire had understood the necessity of getting at this inner reality when he was working on the *Lettres philosophiques*. There, history was what happened at one time in one place to one people, in the various categories of life in which every individual in some degree or other participates. For Voltaire, these categories were religion, politics, and economics, philosophy, including science, literature and the beaux arts, and morality. Voltaire, however, gave more attention to religion, philosophy (including science), and literature than to morality, economics, and politics. And he hardly hinted that there was a category of the self. Still, even in a restricted way, he succeeded in showing that it is possible by the analysis of a category to learn something fundamental about a people. He also discovered that the fundamental characteristic of one category is a trait of the other categories as well. And, by comparing England and France, he came to the conclusion that England had a particular, definable personality which was quite different from that of the French.

It could be readily assumed that the first duty of a historian is to penetrate the historical personality of a people. That particular task is a large order, because there are so many peoples that have not been studied and because we do not, in any case, have a ready method for performing the task. Not many applications of the Voltairean method, used in the *Lettres philosophiques*, have been made to those analyses which we have, and they are consequently descriptive rather than evaluative; and they often consist in uncoordinated, unrelated facts. Even though they do arrive at a modest state of generalization, they rarely bring out the inner reality of these peoples. Voltaire, however, maintained that these studies must be made. The Chinese, the Persians, the Indians, the Babylonians had an inner reality which belonged in a peculiar way to each and to humanity.

In a way, this was the most disturbing discovery which Voltaire made, because it completely upset an assumption which until then reigned supreme—the assumption that man is everywhere the same and, consequently, that there is a uniformity of human nature and of human values. Brumfitt (*Voltaire Historian*, pp. 102-104) has well explained that, in dealing with this problem, Voltaire was caught between his rejection of innate ideas, which was a Cartesian concept, and his acceptance of a fundamental natural law, that is, a universal morality, a notion which had been rejected by Locke. Voltaire liked to identify his thought with Locke's and, of course, scorned the innate ideas of Descartes, which were the only possible source of a fundamental moral law. To rescue this latter notion, he proceeded in *Le Philosophe ignorant* to take Locke to task for his view, insisting that all men have an idea of justice and injustice which is the universal morality created by God and present in us all.

The effect of this stand creates much confusion in Voltaire's historical thinking. How can the historian seek the fundamental characteristic of a people in the categories of its living if the categories are constantly changing while the fundamental moral law is the same for everybody? The simple expedient of method (or, rather, purpose) becomes paramount.

Is it the task of the historian to bring out the changing and diverse attitudes of a people to the categories of living, or is it rather his task to point out the absurdities of these deviations from the fundamental character of men? Voltaire, as usual, tried to have it both ways. As a strict classicist, he wanted human nature to conform to a certain norm; as a strict neoclassicist, he knew that it is constantly changing according to the fluctuations of men's attitudes to the categories. Hence, any custom which does not conform with his norm is false, inexistent, and absurd, but any spirit which is the result of a people's categorical, organic way of living is an inner reality. Voltaire tried valiantly to prove the old French proverb: "plus ça change, plus c'est la même chose." But he also wanted to prove the obverse:

"plus c'est la même chose, plus ça change." Brumfitt attributes this difficulty to a "natural lack of psychological and historical imagination," and it is true that Voltaire along with his age suffered from this lack. Yet it is also true that no amount of psychological and historical imagination can adequately resolve the incompatibility between a God-given natural law and the particular mores of a people. Voltaire (still in conformity with his time) did as well as could be done by clinging to a set of abstract ideas (justice, freedom, beauty, truth, etc.) as ideals, and by devoting his attention to the changing categories and to the changing attitudes of each people in all times to its categories. And, having laid down the rules of prudence that we must not give credence to those things which are contradicted by common sense, that we must not accept those things which are obviously exaggerated, and that we must exercise the same distrust in studying the mores of a people that we employ in examining a peculiar fact, he set to work to study the relationships of a people to its categories.

This was the task which he set himself in the *Siècle de Louis XIV*. Some of the principles which he enunciates as guidelines are perfectly clear. To limit himself to a nation at the peak of its power, to study not only the ruler but the ruled, that is, to transfer the focus from the government to the people, to select not only wars and battles but achievements in economics and politics, and to mark out the great scientific discoveries, the new institutions, and the masterpieces of literature, music, and painting—all these principles represent an honest effort to distinguish between the important events and the mass of facts. Properly speaking, they constitute a clarification of method rather than an expression of a philosophy, but they clear the air so that the next move in philosophy can be made. But there are some real innovations in the *Siècle*. The restriction of a study to a century is, as we have said, one of them. The transference of interest from the ruler to the ruled is another. The desire to lessen the military, foreign affairs category in favor of the scientific, beaux arts category is a third. The attack against the category of religion is a fourth, but questionable one. The determination to shift the focus from what is happening to how it is happening is the really important philosophical point.

This resolve brings up naturally the problem of causation. Bossuet's explanation, which has always been accepted as the traditional Christian one, centers on the working of Providence through the Jewish people and the Church—what Pascal understood by the word "perpétuité." But Bossuet was much less categorical in his answer than we usually think, and Voltaire, whom we often quote to stress his opposition to the doctrine of Providence, was not as far removed from that view as his various statements lead us to believe. For instance, Bossuet's theory of Providence is tempered by his acceptance of free will, a problem that Voltaire struggled with, too. Moreover, inclination played a strong role in the attitudes of both men. Bossuet's fluid statement that Providence moves in unexpected ways, after human decision and human actions have been taken, would not be too unpalatable to the deist Voltaire. In fact, the dilemma of *Candide* in which Voltaire was caught was precisely this unexpected working of Providence in human affairs, or the failure to work when it was expected to do so.

Voltaire, however, did reduce the area where this unexpected interference may occur. Instead of accepting it as a statement of faith, he was inclined to admit it as a matter of fact. Indeed, he often reverted to the power, wisdom, and goodness of God wherever he could not explain an event rationally. Otherwise, he, like all his contemporaries, confined himself, in the problem of causation, to the question of relationships, of which that of man to the Deity is only one. From these relationships there arise problems of causation which he was very interested in examining. The first of these is the great man theory, the second is the disproportion between causes and effects, the third is Voltaire's own theory of categories, and the fourth is the theory of "esprit" and "mœurs."

Great men, according to Voltaire's definition, are "tous ceux qui ont excellé dans l'utile ou l'agréable," as opposed to the great "saccageurs de terre," who are merely heroes. In all probability Voltaire adopted the notion from the Abbé de Saint-Pierre, who had defined the great man in an essay entitled *Observations morales et politiques sur la vie de Charles XII roi de Suède et Pierre 1er, Empereur de Russie*. Voltaire, also, weighed the qualities of these two rulers and concluded that, of a king who ruined his country by useless wars and a ruler who elevated his country by all kinds of reforms, only the latter was a great man. Saint-Pierre had arrived at the same opinion without the hesitation of Voltaire. For him, Charles XII suffered precisely from the errors which Voltaire condemned in *Charles XII*: "Le Roi de Suède n'a jamais connu rien de grand, rien de louable, rien de désirable, à quinze ans que de montrer un grand courage et de grands talents pour la guerre, en donnant une licence effrénée à sa colère, à sa vengeance, et à son ambition pour les conquêtes" (Bibliothèque Nationale, N. Ac. fr., 11231, f. 49). Saint-Pierre noted that Peter, too, wanted to wage war but that he wanted to contribute to the happiness of his people as well (f. 49):

> Le Czar voulait de même faire beaucoup de bruit dans le monde par des conquêtes, mais ce qu'il avait au-dessus du Roi de Suède, c'est qu'il visait aussi à augmenter le bonheur de ses sujets, par établir des manufactures, par creuser des canaux, pour le commerce intérieur, par faire des ports, par construire des vaisseaux pour le commerce maritime, par établir des collèges et des académies pour faire cultiver dans ses états les sciences et les beaux-arts, et surtout l'art de la navigation.

All the same, Saint-Pierre pronounced that both were "hommes injustes qui manquent de lumières." Saint-Pierre applied the criterion of "grand homme" to all those to whom he assigned a role of importance in his *Annales*. His definition, which was based on the concept of "bienfaisance" to which Voltaire also subscribed, is very wordy, but at least quite complete (f. 52):

> J'entends par ce mot *grand homme* tout court, celui qui toujours fortement animé d'une grande ambition digne de louanges, c'est-à-dire, de désir, de la joie de surpasser de beaucoup ses pareils en talens et en vertus, emploie constamment avec un grand succès, un grand esprit, un grand courage, et de grands talents acquis à de grandes entreprises pour procurer selon son pouvoir de grands bienfaits aux hommes en général, ou à sa patrie en particulier, pour imiter l'Etre Parfait, et souverainement bienfaisant, pour lui plaire et pour en obtenir le Paradis.

With this criterion, Saint-Pierre not only weighed the merit of Charles XII and Peter but also contrasted Richelieu with Mazarin. He provided one additional idea, however: one can learn how to become a great man. In the *Annales*, he discussed the same problem in his analysis of Turenne and Condé and still came to a negative conclusion. The master himself, Louis XIV, he presented with some admiration, but his final judgment was that he was, because of his inconsistencies and his injustice, a "grand enfant," not a "grand homme"—a judgment which Voltaire vigorously rejected. However, Saint-Pierre heartily approved Colbert as a "grand homme," and with this opinion Voltaire concurred without difficulty.

The second theory is the disproportion between causes and effects. Pascal had presented the classical case in the remark concerning the length and shape of Cleopatra's nose. But, as Brumfitt points out, Bayle, Fontenelle, and even Montesquieu adopted the position, and, later in the nineteenth century, Scribe and others gave it a literary status. Bossuet went so far as to suggest that the little unknown factors are more important in the unrolling of events than we are prone to allow. In any event, it remains one of the most intriguing problems of modern history. As long as Voltaire was content with the great leader idea, as in *Charles XII*, he could explain events by stressing the importance of the king. But, the moment cultural and social forces became as important as kings and battles, the whole problem of causation was thrown open. This seems to have occurred with the *Siècle*. Voltaire was very anxious to prove that Louis XIV was a great leader, as we can see from, among other things, his letter to Lord Hervey. But he was ready to give credit to others also —Colbert, for instance, who was, as Valdruche had already noted, Voltaire's great hero, both for economic and cultural reasons. The thing to note, though, is that accident plays as much a role in the *Siècle* as it does in *Zadig*, with the result that the march of events depends upon two forces. There is, in fact, a third force, determining civilizational factors which operate to elevate a nation to power or to bring about its decline (see *Siècle*, Chapter XXXIX).

The third solution to the problem of causation which Voltaire was finally led to adopt is usually attributed to Montesquieu, and the best expression to that solution is said to have been given in the famous statement at the end of his *Considérations sur les causes de la grandeur et de la décadence des Romains* (1734): "Ce n'est pas la fortune qui domine le monde. . . . Il y a des causes générales, soit morales, soit physiques qui agissent dans chaque monarchie, l'élèvent, la maintiennent, ou la précipitent." Montesquieu endeavored to show in his study that Rome had an unprecedented series of successes as long as it was organized for war and devoted itself to a perpetual conflict. When, however, its boundaries were extended beyond its capacity to defend them, when its soldiers were no longer Romans but allies, when its warlike propensities were supplanted by the love of luxury and the desire for peace, when there occurred a breakdown in the respect for liberty and the love of equality which had been the underlying source of its patriotism, it was doomed by the very force of circumstances to succumb. Montesquieu even went so far as to maintain that, had it not been overwhelmed by the civil war between Caesar and Pompey or overrun by the barbarians of the North, it would have been laid low by some other rebellion and conquered by some other invasion. In reality, as Professor Shackleton has pointed out (*Montesquieu*, p. 75), by the time of the *Traité des devoirs*, Montesquieu had worked out a theory which, though not complete, contained the basic notions for causation in history. According to this concept, every nation develops a particular personality from its manners and customs; consequently, any variation in the "mœurs" entails a change in the personality of the country, and this change jeopardizes its grandeur and may bring about its decline. The theory, which is clearly expressed in Montesquieu's work, was not original with him. Ever since Fontenelle's *Origine des fables* and throughout the historical development of Bayle, Lenglet, and even Voltaire, as we have seen above, there had been the tendency to draw the personality of a society from its manners and customs.

The theory was, in reality, best expressed, not by Montesquieu or by Voltaire, but by Espiard in his *Essais sur le génie et le caractère des nations, divisés en six livres* (Bruxelles, 1743). The original work was issued in three volumes. In 1752, it was reworked and issued in two volumes at The Hague under the title *L'Esprit des nations*. The following year, another edition appeared at The Hague, again in two volumes. In 1769, it was taken over bodily by M. L. Castilhon, revised, and reprinted under the title *Considérations sur les causes physiques et morales de la diversité du génie, des mœurs, et du gouvernement des nations*. The work must have been known to Montesquieu, since a copy of the 1743 edition in three volumes now exists at the public library of Bordeaux, having belonged originally to one of Montesquieu's closest friends. Only the third volume of the 1743 edition is possessed by the Bibliothèque Nationale (R. 20581). Both the 1743 edition of three volumes and the 1753 edition of two volumes are in Voltaire's library. Indeed, of all the contemporary historians used by Voltaire, Lenglet and Espiard were certainly the two most influential, the former for establishing the historical method and the latter for showing how essential it was to apply this method in the study of civilization.

Espiard's treatise took its origin in the voyage literature of the sixteenth and seventeenth centuries, where the explorers endeavored to give a description of the manners and customs of the peoples they had discovered. Although many of these descriptions were too imaginary to be of great use in a scientific way, some were founded on close observation and intelligent reporting. Irrespective of the accuracy of the accounts, however, these analyses of foreign peoples left the impression that it was essential to find ways of getting acquainted with the various peoples of the world. No better means of doing this was discovered than analysis of the manners and customs of each country. An age deeply interested in how others lived could not resist this literature. In due time, there was assembled a whole body of documents upon the Persians, the Chinese, and the Indians. It became a game to characterize the citizens of a neighboring country. England, Holland, Italy, Germany, Spain—all were presented, each with its distinctive traits. A curious phenomenon occurred. The techniques developed in designating the manners of a primitive or exotic race were put to use also in defining the characteristics of the European peoples. It was a clear-cut case of learning to know one's self by knowing others.

Espiard's *Essais* constituted the fullest attempt to bring all this material together in some systematic way. The fundamental idea of this work is that every society has its own special "génie" around which is built all its activities. This "génie" is subject to four forces: climate, institutions, government, and, above all, manners and customs. Espiard judges that among these forces climate has a great bearing upon the spirit of a race and upon its manners. The effect of climate was not a new discovery. Bodin had discussed it at length long before in his *République* (1576), and, with the appearance of Du Bos's *Réflexions critiques sur la littérature et la peinture* (1719), it had become anew a widespread subject of discussion, which culminated in Montesquieu's *De l'esprit des lois*. On the strength of the great influence of climate upon customs, Espiard already feels justified in dividing the countries of Europe into Northern and Southern. The nations situated in warm climates—for example, Spain and Italy—are known for their sobriety and their temperance. In contrast, those who live in the colder regions seek to escape the melancholy to which they are condemned either by a "police ingénieuse et savante" or by trade, war, or invasions. Espiard concludes that, of all the influences upon the personality of a country, climate is the most important, "quoique ses influences puissent être adoucies et corrigées même."

The other influences are less constant. Institutions, for instance, which the author regards as a set of traditions, exercise a much greater authority upon Orientals, whereas European societies have merely preserved the fundamentals of their former customs. Education is everywhere a much weaker influence in modern than in past societies. Generally speaking, the author finds that in Europe the principles underlying the manners and customs of the inhabitants of one country are held in common by those of the other countries. They thus become characteristic of a European, rather than a particular, culture. A gradual merging of these principles occurs throughout the countries of Europe because of the universal freedom, the arts, trade, and travel. Espiard is one of the early theorists who are inclined to regard the civilizations of Europe as parts of one civilization. The particular institution of government, he finds, is less important for Europeans than for Asiatics. In France this is especially true, since there is hardly any relationship between the French government and French manners. The women, in fact, play a more important role in France in directing the manners and customs than the government. Religion is likewise of minor importance in Europe, whereas it is of paramount importance in Oriental, particularly Mohammedan, countries. Christianity, he observes could never influence the "génie" of the races as Mohammedanism, much more favorable to nature, has done. The author stresses that Christianity, in fact, with its insistence upon peace, is in contradiction with the warlike humor of European nations, "une contradiction qui n'a que trop contribué à limiter le pouvoir de la véritable religion." He notes as an aside (but it is an important observation) that in England the idea of freedom is the fullest that can be found in any place in the world.

It is Espiard's view that the character of a race—what he calls "le fond des mœurs"—does not change. However, in the nation itself, there are all kinds of variations in habits, amusements, styles. These particular variations are of little interest to him; it is the larger generalization which he is seeking. He concludes, for instance, that in the manners of the ancients are to be found two particular resources for virtue: application to study, and work in the fields. After careful discussion, he chooses honor as the sovereign law of European nations, particularly France. He remarks that there was among the Romans a strong tendency to suicide, and he adds—what was a commonly accepted myth of the time—that the present-day British have a similar inclination, whereas the French, "plus sage et plus religieux," have a horror of this solution. These general observations of nations chosen more or less at random lead him to the conclusion that each people adopts a characteristic quality or qualities which it endeavors to have accepted by others as its peculiar traits: the Romans affected gravity, a knowledge of organization, and a deep sense of decency; the English pride themselves on their freedom of thought; the French boast of social graces and the social virtues of gentlemen. Once a nation has adopted its peculiar national trait, says Espiard, it is forced to cultivate this image to a certain extent. It is not easy, though, for the student of civilization to select these characteristic traits: to do so successfully requires a rather close examination, not just of one period—certainly not its period of glory or that of its decline—but of a relatively long sweep of periods. In this way, one gets a better perspective upon the "génie" of the people. One will understand then that there is no period absolutely sterile in arts and talents and that decline is not at all attributable to a weakening in the "génie" of the race but must be ascribed rather to the circumstances or to a change in the climate.

Espiard here makes a study of the causes underlying the sterility of the French in his day. It was a problem with which both Montesquieu and Voltaire were preoccupied. He concedes that undoubtedly the quality of the arts has diminished, "sans qu'il soit survenu de changement dans l'air" (III, 67). He argues that to each example of a decline can be assigned different causes—that is, it is difficult to ascertain a general cause for the whole phenomenon of deterioration. This does not mean that a general cause does not exist. Indeed, he proposes that it be sought in some scientific proof: "il faudrait après ici une preuve directe tirée de la physique, plutôt que des exemples qui peuvent recevoir diverses explications." Then, too, even if there has been a diminution in talent, which he is all too ready to concede, he insists that there is also compensation: physics and experimental science are now developed at a much higher level than in the past, and, in the arts themselves, music is now much improved by the skill and the large number of musicians. He admits that letters have deteriorated but points out that philosophy has become more important: "Généralement parlant, on raisonne aujourd'hui et même dans les cercles brillants formés pour le plaisir" (III, 71). Espiard does not differ from the position Voltaire held around 1736-1746: the decline is in the area of literature and the arts. It is fully, or to a great extent, compensated by a development of science and philosophy and even, adds Espiard, by an increase in erudition and progress in morality—"dans les mœurs et les vertus," as he puts it (III, 78). The whole theory of decline and compensation is here united with the doctrine of progress: "Que si l'on voulait suivre les compensations et les progrès de la raison et de la vertu dans tous les siècles, on trouverait de nouvelles preuves de cette vérité" (III, 78). Briefly stated, Espiard lays down two rules for the change in the spirit of a nation. First, although the spirit, and even the character, of a people may be modified in some of its aspects by a loss in its talent, there will be compensations. A decline in art may be counter-balanced by an increase in science, poverty of good literature may be compensated by an increase in philosophy; one art, such as the theatre, may appear momentarily exhausted, while another, such as music, may appear very flourishing. Second, the measure of civilization lies not so much in the description of the decline as in the seizing of the pulsating rhythm of change and progress. From this point of view, it will be understood that men have always begun in great simplicity, in their manners and customs, that they then perfect in time their society, their commerce with other societies, their morality, war, and the arts, and that superiority in these areas passes from one nation to another. From the Orient, which had the talent to invent the arts, it passed to Greece, which was endowed with the talent to perfect them: "L'Orient propre à l'invention des arts, ne semble pas destiné à les perfectionner. Ainsi la Grèce ajouta aux éléments qu'elle avait reçus de l'Asie, la philosophie, l'amour de la liberté, la qualité des mœurs, la méthode et la manière d'écrire" (III, 80-81). From the Greeks, hegemony in the arts passed to the Romans, and from the Romans to modern European man. Adding to all that he has received from the ancients, all that their experiences and researches have accumulated, he has far surpassed these ancients in the natural sciences, in method, in history, and, adds Espiard, "dans tout ce qui s'appelle du nom de lumières spéculatives" (III, 85).

It seems to me that the remainder of Espiard's first treatise is given over to the problem of "rapports." What, for instance, is the best government for favoring the arts? What is the government which produces the largest number of extraordinary citizens? What type of government supplies the greatest amount of resources to its citizens? Espiard distinguishes three kinds: two of them monarchies (limited by a senate, as in England, limited by the "mœurs," as in France) and a republican form which is "composée des grands ou des principaux citoyens, avec le peuple." He evidently accepts that each of these types may change into another, since he asserts that the most favorable moment for arts and letters is that which occurs when republican freedom is turning to monarchy (Pericles is his example). On the other hand, the republic not only is capable of producing the maximum number of outstanding citizens but can also offer them a greater abundance of resources.

Espiard's *L'Esprit des nations* (2 vols., La Haye, 1753) is a more complete and better organized work than the earlier *Essais*, although practically all the material of the earlier work appears to have been incorporated in the *Esprit*. In the introduction, the author acknowledges that he has made a study of the conclusions drawn from the travel literature and from the universal histories which he has read. He confesses that the interesting part of this study is not the accumulation of facts but the organization of general reflections. What he wants to achieve is the portrait of the "esprit général des nations." Beneath this "general spirit" he places the physical causes—imagination and climate—and a certain number of what he calls the simple ideas, or the consequences of the moral causes. There are five of these simple axioms: (1) man is born for society and action, (2) society cannot exist without women, (3) all nations are in a general state of war, (4) freedom is the most perfect state of man and exercises the greatest influence upon the intelligence and upon the heart, particularly in science and morality, and (5) prudence, insofar as states are concerned, is preferable to philosophy.

With these general axioms, Espiard now proceeds to define some of his concepts. The "génie" of nations is the spirit which results from the combination of customs, opinions, and temperament; that is, "génie" and "esprit" are the same thing, both being derived from previous traditions, actions, and opinions. The combination of these elements is what we mean by "mœurs." The elements which enter into the formation of "génie" are language, custom, usages, figure, taste, and religion. But climate is the fundamental determinant of "génie." It controls "la qualité du sang, la nature des aliments, la qualité des eaux et des végétaux." These, in turn, are the factors which determine the temperament. They are analyzable only through "la vie des habitans, la sobriété, la préparation des alimens." Combined, they bring out the dominant trait of a social group: Dutch frugality, English melancholy, French gaiety, which comes from the delicacy of wines. France, thanks to its gaiety, presides over festivities in the courts of all Europe.

Espiard gives a careful analysis of this French gaiety. It is as the lightheartedness of woman, entirely on the surface, and, because it is not rooted in the soul, it is easily diffused. Espiard defines it as a "joie publique et tumultueuse." It is manifest not only in the French temperament but in the language and the dress. It has a curious facility for imitating, without being ridiculous, foreign traits, foreign style, even foreign dress. Whatever it adopts immediately becomes a part of its character, whereas a foreign group attempting to imitate its traits becomes at once ridiculous. Its manners and its well-controlled passions, restrained by strict social rules of conduct, as well as its customs and its rules of etiquette, are completely balanced. The Frenchman places his happiness in the opinion which others hold of him. He literally shouts his pleasures to the world. Finally, this gaiety is a "flamme de mille couleurs, passagère, brillante et légère." It resembles, as Voltaire had said in the *Mondain,* those wines "pétillans, légers, remplis d'esprits, mais sujets à s'évaporer." It contrasts with Italian and Spanish seriousness and with English melancholy, "furieux de plaisirs."

Espiard centers his analysis upon these four countries in order to provide examples of the way the scholar may penetrate the reality of a society, but he is far from limiting himself to them. He analyzes the Oriental societies as well. In general, this exercise in the analysis of a nation's personality is only a means to more relevant observations about civilization. One of his striking claims is that the personalities of all the countries of Europe are similar. It is true that each has its own peculiar traits; there is, nonetheless, a "correspondence universelle" established by trade, social traits, intrigues, politics, science, and a general harmony unknown to antiquity. Travelers carry the traits of one country into another and those of both back to their native land. Wars transport not only men but ideas, customs, and even climate. All of these forces contribute to the formation of a European character. "Il ne reste d'inaltérable que le fond, la base du caractère."

However, this base is sufficiently diverse to warrant some distinctions. There is a difference between the inhabitants of the Northern climates and those of the South. The former have "une complexion moins tendre" than the Southerners and the Orientals; they are better qualified for war. Actually, Espiard prefers to Northerners and Southerners those of the temperate zones, to whom nature has given the necessary prudence and justice to preserve empires and govern them well. It is true that they have less skill in science and in mechanical inventions, but they are very adept at affairs. They are less distinguished in the arts, especially music and painting, but very proficient in jurisprudence, medicine, eloquence, dialectics, comedy which reveals the manners of men, military discipline, navigation, and commerce. Espiard tries to picture them in terms of France, but he succeeds only in terms of Rome—these temperate countries are the active powers. By contrast, Southerners delight in the contemplative life, in speculative philosophy, scholasticism, study of the occult, mathematics, religion, and morality. Northerners who are expecially adept in mechanical things have not excelled in any degree until very recent times in the formation of government. Espiard concludes that historians favor the Northern countries, while philosophers favor the Southern. This attempt at classification is interesting as a prelude to both Montesquieu, with his tripartite division, and Mme de Staël. When the theory of climate reached its climax, the characteristics of the different areas turned out to be precisely the opposite of what Espiard saw.

The second book of the *Esprit des nations* is concerned with the moral causes of "génie." Espiard finds them in what he calls the "institutions," defined as the "première législation ou la forme que donnent les anciennes lois et coutumes à une nation." According to his view, the legislators imprint upon a people a virtue which in time becomes a "passion publique." It is what Montesquieu liked to think of as the education for the principle of a society. In Rome, for instance, education for the military life of the state was a physical, agricultural education; in modern times, it is directed entirely to science. Like Montesquieu, Espiard is led to inquire what the fundamental principle of Rome is, and he answered, just as Montesquieu did: "Rome naquit dans la religion de la guerre." This principle never varied throughout the history of the Empire. In the beginning, it operated in the training of the soldier and the farmer; in later years, it worked when the Romans wanted to be known for their seriousness, for their science of government, and for the decency of their morals. Hence, the objectives of a civilization may vary, but the fundamental principle remains. There was, however, a difficulty: at a given moment the style of expression, which ordinarily reveals the way of thinking, changed. It is here that the law of compensation was brought into play. The style of literary expression weakened, but architecture and sculpture achieved its climax, and jurisprudence flourished. "Cette bienséance et ce sérieux qui étaient le fond du caractère romain, ne se perdirent jamais."

Espiard now risks some general observations on the study of a nation's "esprit." It is certain that that which characterizes a nation does not vary, though its ways of manifesting itself may change. If perchance it did undergo alteration, the change would destroy that society. It is the key to an understanding of the characteristics and explains all the contradictions of history.

Returning to his analysis of France, Espiard notes that many foreigners visit France to complete their education. They are attracted to France because it has spread its "grâces, les douceurs des mœurs, et donné l'esprit de société à toute l'Europe." This, properly speaking, is what we call "urbanity," which consists in a suppleness of spirit, enabling the French to assume the characters of others, and the appearance of virtue. It is a natural inclination to oblige our neighbors when our interests are not involved. (See also Book II, Chapters X-XV.)

Espiard is now willing to assert that there are three institutions of great importance in characterizing a nation: politics, religion, and the arts.

The section upon politics as an element of a nation's spirit is extremely important. The development which Espiard gives the subject has much in common with Montesquieu's approach. The author examines first the nature of small republics, moves on to a comparison between ancient and modern polities, and devotes some time to studying the governments of China and Japan. He notes that some nations possess an inclination to despotic government, whereas in others the love of liberty is very strong. He asks, finally, what would be the most suitable government for Europeans, but he apparently could not give a clear answer to this question.

He agrees with Locke that the state of nature is a state of freedom. He is committed to the idea of the growth of a European political society, a real European community. The Greeks first laid the foundations of public law for such a society, but the invasion of barbarians threatened the whole structure. In time, however, public law reappeared, and a form of government developed unknown to antiquity. From feudalism was derived both the point of honor and the social instinct. In the Orient the harem was the precursor of despotism, whereas in Europe the union of masculine virtue and feminine charm made possible gentler, freer "mœurs." The countries of Europe submitted to the constant change, unlike the ancients, who resisted all change.

From this description, the author derives the following principles. In a despotism there is a sterility of customs because woman has no freedom, the point of honor is unknown, the dominating principle is pride, property rights are scarcely ever sanctioned, and no permanent nobility exists. As a result of these traits, the country is subject to constant revolutions, and the various parts of the government are in a continual languor. In a European country, on the other hand, the distinct difference lies in the love of freedom, which does vary according to the form of government but exists in a degree in all. Espiard attempts to deduce these necessary principles of freedom. A large monarchy to be solid must appear natural; a little republic must appear unique. There can be no liberty without a recognition of equality. There are, in fact, three kinds of liberty: a philosophical freedom, founded upon principles of humanity, especially by the Greeks; political liberty, characteristic of Rome, Venice, and aristocratic states, organized with the preservation of a state's laws in view; and, finally, natural liberty, founded on the equality among men. This latter Espiard sees as the freedom of the European peoples.

It should be stressed that all the historians of the time, including Espiard, really set themselves an impossible task. Not only did they want to establish a priori the notions of a true government, that is, an ideal government; they were also very anxious that these notions conform to the actual conditions of government as it existed. Moreover, they insisted that this ideal state and the actual state should both be derivatives of the governments of antiquity. They really exacted that the theory, practice, and historical development of government should be in harmony. They wanted to show an evolution of the state, to justify at the same time a scale of values, and to establish some general, but solid political principles. It was this preoccupation which led Espiard to see in natural liberty the core of all political phenomena, which in his opinion was phenomenologically exact, necessary to all nations, and essential to all freedmen. This analysis led then to the conclusion concerning the best government for a European: "généralement parlant, on peut assurer, que tous les peuples de l'Europe ont un germe de principes républicains, et que jamais aucun n'est tombé dans l'idolâtrie civile et politique, que nous présente l'histoire des Grecs, et celle des Romains en monarchie" (I, 232).

Espiard offers the French government as the characteristic European state. It is founded on a background of reasonable obedience, and everything about it, except the sovereign, may be questioned. The Frenchman believes he is free and wants others to believe it. He has a fitting respect for his sovereign and a keen desire to be rewarded by some appointment. French honor is an excellent principle of government, but it is subject to some vice: it dissipates the public funds, it is immoderate in its gifts, and it is naturally "frondeur" as regards the law. The author concludes that there is an incompatibility between the French character and a republican constitution. Consequently, we would have to hope that a republican constitution would cure the political weaknesses in the French character, or we would have to admit that the French nation is incapable of governing itself.

Religion is the second great factor in establishing the personality of a people. In fact, Espiard notes that, "de toutes les causes des mœurs, il n'en est point qui ait autant d'efficacité que la religion." He conceives of the development of civilization very much as Fontenelle had and as Voltaire did in the *Philosophie de l'histoire*. At the beginning, everything was mythical, and then the earth became populated with divinities. The two primary instincts were love and the social urge. Man was by nature a farmer. Those of the North were busied with war. Those who stood out were called "enfants des Dieux." Then came metempsychosis, which spread throughout the Orient. Everything became "merveilleux," and superstition was rampant everywhere. Outside of Europe, all religions were flooded with miracles. All religions came out of the Orient. But a distinction must be made: Oriental nations have insisted that the highest point of wisdom lies in silent contemplation; Europeans, for their part, believe that the highest wisdom lies in the administration of public affairs. Mohammed came forth with the most terrible religion of all. All ancient religions were filled with symbolism, since every event was the prefiguration of another. But eventually a spirit of tolerance arose. Espiard notes that republics lend themselves better than monarchies to the spirit of universal religion. He concedes that there is a relationship between the character of a religion and tolerance, and, although he is not a partisan of that doctrine himself, he notes that the Dutch, with their spirit of tolerance, know how to turn out good citizens.

The last of the important factors in bringing out the spirit of a race is art. After some factual observations—for instance, that Homer's imagery is impossible in modern poetry, that France is superior to all countries in eloquence—Espiard attempts to define the outstanding artistic quality of the French. He finds that they have the art of saying just what is necessary, free from poverty of expression and from superlative enthusiasm. This "juste mesure" is contrasted with the unrestrained expression of the English, which can be best seen in the theatre. It is clear that they lack all "bienséances," conduct, gentle passions. France is free from these defects with its elegance of form. Espiard does not say so in so many words, but he seems convinced that what characterizes French civilization most is its art.

I have presented a detailed exposition of Espiard's two works because of my conviction that they not only represent the climax of historical thinking in the eighteenth century but give the clearest theoretical organization to that thought. Espiard's theory of history sums up the whole development of history from Bayle and Fontenelle to Montesquieu and Voltaire. His two works give a clear structure to the theory of history and provide ample illustrative material, with facts collected from travel literature and continual reference to the major European countries, to support the theory. They are not histories, but they lay the groundwork for historical thinking.

Voltaire, whose interest was in the writing and the making of history and whose one special desire was to avoid any systematic organization of theory and, above all, a system of philosophy in history, could profit by Espiard's efforts. Indeed, one of the curious facts of the time was the way Espiard explained, without knowing it, what both Montesquieu and Voltaire were doing. Voltaire, as we have seen, made numerous attempts in his prefaces, introductions, and short articles to explain his own activities. When collected and analyzed, as we have tried to do in this essay, they offer an impressive demonstration of what underlay this "new" history.[17]

The fundamental idea in Voltaire's concept of history is that man has the responsibility to make and to enjoy his world. He can only do so by using his mind. But the human mind is not free to make the world *ab ovo*, so to speak. It is always conditioned by the three factors of climate, government, and religion, and the way it coordinates these factors will produce the "génie" of the person—that is, what he is as an active personality responding to his conditions. The response is what history is. Voltaire insists that it must always be consistent, continuous, and organic. Its one active quality is that it produces revolutions—that is, change—which offer additional challenges to the human mind. The revolution which is constantly occurring in one

---

[17] See J. H. Brumfitt, *Voltaire Historian*; C. Rihs, *Voltaire, Recherches sur les origines du matérialisme historique*; and Pomeau's introduction to his edition of Voltaire's *Essai sur les mœurs*.

human mind is present in the aggregate human mind of a society. This collective revolution also creates a collective personality, a "génie" of the people, and its response to its conditions is the origin of its "mœurs," its usages, its "esprit." There are thus two histories of the human mind, one for each human mind and one for the collective human mind of the society. There are two "génies," one for each personality and one for the collective personality of the group. There are likewise two "esprits," the "esprit humain" of each individual and the "esprit des nations." By responding to its conditions, that is to say, to the categories of its living—each "esprit" creates new conditions: these are the revolutions which change constantly man's manners and customs, his political and social institutions, his artistic creations. These changes are the source of a new spirit, which is no longer the drive to creation but the resultant creation itself. Thus, the human mind is not only the power to act but also the resultant action. The thought is the drive to creation, but it is likewise the thing created. History, therefore, is literally the movement of ideas as they create ever new possibilities for living, which we call revolutions. It always involves two things: the release of creative energy, and the drive for power. History is that life which is striving for its utopia and that utopia which progress in the striving makes possible. This is what, in his Introduction to the *Essai*, Voltaire seems to mean by "l'énigme du monde." The mystery is no longer man's place in the divine plan—which, of course, is not to be denied, even though this mystery can have no meaning for the human mind. Its mystery lies now in the transformation of human thought into creative energy. What man thinks is what he is; what he is, he says; and what he says, he does. In the final analysis, history is an artistic process in which the living of a life is to be equated with the making of a work of art. This work of art is likewise two things: it is, first of all, the art product, the good things of life, and, as such, it is also, collectively, the "art" of living. We have a word for that now: we call it "civilization." In Voltaire's day, the thing, but not the word, existed.

9. BIBLICAL CRITICISM

WE COME NOW TO AN ACTIVITY at Cirey which was of paramount importance to Voltaire's subsequent career but which has hitherto been ill-defined: critical deism. The whole movement of critical deism in France was, in fact, shrouded in clandestinity because of the censorship. Voltaire was merely one of the many individuals who were interested in the movement but were unwilling to accept the risk of openly expressing that interest. We now have a fairly good record of critical deistic works which circulated in manuscript during the first half of the century.[18] Although we do not yet have a complete list of these clandestine manuscripts, we do know well over a hundred in France which were copied and distributed among the public, sometimes in surprisingly large numbers. We have a fairly good idea of the manner of distribution, the names of the writers, and the period in the century (1720-1740) when they became most frequent and apparently most popular. For the most part, they were derived from Spinoza's *Tractatus theologico-politicus* (1670). The *Tractatus* was, at any rate, the model of the genre, and, in fact, one of the manuscripts which circulated was a translation of the *Tractatus* itself. The writers whom we know to have dabbled or even become thoroughly committed to this kind of activity were Boulainvilliers, Meslier, an individual whom we can identify only as "Le militaire philosophe" and who has sometimes been thought to be Saint-Hyacinthe, Fréret, Mirabaud, Dumarsais, and Lévesque de Burigny. The manuscripts which were of major importance to the movement, from the point of view both of the quality of the criticism and of popularity with the public, were *Le Militaire philosophe*; Meslier's *Testament*; the *Vie et Esprit de Spinoza* (often called *Les Trois imposteurs*), the *Examen de la religion*, and the *Analyse de la religion*, with the *Notes* and the *Preuves* attached thereto, these three last works being often attributed to Dumarsais; the *Examen critique des apologistes de la religion chrétienne* and the *Lettre de Thrasibule à Leucippe*,

[18] See G. Lanson, "Questions diverses sur l'histoire de l'esprit philosophique en France avant 1715"; I. Wade, *The Clandestine Organization and Diffusion of Philosophic Ideas in France, 1715-1750*; J. S. Spink, *French Free-thought from Gassendi to Voltaire*; N. L. Torrey, *Voltaire and the English Deists.*

thought to be by Fréret; and a series of *Opinions des anciens* on matters taken up in the *Bible* (the nature of the soul, the formation of the world, the divinity of Christ), attributed to Mirabaud. Of the hundred or so manuscripts which circulated, a score contain practically all the pertinent criticism, which was repeated in the others. A manuscript of a foreign work of this sort which had a very significant influence was a French translation of Woolston's *Six Discourses on Miracles*. A few other manuscripts were also translations of English deistic treatises, notably, Toland's *Panthéisticon* and a treatise attributed to Mandeville.

There are several traits of the movement which should be stressed. It has been shown that it was a bona fide, well-organized intellectual movement, at the center of which were a number of people belonging to a coterie, which formed a loosely connected nucleus. The writers were prepared to discuss either a particular aspect of religion (miracles, prophecies, the establishment of the Church, the divine mission of Christ, the morality of the Scriptures, the Christian martyrs, the continuity of history in the Bible) or all of these aspects together. Since these special features had been presented as proofs of the divinity of Christianity, these clandestine writers submit them to a rigorous examination, by testing the accuracy and credibility of the facts as they are related in the Scriptures. Taken together, the combined essays offer evidence of an unconscionable number of errors in the Bible—errors in scientific fact, in computation, in geography, in chronology—as well as all kinds of false miracles and false prophecies supported by false martyrs. The general conclusion reached is, like the Spinozistic conclusion of the *Tractatus*, that the Bible is a work directed to the spiritual needs of one race, the Jewish race. It has to be interpreted in the light of the "mœurs" of that race. It cannot be accepted by others as the foundation of morality or of political and religious organization. Whenever it is so used, it will prove to be filled with factual errors and prejudices common to one people. Its support of one religion should not be permitted to invalidate natural, universal religion. Its dogma, its organization of the Church, its priesthood, and its ceremonies should not be accorded any validity beyond its community. Persecutions by its devotees should not be permitted, since it lacks all authority for these acts. Real religion is natural religion; real morality is founded upon fraternity and the Golden Rule; real law is the extension of natural law.

These conclusions carried with them implications of a far-reaching nature, which we are wont to forget. For instance, the whole institutional organization in Christian countries had for centuries depended for its authenticity upon the divine character of the Scriptures. There is no exaggeration in insisting that the Bible embraced all aspects of Christian life with as much thoroughness as the Koran now embraces all aspects of Mohammedanism. The foundations of morality were derived naturally from the Ten Commandments. The nature of all economic activity, the divine right of kingship, the whole institution of religion in its organizational hierarchy, the cult, the ritual, the dogma, and the continuity of history and knowledge, as well as belief, were all derived from the Bible. Any attempt to invalidate its authenticity could bring about inevitable modifications in all the categories of living. For instance, Bossuet's *La Politique tirée de l'Ecriture Sainte* is a clear-cut statement of the way politics depended upon the Bible. If the Bible was questioned as a relevant source of political theory, a whole new concept of political theory and practice would have to be devised. Thus, the questioning of the accuracy, the validity, the reliability of the whole Bible could easily upset the accepted order of things. Just as it was thought to give the history of events, so it was thought to provide the standard of moral conduct and to be at the fountainhead of all legitimate human institutions. An attack against its veracity, therefore, could transform the whole Christian way of life. In many respects, this is just what happened. Thus, we commonly interpret the whole movement as a destructive blow at Christianity, as, indeed, it was. Entailed in it, however, was not only the destruction of a way of life which had served humanity for centuries but also the creation of another way of life which was judged more acceptable than that of the past.

In addition to threatening the destruction, or the impairment, of previous institutions, this movement brought into sharp focus a whole long line of problems which had been discussed off and on in the past but had not yet been resolved. The question of tolerance in religion, for instance, which had been debated back and forth, was put in a prime position in the title of Spinoza's *Tractatus*. The mere assertion that it is the obligation of the state to enforce tolerance among religious sects removes a certain amount of authority from the religious sphere and gives it to the political sphere. Moreover, if a change of this sort were made, other questions would have to be answered. If the state has the obligation to enforce tolerance, does it have the authority to support a religious organization or to reject one? Does it have the authority to declare that civil, political life is entirely free from religious life and that these two aspects of living should be kept separate? If the institutions are separate, which one should be entrusted with the education of the citizens? Which should be in charge of directing moral conduct? These questions of relationships, once started, are limitless. Each revision extends to other relationships until finally the whole set-up is reconstituted. It is this type of chain reaction which makes a work like Spinoza's *Tractatus* of supreme importance.

The *Tractatus* was the greatest single influence on the writers of the period. So great was its impact, in fact, that one is tempted to see in the whole movement a gigantic manifestation of Spinozism triumphant over other forms of thought. When one reflects that Spinoza's reaction to the Jewish and Christian religions—if one may judge by Spinoza's correspondence with Oldenburg—was rather analogous to Voltaire's attitude toward the Christian religion, it is easy to understand why the *Tractatus* became the model for this movement. Spinoza regarded the religion of his day as a threat to the development of philosophy. He resented the persecution to which theologians subjected philosophers, and he decided that the "superstition" which motivated their activity would have to be attacked. He set out singlehandedly to analyze, in as scientific a way as possible, the facts of the Bible, using not only his knowledge of the Hebrew tongue and his close acquaintance with the manners and customs of his forebears but every conceivable technique of history and geography as well.

We have studied in a previous work the way the Spinoza of the *Tractatus* first attracted the attention of Boulainvilliers, who was led to investigate the *Ethica*, and even to compose an *Essay de métaphysique* with the *Œuvres posthumes* as his guide, as well as a short *Traité des trois imposteurs* which summed up Spinoza's main philosophical points. Moreover, we have seen how Boulainvilliers introduced the *Tractatus* to his group and how first one and then another—Fréret, Dumarsais, Mirabaud, Lévesque de Burigny—entered into the sort of investigation Spinoza had inaugurated. When we realize that more than a hundred of these treatises were composed along similar lines, some of them extremely long and full, others very short and dealing with one or two problems, we can have no difficulty in understanding why, taken together, they had such far-reaching consequences and gave such a powerful impetus to the movement. What is more, they could easily be copied and distributed to an influential public, for French society was organized precisely so that a small but powerful elite could be reached.

There was an English deism, also, which had arisen long before this critical deism of the last third of the seventeenth century in France. It began with Herbert of Cherbury and in many respects corresponded to the libertinism of Gassendi, La Mothe le Vayer, and Naudé in France. Lord Herbert's *De Veritate* had, indeed, attracted the attention of Gassendi, who had submitted it to rather stringent criticism. Voltaire frequently referred to Lord Herbert's work, but, to all intents and purposes, it was of little use to him. Torrey (*Voltaire and the English Deists*, p. 2) notes that Voltaire's constructive deism was undoubtedly French in origin. It is well to recall, however, that the constructive deism of Lord Herbert can be traced in the works of Dryden, Shaftesbury, Tindal, Trenchard, Gordon, Pope, and Bolingbroke and that, insofar as it penetrated the works of these writers, it exercised, though indirectly, some influence on the formation of Voltaire's thought. Its most important contribution was the establishment of a natural religion, or rather a natural law, and a natural morality which made deism a possible replacement for the presumed defects in Christian thinking. The argument ran as follows: the seven proofs of the divinity of Christianity are no longer valid (or at least one of them is invalid); consequently, with the breakdown in the arguments drawn from miracles, prophecies, martyrs, morality, and so on, it is now impossible to attribute validity to Christianity; therefore, one should fall back upon natural religion, which is the religion of all, supported by the law of reason, which is the law of God, that is, natural law. In this roundabout way, the English constructive deists, just as the French "libertins," found in the threatened breakdown of formal religion justification for the establishment of a natural, universal, moral religion. Although the whole movement was built up along these lines in both England and France,[19] one should not forget the tremendously important role Locke played at the end of the seventeenth century not only in uniting English constructive deism to French constructive deism (through Sir Herbert, on the one hand, and Gassendi-Bernier, on the other) but also in fostering a kind of critical deism.

Voltaire does not seem to have stressed Locke's deistic tendencies, having given only a casual notice to the *Reasonableness of Christianity*, with the statement that Locke was talking about another kind of religion. He does not seem, either, to have used to any great extent Toland, whose contribution to the deistic debate consisted chiefly in his use of the historical argument in connection with the apochryphal works and his theories on the origins of belief. Indeed, although Voltaire gives a sketch of Toland in the *Lettres sur Rabelais*, it is doubtful that he ever knew the *Christianity not Mysterious*, the *Life of Milton*, or the *Amyntor*. Although he does make a reference to the *Lettres à Seréna* (1768), he shows but little interest in it, while the *Panthéisticon*, which actually circulated in translation in France, and the *Tetradymus* left no impression whatever upon him. All told, Torrey is quite correct in judging that Toland had a negligible influence on the development of Voltaire's thought and writings, even though he did occupy a position of prominence in English deism.

Anthony Collins, on the other hand, was much better known to Voltaire. Four of the Englishman's works—the *Recherches philosophiques sur la liberté de l'homme* (1720), the *Discourse on Free-thinking* (1713), the *Discourse on the Grounds and Reasons of the Christian Religion* (1737), and the *Scheme of Literal Prophecy Considered* (1727)—had considerable influence on him. The *Recherches,* which he doubtless knew in Desmaizeaux's translation in the *Recueil,* was useful to him in putting in order his ideas on free will, which he had borrowed from Locke. He was impressed by the *Discourse on Free-thinking* because of its audacity. Torrey notes that Voltaire almost certainly read this discourse in the late thirties

---

[19] See L. Stephen, *History of English Thought in the Eighteenth Century,* and R. Pintard, *Le Libertinage érudit dans la première moitié du XVII⁰ siècle.*

"during the period of his metaphysical researches, along with Newton, Locke and Clarke, but [that] the influence was general rather
than detailed, early rather than late" (*Voltaire and the English
Deists*, p. 47). In spirit and in method, the two were similar in their
attacks on miracles, their belittling of the Jews, and their treatment
of contradictions in the early history of the Church. The crux of the
influence, however, lay in the *Grounds and Reasons* and the
Scheme of Literal Prophecy, both of which Voltaire annotated.
There are some ambiguities, however. Although he had these books
and annotated them, nowhere did he connect Collins's treatment of
the prophecies with his own discussion of the subject. More interestingly still, Voltaire's prophecies, which he treats in the *Dictionnaire philosophique*, differ from those selected by Collins. But they
do not differ from those selected over and over again by the French
deists. Indeed, what interested Voltaire in Collins's books was, not
the treatment of the prophecies, but the inquiry into the authenticity of the Pentateuch.

The situation with Thomas Woolston is entirely different. Voltaire
knew that the *Six Discourses on the Miracles* (1727-1729) were being published when he was in England. He had the French translation of them in his library. Mme du Châtelet's mind was saturated
with the Englishman's comments on the miracles, and she and Voltaire used them to the fullest. Torrey remarks, for instance, that borrowings from the *Discourses on the Miracles* can be found in nearly
every work that Voltaire wrote against Christianity. Voltaire re-
sorted to quoting Woolston in the original English, apparently so
that he could not be accused of having invented such crude, blas-
phemous expressions. Torrey, who has studied carefully the use of
these miracles, finds that it occurs for the first time in the *Sermon des
cinquante*, where a whole page is given over to six Woolston miracles. Applications of Woolston's treatment of the miracles reappear
in the *Catéchisme de l'honnête homme* (1763), the *Traité sur la
tolérance* (1763), the *Questions sur les miracles* (1765), the *Questions
de Zapata* (1767), and the *Examen important de Milord Bolingbroke*
(1767), and over and over again thereafter. Some miracles are employed over a score of times. Voltaire had favorite ones, such as the
fig tree and the swine, to which he added the temptation on the
mountain, one that did not occur in Woolston's work. In addition,

Voltaire showed some predilection for Woolston's spirit, as well as for his material.

Along with Woolston, Voltaire and Mme du Châtelet showed a special preference for Tindal, the author of the *Rights of the Christian Church Asserted* and *Christianity as Old as Creation*. Here the influence was restricted for the most part to Chapters XII and XIII of the *Christianity as Old as Creation*. Voltaire put place markers in his copy at these chapters, and Mme du Châtelet, as Pomeau has shown, took a particular interest in this section, too. The argument proposed by Tindal was simple: we should learn to distinguish between religion and superstition; the only way we can do so is by using our reason, which will disclose that God gave laws to all mankind; thus, the only authentic religion is natural religion. With this firm conviction, Tindal set out to present the episodes of the Bible as either ridiculous or immoral. In this moral argument rested Tindal's special strength. Torrey concludes that he influenced Voltaire profoundly, both in his destructive criticism of Christian revelation and in his constructive appeal to natural religion.

It would seem that, in this respect, both Chubb and Bolingbroke exercised but little influence on Voltaire. On the other hand, Conyers Middleton, the author of *Letters from Rome* and the *Free Enquiry into the Miraculous Powers of the Christian Church*, was a major influence on Voltaire. Voltaire read Middleton's writings carefully and borrowed abundantly from his material concerning miracles, the martyrs, the Church Fathers, the lack of originality in Jewish customs, and the weakness of the authority of Scripture. Torrey concludes that Middleton, rather than Bolingbroke, must be regarded as the most important English source of Voltaire's refutation of the historical argument of the truth of Christianity.

The only remaining English deist who had a serious effect on Voltaire's thinking was Peter Annet, whose work on *David, the Man after God's Own Heart* (1761) was one of the violent, radical attacks against Christianity. Voltaire knew this work and imitated its ideas in the *Saül* which he wrote. Annet's attitude toward Christianity was one of great antipathy, reminiscent of the virulence of Meslier of the preceding generation in France. Not only did the Englishman actually think that the Christian was deceived because he refused to apply his reason to the phenomena of the Bible, but he judged this refusal immoral. He applied the type of rational analysis he espoused in the *Resurrection of Jesus Considered* in 1744 and again in the following year in a sequel, *Resurrection Reconsidered*. Voltaire does not appear to have made direct use of these tracts. But his own references to Christ's death are often as radical and as disrespectful as Annet's. And much the same attitude as that which underlies Annet's *History and Character of St. Paul* (1747) can be found in Voltaire's *Dialogue du douteur et de l'adorateur* and the *Examen important*: both critics present Paul as an imposter and a schemer, and they both attack the contradictions in his doctrines. Finally, Voltaire procured the *Life of David*, written with the same truculence that characterized Annet's attacks against Paul, almost as soon as it appeared and found it to be infinitely more violent than Bayle's article on David in the *Dictionnaire historique*. It gave a broader picture of horror, crime, and immorality, and it incorporated the story of Agag, as well as the tales of David's love affairs. Torrey concludes that Voltaire favored Annet's work over Bayle's as a source for his criticism of David, although Torrey concedes that Voltaire did take some material from Bayle. The most interesting assertion Torrey makes, however, is that the twenty-five page article on "Saul and David" in the *Bible enfin expliquée* was drawn almost entirely from Annet.

Voltaire had already been in contact with this English critical deism—at any rate, we surmise as much. He had been in England when it had been in the full bloom of its development. How much interest he had shown in the movement we cannot say, because we have no documents upon which to base a judgment. The references to his English sojourn in the correspondence give us no clue whatever to the extent of this interest. The *Notebooks*, also, are remarkably unhelpful. A short, inconsequential statement on Locke's *Reasonableness of Christianity* and a few unimportant remarks on deism in the second *Notebook* are all the hints they contain. No reference is made to any outstanding English deist save Woolston, and then only to record in the early, tentative *Lettre philosophique* that Woolston had brought out the fourth part of his *Discourses*. Otherwise, there is only silence. Critics have had some difficulty in explaining this silence. Usually, it is attributed to prudence. Bonno believes it to be, instead, a sign that Voltaire simply had no interest in English deism at this time. In view of the important role which English deism played in the Ferney period (see Torrey, *Voltaire and the English Deists*), though, it seems incredible that Voltaire should not have manifested more interest between 1728 and 1762.

During the past few decades, however, we have been assembling some evidence that Voltaire's interest was more active in the Cirey period. We are fairly certain, for instance, that he read and used in connection with his *Traité de métaphysique* Collins's *Treatise on Human Liberty*. We now know, too, that Woolston was a most important source for Mme du Châtelet at Cirey (see I. Wade, *Voltaire et Mme du Châtelet*, Appendix), and it is only natural to infer that, if Mme du Châtelet used his writings so liberally, Voltaire must have been familiar with them, also. In addition, already in the edition of the *Lettres philosophiques*, Voltaire had given slight indications of being acquainted with Tindal's *Christianity as Old as Creation*. Since Mme du Châtelet drew from Tindal's work in a whole series of remarks in the *Examen de la Genèse*, it has been assumed to have been, along with the Woolston's *Discourses,* one of the basic texts. We have a good many pieces of evidence here and there that both Mme du Châtelet and Voltaire were becoming more active in the field of biblical criticism.

We also have a few indications that Voltaire had some interest in the French deists. There is a note referring to Meslier in the Leningrad *Notebooks*, for instance, and a letter to Thiériot in 1735 making some inquiries concerning Meslier. Voltaire's library contained manuscripts of the *Examen de la religion*, the *Analyse de la religion*, the *Elie et Enoch*, and the *Trois imposteurs*, and, since these manuscripts were circulating during the first half of the century, it is assumed that it was during the Cirey period that they found their way there. At a later date, as we shall see, Voltaire was very active in publishing these as well as other clandestine manuscripts. Another piece of evidence is furnished by Mme de Graffigny, who notes, in her letter of January 1739, that the occupants of the château were reading Dom Calmet's *Commentaire littéral sur tous les livres de l'Ancien et du Nouveau Testament*. Since Dom Calmet became one of the most important sources for the *Examen de la Genèse* and of interest to Voltaire in his *Bible enfin expliquée*, the conclusion has been drawn that both Mme du Châtelet and Voltaire were actively engaged in this kind of work. Voltaire's library was rather well supplied with Dom Calmet's works, since it had two copies of the *Commentaire littéral*, one an edition of 1714-1731, the other of 1720, both, apparently, in twenty-eight volumes. In addition, there were three copies of the *Dissertations tirées du Commentaire de Dom Calmet*: an edition of 1750 in fourteen volumes, an edition of 1767 in seventeen volumes, and an early edition of 1720 marked *Nouvelles dissertations*. The library also contained a *Dictionnaire historique de la Bible* of four volumes, published in 1730, and a *Traité sur les apparitions des esprits*, published in two volumes in Paris in 1751. It has been noted that, in the correspondence of both Voltaire and Mme du Châtelet, quotations from the Bible and sly allusions to incidents related therein become more numerous after 1735. Pomeau, to whom we are indebted for this observation (*La Religion de Voltaire*, p. 159), adds that, in some cases, these biblical references indicate more than a banal acquaintance with the texts of the Bible. Some of these remarks go back to the early period— alluding to biblical incidents seems to have always been common practice with Voltaire, indeed, something of an obsession. Even in England, he had observed that Solomon apparently believed in the mortality of the soul. The *Lettres philosophiques* likewise contain a few references to biblical matters. Voltaire notes there that the Scriptures contain scientific errors. He also remarks that the Jews are silent in regard to the problem of the immortality of the soul. But the most important piece of evidence of this sort is to be found in the Leningrad *Notebooks*, which, aside from the scattered and not very important references to deism, include a lengthy series of notes collected from the works of Maillet, along with a sizable list of quotations apparently selected from the Vulgate.

Among these clandestine works of criticism was a large (738-page) manuscript entitled *Examen de la Genèse*, which actually examines all the books of the Bible. The manuscript, in six volumes, now in the public library at Troyes, comprises not only the *Examen de la Genèse* itself but the *Notes* and the *Preuves* of *La Religion chrétienne analysée*. It is attributed to Mme du Châtelet and said, though erroneously, to be an autograph. There are, in reality, two extant manuscripts of this *Examen*. The second copy, offered publicly for sale some thirty years ago in Paris, is likewise in an unknown hand and has been attributed to Voltaire. There may even be a third one at the Public Library in Leningrad: G. Bertrand (*Catalogue des manuscrits français de la Bibliothèque de Saint-Pétersbourg*, in-8°, Paris, 1874) lists a 409-page manuscript entitled *Commentaire sur la Genèse et l'Exode*. The Troyes manuscript, though, has always been considered the authentic copy of the *Examen de la Genèse*.

We have some evidence that Mme du Châtelet was interested in these clandestine manuscripts. Voltaire himeslf is the authority, in a letter to Mme du Deffand (17 September 1759), for the statement that Mme du Châtelet had commented on the Old Testament from beginning to end. Beuchot (*Œuvres*, LVIII, 179), in a note to this letter, wrote that the manuscript was an autograph, entitled *Examen de la Genèse et des livres du Nouveau Testament, preuves de la Religion*. He said that it comprised six little octavo volumes and added that it had been in the library of L. S. Auger until it was sold on 14 October 1829. I have always assumed that Beuchot was referring to the Troyes manuscript, but, on second thought, it seems to me probable that Beuchot was talking about still another manuscript. The Troyes manuscript, though in six octavo volumes, does not have this title. It is not an autograph (and it seems absolutely inconceivable that Beuchot would be mistaken in Mme du Châtelet's handwriting). And, although he undoubtedly owned the Troyes manuscript at one time, since the *Coll. B.* which appears in his books is in the manuscript, I have found no evidence to indicate that L. S. Auger ever owned it.

Grimm added two additional details in the *Correspondance littéraire* (XI, 348), in 1776, on the occasion of the appearance of Voltaire's *Bible enfin expliquée*. He there related on hearsay ("on nous a assuré") that the manuscript of the *Bible enfin expliquée* had for a long time been in the portfolio of the author and that it actually dated from the Cirey period. At that time, every morning at breakfast a chapter of the Bible was read, and each of the participants made his own observations on the chapter according to his particular interest. Grimm added that Voltaire had undertaken to put his observations together into a coherent commentary in the *Bible enfin expliquée*. This extra information Grimm also related upon hearsay.

The story persisted, with some modifications in the nineteenth century. George Avenel, according to Moland (XXX, 2), alleged that Mme du Châtelet and Voltaire both "prirent note de ces commentaires impromptus," and that, consequently, two such manuscripts were written. Avenel added that the Marquise's manuscript was never published, while Voltaire's "servit de noyau" to the *Bible enfin expliquée*. Beuchot supplied the information that the Mme du Châtelet manuscript was still in existence in 1829. It was Beuchot, too, who surmised that it would not be unusual, under the circumstances, if similar remarks occurred in both works.

It is often said that the *Examen de la Genèse* is a chapter-by-chapter commentary on the Bible. The origin of that assertion is doubtless the story that the two Cirey lovers read and commented on a chapter each day. Although, in the main, this story is probably an accurate reflection of what actually happened, it is not true that each chapter was thoroughly examined. As far as the books of the Old Testament are concerned, it is more likely that they were scrutinized point by point, rather than verse by verse. The pertinent verses are quoted in Latin, then translated into French, and subjected, finally, to comment. But the commentary, it should be noted, is a running commentary, and it is interspersed with personal remarks. In contrast to the treatment accorded the four Gospels, which are taken up one by one and examined chapter by chapter, the stories of the Old Testament are studied as a unit, with remarks thrown in on the side, not without wit and irony.

The nature of the commentary is so diverse that it is difficult to show in a short space how it is conducted. One question often raised is the authorship of the work. Who, for instance, wrote the Pentateuch? Mme du Châtelet claims that it could not have been Moses, since he would have had to relate his own death. Impossible statements are underscored immediately—for instance, that Moses was on the other side of the Jordan. Mme du Châtelet explains that the Hebrew word, according to Dom Calmet, means both "on this side" and "on the other side." Voltaire makes the same point in his works. Another criticism often voiced is that the portrait the Bible presents of God is altogether unworthy of Him. The opening remark of the *Examen* is, in fact, just this—that the depiction of God as jealous, choleric, and subject to repentance does not do Him justice. Time and again thereafter, wherever the Bible states that God instructed the Israelites to kill, murder, or plunder, Mme du Châtelet revolts against this portrayal. This was a view Voltaire had commonly expressed ever since the *Epître à Uranie*, and it occurs frequently in the clandestine essays, particularly in the *Religion chrétienne analysée*. A third type of comment in the *Examen* concerns the miraculous incidents in nature—the stopping of the sun, the separation of light from darkness, the formation of the sun four days after the creation of the earth, and Hezekiah's sundial. Mme du Châtelet is quite quick to point out the unscientific aspects of the Old Testament. All contradictions are immediately picked up: the double creation of woman, Cain's fear of being slain in a world which had no other inhabitants, the reference to God in the plural (*Dii creaverunt*). She not only seizes upon such contradictions but notes whatever she considers ludicrous, confusing, or absurd—the serpent who tempts Eve or the Fall, for example. She finds that, if the story of the Fall is absurd, the story of the flood is full of difficulties, too. Where did all the water come from? What were the cataracts in the sky? Where did the water go after the flood? How did the rainbow become a sign of the Covenant? Where did Noah get all the American animals, and how did they get back to America after the flood? Mme du Châtelet is fairly bursting with rationalistic questions. Moreover, she adds, there are many events in the history of the Patriarchs which are absurd, contradictory, immoral, or unjust. Moses, for instance, said to be the gentlest of men, waxes wroth, breaks the stone tablets of the Law, orders 24,000 Hebrews to be slain, and has whole Canaanite towns, including old men, women, and children, obliterated. All of the Patriarchs use subterfuge, trickery, deceit, guile, and even cruelty: Abraham passing Sarah off as his sister before Abimelech and before the King of Egypt, Jacob's deception with Esau, the horrible affair of Simeon and Levi, the cruelty of Jacob's sons in their treatment of Joseph, David's escapades. Mme du Châtelet's list is well-nigh interminable, as she moves from physical impossibilities through moral opprobrium to useless miracles and absurd contradictions. Long before the 738 pages of cruel absurdities have been exhausted, the Old Testament as well as the New has been shown to be untrustworthy, erroneous, morally corrupt, and scientifically ridiculous, presenting stories which surpass in extravagance anything in the *Arabian Nights*.

Thus, in her long *Examen*, Mme du Châtelet continues her witty, ironic comments and offers her rationalistic criticism. It is not always reasonable or in particularly good taste. She is not reverent or tolerant, though certain of the biblical stories—Job, Tobias, Jonah, and Daniel—are related with verve. It is evident that she had become familiar with the methods of Spinoza, but nowhere does she display either his seriousness or his critical spirit. Every action or incident she characterizes as absurd, ridiculous, contradictory, barbarous, brutal, unreasonable, or immoral. The outstanding flaws of the Bible, in her view, are its contradictions and its immorality. The inevitable conclusion is that a work as contradictory and immoral as this one cannot have been divinely inspired and, therefore, is unacceptable as the basis for religion. The result is an expression not only of irreverence and disrespect but also of frank hostility. One senses on her part an almost fanatic revulsion for a work which has proved so little worthy of acceptance. One would think that sooner or later she would have asked, assuming that the Bible must be rejected as divine for rational reasons, if it might not have real human value as the historical account of a nation's struggle to reach a higher level of human reality or if it might not actually be a magnificent expression in poetic form of man's search within his own being for some means of knowing himself. But no, with the denial of its religious significance, all the other human values in the work seem to have been destroyed for her, also. It would not take too much effort to persuade oneself that, as far as Mme du Châtelet was concerned, *l'Infâme* was already a reality.

Among the clandestine writers, the one who exercised the greatest influence upon Voltaire, after Woolston and Mme du Châtelet, was Jean Meslier, the curate at Etrépigny who, on dying in 1729, left three autograph copies of a *Testament* (one with the Grand Vicaire at Rheims, one with Chauvelin, the Garde-des-Sceaux, and one with the clerk of the court at Mézières) which contained the strongest indictment of religious and political institutions of all the clandestine treatises written—stronger even than Spinoza's *Tractatus*, which at least transferred the authority formerly exercised by religion to the state.

Meslier's career had begun under rather favorable circumstances.

The son of a merchant at Mazerny, he had eventually enrolled as a theological student in the Rheims Seminary, with the announced intention of becoming a priest as soon as possible. Tonsured at Rheims on 20 April 1685, he became *sous-diacre* in 1687, deacon in 1688, and priest at Châlons at the end of that year. We do not know exactly when he transferred from Châlons to Etrépigny—whether it was in 1688 or in 1692—for the record of his Archbishop, Le Tellier, is contradictory. It is certain, though, that he was performing his duties satisfactorily. The commendation of Le Tellier was not unqualified, but he noted, on various occasions, that the young priest was doing well. An inspection made on the premises at Etrépigny observes that "Mr le Curé a la Sainte Bible et d'autres bons livres." It is obvious that the priest had the confidence of his Archbishop between 1688 and 1716. Then, curiously enough, everything changed. Archbishop Le Tellier died and was succeeded by Cardinal de Mailly, who had less confidence in the Etrépigny curate. Meslier was now judged "ignorant, présomptueux, très entêté et opiniâtre, homme de bien, négligeant l'Eglise à cause qu'il a le plus de dismes. Il se mêle de décider des cas qu'il n'entend pas, et ne revient pas de son sentiment. Il est fort attaché à ses intérêts, et d'une négligence infinie avec un extérieur fort dévot et Janséniste." It appears that his church had been allowed to run down and that he was now involved in a bitter discussion with his "Seigneur." An attempt at discipline only made matters worse. The truculence of the former model priest led to a revolt against his superior, open war against Mr. de Cléry, his "Seigneur," and a thorough denunciation of all religions and all political institutions, which, said Meslier, support each other like "deux coupeurs de bourse." The old priest, now threatened with blindness, found no joy in living, and penned, at the end of his *Testament*, a legacy to humanity which is one of the bitterest farewells ever written by man.

It was quite probably the political and religious persecution, coupled with bouts of ill health, that turned the priest away from the exercise of his piety and robbed him of the joy of his priesthood. There are some indications, however, that, in spite of his altercations with his superiors, he retained to the end, especially among his parishioners, his reputation for piety. There are also indications that he had been reading assiduously those "good books" which had been found in his library. We can only identify them by the way they enter into his *Testament*, for the old priest never refrained from quoting interminably from others, probably because he found his own style trying—Voltaire characterized it as a "style de cheval de carrosse." Still, although rambling, diffuse, and terribly repetitive, it was not at all colorless or lacking in vigor. The long excerpts he extracted from others show that he had a close familiarity with Montaigne, the *Espion Turc*, Bayle, La Bruyère, Naudé, Pascal, Comines, Fénelon, and Malebranche. The curate had apparently done everything he could to unite the theologians, the philosophers, and the free-thinkers of the previous century. When, in 1718, a copy of Fénelon's *Démonstration de l'existence de Dieu*, followed in the same volume by the *Réflexions sur l'athéisme*, composed by Voltaire's old teacher Tournemine, fell into his hands, Meslier was so moved by his opposition to the Archbishop of Cambrai and the Jesuit priest that he composed a set of notes to the volume. Copies of these notes were made and circulated during the century. Their general tone was one of violent opposition to Fénelon's orthodox beliefs, accompanied by active affirmation of Spinozistic leanings and negation of Christian metaphysics, with a firm Lucretian conception of the cosmos.

The whole turn of Meslier's thought can be divined from these notes. Like his predecessor Spinoza, he, too, was "drunk with God." He lived in apparent dread of accepting a false, anthropomorphic conception of the Deity and thereby of falling into an idolatry he roundly condemned. To avoid this error, he preferred to rest his beliefs upon a naturalism which satisfied his reason but offered slight consolation to his emotions. This naturalism he opposed firmly to orthodox Christianity, which he ended by judging a false metaphysics, a false rationalism, a false emotionalism. In many respects, he reminds one of Pascal: sincere, suffering, highly rational in an emotional way, ever assailed by impulses of emotion, bitter, obstinate, unresigned, but honest. Meslier, however, never found the deep serenity of Pascal.

Fénelon's treatise gave him the opportunity to organize his Spinozistic philosophy. To what he considered a "vain" or a "faux" reasoning of his predecessor, he opposed a stern assertion of the power of Nature. He categorically contradicted the opinion that the universe bears witness of a cause "infiniment puissante et industrieuse," because of its defects. He, like Voltaire, argued that matter, in man as in the animals, is capable of thought. Consequently, he rejected Fénelon's notion that the faculty of thought is distinct from the body, as well as the notion that thought in man is distinct from thought in animals. He opposed Fénelon's ideas of free will, maintaining that, if it is God who gives us the power to will, we cannot will except in accord with what He makes us will, nor fail to do what He makes us do.

The whole tendency of Meslier's thought was in the direction of naturalism. His arguments were not arranged to prove a Christian God but a God who is Nature. He rejected the ontological proofs, as well as all proofs from final causes. The one power which he did admit is the power of Nature; he denied that it is difficult to believe that nothing can come from nothing, that Being is eternal and has never ceased to be. Being can of itself move, and it does. Besides, Being is everywhere, extended, having parts, combining them, dividing them, constantly producing new forms and figures. Thus, Nature is identified with matter. She is all-powerful; she has her being, existence, and laws within herself. She is also eternal: "C'est elle-même qui inspire les bons conseils, qui règle les lois de justice, qui donne la prudence et la force et qui fait régner sagement les princes et les Rois."

The fundamental idea in the *Testament* is that all religions in general, and the Christian religion in particular, are filled with errors, illusions, and impostures and are therefore false. Meslier attributed their falsity to their origin, which he saw in the pact between the political and the religious authorities, and to the deep superstitious character of the people. He protested also the insistence of all religions upon faith, rather than reason. The priest was undoubtedly one of the strictest rationalists in the deistic movement. He refused categorically to accept the divine character of Christianity, established upon what he called false visions and revelations which had never occurred. He rejected caustically all prophecies offered as proof of divinity, pointing out that these prophecies had never been fulfilled. He assailed errors of doctrine and accused them of having fostered a spurious morality. They had failed, moreover, to eradicate unjust abuses in government and society, they gave a wrong idea of

God's existence, and, lastly, they presented untrue teachings concerning the spirituality and the immortality of the soul. These examples of misrepresentations in all religions he offered over and over again as particularly pertinent to establishing the falsity of the Christian religion. Meslier stressed that his world was infamous because it was founded upon an erroneous conception of the Deity and that this distorted conception was responsible for the falsity of society, of the state, and of life itself. Meslier's final purpose was to show that man in society is surrounded by both moral and physical evil. By his fellowman, he is oppressed and unjustly persecuted; by kings, he is tyrannized; by magistrates, he is victimized. Everywhere he has been robbed of the justice which is his due. Worst of all, there is for him no appeal: not only is there no justice, but justice is impossible. One by one he ticked off, in derision, the utter uselessness of the sanctions of justice which a groping humanity had devised: the doctrine of rewards and punishments, the belief in immortality, theism, the efficacy of a state police, and, above all, religion.

His revolt was therefore total and embraced the attacks of all the critical deists. The remarkable thing about this priest, who by training knew all the arguments of seventeen centuries in favor of Christianity, was that he turned them around and threw them back against religion itself. Like Boulainvilliers, he denied that the origins of religion were divine. He asserted, also, that religion was imposed by the powerful and the astute upon the humble and the ignorant. Finally, he, too, traced its source to the vanity of heroes who encouraged their own deification. Like Dumarsais, he drew up an imposing list of contradictions in both the Old and New Testaments and attacked viciously the divine revelation as it is represented in the Bible. Like Mirabaud, he repudiated miracles, on the ground that all religions had miracles to support their pretensions, and he made parallel lists of Christian and pagan miracles to show the vanity of these pretensions. Like Dumarsais, he affirmed that the prophecies had never been fulfilled. Like Fréret, he declared the impossibility of a spiritual, immortal soul and the uselessness of a doctrine of rewards and punishments. Like the *Préface d'un traité*. . . , he analyzed the dogma of the Church, particularly the doctrines of Trinity, original sin, and transubstantiation, and rejected it. Like the *Militaire philosophe*, he refused to believe that faith was superior to reason as a criterion of truth. Like Mirabaud, he proclaimed the eternity of matter, the impossibility of the creation, the ability of animals to think, and hence the inherent quality of thought in matter. And, like all the critics in both England and France, he condemned the priests for their idleness.

His diatribe was thus a complete arraignment of the Christian religion. It embraced in one single work the whole movement of critical deism and went beyond that movement in its ultimate consequences. Meslier transcended the simple advice of his fellow critics, that natural religion was the answer to the falsity of Christianity. It is true that he approved the Golden Rule in one of his violent passages, but he had scant faith in its efficacy. There was, he believed, no hope of ever organizing among mankind the social beneficence of man. Nor did Nature itself offer any final hope to man: the universe is composed of matter, there is no spiritual force, no final cause, there is no virtue nor vice, no good nor evil. Meslier's declaration of war against *l'Infâme* was absolute, his revolt epic in its grandeur.

Voltaire heard of the priest in 1735, when he inquired of Thiériot who Meslier was. Thereafter, he secured the *Testament*, which was circulating in manuscript form in unusually large numbers in Paris. He also learned that it had been abridged. The first five proofs of the falsity of the Christian religion had been extracted, and these *Extraits* were also circulating in Paris. There were, as we have shown, four different sets of these *Extraits* being made at the time, some of them, and probably all of them, circulating around 1742. They differed considerably in their composition, but they all agreed in limiting the content to the critical deism of the *Testament*. Did Voltaire make one of them? I do not know. I have shown that the *Extrait* which he published could not have been made from any one of the four sets, although it resembles most closely a manuscript like Orléans 1115, or others of that group. It likewise bears some resemblance to those belonging to the group of Rheims 653. In view of these resemblances, I concluded that Voltaire made the text of his printed *Extrait* by extracting it from a ready-made *Extrait* like Orléans 1115 and adding some things of his own, along with one or two items from an *Extrait* like Rheims 653. His contribution, therefore, consisted in dressing up an already formed *Extrait*.

Professor Morehouse, who has published a splendidly perceptive study on *Voltaire and Jean Meslier*, does not agree. It is possible, of course, that Voltaire first made one of the *Extraits*, like Orléans 1115, then reduced it to the smaller proportions of the printed *Extrait* by making a few changes, and finally published this shortened version. At all events, Voltaire never adopted the whole of Meslier. The Etrépigny priest made a deep impression upon him, and, as Morehouse has shown, his work was used extensively in all of Voltaire's critical deism. Most important, though, was his presence. Voltaire was terribly awed by a priest, who, upon his death, asked pardon of God for the religion which he had served all his life. It is quite possible that Meslier showed Voltaire the way to combat *l'Infâme*. Voltaire, however, was determined that *his* war against *l'Infâme* would be a more limited affair.

There is no disagreement among Voltaire scholars about these facts. On the other hand, they do show some hesitation when it comes to admitting that this kind of biblical activity could have been concentrated in the Cirey period. The normal way of regarding the activity is to place it rather in the Ferney period, usually after 1762. This is the opinion Professor Torrey expresses in his *Voltaire and the English Deists*, and it is one that the majority of Voltaireans would accept. In fact, Professor Vernière, in his *Spinoza et la pensée française avant la Révolution* (II, 507), argues that the deistic criticism, the cry against *l'Infâme*, the suppression of the Jesuits, and the weakening of the monarchy all coincided around 1762. The same attitude, somewhat modified, is held at the present time by Pomeau (see *Religion*, pp. 174-179). I suspect that the reason for this hesitation is the reluctance to grant authenticity and influence to a work until it is published, and it is certainly true that in Voltaire's case—and, to a large extent, in the case of the deistic writers of clandestine manuscripts—publication took place in what has become known in the study of Voltaire as the Ferney period (1759-1777). This is the decisive consideration, for instance, in Torrey's *Voltaire and the English Deists*.

There is, however, another side to the problem: a clandestine work by its very nature has to conceal its authenticity and even its influence. It is important in its first stages in that it is directed to a small, but powerful intellectual elite, and it achieves its purpose by eluding censorship and all public appeals. It is also important in this stage because the movement it creates is in the very vanguard of the intellectual development of its time. As a consequence, its history as a living evolution of thought is crucial before the period when it becomes a published work. For Voltaire's intellectual growth, the decisive point was reached at the time of his clandestine participation in critical deism, rather than at the moment of his cooperation in the widespread circulation of its results. Or, rather, both periods were important, the first being of greater consequence for Voltaire's intellectual development, the second for the historical spread of deism and for the effect it had upon the public. The thing to stress, I suppose, is that Voltaire participated in both in a particularly effective way.

Perhaps if at this point we looked at the rise of critical deism in fuller perspective, we could get a clearer conception of Voltaire's connection with it. It should be pointed out that, in the development of Enlightenment thought, the organizational stage of deism certainly extended from the publication of Bayle's *Dictionnaire historique* (1697) to the period around 1761, when Peter Annet's *David* appeared. (See the table of publications in Torrey, pp. 207-208.) To all intents and purposes, it seems to have reached its climax by 1730 in England, where, because of a relatively mild censorship, it was permitted to develop along the seven points of attack we have outlined above (miracles, prophecies, martyrs, establishment of Christianity, etc.) and to circulate its material in the public in printed form. Between 1730 and 1760, about the only modification that occurred was the appearance of a more radical form of deism. Annet seems the most characteristic English deist in this respect, but the radical aspect of Woolston's attack, which was at least a generation earlier, should not be overlooked. On the continent, critical deism had a longer period of gestation, extending from 1670 (the date of the *Tractatus*, which was published, circulated, and translated into French within a decade or so afterward) to 1697 (the date of Bayle's *Dictionnaire historique*, where biblical criticism was one of the subjects seriously treated, which was similarly published and then distributed among the public) to 1749. The development during this latter period, 1697-1749, where the focus was now France, rather than England or Holland, was distinguished by the organization of a more or less loosely united group of writers, who espoused the views of either Spinoza or Bayle or both and who were forced, because of censorship, to produce their material in manuscript and circulate it clandestinely. After 1743 (and, once again, after 1760), when censorship had been relaxed and the authorities had become for a short time more lenient, some of the manuscripts began to appear in print. The peak of the clandestine period in France was 1720-1740, the climax being somewhere between 1735 and 1742—precisely, that is, in the Cirey period. Thus, while in England, Voltaire had access to all the advantages of the English movement and, similarly, while at Cirey, had access to all the advantages of the French movement. Finally, in France, the clandestine period, which extended, as we have said, to around 1749, was only a part of a larger period, from 1740 to 1760, when there was a tendency for the manuscript treatises to be published and a general trend during the publishing period, from 1740 to the end of the century, toward more and more radical publications. Whereas in England, then, the movement was, to all intents and purposes, completed with Annet, in France it continued with Voltaire to the end of his life and with Holbach even later (see D. Mornet, "Bibliographie d'un certain nombre d'ouvrages philosophiques du XVIIIᵉ siècle et particulièrement de D'Holbach"). The high point of the radical period in France, with Voltaire and Holbach, was 1764-1774, after the movement had lost its significance in England.

In reality, the best way of presenting this confusing chronology is to note, first, that the period of intense deistic activity in England was from 1700 to 1761—that is, from Toland to Annet. The climax of the movement occurred in the decade 1728-1738. After that, the movement dwindled and lost, with Annet, all importance as an intellectual activity. Second, we must note that the period of greatest energy in the clandestine organization of deistic ideas in France extended from 1700 to 1750. The medium through which this energy was displayed was the manuscript, which reached its highest level as a manifestation of the deistic spirit in the period 1720-1740, with the peak occurring in the decade 1732-1742, precisely, that is, at the very center of the Cirey period. This period of clandestine organization was followed in the second part of the century (1750-1788) by a period of clandestine diffusion, which attained its peak in the decade 1764-1774.

It is thus evident that, by the early years of the Cirey period, Voltaire had access to a whole mass of material arising out of English critical deism—works by Toland, Collins, Tindal, Woolston, Middleton, and Annet. Torrey (p. 199) concludes that these were the deistic disciples of Locke and that Voltaire, in his attack against the Christian religion, "adopted every method that was used by his English predecessors." Voltaire did have his favorites, however, he preferred in the group those who used the ethical, rather than the historical argument, and those who were radical in their attack, rather than those who were more moderate or more scholarly. Thus, Toland was undoubtedly helpful with his list of apochryphal works, but Voltaire had Fabricius to refer to also. Collins was helpful with his presentation of the argument drawn from the prophecies, but he was more helpful still with his defense of free-thinking and in putting Voltaire more in accord with himself on the matter of free will, which Clarke's work on the existence of God had distorted. The deistic influence of Tindal was even more pronounced, especially his *Christianity as Old as Creation*, which was, says Torrey, "a very important source of Voltaire's deism." The particular focus of this influence was the group of ethical arguments in which Tindal stressed the barbarities of the Jews, their cruelties to others, the ridiculous conduct of the prophets, and the contradictions in the morality that Christ taught. These arguments, as Torrey has shown, appealed greatly to Voltaire. Voltaire, however, was much more aggressive in his use of them than Tindal, probably because, Torrey suggests, Voltaire was trying to pattern his style after that of Woolston and Annet. It is certain that these two writers meant much to Voltaire. He himself admitted freely by direct quotation his indebtedness to Woolston, and a comparison of his *Saül* with Annet's *David* makes the impact of Annet equally evident, although Voltaire never referred to Annet by name. As Torrey sees the situation, Annet summarized the most valid arguments of his predecessors and "transfused them with the spirit of Woolston for Voltaire's use" (p. 202). In spite of the difficulty of determining the precise amount of influence each of these English deists had upon the Frenchman, one could argue reasonably that Woolston's was the paramount influence. Annet, nonetheless, played a significant role, and so, surprisingly enough, did Conyers Middleton, who used, not the ethical, but the historical argument. Torrey views Middleton's influence as at least equal to Van Dale's. He admits that not all the influences on Voltaire's deistic thought were English. Meslier's influence, for instance, he notes in passing, but he depreciates its value with the remark that we must not forget that Voltaire, by the time he knew Meslier, had already read Tindal, Woolston, and Annet. This opinion needs now to be revised, since it is more probable from the evidence that, with the exception of Annet, he was reading all these deists in the Cirey period. Nor does Torrey forget the more consistent French "précurseurs"—Bayle, Fontenelle, and Perrault. Yet he argues that they "were not felt directly to any extent by the later French School" (p. 203). In his explanation, they crossed over to England only to return "greatly augmented" by Toland, Collins, and the other English deists. Torrey concludes that English deism was a primary factor both in Voltaire's constructive and in his critical deism. He became convinced that the Christian religion, like all religions, was founded upon imposture and fraud and that the Church's history was no proof of its divinity. He rejected both its miracles and its prophecies as proofs of this divinity.

Although this analysis is substantially correct, we still do not have a clear and accurate picture of the chronology, of the place of the development of French critical deism in the evolution of European deism, and of the way English and French deism were fused. We have failed, moreover, to distinguish between a period of clandestine organization and limited diffusion of manuscripts—the Cirey period—and a later period of more widespread diffusion of published works—the Ferney period. I think that the same criticism could be made against those studies which have tried to assess the role of French deism in the movement without giving careful attention to English deism. It appears that the proper approach would be, not to attempt to stress the role of one of these countries over that of the other, but to try to understand more clearly the merging of these two movements in Voltaire and others. Pomeau, for instance, has shown that Tindal's work was important not only for Voltaire but for Mme du Châtelet also, especially Chapters XII and XIII of *Christianity as Old as Creation*. Woolston's work, also, had a significant

impact on Mme du Châtelet, as we have seen by comparing statement after statement from the *Discourses* with similar statements in
the *Examen de la Genèse* (see my *Voltaire and Mme du Châtelet*,
Appendix, pp. 212-227). We may conclude, then, that Tindal and
Woolston, who are said to have had an effective influence on Voltaire after 1762, had just as effective an influence on Mme du Châtelet
and Voltaire before 1749. Moreover, there were among the pre-
cursors of Voltaire and Mme du Châtelet a whole line of French
critical deists—"Le militaire philosophe," Boulainvilliers, Meslier,
Mirabaud, Fréret, Dumarsais, etc.—who presented arguments
against Christianity similar to those so abundantly deployed by the
English but offered them in a different context and with a differing
intent. One of the most detailed of these treatises was Jean Meslier's
Testament, which was as radical as any produced in England and
more rounded in its point of view than all of them put together.
Morehouse has shown that no deistic treatise has exercised more influence upon Voltaire's works than Meslier's. His work was also
known to Mme du Châtelet. According to Pomeau, she used it but
sparingly. She does, indeed, quote him very sparingly, but, if her
points are compared with Meslier's, it will be found—even though
Meslier's treatment is a systematic study of the Bible and Mme du
Châtelet's is more verse-by-verse commentary—that there is much
similarity in the comments of the two critics. Lastly, Pomeau has
shown that both Voltaire and Mme du Châtelet used the *Commentaire littéral* and the *Dictionnaire de la Bible* of Dom Calmet. There
are other studies—mostly unpublished, it is true—which show that
Voltaire used the Dumarsais treatise he had in his library, which
Mme du Châtelet had copied in her treatise, as well as the works of
Fréret, Mirabaud, and Boulainvilliers.[20]

Both Voltaire and Mme du Châtelet, then, were abundantly supplied with the writings of English and French critical deists alike.
Their thinking was saturated in particular with the ideas of Woolston, Tindal, and Meslier. With the writings of these three, plus the

[20] See A. Hole, "J. B. de Mirabaud: His Contribution to the Deistic Movement
and His Relation to Voltaire," Ph.D. dissertation, Princeton University, 1943;
J. Humeston, Jr., "Voltaire, the *Examen*, and the *Analyse*: A Comparative Study,"
Ph.D. dissertation, Princeton University, 1943; and C. Crist, *The* Dictionnaire
philosophique portatif *and the Early French Deists*, New York, 1934.

scholarly works of Dom Calmet and Bayle, they had all the material they needed to carry on their campaign. Since Mme du Châtelet completed her *Examen* before 1749, Voltaire, for his part, could profit not only from the other manuscripts which were circulating but also from her manuscript.

In spite of these conclusions, the belief that Voltaire practiced his critical deism only in the Ferney period still persists. Surely, though, he could not have waited until Ferney to compose all of these deistic treatises. The *Notebooks*, Mme du Châtelet's *Examen*, and the whole rhythm of the French deistic movement all provide evidence contradicting the notion that Voltaire waited until after his return from Berlin before entering upon the deistic controversy. Besides, the temperament of Voltaire renders such a likelihood unthinkable. It is, however, not easy to determine which of Voltaire's works were composed clandestinely at an earlier time and published only at a later date.

There are only two ways to approach this problem: either one has to inquire diligently whether Voltaire, or Voltaire and Mme du Châtelet, became engaged in the actual composition of works of this nature, which were allowed to circulate clandestinely with the other treatises we have collected; or one has to consider the possibility that several of the treatises which Voltaire published in the Ferney period were actually composed as clandestine deistic treatises in the earlier Cirey period. Of the hundred or so treatises which were known to have circulated clandestinely during the earlier period, there is one which could have had its origin in the Cirey activity: the *Analyse de la religion* or, rather, the *Religion chrétienne analysée*. The possibility is suggested first of all because the *Notes* and the *Preuves* were copied in the same hand and united with the *Examen de la Genèse* in the Troyes manuscript. These *Notes* and *Preuves* were appendices to the *Religion chrétienne analysée*, which has always been judged a revised version of the *Analyse de la religion*, and almost always attributed to Dumarsais. It has been suggested (see Pomeau, *Religion*, p. 165n) that, since Mme du Châtelet's manuscript of the *Examen* at Troyes was a copy, not the original, there is no reason it could not have been made after her death in 1749. Still, one must admit that, so far as the evidence goes, there is no reason it could not have been made before her death, either. This merely proves that we cannot base an argument for its date upon the manuscript itself. All we can do is to state that the ideas contained therein were her own and were circulating before her death—unless, of course, we accept Beuchot's statement that there was a manuscript of the *Examen de la Genèse* in Mme du Châtelet's hand and that it was still in existence in 1829 in the library of Auger. It is, nevertheless, conceivable that the *Notes* and the *Preuves* could have been added by some other person than Voltaire and Mme du Châtelet, at any later date.

However, it is not entirely correct to say that the ideas contained in the six-volume manuscript at Troyes were all her own, because the second manuscript of the *Examen,* which was sold privately some years ago, was attributed (but without any proof) to Voltaire. It seems reasonable then, to start all over and see what evidence can be collected that will justify assigning the Troyes manuscript either to Voltaire or to Mme du Châtelet.

All we know about the *Religion chrétienne analysée* is that it circulated as a clandestine manuscript, that it is sometimes dated 1748, sometimes 1749, that it bears a strict relationship to the *Analyse de la religion* (the important difference being that the eleven initial paragraphs of the *Religion chrétienne analysée* often do not appear in copies of the *Analyse*), and that the *Religion* usually, but not always, is accompanied by a set of *Notes* and *Preuves*. We have shown that there is a close similarity between the *Examen de la religion* and the *Religion chrétienne analysée*, especially in the early part of the latter treatise where there is a distinct pilfering of the former during the first eleven paragraphs. We have also pointed out the close relationship between the *Religion chrétienne analysée* and the *Examen de la Genèse*. Finally, we have noted that there are distinct parallels between the latter work and several of Voltaire's deistic treatises, not only in the points treated, but in the sequence of similarly expressed ideas when each takes up similar points. Moreover, we have shown that there is a surprising conformity of tone between the *Religion chrétienne analysée* and the *Epître à Uranie*, not so much in expression, but in actual content of thought. We may conclude, then, at the very least, that the *Examen de la religion*, the *Religion chrétienne analysée*, the *Examen de la Genèse*, the *Epître à Uranie*, and several of Voltaire's deistic treatises all belong to the same current of thought, in which the sources are often the same, the attitudes surprisingly similar, the subjects treated closely related, the conclusions comparable, and the manners of expression frequently strikingly alike. These resemblances are especially noticeable when we juxtapose the *Examen de la Genèse* and the treatises of Voltaire, to which we shall return shortly. This congruity is perfectly understandable, since, according to the evidence we have produced, Voltaire and Mme du Châtelet were working together. The relationship between the *Examen de la religion* and the *Religion chrétienne analysée* and the striking similarity between these two works (especially the *Religion chrétienne analysée*) and Voltaire's works (especially the *Epître à Uranie*) have been studied by Pomeau and myself, but we have as yet reached no firm conclusions.

Since my own treatment of the problem is the least important, perhaps I should begin with it (see *Voltaire and Mme du Châtelet,* pp. 136-138). "When we begin to examine various treatises which might fall in the first category [that is, treatises written by Voltaire but never published under his own name] we are immediately confronted with the *Religion chrétienne analysée* published in the *Recueil nécessaire* and in the *Evangile de la raison*. Its authorship has never been definitely determined, and although there have been suggestions that Voltaire wrote it, no one has ever proved that he did. The strongest evidence in support of his authorship presents itself in some until recently unpublished notes of Beuchot which I have published elsewhere. It might be added, in partial support of Beuchot's contention, that there is a close parallel between portions of the *Religion chrétienne analysée* and the *Epître à Uranie*. There is an even closer connection between it and Mme du Châtelet's *Examen de la Genèse*. And the fact that the sixth volume of Mme du Châtelet's collection was devoted to the *Notes* and the *Preuves* of the *Religion chrétienne analysée* at least renders plausible the assumption that the whole series, *Religion chrétienne analysée, Notes,* and *Preuves,* is a product of the Cirey atmosphere. Moreover, it should be noted that the date of composition of the *Religion chrétienne analysée* (1737-1742) coincides with that of the first three volumes of Mme du Châtelet's *Examen de la Genèse*. Although there is no conclusive evidence that Voltaire was not the author of the *Religion chrétienne analysée,* there is still no conclusive evidence that he was its author. And for the time being, it is impossible to say whether the *Religion chrétienne analysée* furnished inspiration for or was a product of the critical deism at Cirey. Voltaire's connection with the work is still problematical save in one respect. It is known that he first published it, or rather the *Analyse de la religion,* which derives from it. Did he prepare *his* draft of it during the Cirey Period? There is no definite proof, although there is a strong presumption that he did so, when the date 1742 which was attached to the *Extrait* of Meslier is recalled. And if he made his draft of the *Analyse,* it becomes more plausible that he made his drafts of the *Examen* and the *Meslier* in and around the same time."

This discussion in *Voltaire and Mme du Châtelet* was occasioned not only by some parallels between the ideas in the *Religion chrétienne analysée* and those in the *Epître à Uranie,* which I had already noted when I was looking for the latter's possible sources, but also some notes written by Beuchot and inserted in manuscript form in his copy of the *Recueil nécessaire* (Z Beuchot 742 at the Bibliothèque Nationale). In these notes, Beuchot declares his belief that Voltaire was also the author of the *Analyse,* and not merely its editor. The evidence he offers in support of this conclusion is drawn from Voltaire's correspondence and a reference from Grimm's *Correspondance littéraire* (IV, 233). The main points made by Beuchot in his analysis of the Voltaire letters for 1764 are the following: Voltaire frequently refers to the *Analyse* as a work by Dumarsais which has been attributed to Saint-Evremond. On 13 December 1763, he states that he has received the printed edition and that it is "très mal imprimé." Two days later, he declares to the same correspondent that he has not seen the work. Beuchot infers that this sort of coquetry betrays a connection with the work. His suspicion is strengthened by a letter of 8 January 1764, which reads: "L'ouvrage qui est *en partie* de Dumarsais et qu'on attribue à Saint-Evremont se débite dans Paris; et je suis étonné qu'il ne soit pas parvenu à vous. Il est écrit, à la vérité, très simplement, mais il est plein de raison." Beuchot apparently reasons that the expression "en partie" betokens Voltaire's authorship. Citing several statements made by Voltaire in his letters to Damilaville at the time, he goes on to note the interest which Voltaire took in the success of the published *Analyse.* This repeated inquiry Beuchot likewise interprets as the expression of an authorly interest. Further, Beuchot mentions, but does not discuss, a letter which Voltaire wrote to Damilaville on 26 December 1764, in which he speaks of an edition printed by M. M. Rey "avec son nom." Finally, Beuchot quotes an extract of a letter to Damilaville of 9 August 1764, which reads: "Vous souvenez-vous du petit ouvrage attribué à Saint-Evremont? On le réimprime en Hollande revu et corrigé avec plusieurs autres pièces dans ce goût. On m'en a promis quelques exemplaires." Beuchot remarks that the content of this letter furnishes "une conjecture de plus." The bearing of this remark is not completely clear. I take it he means that it was Voltaire who had taken the *Analyse* as composed by Dumarsais and published an edition "revue et corrigée."

To sum up Beuchot's stand, he was convinced that Voltaire's enigmatic remarks to D'Alembert, together with the unusual interest in the success of the printed *Analyse* which he disclosed in his letters to Damilaville, constituted good evidence that Voltaire had written the work. It seems to me, however, that Beuchot's notes, although they suggest the possibility, do not prove Voltaire's actual authorship. Indeed, the Damilaville letters reveal an interest, not in the success of the work itself, but only in the success of its publication. It was not ownership that Voltaire was expressing, but rather his role in publishing the work.

It is still possible to put these references together and advance another interpretation. The assertion that M. M. Rey published an edition of the *Analyse* under Voltaire's name, though not necessarily correct, is important, for knowing that Rey was the publisher of some score of these clandestine works at the instigation of Voltaire through Dupeyrou gives some weight to the significance of Rey's knowledge about the publication of clandestine works. More important still is the constant reference to the *Analyse* of Dumarsais as mistakenly attributed to Saint-Evremond. I have always assumed in the past that Voltaire was hopelessly confused about the *Examen* and the *Analyse*, that he sometimes talks about the *Examen* when he really means the *Analyse*, sometimes about the *Analyse* when he really means the *Examen*. It seems to me now more likely that I was the one confused and that this effect is precisely what Voltaire wanted to achieve. The correspondence suggests that he is clearly talking about the *Examen*, which is, indeed, constantly "attribué à Saint-Evremond" and which could very well have been "en partie" by Dumarsais. What is certain here is that Voltaire constantly denies that the *Examen* could be by Saint-Evremond. If this interpretation is accepted, it is plausible that, in continuing to talk about the *Examen* in his letter of 9 August 1764 to Damilaville, he is referring to it, not as written "en partie" by Dumarsais, but as "revu et corrigé" by himself—in effect, that he does accept the authorship of the *Analyse* as derived from the *Examen*.

Pomeau (*Religion*, p. 175) has meticulously reviewed Beuchot's notes and has conceded that in favor of his hypothesis can be alleged the fact that the work, closely knit, well-organized, develops ideas which are characteristically Voltairean: the Bible is not inspired, it has no historical value, the prophecies and the miracles do not prove the divinity of the Christian religion, Christian dogma is totally opposed to reason and is an insult to the majesty of the Deity. But Pomeau argues that these ideas are not uniquely Voltairean, and that they may be found in scores of treatises composed by others. Against the attribution of authorship, on the other hand, can be found several objections. First of all, Pomeau notes, Mme du Châtelet's *Examen* does not make use of this treatise. Besides, what little we know about the author of the treatise does not square with what we know about Voltaire: several of the copies of the manuscript are signed with the initials CfCDf or CfCDt; a note found in a Beuchot copy indicates that the author died around 1751; a passage Pomeau has unearthed in the *Anti-Uranie* states that the author was a Chevalier d'E——. Lastly, Pomeau points out that the manuscript discloses a notably richer documentation than Voltaire could have had at his disposal before 1749. For these reasons, he proposes to reject the idea that Voltaire could have composed the *Religion chrétienne analysée*.

Although Pomeau's facts are disturbing, they do not prove very much one way or the other. As we shall see, it is not very accurate to say that Mme du Châtelet did not use the treatise, and, even if she failed to take advantage of its existence, that would hardly constitute a proof that Voltaire was not its author. The signed initials certainly do not remind us of Voltaire's name, but neither does the attribution of the *Sermon des cinquante* to Dumarsais remind us of Voltaire. If he wished to throw the public off the track, he chose a most effective way. But we have no specific information to warrant any inference from these initials. The statement that the author was dead by 1751 could be an error, and probably was; so was, no doubt, the information that the Chevalier d'E—— was the author. I do not know how one can judge whether Voltaire was or was not capable at the time of providing the manuscript with its rich documentation. It is hardly conceivable, though, that the *Analyse* was any more richly documented than the *Sermon des cinquante*. While the reasons are interesting, then, they are by no means conclusive, and, even when they do seem to be true, explanations can be offered for their unimportance.

There are two observations of a general nature which could be made regarding the *Religion chrétienne analysée*. The first is that it seems to have been the intention of its author to write a compact, undivided treatise on the authenticity of the Bible. In content, the work resembles to an extraordinary extent the *Tractatus* of Spinoza, but it recalls even more the *Sermon des cinquante*. It not only deals with point after point taken up in the *Sermon* but somehow leaves the impression that it has dealt with each point in the same way. It analyzes, in fact, in a very detailed way the authenticity of the books of the Old and New Testaments, but without cramming too many observations into the discussion. This tendency reminds one often of the *Examen de la Genèse*. In addition, it is one of the very few manuscripts which take up the matter of Phlegon and the sun's eclipse at the time of Christ's crucifixion. It places much emphasis upon the discrepancies in the chronology of events and errors of computation in the Old Testament. It also frequently refers to Dom Calmet, who, as we know, was a favorite commentator of both Voltaire and Mme du Châtelet. One could easily see in these characteristics that the *Religion chrétienne analysée* assembles in abridged form the material of the *Examen de la Genèse* and expresses it in a way reminiscent of the *Sermon des cinquante*. It is doubtless because of these two similarities that we have constantly wavered between attributing it to Mme du Châtelet and assigning it to Voltaire. The most recent attempt to analyze the relation between these works was made by Professor E. J. Humeston, Jr., in his unpublished doctoral dissertation entitled "Voltaire, the *Examen* and *Analyse*: A Comparative

Study." By comparing, in respect to both substance and manner of presentation, the ideas contained in the deistic treatises of Voltaire—such as the *Sermon des cinquante,* the *Examen important,* and the *Bible enfin expliquée*—the *Examen de la Genèse* of Mme du Châtelet, the *Examen de la Religion,* and the *Religion chrétienne analysée,* he has established beyond a doubt that there is a close affinity between these works—so close, in fact, that he is prepared to see in it either a collaboration or a very careful imitation. More particularly, the *Religion chrétienne analysée* is so obviously a revision of the *Examen de la religion* that it could have come directly from no other source. Even so, the revision of it was strongly influenced by the *Examen de la Genèse,* and more strongly still by Voltaire's works. Humeston has cited twenty special points made by the *Analyse* that were likewise made by Voltaire and Mme du Châtelet. In each case, the resemblance between the *Analyse* and Voltaire's works is closer than that between the *Analyse* and the *Examen de la Genèse.* Humeston (pp. 217ff.) concludes that Voltaire must have been its author.

I am not prepared to go as far as Humeston, although I think his findings are extremely interesting. I doubt that Voltaire was the author of the *Religion chrétienne analysée,* but I do think he was responsible for its "remaniement." The eleven initial paragraphs lifted bodily from the *Examen de la religion,* the more or less direct incorporation of other material from the *Examen,* the selection of many factual points treated in the *Examen de la Genèse,* the stress placed upon errors in chronology and errors in computation, which is so characteristic of the *Genèse,* the close parallel between the "portrait naïf" of the *Analyse* and the first third of the *Epître à Uranie,* parallel not only in material selected but often in actual expression—all these things betoken that Voltaire had a hand in its confection. That it was Voltaire who first published the work adds a presumption that he was at least as implicated in the *Religion chrétienne analysée* as he was in the *Abrégé du Testament de Jean Meslier.*

There is more evidence which could give confirmation to this hypothesis. From the *Religion chrétienne analysée* was developed a set of *Preuves que l'auteur de la Religion chrétienne analysée a simplement indiquées dans l'ouvrage* and a set of *Notes.* The *Notes* are devised to give supplementary material on special subjects; the *Preuves*, on the other hand, offer confirmatory material on the points already discussed. There are five (in some editions, six) of these *Preuves*: (1) the history of Cain, (2) the flood and Noah's ark, (3) Jacob's marriage and the sack of Salem, (4) the fourth age of the world (that is, from the departure from Egypt to the building of Solomon's temple), and (5) Solomon's riches. The sixth, when it occurs, is on the number of Israelites who returned from captivity. These proofs are arranged in a rather unique way: in one column at the right the "textes" from the Scriptures are quoted, while on the left is a corresponding column of "observations." Eventually, after the "textes" have been exhausted, the commentary extends over the whole page. This technique is precisely the technique Voltaire followed in the *Bible enfin expliquée*, the only difference being that in the *Preuves* the two parts are arranged laterally, while in the *Bible* the "textes" occupy the upper part of the page and the "observations" the lower part. In the *Examen de la Genèse*, the "textes" mingle with the "observations."

Moreover, the *Preuves*, which often accompany the *Religion chrétienne analysée*, form Part I of a manuscript entitled *La Foi anéantie ou démonstration de la fausseté des faits principaux qui sont contenus dans les deux Testaments*. The manuscript is marked "translated from the Latin of Hobbes" and is dated 1763. Only one copy is known to exist: Mazarine 1189. It is, however, a complete work, of which the *Preuves* constitute only Part I. Part II takes up the life of Christ as it is related in Matthew; Part III is an analysis of the other three Gospels; and Part IV is an analysis of the Epistles of St. Paul. The Mazarine manuscript is not the original, since on page 35 of Part II there is an "Avis" which begins "Dans le manuscrit original." The subjects treated in each of the parts are taken up topically, and each article is devoted to a discussion of the facts of the text; the technique, in other words, is the same as that followed in the *Notes* and *Preuves*. Part IV is particularly interesting because it treats St. Paul, who was criticized in the fifth volume of the *Examen de la Genèse*. There can be no doubt that the work formed a unity and that Part I was not added arbitrarily. At the end of Part I, there is a short conclusion which begins: "Avoir prouvé que le Vieux Testament est un ouvrage purement humain. . . ." The

opening sentence of Part II—"Nous sommes convenus, dans la première partie de cet ouvrage . . ."—clearly indicates that the parts fit
together naturally. I should mention, as I have already in my *Clandestine Organization* (pp. 181-182), that the criticism in the last three
parts is both violent and bitter and recalls the bad taste of the worst
parts of the *Examen important*. The treatment of Paul, moreover,
not only shows analogies with Mme du Châtelet's treatment but is
also in accord with Voltaire's, as expressed in other deistic treatises.

From the observations we have made, it should now be possible
to construct at least a tentative hypothesis. Mme du Châtelet made
at Cirey a complete analysis of the Bible, to which was added *Notes*
and the *Preuves* of the *Religion chrétienne analysée*. While she and
Voltaire were preparing the critical material for this lengthy analysis, they apparently used a certain amount of time to get acquainted
with other clandestine treatises of this type. We are not able to assess,
though, how many of these treatises they actually knew at this time.
In her papers, which are in the Voltaire collection at Leningrad,
there is a fragmentary *Analyse*, consisting of the *Preuves* and an
Elie et Enoch. It seems reasonable, therefore, to assume that she
knew the *Analyse*, along with the *Notes*, the *Preuves* and the *Elie
et Enoch*. Voltaire, for his part, published the *Analyse*, and there is
a strong probability that he actually wrote the *Preuves* and the
Notes, particularly the *Preuves*. He inquired about Meslier's work,
got acquainted with it, and eventually published it, also, in abridged
form. As a matter of fact, the *Examen*, the *Analyse*, and the *Extrait
de Meslier* were often published together after 1764, either in the
Recueil nécessaire or in the *Evangile de la raison*. There are some
grounds, therefore, for believing that, while Mme du Châtelet was
making her analysis, Voltaire was at least devoting some of his
time to aiding her and some to getting acquainted with clandestine
manuscripts and preparing them for publication. In this way, he
undertook the revision of the *Religion chrétienne analysée* into
the *Analyse de la religion*, the *Extrait de Meslier*, and probably the
Examen de la religion, from which the *Religion chrétienne analysée* was largely derived. It is possible to construct even a tentative
chronology: the *Meslier* was, in all probability, ready in 1742, the
Religion chrétienne analysée between 1742 and 1746, the *Notes* and
Preuves in 1748-1749. These were preceded or accompanied by some

sort of mock-up composition comparable to the *Examen de la Genèse* of Mme du Châtelet and to the Mazarine 1189 manuscript, *La Foi anéantie*—if, indeed, it was not that very document. This mock-up was to serve henceforward as a collection of notes for all the subsequent treatises Voltaire composed in the area. Already, long before the end of the Cirey period, he had begun looking in earnest for weapons to equip his arsenal in the struggle against *l'Infâme*.

We must insist, though, that none of this material was published at the time, for the simple reason that Voltaire and Mme du Châtelet understood very well that none of it would be tolerated. That interdiction did not prevent the two from preparing themselves in the field of Biblical criticism, however. The preparation consisted in a day-to-day analysis of a chapter or so of the Bible, which was then commented upon orally by the two and, in all probability, checked against Dom Calmet's *Commentaire littéral*. Afterward, each recorded the comments in a dossier as he or she saw fit. Mme du Châtelet's manuscript was more orderly, more thorough, and more complete. Voltaire apparently respected it sufficiently to retain a copy in his library. He was totally unable to sustain this method himself. Even before Genesis had been covered in the *Bible enfin expliquée*, he had shifted to another procedure, and, by the time Solomon was reached, he had adopted a technique of the sort used in the *Notes* and *Preuves*. The model must have been something which first looked like *La Foi anéantie*, but I think it very soon resembled more closely the present *Bible enfin expliquée*. In the meantime, both Voltaire and Mme du Châtelet assembled a certain number of these clandestine essays as they were composed and circulated —the *Examen*, the *Analyse*, the *Meslier*, Woolston's *Discourses*, Spinoza's *Tractatus*, and the treatises by Fréret, Mirabaud, Dumarsais, Boulainvilliers, Lévesque de Burigny, Middleton, Gordon, and Annet. Cirey became a stronghold of English and French critical deism, at least potentially so.

There are indications that Voltaire actually entered upon the composition of some of his treatises at this time. Three of them I have examined in *Voltaire and Mme du Châtelet*: the *Sermon des cinquante*, thought to have been published for the first time in 1762, the *Examen important de Milord Bolingbroke*, published in 1766, and the *Bible enfin expliquée*, published for the first time in 1776.

If the *Sermon* appeared in print for the first time in 1762, it is certain that it was circulating in manuscript in 1760, when Barbier took note of it in his *Journal*, and even in 1759 when Mme de Fontaine mentioned it in a letter. Further, it was known to La Beaumelle by 1754, for he referred to it in his *Réponse au supplément du Siècle de Louis XIV*, which was published in that year. Grimm (*Correspondance littéraire*, VII, 147) stated that it was read publicly at Frederick's court. La Beaumelle, who was there in 1752, must have heard it then; hence, the manuscript existed already at that time. There is a copy of the printed *Sermon* dated 1753. As a matter of fact, Voltaire in the title ascribed to it the date 1749. With this evidence, it seems entirely possible that 1749 is the correct date of the composition, since it is difficult to understand why Voltaire would want to antedate a work published in 1752 or 1753 by three or so years. There could have been nefarious reasons for antedating it thirteen or so years when we thought that it was first published in 1762. But it seems to me now that we can accept that the *Sermon* was certainly written by 1749, that it was known to a select circle at Potsdam by 1752, that it was apparently discreetly printed abroad by 1753, that it was circulating in manuscript in Paris by 1759-1760, and that, by 1762, it was in open circulation. Voltaire, it is true, was very touchy about it, even later in 1764, as well he might be, because it was one of the deadliest of his deistic diatribes. When La Beaumelle insinuated that he was the author, he treated the insinuation as casually as he dared, but, when Rousseau attributed the *Sermon* to him, he reacted violently. It showed at least to what extent he appreciated the reputation Rousseau had with the public for integrity.

The *Sermon* has now been shown to be a product of the atmosphere of Cirey. When it is compared with the *Examen de la Genèse*, it will be seen that Voltaire has given his "rogaton" a different form. Instead of picking out miscellaneous discrepancies in the Bible, he has focused on two kinds of defects: moral perversities and false statements. Instead of packing his *Sermon* with long lists, he has made judicious selections and presented his items in points, as one would expect of a technique characterized by *Notes* and *Preuves*.

That is the reason the *Sermon* smacks not only of the *Examen de la Genèse* but of the *Religion chrétienne analysée* also, although it is even more compact than the latter treatise. Nonetheless, if it is examined closely, it will be found that Voltaire's reactions to the items selected are very similar to Mme du Châtelet's reactions to those same items. Indeed, in eleven cases, not only are the reactions to the items similar, but the actual objections are made in similar language and arranged in similar sequence. The model of this similarity of treatment can be seen in the two following examples.

 1. Joshua commands the sun to stand still.

Sermon: . . . le Seigneur Adonaï fait pleuvoir sur les fuyards une grosse pluie de pierres. . . .
Examen: Dieu faisoit pleuvoir sur eux une pluye de pierres.

Sermon: . . . le soleil s'arrête à Gabaon, et la lune sur Aialon.
Examen: . . . il se met à commander au soleil de s'arrêter sur Gabaon, et à la lune de demeurer sur Ajalon.

Sermon: Nous ne comprenons pas trop comment la lune étoit de la partie.
Examen: Au reste on ne sait trop ce que la lune fait là; ni le besoin que Josué en avoit. . . .

Sermon: . . . et il cite, pour son garant, le livre du Droiturier.
Examen: L'auteur pour faire croire un fait si extraordinaire, dit qu'il est écrit dans le livre des Justes.

Here, the criticism and language are similar, the sequence of ideas impressively so.

 2. The genealogy of Christ.

Sermon: . . . Matthieu compte quarante-deux générations en deux mille ans; mais dans son compte, il ne s'en trouve que quarante et une. . . .
Examen: . . . car il est absurde qu'en près de deux mille ans il ne se trouve que quarante-deux générations. Mais ce nombre de quarante-deux générations que St. Mathieu a choisi de préférence, il ne le remplit pas, et il n'en rapporte que quarante et une. . . .

Sermon: . . . il se trompe . . . en donnant Josias pour père à Jéchonias. . . .
Examen: . . . Josias n'a jamais eu de fils appellé Jéchonias. . . .

Sermon: . . . ces généalogies sont celles de Joseph.
Examen: . . . cette généalogie se trouve être celle de Joseph.

In this case, the ideas are similar, both in content and sequence.

The *Examen important,* which was published in the *Recueil nécessaire* (1766), was marked "ecrit sur la fin de 1736," apparently by Voltaire himself. However, in the "Avis" to the editors, apparently also written by Voltaire, was the following note: "Ce précis de la doctrine de Milord Bolingbroke, recueillie tout entière dans les six volumes de ses *Œuvres posthumes,* fut adressé par lui, peu d'années avant sa mort, à Milord Cornsburi." Since Bolingbroke died in 1751, it would seem that the "peu d'années" could be interpreted as around 1748. That means that we have two possible dates proposed by Voltaire for the *Examen important*: 1736 and 1748. This time the difference is considerable. But, whichever date we choose, the work still lies within the Cirey period. The two dates, though, are always rejected as fabrications devised by Voltaire. The arguments given are never very cogent. Either it is pointed out that the work was certainly not published until 1766 and that, consequently, it is unthinkable that it should have been written thirty or twenty years before, or it is recalled that Voltaire is known to have falsified dates, or, finally, it is stressed that the work is far too mature a one to assign to the Cirey period. Why Voltaire antedated the work is seldom discussed, the usual assumption being that Voltaire must have had his reasons. In this particular case, however, I cannot see that there was any advantage whatever Voltaire could have gained from antedating the composition of the work by thirty, or even twenty, years. In fact, I think it was a mistake for Voltaire to have given two dates twelve years apart, since such irresponsibility merely invites skepticism without creating any presumption in the author's favor. It can be argued that, if Voltaire wanted to lay the work at Bolingbroke's door, he would have had to write it before 1751. But, then, 1748 would do as well as 1736, and vice versa. If he wanted to leave the impression that the work was compiled using extracts from the manuscripts of the *Œuvres posthumes,* which were published in 1754-1755, either 1736 or 1748 could have been chosen without creating any difficulty.

If one scans the treatise for contemporary allusions, one can find an impressive number which would justify either of these dates, though particularly 1736. I have assembled them in *Voltaire and Mme du Châtelet* (pp. 153ff.). The idea that one's religion depends upon the place of one's birth, which was taken from Dryden, was used in *Zaïre* (1732). The attack against Pascal for revolting his readers recalls the attack of the twenty-fifth *Lettre philosophique*. The reference to Meslier, "mort depuis peu" (Meslier died in 1729, but Voltaire, who heard of him in 1735, thought he died in 1733), fits perfectly with 1736. The reference to the Dorsetshire curate which comes immediately thereafter is a strange case, since the only other places I know of where it exists are in two extracts to Meslier (Orléans 1115 and Arsenal 2559). I have shown (*Modern Philology*, XXX [1933], pp. 392ff.) that Voltaire's printed *Extrait* resembled an *Extrait* drawn from a manuscript of this kind. Since some of the *Extraits* in manuscript, as well as Voltaire's printed *Extrait*, are dated 1742, the allusion seems to belong to the Cirey period. The only reasonable explanation here is that Voltaire heard of both Meslier and the curate at the same time. Further, the mention of Lady Blackacre, a character in the *Plain Dealer*, used by Voltaire in *La Prude* (1740), should be added. The phrase "mais à la fraude ajoutons le fanatisme" recalls the subject of *Mahomet*. The reference to Fox brings to mind a similar reference in the *Lettres philosophiques* (1734). The two lines quoted from Ablavius remind one of the opening lines of the *Mondain* (1736), while the remark of Valentinien concerning the activities of two or thirty sects in a state was apparently echoed in a similar statement in the *Lettres philosophiques*. Once more, the question of the significance of these reminiscences arises. It can, of course, be argued that Voltaire was trying to make the statement "écrit sur la fin de 1736" look authentic by dubbing in these contemporary references, and it is certainly possible that he was. But why go to all that trouble? Just what would he have gained by making it look authentic? Moreover, having gone to the trouble of authenticating 1736, why would he have then suggested 1748? One can hardly escape the feeling that the Cirey atmosphere pervades the *Examen important*.

The impression is strengthened when the statements of the *Examen important* are set alongside the corresponding statements of the *Examen de la Genèse*. The sheer number of matching statements is striking but the similarity between the reactions of Voltaire and Mme du Châtelet is more impressive still. These parallel passages have been presented in *Voltaire and Mme du Châtelet* (pp. 156ff.). Some of the most significant are the same as some of those we quoted above in comparing the *Sermon* with the *Genése*.

    1. Joshua commands the sun to stand still.

Examen: ... et c'est en faveur de ces monstres qu'on fait arrêter le soleil et la lune en plein midi! et pourquoi? pour leur donner le temps de poursuivre et d'égorger de pauvres Amorrhéens déjà écrasés par une pluie de grosses pierres que Dieu avait lancées sur eux du haut des airs pendant cinq grandes lieues de chemin. (XLIII, 67)

Genése: ... et pendant qu'ils fuyoient devant Israël, Dieu fit pleuvoir une pluye de pierres sur eux qui en tua encore plus que n'avoit fait Josué. Qui croiroit après cela que Dieu eut eu encore quelque chose à faire dans cette occasion pour les Israëlites contre les Amorrhéens, cependant Josué ne fut pas encore content, et dans le tems que ses ennemis s'enfuyoient devant lui et que Dieu faisoit pleuvoir sur eux une pluye de pierres, il se met à commander au soleil de s'arrêter sur Gabaon. ... (II, 11-12)

    2. Zachariah, son of Barachiah.

Examen: On a une preuve bien sensible dans celui qui est attribué à Mathieu. Ce livre met dans la bouche de Jésus ces paroles aux Juifs: "Vous rendrez compte de tout le sang répandu depuis le juste Abel jusqu'à Zacharie, fils de Barachie, que vous avez tué entre le temple et l'autel." Un faussaire se découvre toujours par quelque endroit. Il y eut, pendant le siège de Jérusalem, un Zacharie, fils d'un Barachie, assassiné entre le temple et l'autel par la faction des zélés. (XLIII, 101)

Genèse: [The same verse is quoted.] Ce verset est une preuve que l'Evangile de St. Mathieu a été écrit depuis la prise de Jérusalem; et que par conséquent il n'est point de cet apôtre: car il n'y a point de Zacharie fils de Barachie tué entre le temple et l'autel, que celui dont parle Joseph dans son histoire, qui fut tué pendant le siège de Jérusalem par Titus. ... (IV, 88)

    3. The money-lenders.

Examen: Il entre dans le temple, c'est-à-dire dans cette grande enceinte où demeuraient les prêtres, dans cette cour où de petits marchands étaient autorisés par la loi à vendre des poules, des pigeons, des agneaux, à ceux qui venaient sacrifier. Il prend un grand fouet, en donne sur les épaules de tous les marchands, les chasse à coups de lanières, eux, leurs poules, leurs pigeons, leurs moutons, et leurs bœufs même, jette tout leur argent par terre, et on le laisse faire! (XLIII, 87)

Genèse: Quand Jésus fut entré à Jérusalem, il alla au temple, et il se mit à chasser les marchands qui étoient dans le parvis, v. 12, à renverser leurs marchandises, et à leur citer les prophètes. . . . Assurément il n'y a rien si surprenant que cette action de Jésus et de voir un homme seul, sans autorité, et un homme méprisé chasse cette foule de marchands qui étoient dans les galleries extérieures du temple. (IV, 76)

4. The Jews in Egypt.

Examen: C'était bien alors que le prétendu Moïse devait s'emparer de ce beau pays, au lieu de s'enfuir en lâche et en coquin . . . avec deux ou trois millions d'hommes parmi lesquels il avait, dit-on, six cent trente mille combattants. (XLIII, 54)

Genèse: Il faut avouer que c'étoit bien la peine de faire tant de miracles et tant de mal aux hommes pour faire sortir les Israëlites d'un beau et bon pays comme l'Egypte, pour les faire errer quarante ans dans les déserts de l'arabie; et qu'il est plaisant de voir plus de six cent mille hommes fuyant devant pharaon, et errans dans les déserts pendant quarante ans, le tout par les soins du Dieu tout puissant. N'était-il pas plus court et plus expédient de leur donner tout d'un coup l'Egypte dont Dieu avoit presque détruit tout le peuple à force de miracles. (I, 116-117)

5. Rahab.

Examen: Et remarquons en passant que cette femme, nommée Rahab la paillarde, est une des aieules de ce Juif dont nous avons fait depuis un Dieu. (XLIII, 67)

Genèse: Au reste, cette Rahab eut non seulement l'honneur d'être incorporée au peuple hébreu, mais encore celui d'être ayeule du Messie, et rappellée dans sa généalogie. (II, 2-3)

6. Saul's swords and lances.

Examen: Il n'y avait dans leur petit pays ni épée ni lance; les Cananéens ou Philistins ne permettaient pas aux Juifs, leurs esclaves, d'aiguiser seulement les socs de leurs charrues et leurs cognées . . . et cependant on nous conte que le roi Saül eut d'abord une armée de trois cent mille hommes, avec lesquels il gagna une grande bataille. (XLIII, 71)

Genèses: Il n'y a rien de si extraordinaire que ce qui est marqué au v. 19, "qu'il n'y avoit point de forgerons alors dans Israël; que les Philistins les avoient ôtés aux hébreux, crainte qu'ils ne se forgeassent des épées et des lances, et qu'il n'y avoit que Saül et Jonathas qui eussent des armes . . ." où les Israëlites prenoient-ils donc des armes pour combattre? de quoi les trois mille hommes que Saul choisit au commencement de ce chap. 11, v. 11, avoient secouru Jabés de Galaad. . . . (II, 49-50)

7. Hosea and his prostitute.

Examen: Ici c'est Osée à qui Dieu ordonne de prendre une p. . . et d'avoir des fils de . . . Vade sume tibi, etc. . . . dit la Vulgate. Osée obéit ponctuellement. . . . (XLIII, 77)

Genèse: Dieu lui ordonne de prendre pour sa femme une prostituée, et d'en avoir des enfans de prostitution . . . Vade sume tibi, etc. . . . On ne sait guères comment des enfants de Prostitution sont faits; mais apparemment qu'Osée le savoit, car il obéit. (III, 130)

8. The Roman census.

Examen: Je dirais à Luc: Comment oses-tu avancer que Jésus naquit sous le gouvernement de Cyrinus ou Quirinus, tandis qu'il est avéré que Quirinus ne fut gouverneur de Syrie que plus de six ans après? Comment as-tu le front de dire qu'Auguste avait ordonné *le dénombrement de toute la terre* et que Marie alla à Bethléem pour se faire dénombrer? Le dénombrement de toute la terre! Quelle expression! (XLIII, 105)

Genèse: Premièrement aucun historien ne parle de ce dénombrement, qui eut été cependant assés remarquable; secondement il n'y a jamais eu de Cyrinus gouverneur de Syrie. Mais en supposant que le nom de Cyrinus fut celui de Quirinus corrompu, on n'en est pas plus avancé; car il n'y eut point de Quirinus gouverneur de Syrie pendans le règne d'Hérode, ni par conséquent du tems de la naissance de Jésus Christ. Enfin, pour comble de ridicule, St. Luc dit v. 2 que ce dénombrement fut le premier qu'on fit sous le gouvernement de Cyrinus, comme si Auguste avait fait faire tous les jours le dénombrement des habitans *de toute la terre*. (IV, 139)

Pomeau, who has discussed (*Religion*, pp. 175-176) very intelligently these cases I proposed, has hesitated to accept that the *Examen important* was written either in 1736 or 1748. If by "written" is meant "completed," then I would agree. What I suggested was that a draft of the first half of the *Examen important* was made at this time, and I offered these similarities as evidence. Pomeau concedes that several critical points examined by Voltaire were also taken up by Mme du Châtelet. In fact, there are not simply several of these points, but many of them. One of the excellent stylistic qualities of the *Examen important* is its condensation of the material into concentrated points. The effect engendered by this condensation is the opposite of the impression created by the *Sermon*. It is true that in both works the technique of the *Notes* and *Preuves* is used. But, whereas in the *Sermon* the necessity of restricting the length was made into a virtue by a judicious selection of the items to be treated, the *Examen important* gives the impression that an attempt was deliberately made to pack as many biblical items into the treatise as possible. It is as if the writer tried to summarize all of Mme du Châtelet's treatise. Pomeau states further that the contemporary allusions do not prove the early date, since it often happens that Voltaire dates a work "en fonction de la présentation qu'il a choisie." On this point he is surely correct, for, with a literary artist, this practice can easily become almost second nature. But that does not explain why the work came to be given two dates. Nor does it account for the fact that either date can be easily justified by these contemporary allusions, though only the date 1736 is fully justified by them since they extend from 1732 to 1742, but not from 1742 to 1748. Pomeau suggests that Voltaire was probably not even aware that he had given two dates. Such a lapse of memory would have been very strange, indeed, particularly if he was deliberately suggesting one or two false dates. And, if they did not have a "signification précise" (as Pomeau also suggests), there would have been no reason for giving a false date. Avenel's remark that 1736 was chosen because it was the year Bolingbroke withdrew to France and began his historical studies will not do, both because there is no suggestion that this *Examen* was connected with Bolingbroke's newly undertaken historical studies and because there is a suggestion that this *Examen* was connected with the termination of those studies, the *Œuvres posthumes*. That might justify the 1748 date, but not 1736. Pomeau has found the really significant document which gives a clue to what actually took place. Voltaire wrote a letter to Mme du Deffand in 1759 in which he said: "Je voudrais que quelqu'un eût élagué en France les *Œuvres philosophiques* de feu Milord Bolingbroke. C'est un ouvrage bien terrible pour les préjugés, et bien utile pour la raison." That seems to indicate that, before 1759, there may have been an *Examen important* (that is, the first half of the present treatise, albeit only in a preliminary draft) but that there was not an *Examen important de Milord Bolingbroke* until after 1759. Bengesco or Beuchot had already suggested that the "Milord Bolingbroke" was not added to the title until after the Mallet edition (1754-1755).

Pomeau, moreover, does not accept the analogies between Voltaire's and Mme du Châtelet's treatments of the various items, in the first place because they come from Dom Calmet. I do not understand what difference that makes. He does concede that the analogy between the two sets of remarks which do not derive from Dom Calmet is "probante," but he maintains that it does not prove the existence of a tentative first draft of an *Examen important* at Cirey. He admits, though, that the *Examen important*, like the other pamphlets written at Ferney, "utilise les matériaux de Cirey," but enriched by other research. I am not too opposed to this way of looking at things. I would like to know more definitely, however, since I am concerned with the development of Voltaire's intellectual outlook, how he proceeded.

Pomeau is likewise unwilling to grant that the *Bible enfin expliquée*, also, had its origin in the Cirey atmosphere, citing Wagnière's remark that the composition dated from 1776 and Du Pan's comment ("son nouvel ouvrage est, dit-on, un commentaire sur la Bible") that it dated from 1774. Pomeau thinks that Voltaire had only to assemble the numerous notes which he had accumulated over the previous decades, and certainly nothing would have been easier. But it seems likely that, had he done so, the work would have been more solidly constructed. Pomeau grants that some of the points come from notes accumulated at Cirey, and these are the ones, he says, which I can quote as resembling the *Genèse*. For him, the *Bible enfin expliquée* is a "pastiche" of Dom Calmet, a sort of "à la manière de . . ." This would seem to me an unlikely hypothesis. In the first place, I have shown that the technique used in the *Bible* is that of the *Notes* and *Preuves*, which was a product of the Cirey atmosphere. Moreover, Calmet, who certainly was important to the Cirey pair, was yet no more important than many others. The only difference was that he was more carefully quoted. But that care indicates an earlier date of composition, when the two were studying Calmet, rather than a later date. However, just as I think the evidence indicates that only a part of the *Examen impor-*

tant was composed at Cirey, so I also think the evidence indicates that the *Bible* was revised before publication, and Pomeau (*Religion*, p. 177) seems ready to grant that the *Bible* as well as the *Examen important* did use the materials assembled at Cirey, along with other materials assembled at Ferney. In the final analysis, our views are not so far apart. The greatest divergence appears in our estimates of the amount which was done at Cirey: I think about two-thirds of the *Bible* was composed there and one-half of the *Examen important*; Pomeau would reduce that figure considerably, if not to zero.

Nonetheless, the extent to which the *Bible* is in accord with the *Genèse* is very impressive indeed. I shall not repeat the details here, having already recorded them elsewhere (*Voltaire and Mme du Châtelet*, pp. 170-189). The immense number of these similar treatments could be used to lend weight to the thesis that the two works were prepared under similar circumstances. More important still are the few comments which occur in these two works but occur never, or very rarely, elsewhere: the statement that the Hebrew text differs from the Vulgate in the reference to plural Gods, the insistence upon the primitive vulgarity of the Bible, the concern about the "cataracts" of the sky at the time of the flood, the remark that after the Fall, God treats Adam with "bitter irony," the stress on the point that in the Old Testament man and beast share and share alike and that God even made a pact with both man and beast, and the observation that, since the time Jacob struggled with the angel, the Jews have removed the nerve in the "cuisse" of animals they eat, although there is no law to that effect.

Another source of support for this thesis is to be found in the technique Voltaire invented, which consists in using some such phrase as "Les critiques disent," or "à ce que disent les critiques," or "nos critiques," or "les critiques." There are many occurrences of phrases of this sort in the *Bible*, and, in the vast majority, the remarks appear in precisely this form in the *Examen de la Genèse*.

Still more evidence is provided by the many instances where, in the choice of event, manner of expression, points made, and sequence, the two are decidedly similar. One example should suffice here: Joshua commanding the sun to stand still. Each of the authors makes four comments upon the event in exactly the same order:

there was no need for the miracle after the hail of stones had killed the Amorrhéens; there was no need for the miracle, since the sun was in the middle of the sky and there was ample time to complete the rout of the few remaining Amorrhéens before nightfall; the miracle could not have happened, since the sun does not turn around the earth; and the Book of the Just, which is mentioned as proof of the miracle, proves, on the contrary, that Joshua did not write the Book of Joshua.

Bible: On remarque seulement ici que ces pierres . . . durent écraser tous les Amorrhéens . . . c'est ce qui fait que plusieurs savants sont étonnés que Josué ait encore eu recours au grand miracle d'arrêter le soleil et la lune. (I, 225)

Genèse: Qui croiroit après cela que Dieu eut eu encore quelque chose à faire dans cette occasion pour les Israëlites contre les Amorrhéens. . . . (II, 12)

Bible: Mais tous les autres commentateurs . . . conviennent tous que le soleil et la lune s'arrêtèrent en plein midi. On auroit eu le temps de tuer tous les fuyards depuis midi jusqu'au soir. (I, 225)

Genèse: Il étoit selon les interprêtes environ dix heures du matin, et au plus midi, selon le texte *in medio cœli* quand Josué commanda au soleil de s'arrêter pour lui donner le temps de deffaire des ennemis déjà vaincus, il faut avouer qu'il étoit d'une grande précaution. (II, 12)

Bible: Les physiciens ont quelque peine à expliquer comment le soleil, qui ne marche pas arrêta son cours, et comment cette journée, qui fut le double des autres journées, put s'accorder avec le mouvement des planettes et la régularité des éclipses. (I, 226)

Genèse: Je ne parle pas de l'absurdité physique de ce miracle. . . . On est aussi un peu embarrassé à expliquer cet ordre que Josué donne au soleil, depuis qu'il est prouvé que ce n'est lui qui tourne, mais la terre. . . . (II, 13)

Bible: A l'égard du livre des justes, qui est cité comme garant de la vérité de cette histoire, le Lord Bolingbroke insiste beaucoup sur ce livre. . . . Cela démontre, dit-il, que c'est du livre du droiturier que l'histoire de Josué est prise. (I, 226)

Genèse: Ce que Josué cite ici du livre des Justes, fait voir évidemment que le livre que j'examine et qui porte son nom n'est pas de lui, car comment pourroit-il citer un livre où l'événement dont il parle, est marqué comme passé. (II, 14)

All of this grubbing and splitting of hairs can be justified only on one score—that it makes a difference to the interpretation of Voltaire's role in the deistic movement whether he entered it in the period of its clandestinity or whether he did so later in the stage of its expansion. At first glance, it does not seem that there is much to be gained from knowing what really happened. It could be argued with some cogency that, as far as the overall effect goes, all of these deistic treatises played some role in the changing of religious thought during the second half of the century. However, from another point of view, the problem has more significance than would at first appear. As in all problems concerned with clandestinity, determination of the timing is very important; otherwise, it is very easy to become confused about the motive for the event and the actual relationship between the event and the surrounding circumstances—not to mention the way the event shaped the evolution of the protagonist's thought.

For instance, if Voltaire started his deistic campaign as an attack against *l'Infâme*, in 1762, as we have always thought, we have to explain why he refrained from doing so, as all logic would seem to dictate, between 1730 and 1762. And, if despite that logic, Voltaire did have reasons for delaying the attack, we must then perforce explain how in 1762, or thereabouts, he prepared for that attack, because a movement of ideas of these proportions cannot be mounted in short order. Therefore, if, despite his seeming silence, he was going through a period of preparation between 1735 and 1760, we have to explain the general direction of that preparation and at least how it united with his other more open intellectual activities—his development of history, for instance. Once we clearly perceive the general outlines of his activity, we can understand better that it is not correct to say that the Potsdam experience emboldened Voltaire and made him more radical in his thought and action, as Lanson suggested. What really occurred was that Voltaire had all along the line combined his deistic experiences (English and French) with his deistic inclinations and had thus prepared himself to become the leader in eighteenth-century theism, so that, when the moment was ripe for the attack of theism against organized Christianity, he was ready, in every sense of the word, to join battle.

That does not mean that we do not need to appreciate fully the general outlines of the battle. Certainly, it is important to know the main points of his preparation. And it is equally important to know how he organized his campaign and conducted his assault. It seems perfectly plausible that Voltaire postponed the assault until the political and social circumstances offered a most propitious moment for anyone who judged that a new start in these areas was indicated. Nor should we forget that Voltaire followed, as Pomeau has shown, a more or less definite timetable in developing the movement. Lastly, we must not fail to note either the rhythm or the variety or the completeness of the attack.

If one will scan carefully the voluminous section in Voltaire's work usually marked "mélanges," one will discover eventually that it consists entirely of works dealing with the aspects of life which will have to "merge" in order to open up a new approach to life: science, philosophy, history, morality, aesthetics, religion, and politics (including economics). These categories really comprise the categories of living. If one tries to understand what characterizes these categories as Voltaire discusses them, in every case it is change, revision, reform. These three things, however, are not equivalent. Change is regarded as something endemic, like a disease, and as something that transcends human existence. The other two characteristics, on the other hand, are definitely human responsibilities; they merely take advantage of the endemic quality of change. But the important point is that they are really connected with "vision," with "form." Owing to the inevitable change, man gets a chance to remake, to plan anew, to live otherwise. To accept the challenge, he has to accept certain conditions: he cannot "revise" without changing the "vision," nor can he "reform" without doing away with the old "form."

What concerns us here, however, is not the whole human picture, but the category of religion in Voltaire's thought. The striking thing is the immense amount of space Voltaire accorded to the category. Beginning with the *Sermon du Rabbin Akib* (1761), Voltaire literally poured forth treatise after treatise devoted to this category. The mere enumeration of these "rogatons" is impressive: *Sermon des cinquante* (1762), *Catéchisme de l'honnête homme* (1763), *Dialogue du douteur et de l'adorateur* (1763), *Questions sur les miracles* (1765), *Examen important de Milord Bolingbroke* (1766), *Ques-*

tions de Zapata (1767), *Homélies prononcées à Londres* (1767), *Le Dîner du Comte de Boulainvilliers* (1768), *Sermon prêché à Bâle* (1768), *Entretiens Chinois* (1768), *Profession de foi des théistes* (1768), *Homélie du pasteur Bourn* (1768), *Collection d'anciens Evangiles* (1769), *Dieu et les hommes* (1769), *Les Adorateurs* (1769), *Sermon du Papa Nicolas Charisteski* (1771), *La Bible enfin expliquée* (1776), *Histoire de l'établissement du Christianisme* (1777)—without insisting upon the *Dictionnaire philosophique* (1764), the *Traité sur la tolérance* (1763), and the *Questions sur l'Encyclopédie* (1771-1772).

It would be superfluous to recapitulate the contents of all these works, particularly since we of the twentieth century are neither interested nor amused by Voltaire's sallies against religion. They probably best correspond to the bitter and sometimes intelligent discussions at the present time in the political arena, particularly in the struggle which goes on relentlessly between communism and democracy. What was at stake in the eighteenth-century struggle between deism and Christianity in the category of religion, indeed, is rather analogous to what is at stake in the struggle between communism and democracy in the category of politics. We must keep in mind, though, the general law that one cannot upset or modify one category of life without involving all of the other categories.

For Voltaire, the category which had to be revised was the Christian religion, specifically, since he was a Catholic, the Catholic Church, but more specifically still, the "superstition" which had, in his opinion, become the poisoned root of all religion. It was this superstition, he felt, which was the cause (the historical cause) of the errors, the contradictions, the absurdities, and the vices of contemporary life. Moreover, since the end of the fifteenth century, it had produced interminable turmoil, rank injustice, unending persecution, and wars. Voltaire looked upon it as the great evil of this world. Much of his reaction was motivated by the same considerations that prompted Spinoza's attack, or, at any rate, Spinoza's explanations of his reasons for undertaking the *Tractatus* fit well with what we know about Voltaire's underlying motives for his savage denunciation of religious superstition. There were, however, two points on which Voltaire differed from Spinoza. The latter deeply resented the accusation of atheism which the religious were constantly bringing against him, and he set out with cool determination to replace religious thought by philosophical thought. Voltaire did not escape a similar accusation, particularly after the publication of the *Lettres philosophiques*, but his revolt against the Christian devotees was less a personal resentment for his own persecution than an almost fanatic condemnation of the persecutions the Church carried out in the name of human justice. It is as if Voltaire suddenly became aware of the inherent evil of man, of Hobbes's reminder that *homo hominibus lupus est*. He became convinced that the source of that evil was the religious wars, the persecutions, and the injustices of Catholics and Protestants. His first objection to Christianity was that it was not Christian: the idea of brotherly love, he thought, had long since been abandoned. We must believe Voltaire perfectly sincere when he insisted that all men are "frères." Hence, he had no such ambition as Spinoza did to replace religious thought by philosophical thought—although, as we shall see, circumstances forced him to do so. He was, as a matter of fact, totally incompetent in the realm of systematic philosophy, as we shall also see. What he wanted in the place of Christianity was, paradoxically enough, "real" Christianity. The old fight between verisimilitude and truth entered the debate: contemporary religious discussions seemed to him frankly to manifest only the appearance of truth, while "true" religion was something else. Voltaire, like all his deist friends, called this "true" religion "natural"; he, too, based it upon some form of the Golden Rule. He required an open confession of the brotherhood of man, and he constantly reiterated that the test of that brotherhood was human justice. It was this reign of justice, this Golden Age, this Utopia, this "real" Christianity which he envisioned, and, since his "vision" was sadly out of tune with reality, he savagely lacerated the institution which, in his opinion, was mainly responsible for this state of affairs. His cry became "Ecrasons l'Infâme." It was repeated over and over and became as audible as that other protest which he launched: "Le mal est sur la terre." We must not delude ourselves by the abstraction of the war cry, nor attempt to palliate Voltaire's intentions. Ever since the beginning, since the *Epître à Uranie* (1722), he had been conscious of an incompatibility between what Christianity was and what Christianity should be. He probably was totally lacking in the insights of Meslier, but he ultimately saw things the way Meslier did: Christian dogma was false, Christian ritual was useless, the organization of the Christian Church was totally evil, the representatives of this religious form were untrustworthy and hypocritical. Voltaire felt that these opinions could be proved by a constant assault against all the reasons given for the divinity of the Christian religion.

An attack of this sort could be expected to raise havoc with the organic unity of life as the Enlightenment inherited it from the seventeenth century. The logical conclusion one would think Voltaire and his contemporaries would naturally have come to is that the category of religion needed to be reformed, and indeed, as we have seen, practically every one of these treatises concluded with an exhortation to replace the present-day religious order with "natural" religion. Voltaire very carefully wrote a long poem, *Poème sur la loi naturelle,* to provide for that reform. His moves to replace orthodox Christianity with deism were genuine, but they were not very successful, as we now know. The reasons for this lack of success need further study. It is already evident, though, that, of all forms of religion, deism is the most unstable and the weakest. Voltaire became aware of its shortcomings around 1770, when Holbach, Diderot, and others pushed on intellectually to atheism. Voltaire's defense may appear heroic, but, as a matter of fact, it was totally inadequate. It should be stated clearly, however, that he was well aware all along that a new strength had to be given to the category of religion. There were four ways he felt this could be done: (1) by a history which justified the making of civilization and a philosophy of progress, (2) by a strengthening of the category of politics, which would share its strength with a weakened religion, (3) by remaking the category of morality along the lines of brotherly love and "bienfaisance," and, finally, (4) by giving a philosophical, rather than a religious, foundation to all the categories of living. The remainder of Voltaire's intellectual life was employed in all of these operations, but the thing which united them was the search for an organic philosophy.

10. THE MEANING OF THE CIREY EXPERIENCE

B Y THIS TIME WE should be able to draw a relatively accurate picture of Voltaire's entry into philosophy. The initial act was undoubtedly Voltaire's own: it consisted in a close reading of Malebranche's *Recherche de la vérité*, around 1722, and a rather more casual surveying of Bayle's historical writing in a search for some confirmatory material for the *Henriade*. This initiation into philosophy was supplemented by some curiosity concerning Fontenelle's *Entretiens sur la pluralité des mondes* (see the letter to Fontenelle in 1721) and at least some slight connection with the contemporary critical deists (see the *Epître à Uranie*), which could have grown out of the experiences of the Temple. Then came the letter of 1724 from Bolingbroke which counseled a study of Locke and Newton and suggested that study of these two would throw the philosophy of Descartes and Malebranche more into perspective. Once in England, Voltaire availed himself of the opportunity to acquaint himself with the *Essay concerning Human Understanding*, which he apparently read at the time, and with Pemberton's introduction to Newton's philosophy, which he evidently had seen in manuscript. We do not know, however, how deeply he entered into these works at the time. There are reasons to believe that he waited until his return before pursuing his study of them vigorously, under the guidance of Maupertuis and Pitot. At the same time, he seems to have delved into Bayle with some assistance from Des Alleurs and the society around La Popelinière. The *Lettres philosophiques* bring together these varied philosophical interests. Lanson has shown in his notes to the critical edition of the *Lettres philosophiques* that they are filled with reminiscences from Bayle, and the *Lettres* themselves are devoted to Bacon, Locke, Descartes, Newton, and Pascal. Viewed in this perspective, they are, as we have seen, truly "philosophical." One can readily understand why the next step Voltaire took was to deepen his acquaintance with these philosophers. This, of course, was the meaning of his *Traité de métaphysique*, where he attempts to clarify for himself his own philosophical position. While doing so, though, he discovered, in 1735, that one cannot adopt Locke and Newton without giving some consideration to Descartes, Pascal, and Gassendi. He learned further that one cannot treat philosophy lightly and that science requires careful training, precise thinking, and a solid grasp of fundamental principles. He hoped that Formont would aid him in becoming a philosopher, as Cideville had helped and encouraged him when he was developing his poetry and drama.

It was his old teacher Tournemine who taught him that he could not hope to achieve his ends if he only discoursed pleasantly upon metaphysical subjects. The criticism in the *Journal de Trévoux* and the subsequent exchange of ideas between Voltaire and the Jesuit did much to clarify Voltaire's position, but it did even more to show him how terribly superficial he was in philosophy. This realization led him to undertake a second draft of the *Traité de métaphysique,* in which his goal was no longer to espouse a set of philosophical principles but to put forward a single principle, the existence of God, which would guarantee a "métaphysique morale" and at the same time justify the Newtonian universe. It was at this point that Frederick intervened with his announced enthusiasm for Leibniz. Once more, a lengthy exchange of views took place, between the Prince whom Mme du Châtelet called an "assez bon métaphysicien" and Voltaire whom she now conceded was "un grand métaphysicien." This discussion coincided with a third revision of the *Traité.* In the meantime, Algarotti had visited Cirey, bringing with him his *Neutonianismo per le dame.* The two erstwhile philosophers were too involved now to let matters stand at a personal treatise on metaphysics, which could not be published anyway. It would be much better, they felt, to redo Algarotti's superficial *Neutonianismo* in a serious way, much better to give a metaphysical background to the Newtonian discoveries. The result of these efforts was the *Eléments de la philosophie de Newton.* Amidst all of this activity, Voltaire was structuring his own thought, but he was also giving focus to the thought of his time. He himself recorded in 1735 that a humanistic, cultured, artistic society had become scientific and philosophical. He announced that he would have to adapt himself to that change but that he refused to abandon one society for the other. Instead, he would merge the two.

To understand how this merging took place, we have to get

some general perspective on Voltaire's production during the Cirey period. This production comprised a set of additional plays—*Alzire* (1735), *L'Enfant prodigue* (1736), *Mahomet* (1740), and *Mérope* (1743), which, incidentally, are among the best that Voltaire wrote. He also produced a set of philosophical poems—*Le Mondain* (1736), *Défense du mondain* (1737), and *Discours en vers sur l'homme* (1738)—in which he subordinated the poetic content to the thought content. To the field of philosophy, he contributed the *Traité de métaphysique* (1734-1739), which attempted to continue the philosophy of Locke, along with the thought of Shaftesbury and Mandeville. His study of science resulted in the *Eléments de la philosophie de Newton* (1738, rearranged in 1740, with a new Part I), which was designed to present the essential importance of Newton's theories of attraction and optics. These latter two works were most important, for they introduced into French civilization the two outstanding thinkers of English civilization—Newton and Locke. A whole set of histories came out of this period, beginning with a revised *Charles XII* (1738) and including the *Siècle de Louis XIV* (begun in 1732, first draft completed apparently in 1737, some chapters published in 1739 in a *Recueil de poésies*, published as a whole in 1751), the *Essai sur les mœurs* (begun in 1739 as a *Histoire universelle*, some chapters published in the *Mercure* in 1746-1747, published as a whole in 1753), and the *Précis du siècle de Louis XV* (begun in 1746, published in 1754). At the same time, Voltaire and Mme du Châtelet began a study of the Bible which culminated in the *Sermon des cinquante* (1746), the writing of the first part of the *Examen important de Milord Bolingbroke* (1766), and the *Bible enfin expliquée* (1776). Finally, he undertook an excursion into a new kind of fiction, called the *conte philosophique*. The first attempt at this sort of *conte* occurred around 1736 or 1737 with the *Comte de Boursoufle,* of which we have only a fragment. A more serious effort was the *Gangan,* which Voltaire sent Frederick in 1739. Indeed, there is every indication that the *Gangan* was the original draft of *Micromégas,* so finished that it took but very little revision when it was published in 1752. It is very likely that *Le Crocheteur borgne* belongs to the same time (1739-1740), and *Memnon* and *Zadig* were soon to follow (1746-1748). In fact, far from being an epoch of sterility, as Lanson would have it, Voltaire used the decade 1739-

1749 to create and develop a new art form which was destined to become his characteristic artistic genre.

We are now in a position to draw some very definite conclusions concerning the importance of Voltaire's activity in the Cirey period. The first thing to note is its tremendous diversity: it embraced theatre, light verse, and philosophical poems, it definitively merged the English civilization with that of France, and it showed the necessity, for the betterment of European civilization, of uniting English thought with French art. To that end, Voltaire adopted a procedure whereby French art could be made more philosophical and gave his enthusiastic support to the movement in which English thought, and, indeed, European thought, tended to become more artistic. He made every effort to coordinate his artistic genres with the new thought content, and, when they appeared inappropriate, he either recast them or invented new genres. To the historian of ideas, two problems seem to have been paramount for Voltaire: how to put philosophical and scientific content into old accepted genres, and how to create new and vital genres which would adequately contain the tremendous vitality of the new philosophical and scientific content.

It was the situation created by these two problems which required the poet to reeducate himself. It is as if the humanistic training the Jesuit fathers had given him was no longer adequate to the changing conditions. The epic, drama, and Horatian verse were no longer deemed a worthy justification for the career of a man of letters. Certainly, as Voltaire saw these changing conditions, the predominant pursuits of the time were science and philosophy—more specifically, Newtonian science and Lockean philosophy. But, though dominantly Newtonian and Lockean, that is, English, this science and philosophy could not be separated from the body of seventeenth-century philosophy and science that was European. Voltaire, in 1734-1739, could not very well study these two outstanding English philosophers without taking Leibniz, Bayle, Fontenelle, Malebranche, and Spinoza into consideration, too. Philosophy, in addition, incorporated "la morale," the science of man, and that included biblical criticism, history, politics, economics, and psychology. Voltaire involved himself in these embryo sciences, the "sciences humaines," as we now call them, either to the point where he kept abreast of their development or to the point where he became a leader in their expansion. His intellectual growth was thus strictly coordinated with the intellectual growth of the Enlightenment.

This latter point is very important. In a striking way, Voltaire was preparing himself for the changing times in the same manner as his century was doing. At the same time, he was engaged in preparing his contemporaries to adapt themselves to these changing times. The expansion of science, both physical and moral, which was taking place between 1680 and 1750 and which brought about the need for the *Encyclopédie*, transformed Voltaire, through his reeducation, from a poet into an encyclopedic man. His efforts in reaching out into other intellectual domains were similar to those of many of his contemporaries. His personal problem was the century's problem, too: how to grasp the new learning and turn it into an instrument for remaking the world. It is not easy for us to understand this operation. In the first place, it was carried on clandestinely. Then, too, it involved four other distinct problems: the problem of *influence*, the problem of *organization*, the problem of *expression*, and the problem of *expansion*. Viewing the matter from this perspective, we can see why Voltaire had to hark back to his philosophical ancestors in order to orient himself. He had to discover the sources of this new thought in the twelve great seventeenth-century philosophers. He had to sift that thought, rid it of unnecessary contradictions, and, above all, gather it together into some sort of a coherent structure. Essentially, what the task involved was the organization of thought. The accomplishment of this task, however, presupposed other very important activities. Voltaire had to seek means of accumulating this thought, and he had to invent ways of refining the instrument of thinking and the stream of thought itself. He was not exaggerating when he talked of producing the history of the human mind. Lastly, he had to seek methods for putting this thought at the service of the public.

These preoccupations seem to us at this late date to be mere technical procedures, and we are inclined to give them only slight consideration. There are some very interesting studies of Voltaire and Bayle, Voltaire and Leibniz, and Voltaire and Hobbes, but really no one has so far adequately dealt with the position of Voltaire vis-à-vis the philosophers. And yet the significant feature of the Cirey activity was the basic philosophical foundation which Voltaire had to give to his thought. It is not so much that he had to consider in detail the separate philosophical contributions of Locke, Leibniz, and Spinoza as well as all the other philosophers of the preceding age; rather, he was forced by circumstances to coordinate these philosophical approaches to life in such a way as to create organically a valid eighteenth-century philosophy. He literally had to create in a living way what D'Alembert attempted to describe in his "Discours préliminaire" to the *Encyclopédie*, and, since he was terribly allergic to systematic philosophies, he was forced to do his merging unsystematically and eclectically, in the manner Diderot explained in the article "Eclectisme." Voltaire, in fact, had to submit to the influence of these philosophers in a coordinated way, just as the *Encyclopédie* had to also.

Submission to the will of the philosophers entailed likewise devising some way of dealing with the tremendous expansion of factual knowledge which had taken place and which was still taking place between 1730 and 1750. Voltaire's preoccupation with facts, which Diderot proclaimed "la vraie richesse des philosophes," did not at all differ from that of the other Encyclopedists. He, as well as they, was overwhelmed in his efforts to become an encyclopedic man. In a way, he was especially distressed by the sheer mass of facts, because of his allergy to systems. He therefore had to devise a method of sorting out essential from nonessential facts, and, since he could not very well systematize them, he had to seek means for coordinating them. This was what Voltaireanism was supposed to do. Moreover, he had to discover some means of extracting basic ideas from this mass of facts and of establishing primary theories and doctrines upon these basic ideas. For he, like all the Encyclopedists, had to find a way of passing from facts to ideas, from ideas to theories, from theories to an organic attitude toward life, and from organic attitude to action. This also is what Voltaireanism was designed to do. Essentially, it consisted in seeking the correct method of moving from the critical suppression of prejudices to the creation of new and fruitful intellectual relationships.

The third move was concerned with selecting a correct medium for conveying the facts, the ideas, the theories, and the new philosophy to the public. Drama, Horatian poetry, and the philosophical poem, though possible vehicles for this purpose, were largely imperfect. Poetry could carry the inner meaning of things but could not very adequately deal with facts, an insufficiency Voltaire became aware of in writing his *Epître à Mme du Châtelet sur la philosophie de Newton*. Drama was more inadequate still. And, although Horatian poetry was devised to express an ancient philosophy and did so beautifully, it could not be expected to convey the ideas of modern science. Moreover, there was already a drive to substitute prose for poetry, fostered precisely by what was called the movement in geometry. Voltaire was well on his way to changing the manner of his presentation. Drama was retained, but it became more arid, more incapable of supporting philosophic ideas. Dramatic effect was transported to history. Voltaire actually decided that history could best be structured as drama. The poetic *Epître* became the prose letter. The philosophical poem lingered on, but it was not rich in possibilities, and already it had been superceded by the prose essay. In reality, all that Voltaire retained of the old poetic genres was the dialogue, the wit, and the dramatic effect. These things were perfectly adjusted to the needs of science and philosophy, although in the readjustment they were likely to lose their artistic qualities.

Voltaire and his contemporaries were really attempting two incompatible things: they wanted a genre which would put the advantages of the new science at the service of everybody, and, at the same time, they also wanted to put these same advantages of science at the service of art. Unfortunately, what would best carry the content was not necessarily the most artistic genre. For the dissemination of thought, Voltaire chose the philosophical essay, what he came in time to call his "petits chapitres." Montaigne had used it already, it was the normal expression of encyclopedic thought, and its qualities of clarity and succinctness made it very suitable. On the other hand, it was more informative than rich in artistic effect. For the latter effect, Voltaire was forced to create the genre of the *conte philosophique*. That is to say, he needed a genre which would at the same time be witty, lively, and all-embracing. The *conte* fulfilled this need. Both genres were normally the genres of journalism and the best vehicles for ideas. Voltaire, as we shall in time try to show, suffused them with his wit, his spirit, his Voltaireanism. For the moment, we must return to his relationship with the philosophers.

PART IV

THE PHILOSOPHER

"But one thing at least is certain, that spirit, whether it was admirable or whether it was odious, was moved by a terrible force. Frederick had failed to realize this; and indeed, though Voltaire was fifty-six when he went to Berlin, and though his whole life had been spent in a blaze of publicity, there was still not one of his contemporaries who understood the true nature of his genius; it was perhaps hidden even from himself. He had reached the threshold of old age, and his life's work was still before him; it was not as a writer of tragedies and epics that he was to take his place in the world."[a]

1. VOLTAIRE AND THE PHILOSOPHERS

SINCE VOLTAIRE ULTIMATELY turned from poetry to philosophy, it seems perfectly reasonable that he should have addressed himself to the philosophers of the seventeenth century as a means of acquiring a philosophical foundation. Even at the time he was primarily interested in poetic values, he was not totally unmindful of the importance of thought. The content of his thought at this time, however, was philosophical only in a general way, expressing, in turn, an epicurean appreciation of the joys of living, a firm stoicism before the trials of life, and an attitude of constructive deism. The sources of this general philosophical content are already well known: the long line of poets beginning with Théophile de Viau and extending through Des Barreaux, Blot, Malherbe, Dehénault, Mme Deshoulières, Saint-Evremond, and the early La Fontaine down to La Fare and Chaulieu. As far as thought content was concerned, Voltaire consciously imitated these poets in their epicureanism, their stoicism, and their constructive deism. It is in this sense of the word that his poetry had a tendency to be "impure," because it was consciously philosophical.

On the other hand, when Voltaire, around 1738, finally decided to make a shift from poetry to philosophy, he cast about in search of a medium for continuing the artistic content along with the now all-important thought content. He tried both "philosophical" poetry and "philosophical" drama, but, although he did not totally reject them or find them entirely unworthy, he must have concluded that they were unable to express beyond a modest limit the moral content which he always affirmed lay at the root of his philosophical thinking. It was this dilemma which led him to adopt, also around 1738, the *conte philosophique* as the best medium for this kind of expression. The *conte* was derived from the utopian tale developed by Rabelais, Cyrano de Bergerac, Vairasse, Foigny, Gilbert, Fénelon, and Tyssot de Patot. Not only did it unite satire with idealism and destructive with constructive criticism, but it was devised to unite as well thought with action, and even an art form with philosophy. As Voltaire developed the genre, it became capable of expressing

[a] L. Strachey, *Books and Characters*, p. 180.

· 573 ·

any content within the framework of fiction. This is important, because it actually made philosophy submit to verisimilitude, rather than to truth. It is thus evident that, during the first two decades of Voltaire's career, he was not deprived of a medium of expression, as he identified himself, first, with the lyric, epicurean poetry, then, with the epic, drama, the philosophical poem, and, finally, with the satiric, utopian novel. As the content became more important than the lyricism and as the poetry gradually yielded to prose, Voltaire still retained a medium of expression which was essentially adequate to his needs. Or, rather, it would have proved satisfactory had he known how to restrict his needs. When, however, along with his contemporaries, he expanded the thought content beyond all proportion, so that it embraced all kinds of philosophy from metaphysics to aesthetics, from science to history, and from ethics to biblical criticism, he could no longer find an art form which would contain all these excursions into thought. Since the thought had become finally encyclopedic in scope, Voltaire could only cast it, as his contemporaries did, in the encyclopedic mold.

It should be stressed that he was not content to bring together the epicurean poetry and the utopian novel of the seventeenth century, or even these two literary expressions of philosophy with the free-thinking essay of the "libertin." These three currents appeared in his own literary production of 1738, it is true, but this essentially literary production of the time represented less than half of his activity. Voltaire set out to incorporate in his total expression the whole philosophical movement of the preceding century. At first blush, it appears that he was actually deliberately turning from literature to philosophy. The *Traité de métaphysique*, the *Eléments*, the *Lettres philosophiques*, the histories, and the deistic articles became overwhelmingly "philosophiques." Indeed, along with the *poèmes philosophiques* and the *conte philosophique*, everything was suddenly taking on the appearance of philosophy.

The first problem, though, is not how he found the proper medium for the expression of his thought but why he turned to the philosophers in the first place. Some explanation for the move can be found in the drying up of poetry, as well as in the sterility which overtook drama. The continual development of scientific and metaphysical thought throughout the seventeenth century was now undoubtedly beginning to take its toll in the field of literature, particularly as it adopted the vernacular rather than the Latin language as its medium of expression. A more likely reason is that science and philosophy had become, as Voltaire said in his famous letter of 1735, the fashion, for Voltaire could never resist the movements of his day which were in style. The main reason, though, was the threatened breakdown in religion.

It would be interesting to know in what way and at what time Voltaire became acquainted with these philosophers. It has been assumed that he could have been introduced initially to some of them by his teachers at Louis-le-Grand. The exception which Tournemine, one of these teachers, took to his espousal of Newton's philosophy might reasonably be interpreted as a gentle rebuke given a former pupil by an old philosophy professor. We really do not know anything about Voltaire's philosophy studies at Louis-le-Grand. He possibly progressed no further than the rudiments of the subject and, in all probability, was never introduced in his classes to the philosophers of the previous century. It is conceivable that he discussed philosophers and philosophical matters with some individual professor—Tournemine, for example—although even that is not very likely. The priest showed no particular interest in the pupil. Indeed, he was reputed, in contrast with Voltaire's other teachers, to have been peculiarly cold to him.

It has been assumed likewise that the young Arouet could have learned about some of these philosophers from the frequenters of the Temple. This, too, was possible, although the epicureanism of the Temple does not seem to me to evidence a very profound knowledge of these philosophers, unless it be Gassendi and, of course, Gassendi's interest in Epicurus, as it was interpreted through Bernier via La Fontaine. It is more likely, though, that the epicureanism which the youthful Arouet imbibed at the Temple was a mode, an attitude, rather than a philosophy.

He had a greater opportunity to get acquainted with some of these philosophers through his own personal reading, but we do not have a very accurate knowledge of his early readings, and there are no notebooks which seem to date before his sojourn in England. Such authors as he is known to have consulted in the early days are Fénelon, Houtteville, and possibly some early clandestine deists. Of these writers, only Fénelon offers a possibility, though slight, of having been able to interest the young Arouet in seventeenth-century philosophers. Not that Voltaire did not give many indications of free-thinking in this early period. In truth, he was perfectly willing to discuss any of the philosophical problems in his early poetry which he discussed ten or twelve years later in his *Traité de métaphysique*. The discussion at this time, however, gave no evidence of being grounded in any knowledge of either ancient or modern philosophy.

The first document of a positive nature we possess that is related to this problem is Bolingbroke's letter of June 1724 (B. 185), to which we have often referred:

Si vous lisez l'Essay sur l'Entendement humain, vous lisez le livre que je connois le plus capable d'y contribuer. Si vous n'y trouvez que peu de choses, prennez garde que ce ne soit votre faute. Vous y trouverez des vérités prodigieusement fertiles. C'est à vous à en faire les applications, et à en tirer les conséquences. Il est sûr que vous n'y trouverez pas les profondeurs de Descartes ni le sublime de Mallebranche. . . . On a découvert par exemple que Des Cartes dans la physique et Mallebranche dans la métaphysique ont étez plûtost poètes que philosophes. Les bornes des observations et de la géométrie étoient trop étroites pour le premier, il a voulu les franchir. Il les a franchis [*sic*] en effet, mais elles se sont cruellement vangées. Elles ont suscité des Huygens et des Newtons qui ont démontré, car il ne s'agit pas d'opinion, ou de probabilité, que la nature n'agit pas comme il l'a fait agir, que presque toutes les loix du mouvement qu'il établit, sont fausses; et que ces fameux tourbillons sont des chimères. Les bornes des idées que l'esprit humain est capable d'avoir étoient trop étroites pour le dernier. Il en est sorti, et il a fait des livres remplis du plus beau galimatias du monde, mais dans les quels on ne voit pas plus qu'il voyoit en Dieu.

Bolingbroke's letter is at least an exhortation to the youthful Voltaire (who had already turned thirty) to get acquainted with Locke and Newton. It carries also a faint implication that Voltaire already had some knowledge of Descartes and Malebranche and a strong admonition that he would be wise to transfer his interest to the two English philosophers. The context in which the two English philosophers are approved, while the two French are treated rather as poets who have exceeded the limits of philosophical thought, lays the groundwork of what was to become the Descartes-Newton quarrel. Even the fact that Huyghens was to be the intermediary in that quarrel is already faintly intimated. The frame of reference, however, extended beyond Descartes and Newton, as we have already seen. Implied in the Bolingbroke letter are really two different approaches to life: one, realistic, pragmatic, commonsense, English; the other, idealistic, metaphysical, poetic, French.

PASCAL

These considerations in a way explain the necessity of Voltaire's attack against Pascal: the "sublime misanthrope" was anything but a commonsense rationalist. It would take a lot of exegesis to make of him a Lockean, and he could never be considered under any circumstances an Englishman. For Voltaire, though, Pascal must have appeared to sin because he was literally an *anti-mondain*. Voltaire saw him, not as a philosopher at all, but as a rigorist totally lacking in charity toward his fellowman. One could suspect that Voltaire had invoked the spirit of Shaftesbury (and, indeed, he had, I imagine, through the elder Shaftesbury's sometime secretary) in his defense of the normal joys of living. This is why Voltaire's remarks appear to have been extracted from divers contemporary writers: sometimes he would support the positivistic factualism of Houtteville against the faith of Pascal. But his thesis that Christianity, in the Bible, teaches only the how of living, that it contains the rules of manners and not philosophical truths, was also the point of Saint-Evremond, as well as of Spinoza. His optimism—what Lanson and Pomeau call his deistic optimism—which consisted in maintaining that the evils of life can be grossly exaggerated, that there are many pleasures, and that, in reality, some pain is necessary in order to maintain an equilibrium in the laws of the universe, seems to come straight from King. The incompatibility of reason and faith, which Pascal would not have objected to, if properly resolved, seems to have been suggested by Bayle. Even Shaftesbury's "Ask not merely why man is naked . . . ? Ask why he has not wings also for the air, fins for the water, and so on," entered into Voltaire's position. His possible sources are thus so very diverse that Lanson concludes that it was the morality of deism and its optimistic rehabilitation of pride and passion which Voltaire adopted and which was the contrary of the Christian view of corruption. Lanson quotes Shaftesbury: "The question would not be, who lov'd himself, or who not? but who lov'd and serv'd himself the rightest, and after the truest manner." He also mentions Nicole (*De la grandeur*, Chapter VI) who admits, in giving precisely Voltaire's examples, that the morality of personal interest (which came originally from Hobbes) can produce the same effects as the morality of Christian charity and, in certain cases, can produce them more effectively. The important point here, though, is that Voltaire was strengthening his view by merging an Englishman and a Frenchman. The purpose of all this search for possible sources is not to mark the diversity so much as to show the innumerable currents of anti-Pascal feeling which were blowing in the period of Voltaire's English experience.

This anti-Pascal movement has been the subject of much discussion since Lanson first gave a summary description of it in the "Questions diverses" (pp. 309-313) in 1912. In 1932, J. T. van Konijnenburg presented a thesis entitled *Courant Pascalien et courant anti-pascalien de 1670 à 1734*.[1] It is certain that between 1700 and 1734 there were numerous works which attacked Pascal: Gilbert's *Histoire de Caléjava* (1700), De Lassay's *Recueil de différentes choses* (1727), Fréret's *L'Examen critique des apologistes de la Religion Chrétienne* (1729), to name only a few.

There are certain preliminaries which should be established before the position of Voltaire vis-à-vis Pascal is discussed, the first being the date of the *Remarques sur Pascal*. Voltaire, in introducing them, stated that they had been composed "depuis longtemps." Lanson concedes that Voltaire wished to suggest that they went back to a period antecedent to the moment in which he was writing. He thinks that the remark was made to coincide with the fiction that the *Lettres philosophiques* were composed in 1728. He asserts, though, that it is impossible to know how authentic this statement is. What is certain is that when, in June 1733, Voltaire consulted Formont about adding the reflections on Pascal to the *Lettres*, they were by then already written. Finally, Lanson calls attention to the poem written in 1732 to Mlle de Malcrais where the poet describes his philosophical activities:

---

[1] See also J. R. Carré, *Réflexions sur l'anti-Pascal de Voltaire*, pp. 37-43; M. Waterman, *Voltaire, Pascal and Human Destiny*; and N. L. Torrey, *The Spirit of Voltaire*, pp. 208-216.

De ces obscurités [science] je passe à la morale;
Je lis au cœur de l'homme, et souvent j'en rougis.
J'examine avec soin les informes écrits,
Les monuments épars, et le style énergique
De ce fameux Pascal, ce dévot satirique,
Je vois ce rare esprit trop prompt à s'enflammer;
   Je combats ses rigueurs extrêmes :
Il enseigne aux humains à se haïr eux-mêmes;
Je voudrais, malgré lui, leur apprendre à s'aimer.

Lanson finds that the *Epître à Uranie*, which was published in 1732, offers a substantiation for that date. On the other hand, Beuchot, basing his opinion on the reference to Falkener's letter in Remark VI, gives 1728 as the date; Moland, for the same reason, gives 1729. Pomeau suggests 1719 and 1725 as possibilities (see M. II. 45-46, 162-163). It would be interesting to know the date. It would be rather embarrassing to maintain that the English experience ripened Voltaire's antagonism to Pascal and then find that it was already vigorous before he went to England. On the other hand, if, as we have pointed out above, Voltaire responded to Pascal's *Pensées* with ideas which were analogous to those found in such divers thinkers as Bayle, Hobbes, Saint-Evremond, Houtteville, Montaigne, and Shaftesbury, not to mention Claude Gilbert and the utopian writers, then his acquaintance with the thinkers of his time was much richer before 1726 than any other evidence we possess would indicate.

The second preliminary problem to consider is that proposed by Pomeau. "*Les Lettres philosophiques*," he wrote (*Religion*, p. 141), "font date dans l'histoire du siècle et dans la biographie de leur auteur, parce qu'elles ont révélé un nouveau Voltaire. Avec cette œuvre, l'impertinence anti-chrétienne du versificateur devenait philosophie." If this judgment is correct, Voltaire's letter on Pascal would have been, along with the center chapters (XII-XVII), the first real manifestation on Voltaire's part of an interest in philosophy, as opposed to theology. It is more probable, though, that the factors involved in Voltaire's shift from poetry to philosophy were much more complicated than Pomeau suggests here. The opposition would have been between deism and Christian theology, which certainly went back to the *Epître à Uranie*, and between libertinism (free-thinking) and Christian faith, which certainly went back to his early Horatian poetry, as well as between philosophy and theology.

Voltaire's objections to the opinion of Pascal in the *Pensées*, though clearly expressed, are not well-organized. It seems that the author of the *Lettres* wished to leave the discussion in the same fluid state as the author of the *Pensées* had. One of the effects of this kind of composition—if it can be called by so formal a name—is that Voltaire's ideas constantly have the appearance of being not only disorganized but niggling and picayune. He must have been aware of this danger, since he often tries to show the difference between his idea and Pascal's and takes some pains to point out the consequences which derive from these differences.

From the very first, he notes that the core of the problem is the nature of man. Pascal, in his opinion, had presented man in an odious light, writing against human nature as he wrote against the Jesuits. He attributed to human nature what can be found only in certain men, thereby insulting the whole human race. Voltaire proclaims that he intends to take the side of humanity: we are neither so wicked nor so unhappy as Pascal pretended. It was Pascal's custom to deduce from the misery of man a proof of the Christian religion, a tactic which had been adopted by subsequent apologists. Voltaire protests against this tendency, which represented a metaphysical way of proving the verity of Christianity by the contradictions of our nature. For him, Christianity teaches simplicity, humanity, and charity; any attempt to reduce it to a metaphysics would only result in a set of errors. It should be regarded as the source of morality, not as the foundation of philosophical truths. Voltaire, like Saint-Evremond and Spinoza, maintains that religion teaches man how to live; it is a morality, not a philosophy.

This divergence between Pascal and Voltaire stemmed from a misunderstanding attributable to the evolution of thought throughout the seventeenth century. Pascal, as is well known, did not assume that theology and philosophy are one and the same. He did not believe that philosophy can teach religion. It can, to be sure, offer a "summum bonum," but it is a "béatitude" which has nothing to do with the glory of eternal life. Indeed, it does not even cure the ills of this life, or reduce the pride of man, or take away our sinful desires. Pascal would have cheerfully concurred with Voltaire's assertion, in reply to this stand, that philosophers have not taught religion.

He would naturally have agreed, too, with Voltaire's opinion that philosophers are not inspired men. And he would not have disagreed with Voltaire's claim that the problem is not to compare the teachings of Christ with the thought of Aristotle. Confronted with Voltaire's conclusion that the task is to prove that Christianity is the one true religion, Pascal would have declared that that was precisely what he had been trying to do.

It is nonetheless true that there was in the period 1670-1730 a confusion in the uses of philosophy, theology, and morality. In the shift which had taken place even as early as Descartes, philosophy had arrogated to itself duties which had previously belonged to theology. Metaphysics had understood that it was its duty to prove the existence of God, the immortality of the soul, the nature of the material universe, and the rules of right action. When difficulties had thrown into question the ability of philosophers to prove these things, there arose two attitudes. On the one hand, some proclaimed that religious truths could not be proved by reason and must, as always, be accepted on faith. This was primarily Bayle's position. But Pascal would not have disagreed; on the contrary, he had made a very pertinent remark about the insufficiency of the metaphysical proofs of God's existence. On the other hand, some sought to discredit metaphysics as a subject useful to man, holding that only physics was the proper sphere of philosophy. Very quickly, physics was thought to provide knowledge not only of the physical world but of man's place and his role in its organization. Hence, philosophy was now concerned primarily with science (the outside universe) and morality (the inside world of man). It was this attitude which accounted for the tendency to trust what the human mind could know and the corresponding tendency to distrust what appeared mysterious.

The vast distance which existed between Pascal and Voltaire thus becomes clarified. Where Pascal wrote for instance, that original sin is the most incomprehensible of things and yet that, without acceptance of the notion of original sin, man is incomprehensible to himself, Voltaire accuses him of reasoning badly—and, indeed, he was not reasoning at all in Voltaire's sense of the word. When Voltaire maintains that making original sin a necessary but incomprehensible support of the Scriptures is sustaining them with "idées philosophiques," he is not even talking the same language as Pascal. That he recognized the absurdity of his reply is evidenced by the fact that, after 1748, he wrote here: "C'est bien assez de ne rien entendre à notre origine, sans l'expliquer par une chose, qu'on n'entend pas. Nous ignorons, comment l'homme naît, comment il croît, comment il digère, comment il pense, comment ses membres obéissent à sa volonté." He complains that Pascal was only explaining things which were not understandable by something which was incomprehensible; it would be better had he said, "I just don't know." "Un mistère ne fut jamais une explication, c'est une chose divine et inexplicable." Pascal would have heartily agreed, although, of course, he would have attached no importance to the confession that "I just don't know." He would merely have replied that, in view of the conditions Voltaire lays down, "Le Pyrrhonisme est le vrai."

Voltaire, however, thinks it is not at all possible to grant that Pascal was right. Pascal's explanation, insofar as he insisted upon the misery of man as the *sole* cause of his despair, does not explain away that despair. But Pascal had not insisted solely upon the misery of man; he had insisted also upon his grandeur. Voltaire, however, ignores that side of the argument. In fact, whereas Pascal had balanced off man's misery against his grandeur, Voltaire is inclined to take a more commonsense view of the matter. Man is born in the way all the other animals are born; he is only a little higher than they are. Like some, he is badly organized; like others, he is well-proportioned. Those who have the keenest passions are the best organized. "Amour-propre" is, however, equally shared by all. It is a gift from God which provides for our self-preservation. He has also given us religion to control this state of affairs. We are determined by the conditions which surround us. All of this does not prove, though, that man is a riddle to himself. He occupies his place in nature, above the animals, to whom he is superior, below higher beings, to whom he is inferior but whom he resembles in thought. He is, like everything, a mixture of good and evil, of pleasure and pain. He has passions which drive him to action, reason which governs his deeds. If he were perfect, he would be God; all these so-called contradictions are necessary ingredients which enter into the composition of man. He is as he should be. Voltaire here seems to be paraphrasing King, though, fundamentally, his attitude is not far from the Jesuit position. Bayle, however, who was at the very center of the discussion was not content with this conclusion. Pascal, who was not concerned with the problem of evil except insofar as it drove man to seek God, would not have disagreed with this exposition; he would only have found it irrelevant.

Pascal did suggest that man is double, that he has two natures, that he is a creature characterized by his *duplicity*. Bayle, who was terribly preoccupied with this problem of evil, feared that it could only be solved after the fashion of the Manicheans, by admitting that two natures are not only in man but permeate the whole universe. Voltaire, who later had something to say about Bayle's fear, for the moment rejects the interpretation of both: "Cette prétendue duplicité de l'homme est une idée aussi absurde que métaphysique." He does so, however, at the expense of a concession which gives the whole commonsense case away. "J'avoue que l'homme est inconcevable [which was Pascal's point], mais tout le reste de la nature l'est aussi [which was also Pascal's point], et il n'y a pas plus de contradictions aparentes dans l'homme que dans tout le reste."

Voltaire nonetheless makes the point that there are in this world happy men or, at any rate, those who say they are happy. He quotes Falkener to prove this and generalizes by affirming that there are many who resemble Falkener. If one looks carefully at Paris or London, he will find no reason to enter into this despair which Pascal noted. These are not deserted islands, but populated, opulent, policed lands, where men are as happy as human nature will permit. Voltaire asserts that the wise man will know how to enjoy these good things of life which the metropolises of the world offer. Here, suddenly, is injected into the discussion the joys and pleasures of the worldly man, the "mondain" whose praises Voltaire was to sing only a few years later. Voltaire concludes against Pascal that he can find no reason for despairing just because he knows no way of seeing God face to face and because he knows no solution for explaining the doctrine of the Trinity. Here the positions of the two are clear. Voltaire's worldly man does not need the intricate explanations of theology to be happy; for this sort of man, theology is totally irrelevant. Once more, Voltaire opposes to Pascal the commonsense view:

Pourquoi nous faire horreur de notre être? Notre existence n'est point si malheureuse qu'on veut nous le faire acroire. Regarder l'univers comme un cachot, et tous les hommes comme des criminels qu'on va exécuter, est l'idée d'un fanatique; croire que le monde est un lieu de délices où l'on ne doit avoir que du plaisir, c'est la rêverie d'un Sibarite. Penser que la terre, les hommes et les animaux sont ce qu'ils doivent être dans l'ordre de la Providence, est, je crois, d'un homme sage.

It is evident by now that Pascal and Voltaire were talking about two different men, not man. Pascal assumed that the purpose of man is to seek God, Voltaire assumes that his purpose is to enjoy the pleasures of this world. The difference is really between the "saint" and the "mondain." Consequently, it is not surprising that the divergence between the two was so great. The "saint" places his goal in what is beyond this life, the "mondain" endeavors to partake of all the possible pleasures of this world. The "saint" mortifies the love of self, the "mondain" sees in it the foundation of all society. Without it, there would be no art, no social order, no respect for one's fellowman. Since it is at the basis of the social organization, law directs it and religion perfects it. This is the orderly way in which God has ordained things. We should accept His decrees, adore Him, without trying to pierce the obscurities of His mysteries.

Fundamentally, where Pascal condemned the search for pleasure, Voltaire approves it, for it, too, is the product of self-love. It is rather the instrument of our happiness than the symbol of our misery. Inactivity and contemplation are both totally incomprehensible, as far as Voltaire is concerned. It is absurd, he states, to believe that our first parents were given perfect senses—that is, perfect instruments for action—uniquely for contemplation. Man is a creature of the senses. He can be occupied only with the outside world, because that is the source of his ideas. To conceive of him as remaining in a state of apathy, which, for Voltaire, is represented by the state of contemplation, is absurd. He was born for action; it is as natural for him to act as it is for fire to rise and stones to fall. He was born to look to the future; otherwise, he would perish in misery today. This, too, was precisely Pascal's point, but not his conclusion.

On three points Voltaire stands in direct contrast to Pascal. He finds the "Wager," as he says, "indécent et puérile." Further, he very aptly remarks that the fact that it is in one's interest to believe a thing exists is not at all a proof of its existence. To convince anyone, it is not enough to show him that there is an advantage to be gained from believing; it is necessary also to convince his reason that what the belief asserts is precisely true. Besides, it is totally inconsistent to say that it is in one's interest to believe in a certain thing and then to add that the salvation which comes from this belief is accorded to only a very small number of men. How attracted would someone be to a "bonheur infini" if he is told that, of a million persons, scarcely one will qualify for it? This argument which, in the beginning of the debate between the Jesuits and the Jansenists, so disturbed the Jesuits because they feared it would discourage piety, looms large in the thought of this Jesuit pupil. Moreover, Voltaire seems sincerely convinced that this way of thinking, far from attracting men, would succeed only in making atheists of us all. It would be unwise to put Voltaire's arguments against the "Wager" on the footing of its mathematical accuracy. Carré has shown that Voltaire, following particularly such predecessors as Gilbert, De Lassay, and Boulainvilliers, pointed out the incongruity of placing an infinite gain against an infinite loss when the contents of gain and loss are unequal and when the quality of what is gained or lost is not consistently weighed. Voltaire developed this argument later; for the period of the *Lettres*, he placed his emphasis upon the absurdity of offering salvation to so many who could not, according to Jansenist theology, be saved.

The second point on which the two differed was the question of the value of reason and the heart. Here Voltaire's misunderstanding of Pascal is complete. It is doubtful if he had any conception whatever at this time about the heart as a means of knowing reality. For him, reason was a matter of logic, discourse was a matter of logical arrangement of ideas, proofs were of a geometric order exclusively. He never refers to Pascal's famous remark that "Le cœur a ses raisons que la raison ne connaît pas." It is doubtful if he could by temperament understand the value of intuition. He could, however, appreciate the value of logical disquisition. Thus, in the face of Pascal's bold remark that "Selon les lumières naturelles, s'il y a un Dieu, il est infiniment incompréhensible . . . nous sommes donc incapables de connaître, ni ce qu'il est, ni s'il est," Voltaire is properly scandalized, since, in his opinion, it is dangerous to admit that the human mind cannot prove the existence of God. Pascal, however, pushed on further and spoke of "Dieu sensible au cœur," but, in these terms, Voltaire is completely lost.

The third point of difference concerns the prophecies and miracles. Pascal proclaimed their authenticity, but, in speaking of prophecies, he stated that they must have two senses or else they are not a proof of the coming of Christ. Voltaire protests violently against this view. The Christian religion is so true that it has no need of doubtful proofs, he says; if anything can upset it, it will be this opinion of giving two meanings to the Scriptures. Such an interpretation would give free rein to any free-thinker.

It is obvious that there were fundamental points of difference between Pascal and Voltaire. It is more obvious still that there was a fundamental difference in temperament. Between the "misanthrope sublime" and the "optimiste à toute épreuve," there was a whole world. Pascal's deep, tragic sense of life was totally incomprehensible to a man like Voltaire; on the other hand, Voltaire's views would have seemed to Pascal inconsequential, irrelevant, and fickle. I doubt, however, that he would have attacked them in any polemical way; he would have been more apt to use the art of persuasion which he employed with his contemporaries. I doubt, also, that Voltaire understood the basis of Pascal's thought or the subtleties of his argument. What he did understand was that his own conception of man differed radically from Pascal's. Voltaire's view at this time was that man is a normal, fairly well-integrated creature who has his place among other creatures. The aim of existence is pleasure. Worldly, social pleasure is more attractive than future bliss. The universe is, in general, orderly and friendly (at any rate, that is the way it appeared to him until the earthquake struck Lisbon). There is a limited free will; or, rather, rational action is possible. Finally, we are more happy in practicing humanitarianism than in condemning man. This is the road to confidence in the future, at least the immediate future. Voltaire had developed these views continually in the poetry of his early days. They were, for the most part, the libertine views of Chaulieu and La Fare. He now set them in opposition to the contrary view of Pascal.

He disclaimed that they were grounded in anything other than in a commonsense faith in reason. He was not ready to admit that there was any philosophical content underlying them. Nor would he admit that they presupposed certain metaphysical tenets. Nevertheless, as he quickly discovered, even before the *Remarques sur Pascal* were published, they were in fact supported by five metaphysical presuppositions: the existence of God; the materiality, rather than the spirituality and immortality, of the soul; faith in rational action, that is, in thinking matter; freedom of action, although limited; and, finally, the key definition that moral action is social action.

The relationship between Voltaire and Pascal is thus an ambiguous one. It is evident how the author of the *Lettres* felt about the author of the *Pensées*. But it is not clear from the arguments which Voltaire presented why the author of the *Pensées* was the enemy. It is true that the two held distinctly separate views of man—or, rather, that they drew distinctly different conclusions concerning man's destiny from the way they regarded him. But we have seen that Voltaire was not always correct in drawing distinctions between himself and Pascal. Nor is it so very clear that Pascal was always opposite in opinion to his opponent. It is, on the contrary, often apparent that Voltaire's presentation was fundamentally the same as Pascal's, with the important distinction that Voltaire was determined to give a commonsense interpretation to the phenomena, whereas Pascal was determined to give a religious one. So striking is this discrepancy in intentions that one can hardly avoid the suspicion that Voltaire was attacking Pascal solely because, as Brunetière suggested in the *Etudes critiques*, the "sublime misanthrope" was the stalwart obstacle to all attempts to give a commonsense interpretation to man's world. However, we can easily exaggerate that point of view. Pomeau has a section in his *Religion de Voltaire* (pp. 232ff.) where, after conceding that Pascal was concentrated, interior, inclined to the tragic— that is, just the opposite of Voltaire, who was diffuse, exterior, and inclined to buffoonery—he remarks that the two men resembled each other, too. One could readily grant that there is a bit of Voltaire in the *Provinciales* and certainly a bit of Pascal in the *Lettres*. Pomeau has drawn up a list of these resemblances which lead to the conclusion that one was a "dévot satirique," the other a "satirique impie." He notes that, even in Voltaire's replies to Pascal in the *Remarques,* there are expressions which are "inconsciemment pascaliennes." Pascal had his revenge in the closing days of Voltaire at Cirey, where the latter wrote: "Me voici dans un beau palais, avec la plus grande liberté (et pourtant chez un roi), avec toutes mes paperasses d'historiographe, avec Mme du Châtelet, et avec tout cela je suis un des plus malheureux êtres pensants qui soient dans la nature. Je vous trouve heureux si vous vous portez bien. *Hoc est enim omnis homo.*" All it took, apparently, to make Voltaire resemble Pascal in attitude was a run of relatively bad health. To resemble the "sublime misanthrope" in his search for a true inner reality, however, Voltaire would have been forced to sacrifice his "esprit" for the "genius" of Pascal. There they were worlds apart.

DESCARTES

One of the puzzles in the history of ideas is the fortune of Descartes's physics. It is well to keep in mind that, for Descartes himself, this physics formed the indispensable center of his method and his thought. Some of its difficulties were occasioned by the peculiar circumstances surrounding its formation. It would seem idle to speculate upon its original state if it were not for the fact that it was created at the moment when Galileo and his ideas upon the nature of the universe were condemned. Undoubtedly, in view of Descartes's natural timidity, this condemnation, caused him to give a different orientation to his metaphysics and to modify his physics. But we are very unclear as to the nature of this reorientation and totally ignorant as to the nature of the modification. We do have, though, in the *Discours* and the annexes, the product as Descartes wished it to be known, and its natural or, rather, normal development in the *Méditations* and the *Principes* only served to round out his physics.

One problem about Cartesian physics is the difficulty Descartes experienced in getting it established. Hardly had it appeared when it was attacked by his contemporaries, especially Gassendi. Gassendi, however, was not alone; Hobbes and Mersenne and his group produced a whole array of objections, which focused particularly on the theory of the vortices, the plenum, the laws of movement, and the nature of matter, not to mention the arbitrary, dogmatic method by which Descartes sought to support these hypotheses. Indeed, from 1647 to 1687, in spite of Descartes's efforts during the last decade of his life (1596-1650) to have his physics adopted in Jesuit schools, it always met with opposition. Every philosopher of note from Pascal to Fontenelle—that is, from 1662 to 1680—criticized it. Pascal, Spinoza, Leibniz, and even Malebranche found serious difficulties in his fundamental physical ideas and in his method. And yet, strangely enough, every one of these seventeenth-century philosophers, though eventually opposed to Cartesian physics (and this was equally true subsequently of Locke and Newton), found his starting point in Descartes's work, and was inspired to enter upon the study of physics by the father of modern philosophy. More strange still is the fact that, when the Jesuits issued their famous decree forbidding the teaching of Cartesian physical principles in their schools, Cartesianism, which one would expect to have completely disintegrated and disappeared, in the face of all this opposition actually reached the peak of its popularity, with Rohault's *Traité de physique* (1671, but it remained the only serious French textbook on science until 1730), Régis's *Système de philosophie* (1690), and Fontenelle's *Entretiens* (1686). It was at this moment of maximum effect that Newton and Locke arose to challenge, between them, every scientific principle proposed by the founder of modern philosophy. Thus, not only the vortices, the plenum, the nature of matter, and the laws of movement but Descartes's method of speculative reasoning upon the nature of things were put in question. Newton, for instance, showed beyond any possibility of doubt that the laws which regulated the movements of the vortices were in opposition to Kepler's laws.

Voltaire entered upon a study of Descartes's work just when the Descartes-Newton quarrel was ready to explode. To judge by Bolingbroke's letter of 1724, he had already some acquaintance with Descartes and Malebranche. Indeed, a reference to his annotations in the *Recherche de la vérité* makes very plausible Bolingbroke's assumptions, at least with regard to Malebranche. The problem is somewhat more complicated with regard to Descartes. Voltaire's library contained the *Discours de la méthode*, 2 vols., Paris, 1724; the *Lettres qui traitent de plusieurs belles questions, concernant la morale, la physique, la médecine, et les mathématiques*, 6 vols., Paris, 1724-1725; *Les Méditations métaphysiques*, 2 vols., Paris, 1724; *Les Passions de l'âme*; *Le Monde, ou traité de la lumière*; *et la Géométrie*, Paris, 1726; and *Les Principes de la philosophie*, Paris, 1723. There is a curious fact in the dates of publication of the works of Descartes he possessed: only the *Principia* clearly preceded the Bolingbroke letter; all the other works dated from 1724 or shortly thereafter. One could easily be persuaded that Voltaire was already launched upon an investigation of Descartes's philosophy when Bolingbroke's letter arrived, or, more plausibly still, that he knew the *Principia* (which, incidentally, was Descartes's textbook of his philosophy, as he conceived it) and was encouraged to secure the other essential works immediately thereafter. Since, however, he was soon engaged in the Rohan affair and preparations for his trip to England, it is probable that he did not get around to undertaking a thorough investigation of Descartes's ideas until during the early months of his stay in England.

The *Notebooks* seem to offer some slight confirmation of this hypothesis. The early English *Notebook* makes no reference whatever to Descartes. The second English *Notebook*, on the other hand, has a section entitled "Erreurs de Descartes dans le livre de l'homme." A note mentions that Descartes was the first to discover the rule for refraction of light. I find only one more reference of importance: "Preuves contre les tourbillons de Descartes" (I, 227). The few other references are rather inconsequential.

Descartes became, immediately after the English sojourn, a subject of discussion for Voltaire. One would suspect that he had been studied as a foil for Newton. There is some evidence to suggest that this interest in Descartes and Newton dated from Voltaire's early years in London. In 1728, he wrote Thiériot that Pemberton's book on Newton would soon appear and that he advised its translation. He indicated that he was already acquainted with the substance of Pemberton's manuscript, to the extent that we often assume that he saw it before the work appeared in print. It is certain, however, that the intensive work which Voltaire did on Descartes and Newton took place at the moment when he was composing the letters about them for the *Lettres philosophiques*. This period seems to have extended from October-November 1732 to the end of February 1733. In November 1732, he wrote Formont that he had revised the letters where he talked about Newton and that he now was undertaking to give a sketch of the whole Newtonian philosophy. "Je fais son histoire, et celle de Descartes," Voltaire added. On 24 February 1733, he wrote to Thiériot: "Enfin j'ai passé deux mois à m'ennuyer avec

Descartes." Apparently, he was anxious to avoid any misunderstanding. For studying Descartes, he used Baillet's biography (Lanson has clearly shown the relationship), while Pemberton's book (London, 1728) served as the foundation for his work on Newton. For contrast between the two, he referred to Fontenelle's *Eloge*, written on the occasion of Newton's death, and the account of that essay as it was commented upon in the *Present State of the Republic of Letters,* January 1728 (I, 52-84), and, above all, to Maupertuis's *Discours sur les différentes figures des astres* (Paris, 1732), where the parallels had already been drawn between Descartes and Newton and a clear pronouncement made in favor of the latter, although Maupertuis also laid claim to an air of objective neutrality.

In the fourteenth of the *Lettres philosophiques*, Descartes is presented as the counterpart of Newton, Voltaire readily hypothesizing that the two philosophers exemplify the intellectual differences of France and England. In France, one has vortices and subtle matter; the tides are caused by the pressure of the moon; everything is explained by impulsion; the earth has the shape of a melon; light exists in the air; chemistry is a combination of acids, alkalis, and subtle matter. In England, these things are rejected: vortices and subtle matter do not exist; tides are caused by attraction, and the sun plays a role as well as the moon; everything, including chemistry, is explained by attraction; the earth is flattened at the two ends; light comes from the sun in six minutes. More important than these explanations, Voltaire declares, are their opinions on the essence of things: Descartes and Newton disagree completely on the nature of the soul and the definition of matter.[2]

The dissimilarities are derived, by Voltaire, from the temper of the two men. Descartes had a powerful imagination, which directed his private life as well as his manner of reasoning. It is present even in his philosophical works, where appear at all times "des comparaisons ingénieuses et brillantes." Nature made him almost a poet. He withdrew to Holland at a time when his French compatriots condemned philosophy and persecuted him. He was accused of atheism, although he used all his penetration to acquire new proofs of God's existence. Voltaire concedes that he acquired deservedly a

[2] Voltaire later, in the *Eléments*, modified this last statement, which was incorrect.

"très-grand mérite" and "une réputation éclatante." Finally he died prematurely at Stockholm. Newton's life was entirely different, "toujours tranquille, heureux et honoré dans sa patrie." He was devoid of passion or weakness and unbelievably ascetic in his manner of living. The English believe him a "sage," while they call Descartes a "dreamer." Still, Descartes carried geometry to its highest point. He taught how to apply algebraic equations to curves. He carried algebra into optics, which therewith became a new art. It is true that all his other works are full of errors. He adopted "l'esprit de système, and his philosophy became "un roman ingénieux." His views on the nature of the soul, the laws of motion, the nature of light, and innate ideas proved to be wrong. Voltaire concludes that Descartes created a world which has never existed and placed in it a man who was but the figment of his own imagination. But, at least, he destroyed the old errors of scholasticism and taught his contemporaries how to reason.

In the catalogue of writers at the head of the *Siècle de Louis XIV,* Voltaire returns to practically every point he had made in the fourteenth *Lettre philosophique*. Descartes was the outstanding mathematician of his time but a most ignorant philosopher in regard to nature. He spent his life in seclusion outside his native land, and he was accused of atheism and persecuted by the Dutch. His *Méditations* and his *Discours* are still esteemed, but his whole physics has been discarded because it was not established empirically nor mathematically. His *Dioptrique* is the work of an excellent geometer; his laws of the impact of bodies are indicative of an extraordinary genius; and his geometry assures him a superiority as mathematician over all his contemporaries. Only since 1730 has his philosophy been declared chimerical.

Over and over, Voltaire tirelessly defends his judgment on Descartes, sometimes by citing a particular phenomenon on which the latter was in error—primary matter, light and the way it comes to us, the nature of colors, the plenum which is "inadmissible," vortices, comets. Throughout the *Eléments*, the eighteenth-century philosophe criticizes point by point the views of his seventeenth-century predecessor. We have already seen some of this activity in his major controversy with Tournemine. Voltaire, from 1738, not only attacked Descartes but asserted stoutly that he had every right to do so, since

Descartes had likewise attacked the errors of Aristotle. In the *Eclaircissements nécessaires sur les éléments de la philosophie de Newton*, he asserts that there is no philosopher alive who would now defend Descartes's elements, his laws of motion, his vortices, his views on man. In the article "Cartésianisme" of the *Questions* (M. XVII, 56), Voltaire has given a list of twenty-seven errors:

1. He has imagined three elements which are by no means evident.
2. He has said that the sum total of motion in the universe is constant.
3. Light does not come from the sun; it is transmitted to our eyes in an instant.
4. He has admitted the plenum.
5. He has explained the rainbow by imaginary whirling in small bits of light.
6. He has invented vortices of subtle matter.
7. He has assumed that comets are pushed by these vortices.
8. He has assumed that in rotation heavy bodies tend to the center and the subtle matter to the circumference.
9. He has imagined that vortices will not come together.
10. He has explained tides and magnetic attraction by these vortices.
11. He has judged that the sea flows constantly from east to west.
12. He has imagined that matter of the first element and that of the second will produce mercury.
13. He has said that the earth is an encrusted sun;
14. He has stated that there are great cavities beneath the mountains which fill with sea-water and produce fountains;
15. That salt-mines come from the sea;
16. That the third element composes vapors which produce diamonds and metals;
17. That fire is the product of the first and second element;
18. That pores of the magnet are filled with "matière cannelée";
19. That quick lime bursts into flame only because the first element chases the second from its pores;
20. That digested food passes through an infinite number of openings into a main vein which carries it to the liver;
21. That chyle turns to blood in the liver;
22. That blood expands in the heart by a fire without light;
23. That the pulse depends upon 11 little skins which open and close the entrances to the two cavities of the heart;
24. That when the liver is pressed by nerves, the subtle part of the blood rushes straightway to the heart;

25. That the soul is in the pineal gland;
26. That the heart is formed by distended semen;
27. That animals are automata.

Voltaire concludes with the remark that there is not one single novelty in Descartes's physics which is not an error. It was not that he was deficient in genius; in fact, his mistake lay in consulting his genius, rather than experience and mathematics. He was the greatest geometer of his time, but he abandoned geometry to trust himself to his imagination and thereby delayed the progress of the human mind for fifty years.

It is evident that both Mme du Châtelet and Voltaire became involved in the Cartesian-Newtonian quarrel. To understand their attitude toward it and the way in which all their scientific activity was modified thereby, it is necessary to grasp the points of view of both the Cartesians and the Newtonians, especially the former. In the evolution of thought, what customarily happens is that a theory once proven in error is abandoned for what is taken to be a more correct theory. But it is possible that a body of thought may be condemned and yet an attempt made to preserve the method whereby this thought was reached. This seems to be precisely what took place in the case of Descartes's ideas. The more he was proved in error, the more tenaciously Cartesianism persisted—and not only in the seventeenth and eighteenth centuries, but even down to the present day.

Some of this durability is attributable to the historical position which he has always occupied in modern philosophy, of which he has always been considered the founder. Indeed, much of Descartes's reputation from the very beginning derived from the general acceptance of him as the philosopher who destroyed the prestige of the father of ancient philosophy, Aristotle. His undoubted claim to recognition is based upon the belief that he introduced (1) the concept of quantity, (2) mathematical physics, and (3) mechanism against Aristotle's physics of quality. It does not really matter that Gassendi, as well as many others, was as opposed to Aristotle's physics of quality as Descartes; it is the latter who receives the credit for changing the course of science.

The essential point of Aristotle's philosophy was that the idea of an object, its substance, constitutes its reality. God creates the idea, and the idea forms the matter into the object. Moreover, for Aristotle, movement is an alteration, not a change of place. In mathematical physics, in contrast, movement is a change of place. For Aristotle, the alteration does not change the substance: there are all sorts of men, but the idea of man remains constant.

Aristotle's view encountered difficulties in the twelfth century with the rise of the nominalists. The question they posed was how a substance, which is a reality, can be found in an infinite number of different subjects, which are likewise realities. The solution of this question was found by replacing the concept of substance by the concept of phenomenon and by introducing the idea of causation. There followed, in a perfectly logical way, the idea of an experimental science, for which Francis Bacon receives much credit, and the notion of the interrelationship of phenomena. These new steps to a different physical world made Aristotelian classification unnecessary. But this was only the first breakthrough. There arose from the notion of the interrelationship of phenomena the further idea that hidden in all the diversity of nature is a mathematical harmony. Galileo best expressed this conviction when he stated that nature answers our questions when we address them to her in the right language and that the language of nature is mathematics. Galileo however, sought dynamic, rather than static, laws in nature. He sought these laws by setting up experiments and generalizing from the observations he made. In a way, these were false experiments, since they were based on theory without any prior inquiry into whether the phenomena exist. Descartes, still holding to theory, substituted a quantitative rationalism for Aristotelian qualitative rationalism and mechanics for substance. He insisted that physics must have a metaphysical basis. God guarantees the verity of the deductions, chief among them being His own existence, the existence of thought, the existence of space and extension, and the constancy of the quantity of movement.

Cartesianism was known to have willfully combatted Aristotelianism. But Descartes's philosophy was combatted even by those who accepted his mathematical rationalism and his mechanism. What they rejected was his insistence that physics is dependent upon metaphysics. They also criticized him for not completing his quantitative rationalism with an experimental rationalism.

It was Newton who finally provided a solid ground for the views of the mechanists and who, by his discoveries, gave a totally different explanation of the world, which discredited the whole of Cartesian physics. Cartesian method, however, survived. The result was that Newton was opposed because he could not explain gravitation, which to many appeared an occult phenomenon. Both Huyghens and Leibniz questioned Newton's theories. Ultimately, though, it became known from practical observation and reiterated experiments that Newton's observations, calculations, measurements, and conclusions were correct and that Descartes's were in practically every case erroneous. For this reason, the Newtonians were prepared to reject Descartes's thought.

If his thought could be easily rejected, however, his way of thinking could not. His assumptions, his explanations, his positive statements might all be wrong, and still his way of thinking could lead to truth. It had the added security of possessing a metaphysical guarantee, which many suspected Newton's attraction did not possess. Descartes was thought to have invented mechanism, and mechanism was true. He was credited with having discovered the proper uses of mathematical rationalism, and mathematical rationalism was true. He was said to have initiated metaphysical empiricism, and this, too, was true. His view of the universe and of man was a fully developed view, and his scientific thinking had not only a metaphysical background but also a moral tendency: what one knows about this universe is known for the greater glory of God and the greater benefit of man. It was not easy to discredit the philosophy of a man whose scope was so broad and whose insights were so deep.

It is for these reasons that Mme du Châtelet made an initial obeisance to Descartes in her "Avant-propos" to the *Institutions*. And, though she was just as ready as Voltaire to discard him, she was also as firmly convinced as Voltaire that no physics can be valid which is not grounded in metaphysics. For this reason, she adopted the new metaphysics of Leibniz, because she wanted a control over Newtonianism. Her action consequently changed the Descartes-Newton quarrel into a Leibniz-Newton quarrel, or, rather it united the two quarrels.

Voltaire's first reaction to the Descartes-Newton quarrel was, as we have seen, a fairly strong condemnation of Descartes and a thorough espousal of Newton. From the *Eléments*, the *Lettres philosophiques*, and the correspondence with Tournemine, the impression is easily gained that nothing favorable can be said for Descartes and nothing unfavorable for Newton. Voltaire's personal position seems to have been that anyone defending Descartes's ideas against Newton was guilty, if a Frenchman, of intellectual chauvinism. He did not admit of an honest difference of opinion, or even a possible merit balanced by a considerable demerit. Any support given the French philosopher was *ipso facto* suspect. However, under the more balanced judgment of Mme du Châtelet, Voltaire became more tractable. He had understood, in the fourteenth *Lettre philosophique*, that Descartes and Newton were at opposite poles. He subsequently modified this extreme view and became more tolerant.

The judgment on Descartes expressed in the *Lettres philosophiques* is more or less repeated in the *Siècle de Louis XIV*, but here it is more balanced. All the unfavorable criticisms occur. Descartes did the very opposite of what he was supposed to do; instead of studying nature, he tried to guess its secrets. He overemphasized inventions, scorned experiments, and composed scarcely more than philosophical novels. He never mentioned Galileo. Nonetheless, the whole romanesque part of his philosophy succeeded. We must not forget that he was the greatest geometer—in fact, the outstanding mathematician—of his day. Although he is the philosopher who knew the least about nature, compared to those who followed him, his *Méditations* and his *Discours de la méthode* are still highly valued. It is true that all his physics has been rejected, because it is founded neither upon geometry nor upon experiments. But his studies in optics and his laws for the impact of bodies in motion will always be monuments of an extraordinary genius. Voltaire reproaches him most severely for his failure to apply mathematics to nature, even though he was superior in this field to all his contemporaries. Voltaire records that Descartes's truths finally prevailed thanks to his method; before him, there was no such thing as a method. And he did destroy the foolishness of the peripatetics, although he put in place of their nonsense follies of his own. This Voltaire recognizes as a merit, the only real merit remaining to Cartesianism. Since 1730, he adds, when geometry in science and experimental physics began to be cultivated more, there has been a strong reaction against the errors of this chimerical philosophy.

It would seem reasonable that this general judgment on Voltaire's part would be sufficient to preclude further discussion of Descartes. Yet this is not the case. Voltaire goes to infinite pains to explain what is wrong with specific ideas of Descartes. Where the seventeenth-century philosopher shows, for instance, how the body is the occasional cause of our ideas, Voltaire elucidates that matter makes an impression upon our body, and then God produces an idea in our soul, or, vice versa, man produces an act of will, and God acts immediately on the body in consequence of this act of will. Therefore, man does not act, does not think, except in God. This notion possessed some attractiveness for Voltaire; it was a constant practice of his to resort to God when he could not find a satisfactory explanation of a physical phenomenon. He had apparently learned the tactic in England, probably from Locke. Mme du Châtelet rejected this way of approaching physics. In this particular place, Voltaire himself senses a difficulty. How can man be said to will for himself and not think for himself? Moreover, he states, if God has not given us the faculty of acting and thinking, if He alone acts and thinks, then it must be He who wills. Thus, man is not free; he is only a modification of God, who alone exists. This mild Spinozism Voltaire, anxious to prove free will, at first finds repugnant.

He is more open to Descartes's notion on matter. The most plausible theory is that there is a primary matter indifferent to everything, uniform, and capable of taking all forms. Differently combined, it constitutes the universe. The elements of this matter are the same, but matter is constantly modified in becoming any object. Since this was the opinion of both Descartes and Newton, Voltaire adopts it as his own.

He discusses at some length Descartes's ideas on light. He rejects the notion that light is a "matière fine et déliée." Over and over, he returns to the foolishness of making light an element of matter and scoffs continually at the "three elements" of Descartes. He rejects, also, the explanation that light is pressed instantaneously against our eyes. He condemns Descartes's notion that the spinning of bits of light particles is what produces different colors. Finally, he notes that Descartes, who could not know the real cause of refrangibility, invented explanations which were not explanations at all.

The greatest nonsense Descartes came forth with was his "tourbillons," which do not exist and which, says Voltaire, cannot exist, since they cannot in any way explain the movements of the planets, or the weights of the planets, or the movement of light. Voltaire condemns the whole notion of the plenum: "tout est impossible dans le plein."

In summary, Voltaire's treatment of Descartes, though more "nuancé" than has been supposed in the past, can hardly be said to have given full consideration to his illustrious predecessor's philosophy. After reading his comments, one is a little disturbed to see that Descartes is expected to be scarcely more than a scientist, a mathematician with an interest in the phenomena of the physical world. Voltaire felt that Descartes's mathematical equipment enabled him to put the questions to nature which should have disclosed nature's secrets, and he was shocked that Descartes seemingly had no interest in proceeding along these lines. Since Voltaire's mathematical ability was practically inexistent, one wonders on what grounds he formulated this judgment. Still, his observation is thought to be correct in general: Descartes did not show any great interest in applying geometry to natural phenomena, nor was he particularly interested in experimental physics. But he did have a consuming interest in philosophy, that is, metaphysics. One would think that Voltaire would have wanted to know something about the validity of this metaphysics, since he believed that it constituted the foundation of physics. But there is no evidence anywhere that he understood the metaphysics of Descartes even in a superficial way. More serious still was his failure to see any connection between the metaphysics and the "morale" of Descartes, although he stated grandiloquently that he reduced all metaphysics to "la morale." That leaves the method of Descartes. What importance did that have for Voltaire? There is no evidence that he attached to these relationships the slightest significance.

The purpose which Descartes seemed to serve in Voltaire's intellectual formation was a historical one. He was the philosopher who overthrew the philosophy of Aristotle. In the *Eclaircissements sur la philosophie de Newton* (M. XXII, 276), Voltaire affirms that no philosopher would now support Descartes's elements, his laws of movement, his vortices, or his conception of man. He concedes that Descartes's one claim to fame was his destruction of Aristotelian philosophy but insists that Descartes would have been wrong to combat Aristotle without respecting him, since Aristotle was a genius who, far surpassing Descartes, Malebranche, or Newton, had united with an immense intelligence the philosophy of his time and a profound knowledge of eloquence and poetry. Voltaire infers that it is as proper to dethrone Descartes with respect as it was fitting for Descartes to dispossess Aristotle. Fundamentally, all he represented for Voltaire was the merit of having been opposed to the errors of antiquity. When he attempted to replace those errors with the truth, he succeeded only in establishing a new set of errors. Voltaire sums up Descartes's achievement in a rather remarkable statement: "Il voulut créer un univers. Il fit une philosophie, comme on fait un bon roman; tout parut vraisemblable, et rien ne fut vrai" (M., XXII, 134). For a person who had spent almost two decades trying to be France's greatest poet and who had just praised the genius of Aristotle because the latter possessed a profound knowledge of poetry, Voltaire is a little severe with his French predecessor. He deserves perhaps some commendation for perceiving in Descartes poetic qualities. His condemnation of these same poetic qualities because they were exercised by a philosopher shows a rather nonpoetic, niggling spirit.

This niggling spirit is all the more surprising since it is difficult to accuse Voltaire of being ignorant of Descartes's works. From his library catalogue, we know that he possessed all the principal works. From the dates of their publication, we have inferred that Voltaire must have undertaken a serious study of them after arriving in England. In the light of Bolingbroke's letter, we have been tempted to state that Voltaire carried out the directions of his English friend by first securing and reading Descartes before attempting to get acquainted with Newton. If, as Pomeau suggests (*Religion* p. 187), Newton supplanted Descartes in Voltaire's estimation from 1727 to 1732, it was because Voltaire did not have too much time to make a careful study of the French philosopher. The evidence indicates that, having prepared to make a study of Descartes, Voltaire, because of the circumstances of his English trip, quickly switched his attention to Newton and thereafter spent practically no more time trying to understand the philosophy of the French philosopher. That does not underestimate, however, the effect that Mme du Châtelet's balanced judgment upon Descartes had upon her famous poet-philosopher friend.

NEWTON[3]

Voltaire decided at the end of 1733 to throw in his lot with Newton in the quarrel between the Newtonians and the Cartesians. His conversion was at least supported, if not actually fostered, by Maupertuis, who had also spent some time in England and who had been attracted to Newton. As a matter of fact, Voltaire had already manifested a lukewarm adherence to the Englishman. There is a reference in the second English *Notebook* to his espousal of Newtonianism, but it occurs without any particular enthusiasm, Voltaire merely stating that his support was given with the same reserve with which a Catholic gave money for masses—if the desired end is not achieved by the masses, the giver will use his money elsewhere. The letter to Thiériot on Pemberton's *Introduction* to Newton indicates a certain amount of curiosity concerning the *Principia* and the *Optics* while he was still in England. The mild flurry in Britain occasioned by Fontenelle's *Eloge* and the protest against it in the *Present State of the Republic of Letters* also attracted his attention.

The section in the *Lettres philosophiques* which he now intended to devote to Newton, Locke, and other English philosophers brought matters to a head. He enlisted Maupertuis's collaboration, declared himself a most enthusiastic "novice," as we have seen, and read carefully the *Discours sur les différentes figures des astres*. The immediate result of all this activity was the series of letters in the *Lettres philosophiques* on Newton. Henceforward, all his energy was directed to the support of the Newtonians against the Cartesians. It was not an easy path. Besides finding comprehension of the *Principia* very difficult, Voltaire felt that he had to understand the evolution of scientific thought from the Renaissance to his day in order to place Newton's discoveries in true perspective. That entailed some knowledge of Galileo, Kepler, and Huyghens, at the

[3] See P. Brunet, *L'Introduction des théories de Newton en France au XVIIIe siècle avant 1738.*

very least. This was a difficult task, too. Added to it was the controversy in which he became involved with Tournemine. Altogether, he had entered upon an undertaking of rather formidable proportions.

Newton's position was diametrically opposed to Descartes's. There is a story that, in his early years, when he undertook to read Descartes's works, Newton entered beside each statement of the beginning pages "error" and, having assembled in a few pages an inordinate number of errors, laid the work aside and never returned to it. But there is also a contrary legend which has it that Newton found the starting point for his scientific thought in the writings of his French predecessor. However that may be, it is certain that the Englishman rejected innate ideas, the plenum, and the automatism of animals. In fact, as Voltaire was shrewd enough to see, Newton seemed to take point by point a stance opposite to Descartes's.

The one work which Voltaire devoted to Newton, *Les Eléments de la philosophie de Newton* (1738), appeared at a moment when many French scholars still supported Descartes. With the exception of Maupertuis and Clairaut, the whole Académie des Sciences was composed of Cartesians. In general, the support was founded upon national interest, rather than upon scientific scholarship. One of Tournemine's prime arguments against Voltaire's work was, as we have seen, that it was indecorous for a Frenchman to prefer an English to a French scientist. It is important that Voltaire took the unequivocal stand that the discovery, not the nationality, of the scientist is what should be judged. Moreover, he was acutely aware that the whole quarrel was being carried on by those who understood little about scientific matters and who were debating from general attitudes rather than from knowledge of Newton's, or even Descartes's text. There was not only the public of scientists, but the general public, to enlighten. Once more, it is to Voltaire's credit that he endeavored first of all to inform himself and then to cast his understanding of scientific matters in language comprehensible to the layman. What was scoffed at as a joke—the "mis à la portée de tout le monde"—was the very center of his policy. Finally, it should be noted that Voltaire was genuinely impressed by Newton's discoveries. To him they made sense, both in content and method. The "conversion," like everything connected with Voltaire's biography, had its comic and especially its superficial side; but it was genuine. The conclusion of the Kehl "Avertissement" would thus seem a perfectly proper one: "L'ouvrage de Voltaire fut utile: il contribua à rendre la philosophie de Newton aussi intelligible qu'elle peut l'être pour ceux qui ne sont pas géomètres" (XXII, 393).

It is not easy to get at this intelligibility of Newton because of the three directions the discussion takes: Voltaire attempts to be at the same time informative, scholarly, and defensive. When he is simply informative, as he is in the fifteenth *Lettre philosophique*, he is clear and, for the most part, useful and intelligent. On these occasions, he is usually uncomplicated and leaves the impression that the subject is important and not too difficult. When, on the other hand, for scholarly purposes, he undertakes a Newtonian demonstration, he is less clear and is inclined to fall into a kind of Cartesian rationalism which complicates the subject and leaves the impression that the end result either is difficult to comprehend or, when rightly grasped, does not seem very rewarding. It is when he becomes defensive, though, that he is the least attractive. On all such occasions, he immediately reverts to a comparison between Descartes and Newton, speaks with contempt of Descartes's philosophy, while usually professing unlimited respect for the man and his time, and at the same time rejects any suggestions that Newton could be in error. In fact, at these times, he defends Newton with a zeal which recalls Mohammed's defense of Allah. Fortunately, his zeal is genuine enough.

There can be no doubt that Newton's philosophy represented everything which Voltaire required in a philosopher. It comprised a simple method, well-adapted to the limited scientific capabilities of human beings; it described what was observed, it weighed, calculated, and measured; it refused to explain, to conjecture, to pass from the phenomenon to its human meaning. Voltaire insisted to the point of embarrassment upon Newton's "hypotheses non fingo." When it came to penetrating the precise rules for scientific investigation which Newton gave, Voltaire seems to have been totally unaware of their importance. For him, empiricism was the opposite of imagination; observation of phenomena was the opposite of rational logic; natural science was the opposite of literary art; *ergo*, the philosopher, that is, the scientist, was the opposite of the poet. Voltaire's capitulation to Newtonianism as method was total.

He saw undoubtedly not only a method but a metaphysic, at least of sorts. Here we have to be extremely careful. Voltaire always seemed to make some room for metaphysics even while decrying it. His statement to Frederick that metaphysics comprises a small number of things which everybody knows and a large number which no one will ever know measures exactly the kind of metaphysics which interested him. When he added that he always reduced metaphysics to "la morale," he meant precisely that a small number of metaphysical facts which everybody knows are facts of relationship: man's relations to God, to his fellowman, to society, to nature, to himself. Hence, for him a physics which clarifies these relationships was a physics of the right order. Voltaire was genuinely persuaded that Newton's discoveries of nature's secrets proved conclusively the existence of God, and he assumed that this one metaphysical fact guaranteed the right relationships of man in all the other necessary metaphysical, that is, moral, problems. He was, in all probability, convinced that Cartesianism led to atheism while Newtonianism confirmed deism. Both philosophers would have been profoundly shocked at this interpretation. It remains nonetheless true for Voltaire that Newton's few metaphysical assumptions—the existence of God, space and time as properties of God, God's freedom, man's limited freedom, natural religion, the origin of ideas and the nature of the soul, atoms, the first principles of matter, the elements of matter, and the nature of energy—were satisfactorily presented in Newtonian philosophy. Voltaire assembled them in the *Eléments* in Section I, which was not published until 1740.

The Newtonian proofs of the existence of God are drawn from the doctrine of final causes. The whole of the Englishman's philosophy leads inevitably to the knowledge of a Supreme Being, who has created and put in order all things. These things, in the language of the Psalmist, declare the glory of God. For if the world is finite, if the vacuum does exist (as Newton supposed), matter cannot exist by itself and must therefore have received its existence from a free Power. If matter gravitates, the gravitation must be a gift of God. Voltaire, who concurs with Newton's view, looks to God for all the phenomena of this universe much like children who look to

Guignol for order in their troubled world. It is not an accident, or even a joke in bad taste, that the Frenchman thinks of the Deity in terms of Brioché, the seventeenth-century puppeteer. Newton differs from Descartes in his apprehension of the Deity. The latter's thought leads naturally to Spinoza, who recognizes no other God, says Voltaire, than the immensity of things. Voltaire willingly ascribes to Descartes an atheistic tendency, because the latter judged this universe infinite, deemed movement always a constant, and was reputed to have said: "Give me matter and movement, and I'll make you a world." It is evident that Voltaire was not so much committed to the mechanical aspect of the universe as he was to the view of the whole existing necessarily and eternally. But he objects most strenuously to the atheist who stressed the infinite flow of evil as proof of the powerlessness of the Deity.

Voltaire replies to this attack against the all-powerfulness of God with arguments which resemble those of King and Leibniz, rather than Newton's. The word "good," he says, is equivocal. What is bad for the individual is good in the general arrangement. Man demands absolute happiness, but he is finite and his ills are proportionately less than his joys. Voltaire asserts that there are more good than evil things in this world. God is such a clever artisan in the design of His creatures that it would be foolish to revolt because spiders eat flies or wolves devour sheep. Moreover, a moment of suffering is more than compensated by an eternity of happiness. Voltaire concludes that the doctrine of absolute necessity does not explain things as well as the theist's doctrine. The latter offers difficulties, it is true, but the former offers only absurdities: "La philosophie nous montre bien qu'il y a un Dieu, mais elle est impuissante à nous apprendre ce qu'il est, ce qu'il fait, comment et pourquoi il le fait."

Voltaire accepts the Newtonian concept of God, rather than the atheist concept of necessity, and he derives from the former the two concepts of time and space. The opponent of Newton in the problem of time and space was not Descartes, however, but Leibniz. It was one of the major issues in the Leibniz-Clarke debates. Essentially, the problem concerned the reality of space and time. Implied in this reality, Voltaire asserts, is the existence of matter and of God. For instance, if space is infinite and exists necessarily, why should matter not be infinite and exist necessarily? The old bogey of atheism again raises its head, and Voltaire takes fright as usual. This, of course, was not what was at issue in the Leibniz-Clarke debate. There, only the question of the reality of time and place was involved, along with the problem of Providential intervention in the workings of the universe. Voltaire adds but little to clarify that debate. He does stress, though, that Newton drew his notions of space and time from Democritus and Epicurus, as they were interpreted by Gassendi, and that the English philosopher stated that, in these problems, he was altogether of the opinion of Gassendi.

Newton is presented as having accepted the view that God is infinitely free just as He is infinitely powerful. Many things owe their existence to God's will alone. Voltaire notes that Leibniz, who stressed the law of sufficient reason, asserted the opposite. Clarke therefore accused Leibniz of presenting a God of fatality, while Leibniz retorted that Clarke presented a capricious God who acted without reason. Voltaire gives his reasons, which are anything but impressive, for adopting on this point the view of Newton and Clarke.

Newton and Clarke held that God has granted to man a limited portion of His freedom. Freedom in this sense is not the ability to apply thought to a particular object, and to initiate motion, or the faculty of willing, but the faculty of freely willing, with a full efficacious will, and willing without any other reason than the will provides. Voltaire adopts provisionally a freedom of indifference and a freedom of spontaneity (a term he took from Collins). He explains that freedom is a kind of health. But he admits that one is very right to question the efficacy of an indifference where one has no reason whatever for making the choice and where the choice only leads to frivolous consequences. He questions the validity of a freedom which is dependent on the last idea; and he admits that he knows no way to reconcile free will with God's prescience. He agrees with Locke that one is free when one can do what one wishes.

In reality, Voltaire's whole discussion derives, not from Newton, but from Locke tempered by Clarke, and especially from the debates of Collins and Clarke and of Clarke and Leibniz. It was considerably readjusted by Voltaire's own exchange with Frederick. Essentially, his conclusion expresses more a desire for freedom than a conviction that freedom is possible. He defines free will more or less as Locke did, that is, as power, maintaining that, when one has the power to do what one wants to do, one is to that extent free. The accordance of will and power he calls health. But, in the end, in spite of much irrelevant or at least unclear argument, he is inclined already in this early stage (1740) to admit that, although he very much desires to prove free will in man, he has not any firm way of establishing his belief. The freedom of indifference, he argues, cannot be very relevant, since, even if it is possible, it only leads to a choice which precisely is of no consequence. It is difficult to argue that one has free choice when choosing does not really matter; one has free choice only when it does matter. Voltaire's freedom of spontaneity, which he adopts on all occasions when the freedom is not one of indifference, is scarcely free, as Collins has shown, since it is the result, not of spontaneity, but rather of the last judgment (that is, the *dictamen*) of the understanding. Voltaire, while insisting that the great utility of free will lies in the effective way our will combats our passions, concedes that our freedom is severely limited in all cases, not excepting this particular case. His real conclusion in the *Eléments* is that the arguments against free will are frightening. Voltaire sums them up in one final statement: (1) the liberty of indifference leads to no effective expression of free will; (2) since everything has its cause (which was precisely Leibniz's first principle), will must have one, too, and our action is therefore determined by our most recent idea; (3) nobody is master of his future ideas, and, hence, no one is free to will or not to will; (4) besides, if one were free, one could act against the will of God and disrupt the chain of events already arranged by God, and thus the whole eternal order could be upset. Voltaire takes refuge behind Locke and Collins, while using the arguments of Leibniz and Frederick. He is not extraordinarily honest, though, since he started out arguing that Newton and Clarke had the best manner of explaining the necessity of free will. Instead of ending with some evidence that such was the case, he winds up his irrelevancies with the remark that, no matter how we must submit to our fate, we will always act as if we are free.

The real importance of his treatment of the problem of free will is the way he adjusted the English interpretation of the problem with the German interpretation and came up with a pragmatic French conclusion. Critics are wont to stress the change in his views on free will between 1738 and 1762. Voltaire himself thought that he had changed ("L'ignorant qui pense ainsi ne l'a toujours pensé"). In reality, he had not changed his view one iota.

Voltaire made some effort in the following chapter to defend Newton's ideas on natural law. The discussion here grew out of Leibniz's accusation that Newton had destroyed all natural law. It stemmed, also, from the Leibniz-Clarke controversy, where Leibniz attacked the concept of the *Sensorium* as tending to make God corporeal. Leibniz, in addition, objected to Newton's notion that the Deity created an imperfect world which is constantly running down, holding that Newton's God was an imperfect artisan. Implied in this discussion was the idea that, if there is no regularity, no constancy, and no universality in the law of nature, there can be no stable science of the physical world and no security in the moral world. There was thus posited the notion that natural law is the guarantee of natural science as well as of natural morality. A misconception of its nature would transform the relationship between man and religion, nature, and morality. A natural law which did not conform with positive, scientific laws, or with positive, scientific moral laws, or with positive, scientific, religious, or metaphysical laws could upset the whole foundation of contemporary life, since it would bring into question the relationship of man to God, to nature, and to his fellowmen. It was undoubtedly in this sense that Voltaire talked of reducing all metaphysical and physical problems to "la morale."

The question of natural religion, therefore, becomes for Voltaire a central point. He takes the position that Leibniz's reproach to Newton was unfounded, since the law of nature or, rather, the law of God is not amenable to a constant, eternal world. As for natural religion, "les principes de morale communs au genre humain," Voltaire contends that Newton subscribed to that principle almost as fully as Leibniz. However, he stresses that Newton rejected all notion of "innate ideas." The problem is thus shifted from the universal existence of natural laws, from principles of conduct common to all humans, to the origin of these principles. Voltaire explains that Locke (and he implies that Newton was in agreement) rejected all notion of innateness. All ideas come through the senses. God having given the senses to all, there develop everywhere the same needs, feelings, and primitive rules of conduct. Voltaire adds that, since God gave man senses which lead to needs which, in turn, lead to social laws, He must have given man principles necessary to the constitution of society. That is why everybody respects gratitude and honor. But Voltaire recalls that Locke asserted that there is no notion of good and evil common to all men, which literally means that there is no fundamental natural law. Voltaire protests against this stand. It is true that travelers report moral actions which appear immoral, as Locke said. Voltaire explains that they have observed badly or misunderstood the underlying motives of these actions. He himself proclaims that every human bases his moral conduct on the Golden Rule: "fais ce que tu voudrais qu'on te fît." He concedes that the rules derived from this law vary interminably, but he argues, rather lamely, that the variations in the rules prove the existence of the general law. Voltaire adds that Newton thought that all men had a "disposition" to live in society and that this "disposition" was the origin of natural law, which Christianity perfected. Voltaire concludes that this is the source of our "humanity," as well as our belief that God has given beasts the same feelings and the same ideas as man, although in lesser degree.

The following chapter concerns the soul. Voltaire presents Newton as having accepted the notion of Locke that we are not sufficiently acquainted with nature to be able to say that it is impossible for God to give thought to any extended being. Newton did not pronounce, however, on the manner in which this could be done, since he believed the soul, says Voltaire, to be "une substance incompréhensible." Voltaire suggests, for his part, that God can as easily add thought to matter as movement, gravitation, and "life." If the smallest portion of matter is indestructible, he argues, the smallest portion of thought accorded by God could be immortal. He rejects the argument that, if matter can think, the soul must be mortal. The only alternative to thinking matter, he urges, is to assert that what we call "l'esprit" is a being whose essence it is to think, to the exclusion of all extension. This, of course, is the Christian view, but Voltaire argues that "l'esprit" should then always "be thinking," and it always "must be thinking." Voltaire denies both premises on grounds of experience. His confusion seems complete. He understands, for instance, that, if there is a substance which moves, the gift of movement comes from God; but he holds that, if there is a substance which thinks, the thought comes from itself, since it is its own essence. It does not occur to him that God can give thought to a substance that thinks in the same way that He can give movement to a substance that moves. Voltaire attacks eloquently those who reject the latter possibility, accusing them of limiting the power of God, totally unaware that he is doing the same thing. Notwithstanding, he approves Newton's refusal to define the soul and asserts that the English philosopher understood that there could be millions of other thinking substances. Therefore, he adds, the simple division of the universe into "body" and "spirit" was regarded by Newton as entirely too restricted. Newton consequently had no systematic theory of the way the "body" and "spirit" are united; he did not like systems anyway.

Voltaire next presents the four systems on the formation of our ideas: (1) the opinion of ancient philosophers (*l'impression du cachet sur le cire*); (2) those philosophers who believe that matter thinks by itself; (3) Locke's opinion; and (4) the notion of two separate realms as presented in Malebranche's system of occasionalism and Leibniz's system of preestablished harmony. Voltaire objects to Leibniz's system on the grounds that it allows no room for any notion of free will and, moreover, runs counter to Leibniz's own principle of sufficient reason, since no reasonable explanation can be given of God's manner of coordinating the ideas of the soul and the movements of the body. Voltaire then attempts to explain Leibniz's monads, his "êtres simples," finally rejects all these notions, and finishes his chapter by praising Newton for having no fixed notion of the nature of the soul and for his ability to know when to doubt.

In the following chapter, Voltaire deals with the nature of matter. He accepts as the most plausible explanation the one which affirms that there is a primary matter indifferent to everything, uniform and capable of assuming all forms, which, differently combined, constitutes the universe. Voltaire notes that both Newton and Descartes had similar views upon matter, stressing that Newton founded his opinion only upon experience and observation.

This leads Voltaire to examine more carefully the problem of method. For him, there is only one way of reasoning about objects: the method of analysis. If this method is applied to the study of matter, there arise several difficulties. First, it is impossible to conceive how a primary matter which is nothing is the source of everything. In addition, if this primary matter can produce anything, there seems no reason why it cannot produce men as well as trees and why, when it produces one thing, it should not produce some other thing. From this dilemma, Voltaire concludes that, since matter has no design, there must be a Master of the World who furnishes the design and prevents matter from being an eternal chaos. That is to say, God has formed an infinite number of creatures. This does not prevent a creature from being an agglomeration of atoms. Voltaire accepts this possibility along with Newton and Descartes, and even Leibniz. He rejects, however, Newton's notion that these atoms are constantly changing into atoms of another nature, and he confesses that he cannot understand what produces the change unless it is the same principle of attraction.

The subsequent chapter is devoted to a discussion of Newton's and Leibniz's conceptions of the elements of matter. In Newton's view, matter is an extended, impenetrable being which the human mind cannot investigate and which God can divide infinitely and, if He wishes, annihilate. These infinitely small particles serve as a basis for all of nature's productions. Leibniz seems also to have accepted that everything is composed of extended particles, infinitely divisible. At first glance, this view seems to contradict the law of sufficient reason in making extension its own cause. To obviate this difficulty, Leibniz proposed that the cause of extension is to be found in beings devoid of extension, which he calls "simple beings" or "monads." Matter thus is always an assemblage of particles. Each monad is subject to change, but the determinations of this change cannot come from without since, having no extension and occupying no place, monads have no connection with the outside world. Its changes come from within, from its own ideas which are in necessary relationship with all the parts of the external world. Voltaire rejects monads because they, without extension, may be parts of objects which possess only extension. He concludes that Leibniz's system is impossibly imaginary and takes too much for granted. For instance, it is built upon the concept of the plenum, but what proof, Voltaire asks, is there of a plenum?

It is superfluous to attempt an analysis of the *Eléments*, a work which is more concerned with the history of ideas than with the history of science. It should suffice to point out the aim of Voltaire and the method whereby he succeeded in achieving that aim. Voltaire asserts that his intention in composing the work is to attain, for himself as well as for the benefit of other readers, a clear idea of the primitive laws of nature which Newton discovered. He adds that he intends to mark out the history of the problem before Newton undertook his investigation, how he set to work to achieve its solution, at what point he stopped his research, and, in some cases, what was done subsequently to advance this research. Voltaire promises to discuss two Newtonian problems, light and weight, but he promises he will stress at the end the law of gravitation or attraction, the universal law of nature, which Newton alone was responsible for having uncovered. Voltaire concludes that he will attempt to present these *Eléments* in a way which will be understandable to all those who are unfamiliar with science and philosophy. He expresses the belief that the science of nature is the property of all men. He concedes that it may seem as unintelligible as Greek science but says he hopes to be able to clarify these Newtonian discoveries.

The clarification is attempted in three stages, but they are not arranged in a historical sequence. Voltaire dismisses summarily the Greek ideas on light. He stresses that Descartes correctly defined light and explained the nature of colors but, being possessed of the desire to establish his system, invented, rather than observed, his three imaginary elements and incorrectly taught that light did not come from the sun. Voltaire gives reasons for rejecting Descartes's theory and hastens to explain Rœmer's demonstration that light comes from the sun "en sept ou huit minutes." From there, he proceeds to a description of Bradley's experiment, which confirmed fully Rœmer's discovery. Bradley had profited from the scientific activities of the famous Hooke and the astronomer Flamsteed, discoverer of 3,000 stars, and the chevalier Molineux, aided by the "mécanicien" Graham, who invented the parallactic telescope so ably described in Smith's excellent *Traité d'optique*. We are slightly overwhelmed by such control of authorities, but somehow we get the main points Voltaire is trying to put across, that light comes from the sun in seven or eight minutes and that it was discovered by scientists who trusted only observation and experiment, unlike Descartes, who trusted only his imagination.

Voltaire attacks another "dreamer"—Malebranche—for having believed that the vibration of luminous bodies impresses motion upon small and gentle vortices. Voltaire now produces proof that these gentle vortices do not exist. Having eliminated the Cartesian explanation, he turns to give an account of the true nature of light. It is fire, it weighs very little, it travels a thousand million feet a second. It is characterized by three phenomena: reflection, refraction, inflection. The interesting point about reflection is that light is not reflected from the solid surfaces of bodies but rebounds without touching the surface because of some unknown power. In a mirror, light is not sent back by the solid surface of mercury but from the bosom of the pores of the mirror and the mercury. Voltaire makes the assumption that light enters the eye under circumstances described in the theory of reflection and refraction. Consequently, he devotes a chapter to the anatomy of the eye. The succeeding chapters take up various problems of vision: distances, magnitudes, and situations. We cannot determine these things except by experience. Voltaire defends this point by relating again Cheselden's operation upon a blind person in 1729 (it was the standard example). He suggests that it is an error to state that our senses deceive us. In reality, they alone can aid us, but they must work together—touch with sight, for instance. Voltaire concludes this aspect of the problem by condemning Malebranche for having rejected the evidence of the senses and by lauding Berkeley for his new theory of vision. A minor problem taken up by many theorists was the size of objects seen on the horizon in comparison with those same objects seen at the zenith. Voltaire undertakes to give a solution, which he derives from Smith. He is now prepared to enter upon a discussion of refraction. It is on this occasion that he strongly suggests that both reflection and refraction are the result of attraction, and in the following chapter (X) refrangibility is attributed to the same cause. Voltaire now undertakes the explanation of the rainbow, where he gives ample credit to De Dominis and, for once, metes out some praise to Descartes for having rectified De Dominis's measurements. The twelfth chapter is a kind of summary of the section on optics, particularly on the problem of colors. Voltaire adds, in a Chapter XIII, later suppressed, that the theory of light has a very close connection with the theory of the universe. Matter, he states, has many more properties than is thought possible (M. XXII, 503):

Pour moi, j'avoue que, plus j'y réfléchis, plus je suis surpris qu'on craigne de reconnaître un nouveau principe, une nouvelle propriété dans la matière. Elle en a peut-être à l'infini; rien ne se ressemble dans la nature. Il est très probable que le Créateur a fait l'eau, le feu, l'air, la Terre, les végétaux, les minéraux, les animaux, etc., sur des principes et des plans tous différents. Il est étrange qu'on se révolte contre de nouvelles richesses qu'on nous présente: car n'est-ce pas enrichir l'homme que de découvrir de nouvelles qualités de la matière dont il est formé?

Part III of the *Eléments* is devoted to the problem of attraction. Voltaire opens the discussion with an assault against the Cartesian theories on weight, subtle matter, vortices, and the plenum. Showing that light objects or heavy objects drop with the same speed in a vacuum, he asserts that, if the vacuum contained subtle matter, there would be no reasonable explanation for this phenomenon. Therefore, he concludes, subtle matter does not exist, for otherwise its resistance to the objects dropped would cause them to drop at different rates. Voltaire deduces two facts: an object weighs according to its mass, not according to its surface; a vacuum exists, while subtle matter does not. If these two points are accepted, it is readily seen that the vortices composed of this subtle matter cannot exist either. Nor, in that case, can propulsion, which, according to Descartes, comes from the rapid whirling of this subtle matter around the globe, thereby driving objects through pressure toward the earth. Therefore, objects have weight, not because they are pushed, but because they are pulled. Voltaire, having eliminated the system of Descartes in the first chapter with one experiment and a series of logical deductions, uses the second chapter to review the arguments which can be advanced against the vortices and the plenum. He details these arguments in true systematic order: eleven which show the impossibility of the vortices, six which prove the impossibility of the plenum. We shall not stop to repeat them, since Voltaire copied them from Pemberton and elsewhere. The one important point he makes is that Descartes's explanations will not square with Kepler's laws, which everyone admits are incontrovertible. Having demolished both notions, he is now ready to return to the experiment of the pneumatic tube, which indicates that there is a force which makes objects descend toward the center of the earth.

Here, true to his method of giving a little historical background to the problem discussed, Voltaire presents Galileo's discoveries on falling bodies. He notes that already, in Galileo's time, there existed the suspicion that falling bodies were drawn to the center of the earth. Copernicus himself had "quelque faible lueur de cette idée." Kepler had already adopted it, though in disorderly fashion. Bacon said that it is probable that there is an attraction of bodies in the center of the earth. Descartes had heard of Bacon's experiments, but he rejected them because they had not produced the desired results and because, in creating his system, he attributed the cause of weight to subtle matter. It is true that Gassendi protested against the Cartesian system, but with undue timidity. Only Newton, pondering the whole phenomenon of falling bodies from a simple observation of falling fruit, surmised that the force which attracted the fruit would attract the moon and thus all the planets which gravitate toward the sun. This observation, which Voltaire is careful to emphasize, is in no sense of the word a hypothesis, led Newton to make the necessary measurements, the precise calculations, the exact weighing. Voltaire dramatizes the efforts Newton made to obtain these accurate measurements, his disappointment when they did not square with other accepted measurements, and, finally, his success when these latter were discovered to be in error, revised, and then squared with his own measurements.

Voltaire now undertakes to explain the law of inertia, the effect of this upon bodies moving in a circle around a center, and the tendency to be drawn to the center. To this discussion he adds a simple explanation of Kepler's laws and, finally, a very simple demonstration of Newton's theory which, he states, will be understood by everybody, "car les hommes ont une géométrie naturelle dans l'esprit, qui leur fait saisir les rapports quand ils ne sont pas trop compliqués" (Beuchot, Œuvres, XXXVIII, 204). A fuller demonstration is given to Chapter V, beginning with a careful enunciation of Kepler's laws and including a complete recapitulation of the proofs of gravitation and a conclusion concerning the movement of the earth drawn from these laws. Having proved the universal necessity of gravity, both in explaining the irregularities in the movement of the moon, the elliptical orbits of the planets, and the movements of the planets around the sun, the common center, Voltaire now feels that he can challenge the Cartesian theories of vortices upon real, scientific grounds because, if they actually existed, they, too, would have to be subject to the law of gravity.

Voltaire suggests at the beginning of Chapter VII that this attraction may be a first principle established in nature. At all events, he notes that centripetal force, attraction, gravitation, is the one undoubted principle that accounts for the movement of planets, the fall of heavy bodies, and the weight which is present in all bodies. Gravitation operates in reaction as well as in action, so that, if the sun attracts the planets, the planets also attract the sun. Further, it occurs not only in the mass of each planet but in each part of the mass, so that there is not one single atom of matter in this universe devoid of this property. Voltaire next undertakes, using Newton's measurements, to give a "theory" of the world. There ensue a whole series of comparisons of weights, densities, quantities of light and heat, distances of the individual planets of the solar system from each other. The overwhelming set of statistics is followed by a chapter devoted to the shape of the earth, which results from the laws of attraction and its rotation on its axis. This gives Voltaire an opportunity to relate the history of those who have sought the shape of the earth and to recount Maupertuis's expedition of 1736 to measure a meridian. Voltaire now considers three special cases subject to attraction: the precession of the equinoxes, tides, and comets. Chapter XIV, the last, is a kind of general summary. Here he asserts that attraction plays a role in all the operations of nature. It is a principle which acts from one end of the solar system to the other, on the largest mass as on the smallest atom, on the sun as on the thinnest ray of light. Voltaire wonders if it is not the cause of the continuity and the adhesion of bodies. In a final summary, he lists: (1) There exists an active force which impresses on all bodies a tendency to be drawn to each other. (2) This force acts in inverse proportion to the squares of their distances and in direct proportion to their mass. We call this force attraction in relation to the center of the movement, and gravitation in relation to the bodies which tend to the center. (3) The same force makes falling objects descend toward the center of the earth. (4) A similar force is the cause of adhesion, continuity, and hardness. (5) It also acts between light and bodies. The cause of this force is unknown. One can say, however, with Newton, that it is not a mechanical force. Voltaire adds that it is not the only principle of physics, that there are probably a lot of other secrets which we have not divined in nature and which work with gravitation to maintain the order of the universe. He predicts that in time we shall discover some of them.

It is necessary now to inquire what Newton meant to Voltaire as a philosopher. First of all, it would seem that he offered the Frenchman a whole new field of intellectual endeavor, which extended far beyond a simple investigation of Newtonian discoveries. The activity displayed by Voltaire in getting acquainted with the meaning of Newton was intense. A simple enumeration of the authors whose writings he perused is very impressive: Fontenelle, Maupertuis, Mairan, Bernouilli; S'Gravesande, Musschembrœck, Boerhaave, Huyghens; Keill, Gregory, Hooke, Smith, Pemberton. He consulted as well the *Transactions* of the Royal Society, the *Mémoires* of the Académie des Sciences, the *Journal des savants,* and the *Mémoires de Trévoux.*[4] He also made every effort to acquaint himself with the line of seventeenth-century giants who set the stage for Newton: Galileo, Kepler, Kircher, Huyghens, and others. In a way, he reviewed the whole history of modern science from Galileo to his own day. In a two-year span, or four years at the most, Voltaire made serious efforts to keep abreast of important English, Dutch, and French works on Newtonian physics. He tried intelligently and with remarkable assiduity to see this "modern" interpretation of the world in the right perspective; that is, he proceeded first of all to inquire into what it was, reducing it on occasion to the simplest terms possible and describing it with a clarity which could be grasped by all. The initial aim, though, was to comprehend clearly himself what it was all about; only after he had some grasp of the facts did he undertake to transmit his "new" knowledge to others. The earnestness with which he learned his lesson, the sincerity with which he entered upon his study, and the straightforward tone with which

---

[4] Cf. M. Libby, *The Attitude of Voltaire to Magic and the Sciences,* p. 271: "One of the most admirable traits of his work is the number and quality of the texts and specialized studies praised or discussed."

he communicated his results to the public at large attest to a curious change of attitude. Voltaire was genuinely scandalized at the flippancy of a Fontenelle and the airiness of an Algarotti. He was shocked that such a profound subject as the meaning of the physical universe should be discussed in a language which pretended to be poetic, metaphorical, and imaginative. He had a tendency to denounce all imagination in connection with science as bad taste. When he wanted to condemn a philosopher who discussed science, he would attack his imagination (cf. his treatment of Descartes, Malebranche, Leibniz), call him simultaneously a "poet" and a "dreamer," and dismiss him as no scientist at all. Curiously, he felt, though, that these new discoveries must, to be presented effectively, be "égayées," and the poet in him still persisted to the point where he wanted to explain Newtonian philosophy to Mme du Châtelet in rimed couplets and an Horatian *épître*. The trip to Lapland to measure a meridian he tried to celebrate in something resembling an ode. When the poetic value of his efforts was almost nil, he complained that it was incongruous to sing the Newtonian synthesis in rimed strophes.

The question naturally arises what motives lay behind Voltaire's sudden interest in Newtonian science. There were, as we have seen, historical reasons for this interest. But it is more important to discover what made Newton great in Voltaire's opinion. Even in 1776, Sherlock recorded the old Patriarch's profound veneration for the English scientist. In 1736, that veneration was already present. In a letter to Olivet (18 October 1736), Voltaire wrote: "Mon cher ami, mon cher maître, Newton est le plus grand homme qui ait jamais été, mais le plus grand, de façon que les géants de l'antiquité sont auprès de lui des enfants qui jouent à la fossette." It is true that Voltaire told Sherlock that Locke, also, was "le plus grand homme." What is clear is the lasting enthusiasm Voltaire had for the two English philosophers. He could find all kinds of reasons for Newton's greatness. Newton destroyed the "rêveries" of Descartes, as Descartes had suppressed the banalities of Aristotle. He proved against the French philosopher that the vacuum exists, that innate ideas do not exist, that vortices likewise are inexistent, and that Descartes's whole universe was a figment of the imagination to which nothing in reality corresponded. He discovered the only way to approach the phenomena of nature. He espoused analysis and experimental procedures built on observation. He proscribed a priori thinking, general principles devoid of experience, and hypotheses. He marked out the limits of science, showing his contemporaries that man can measure, calculate, weigh the phenomena of nature but must not expect to reach the general principles which govern our universe. He dared acknowledge that a force which he had discovered, which is universal and which transforms our conception of the whole universe, is unknown to us in its origin and its causes. Rather than surmise whence it comes and what it is, he preferred modestly to assert that he did not know the answer to these questions. "Il savait douter," Voltaire said, in according him one of his highest compliments. All the same, he had penetrated one of nature's secrets and thereby had discovered a universal law of nature which opened up infinite possibilities and limitless horizons. Voltaire concluded with fervor his paean of Newton in the article "système" of the *Dictionnaire philosophique* (M. XX, 470): "Admirons encore davantage la profondeur, la justesse, l'invention du grand Newton, qui seul a découvert les raisons fondamentales de ces lois inconnues à toute l'antiquité, et qui a ouvert aux hommes un ciel nouveau." If one will compare Voltaire's ultimate estimate with those of our present-day historians of science (see A. E. Bell, *Newtonian Science*, London, 1960), it will seem surprisingly accurate and hardly excessive.

LOCKE[5]

Of all the philosophers with whom Voltaire associated himself, Locke was undoubtedly the one to whom he accorded the greatest respect. Faguet, who likes to make profound judgments in "bons mots," called him "le grand homme" of Voltaire, and his remark seems very apt. In many respects, this adoration of Locke even transcended that of Newton, although in the mind of the French poet the two were so highly esteemed that he often had difficulty in expressing a preference. He had, following Bolingbroke's letter of

[5] See E. Sonet, *Voltaire et l'influence anglaise*, pp. 75-115; C. Dédéyan, *Voltaire et la pensée anglaise*, pp. 120-136; G. Bonno, *La Culture et la civilisation britannique devant l'opinion française au XVIIIᵉ siècle de la paix d'Utrecht aux* Lettres philosophiques, pp. 80-96.

1724, come in contact with both of them simultaneously, and they had represented for him the two kinds of philosophers whom he knew—the scientist and the metaphysician. Bolingbroke had presented them as counter-balancing Descartes and Malebranche, but there are reasons to believe that Voltaire thought of them as being the opposite numbers of Descartes and Pascal, respectively. It was not easy, though, to pair them off. Ultimately in Voltaire's mind, as we shall see, Bacon, Newton, and Locke represented English philosophy (both physics and metaphysics), while Descartes, Pascal, and Malebranche represented French philosophy (both physics and metaphysics). The sharp distinction which Voltaire thought he could make between the physicist Newton and the metaphysician Locke in England he found impossible to make in France, because of the assumed preeminence of Descartes in both areas and the intrusion of theology (Pascal and Malebranche) in the field of philosophy. For him, though, Locke was an excellent example of a metaphysician who reduced all metaphysics to "la morale." He possessed an added advantage in that he presented his metaphysical "morale" in the clearest of terms. Voltaire felt he could read and understand Locke because of this simple clarity, while he was never quite confident that he understood Newton.

Consequently, he is very lavish in his praise of the author of the *Essay concerning Human Understanding*. To Walpole (B. 14179), he calls him another Hercules who, in metaphysics, has laid out the boundaries of the human mind. In the *Siècle de Louis XIV* (M. XIV, 562-563), he finds Locke is an excellent example of the superiority of the seventeenth century over the Golden Age of Greece. There is no one between Plato and him who attempted to trace the operation of the soul. Indeed, he is far superior to Plato. He has alone traced the movement of the human understanding in a work in which there are nothing but truths, all clearly expressed. To Formont, he confides that Locke is "l'homme le plus sage" (B. 625). What Locke has not clearly seen will probably never be divined. He is the only philosopher who does not take for granted the problem at hand. To S'Gravesande (M. XXXIII, 65), he asserts that Locke has restricted the confines of knowledge in order to strengthen it. Voltaire urges everyone to read him. His enthusiasm was not the exuberance of a sudden acquaintance: three decades later in the *Philosophe*

ignorant (M. XXVI, 74), he praises Locke for his modesty and recalls that the Englishman never pretends to know what he does not
understand. He concedes gracefully that his hero is not overly
wealthy in ideas but insists that the ideas he possesses are solid, sure,
and not offered as a display. He proceeds, says Voltaire, like an
excellent anatomist in detailing the springs of the human mind. Voltaire remarks that the Englishman has been accused of being opposed to religion. Some theologians have stated that he has openly
denied the immortality of the soul and destroyed the foundations of
morality. Needless to say, Voltaire vigorously denies both charges
(M. XXII, 126):

> Ne vous révoltez donc plus contre la sage et modeste philosophie de
> Locke; loin d'être contraire à la religion, elle lui servirait de preuve, si la
> religion en avait besoin: car quelle philosophie plus religieuse que celle
> qui, n'affirmant que ce qu'elle conçoit clairement et sachant avouer sa
> faiblesse, vous dit qu'il faut recourir à Dieu, dès qu'on examine les pre-
> miers principes.

Voltaire praises not only the man but his ideas, too. In the *Philosophe ignorant*, he points out the most important of them. Nothing enters the understanding except through the senses. There are
no innate ideas. We human creatures cannot conceive of infinite
space or even an infinite number. Thought is not the essence, but the
action of the understanding. I am free when I can do what I wish.
This freedom does not abide in the will. Thus, it is absurd to say
that the will is free, for I can only will as a consequence of the
ideas in my mind. I am forced to determine myself as a consequence
of these ideas. Being finite, I have no idea of infinity. I cannot know
any substance, only its qualities. Memory makes me a "person." I
am never the same person. I am always gaining a new identity, with
tremendous consequences. Thinking and feeling do not essentially
belong to being. We do not know any being thoroughly. So we do
not know whether a being can receive feeling and thought. The
words "matter" and "spirit" are only words. We have no idea what
they are. Hence, no one can say that matter cannot receive the gift
of thought from God.

Voltaire's library was fairly well stocked with Locke's works. Besides the *Œuvres diverses*, 2 vols., Amsterdam, 1732, he had two

editions of *Le Christianisme raisonnable*—one 2 vols., Amsterdam, 1731, and a second the translation by Coste, also 2 vols., Amsterdam, 1740. Voltaire also had a copy of *Du Gouvernement civil*, Amsterdam, 1691, and the 1710 London edition of the *Essay concerning Human Understanding*, along with Coste's translation, *Essai philosophique concernant l'entendement humain*, 4 vols., Amsterdam, 1748. I do not know what use Voltaire made of the *Histoire de la navigation*, 2 vols., Paris, 1722, or of the autograph letter of Locke which he was said to have possessed.

Voltaire's first contact with Locke undoubtedly took place following the famous Bolingbroke letter of 1724. There are indications that, while he was in England, he began his study of Newton and Locke, as the English Lord had recommended. There are two notations in the English *Notebooks*: one which marks out a program of philosophical subjects he would like to pursue and the way in which he intends to pursue them, and a second which recalls that we know nothing about the nature of the soul and therefore should not acknowledge its existence. Both notes bespeak already a close interest in Locke and stand as the focus around which Voltaire intended to organize his metaphysics. For Locke was a metaphysician who approached his subject in a way which received Voltaire's unreserved approval. There really is nothing unusual about this approval, though, since Voltaire, even before knowing Locke and before the English sojourn, had undertaken a review of his own metaphysics. We have already pointed out how closely his metaphysical preoccupations before the English visit resembled his Lockean interests after his return. There was a natural conformity of intellectual interests between the two, which first manifested itself in the thirteenth letter of the *Lettres philosophiques* "on the soul." This letter not only carries out a presentation of Locke but practices the injunction in the *Conseils à un journaliste*. Voltaire outlines a history of the idea of the soul from earliest times to Descartes and Malebranche. He concludes that everyone before Locke had written the romance of the soul but that only Locke had endeavored to write its history. Voltaire praises highly this historicization of metaphysics and applauds fully Locke's efforts to trace step by step the operations of the mind.

The result of this careful, experimental method was that Locke could make three very significant points. In the first place, our ideas are not derived from a set of innate ideas. The mind at birth is like a blank sheet of paper, on which are inscribed only those things which enter it via the senses. It is true that Locke had also insisted upon the way in which reflection is likewise a source of our ideas, but Voltaire does not now stress this. The important point is the elimination of innateness and the insistence that our ideas are derived from our experience. What we experience we know, as Locke said.

This experience as the source of ideas does not differ fundamentally from that of other living creatures. They, too, receive their impressions through the senses. Since God gave them these senses, Locke (seconded by Voltaire) assumes that they were meant to be used. Whatever difference exists between animals and humans in this respect is one of degree. Animals have more simple ideas, but they are developed the same way in animals as in men. Voltaire does not follow readily the evolution of ideas, the distinction between simple and complex ideas, the relationship between abstract and concrete ideas, and, above all, the relationship between ideas and actions. For the moment, he limits himself to the simple exposition of the development.

The third point concerned the relationship of matter and spirit. In the thinking of Cartesianism, matter was distinguished by extension, the soul by thought. Extension and thought were held to be two incompatible qualities. Locke had suggested that no one can say that God could not give thought to matter. This point, which was merely an English prudent restriction, had been touched upon by Locke in passing and was not a capital point in the elaboration of his thought. It had, however, been severely challenged by Stillingfleet in the famous controversy which ensued. For Voltaire, it carried implications out of all proportions to Locke's intentions, so that thereafter it became for the Frenchman the central point of all of Locke's thinking. For the rest of his life, Voltaire could never refer to Locke without reverting to this idea and without defending its truth. The arguments are simple—too simple, indeed, to carry much philosophical significance. God can, if He wishes, endow a portion of matter with thought, as he has endowed matter with attraction. There is no impiety involved in this belief, since it is based simply on the all-powerfulness of the Deity. Besides, we talk about matter and spirit as being opposed things, but we have no notion whatever of what matter and spirit are. This point, already stressed by Pascal, was echoed by Locke and interminably repeated by Voltaire. For the moment of the *Lettres philosophiques*, the scandal arose from the consequences of this view. If God can (and does) endow a portion of matter with thought, then the soul, whatever it is, can only be something material, or there would be two kinds of thought—one material, one immaterial. Voltaire was perfectly right when he wrote to Formont that the letter on Locke involved only the simple matter of immateriality. If material, the soul must exist in the same terms as all material things; that is to say, it is not eternal. This assertion gave rise quickly to the impression that Voltaire was defending the materiality and the mortality of the soul. Since this was precisely in accord with the note upon the soul in the *Notebooks*, since it was given the priority in being placed as the third of three points which Voltaire noted in Locke, and since far more space was accorded to it than to the other two points, it is obvious that, for Voltaire, it was the central notion of the *Essay*. Whether it became so important because of the Stillingfleet-Locke discussion, or because it represented for Voltaire, if not for Locke, the indispensable metaphysical problem, or because, finally, it was a point from which Voltaire decided to combat both materialism and spiritualism, I do not know. I suspect, however, that all three reasons entered into the act. At all events, as Bonno has shown, the stand was severely criticized by those who saw its possible deleterious effects and those who suspected the nature of the ruse. From then (1734) until the end of his life, Voltaire wrote innumerable articles upon the soul. He hardly added anything of consequence, though, to his original statement, which he presented as Locke's.

He must have known, however, that this did not constitute a valid presentation of Locke. Even before the publication of the *Lettres philosophiques*, he was busily engaged in mastering the Englishman's ideas. He accorded Locke a first reading while in England, a second reading around November 1732 while he was rewriting the thirteenth letter, and still a third reading before 1734, the latter accompanied by a letter to Formont announcing that he was now putting in order his own views in metaphysics, what he called his "songes métaphysiques." We are accustomed to give Mme du Châtelet credit for the inauguration of the *Traité de métaphysique,* and there is no doubt that she was interested in it. But the evidence is firm: it was the reading of Locke's *Essay* which gave the initial impulse to the *Traité.* In that respect, it was another attempt to summarize what was important in the *Essay.* Dédéyan (see *Voltaire et la pensée anglaise,* pp. 120-136) has noted, with admirable precision, these subjects: (1) innate ideas, (2) matter, (3) God, (4) the soul, (5) free will, (6) natural law, and (7) tolerance. However, in the *Traité* itself, Voltaire arranged these subjects a little differently: (1) God, (2) the senses, (3) ideas, (4) the soul, (5) matter, (6) free will, and (7) natural law. In the *Discours en vers sur l'homme,* which in a way was a poetic rendering of the *Traité,* the emphasis was shifted almost entirely from the abstract subjects to the nature of man. Thereafter, whether in the *Philosophe ignorant,* the *Dictionnaire philosophique,* or the *Questions sur l'Encyclopédie,* these problems constituted for Voltaire the basic metaphysical subjects. However, though Locke furnished the subjects, he did not necessarily furnish the answers. The *Traité,* in Voltaire's own mind, represented an attempt to bring together in synthetic form what he had learned from Hobbes, Locke, Clarke, Descartes, Bayle, Malebranche, and Pascal.

After an Introduction on the diversity of the human race, Voltaire announces that we must now examine what the faculty of thought is in these different races, whence come one's ideas, whether one has a soul distinct from the body, whether it is eternal, whether it is free, whether it is subject to vice and virtue. Obviously, these are the basic problems of Locke, as Voltaire saw them; indeed, not only are the problems Locke's, but the method of handling them is Locke's also. Voltaire, however, makes them all dependent upon the one problem of the existence of God.

Our understanding of the *Traité*[6] is colored by the fact that we know no other than the second redaction. We therefore assume that the completed first redaction was similar. In all probability, this is a mistake. I doubt that Chapters VIII and IX, which are closely allied in thought to Shaftesbury and Mandeville, occurred in the first draft, simply because Voltaire did not know Mandeville at

[6] See H. T. Patterson, ed., *Traité de métaphysique,* and I. Wade, *Studies on Voltaire.*

that time. When these two chapters are removed, the remaining seven resemble even more closely Locke's problems, though now somewhat modified by Clarke and Bayle. Voltaire, making a synthesis of his opinions and still not very adept at this sort of thing in philosophy, picked up any assistance he could, from Clarke and Bayle as well as from Locke.

The first of these problems concerns innate ideas. Locke's initial preoccupation, as everyone knows, was the extent and limits of the human understanding. In Book I, he undertook to mark out these limits. Against those who proposed that man was born into this world with a certain body of essential truths upon which he could build, Locke asserted that man appeared with a mind as blank as a sheet of paper upon which, in time, his experiences were engraved. Historians of philosophy have had some difficulty in naming those who, in Locke's opinion, held a positive view of innate ideas. One usually thinks of Herbert of Cherbury, the Cambridge Platonists, or Descartes, but, in truth, these thinkers held rather a dispositional view of innate ideas. Voltaire, who was trying to distinguish between English philosophy and French philosophy, was certain that Descartes was the supporter of innateness, and he ironically presents arguments, in the *Lettres philosophiques*, which Descartes never espoused. Voltaire himself was fully in agreement with Locke: "Je conviens avec le sage Locke qu'il n'y a point de notion innée, point de principe, de pratique innée" (M. XXVI, 74ff.).

If there are no innate ideas, no matter how they may be defined, whence come our ideas? Locke proposed the senses and reflection: that is, external objects are picked up by the senses; internal objects, by reflection. Voltaire follows Locke closely in this step, with the exception of reflection, which he is incapable of treating. There is nonetheless a difficulty: what is the mechanism whereby an object initiates an idea which arrives through a sense organ to our perception? Both Locke and Voltaire propose that God gives the idea to the sense. In Malebranche's phrase, we see all things in God. Thus, the elimination of innate ideas does nothing more than postpone the moment of the origin of ideas to post-natal experiences, rather than at birth. Whatever the time, they come from the same source. There are, however, two remarks to make. Ideas have their origin in the Deity, but they come by way of experience. The limit lies within the experience. There are thus many things which we do not know, not having had the relevant experience; and there are many things we cannot know, since our senses are limited in the knowledge they can bring us. The great advantage of Locke's way of presenting the origin of ideas lies in the modesty with which he restricts them and the simplicity with which he admits his ignorance. Hence, the one fundamental idea with Locke—and with Voltaire—is that the human understanding is very limited. The consequences of this stand are very important. They have been discussed in Section XXIX of the *Philosophe ignorant*: (1) man can only will as a consequence of the ideas he has received, (2) he cannot have any idea of the infinite, since he is a finite creature, (3) he can have ideas of the qualities of an object, but not of its substance, (4) he himself has no identity, except through memory and feeling, that is, he does not know his own substance, (5) he is therefore profoundly ignorant of the principle of things. It is this condition of restricted knowledge which makes Voltaire a "philosophe ignorant."

The second Lockean problem taken up by Voltaire is the nature of matter. Voltaire connects it almost entirely with the problem of thought. The context in which it is cast is the view that it is perfectly plausible that the capability of thought should be given to matter, just as the power of attraction has been accorded to it. Since we cannot know whether a being has the capacity of thinking or not, the words "matière" and "esprit" have no meaning. Voltaire argues that it would be rash to assert that God cannot attribute thought to matter. It is certain, for instance, that animals have been given sensations, memory, and ideas. If animals, being organized matter, have this capability, why should not bits of unorganized matter possess it? Voltaire returns to this argument over and over. One feels that he is forced to remain within the narrow confines which Locke has laid out for him and that, although he is prepared to respect these limits, he nevertheless feels cramped, harassed, and tortured by them. In this connection, Dédéyan has quoted an extract from a letter of Mme du Deffand (19 February 1766) apropos his own *Philosophe ignorant (Voltaire et la pensée anglaise*, p. 125):

Voyant dans ce traité qu'un nombre prodigieux d'hommes n'avait pas seulement la moindre idée des difficultés qui m'inquiétent . . . , voyant même qu'ils se moquaient souvent de ce que je voulais savoir, j'ai soupçonné qu'il n'était point nécessaire que nous le sussions. Mais, malgré ce désespoir, je ne laisse pas de désirer d'être instruit et ma curiosité trompée est toujours insatiable. . . . Ne méditez-vous pas aussi, Mme., ne vous vient-il pas cent idées sur l'éternité, sur la matière, sur la pensée, sur l'infini? . . . Je trouve d'ailleurs dans cette recherche, quelque vaine qu'elle puisse être, un assez grand avantage. L'étude des choses, qui sont fort au-dessus de nous, rend les intérêts de ce monde bien petits à nos yeux; et quand on a le plaisir de se perdre dans l'immensité, on ne se soucie guère de ce qui se passe dans les rues de Paris.

Voltaire also follows Locke's proofs of the existence of God, agreeing with the Englishman that we have no innate idea of God but that, as Locke put it, "If God has given us no innate ideas of himself, though he has not stamped original characters on our minds wherein we may read his being: yet having furnished us with those faculties our minds are endowed with, he has not left himself without witness." Voltaire uses the finalistic argument to prove the existence of God.

To the metaphysical problems of innate ideas and the limits of human intelligence, the nature of thinking matter and the immortality of the soul, and, finally, the existence of God, Voltaire, following Locke closely, joins four moral problems: the nature of free will, natural law as the basis of all morality, the nature of morality, and tolerance. It is evident from these eight points that Voltaire sees in Locke a satisfactory attempt to create a metaphysics which will justify an ethic. His understanding of Locke is an excellent commentary upon his announced tendency: "Je ramène toujours la métaphysique à la morale." The one fundamental metaphysical problem which gives the key to all the metaphysical and moral problems is the existence of God. The one fundamental moral problem which furnishes the key to the other moral problems is the nature of free will. It is in that sense that Voltaire wrote to Frederick (October 1737): "La question de la liberté est la plus intéressante que nous puissions examiner, puisque de cette question dépend toute morale."

The problem of free will is debated in such puerile details, especially in the correspondence of 1737-1738 with Frederick, that what is involved in the debate is easily lost from view. Voltaire attempts in the second of the *Discours en vers* to express the problem in simple terms:

> Suis-je libre en effet? ou mon âme et mon corps
> Sont-ils d'un autre agent les aveugles ressorts?
> Enfin ma volonté, qui me meut, qui m'entraîne,
> Dans le palais de l'âme est-elle esclave ou reine?

Thus, the three factors involved are body, soul, and will. Voltaire defines the word "freedom," in line with Locke, as "the power to act." In the second *Discours*, he adds to the definition: it is the power to do what one wishes to do. With these definitions, it is evident that Voltaire can conclude that, if a man can move, act, and will, he is, in acting, free. This freedom is a gift from God; it is, indeed, a part of God's freedom. It comes, Voltaire seems to say, along with the gift of thought: it is the thought which guides the action. Up to this point, Voltaire has adopted Locke's statement (*Essay*, Book II, Chapter XXI, Section 8): "So far as man has the power to think or not to think, to move or not to move, according to the preference, or the direction of his mind, so far he is free." But Locke, it will be recalled (see letter to Molyneux, 15 July 1693), was discontented with his explanation and in a subsequent edition of the *Essay* made revisions. The crux of the problem, according to the revised view of Locke, is not whether we are free to move, or even whether we are free to think, but whether we are free to will. Locke answered that this part of the question is absurd because it reduces itself to the possibility of willing to will. The will, he now suggested, is not free in the sense that it is devoid of determinants. The thing which determines is not the goal of the good, or the greatest good, or happiness or pleasure, but "uneasiness" which springs from desires; that is to say, the determining factor precedes the will, it is not the goal to which the willing tends. Desires tend to happiness, however, or, at any rate, to the diminution of pain. The action which follows the will which follows the "uneasiness" which follows the weighing of these desires is thus determined by the last judgment one forms before action. In other words, we are free to weigh, calculate, and measure our desires. But we are not free to prevent them from exercising an effect upon our response or to prevent the response from leading to a certain act which we perform in consequence of a final judgment. It is obvious that, in one sense, the ability to weigh, measure, and calculate our desires is a freedom; but, in another sense, this freedom is no guarantee whatever of the freedom of the will. Voltaire tries to be very precise about this freedom in a letter to Frederick: "A peine pourrions-nous concevoir un être plus libre qu'en tant qu'il est capable de faire ce qui lui plaît, et tant que l'homme a cette liberté, il est aussi libre qu'il est possible à la liberté de le rendre libre, pour me servir des termes de Locke." I suppose this is the sense of Voltaire's letter to Helvétius (11 September 1738) where he states that, no matter how many restrictions are placed upon man's freedom, he will always act as if he is free. In the *Philosophe ignorant* (M. XXVI, 56), Voltaire gives practically a literal translation of Locke's final view:

Ma liberté consiste à ne point faire une mauvaise action quand mon esprit . . . m'en fait sentir le danger et que l'horreur de cette action combat puissamment mon désir. Nous pouvons réprimer nos passions comme je l'ai déjà annoncé, mais alors nous ne sommes pas plus libres en réprimant nos désirs qu'en nous laissant entraîner à nos penchants: car, dans l'un et l'autre cas, nous suivons irrésistiblement notre dernière idée, et cette dernière idée est nécessaire; donc je fais nécessairement ce qu'elle me dicte.

We usually interpret all this as a reversal of opinion on Voltaire's part. We note that, having started out to affirm free will, Voltaire gave it a simple interpretation: freedom is the power to do, in effect, what we want to do: If I want to walk, if I have two legs and can walk, I am free to walk. Things are not quite so simple, however. It is possible for me to think that "I will to walk." It is not at all possible "to will to will to walk." The walking may be free, but the willing is certainly determined. Determined by what? Uneasiness, said Locke. God's prescience, said Frederick. At all events, it is evident that man is precisely an "impuissante machine," an "automate pensant," subject to fatalism. Voltaire would have none of these philosophical truths; in the letter to Helvétius, already referred to, he returned to his "raisons de bonne femme." Man acts as if he is free. The good of society requires that he believe he is free. He does not know anything about the Newtonian universe, except that he can weigh, calculate, and measure it. Indeed, one is well called a "philosophe ignorant." But, if freedom is diminished, at least morality is saved.

It is disturbing to learn that one is ignorant and that there is no first principle of morality. Voltaire was interested in freedom because of the relationship between thought and action, on the one hand, and good and evil, virtue and vice, rewards and punishments, on the other. The argument was that, if man is not free, how can he be held responsible for evil? Voltaire attempted to account for this responsibility by the theory of natural law. Precisely Locke seemed to Voltaire to deny this natural law, and thereupon the Frenchman for once found himself in disagreement. Locke, who had already condemned innate ideas, condemned an innate sense of justice on the score that there are crimes committed without the slightest subsequent remorse. He was an omniverous reader of travel literature, and he could therefore recite cases in which parents killed and ate their children, children killed and ate their parents, whole races had no idea concerning the existence of God, no religion, no cult. Locke's demonstration of evil in our world joined Bayle's here, but it was much more thorough. The explanation of evil is that no universal moral law exists. Voltaire, who had approved the suppression of innate ideas, took violent exception to the attempted elimination of a moral law. He argued that, even though one is born without the idea of justice, everyone does possess from birth those organs which, properly developed, arrive at a moment of maturity and support this idea of justice. Voltaire defined it in one line of his *Loi naturelle*: "Adore un Dieu, sois juste, et chéris ta patrie." To the long list of examples Locke cited against this universal law, Voltaire opposed the simple objection that the savage acts Locke presented were badly observed, wrongly motivated, or erroneously interpreted. The full idea concerning this natural universal law was contained in the poem *La Loi naturelle* (see F. J. Crowley, *Voltaire's Poème sur la loi naturelle*). The law is based on human nature itself, which is everywhere the same. Voltaire had stressed this equality of condition in the first of the *Discours*. He now stated that all men receive impressions from their senses and possess a faculty called reason. We all admit that there is a superior Power, who has endowed us with necessities. Since we are endowed with a social instinct, He must have given us a rule of conduct, engraved in our heart. Voltaire maintained that it is a law universal not only in space but in time also. All the virtuous pagans respected it, and, indeed, it makes itself felt, through remorse and conscience, in the hearts of all.

BAYLE

If Voltaire had some slight early acquaintance with Descartes and Malebranche, it is likely that he also knew Bayle. We are not very well informed about this relationship, however, and, in fact, we can do no more than guess how he became acquainted with Bayle's work. Some have surmised that he was led by the frequenters of the Temple, or possibly by his friend Lévesque de Pouilly, to undertake the reading of Bayle. A far more likely person would be Des Alleurs, whose interest in Bayle was noted in Voltaire's letters to him. At all events, once launched upon his enterprise, Voltaire seems to have made plans to pursue it methodically. By 1723, he had used the *Œuvres diverses* to furnish a note to the *Ligue*; by the spring of 1725, he owned the *Dictionnaire historique et critique*. In due time he acquired: *Pensées diverses sur la comète*, 2 vols., Rotterdam, 1683; *Nouvelles de la République des lettres*, 14 vols., Amsterdam, 1686; *Avis important aux réfugiés*, Paris, 1692; the 1697 Rotterdam edition of the *Dictionnaire* in 4 vols.; the *Lettres choisies*, 3 vols., Rotterdam, 1714; and the *Œuvres diverses,* 4 vols., La Haye, 1737. In addition to the full works, Voltaire possessed several abridgments of the *Dictionnaire historique et critique*: one entitled *Bayle dégagé de ses inutilités*, a folio manuscript of 180 foll. by A. J. Le Bret; an *Extrait du Dictionnaire historique et critique*, 2 vols., Berlin, 1765, by Frederick II and D'Argens; the *Dictionnaire historique et critique . . . recherches sur plusieurs hommes célèbres tirées des Dictionnaires de Bayle et de Chauffepié*, 4 vols., Lyons, 1771, by the Abbé de Bonnegarde; and, finally, an *Abrégé de Bayle*, 4 vols., in manuscript, of which the fourth volume is said to be dated 1736. Voltaire also had several manuscript dissertations: *Préface aux Remarques critiques sur le Dictionnaire de Bayle*, by the Abbé P. L. Joly; a *Dissertation sur le dit ouvrage de M. l'abbé Joly*; some *Remarques en forme de critique insérées dans le Journal de Trévoux sur l'Analyse de Bayle*; and an *Abrégé de la dissertation concernant le livre d'Etienne Junius Brutus*, "imprimé l'an 1579." The impressive thing about these holdings is that they fully cover not only Bayle's production but also the abridgments which makes Bayle's contribution more readily useful.

We are still not clear about when Voltaire turned to Bayle. H. T. Mason (*Pierre Bayle and Voltaire*, p. 2) surmises that Voltaire must have been acquainted with Bayle's work long before his first mention of him in 1723. It is certain, however, that his first note on the *Dictionnaire* dates from 1725. If Bolingbroke gave Voltaire his initial impulse to become competent in philosophy and if the latter set to work to prepare himself by studying the development of seventeenth-century philosophy, he turned to Bayle, not to absorb his philosophy, but to glean information from his *Dictionnaire*, which was the best compendium of seventeenth-century, or rather of modern, philosophy in existence. As a matter of fact, it was the best history of philosophy (old as well as new) which had ever been written. If Voltaire needed a work of this sort to guide him in his new enterprise, he could not have selected a better one. Indeed, Bayle's popularity, as Lanson has shown ("Origines . . . ," p. 409), was enormous. Moreover, it continued throughout the eighteenth century, to judge by Mornet's "Enseignements des bibliothèques privées" (pp. 463-464), where the *Dictionnaire* turned up more than any other eighteenth-century work (288 times) in the five hundred contemporary library catalogues examined. It is probable that Voltaire was first motivated by a desire to be philosophically informed and then, being by nature curious, was attracted to this work because it was so widely known and respected.

Haxo in "Pierre Bayle et Voltaire avant les *Lettres philosophiques*," has carefully examined the early influence of Bayle upon Voltaire. But, beyond the reference to Bayle in a note in the *Henriade*, in 1723, and a reference to him in the *Temple du goût* in 1733 he has been unable to locate any evidence of a connection between the two. Bayle's name, according to Haxo, does not appear in the correspondence of Voltaire before 1733. Haxo (p. 468) argues that this silence does not prove that Voltaire did not avail himself of Bayle every time he needed him. But it must be admitted that it does prove at least that we have no evidence of any close connection between the two during that decade, 1723-1733. Later on, Voltaire spoke of conversations which he had had at the Hague with Basnage de Beauval concerning Bayle. These conversations could only reasonably have taken place in 1722. They can be cited not so much as evidence of an intimate acquaintance with Bayle's works as an expression of curiosity on the part of a young man always eager to learn something interesting about his literary forbears. Voltaire always had this type of curiosity. As for the remark concerning Bayle in the *Temple du goût*, it at least discloses that Voltaire was now sufficiently familiar with Bayle's works to find them excessively prolix—a conclusion which indicates that he recognized they could be useful but that he still did not know, because of their prolixity, how he could use them. I think, though, that he soon discovered to what use he could put them.

It comes thus as no surprise that Voltaire, once he had become acquainted with Bayle's works, saw in them the link which united the seventeenth-century movement of ideas with the eighteenth century. He saw, further, that these works treated the whole range of theological discussion, as well as philosophical principles and even the relationships of the ideas with arts and letters. He recognized in Bayle a storehouse of information upon specific philosophers from antiquity to the beginning of the eighteenth century, as well as upon the libertine poets and the utopian novelists. Consequently, whenever he wanted to learn about the important writers, philosophers, and free-thinkers of the sixteenth and the seventeenth centuries and whenever he needed guidance on the wars of religion and the theological discussions, he would address himself to Bayle. Likewise, when in the footsteps of Bayle he wanted to understand the march of the human mind—and the phrase actually occurs in Bayle—he turned to the *Dictionnaire historique* and the *Œuvres diverses*. Beginning in 1738, Bayle must have become his mentor for religious discussion, philosophical matters, and history. But, even earlier, by 1732, he was being used rather extensively, as Lanson has shown, in connection with the composition of the *Lettres philosophiques*.

Voltaire, in a way, rendered Bayle the same service which the latter in his *Dictionnaire historique et critique* had performed for others. There is an article on Bayle in the *Siècle de Louis XIV* (M. XIV, 37-38) of more than modest length where he is specifically represented as having withdrawn to Holland as a philosopher, rather than as a Calvinist, though much is made of his persecution. Voltaire pictures him as modest, unassuming, and stoically content with bare necessities. His *Dictionnaire* is said to be overly filled with obscure names. It is all the same highly recommendable, says Voltaire, but more for Bayle's excellent method of reasoning than for his manner of writing, which is diffuse, careless, incorrect, and often vulgar. He was, said Voltaire, a splendid dialectician, rather than a profound philosopher. He was almost totally ignorant of physics and seemed to have never heard of Newton's discoveries. He derived his philosophy from Descartes and, like Descartes, attributed extension to matter, though he failed to recognize any other properties which had been responsible for the development of modern philosophy. Since his time, this modern philosophy has presented new approaches and additional doubts, with the result that his skepticism has become entirely too timid. He was nonetheless a "sage." His life has been related at length in Desmaizeaux's volume, although six pages would have sufficed since the life of a writer is in his works. No one has ever been able to imitate the *Dictionnaire* because no one possesses Bayle's genius or his talent for disputing. Voltaire concludes by adding a remark or two about the persecutions Bayle suffered, especially at the time of the article on "David."

Voltaire devoted a second article to Bayle in the *Lettres à S. A. Mgr. le Prince de* —— *sur Rabelais, . . .* , 1767 (M. XXVI, 502). Here he is presented as foremost among the skeptical philosophers and the dialecticians. Voltaire is careful to note that Bayle's bitterest enemies are forced to admit that there is not evident in his work a single line which is a blasphemy against the Christian religion, but his staunchest supporters will have to confess that there is not in his controversial articles a single page which does not induce the reader to doubt and often to disbelieve. Thus, he was not impious, but he contributed to the making of unbelievers. Voltaire suggests that there is a long line of free-thinkers—Maillet, Boulainvilliers, Boulanger, Meslier, Fréret, Dumarsais, La Mettrie, "et bien d'autres," all of them admirers of Bayle—who have gone much further. He stresses, however, as always, the purity of Bayle's morals, "un vrai philosophe dans toute l'étendue de ce mot."

Throughout the works of Voltaire, there occurs at intervals an enthusiastic commendation of the Rotterdam philosopher. He is a "génie facile," a universal savant, a dialectician "aussi profond qu'ingénieux" (M. XXXV, 287). He is a judicious philosopher, the eternal honor of the human mind (M. VIII, 477). He is the greatest of dialecticians, and he uses his dialectics to combat even himself. He is, Voltaire adds shrewdly, the "avocat général" of philosophers, but he never draws conclusions (M. IX, 468, 476). Voltaire calls his *Dictionnaire* a novelty and declares that it is the first work of its kind which can teach one how to think. In the article "philosophe" of the *Dictionnaire philosophique*, he is the "immortel Bayle, l'honneur de la nature humaine" (M. XX, 197).

In view of this continual enthusiastic commendation of Bayle, one would naturally expect that Bayle had a marked influence upon Voltaire. Mason, whose study we have already mentioned, has presented evidence of a consistent reference to Bayle by Voltaire, beginning with the *Temple du Goût* in 1733 and continuing with the *Lettres philosophiques* of the following year. Lanson, in fact, in his critical edition of the latter work, has noted many passages which are reminiscent of Bayle. Voltaire put the *Dictionnaire* to use in planning the catalogue of writers in the *Siècle de Louis XIV*. Still, even though he seems to have formed a fairly definite idea of Bayle's importance by 1750, he used him rather sparingly. This was the period of the Locke-Newton influence, when Voltaire was striving to put in correct perspective the science of Newton and the "metaphysics" (as he called it) of Locke. In comparison with these two English philosophers, Bayle, as a philosopher, must have seemed relatively minor. Indeed, Voltaire not only spoke with some asperity about his prolixity but condemned him for failing to know Newton's great discoveries and for deriving his scientific knowledge from Descartes. He insisted, it is true, upon Bayle's rectitude, deplored his persecution, and encouraged his friend Des Alleurs, who was a confirmed Baylist. All in all, though, Bayle's philosophy did not loom large in Voltaire's work during the period. Frederick and Mme du Châtelet, however, must have encouraged Voltaire to continue his acquaintance with the Rotterdam philosopher.

Mason finds that Bayle did not attract Voltaire's attention to any extent during the forties. On the contrary, the enterprise of writing a *Dictionnaire philosophique*, begun at Potsdam, brought back into favor the Rotterdam philosopher, since the *Dictionnaire philosophique* was to be modeled upon the *Dictionnaire historique*. The *Essai sur les mœurs* also evidenced a constant use of Bayle. The disaster of Lisbon completely restored him in Voltaire's interest, since the Rotterdam philosopher, too, had been haunted with the problem of evil. This time, it was not a question of imitating him. Rather, Voltaire was earnestly seeking an explanation of the presence of evil which would give him some comfort in his distress. Thereafter, Voltaire reexamined the article "David" under the impulsion of Peter Annet's *Life of David* and in preparation for his *Saül*. And, when he was working on his *Traité sur la tolérance*, he asked for Bayle's *Commentaire philosophique*. Some three years later, sensing the movement toward atheism, he turned all his interest to Bayle's article on "Spinoza." All of this heterogeneous activity he deposited in the *Questions sur l'Encyclopédie*, where he allowed his case to rest.

There is thus some difficulty in assessing accurately the impact of Bayle upon Voltaire. There can be no doubt that the *Dictionnaire historique* and the *Œuvres diverses* became a storehouse of information for Voltaire, who had reached the age of forty and was on the point of shifting from a literary career to a philosophical one. He must have found in Bayle a rich mine of resources, which saved him a tremendous amount of labor. This was especially true for his work on history. Mason has noted that Voltaire frequently turned to the *Dictionnaire* for readily accessible material for the *Essai sur les mœurs*. This fact would indicate that Bayle was more useful to Voltaire in the forties than Mason seems willing to admit, since the *Essai* certainly held Voltaire's attention from the late thirties to the late forties. Indeed, we have already stressed the close parallels between Bayle's ideas on history and Voltaire's (see above, pp. 456ff.), while Lanson has noted in addition the frequent use Voltaire made of the *Dictionnaire*, as well as the *Œuvres diverses,* for the *Lettres philosophiques*.

It has often been suggested that Voltaire gathered much of his biblical criticism from the *Dictionnaire*. Specifically, it is known that he took his material for the article on "Abraham" in the *Dictionnaire philosophique* from the *Dictionnaire historique*. Bayle's stress upon the patriarch's idolatrous upbringing and his mention of Suidas and Philo as his authorities were taken over by Voltaire. Bayle, as well as Voltaire, makes sport of Sarah's abduction by Abimelech, and both make incongruous comments on the whole episode. Both likewise remark upon Sarah's age. In the matter of "Adam," both refer to Antoinette Bourignon's beliefs about the nature of the first father. Both note that Cain feared to be killed by strangers in a world where there could not reasonably have been any people outside of Adam's family. One could continue indefinitely to point out similarities in attitude between Bayle and Voltaire where the details of Old Testament history, particularly in its relationship to the early Fathers, are given by both writers. There are so many places where Voltaire could have found this material, though—from the clandestine French deists, from the English deists, and especially from Spinoza and Dom Calmet—that it is difficult to say which source was the most important. Here, however, the plurality of the sources merely magnifies the extent of Voltaire's interest.

At all events, Bayle undoubtedly was a source for Voltaire in this field. To measure the extent and, indeed, the direction of this influence, one has only to take the single case of David. Mason has shown how Voltaire took an especial delight in this case, perhaps because of the raciness of some of the episodes. It is not entirely clear, though, why Bayle delivered his attack. Most recently, Rex (*Essays on Pierre Bayle and Religious Controversy*, p. 204) has endeavored to show that the Bayle assault was more connected with Calvinist dialectics than with biblical deistic criticism and that, fundamentally, Bayle's presentation of David's lapses does not ill accord with the doctrine of Calvinist predestination or with the Calvinistic tendency to explain this doctrine by citing David's antics. It is certain that, irrespective of Bayle's intent and its conformity with Calvinist dogma, Voltaire saw in his demonstration a clear example of the immorality of the Old Testament, and he reverted to it over and over. Mason insists particularly on the recurrence of the theme after 1761, that is, after Peter Annet's onslaught in the *History of the Man after God's Own Heart*. From this he seems to infer that Voltaire needed Annet's work to support his own attack. It could well be that Voltaire was encouraged by the virulence of Annet's attack to increase his own condemnation of David, although he had long before been rather vigorous in his criticism.

One would like to get some sort of perspective on all this biblical criticism. We know that Spinoza devoted his *Tractatus theologico-politicus* to an examination of the Old Testament. We know, too, that Bayle, who would have none of Spinoza's metaphysics, indulged in examinations of some of the very points which came under the scrutiny of Spinoza's work: the identity of the author of the Pentateuch, the morality of certain acts of the Jews, and the authenticity of specific statements. Bayle, if anything, examines these points in a more positive way than Spinoza, in the sense that Spinoza tends to explain biblical material as peculiarly characteristic of the Jewish race while Bayle regards it in the framework of universal right and wrong, from which he deduces theological positions. Bayle concentrates more upon the actors, Spinoza more upon the action. The conclusions, Spinoza drawing political conclusions and Bayle moral ones, seem miles apart. But the effect of the criticism seems similar. Voltaire was subjected to both currents; indeed, he seems to have borrowed extensively from all of them.

In actual Old Testament criticism, Voltaire seems to have selected the biblical characters treated by Bayle for his own investigations: Adam, Abraham, David, Cain, Jonah. Curiously enough, Voltaire was inclined, also, to put them in his *Dictionnaire philosophique* and to deal with them in a way similar to Bayle's. The composite biblical criticism which he indulged in came from more indiscriminate sources and was used more or less cumulatively. Mason has already remarked that Bayle's New Testament criticisms were severely limited. All told, there seems no doubt that Voltaire made some use of Bayle's commentary, although Bayle was only one source among many and probably not a very important one, comparatively speaking; Spinoza had much more significant influence on Voltaire's biblical criticism.

On the other hand, in the history of early Christianity and matters concerning the Church Fathers and all details of disputes, Bayle, the historian, was extremely helpful to him. Voltaire's discussion of false messiahs, for instance, especially Barcochebas, owes much to Bayle. The role of Cerinthus in creating an early heresy is accorded an article by Bayle in the *Dictionnaire historique* and three articles by Voltaire in the *Dictionnaire philosophique*. There are resemblances between Bayle's and Voltaire's treatments of the Adamites. Voltaire seems to have studied Bayle's article on "Socin" when he was preparing his remarks upon Socinianism. Likewise, the two stress the continuity of superstitions in the transition from the pagan

to the Christian world. They agree that Christianity was successfully established because of its union with Platonism, and both reject the view that its success stemmed from the death of its martyrs,
arguing that there are martyrs in all religions and that Christian
martyrs were not nearly as numerous as has been supposed. Neither
Bayle nor Voltaire wish to accept miracles; Bayle, however, like
Malebranche, grants them a certain utility, whereas Voltaire, who
accepts the criterion of utility, declares them utterly useless. They
both treat the story of Apollonius of Thyanus as proof of the
presence of pagan miracles. In all these cases, the point of common
interest is the analysis of four of the seven proofs of the divinity of
Christianity: its establishment, miracles, martyrs, and prophets.
The influence is manifested more in a similarity of approach than
in the imitation of specific arguments. Seen together, these observations furnish a defense of deism, rather than a closely knit attack
upon Christianity. This is perfectly logical, of course, since Bayle,
as well as Voltaire, was presenting the historical argument against
the development of Christianity.

In reality, the approach of Bayle and Voltaire to these deistic
assertions grew out of a situation to which each reacted in his own
way. The basis of this reaction reaches back into the sixteenth and
seventeenth centuries to the quarrels of Catholics and Protestants,
Jansenists and Jesuits, the dispute between Bossuet and Fénelon over
Quietism, and the struggle between the orthodox and all tendencies
toward free-thinking. These quarrels gave rise to a subtlety of discussion, an odious persecution of one's enemies, and, ultimately, a
search for tolerance. Bayle, as a Protestant, had been caught up in
all these movements. He had not only developed a sense of religious
history, as it moved from the beginning of schism down to his day,
but had forged also a dialectical method which would protect his
position and, he hoped, advance the cause he represented. This was
the source of his great quality as a dialectician which Voltaire admired, not so much because of the Protestant position Bayle was
defending as because of the deistic position to which this defense
inevitably led.

It is for this reason that many parallels exist between Bayle's
Œuvres and Voltaire's *Essai sur les mœurs*. Beginning with the
crusades and continuing to the dragonnades, both historians trace

the miseries, the superstitions, the cruelties, the deceits, and the inhumanities which signaled the struggle of mankind in search of its own inner integrity. The struggle symbolizes for them the workings of injustice, the expression of human folly and ignorance, and the bolstering of an institution which proved unworthy of its mission. It is, consequently, not surprising that, time after time, Voltaire borrows from the *Dictionnaire* or the *Œuvres diverses* facts which demonstrate these injustices and follies.[7]

Another point at which Bayle and Voltaire meet is the problem of evil. Historically, Bayle was at the very origin of the eighteenth-century discussion. It was he who started the debate in the article "Manichéens" in the *Dictionnaire historique*. Man, says Bayle, is "méchant" and "malheureux." One needs no proofs of this statement; one can always find it in the experience of living. Everywhere can be seen the monuments of wickedness and misfortune: hospitals and prisons, scaffolds and beggars, once flourishing towns now in ruins. History is a collection of mankind's crimes and miseries. But history contains examples not only of moral and physical evil but also of moral and physical good. Good does exist, Bayle affirms, and that is what causes the difficulty. Further, unhappy man is the creation of a perfect Deity, whose handiwork, reason tells us, should be perfect, too. Bayle wonders how, being the creation of a perfect God, man can be held responsible for sin. He asks why an all-wise God would grant man free will if the end result is evil. He does not attempt an answer, but he does observe that the human mind is incapable of fathoming this problem and should not seek rational solutions to the nature of Providence and free will; it would be far better to "captiver son entendement sous l'obéissance de la foi." He was too confirmed a dialectician, however, to let the case rest there. In the article "Pauliciens," he explains the interpretation of the problem of evil proffered by the Manicheans and declares that, in spite of its absurdity, it is, rationally speaking, a better explanation of human experience than the orthodox view of a "premier principe infiniment bon et tout puissant."

Bayle's dictionary articles on evil were followed in 1702 by King's *De Origine mali*, which was translated with an abundant commen-

---

[7] See H. Mason, *Pierre Bayle and Voltaire*, Chapter II, sections entitled "Later Christianity" and "Christian Institutions and Beliefs."

tary in 1732 by William Law. Lanson (*Lettres philosophiques*, II, 229, n. 8) has noted the impact of King's argument upon Voltaire in his twenty-fifth *Lettre philosophique*. It should be pointed out, though, that neither King's work nor Law's translation appears in Voltaire's library, nor does he seem to have referred to either. In all probability, he knew King only through the notice in the *Nouvelles de la République des Lettres* and Bayle's reply in the *Réponse aux questions*. Nevertheless, King stressed three ideas which Voltaire, also, was eventually to adopt: God made the world as well as it could be made by the highest power, goodness, and wisdom; there is more good than evil in the universe; and all created things are necessarily imperfect, since they do not exist of themselves. On the other hand, King was a strong believer in a freedom of indifference, a point of view which Voltaire came to reject. The work itself was reviewed in the *Nouvelles*, and Leibniz also wrote a commentary upon it. Bayle, who also appears, like Voltaire, never to have seen it, on the strength of the review undertook a general work upon evil in Volume III of the *Questions d'un provincial*.

Bayle, in his reply to King in the *Questions*, makes certain points which were to be of interest later on to Voltaire. For instance, the Rotterdam philosopher does not accept King's statement that God created this universe for His glory; he believes, rather, that the creation of the universe can be attributed to the superabundant goodness of God. What was designed was the happiness of man, a happiness which was to be supported by divine and brotherly love, from which would spring all the virtues. Bayle, however, stresses that these virtues did not develop, that the brotherhood of man turned out to be a failure, and that happiness became impossible because of the prevalence of evil. Bayle assumes that there is much more good than evil in this world, but he notes that an evil is much more an evil than a good is a good. He can see no justification for King's idea that matter is necessarily subject to suffering. Nor can he understand the usefulness of suffering. For what, he asks, is it useful? King's assertion that God has chosen for the best he denies. Had He done so, He would have selected a plan which would have insured constant virtue and constant happiness. Bayle laments that holding the creation to be dependent upon a single principle makes it impossible rationally to maintain all the attributes of the Creator. This was the dilemma which had so forcefully been expressed by Lactantius. Finally, Bayle does not believe in a "liberté d'indifférence." He can explain only the source of evil as the result of two principles—one good, the other bad. Freedom is not unmotivated, it is merely freedom to act without constraint. Bayle concludes his demonstration by listing a set of theological propositions which must be true. He then shows that these theological statements are countered philosophically by a set of equally true statements. The theological statements are all built around the power of God and the doctrine of original sin. The philosophical assertions are, on the contrary, built around the goodness of God and the moral obligation to prevent evil.

Leibniz also entered the discussion with a *Remarques sur le livre de l'origine du mal, publié depuis peu en Angleterre*. His arguments do not concern us here. The *Remarques*, however, were often published with his *Essais de théodicée*, which does interest us, since it was in large measure inspired both by Bayle's dictionary articles and by the *Questions d'un provincial*. The German disagreed vigorously with Bayle's insistence upon the inadequacy of human reason. He felt that, if accepted, such an attitude would nullify human energy. The one essential difference between Leibniz and Bayle was that the German tended to unite, to harmonize, to integrate, while the Frenchman had a tendency precisely to separate, to disunite. Leibniz distinctly disapproved of Bayle's statements arranged theologically, since they were contradicted by his statements arranged philosophically. Such an arrangement indicated a sharp distinction on Bayle's part between reason and faith, between philosophy and religion. Leibniz, however, whose introductory essay in the *Théodicée* was on the conformity of reason and faith, would accept none of Bayle's dialectical arguments. That is why, for the German, the whole question of evil depends upon one fundamental problem— the nature of God. Once that nature is clearly understood, the problem of free will and what we call evil can be understood, too. Therefore, Leibniz's attack is directed against Bayle's skeptical restriction upon the goodness, power, or wisdom of the Godhead. Leibniz thought that this skepticism produces, through apathy and indifference, a kind of fatalism. What one must have is faith, but what one must use to support faith is reason. Once again, the German differs from the Frenchman. Reason, for Leibniz, is a constructive force; for Bayle, a destructive force. Bayle believed that the human mind cannot penetrate many problems and, consequently, cannot do anything to establish the reality of these things. The same old fight between Pascal and Descartes over the ability of the human mind to push to the incomprehensible was continued here, with Leibniz taking the position of the mind's unlimited powers and Bayle sticking more closely to the conception of a limited human intelligence.

In this debate, one would expect that Voltaire would have been hard put to accept unqualifiedly either side. On the relationship of faith and reason, as well as in the view that reason is a destructive, rather than a constructive, force, he would be expected in the Cirey period to have sided with Bayle. He would also be expected to have believed that this reason has a limited capacity and is not predominantly a creative faculty. On the other hand, he would be expected to have had no stock in apathy, indifference, or fatalism. He did not feel, indeed, that Bayle had any standing as a philosopher; he judged him a superb dialectician, but certainly not a creative thinker. In view of this opinion, one can expect there to have been in the Cirey period no more than a general agreement between Bayle and Voltaire concerning God, free will, and evil. Mason has suggested, after a serious study, that whatever resemblances can be found in the Cirey period between the two are trite, and he concludes that "Bayle was not, with one important exception (Manicheism), representative of any particular viewpoint of Voltaire in this field of debate. Here and there we find an obvious parallel but more often Voltaire is deriving his background from a tradition in which Bayle's influence is not clearly distinguishable, or is overshadowed by others" (*Pierre Bayle and Voltaire*, p. 67). This conclusion seems reasonable. Given the general tone of Cirey, Voltaire would be expected to have treated lightly Bayle's concern with evil. What causes more surprise, in the debate between Bayle and Leibniz, is the importance which the latter's interpretation of the problem seemed to assume for both Mme du Châtelet and Voltaire.

In the fifties, however, the situation developed to the point where the problem of evil became a personal preoccupation, and almost an obsession, with Voltaire. More and more, he felt impelled to come to a firm stand. The Lisbon earthquake shook him into the necessity of making choices. At first, the choice was between Pope, Shaftesbury, Bolingbroke and Leibniz. Voltaire tried to elect the English empiricists, rather than the German metaphysician. But Leibniz held a priority. He had originally taken part in the debate on the origin of evil between himself, a Frenchman, and an Englishman. Voltaire's second choice was between these three. There is every evidence to indicate that, in his hesitation, he turned directly to Bayle. The verses in the *Désastre* state explicitly that he did so:

> La balance à la main, Bayle enseigne à douter,
> Assez sage, assez grand, pour être sans système
> Il les a tous détruits, et se combat lui-même.

What must have appealed to Voltaire at this moment of distress was Bayle's pyrrhonism: all during the forties he had praised first one and then another because "il savait douter." Even Newton did not escape this commendation. Now, at a time when he did not know what to believe, Voltaire returned to the old "Questionneur fâcheux." But simple reflection would show that the dialectician Bayle had nothing to offer to the philosophe Voltaire. At a later date, Voltaire actually censured his predecessor for his impartial weighing of others' opinions. Why did he not, asked Voltaire, state his own views, instead of discussing those of everybody else? What Voltaire had at first thought a recommendation for Bayle now appeared a defect, and, just at the moment when Voltaire was on the point of adopting Bayle, he rejected him. Bayle's apathy, indifference, and fatalism appealed to him as little as they did to Leibniz, and for precisely the same reasons.

More reflection, however, would bring out that, although Bayle had offered no explanation of his own, he had, in his series of dictionary articles, certainly favored the arguments of the Manicheans and those others (Socinians, Paulicians) who adopted the theory of the two principles, one good, one bad. There is some evidence that Voltaire gave close consideration to this solution between 1756 and 1758. In *Candide*, Martin confesses that he is a Manichean, and he argues with his "détestables principes" that this world is subject to a constant war between good and evil, in which the wicked may flourish but the innocent certainly suffer. Martin's views of this universe are as extremely pessimistic as Pangloss's are optimistic. Indeed, there have been critics who have seen in the contrast between these two extreme points of view Voltaire's acceptance of a supremely pessimistic world. Some critics have actually drawn up a list of resemblances between Martin and Bayle, which ends by suggesting that Martin-Bayle is the opposite of Pangloss-Leibniz and that, since Pangloss-Leibniz is obviously a fool and Martin-Bayle is at least serious, satirical, and skeptical, Voltaire must have created him to carry the meaning of the *conte*. This sort of interpretation, as Morize, Bottiglia, and Mason have shown, is undoubtedly one-sided. In *Candide*, neither Martin-Bayle nor Pangloss-Leibniz is permitted to have the final judgment—that is given to Candide-Voltaire.

After the purge of *Candide*, the validity of the Manichean position was explored carefully by Voltaire (see, especially, Mason) and found wanting. In the *Dictionnaire philosophique*, Voltaire characterized it as one of the great absurdities of this world; and he continued to hold this opinion throughout the later part of his life. His objection was drawn from the principle of final causes. The order which Voltaire saw in the universe made the doctrine of the two principles appear foolish. Curiously enough, this particular argument was used also by Bayle in his "Eclaircissement sur les Manichéens."

One of the outstanding ideas which Bayle launched in the eighteenth century and which scandalized orthodox believers and philosophers alike was the possibility of a "state of atheists." In the *Pensées diverses*, where the paradox (as it was called by everybody) is discussed, Bayle makes three points. First, atheism is preferable to idolatry. Bayle supports this idea by redefining atheism: "Je parle de ces athées qui ignorent l'existence de Dieu, non pas pour avoir étouffé malicieusement la connaissance qu'ils ont eue, afin de s'abandonner à toutes sortes de crimes sans nul remords, mais parce qu'ils n'ont jamais ouï dire qu'on doive reconnaître un Dieu" (*Œuvres diverses*, III, 77). That is to say, the atheist about whom he is thinking is not the contemporary libertine but a primitive, innocent pagan. The atheist does not appear so primitive as all that, though, when Bayle proceeds to talk about the Epicureans, Spinoza, and the Chinese, who, he maintains, were all virtuous. Furthermore, since atheists are guided by reason and virtue, they are more amenable to persuasion than idolaters, who accept the idea of false or plural Gods, and superstitious people, who obstinately or fanatically refuse to change. The opposite of these atheists, then, would be the idolaters, who worship plural Gods and false images of the Godhead, and the superstitious, who support their conduct by prejudices and false piety. It should be remembered, though, that not only virtuous pagans (Epicureans) were atheists, but also virtuous, nonbelieving moderns (Spinoza). Bayle gives several reasons for preferring them to idolaters: their sincerity, their virtue, their reasonableness. Bayle's next point is that man does not conduct himself according to his religious beliefs—what Bayle designates as the "connaissances générales qu'il a de ce qu'il doit faire"—but, rather, by his private opinion. This "jugement particulier" is practically always determined by his dominant passion, the kind of character he has, the habits he has contracted, and his peculiar attraction to certain things. Bayle argues that, since action is not derived from special principles or precepts, moral action of the atheist can be more virtuous than any spontaneous action by the idolater. Such being the case, finally (and Bayle gives numerous examples drawn from the history of Christianity to show that the problems of belief and morality are not indissolubly united) a "state of atheists" is entirely possible. It would be on the order of the Greek schools, like the Epicureans and Stoics, and it would direct the actions of the community by active policing.

Bayle's theory became the scandal of the eighteenth century, and even the philosophes took fright at the prospect. The Abbé Yvon, who wrote the article on Bayle in the *Encyclopédie*, criticized him there for the kind of atheists he envisaged (I, 798^b-815^a):

On peut observer qu'il règne un artifice uniforme dans tous les sophismes dont M. Bayle fait usage pour soutenir son paradoxe. Sa thèse étoit de prouver que l'athéisme n'est pas pernicieux à la société; et pour le prouver, il cite des exemples. Mais quels exemples? De sophistes, ou de sauvages, d'un petit nombre d'hommes spéculatifs fort au-dessous de ceux qui dans un état forment le corps des citoyens, ou d'une troupe de barbares et de sauvages infiniment au-dessous d'eux, dont les besoins bornés ne réveillent point les passions; des exemples, en un mot, dont on ne peut rien conclure, par rapport au commun des hommes, et à ceux d'entr'eux qui vivent en société.

It has been pointed out that Voltaire was inclined to accept Bayle's paradox in the days of the *Traité de métaphysique* (1734). He had no objection to the existence of uncivilized, atheistic savages. Like Bayle, he argued that society could police a group of primitive atheists. He felt, indeed, that the desire to be respected by one's fellowman was a powerful force for morality. As for the Greek schools, he readily assented to their sincere interest in virtue, and one of his constant tenets was that contemporary so-called atheists were naturally high-minded, virtuous men. He actually maintained that the contemporary elite, living the ideal life of the ancient Epicureans, would have no need to be coerced into morality by a doctrine of rewards and punishment. This view he held constantly even after Holbach (1770). There was, however, another side to his opinion. From the first part of his career, he seems to have had a horror of atheists, and there is no reason to assume that it was anything but genuine. One of his reasons for supporting Newtonian over Cartesian physics, for instance, was his conviction that Cartesianism encouraged materialism and atheism, while Newtonianism did not.

It was the latter attitude which prevailed throughout Voltaire's life. Whenever any crisis developed which could lend comfort to the atheists, such as the Lisbon earthquake or the later attacks of Holbach and his coterie, Voltaire responded energetically to prevent them from making any gain. And the very end of his life saw him unremittingly committed to rejecting any form of atheistic thinking. His opposition to Bayle's paradox is expressed in the article "Athée, Athéisme" of the *Dictionnaire philosophique* (1764) and the additional article in the *Questions* (1770). Voltaire insists that, in any community, it is far more useful to have a religion, even a bad one, than none at all. He is not interested, though, in the relative merits of atheism and idolatry but rather in the more significant problem of the relative perils of atheism and fanaticism. Voltaire is prepared to state that fanaticism is much more dangerous. But an atheistic prince, he feels certain, could work havoc with the state, and a society of atheists would wind up with an unscrupulous morality. In the second article of the *Questions*, Voltaire repeats his stand for a firm government based on religious beliefs and a society committed to a religious morality. He rejects the idea that the pagan conception of plural Gods has anything to do with the problem. He comments, finally, that, when one is a responsible "seigneur de village," one becomes more practical and less speculative, and he expresses the opinion that this settles the matter as far as society and politics are concerned. The rest of the article, which is lengthy, is given over to a defense of many previous writers—Vanini, Des Barreaux, Fréret, and others—accused of atheism.

This, however, does not end the debate, because the foreseen consequences of Bayle's paradox appeared to Voltaire more significant than the paradox itself. The solution demanded not only a firm belief in the existence of God but a firm conviction regarding the doctrine of rewards and punishments and a firmer insistence still upon the source of moral law. The necessity of a God to keep social and political order is what convinced Voltaire that His existence must not be questioned. In this respect, he went much beyond Bayle's paradox. The Rotterdam philosopher held that a society of atheists would police its morality more strictly than a Christian society. Voltaire, however, who had as little confidence as Bayle did in the morality of the masses, was certain that many secret crimes would be prevented by instilling in them the idea of a rewarding and avenging Deity. This he deemed necessary for the masses; the enlightened few could, if they wished, dispense with the idea. But Bayle, in the article "Spinoza," Remark E, noted that all religions insist upon a supreme judge who rewards and punishes after this life. Where Bayle differed was in the idea that it is possible to have a society in which, not having a religion, there is no religious morality. Here, in spite of inconsistencies, Voltaire refused to yield his consent.

Both agreed, nonetheless, that there is a universal moral law. For Voltaire, this moral law, which obliges one to worship the Deity, be just, and accept one's responsibilities toward one's fellowman, is closely identified with the law of God. For Bayle, there is an unquestioned moral principle universal in scope, such as the Golden Rule, to which a whole set of laws conform. For both, it is the "dictamen" of the moral code. Its control is in the "conscience," or, as Bayle would say, in the "lumière intérieure." There is a slight difference, however, in their views of the way the control is exercised. For Voltaire, it is God who commands the judgment; for Bayle, it is the moral reason which gives the command and which would support an atheistic society as readily as a Christian one. Both Bayle and Voltaire agreed that a moral relativism exists everywhere. As Voltaire explained, there is a law of nature, which is everywhere the same, and there is a law of custom, which differs from society to society.

Any attempt to assess the impact of Bayle's ideas on the thought of his time is bound to leave the impression of rambling, because of the encyclopedic, dialectical nature of Bayle's thought. It therefore seems wise to give here a short summary of the respects in which the Rotterdam recluse exercised an influence on Voltaire. The chief way Bayle aided Voltaire was through the information he compiled. The *Dictionnaire historique* was the repository of all the important ideas and actions which had taken place between the end of the fourteenth century and the beginning of the eighteenth. It was especially full in its treatment of philosophers and free-thinkers (essayists, poets, and utopian novelists). It discussed at great length the problems which had arisen in the discussions of the theologians and the philosophers and the free-thinkers. The general aim of the work was the establishment of a lay morality, which precisely fit in with the intellectual goal Voltaire set for himself. Moreover, Bayle carefully defined the proper historical method for analyzing ideas and events, and, in many respects, he was for Voltaire the model historian. In addition, his forays into biblical criticism provided an abundance of material, from which Voltaire certainly profited. On two particular issues, the problem of evil and the "state of atheists," Bayle inaugurated the discussion in the Enlightenment, and, in each case, Voltaire gave careful consideration to his predecessor's point of view. Thus, the effect of Bayle's ideas on Voltaire was important. In a curious way, though, they never seem to have had a full impact, since they were always supplemented or contradicted by the ideas of others. I think this can be explained partly by the fact that Bayle seemed to Voltaire not really a philosopher at all but a compiler and a dialectician. The role he performed was precisely that of "précurseur"; that is, he summed up the relevant ideas of the seventeenth century and made them available to the eighteenth, but he did not organize them into a philosophy of his own. Since Voltaire, who also had this role, was determined to create his own philosophy, he naturally turned to those philosophers who contradicted Bayle, especially Leibniz.

LEIBNIZ

We do not know precisely at what date Voltaire became interested in Leibniz, nor do we know how he came to have this interest. Barber (*Leibniz in France*, p. 178), like everybody who discusses these questions, suggests Tournemine as an intermediary, but we have no evidence that Tournemine introduced any modern philosopher to Voltaire. Bolingbroke has also been suggested, yet, although it is fairly clear that Bolingbroke exerted considerable influence in encouraging Voltaire to turn to philosophy and actually urged his young friend to give more serious attention to Newton and Locke in preference to Descartes and Malebranche, there is no evidence whatever that he acquainted him with Leibniz. Besides, it is well known that, to those who compared his own philosophy with that of the German, the English Lord affirmed that he had never read the German's works. This attitude could have been merely a pose, it is true, but so far it is what the evidence actually indicates.

It is more likely that Voltaire's attention was attracted to Leibniz by his association with Samuel Clarke and that this association led the Frenchman to study (or at least read) Desmaizeaux's *Recueil de diverses pièces, sur la philosophie, la religion naturelle, l'histoire, les mathématiques* (2 vols., Amsterdam, 1720), which published the debate between Clarke and Leibniz on Newton's philosophy. Voltaire, after all, knew Desmaizeaux personally while he was in England and at one time sought his company. It would seem that Clarke and Desmaizeaux offered Voltaire a real opportunity to get acquainted with Leibniz. Still, I think that, beyond a superficial acquaintance with Leibniz through the *Recueil de diverses pièces,* Voltaire did not pursue this interest immediately. There is no doubt, though, that he did advance as far as that, because he depended upon Clarke in the beginning for his first-hand knowledge of Newton; he could not have failed to know of Clarke's intimacy with Newton's ideas and his defense of them against Leibniz. He unquestionably sought out Desmaizeaux's *Recueil* to get some perspective on the debate, which he judged to center around the problem of natural law, as was indicated in Desmaizeaux's title. In fact, it would seem that the *Recueil* also led Voltaire to Collins and his stand on free will. I repeat, however, that, while he was in England, the *Recueil* satisfied his curiosity, but it did not stimulate a deep interest in Leibniz. Voltaire had all he could cope with in his readings of Descartes and Newton. Moreover, his selection of Newton as the core of his philosophical activity precluded any real penetration of Leibniz, at this moment, who thereby remained at best another philosopher—and a metaphysician at that.

In 1733, after a five-year period of silence regarding Leibniz, Voltaire put him in the *Temple du goût*, alongside Fontenelle curiously, although he was a geometrician and a metaphysician. Voltaire assigned him a place there because he had written some Latin verses, and a note adds that no man had brought greater glory to Germany. Voltaire already compared him to Newton, conceding that, although Newton was the better mathematician, the German was a more universal philosopher who united (just as Voltaire was now preparing to do) a profound study of all the aspects of science with a deep interest in belles-lettres. Voltaire remarks, apparently in amazement, that "il faisait même des vers français." But he did not forget that metaphysics seemed to have led Leibniz astray, as it did everybody who became too infatuated with system-building (M. VIII, 566ff.).

In the *Siècle de Louis XIV*, he presents the German philosopher as the most universal scholar in Europe: a "historien, infatigable dans ses recherches," a profound student of jurisprudence, interpreting law in the light of philosophy—which, says Voltaire, is strange, seeing that philosophy is totally foreign to law (a remark that gives us reason to question Voltaire's competence in philosophy at the time)—an extraordinarily subtle metaphysician who devoted his energies to reconciling theology with metaphysics, a poet, and, above all, a mathematician sufficiently profound to vie with Newton in the invention of the integral calculus and even to challenge Newton's prestige in that field. Since these aspects of Leibniz's universality represented the aspirations of Voltaire at the time, one could readily believe that Leibniz was on the point of becoming Voltaire's hero in learning.

In addition, the opening letter of Frederick to Voltaire (1736) conveyed the admiration of the Prince for Leibniz's thought as it was then being assembled and interpreted by Christian Wolff. Frederick announced that the work of the incomparable Wolff was being translated, and he offered to transmit the translation to Voltaire. Leibniz could hardly have been presented to Voltaire under more auspicious circumstances. A prince who recommends a metaphysician whose thought is being systematized by a German logician and translated by a French translator is, indeed, a strange prince. Frederick immediately became, in the opinion of his Cirey friends, an "assez bon" metaphysician. Wolff, the successor of Leibnizianism, who had now organized it into a full system of philosophy, came highly recommended to the Cirey group. In the discussion between the Prince and the poet concerning free will, Frederick showed more aptitude in analyzing the problem "d'après Leibniz" than Voltaire displayed by his analysis "d'après Newton et Locke," as we have seen. Certainly, no metaphysician had ever had a richer introduction.

In spite of all this folderol, though, the poet found many objections to the German philosophers. Their prolixity appeared to him a vice, their thoroughgoing logic soon became a most troublesome geometrical method, and their metaphysics overwhelmed his simple soul, which had already been corrupted by English common sense. He had a hard enough time understanding Newton and Locke, so it was only natural that he should have considered Leibniz confused, irrational, and scholastic. Although he attempted to express his annoyances to his Prince as politely as possible, it was evident that he understood nothing about Leibniz's metaphysics: the "êtres simples," the monads, the preestablished harmony represented to the recently converted Newtonian and the fervent Lockean just so much jargon. He became the center of the old Newton-Leibniz (Clarke) quarrel which Desmaizeaux had published; he tried to resolve that quarrel in the section of the *Eléments* he entitled *La Métaphysique de Newton*, but the best he could do was to pick up five or six "metaphysical" problems and present in each case a parallel between Newton's and Leibniz's thought on that subject, showing what in Leibniz's thought he had already decided was obscure, wrong, or absurd. When one approaches Voltaire's opinion on Leibniz thereafter, one finds such remarks as that Leibniz is a charlatan, his ideas are confused, he is lacking in seriousness. "Il n'a songé qu'à avoir de l'esprit." This is an unfortunate result, because Voltaire's attitude toward the German was much more subtle than that, as we shall see. The charge of the lack of seriousness arose, no doubt, from Desmaizeaux's *Recueil*, where the editor cites the occasion on which, after the publication of the *Théodicée*, the author was asked point-blank if he had not written the book in jest, to which he replied that he had indeed done so and was surprised that no one had taxed him with the act. Metaphysicians are a funny lot, but critics can be queer, too, at least in the eighteenth century.

Voltaire's library does not yield much information concerning his interest in Leibniz. Of the philosopher's own works, he possessed the Raspe edition of the *Œuvres philosophiques latines et françaises*, Amsterdam and Leipzig, 1765; the Dutens edition of the *Œuvres*, 6 vols., Geneva, 1768; the Gruber edition of the *Correspondance*, 2 vols., Hanover and Göttingen, 1745; the *Essais de Théodicée sur la bonté de Dieu, la liberté de l'homme, et l'origine du mal*, with De Jaucourt's biography of Leibniz, 2 vols., Amsterdam, 1747; the *Recueil de pièces*, published by P. Desmaizeaux, 2 vols., Amsterdam, 1720; and P. Sigogne, *Institutions leibnitiennes, ou Précis de la monadologie*, Lyon, 1767. Though not very informative, these items at least tell us that Voltaire was interested enough in Leibniz to acquire most of his works between 1765 and 1768, that he did not possess any of the early editions of the *Théodicée* or the *Monadologie*, that he did not own the *Monadologie* at all, and that what works he did possess dated from 1745-1747, the only exception being the *Recueil de pièces* of Desmaizeaux, which dated from 1720. If one had to trace Voltaire's interest in Leibniz from the books in his library, one would be forced to conclude that he got his information concerning Leibniz at the outset from the *Recueil de pièces* of Desmaizeaux, as we have already surmised, that he did not know intimately either the *Monadologie* or the *Théodicée* at that time, that he displayed a renewed interest in 1745-1747, which, though short-lived, left its mark on *Zadig*, and, finally, that the period of his greatest interest was 1765-1768. Since these results do not at all correspond with what we know from other sources, we have a right to be a bit surprised. There are more astounding facts, however. Voltaire does not seem to have owned a single volume of Christian Wolff's forty volumes of systematic Leibnizianism. He did not possess either the Deschamps translation or the Suhm, or any of Formey's work on Leibniz. In all probability, these works, or, at any rate, a fair number of the Wolff volumes, were in Mme du Châtelet's possession. We do know from Mme de Graffigny's letters that the lady and the lover read some of Wolff's work.

It is customary for critics to stress that Voltaire's reactions to Leibniz were violently and fully negative.[8] No one ever forgets that *Candide* may be characterized as primarily anti-Leibnizian, that Pangloss, who carries the full burden of Leibnizian thought and even the jargon of Leibniz, is cruelly satirized. As is often said, after the Voltairean blast, no one would so much as dare defend the German philosopher. All these things are so picturesquely correct that we prefer relating them over and over to presenting a more pedestrian analysis of what Leibniz's thought meant to Voltaire and how it served his needs. For there is no doubting the fact that Voltaire could not totally divest himself of Leibniz. It is certain that he never understood the theory of the monads or preestablished harmony, chiefly because he did not want to understand them. In addition, there is no gainsaying that he was appalled at Leibniz's system as it was transmitted to him through Christian Wolff. It is evident that he was more than vexed when Berlin defenders of Leibniz pompously and dogmatically attacked the *Eléments de la philosophie de Newton*. Finally, it is sadly true that Voltaire's exasperation at metaphysical systems was sorely tried by one which was more superbly organized and solidly constructed than any seventeenth-century philosophy save Spinoza's. The inexperienced "néophyte" could always find something interesting in other philosophies, even if he did not understand the philosophy as such, but, with the systems of Spinoza and Leibniz, things were a bit different. If their philosophies were not grasped "in a swoosh," the whole project of understanding them had to go by the board. There can be no debating the point: Voltaire did not lack reasons for disliking the German philosopher, heartily disliking him in fact, if only because Mme du Châtelet persisted in finding him intelligent, necessary, and scientifically useful. Voltaire treated the matter lightly, in his epigrams and his letters,

[8] See W. H. Barber, *Leibniz in France from Arnauld to Voltaire*; R. A. Brooks, *Voltaire and Leibniz*; P. Hazard, "Voltaire et Leibniz"; I. Wade, *Voltaire and Candide*, pp. 35-59.

although he smarted under the rule of reason of his mistress. He could have tolerated it had it been dogmatically Newtonian; but Leibniz, "c'est autre chose." Besides, that German who was curious, ambitious, and intellectually volatile, just like Voltaire, had a way of dissolving every philosophy he touched, just as Voltaire did: he had neutralized Hobbes, literally undermined Cartesianism, insinuated Spinoza into oblivion, talked Malebranche almost into recognition of the error of occasionalism, attacked Locke with vigor in the *Nouveaux Essais sur l'entendement humain*, and was now presuming to reduce Newton to an interrogatory. Voltaire, no doubt, was properly horrified and scandalized. Paul Hazard has a charming section on Liebniz in his article (pp. 439-440) in which he describes Voltaire's psychological reaction and sketches his various appeals to the imaginary audience: "Ne sentez-vous pas, etc." I suspect we should all like to penetrate the mind of our hero.

The trouble is that a psychological portrait based on a psychology as elusive as Voltaire's runs the risk of obscuring the facts. Voltaire did write a *Métaphysique de Newton* while Mme du Châtelet was revising the first half of her *Institutions*. Voltaire's treatise did discuss the same philosophical problems that he had presented in the *Traité de métaphysique*. Indeed, I think the reason he never published the *Traité de métaphysique* was that he considered the *Métaphysique de Newton* an adequate revision of the earlier work. And, with one exception, it was. In it, he did use a comparative method in dealing with each of the metaphysical problems, as the subtitle indicates—outlining Newton's ideas on the subject first, then Leibniz's, then his own. This very comparison was an admission of interest, reluctant though it may have been, since there was no great reason, save clandestinity, why Leibniz's views should have been brought into a work designed to deal with the elements of Newton's philosophy. In the comparison, Newton came off very well; on nearly every point, his response was shown to be clearer, more reasonable, more satisfactory. On one or two problems, where Newton seemingly had expressed no opinion, Voltaire rather subtly lent him his own. On only one matter—natural law—did Voltaire concede a quasi-victory to Leibniz. The conclusion certainly imposes itself that, as far as Voltaire was concerned, Newton's metaphysics—assuming that he had one—was superior to Leibniz's.

Granting Newton this superiority (as I think Mme du Châtelet did, too, in the *Institutions*) did not mean, however, that Voltaire, even in the *Métaphysique de Newton*, believed Leibniz to be without merit. Indeed, if Voltaire's statements on Leibniz are divorced from the comparison with Newton, they will be seen to be not so very unfavorable after all. Voltaire still will have nothing to do with Leibniz's monads or his preestablished harmony, he is mildly suspicious of the chain of being, and he tries to argue, rather lamely, that Leibniz's definition of space and time is unsatisfactory. On the other hand, he finds Leibniz's proofs of the existence of God as acceptable as Newton's and for the same reason, since Voltaire is likewise a "cause-finalier." He believes sincerely that the varied designs apparent in the vast universe, as well as in its smallest part, are the works of a supremely skillful Artisan. The heavens and the earth do declare the glory of God. Voltaire concedes that they do not necessarily declare the beneficence of the Deity, at least in the sense we humans attribute to the term. Voltaire explains that the "mot de bon, de bien-être est équivoque. Ce qui est mauvais par rapport à vous, est bon dans l'arrangement général." The remark is already a concession to Leibniz. Voltaire adds that there are proofs that more good exists in this world than evil, since few long to die. He even defends the dispensation of Providence in having each creature serve as sustenance for others. "Changerez-vous de sentiment [that God exists] parce que les loups mangent les moutons?" He further admits that Leibniz's principle of sufficient reason is much stronger than Clarke's liberty of indifference. Although he is confused about Leibniz's acceptance of free will, believing the German philosopher to be in accord with Frederick's deterministic views, he is not entirely opposed to these views. He himself was somewhat confused in his own views on the subject, as we have seen. He is not adamant in his stand for freedom but concludes that, no matter how much we are determined, we will always act as if we are free. He quibbles about Leibniz's defense of a perfect world, but he shows some sympathy for one wishing to establish a better world. As a matter of fact, he is here not too far removed from the attitude he expresses in the twenty-fifth *Lettre philosophique*, where he takes another illustrious philosopher to task for his pessimistic view of man in this world. It would have been ungracious, not to say inconsistent, to condemn someone who could wish more perfection and even believed it possible. All of this does not, of course, add up to unqualified approval of the German, but it does reveal some knowledge of his worth and some sympathy for the general implications of Leibnizianism.

This attitude actually grew stronger in Voltaire's review of Mme du Châtelet's *Institutions*. Usually, we are told that the review approved Mme du Châtelet and condemned Leibniz, and certainly one could get the impression that Voltaire did not adopt Leibnizianism *in toto*, without a demurrer. This, however, need not lead us to the assumption that a discussion of a moot point entails the rejection of that point. It was just Voltaire's way to discuss every point critically, with a consequent modification even when he approved the point. In regard to the Leibnizian points discussed by Mme du Châtelet, Voltaire announced in the title of his review what he intended to do: *Exposition du livre des Institutions physiques dans laquelle on examine les idées de Leibniz.*

Accordingly, he takes up Leibniz's metaphysical principles one by one. He states that the principle of sufficient reason has been self-evident from earliest times. "Il n'y a rien sans cause." He declares the principle of indiscernibles ingenious. He does not agree, though, that this principle constitutes a proof of the infinite power of God, since, he says, it is as difficult to make everything similar as to make everything dissimilar. The law of continuity is a principle "d'une vérité incontestable." But he understands by this "continuity in natural science"; continuity of thought, strange as it may seem, he rejects. The principle of contradiction he accepts unquestioningly: "Il en faut donc toujours revenir au grand principe de la contradiction, première source de toutes nos connaissances" (M. XXIII, 132). He accepts Leibniz's proofs of the existence of God as explained by Mme du Châtelet "par le moyen de la raison suffisante," but he reserves opinion on the further statement that God has created the best of possible worlds. Finally, although he concurs with his companion on the necessity for hypotheses in natural science, he declares monads and preestablished harmony to be more absurd than Descartes's vortices.

To sum up, Voltaire actually assented to each of the six Leibnizian principles. Mme du Châtelet, whom he praised for concision and clarity, had certainly convinced him that science needed principles and that Leibniz's principles were sensible. She undoubtedly had an attraction of her own. Yet it did not extend so far in its influence that it persuaded Voltaire that Leibnizian metaphysics was totally acceptable. To him, monads were incomprehensible, preestablished harmony was inconceivable, and the chain of being was somewhat doubtful.

Leibniz had written a book, though, which announced his interest in three subjects that Voltaire also found very intriguing: *Essai sur la bonté de Dieu, la liberté de l'homme, et l'origine du mal*. Voltaire was, indeed, deeply occupied with each of these questions. In the first place, the English had not neglected them; there was even a book with this title by Chubb, which Voltaire borrowed from Thiériot. Voltaire's English friends took a cheerful view of these matters, though there were exceptions: Swift was always present to play the role of devil's advocate against all optimism concerning man. Bolingbroke, on the other hand, was easily committed to a bountiful God, progress in history, a human nature of promise, and an affirmation of good in nature. Pope, echoing Bolingbroke's cheerful, commonsense acceptance of man's lot, actually undertook to justify the ways of God to man in a poem which offered everything that Voltaire could have wished on this subject; indeed, Voltaire countered with a series of pseudo-Horatian epistles entitled *Discours en vers sur l'homme*, which were originally called *Essais sur le bonheur*. It is evident that the French poet did not await idly all this manifest support of his own point of view. Long before, he had adopted the standpoint of deism and announced in his *Epître à Uranie*, in accord with Chaulieu, his master, a confidence in a "Dieu de bonté." It was a perfectly human attitude growing out of the disposition of a young man eager to enjoy life, living in a period committed to a generous expression of commonsense epicureanism. The poet of 1719-1722, in harmony with his time and his elected models at the Temple, found complete confirmation for this point of view. Much of it was a normal reaction to the Puritanism and Jansenism of the previous age. But the important thing was its deistic origins, because neither Jansenism nor Calvinism was inclined to subscribe to any theory of happiness, or to any conception of a "Dieu de bonté" in the sense which the deists gave it, or to any attempt at justifying man's freedom. Voltaire's declaration against these surviving seventeenth-century religious forces was first expressed in the twenty-fifth *Lettre philosophique*. Although the critique seems out of place there, in reality, it was undoubtedly the existence of a view similar to his own in England that gave him courage to launch his attack against Pascal. The attack achieved its end, but it left Voltaire philosophically defenseless and made him dependent upon Chubb. Chubb, though, could not compare with Leibniz as a philosopher.

This personal dilemma had already long become the predicament of the age. The problem of evil, which necessarily involved the other two problems, had played itself out between 1697 and 1716 in an argument between an Englishman (King), a Frenchman (Bayle), and a German (Leibniz). Voltaire, looking in 1736 for philosophical support for his own interpretation, could find it ready-made in Leibniz. Mme du Châtelet made reference to the *Théodicée* in her *Institutions*, and Voltaire indicated in a letter of 13 March 1739 that he was reading it at the time. Everything suggests that he and Mme du Châtelet were so closely committed to Leibniz that they now had available all the major sources of Leibnizian study. The work which held Voltaire's interest in Leibniz was the *Théodicée*. Mme du Châtelet built her metaphysics on the same book, but she supplemented it with Wolff's *Ontologia*. So did Voltaire, as we have seen from Mme du Graffigny's allusion to the size of the inhabitants on Jupiter.

We are usually so mesmerized by Voltaire's caricature of the German philosopher that we rarely go back to the *Théodicée* itself, and, when we do, it is still in *Candide*'s perspective that we see it. No one can approach that work without finding Leibniz's terminology hilariously funny. We should recall that, even before *Candide*, Leibniz's philosophy was said by Bolingbroke to have had the same effect upon him: "Every time this hypothesis [preestablished harmony] comes into my thought, I laugh as if I was in a puppet-show." We should be properly alerted, however. Leibniz did have a philosophy of optimism, and that philosophy did have a history. The philosophy itself is organic, and its history, like that of all seventeenth-century philosophies, is the account of the attacks against the elements of its organicity, the modifications of these elements, and the defense of the organic system. We cannot here trace the divers steps in the creation of the system any more than we can trace its history. We attempted it previously (see *Voltaire and Candide*, Part I). Unfortunately, very few who take up the matter want to look at Leibniz in this context. Even Lanson, in my opinion, erred in his judgment of *Candide*: "Le but est de démolir l'optimisme. . . . *Candide* n'est ni désolant, ni désolé, ni purement négatif et critique: C'est la parabole essentielle de la philosophie voltairienne qui tend toute à l'augmentation du bien-être." I think this statement, every word of which is true in regard to Voltaire, is a false judgment in regard to Leibniz, and its falsity consists in ignoring what Leibnizianism was and what Voltaire thought it was. The only twentieth-century critic who has made any real headway in this respect is Professor Barber (see *Leibniz in France*).

We must always remember that Leibniz was led to compose his *Théodicée* by his reaction to Bayle's discussion of the problem of evil, just as Bayle was led to present his explanation by his response to what he thought was King's position. Leibniz's starting point was the feeling that both Bayle and King had wrongly judged the problem of evil. King had rightly defined the nature of evil, he thought, and rightly understood the nature of physical evil and metaphysical evil, but he had misunderstood completely the nature of moral evil. The difficulty lay in King's adoption of a freedom of indifference, which, in Leibniz's view, ran counter to the principle of sufficient reason. Leibniz accepted that our souls are always moved by some reason of good and evil but insisted that there are all sorts of little attractive perceptions which lead us to decide. Incidentally, Voltaire's conclusion that a liberty of indifference does not lead very far, since it is exercised only in matters of no importance, was in accord with Leibniz's views on King. Leibniz also felt that King, who had rightly analyzed metaphysical evil, had not insisted sufficiently upon the totality of perfection in the universe. His view here was based upon the opinion that neither God nor his total creation can be imperfect. It is true that the universe is full of unavoidable accidents (even earthquakes, Leibniz added), that creatures devour each other, that there are wicked men, that sin is a reality, and that humans are subject to error. These facts are in accord with the nature of things (which was Voltaire's opinion in his attack upon

Pascal) and change nothing in the universe. Nor do they prove that this is not the best of worlds. Leibniz concluded that King's error lay in his false conception of freedom: "Il n'y a rien de plus imparfait; elle rendrait la science et la bonté inutiles, et reduirait tout au hazard, sans qu'il y eût des règles" (*Théodicée*, Amsterdam, 1734, p. 321). Voltaire could not object to this judgment.

Leibniz also opposed Bayle's view. The grounds on which he rejected it derived from Bayle's insistence upon the separation of reason and faith, philosophy and religion. The German thought this could lead only to a sterile pyrrhonism and a lack of harmony. Moreover, he thought the attack against reason only opened the door to atheism. Voltaire shared these views with Leibniz; even after the *Désastre de Lisbonne*, he refused to follow Bayle in the interpretation of evil, and precisely for these reasons.

Leibniz's concern with King's limitation of man's freedom and with Bayle's separation of reason and faith, with a consequent turn to atheism which he thought he perceived, is reflected in the organization of the *Théodicée*, which deals in turn with the nature of God, the nature of free will in man, and the nature of evil. On all three of these problems, Leibniz differed from Bayle. Whereas the Rotterdam philosopher questioned God's omnipotence, wisdom, and goodness, Leibniz urged that these attempts to limit the powers of the Deity be modified. Further, he objected to Bayle's strictures against reason, holding that it was not, as Bayle declared it to be, a destructive power, but a constructive one. Here, Leibniz joined Pascal, while Voltaire at first joined Bayle. The first two believed that the purpose of reason is to push beyond the comprehensible, the latter two that reason should never go beyond its natural limits. Thus, in Leibniz's opinion, reason has the power to unite with faith. Voltaire did not hold this view. Nor did he understand Leibniz's views on substance. On the other hand, when Leibniz declared that one must turn all his intentions to the common good, which does not differ from the glory of God, that there is no particular interest higher than the pursuit of this common good, and that one must be resigned to the will of God, persuaded that what He wills is best, Voltaire could not but agree, since his whole theory of "bienfaisance" was based on similar sentiments.

The harmony of faith and reason involves, in the preliminary discourse of the *Théodicée*, a distinction between two kinds of truth: eternal truths and positive truths. The eternal truths are the truths of reason and are necessary; positive truths concern facts and are merely contingent. Eternal truths are tested by the principle of contradiction for their validity; positive truths have been bestowed upon nature by God. Therefore, the mysteries of religion are not contradictory to reason; they are merely beyond the reach of reason. But they are not on that account false. In this stand, Leibniz opposed Bayle, who felt that, whenever truths are beyond the grasp of reason in matters of religion, theologians are always at a disadvantage and have to fall back upon supernatural, rather than natural, lights.

This difference of attitude stemmed from the different ways in which the two philosophers looked at reason. Leibniz thought it a constructive force, Bayle a destructive force. Voltaire here took a median position: reason is limited, but it is the only instrument for truth. He would therefore have been inclined to side more with Leibniz, in the view that nothing but enlightenment can result from man's full use of his reasoning power, limited though it be.

The first part of the *Théodicée* proposes to examine two problems: the problem of human freedom, which, though necessary for morality, puts in question God's omnipotence, and the problem of God's power, which involves the existence of evil. Leibniz insists that God's prescience, His omniscience, is unquestioned. Moreover, the chain of cause and effect is also unquestioned. Thus, it would seem that freedom is impossible, man is not morally responsible, and justice is unattainable. God is therefore responsible for the creation of evil and its continuance. This seemingly logical conclusion Leibniz naturally rejects. He posits that God, being perfect in power, wisdom, and goodness, would only have chosen the best world. To the question why, under those conditions, He did not create a world without sin and suffering, Leibniz replies that such a world would not be our world, but a different one, and God has chosen our world as the best. (It is in this statement that faith and reason have to work together for Leibniz. Faith tells us that, many times, good could not exist without evil.) Besides, there are no grounds for asserting that evil surpasses good. We cannot tell whether the evil which often seems paramount here is not more than counter-balanced by the good in the millions of other worlds. Evil in itself is largely privative; it comes from the imperfections of created things. Why God permits it can be easily explained. Sometimes, He permits physical evil for punishment, in order to attain good ends. At other times, He permits moral evil, because it is also required to attain good ends. But, to the statement that God must be held responsible for these imperfections, Leibniz replies that they lie in the nature of things. His final thought is that God is responsible for what is good and positive in man and that whatever is negative and evil results from man's limitations as a human being. One thing is clear: man has a spontaneity of choice, which is freedom. Man is free from constraint and from necessity. And, although he is in a world where future contingent events are determined by God's foreknowledge, the individual is not deprived of the liberty of making choices. Leibniz concludes this first part by pointing out that the individual has the duty of acting, as best he can, in accordance with what he deems God's will to be. But the final dilemma is really whether God Himself is free. Here enters the suspicion that Leibniz himself presents a God who is subject to blind necessity—the *Fatum* of the ancient Stoics.

Thus, several things become clear about the Voltaire-Leibniz relationship. Voltaire, in the late thirties and early forties, acquired a good understanding of the use to which Leibnizianism can be put, by one who was a Newtonian first. He learned from Mme du Châtelet that Leibniz offered a not unjustifiable explanation of the necessary relationship of God to man, faith to reason, metaphysics to physics. Voltaire's work gave a clearer demonstration of the way even metaphysics and physics may be reduced to "la morale." He was certainly not prepared to adopt Leibnizian philosophy; his conviction of Leibniz's incomprehensibility in such matters as the monads and preestablished harmony was genuine and permanent. But Leibniz was more than a German system-builder with an impossible terminology. There were some real advantages that one interested in philosophy could gain from giving him more than casual consideration. The German metaphysician was also, for instance, a historian who looked at the events of his time through the eyes of a jurist and with the experience of a diplomat. He exemplified fully the need, expressed by all the theoreticians of history and emphasized by Lenglet Dufresnoy, of being at the same time a writer, an erudite historian, and an active public official.

These were decidedly primary ambitions of Voltaire between 1738 and 1748. He saw himself not only as a writer and a historian but as one fulfilling a role in the integration of French and German public affairs. Leibniz had had a somewhat similar career. Besides, with his experience, the German had elaborated a sort of philosophy of history which, though certainly not as optimistic as Condorcet's at the end of the century, nevertheless gave some support to the doctrine of progress. If one forgets the darker side of progress and the facts which contradict it in day-to-day living, if one persuades himself that history is not only the description of unending crimes and misfortunes but also the record of human achievements wrought by man's mind, it is possible to believe that through the judicious use of reason man may become happier and more moral in his relationship to other men. Leibnizianism does not contradict Shaftesbury and the English commonsense moralists like Locke and Mandeville. Voltaire, in his adherence to this English, commonsense attitude as early as the letter upon Pascal, but more particularly in the last two chapters of the *Traité de métaphysique*, and with more vigor still in the *Mondain*, the *Défense du mondain*, and the *Discours en vers sur l'homme*, could be expected to look with some favor upon a Leibnizianism which laid a premium upon action, was generally optimistic (although not excessively so), and manifested an idealism tempered with a commonsense view of life.

For Voltaire, the best recommendation of Leibniz was Pope. In the first place, the latter was a poet, an English poet, a true Horatian, too, who wrote satires and epistles after the fashion of his Roman model, whose verses were tinged with epicurean irony and stoic resignation, when they were not filled with virulent satire, who was thought to have the conciseness and purity of expression of a Boileau, and who, by merging the rules of poetic art expounded by the Augustan Roman and the classic Frenchman, had become another poet-critic who succeeded beautifully in uniting artistic structure with "philosophical" content. Voltaire's enthusiasm for Pope was one of those phenomena which only poets can explain; and his admiration would now appear excessive. He declared the English poet's *Essay on Criticism* superior to Horace's *De Arte poetica* and his *Rape of the Lock* superior to Boileau's *Lutrin*. He noted that the *Essay on Man* consists in "épîtres morales en vers," which are a paraphrase of his own *Remarques sur les pensées de Pascal*. He modestly refrained from saying which was the superior work here, but he evidently had an opinion, because he not only claimed to have translated into verse one half of Du Resnel's poetical rendering of the *Essay on Man* but composed his own *Discours en vers sur l'homme* in imitation of it.

Voltaire's first reaction to Pope's *Essay* was one of enthusiastic, though not unqualified, approval. From the very first, he remarks that the total effect is charming but that there are, nevertheless, obscurities (letter to Thiériot, 24 July 1733). He next seems to approve Pope's omission of all comment on original sin (letter to Formont, 22 September 1735). The following year, he observes to Thiériot (9 February 1736), and subsequently to Pallu and the Abbé d'Olivet, that the English poet's ideas on happiness are false. Finally, in a letter to Mme du Deffand (18 March 1736), after clarifying the basis for the "tout est bien" theory and distinguishing between Pope's apparently ambiguous interpretation of "amour social" in the fourth Epistle and Shaftesbury's use of the same term in the *Characteristics*, Voltaire expresses some surprise that Pope should use the term, objects to the use of the concept "love" to explain the dispensation of Providence in having each animal serve as sustenance for other animals, and concludes with the remark that "tout l'ouvrage de Pope fourmille de pareilles obscurités." Notwithstanding these criticisms, Voltaire composed his *Epîtres sur le bonheur* in imitation of the *Essay on Man*, perhaps to show up the "idées fausses" of his English friend.

Voltaire was not the only one to feel disoriented by Pope's poem. It had been thought from the very beginning that Pope's primary intention was, as he said, to justify the ways of God to man. His justification, however, moved with the greatest of ease, from the metaphysical to the moral and from the religious to the moral, leaving some doubt that he was merely, as Bolingbroke disclosed in his letter to Swift (2 August 1731), pleading "the cause of God . . . against the famous charge which atheists in all ages have brought —the supposed unequal dispensations of Providence."

Indeed, there is some reason to believe that Pope himself was aware of the danger. To obviate it, he did everything possible to keep the discussion clear, even to the extent of setting down lengthy arguments at the beginning of his epistles. One can argue that they introduce more confusion still, but, all the same, they bring out very succinctly Pope's major ideas. Briefly put, there are ten of these ideas, arranged in the following order: (1) a God of infinite wisdom exists; (2) such a God would choose to create, out of all possible systems, the best; (3) the best is that which actualizes the maximum number of all possible modes of being; (4) the plenum is real and hierarchical; (5) man's position in the hierarchy is modest and necessary; (6) the good is the good of the organic whole, not of any part; (7) man is motivated by both self-love and social love; (8) self-love has an organizational role in his total personality as a ruling passion; (9) social love has an organizational role in the make-up of a society; (10) virtue, like happiness, is a possibility. To carry out this program, Pope seems to have kept in mind certain tendencies which he wished to stress. It is possible, for instance, that he wished to present a picture of the Deity in accord with the implications of Newtonian philosophy. Moreover, he was desirous of handling the subject philosophically, rather than theologically. The influence of these tendencies undoubtedly led him to present what could easily be thought a deist, rather than a Christian, conception of God and to ignore such basic Christian concepts as original sin, which had always played a major role in any discussion of evil. Moreover, Pope's treatment of man accorded more importance to man's relationships with the universe and with his fellowmen than to his relationship with God. This also suggested a deistic conception of the Deity and, to some extent, an identification of God and nature which smacked of Spinozism. His insistence on the good of the whole could only confirm this suspicion. Finally, in his well-ordered world, with everything in its proper place and man being just what he ought to be, there was not much need to justify the Providence he had started out to exonerate.

It was probably for these reasons that Pope's essay appealed to Voltaire. He readily subscribed to Pope's attempt to justify the ways of Newtonian philosophy by offering a deistic interpretation of the universe, by reducing metaphysics and physics to "la morale" in a well-ordered universe, and by showing that passions which may be bad may lead to effects which are good. These justifications, after Shaftesbury's law of social virtues and Mandeville's assertion that "private vices" may be turned to "public benefits," may have had their paradoxical aspects, but, to Voltaire, they seemed to accord very well with common sense.

The result of these goals and tendencies could easily have been foreseen by anyone acquainted with the movement of ideas. It was evident that Pope was treating the subject philosophically, rather than theologically. It was apparent, also, that his ten major ideas bore a close resemblance to Leibniz's thought in the *Théodicée*. Indeed, they were so close that, when in due time a storm of protest arose against the *Essay on Man*, especially from theologians, the grounds upon which the protest was made were chiefly theological. W. L. MacDonald (*Pope and his Critics*, London, 1951) has noted "the strong traces of infidelity" which several theologians claimed to observe in the poem. Thomas Burnet even interpreted one passage as Lucretian (*Essay on Man*, I, 86-90). Warburton, before he came surprisingly to Pope's rescue, saw manifestations of "rank atheism." In general, the opposition was puzzled about the author's intentions —whether he really was trying to justify the ways of God to man, whether this could be done rationally, whether he was undermining revealed religion, whether he was establishing deism, whether he was attacking Christian morality, whether he taught fatalism. The leading opponent turned out to be Crousaz, a Swiss theologian who, from 1737 to 1748, led an attack against the *Essay on Man* in a whole series of critical brochures. Crousaz judged that the work was fatalistic and that it exaggerated human weakness. Worst of all, he saw the doctrine as coming from Leibniz and Spinoza. This Popian system, he declared, was cheerless in its optimism and false in its ethics. It denied free will and pictured man as a mechanical object. It presented every event as necessary and the whole series of events as unavoidable. Crousaz called it a system of despair. It ignored the Fall (which is just what Voltaire saw in it from the first), declared vice essential to virtue, and made the Deity responsible for moral evil.

Some of us these days think we can distinguish Pope's optimism from Leibniz's.[9] It is, in fact, conceivable that Leibniz hewed more closely to a theological explanation of optimism than Pope, but the

[9] See Barber, *Leibniz in France*. Morize, *Candide*, and Ascoli, *Zadig*, have the same tendency.

distinction is so slim that not much is gained by insisting upon it. The point to stress here is that Pope's contemporaries were unable or unwilling to do so, with the result that Pope, Shaftesbury, and Bolingbroke could be easily associated with Leibniz as co-founders of philosophical optimism without any great distortion of the facts. Consequently, any unfavorable criticism of Pope and his adherents could end with a general condemnation of the English poet for his Leibnizianism. And it was perfectly reasonable for anyone who subscribed to Pope's treatment of the subject to extend his commendation to the German philosopher, also. Or, rather, it became very difficult for anyone to approve Pope and disapprove Leibniz.

This situation causes much embarrassment when we come to make a final assessment of Voltaire's Leibnizianism. For not only did he subscribe to the *Essay on Man* in spite of some obscure points; he actually wrote a series of poems in imitation of his English friend— the *Discours en vers sur l'homme*. In fact, Pope's influence on Voltaire is evident in every major philosophical work from the *Traité de métaphysique* to *Candide*, especially in the *Mondain*, the *Discours, Micromégas, Zadig*, and *La Loi naturelle*. This influence has been studied in considerable detail.[10] We shall not attempt to recapitulate the actual similarities. It suffices to note that these imitations make Pope worthy to take his place, along with Locke and Newton, as one of the three Englishmen who had the greatest influence on Voltaire. We should add that the effect on Voltaire usually manifested itself in the constant repetition of the points of optimism upon which Pope and Leibniz agreed—those ten points which Pope made in his prose arguments to the *Essay*. It is difficult to avoid the conclusion that, between 1733 and 1748, Voltaire imitated the Englishman because he was an Englishman, because he was a Horatian, because he mingled philosophy with poetry, because he interpreted man to himself, and because Voltaire agreed with these ideas. The verses in the *Loi naturelle* (1751) seem still to carry this sort of approval:

[10] See G. Ascoli, *Poèmes philosophiques de Voltaire*; A. Morize, *L'apologie du luxe au XVIIIe siècle et* Le Mondain *de Voltaire*; I. Wade, ed., *Micromégas*; G. Ascoli, ed., *Zadig*; W. H. Barber, *Leibniz in France from Arnauld to Voltaire*; F. J. Crowley, ed., *Poème sur la loi naturelle*.

> Mais Pope approfondit ce qu'ils ont effleuré;
> D'un esprit plus hardi; d'un pas plus assuré,
> Et l'homme avec lui seul apprit à se connaître.
> L'art, quelque fois frivole, et quelque fois divin,
> L'art des vers est, dans Pope, utile au genre humain.

One would swear that Voltaire approved Pope because he was a poet. However, we might add that Pope differed from Leibniz, whom he resembled so closely, not only in being a poet. He differed also in respect to the monads and preestablished harmony, and he did not have a philosophical jargon. Otherwise, they were of the same breed. Thus, Voltaire's own attempt to dissociate Pope's thought from Leibniz's philosophy at the time of the *Désastre* is pure Voltairean trickery, which later critics have sometimes adopted seriously because they could not find any reasonable way out of the difficulty.

We cannot be absolutely sure, though, that Voltaire reasoned in this way, and that makes things particularly problematic when we get to *Zadig* and thereafter, via the *Désastre de Lisbonne*, to *Candide*. Let us take *Zadig* first. Everyone recalls the Hermit chapter, particularly the last page: "Mais quoi, dit Zadig, il est donc nécessaire. . . ." Here Voltaire presents a dialogue between Zadig and Jesrad:

Z: *So* there must be crimes and misfortunes, and the latter happen to good people.

J: Wicked people are always unhappy. They are a trial for good people. *So*, there is no evil which does not produce a good.

Z: *But*, suppose there were only good and no evil.

J: Then it would have to be another world: the chain of events could be another order of Wisdom, and this new order could only be the eternal abode of the Supreme Being, where no evil can exist.

He has created millions of worlds. Not one resembles another. That variety is a proof of His infinite Power.

Even in this world, the same variety obtains. Every object which exists here has to be in a fixed place at a fixed time in accordance with the immutable decrees of the Supreme Being.

So, there is no chance. Every incident is trial, punishment, reward, foresight.

Z: *But. . . .*

J: Yield and adore.

It is this passage which, taken at its face value, offers the Leibnizian and Popian optimism in its purest form. One of its greatest merits is that it reduces the *Théodicée* and the *Essay on Man* to six statements, three by each party. It could easily be reduced to *So* and *But*: Zadig taking the position of *But*, the Angel that of *So*. Coming just before the denouement of *Zadig*, it has been thought to contain its moral, and, since Zadig's *But* is not very explicit and betrays not very cogent arguments and only a foreshadowing of revolt, while Jesrad's *So* is deucedly explicit and Germanic, ending with a command to submit, the judgment of critics has normally been that the conclusion—that is, Voltaire's conclusion—is very Leibnizian. *Zadig*, consequently, passes as the high point of Voltaire's Leibnizianism. Since the subtitle of the story is precisely *La Destinée* and since Jesrad specially states that there is no chance, we conclude that chance is replaced by Providence and that we poor mortals have no alternative but to submit. As the Spaniards of the Middle Ages proclaimed so fervently at Córdoba, *Diós sólo es vencedor*.

These eighteenth-century dialogues are difficult to interpret. Barber—although he wavers somewhat (*Leibniz in France*, p. 221)—finds that Voltaire is imitating Pope, not Leibniz. But we have already seen that it is not easy to distinguish the one from the other. Moreover, insisting that Voltaire's imitation is the actual expression of Pope does not work very well, for Ascoli has shown in his notes that, as often as not, the imitation is the actual expression of Mme du Châtelet's *Institutions de physique*, which is an imitation of Wolff, which, in turn, is an imitation of Leibniz. The presentation of Jesrad is straightforward Leibnizianism, no matter what its immediate origin is. Zadig may not like it, but he has nothing to offer in its place except incredulity. Besides, he is not given much chance to have an opinion. Barber has made another remark which could be important. It does not seem, he says in effect (see pp. 217ff.), that Jesrad's explanations are answering Zadig's questions. Barber details each remark and counter-remark to prove this point and, summing up, says: "One is bound to conclude that he [Voltaire] was himself dissatisfied with his solution." That conclusion, of course, does not necessarily follow, because we do not know his solution. Barber adds that whether chance or destiny is responsible for Zadig's misfortunes is a false problem. The real problem is whether "the purposes of destiny are evil, and why this should be so."

According to Professor Brooks's interpretation of *Zadig*, Voltaire's stand is that the solution of the problem of evil is beyond the realm of human knowledge. "The philosophic *but*, with which 'L'Ermite' concludes, tells the tale" (*Voltaire and Leibniz*, p. 85). One could argue, though, that Voltaire is going to great extremes to oppose the Leibnizian solution of the problem of evil if he is really convinced that the human mind is incapable of penetrating the problem. Brooks's statement that "Zadig's veiled moral and subtle irony were nothing like the audacious pronouncements of Voltaire at Potsdam and Ferney," I take it, means that Voltaire's opinion of the problem of evil in *Zadig* has neither the force nor the significance of his opinion in *Micromégas* (Brooks dates *Micromégas* in the Potsdam period) and in *Candide*. This claim is at least not well-founded: there is nothing audacious in the discussion of evil in *Micromégas,* and we still do not know what Voltaire's opinion concerning evil is in *Zadig*, or in *Candide*, either.

Pomeau, at all events, would not agree with Brooks. He seems to want to interpret *Zadig* (see *Religion de Voltaire*, pp. 234-237) in the light of a crisis which developed in Voltaire's psyche during 1748: "Car le conte voltairien naît définitivement de la crise de 1748. Ce conte [I presume, *Zadig*] dit ce qu'il a à dire, non seulement dans ses formules, mais dans son style." For Pomeau, *Zadig*, with its enigmatic "*But* . . . ," does not dissipate what the illustrious critic calls "le scandale du mal," which took its origin in Voltaire's psychic depression and which was to remain in Voltaire's life a "scandale." Pomeau notes that Zadig "adora la Providence et se soumit," but he suggests that Voltaire's Zadig refused the logical solution of atheism. "Il répète la leçon de Jesrad, sans trop y croire, car il conclut par une défaite" (p. 245). I take it that Pomeau does not know whether to treat the argument of Zadig and the Hermit seriously as a manifestation of Voltaire's depression or whether to regard the argument as an insincere debate proposed by Voltaire to avoid coming to a logical conclusion. "Serré par la logique de l'athée, Voltaire prouve dans cette crise de 1748, combien il tient à Dieu, en continuant à affirmer qu'il est" (p. 245). Pomeau adds that Voltaire, accepting the existence of God and the existence of evil, cannot find any way to harmonize the two and, hence, concludes that one must "adorer et se soumettre." Pomeau comments that Voltaire was never able to find a "better" solution.

Ascoli, in his critical edition, has a chapter of the introduction entitled "La Philosophie de Zadig" (I, p. xlii). Essentially, his argument runs thus: Voltaire thinks that man judges badly the events of this world because he understands neither their purpose nor their consequences; evil, in some obscure way, contributes to the general good; man should, therefore, resign himself to his lot, adore God, and submit. Ascoli thinks this "philosophie" derived from Pope and that only in 1756 in the preface to the *Désastre de Lisbonne* did Voltaire reject it, while trying to preserve his respect for Pope. But Pope's philosophy is, in reality, Leibniz's philosophy. Ascoli (p. xlvi) observes that "dans Zadig même . . . la part avait été faite si belle aux idées de Leibniz, qu'on les avait mises dans la bouche d'un envoyé de Dieu," not forgetting that Voltaire "s'était contenté d'examiner ses réserves par un *mais* plein de sous-entendus." Ascoli takes Zadig's conclusion seriously but notes that Zadig himself has reservations.

In the article by Miss June Sigler Siegel entitled "Voltaire, Zadig and the Problem of Evil" one would expect to find the answer to the meaning of Voltaire's conclusion. Miss Siegel has looked into the problem in a larger context, embracing all of Voltaire's pronouncements on evil. I shall limit myself here to her interpretation of *Zadig*. I pass lightly over the existentialist explanation: "*Zadig*, I think, is something in the nature of an apology for *engagement* and a call-to-arms" (p. 27). I doubt that this inference could be drawn from the last page of the *conte*. I consider less plausible still the hypothesis that the story is an attempt to present an apology for Voltaire's own ambitions as courtier and diplomat. The anti-Versailles aspect of *Zadig*, proposed by Saulnier and more or less accepted by Pomeau, does not help explain the end of the Hermit story. What is involved is, not Versailles, but God. Miss Siegel is nearer to the problem when she states that "the question is whether the Hermit's function in the tale is necessarily dependent on Voltaire's attitude toward the metaphysical doctrines that this messenger propounds" (p. 29). Her own answer is negative. But, surely, it would be very strange indeed if the Hermit did not have something to do with Voltaire's attitude. It is all very well to talk about the "philosophe engagé," the need for abandoning speculation (p. 29), the entrance into the political arena. These things are not at issue. Zadig does not rebel, he questions. Finally, it is not very ingenious to remark that Zadig's *But* signifies that he is not satisfied. The problem is not Zadig's satisfaction or dissatisfaction; the problem is the validity of the argument and, if the argument is not valid, whether there is any better argument and, if there is no better argument, whether the only sensible attitude is not one of submission and respect. It is doubtful, though, that "action is the key word"; one could argue, I suspect, that "submission" and "respect" are more likely the key words. The "go back to Babylon" has all the appearance of a "tip." Miss Siegel's suggestion that Voltaire is probably playing "the cosmological Providence of Leibniz against the particular Providence of orthodox Christianity" could have some merit. But it does not save the embarrassment regarding Voltaire's ultimate conclusion, since it is not at all sure that the Providence of orthodox Christianity can be characterized as "particular" or "general." Moreover, it would appear hazardous to suggest (p. 33) that "*Zadig* represents an early step" in Voltaire's rejection of metaphysical systems. So far we have no evidence in *Zadig* to prove or disprove the rejection of any metaphysical system. I, for one, do not understand how *Zadig* can be viewed as "a milestone in the freeing of man's mind" through the separation of the physical universe from the moral. It is not true that Voltaire wanted this separation; he strove according to his own statement to turn metaphysics and physics into "la morale." Miss Siegel has confused the normal separation of evil into "physical" and "moral" evil as an act of freedom, when it is only a convenience for the purpose of the argument. In reality, no separation is involved. Interestingly enough, her remarks, which do not seem appropriate to *Zadig*, would be very fitting for *Candide*, as we shall see.

Professor Jean Fabre, in a set of complementary notes to a reedition of Ascoli's critical edition, has inserted a note on Zadig's conclusion in which he discusses these various interpretations. He does not proffer any solution himself, save the remark that too much emphasis is perhaps being placed upon the optimism of *Zadig* in contrast to the pessimism of *Candide*. I can only conclude that he infers that Voltaire was indifferent to Leibnizian optimism as well as to Pascalian pessimism. Undoubtedly, we still do not know what *Zadig* means, and Fabre's remark has not aided us very much. But we do know that, if the term "optimism" has any meaning at all, it is correct to apply it to *Le Mondain* and to *La Vision de Babouc* (in spite of Pomeau's hesitation) and less correct to apply it to *Le Désastre de Lisbonne* and to *Candide* (although, regarding *Candide*, I am inclined to be hesitant myself). All of this puzzlement proves, I suppose, that, while Voltaire may not have been confused, he certainly confused the critics. Clandestinity, of course, is a literary device designed to produce just that effect.

Unfortunately, as much as we may admire the literary device, we still cannot move an inch in our discussion of Voltaire's use of Leibniz in *Zadig* until we understand what is involved in the debate between Zadig and Jesrad. Taken at its face value, Jesrad's explanation is an elegant and succinct statement of Leibnizianism. But the question is, did it carry weight with Voltaire? We do not know. We do know that it was not completely convincing to Zadig. And we have a right to assume, if we wish, that Zadig's creator, Voltaire, was not too much impressed with its validity either. Impressed or no, Zadig did not himself have any positive explanation to offer, or, if he did, he never presented it. Again, we have a perfect right to assume, if we wish, that Voltaire had nothing better to offer. As a matter of fact, we can hardly resist the conclusion that Voltaire brought Leibniz into the picture because he knew no other way to end the *conte*, unless he were to return to Christian resignation as a solution to the problem of evil. When we ask whether that conclusion means that Jesrad's explanation in *Zadig* is invalid and that there is a more valid one which Zadig (or Voltaire) could give, we are forced to admit that he does not seem able to offer very much. If we inquire whether this admission does not indicate that, in Voltaire's opinion, Zadig knows no valid solution and deems Leibniz's explanation invalid, too, we are forced to admit that, although Jesrad's replies do not answer Zadig's questions, they do answer the right questions, which Zadig should have asked. Can it be, then, that Voltaire is conducting the whole puppet-show tongue-in-cheek and is spoofing à la Swift, or does it mean rather that, while spoofing, he is at the same time admitting that Leibniz's explanations, silly though they may be, are as good as one can find? We do not know, but it looks very much as if Voltaire is trying to be irresponsible and serious simultaneously. We do know from experience, though, that Voltaire often acted on the belief he shared with Malagrida that God gave man speech to *conceal* his thoughts, and this may well be an example of what resulted. We know, further, that Voltaire was here very close not only to protest but to open revolt. It would not take much more exasperation for Zadig to send Jesrad packing, back to the ethereal realm. But he did not revolt—not this time—and that is the really important thing.

Voltaire's use of Leibnizian optimism in *Zadig* is philosophically irresponsible, but artistically correct. Unlike several other critics, I fail to see any significant change in Voltaire's views on the problem of evil. It seems to me that, at this time, he did not have any particular views. Probably one could grant that it had become a real problem for him, that suffering had become a reality, and that he had perhaps more human sympathy than most for those who suffered. It should not be forgotten, too, that he had just been re-reading Leibniz in 1745-1747. His own misfortunes and the state of his health undoubtedly seemed important (they always loomed large in his mind). But, although they may have brought forth a pessimistic groan, they were just as likely to have made him want to combat an open display of pessimism in others. *La Vision de Babouc* (1748 ?), coming at the moment when, in Pomeau's opinion, Voltaire was going through a state of depression, does not seem to carry any harsh condemnation of social evil. Indeed, the concluding "si tout n'est pas bien, tout est passable" seems rather an amused, commonsense, ironical observation indicative of a return to Voltairean normalcy. It was perfectly natural for him to have these ups and downs.

There are, besides, other indications that Voltaire had returned to a more normal attitude. *Les Deux tonneaux* (1751) begins with a condemnation of "Blaise Pascal, ce pieux misanthrope." Of course, Voltaire's epistle was addressed to Frederick, and he could be expected to assume a joyful attitude. In mock-heroic fashion, he reverted to the conclusion of the *Iliad:*

> Il [Dieu] a deux gros tonneaux d'où le bien et le mal
> Descendent en pluie éternelle
> Sur cent mondes divers et sur chaque animal.
> Les sots, les gens d'esprit, et les fous, et les sages,
> Chacun reçoit sa dose, et le tout est égal.

One could hardly accuse him of seriousness. In his review of Maupertuis's *Œuvres* in the *Bibliothèque raisonnée* (1751), he actually defended the Leibnizian philosophy with perfectly conventional arguments. There is obviously more good than evil in this life; crimes are exceptional. Man is what he ought to be. In the infinite chain of created beings, he occupies a place which is uniquely his own. How can one reproach the Deity if man's place is precisely where it ought to be?

It is nevertheless true that, with the death of Mme du Châtelet, Voltaire entered a period of personal doubt and hesitation, of loneliness, misery, and some ill health, of vexations and uneasiness which were undoubtedly at the root of his philosophical reactions. Such personal afflictions need not color one's philosophy, of course, and up to this point Voltaire, who had had his share of physical ailments and moral suffering, had taken the firm stand that, although one's thought does change with the conditions of one's body and mind, there is no excuse for permitting oneself to reach general philosophical conclusions based primarily upon private experiences. Now, however, he seemed more ready to assume that his misery and suffering were characteristic of the human situation in general. The very thing for which he reproached Maupertuis in the *Bibliothèque raisonnée* he now began to practice himself, at first with some discretion, then with less discretion but more subtlety, and finally with open and unabashed lamentations.

We have all listed the events and the incidents responsible for this change: ill health, the approach of old age, the loss of Mme du Châtelet, the fiasco at Berlin, the day-to-day frustrations, the lessons of misery and foolhardiness he drew from his work in universal history, his unsatisfactory relationship with the French court and with the functionaries of the King, the constant hostility he aroused by his literary, philosophical, and religious indiscretions, the Lisbon earthquake, the Seven Years' War. There is a tendency to arrange the events in such a way as to justify the view which sees in the sequence a progression from a happy, carefree Voltaire in the *Mondain* to a deeply engaged Voltaire in *Candide*, with the extremes of attitude ranging from an irresponsible optimism to a deep despair. And Voltaire's literary production from 1748 to 1758 is offered as proof that this progression can be marked between the *Mondain* and

Candide by *Micromégas*, the *Discours en vers*, *Zadig*, the *Essai sur les mœurs*, and the *Désastre de Lisbonne*. The conclusion generally offered is that Voltaire ran the gamut of life's stages from a sprightly, carefree, optimistic youth to a sickly, wiser, more pessimistic old age.

One can doubtless find some justification for this shift in outlook, for it is perfectly characteristic of human experience that it leads one to see the world more and more critically, or less and less spontaneously, with the passing of time. In that respect, Voltaire does not differ from anybody else. As a matter of fact, though, his enthusiastic optimism was never totally divorced from groans, laments, and protests. And his bitter pessimism was never separated from assertions of supreme happiness. When he was on the threshold of the long, trying experiences which are presumed to have turned him toward a pessimistic view of the world, he wrote: "me voici dans un beau palais, avec la plus grande liberté (et pourtant chez un roi), avec toutes mes paperasses d'historiographe, avec Mme du Châtelet, et avec tout cela je suis un des plus malheureux êtres pensants qui soient dans la nature. Je vous trouve heureux si vous vous portez bien: *Hoc est enim omnis homo*" (B. 3269). And in the days of the composition of *Candide*, when it is obvious that he was wracked with the sight of human suffering, he wrote: "I am so happy, that I am ashamed of it." Some of this seeming inconsistency can be explained, I suppose, by Voltaire's own temperament, which we understand badly. Lanson notes that he was not one to dwell on misfortune; he recovered speedily from the cruel misfortunes which are the lot of any living being. His sister Cathérine's death, for instance, affected him deeply, but we can find no lasting impression of it upon him. Nor can we find any profound effects from his many other misfortunes. His momentary reaction to one of these sad experiences was that of a highly strung, emotional person—Delattre well calls him in his little character sketch "Voltaire l'impétueux," and Torrey points to this quality, too, in the *Spirit of Voltaire*—who feels strongly and deeply, but whose feelings are not "realized," not extended over a long period of time. Voltaire accused Descartes of being unable in his philosophy to distinguish between the "vrai" and the "vraisemblable," with the result that his "philosophy" was a fiction, being in truth neither science nor philosophy. In many respects, Voltaire suffered from the same confusion: he, too, found it difficult to distinguish between the "vrai" and the "vraisemblable" and thereby exercised in his own reactions a clandestinity which fooled, first of all, the creator of that clandestinity and, thereafter, all of us. The result is that he often appeared insincere when he was merely naïve, innocent when he was deeply involved, spontaneous and true when he was calculating every move and lying like a trooper—to himself.

Nevertheless, literary history is a reality, and we are committed to make some sense out of it if we can. It is true that, beginning with the death of Mme du Châtelet (1749) and continuing until the publication of *Candide*, Voltaire went through a series of experiences which not only overwhelmed him emotionally but left him unprepared for the blows that were to follow. I am not too sure about the crisis of 1748: it may have been a genuine crisis, but I suspect it was one of his more ordinary "crise de nerfs." The death of Mme du Châtelet, though, was for him a terrible blow, and I could readily believe that his sorrow was deep and genuine. It was not that he had lost a mistress; he had lost that mistress eight years before and had since taken on another. But he had lost a friend, a close friend, who had undertaken to furnish him a quiet place to work, serenity of mind to pursue his studies, relaxation when the studies became boring and burdensome, travel and court life when he needed more buoyant pleasures, circumspection and judgment when he was on the point of committing one of his impossible indiscretions, and sympathy and tolerance when the way became difficult. She had undertaken to shield him from others and to protect him from himself, and, in spite of Mme de Graffigny's account of wranglings and bickerings as early as 1737, she had performed her task well. It may have been that she had become more and more possessive, and one could be right in believing that life at Cirey had run its course and another phase of Voltaire's career had begun. Clandestinity and the new intellectual preparation had to lead to open revolt and the war on evil. Historians always have difficulty speculating upon what would have happened if something else had not happened. What is certain is that Mme du Châtelet's death left Voltaire unshielded from the public and unprotected from himself. And the result was an incredible number of blunders culminating in the fiasco at Berlin. However, to explain Voltaire's violent reaction to the philosophy of optimism by attributing it to any one of the critical incidents which occurred is probably exaggerating an event. Such a "cause" as the writing of universal history, for instance, does not appear authentic; in the first place, the conclusion of the *Essai sur les mœurs*, which was written around the time of *Candide*, is rather optimistic in tone. Moreover, even the Lisbon earthquake does not clearly qualify as an authentic cause of *Candide*, since there was a relatively long period of time from the event to the composition of the *conte*. The key to understanding Voltaire's response is rather that, having been left by Mme du Châtelet's death with no protection against a whole series of unfortunate blows, which one by one might have been absorbed but one after another exasperated him, he could find refuge only in revolt. This reaction was all the more "reasonable" considering that the last event, the Seven Years' War, which was then two years old, itself had the appearance of a perpetual revolt. To tell the truth, though, each event had evoked on Voltaire's part, if not an open revolt, some sort of violent response which expressed itself in a particular work. The fiasco at Berlin had called forth *Scarmentado*, which was more anti-Potsdam than *Zadig* is anti-Versailles; the earthquake at Lisbon had called forth the *Poème sur le Désastre de Lisbonne*; and the War, which seemed to be the symbol of a total failure in the Enlightenment, had called forth the *Mémoires de Voltaire*, which reflected that sense of failure. There is a curious progression in these works which I have tried to show (see *Voltaire and Candide*, Part II). Each of them is structured after the fashion of *Candide*. Each attempts to respond to a particular kind of evil: *Scarmentado* makes an effort to deal with social evil; the *Désastre* poses the problem of physical evil, but already somewhat in the context of cosmic evil; and *Candide* tackles metaphysically all evil—the only way we human beings can proceed when we become really serious.

This complex situation preceding *Candide* brings us back to the debate between Voltaire, Pope, and Leibniz. The crux of the matter undoubtedly lies in the *Désastre de Lisbonne*. There Voltaire notes that the general disaster always brings up the problem of evil. To explain it by a "tout est bien" is a bit strange. He concedes that one may say that "tout est arrangé" by Providence but insists that there is no way to affirm that everything is arranged for our present welfare. When Pope in his *Essay* developed Leibniz's system, supplemented by Shaftesbury's and Bolingbroke's, a group of theologians, says Voltaire, attacked the poem. They protested that man enjoys as much happiness as is possible. Voltaire objects to this attack. He urges that it would be better to seek useful beauties in the work, rather than to attribute to it a hateful interpretation. The theologians said, though, that, if "tout est bien," there must have been no original sin. If the general order of things is as it should be, human nature must not be corrupt, and a Savior would be unnecessary. If this is the best of worlds, it is useless to expect a happier future. If our ills all contribute to a common good, we are wrong to look for the origin of evil. We are merely a part of a machine, with no more importance than the animals who eat us.

These are the objections which were made to the *Essay*. But the theologians should have rather praised the work for displaying respect for the Deity, submission to His orders, firm ethics, and tolerance. Voltaire states that Pope has said "tout est bien" in a very acceptable way and deserves no condemnation. It is all the same true that "il y a du mal sur la terre." Taken in an absolute sense, "tout est bien" is an insult to human suffering. No philosophy has succeeded in explaining the origin of evil. Bayle only ended by doubting. Voltaire suggests, nonetheless, that he is prepared to accept Bayle's position: there are as many infirmities in the thought of man as miseries in his life. All systems of thought are false; revelation alone can throw some light on all the obscurity which philosophers have produced. We can only be consoled for our present misfortunes by the hope of developing our being in a new order of things. And we can only trust in the goodness of Providence.

It is clear that Voltaire was in some confusion. If, for instance, Pope had said that "tout est bien" in an acceptable way, Voltaire had only to subscribe to his explanation. If Bayle had taught us how to doubt and skepticism was the only answer to evil, then Voltaire should have accepted Bayle's doubts. If Crousaz had correctly demonstrated that optimism is a philosophy of fatalism and despair, then, assuming that Voltaire wanted neither fatalism nor despair, he should have adopted Crousaz's demonstration and rejected Pope and, along with him, Bayle, Leibniz, Shaftesbury and Bolingbroke.

It is evident, at least, that he could not approve Pope while denouncing Leibniz and the Leibnizians, that he could not adopt optimism without abandoning Crousaz and the theologians, and that he could not condemn optimism without replacing it with a certain amount of fatalism and despair of his own. Voltaire clearly wanted to preserve a bit of each explanation. At any rate, he wanted to avoid offending either the Leibnizian optimists, or the theologians, or Pope and the deists. Above all, he wanted to avoid yielding a victory to the atheists, whom he had argued into silence since the days of the *Traité*. And he seems to have been equally anxious not to yield a victory to the orthodox Christians either. But he had a position to defend, too, and it was very precarious: if there is a legitimate explanation for evil in the *Essay on Man*, then there is something wrong with the doctrine of original sin. If whatever is is right, then the old maxim that "il y a du mal sur la terre" has to be wrong. Voltaire knew that it could not be wrong—not in the face of his own everyday experience. If Pope did indeed set out to "justify the ways of God to man," then it is difficult to conceive of a "Dieu de bonté" and original sin simultaneously, and harder still to understand why the innocent, as well as the guilty, suffer. It is even troublesome to make a philosophy which would explain how this is the best of possible worlds and to justify the conviction that it is a philosophy of fatalism and despair. Voltaire's preface seems to say something about evil but contradicts itself at every turn. The three problems of Leibniz—the goodness, power, and wisdom of God, the freedom of man, and the origin of evil—are still inscrutable problems, whether one is Christian, deist, or philosophical skeptic.

Voltaire's rational dilemma is as apparent in the *Désastre* itself as is his genuine feeling for human misery. It is often said that he seriously considered going back to the doctrine of original sin, which he judged preferable to the fatalism and the despair of optimism, and there is some evidence to support this claim. It is certain, however, that he ultimately did not do so. Apparently, he gave some serious thought to Plato and Epicurus in his effort to find a solution, but they gave him little comfort. Certain rationalizations of optimism now appear to him ludicrous. Voltaire simply cannot understand a universe in which innocent and guilty suffer alike, a universe in which the suffering of some contributes to the happiness of all, a

universe which has to destroy cruelly in order to assure the order-
liness of the divine creation. He cannot conceive of a Deity in whom
goodness, power, and wisdom do not work in harmony. He cannot imagine a universe in which the all-powerful Maker would not
want to create the best of possible worlds for man—for all His
creatures, in fact. And yet spiders do eat flies, and wolves do devour
innocent lambs.

Voltaire directs his protest first at Leibniz:

> Leibniz ne m'apprend point, par quels nœuds invisibles,
> Dans le mieux ordonné des univers possibles;
> Un désordre éternel, un cahos de malheurs,
> Mêle à nos vains plaisirs de réelles douleurs;
> Ni pourquoi l'innocent, ainsi que le coupable,
> Subit également ce mal inévitable.
> Je ne conçois pas plus comment tout serait bien....

It is idle to remark that Leibniz never attempted to explain these
specific things. His picture of human misery was fully as pessimistic
as Bayle's and Voltaire's. In fact, as we shall try to show, his explanation was the same as Voltaire's ultimate explanation. For the moment, Voltaire can only blame Leibniz for not having provided a
clear-cut solution; otherwise, he would logically be forced to address
his protest to the heavenly court. This he refuses to do. Specifically,
he writes:

> Humble dans mes soupirs, soumis dans ma souffrance,
> Je ne m'élève point contre la Providence.

Thus, he performs in the *Désastre* the same act of submission and
adoration which *Zadig* performed before Jesrad. To this act of piety,
he adds a conclusion affirming a hope in a future life which would
compensate for the suffering of the present:

> Un jour tout sera bien, voilà notre espérance;
> Tout est bien aujourd'hui, voilà l'illusion.

One could suggest that, to his act of piety, Voltaire has now united
a bit of Christian hope.

When one stops to inquire just what Voltaire has achieved in his
poem, though, the result seems very ambiguous. He has raised his
voice in protest against universal evil. He has rejected the Christian,

the philosophical, and the deistic interpretations of evil. He has offered no positive explanation of his own. And he has declared that he submits to Providence and that he entertains hope for a future life. The *Désastre* is a sort of declaration of independence, without too much to encourage independence. Voltaire flattered himself that he had stated his opinion in the way he had wished. When one seeks exactly what he had to offer, theologically, philosophically, or morally, the answer seems to be almost nothing. His expression of sympathy for human misery in the *Désastre* is surely genuine, but his explanation of its origin is virtually nonexistent, and there is only a faint suggestion that we ought to be looking for some way to alleviate suffering if we can.

Voltaire's next attack against Leibnizianism was in *Candide*, but there is no way in which it can be said that the *conte* owes its existence to a desire to refute Leibniz. What Voltaire is really concerned with here is evil ("le mal est sur la terre"), all kinds of evil—physical, moral, metaphysical. What he is really opposed to are all forces which permit evil, whether the superior powers or the lesser humans. What he expresses is open revolt—revolt against the presence of evil, revolt against those who waste time trying to explain it away, revolt against himself for not acting. In the truest sense of the word, he lives the existential formula of Camus: "Je me révolte, donc nous sommes, et nous sommes seuls." The ringing affirmation of the constant presence of human misery and man's outcry against its existence has never been expressed in more strident, more bitter, more witty terms. But it is more than that. If the *Désastre* is a declaration of independence, feebly expressed, *Candide* is a call to action. The terms in which the call is made are all Leibnizian: "le meilleur des mondes," "la raison suffisante," and all the other paraphernalia of German idealism. But there is no idealism here, for Voltaire transforms in *Candide* every Leibnizian verity into verisimilitude. So convincing is his transformation that no one, as Bellessort has remarked, could ever again hear these terms without bursting into laughter at their unreality. The exorcism which Voltaire performs is terribly complete, but the destruction is practiced in the name of a new creation. The constant cry "le mal est sur la terre" rings loud and true, and the inference is made, without quibbling, that responsibility for this state of affairs must be accepted by every force

connected with this "terre." The implication is loudly and irrever-
ently made that something should have been done about it long
ago. Also affirmed is the thought that something must be done about
it right now. *Candide* is the end of the debate between free will and
grace and the beginning of a rigid affirmation of limited free will
and a reverent desire for grace. Voltaire's revolt is thorough, but it is
not diabolical. He is no angel of light, no Lucifer. He stays
severely within the confines of the human. He refuses all metaphysical problems of determinism. It is not to be debated whether the
human being is modifiable; we must act as if he is, just as we have
always acted as if we were free. Perhaps we shall discover that in the
assumed act—assumed because we have accepted responsibility
for it—we are free, we are modifiable. What we think is what we
are, what we are is what we say, what we say is what we do. One
does not have to be a centaur to storm Olympus, or a Lucifer to
storm Heaven. The simplest little monad is worth no more than its
impertinent defiance. It must not be thought, though, that Voltaire
carries defiance beyond useful human limits. The revolt having released all the human energy of which man is capable, the author
once again submits and bows his head. It was the ultimate solution,
but, before we arrive there, so many other solutions became possible, as we shall see.

It is perfectly natural, in the hullabaloo, to get the impression that
Voltaire sacrificed Leibnizianism to achieve his end and that it was
perfectly all right for him to do so, since Leibnizianism was a
snare, a delusion, a fatalism, a lie. It was its "seeming truth," its
"vraisemblance," which condemned it. There is not much to be
gained in arguing that what Voltaire was excoriating was not Leibnizianism at all. He could have declared his war in the name of a
false progress, and the result would have been the same—Rousseau
in the *Second discours* and Diderot in the *Neveu de Rameau* did
exactly that. Still, we are human beings, and we would like to understand clearly what we are saying and what we mean. Voltaire,
Candide having exploded, tried to clarify his meaning. He had
been trying to do so before *Candide*; in a letter to Bertrand of 28
February 1756, he had said: "L'optimisme est désespérant, c'est une
philosophie cruelle sous un nom consolant." Optimism obviously
meant for him self-complacency, acceptance of the status quo, res-

ignation to one's inevitable destiny of suffering. Essentially, it had become a static conception of life. By asserting that "whatever is is right," one becomes too passive, and one gets to believe that this world of sorrow is an unchanging place. Assuming that this is the best possible world, that evil works for good, that evil is a necessary ingredient to life, one can lose hope and fall into despair. Thus, Voltaire revolted against this kind of optimism, calling it inferentially Leibnizianism, in the same way that Leibniz had revolted against Bayle's Manichaeism and in the same way that Bayle had objected to King's Providentialism. The similarity lay in the protest, however, not in the terms of the revolt.

One has a perfect right to ask, if Voltaire did not like Leibniz's explanations, what did he propose to substitute for them? Since he feared the fatalism and despair of Leibnizianism and since he found Leibniz's metaphysical terminology impossible, he naturally, in *Candide*, posed the problem in terms of fatalism and despair; and, since he used the mode of satire, the satirized expression naturally was Leibnizian metaphysics, which lent itself beautifully to this kind of attack. The fundamental attitude in *Candide* is genuinely antiphilosophical, but it is not for all that theological. Voltaire does not stop to lay down principles; there is no longer any time to discuss the existence of God, the immortality of the soul, free will, the nature of matter, and the basis of good and evil. Voltaire assumes that there is a God and that He is on the side of man, but he is not entirely sure. He does not know whether God is all-powerful, all-good, all-wise, in the human sense of these terms, but he assumes that He ought to be. He does not know the origin of evil, only its presence. He does not know whether free will exists. He knows that man wants to be free, and he assumes that man will always act as if he is free. He does not know what man can do in the face of moral and physical evil, and he is totally nonplussed by metaphysical evil. He does know that evil is too prevalent, and he assumes that something must be done about it. Man must do this himself, and his only prescription is work, the cultivation of one's talents, the acceptance of social responsibility, and some type of human fraternity. He does not know whether by effort and energy evil can be eradicated, but he assumes that something is gained by diminishing vice, need, and boredom. He does not know whether man will ever understand the nature of things or whether, ultimately, there is anything to understand. He assumes, however, that man can measure, weigh, calculate, and that this simple performance carefully pursued may make this world, though certainly not the best of possibly conceived worlds, at least a better world. Voltaire's knowledge has turned to ignorance. The "true" has been conquered by the "seemingly true." Clandestinity has become the science of the verisimilar. Voltaire is already a "philosophe ignorant"; that is, he does not know anything, but he does act—and act violently—from a set of general assumptions which negate fatalism, despair, apathy, and all forms of social and political evil wherever it occurs. In a sense, *Candide* is a multiple utopia to end all utopias, but not to end the quest. In several respects, though, Voltaire is very hesitant. He does not know whether God is friendly, but he wants Him to be. He does not know how far he can trust the human mind, but he assumes that, being God-given, we must apply it to the weighing, measuring, and calculation of our lot. He does not know whether it can be trusted as a creative faculty, but he assumes that it can be used to put in right perspective the phenomenon of man. The last two assumptions, incidentally, are at the basis of the impression that every word, every thought, every act, and every conclusion in *Candide* have been weighed and calculated with the greatest care. It is experimental philosophy in its highest artistic form.

The paradoxical thing about this situation is that Leibniz, in spite of his impossible terminology, would not have been averse to Voltaire's philosophical ignorance, or even to his practical assumptions. He was fully aware that "le mal est sur la terre." He knew only too well how prevalent it was. He urged at all times action, energy, planning, measuring, weighing. No one would have supported more readily than he the doctrine of work or shirked less his social responsibility. Fatalism is the last doctrine he would have espoused. Though he thought times were bad enough, with wickedness everywhere and atheism rampant, he did not despair. Moreover, he was sure that God is all-good, all-powerful, all-wise; he was certain that God is friendly. He never doubted that man is free; the only freedom he denied man was, of all things, a freedom of indifference. The only distinction between Leibniz and Voltaire I can see is that the German had written a book to explain evil's origin, while Voltaire, not comprehending anything about the *Théodicée*, adopted snatches of it over a period of twenty years and now wrote a book to attest evil's presence everywhere. One cannot avoid the feeling that Voltaire held Leibniz responsible because he found his explanation incomprehensible. He condemned the German philosopher because he had formerly accepted much of his interpretation. He all but accused him of having aided and abetted evil by trying to explain it away. And he would have him laughed out of court for having led Mr. de Voltaire to adopt the same stand.

The least that can be said about Voltaire's conduct toward the German philosopher was that it was very strange. But there was more to come. Having buried Leibniz under ridicule, the most natural thing for Voltaire to have done would have been to forget both Leibniz and the problem of evil, remain the "philosophe ignorant" he had become, and work tirelessly under his own assumptions. Instead, Voltaire procured Leibniz's works when they were published in 1765 and 1768 and probably, as Professor Barber (*Leibniz in France*, p. 241) stresses, reread them. He still proclaimed publicly Leibniz's philosophical qualities and privately his charlatanism. Moreover, he kept on trying to conciliate the all-good, all-wise, all-powerful Deity with the freedom of man and sought still the origin of evil. Voltaire had a long article on "Bien (tout est)" in the *Dictionnaire philosophique* (1764); he reverted to the problem in the *Philosophe ignorant* (1766); he touched upon it again in the *Homélies prononcées à Londres en 1765* (1767), in a revision of the *Dictionnaire philosophique* article for the *Questions sur l'Encyclopédie* (1770), in *Il faut prendre un parti* (1772), in the *Fragments historiques sur l'Inde* (1773), and, finally, in the *Histoire de Jenni*. One would say that he had not learned the lesson of *Candide*. Even more surprising is that, as an inspection of these passages will show, he seemed to be approaching more and more the views of Leibniz.

The article "Bien" of the *Dictionnaire philosophique* argues that all attempts to prove the existence of two powers, one good, the other evil, are ridiculous. It states, further, that God is beyond good and evil: "Point de bien ni de mal pour Dieu, ni en physique ni en moral" (M. XVII, 578). What we consider evil is often the natural consequence of living: death is natural, not an injustice, not a punishment, not an evil. Pain is natural, it serves to warn us of dangers, it preserves us from accidents, it governs our activities. "Il n'y a pas de mal moral par rapport à l'Etre Suprême." Moral evil is a relationship between human creatures who have necessary desires, necessary passions, and necessary laws for action.

The article "Tout est bien" of the *Questions* reverts to Pope, rather than to Leibniz. Here Voltaire admits that he is prepared to accept that everything is arranged in order. But that does not mean, he adds, that everybody is happy or that God rejoices in our misfortunes. Voltaire remarks that many Christian philosophers, having adopted the opinion that God chose necessarily the best of possible worlds, did not realize that this idea nullifies the doctrine of original sin. Since then, this world seems to have become the worst of possible worlds. Voltaire states that Leibniz attempted to reconcile the two ideas by pretending that original sin entered into God's plan of choosing the best of possible worlds. Voltaire naturally rejects this view, feeling that human suffering does us no good and cannot have any advantage for God. He acknowledges, though, that evil is everywhere. He next gives the quotation from Lactantius, which is the dilemma quoted by Bayle. He admits the dilemma but rejects the conclusion, declaring that the origin of evil is "un abîme dont personne n'a pu voir le fond." There follow all the standard explanations: the two principles of the Manicheans, all the legends, such as the "charmante" Pandora's Box, the "tout est bien" of Pope, Shaftesbury, and Bolingbroke. Voltaire confesses that he admires the order of the universe, but he claims that order does not disclose the origin of evil. He rejects again the view that particular evil makes for universal good: "Voilà un singulier bien général, composé de la pierre, de la goutte, de tous les crimes, de toutes les souffrances, de la mort, et de la damnation" (M. XVII, 585). This English explanation, he finds, undermines the Christian religion and explains nothing. In his view, this "système du tout est bien ne représente l'auteur de la nature que comme un roi puissant et malfaisant" (p. 586). The opinion that this is the best of worlds does not console, it is "désespérante." Voltaire concludes that the problem remains "un chaos indébrouillable pour ceux qui cherchent de bonne foi." It is a "jeu d'esprit" for those who argue. We know nothing of our destiny "par nous-mêmes." Voltaire adds that there are some who say that things cannot be otherwise than they are. This he calls "un rude système," but he professes that he is too ignorant even to begin to examine it.

Il faut prendre un parti presents a picture of the horrible butchery to which the whole animal world is subjected. Voltaire observes that the same evil which pervades the animal world occurs in the relationship of man to his fellowman. The whole universe is a scene of eternal carnage. Man, however, suffers more than animals from this carnage because he possesses thought and fears death. The definition of man is not consoling: "un être très misérable qui a quelques heures de relâche, quelques minutes de satisfaction, et une longue suite de jours de douleurs dans sa courte vie" (p. 535). Voltaire lists those who have tried to give a more optimistic picture of man—Bolingbroke, Shaftesbury, Pope, and others—and declares that all were quacks, totally miserable. He passes in review all the great miseries of humanity—wars, earthquakes, floods, pestilence—and retraces the magnificent legends (especially Pandora's Box) which sought to explain the occurrence of evil. He then gives a series of speeches by members of various groups: the Manichean, the pagan, the Turk. The three most important are doubtless the "Athée," the "Théiste," and the "Citizen," since they not only represent what he threatened to become in his confrontation with evil but trace in succession the history of his thought as it had evolved. The "Athée" expresses a point of view not unlike Voltaire's in *Candide*: "Faisons comme font neuf cent quatre-vingt dix-neuf mortels sur mille: ils sèment, ils plantent, ils travaillent, ils engendrent, ils mangent, boivent, dorment, souffrent et meurent sans parler de métaphysique, sans savoir s'il y en a une" (p. 539). The "Théiste" in his discourse admits that he will always be a bit embarrassed by the problem of evil. He confesses that he cannot understand how a God who is all-good, all-wise, and all-powerful could have permitted evil. He now believes that God in his goodness has done the best He could. His works—that is, man—cannot be as perfect as He is. Evil is thus the natural result of the imperfections of man: "Enfin il y a nécessairement une si grande distance entre vous et vos ouvrages que si le bien est dans vous, le mal doit être en eux" (p. 548). The "Théiste" concludes that, as long as he respects the Divinity and acts justly toward his fellowmen, he will have played his proper role. The "Citizen" then makes the final remarks. He is convinced that mutual aid, tolerance, and the search for happiness are the goals in life. For the realization of these aims, he counsels the burning of all books on controversy and the rereading of Cicero, Montaigne, and "quelques Fables de La Fontaine." These acts will naturally contribute to peace.

The *Fragments sur l'Inde* (M. XXIX, 170ff.) returns to the discussion of the Hindu interpretation of the problem of evil. Voltaire deems that the Indians were the first to have considered how under a good Deity there can be so much evil in the world. That they were living in most peaceful circumstances makes it all the more remarkable that they should have undertaken this study. Voltaire suspects, however, that they had witnessed the overwhelming misery of other lands, even of the Hindu provinces. They must have judged that, in the weakness of human nature, an immense amount of evil is unavoidable, simply because a perfect Creator could not create more than imperfect creatures, who naturally have desires and passions which give rise to sufferings. The Brahmins, who were inclined by nature to a philosophy of resignation, adopted these views all the more readily as a consequence. They did not, however, have any inclination to an atheistic philosophy, as so many European philosophers seemed to have. Voltaire relates how God first shared his glory with the demigods and how the latter, abusing their freedom, revolted. They were condemned and sent into hell but, after a time, were allowed to establish themselves on earth. They brought with them the germs of vice and the principle of all physical ills. Such was the origin of evil.

In the *Homélie . . . sur l'athéisme*, Voltaire sets forth Leibniz's proof of the existence of God and supports it by the principle of sufficient reason. He further strengthens it with the doctrine of final causes. Voltaire rejects the notion that this universe could be produced by mere movement. He insists there must be an Artisan who works according to a plan. In this scheme, there are those (machines) who "tombent brisées et fracassées dès les premiers pas de leur carrière" (M. XXVI, 388). But there are others who are healthy, straightforward, and upright. There are, it is true, many wretched people, whom we must help. We must admit that we do not understand why they are miserable. "Le mal est sur la terre."

What does the existence of evil prove? That God does not exist? But His existence has just been proved. That He is evil? But that is absurd. That He is not all-powerful? That, too, is intolerable. Should we accept the notion of an evil creature who causes evil? But why should he torture man and leave intact the rest of his creation? Shall we adopt optimism? But that is a philosophy of despair. Pope, Shaftesbury, and Bolingbroke have given views which are false and paradoxical, such as that "le bien général est composé de tous les malheurs particuliers." It is undoubtedly true that evil is the effect of the constitution of this world. And it is true that everything is arranged. But it is not true that things are ordered for the benefit of man, who suffers all sorts of ills or makes others suffer. It is idle to say in the face of evil: whatever is is right, you can expect nothing better. But what can we do? We must accept the opinion of all the sages of antiquity, that we will pass from this miserable life to a better future life. Voltaire asserts that it is evident that we have already experienced other existences. He suggests that "la mort peut nous donner une manière différente d'exister." He concedes, however, that this is but a hope, perhaps even an illusion, whereas evil is a reality.

He undertakes to refute those who raise objections to this hope. We ignore what thinks in us. It is physically possible that we do possess an indestructible monad, "une flamme cachée, une particule de feu divin, qui subsiste éternellement sous des apparences diverses." We have as many reasons to affirm as to deny the immortality of the monad. This is now the generally accepted opinion, and it is perhaps the only one which can justify Providence. One must recognize a just God, or none at all. We have an idea of justice, limited as we are. Whence does it spring, if not from God? Voltaire concludes that "mes pensées et mes actions doivent être dignes de ce pouvoir qui m'a fait naître."[11]

When Voltaire's ideas on evil of a positive nature are added together, it will be seen that he did not really differ very much from Leibniz. Specifically, evil is a limitation, an imperfection. Much of it is caused by man's ill exercise of freedom. It is a human phenomenon, which does not touch God's nature. To accept it as necessary

[11] These ideas are repeated in the *Histoire de Jenni* and the *Philosophe ignorant.*

or to explain it as hopeless merely adds to our misfortunes. Social evil could have been corrected. At any rate, while to err may be human, to act is more human still. Freedom is the fullest expression—no matter how limited it may be—of ourselves. Spontaneity and energy are required to meet the challenge of life. All of these ideas can be found, along with others, in Leibniz's *Théodicée*, especially in Part I. Voltaire even reached the point where he began to think of the human being in terms of a monad. But he adopted the term unenthusiastically. Nor did he ever acknowledge that his thinking on the subject came more and more to conform to Leibniz's. This failure to admit agreement and even a certain tendency to feign reasons for hostility have greatly puzzled some critics. Professor Barber is inclined to assume that Voltaire just did not know the *Théodicée* well enough to realize that his views had much in common with Leibniz's. But he does not exclude the possibility that, once having distorted Leibnizianism, Voltaire was in no mood to make amends when the atmosphere had cleared. These explanations for his attitude are entirely possible, of course. In view of the immense amount of energy he had expended to understand the presence of evil, I would suspect that he knew full well where these ideas took their origin and what was their ultimate philosophical value.

SPINOZA[12]

It has always been assumed that Voltaire was led to an investigation of Spinoza's philosophy by Bayle's article in the *Dictionnaire historique et critique*. There is little reason to question this assumption, made both by Mason and Vernière. It is, of course, true that there is an attempt in the *Notebooks* to give a thumbnail account of Spinozism, which indicates that the ever curious Voltaire was trying to define on his own the philosophy which passed for the most atheistic of the time. But the fact remains that Bayle, over a long expanse of time, was Voltaire's prime source for information about Spinoza and his ideas, as I think he was the source for all the philosophical preoccupations of Voltaire. Outside of Bayle's dictionary and Boulainvilliers's so-called refutation, there were no very satisfactory presentations of the Amsterdam philosopher. Bayle espe-

---

[12] See H. Mason, *Pierre Bayle and Voltaire*; P. Hazard, "Voltaire et Spinoza"; P. Vernière, *Spinoza et la pensée française avant la Révolution*.

cially was to be commended for his work, because, as Vernière has shown (I, 292), the philosopher not only made every effort to know the original texts but spared no pains to become acquainted with all the available commentaries from 1685 until his death in 1706. This devotion to Spinozistic study evinces, according to Vernière, an involvement in Spinozism going far beyond erudite curiosity. Vernière suggests that, for Bayle, Spinoza, with his reputation for virtue and in spite of his reputation for atheism, was an excellent example of the separation of religion and morality. We shall have to return to this problem when we try to assess the direct relations between Voltaire and Spinoza.

For the moment, the thing to note is the ready dependence of Voltaire on Bayle's article. He undoubtedly knew the *Tractatus* at first hand, since he had a French translation of it in his library. He must have had some familiarity with the *Ethica*, too, for he possessed a copy of Boulainvilliers's *Réfutation*, along with Lamy's and Fénelon's. And he certainly knew the *Vie de Spinoza*, written by Colerus, and a second biography by Lucas. Yet, in spite of these works, Voltaire gave virtually complete credence to Bayle's presentation until the sixties. Mason interprets this reliance on Bayle as evidence that Voltaire was relatively indifferent to Spinoza before the Ferney period. Vernière also finds that is was not until 1762 that Voltaire showed a lively interest in the Amsterdam philosopher. Up to that time, according to this view, Spinoza merely represented for Voltaire the virtuous atheist. That this opinion is slightly one-sided is proved by two sets of facts we have cited: the commentary in the *Notebooks* which dates from the period 1735-1750, and the books on Spinoza which Voltaire made some effort to assemble. The one incontrovertible fact is that the *Tractatus* was the source of all critical deism in the Cirey period.

What few references we have from Voltaire's early period, nevertheless, do confirm his dependence on Bayle. Spinoza was virtuous, Voltaire observes, but he was an atheist. Not until the *Philosophe ignorant* (1766) does there seem to be an important change. Voltaire notes that Bayle's presentation of Spinoza's ideas lacks some precision and that this failure could lead to a false judgment of the Amsterdam philosopher. In the *Lettres à S. A. Mgr. le Prince de——— sur Rabelais* (1767), Voltaire again comments that Bayle's judgment on Spinoza must have been biased. He is not too sure anymore that Spinoza's philosophy can be called atheistic: "Peu de gens ont remarqué que Spinoza, dans son funeste livre, parle toujours d'un être infini et suprême" (M. XXVI, 524). That he is now hesitant about Bayle's opinion is seen in two remarks: one, the statement that "Je ne sais si son livre mérite ce nom flétrissant"; the other, the admission that he, Voltaire, has gone back and reread Spinoza, "avec toute l'attention dont je suis capable" (M. XXXI, 167). This reweighing of the evidence leads him to the conviction that, in effect, Spinoza believed in a supreme Intelligence (M. XVIII, 365). Voltaire adds: "J'ai toujours eu quelque soupçon que Spinoza, avec sa substance universelle, ses modes et ses accidents, avait entendu autre chose que ce que Bayle entend, et que par conséquent Bayle peut avoir eu raison sans avoir confondu Spinoza" (Mason, *Bayle and Voltaire*, p. 107).

These references hardly show, though, that Voltaire was ready to adopt Spinoza's philosophy. He may have found it more acceptable than Holbach's *Système de la nature*, and certainly he considered it much less dangerous. All the same, he was far from giving it his own endorsement. He was, in fact, now forced to find reasons of his own for refuting it.

That he sought seriously to understand Spinoza's philosophy is evident. In the *Notebooks*, for instance, Voltaire has a neatly arranged note on Spinoza's ideas: "Spinoza pose pour principes: 1° qu'il ne peut y avoir deux substances de même atribut, c'est-à-dire semblables en tout [to which Voltaire has appended the remark that the Leibnizians have adopted this principle]; 2° qu'une substance ne peut informer une autre; 3° que qui dit substance dit infini; 4° que l'immensité des choses est Dieu; et 5° que tout est propriété de l'être unique" (Besterman edn., p. 273). Elsewhere, in the Picini *Notebook* Voltaire writes: "Les principes de Spinosa sont qu'une substance n'en peut faire une autre; que l'immensité des choses est Dieu. C'était le principe des stoïciens que tout est propriété de l'être unique" (p. 404). This second memorandum is repeated verbatim in a fragment (p. 437). I know of no other philosopher who intrigued Voltaire in the *Notebooks* as much as Spinoza.

It is not only in the *Notebooks* that references to Spinoza occur. Hazard in his article in *Modern Philology* has collected them as they appear first in one work, then in another. The Amsterdam philosopher makes his initial appearance in the *Ode sur la superstition* of 1732 (M. X, 428):

> Spinoza fut toujours fidèle
> A la loi pure et naturelle
> Du Dieu qu'il avoit combattu.

Henceforth, he shows up frequently in the lists of philosophers which Voltaire never tires of drawing up, often for the purpose of proving that philosophers are not a menace to the health of a society. In the *Lettres philosophiques*, for instance, Spinoza is mentioned along with Hobbes, Bayle, Locke, and others as one of the profound thinkers who have never introduced discord into their country. This sort of concession does not carry with it any general approval, for he consistently sets down his opinion that the Amsterdam philosopher was an atheist and (as in his letter of 1737 to S'Gravesande) disclaims any association with him. Hazard points out that, as late as *La Loi naturelle*, Voltaire does not give much evidence of knowing Spinoza's works or of being sufficiently interested to want to study them. Spinoza represented for him the "virtuous atheist" proposed in the Bayle article, nothing more. Even in the *Notebooks,* Voltaire records that "Spinoza, ayant reçu cinq cents livres de rente du père d'un jeune homme qui avait été son disciple, rend les cinq cents livres au jeune homme devenu pauvre" (p. 112).

In the notes which Voltaire inscribed in Nieuwentyt's *L'Existence de Dieu, démontrée par les merveilles de la nature* (Amsterdam, 1760), he cites the life of Spinoza to refute some of the assumptions which Nieuwentyt makes about the atheists. The Dutchman at one point remarks, for instance: "On doit regarder Spinoza comme un de ces athées qui ne l'est que parce qu'il estime pouvoir de cette manière vivre avec plus de plaisir et de contentement d'esprit." Voltaire replies: "Spinoza reconnaît une intelligence suprême, universelle, nécessaire; mais il la joint à la matière: il ne reconnaît dans ces deux modes qu'une seule substance, qui est Dieu. Jamais Spinoza n'a passé sa vie dans la joie" (M. XXXI, 136). Later, the author adds: "Or ceux qui ont lu Spinoza, et qui l'entendent, savent qu'il pose uniquement ses idées et son entendement pour fondement de toute chose." Voltaire rebuts: "Spinoza ne nie point un Dieu; il nie la création, il admet la morale" (M. XXXI, 138).

It was evidently this "morale" which recommended the Amsterdam philosopher to Voltaire. In the *Questions sur les miracles* (1765), he observes that, although Spinoza did not accept a single miracle, he did share his meagre resources with a starving friend. Voltaire exhorts us to feel sorry for his "aveuglément" but to imitate his "morale." In a brochure entitled *La Liberté d'imprimer* of the same year, he mentions that Spinoza's system of atheism is better organized and better reasoned than those of antiquity. His attacks against the Bible are very effective. One has to be a consummate logician to reply to his arguments on substance. And yet, Voltaire insists, he has changed practically nothing in this world.

It was at the time of the *Philosophe ignorant* (1766) that Voltaire first made a close study of Spinoza's views. He confesses that, having made numerous excursions among the other philosophers, he finally wishes to examine the system of Spinoza. Voltaire notes that the only novelty in the system is the geometrical method the Amsterdam philosopher employed. Spinoza, though, has established one incontestable, far-reaching truth: "Il existe éternellement un être nécessaire." Voltaire adds that this truth is so significant that Dr. Clarke used it to prove the existence of God. This Being is everything which exists. For who could limit an eternal, necessary Being? Consequently, there is only one substance in the universe; and no other substance can exist, simply because there is no place for it. There are two reasons why no new substance can come into being. First, how can something be created from nothing? And, second, how can one create another extended entity without putting it in an already existing extension? Thus, God, who is both thought and matter, or, rather, in whose immensity are included all thought and all matter, is everything. God is all different substances, all phenomena. He permeates everything and has no parts. This God, who is necessary, infinite, and eternal, we must love. Voltaire quotes from Boulainvilliers's *Essay de métaphysique* of 1731 a selection which states that everything which exists comes from God, that all those things which I am and all the properties which I possess "Il me les donne libéralement, sans reproche, sans intérêt, sans m'assujettir à autre chose qu'à ma propre nature." It is this thought which banishes all fears, all uneasiness, all distrust.

Voltaire stresses that these ideas attracted many readers. Some who started out to refute them finished by adopting them. Bayle, however, was not one of these. He has been accused of having savagely attacked Spinoza without understanding him. Voltaire denies, though, that he did so unjustly. Bayle merely thought that Spinoza had composed his concept of God out of different parts. However, Voltaire adds, perhaps Bayle misstated the matter; he should have said that Spinoza's God consists, not of infinite "parties," but of infinite "modalités." But the objection that Spinoza incorporated as a "modality" of God the undignified phenomena of nature still holds. On the other hand, Bayle did not object to Spinoza's view that the creation was impossible, since the whole of antiquity had taken the same stand. He only protested the Amsterdam philosopher's views on the nature of God. Voltaire concludes that Spinoza really did not recognize any God, even though he used the term, perhaps to deceive the public. He was certainly not an atheist like Epicurus, who thought the gods useless, or like the Greeks and Romans, who thought them worthy only of the masses. Spinoza did not recognize any Providence; he admitted only "éternité, immensité, et nécessité des choses." He was not a skeptic like Pyrrhon, for he made affirmations like Straton and Diagoras.

For his part, Voltaire reproaches him for having ignored the "designs" of phenomena, the final causes. Spinoza neglected both the magnificent structure of this universe and the mathematical ends which it serves. He refused to trace the effects to a cause; instead, he began at the origin of things and built his "novel," just as Descartes did. Voltaire cannot understand how Spinoza, knowing that intelligence and matter both exist, could have refused to investigate whether Providence had not arranged everything. Voltaire insists that one who does not see in the admirable phenomena of nature the art and design of Providence must be either very ignorant, very stupid, or atheistic.

To the modern followers of Spinoza, Voltaire refuses the interpretation of the existence of God by the heterogeneity of His "modalités." And he sends them back to Bayle: "des philosophes ne doivent pas récuser Bayle." He nevertheless concedes that, if Spinoza was deceived, he was deceived "in good faith," though his system would, if adopted, have upset all the principles of morality, in spite of his unquestioned virtue.

In the first *Homélie prononcée à Londres ... sur l'athéisme* (1767), Voltaire stresses that, although Spinoza admitted a universal Intelligence in the world, he made this Intelligence blind, without design, purely mechanical; he did not accept it as a free, independent, all-powerful principle. For the Amsterdam philosopher, there is only one substance which is the universality of things, thinking, feeling, extended, "figurée." But the slightest human experience proves that everything is arranged in accord with a plan. And there must be a Master in charge of this plan. As far as the nature of this Master is concerned, though, Voltaire admits that, being infinite, He is incomprehensible.

In the *Lettres ... sur Rabelais* (1767), the tenth letter is devoted entirely to Spinoza. Voltaire objects to the accusation which Barral and Ladvocat brought against the Amsterdam philosopher, that he had an extreme desire to immortalize his name by his atheism. On the contrary, says Voltaire, Colerus, who lived with Spinoza and later wrote his biography, testifies that he lived a profoundly solitary life, modest, industrious, never signing a single work, and seeking no glory or renown. Voltaire admits that he has read Bredembourg's refutation, and the curious thing (Bayle had made the same point) is that Bredembourg talks as though he were Spinoza's disciple.

Voltaire here relates the story of Spinoza's difficulties with the Synagogue and his eventual expulsion, in all probability, as he found it in Colerus. He denies that the *Tractatus* contains germs of atheism. On the contrary, it is very profound, full of erudition, the best work the philosopher ever composed. Voltaire gives a few examples: the literal meaning of the Hebrew "ruagh," the authorship of the Pentateuch. This historical part of the work displays an exact chronology and a great knowledge of history, of language, and of the manners and customs of his people. Spinoza has a more scrupulous method than all the rabbis put together. His atheism only appears in his *Œuvres posthumes*. Boulainvilliers translated it from the Latin, apparently with the intention of refuting it, since he called his work *Réfutation de Spinoza*. But he succeeded only in giving the poison, says Voltaire, not the antidote.

It must be observed, though, that Spinoza speaks everywhere of an "Etre infini et suprême." He announces God, adds Voltaire, but with the desire of destroying Him. Voltaire confesses that he himself adopts the point of view of Bayle. There can be no objection to this point of view, if Spinoza does indeed admit a God only as the immensity of everything. Voltaire gives several examples from the *Dictionnaire* article. He adds, however, that Spinoza really does not admit a God but, instead, draws from Descartes the old materialism of antiquity that matter and movement can alone make up a universe. Consequently, his major ideas—the plenum, a unique substance which pervades all space and existence, the eternity of matter, the impossibility of the creation, the lack of any design in the structure of the universe—can all be traced to the ancients. It is, Voltaire concludes, a system built upon ignorance of the physical world and the most monstrous abuse of metaphysics.

Voltaire states that, happily, there are few atheists nowadays. That is well, he writes, since atheism is almost as dangerous as fanaticism and can do immense harm to morality.

In the *Système vraisemblable*, Voltaire seems more open to Spinoza's ideas. He begins to wonder really whether they deserve to be called atheistic. It is certain that he believes in a supreme Intelligence, and he does not deny the existence of God, but his ideas on God appear contradictory. Voltaire confesses that they appear to him absurd. Although he is prepared still to accept Bayle's refutation, Voltaire concedes that Spinoza's idea that a substance cannot create another substance and, consequently, that the creation is impossible has had a tremendous effect upon the thought of his time. Voltaire concludes that Spinoza's geometrical method is absolutely ridiculous. Yet, with it all, he says, seemingly in sincere astonishment, "Il veut qu'on serve et qu'on aime Dieu sincèrement et sans intérêt."

In the *Questions*, there are two articles which refer to Spinoza: "Causes finales," which merely commends Spinoza's notion that there is an Intelligence who presides over the universe; and "Dieu, Dieux" (Section III, "Examen de Spinoza"), which is a summary of all the articles which had gone before. Voltaire emphasizes that Spinoza differs from all the ancient atheists in admitting a supreme Intelligence, in adopting a geometrical method, which he inherited from Descartes, in concluding, like Fénelon, that God requires obedience and love, and in presenting his ideas obscurely. He adds that Bayle perhaps misunderstood Spinoza after all; his greatest error, in Voltaire's opinion, was to have rejected final causes. Voltaire, however, notes that Spinoza, in the section "l'Etre en général et en particulier," seems to contradict himself on final causes.

From this analysis we may conclude that, beginning relatively early, around 1730, Voltaire attempted to grasp the key ideas of Spinozism, perhaps more because of his inherent curiosity than because he had any desire to put them to use. Having reduced Spinozism to five cardinal points in the *Notebooks*, he seemed content to accept Bayle's position that the Amsterdam philosopher was, in fact, an atheist, even though he was noted for his virtue. Voltaire's interests in the thirties and forties, so heavily directed toward English and French deism, were too securely tied to the doctrine of final causes and a strong Providentialism to make it worthwhile for him to pay more than a moment's notice to a philosopher who was reputed to have denied both doctrines. Anyway, Voltaire could not have had at that time more than an indirect acquaintance with the works of the Amsterdam philosopher. It is not certain that he ever studied seriously even the first part of the *Ethica*, much less the subsequent parts. And, at that stage of his career, even if he had desired to have some first-hand acquaintance with Spinoza's texts, he would have been totally incompetent to follow the intricate geometrical method of the philosopher. Indeed, it is probable that he never knew the substance of the *Ethica* except through Boulainvilliers's *Essai de métaphysique* (1731), since even in the sixties and seventies he always gave his references to Spinoza's work in accordance with Boulainvilliers's adaptation. The only other likely sources of information were the refutations composed by Lamy and Fénelon or some chance remark of the more orthodox writers, such as Houtteville. Altogether, the documentation could hardly have been very rich. Considering that Voltaire's other preoccupations were far removed from Spinoza, it is not at all surprising that he evinced at first practically no interest in the Amsterdam philosopher. What is surprising is that, with such meagre information, he was yet able to get the major points of Spinozism and to show, in a very few, but well-placed references, his understanding of what Spinoza's philosophy involved. Lanson has noted that some references in the

Lettres philosophiques (1734) clearly bear the mark of Spinoza's influence. The most striking reference, though, was made elsewhere. In the *Traité de métaphysique,* which, of course, derived from Locke, Voltaire found the time to remark that, if one wanted to reduce Malebranche's system to something comprehensible, one would have to have recourse to a Spinozistic interpretation. Since this is precisely what Voltaire did in the *Tout en Dieu* (1769), the possibility remains that he knew what use Spinoza could have from the very beginning.

The evidence concerning Voltaire's active interest in Spinoza during the Cirey period is thus rather ambiguous. That he knew the possibilities to which Spinoza's offerings could be put is indicated by these remarks here and there. On the other hand, his announced position was that Spinoza, though virtuous, was an atheist, and he wanted nothing to do with atheists. That attitude, though, seen in the light of events, can be interpreted in two ways. It will be recalled that, at the time of Voltaire's stay in Holland after the release of the *Mondain,* he was said to have had a discussion with S'Gravesande which, as reported by J.-B. Rousseau, led to the condemnation of Voltaire for Spinozism. Voltaire, in his own correspondence with S'Gravesande, gave another interpretation, and we still do not know what actually occurred. It is evident that S'Gravesande was knowledgeable about Spinozism; it is possible, but not definite, that Voltaire made inquiries about the Amsterdam philosopher; it is certain that Rousseau did spread the report that Voltaire's Spinozistic interest had been frowned upon; and it is equally certain that Voltaire made haste to cover up whatever interest in Spinoza he may have shown. The whole incident at least shows to what extent Voltaire had to exercise prudence in manifesting any interest in Spinoza. It also has some bearing upon his perpetual silence during the whole Cirey period and even down to 1760. For we cannot very well infer from his silence that he was ignorant of, or lacked interest in, Spinoza when it is just as likely that he was merely being prudent.

On the other hand, it can be stated unqualifiedly that Spinoza did have something to offer Voltaire during the Cirey period and throughout the rest of his career. Irrespective of the philosopher's reputation for atheism, his philosophical position embraced many points which should have had an attraction for Voltaire. Contrary to Descartes, for instance, Spinoza did not stress the seclusion of the contemplative life. Asceticism, he felt, is not at all necessary for the good life. He urged that, to be wise, one should learn to use the world and to delight in it as best one can. He insisted that the highest moral good is social, rather than individual. Man's needs are best satisfied, he thought, by mutual assistance. The Amsterdam philosopher considered the good and evil in this world to be relative. In the world of God, the Great All, things are different, of course, for from the perspective of eternity the cosmic system is beyond good and evil. But here and now, in the finite world of man, Spinoza believed, much can be done to increase the good and diminish the evil, to share the good and shun the evil. This invitation to reform through the acceptance of social responsibility and reasonable activity ought to have appealed to Voltaire—especially after *Candide*. Indeed, when Voltaire eventually insisted upon the "morale" of Spinoza as a counter-balance to his reputation for atheism, if he really understood what that "morale" was, he ought to have approved it with some enthusiasm. There is no evidence, that I can find, however, beyond a similarity between the two, which indicates a direct influence of Spinoza's "morale" upon Voltaire's.

If it is true that Spinoza in the *Ethica* had much to offer Voltaire in the establishment of "la morale," it is truer still that Spinoza in the *Tractatus* had much to offer Voltaire in the field of biblical criticism and the conclusions which must be drawn from it. Critics trying to show particular statements in the *Tractatus* (for example, that Ezra was undoubtedly the writer of the Pentateuch, or that the Hebrew word "ruagh" means "souffle" or "vent") to be the source of similar statements in Voltaire's writings are usually so myopically concerned with minutiae that they run the risk of losing sight of the larger import of the work. Moreover, since direct reference to Spinoza both by Voltaire and by Mme du Châtelet is very rare, for reasons of prudence which are quite understandable, and since the biblical facts discussed are available in many other sources, these same critics are easily persuaded that the relationship between Spinoza's *Tractatus* and the work of the Cirey coterie was a very minor one.

This rationalizing of the situation undoubtedly distorts it. It should not be forgotten that, when Oldenburg inquired of Spinoza whether he was abandoning philosophy for theology in the *Tractatus*, the philosopher replied that, on the contrary, he was motivated by his opposition to the prejudices of the theologians, which were among the chief obstacles preventing men from directing their minds to philosophy, and that he intended to dedicate himself to the task of exposing them. He was annoyed, he said, by the opinion of the common people, who did not cease to accuse him of atheism, and he wanted to defend himself against the charge. He was motivated, he added, by the freedom of philosophizing and saying what one thinks, and he wished to vindicate this freedom in every possible way. Voltaire must have known these motives, since they are all implied in the subtitle of the *Tractatus*—"Containing certain discussions wherein is set forth that freedom of thought and speech not only, may, without prejudice to piety and the public peace, be granted; but also, may not, without danger to piety and the public peace, be withheld"—and are repeated in detail in the preface. There can be no doubt, anyway, that they would have met with his hearty approval. Further, he could only have been favorably impressed by the attack against the prejudices of the priesthood and the insistence upon the freedom of thought and tolerance as a defense of the healthy state. The root of evil for Spinoza, as for Voltaire, was "la superstition." Besides, Voltaire's reputation was so similar to Spinoza's that he must have been drawn to give some consideration to Spinoza's reaction.

It should not be forgotten, also, that Spinoza not only had certain goals in mind in composing the *Tractatus* which must have found favor with Voltaire but announced that he intended to carry out his investigation in accordance with a strict scientific method. It will not vary, he states, in any respect from that used in the interpretation of nature. Just as in the latter case, the method consists in considering the phenomenon as an observer and, after having collected certain data, in deriving therefrom the definition of the objects of nature: "de même, pour interpréter l'Ecriture, il est nécessaire d'en acquérir une exacte connaissance historique, et une fois en possession de cette connaissance, c'est-à-dire de données et de principes certains, on peut en conclure par voie de légitime conséquence la pensée des auteurs de l'Ecriture." Not only is this the sure means of proceeding;

it is the only way. Spinoza recalls that the Scriptures often treat of things which cannot be deduced from known principles by right reason. The stories, revelations, miracles, and moral precepts the Scriptures contain must be interpreted by the Scriptures themselves. Only in this way can one prove their divinity (Pléïade edn., p. 770).

This rule is novel and of extreme consequence: the criterion of truth in history and in human phenomena is the same as that in science and in natural phenomena. Spinoza details at length the elements which condition historical verity. The critic first must understand the nature and the properties of the language in which the Scriptures were written. He must also group the statements made in each book and reduce them to a certain number of leading ideas, point out any contradictions between them, and examine those which are ambiguous or obscure. Under no circumstance should the critic substitute for the meaning of an idea a rationalization of his own. All meaning should be deduced as objectively and as liberally as possible from the text itself. Lastly, all inquiry must take into account the life, the manners, and the customs of the author of each book, his aim in composing the book, and the circumstances surrounding its composition, the history of its acceptance, the modifications of its text, and its incorporation into the Canon. The date of its composition should also be known. Spinoza concludes that all this effort should be directed to the search for universals (p. 775):

De même que, dans l'étude des choses naturelles, il faut s'attacher avant tout à la découverte des réalités les plus universelles et qui sont communes à la nature entière, comme le mouvement et le repos, ainsi qu'à la découverte de leurs lois et de leurs règles, que la nature observe toujours et par lesquelles elle agit constamment, puis s'élever de là par degrés aux autres choses moins universelles; de même dans l'histoire de l'Ecriture nous chercherons tout d'abord ce qui est le plus universel, ce qui est la base et le fondement de toute l'Ecriture.

Spinoza elaborates most carefully the steps of his critical study: one must begin with the most universal principles, then inquire what is a prophet, what is a revelation, what is a miracle, what is the opinion of each prophet. He examines carefully the intricacies of Hebrew. To those who contest the use of right reason, affirming that one can approach the Bible only with a supernatural gift, he replies that they are mistaken, and quotes Maimonides. He insists, further, that "cette méthode ne doit donc pas être ardue au point que seuls des philosophes à l'esprit très aigu puissent la suivre; elle doit être en rapport avec l'esprit commun des hommes et leur pouvoir" (p. 790).

Finally, it should not be forgotten that the works of Spinoza do not deal only with the metaphysical principles concerning the existence of God. It is true that Spinoza was very proud of having based his metaphysics, his morality, and the rest of his thinking upon God. As we shall see, it was this "tout en Dieu" which ultimately made Spinoza more than a curiosity to Voltaire. But there was, besides, a theory of natural law which the Amsterdam philosopher regarded as the basis of his universal morality. Voltaire could have benefited immensely from a study of this aspect of the *Tractatus*. Spinoza's defense of tolerance, too, could have taught him much.

Whether or not Voltaire absorbed any of Spinoza's ideas on these subjects, he surely must have learned something from the Amsterdam philosopher about biblical criticism in the Cirey period. Both he and Mme du Châtelet were very interested in the field during the thirties and forties, as we have shown, as were many of their English and French contemporaries. The first manifestation of this interest, it is true, occurred in the *Epître à Uranie* (1722), which certainly antedated any knowledge Voltaire could have had of the philosopher and which grew out of the free-thinking epicureanism of the Temple, especially that of Chaulieu. It is to be doubted, therefore, that this poem or, indeed, the libertine movement of the end of the century owed anything to the *Tractatus*. It is also very doubtful that Voltaire met with any Spinozistic current in England which could have attracted his attention between 1726 and 1729. There are, of course, a few passing remarks in his poems or his correspondence which display a tendency, before 1730, to make witty references to the Bible, but they are relatively rare and not of any great moment (see Wade, ed., *L'Epître à Uranie*).

On the other hand, the *Tractatus* was not only the earliest of the treatises concerned with biblical criticism but the model of all those which came after. Admittedly, as far as Voltaire and Mme du Châtelet[13] were concerned, there were other sources, too: Dom Calmet, Richard Simon, Jean Meslier, to name a few. But the work of Meslier, Mirabaud, Fréret, Dumarsais, and the rest was at least derivatively Spinozistic. Moreover, Voltaire's library itself contained a translated manuscript of the *Tractatus*, and, eventually, the Boulainvilliers's adaptation of the *Ethica*.

It was in the *Poème sur la loi naturelle* that Voltaire seemed to begin a new phase in his association with Spinoza—initiated clandestinely, to be sure. To all appearances, it was an attack against Spinoza's theory of remorse, which Voltaire condemned along with La Mettrie's. He had some difficulty in keeping his exposition of Spinoza's theory correct, which leads Vernière to judge that he had heard the theory discussed but had not studied it in the text. The important point, however, is the similarity which can be drawn between Spinoza's universal moral law and Voltaire's in his *Loi naturelle*. This becomes all the more significant when we realize that Voltaire found himself on this particular subject in strong disagreement with Locke. For, by judicious reference to Spinoza's *Tractatus*, Voltaire could have strengthened his own views on the necessity of a universal moral law, on the use to which it could be put in approaching the practical problem of the relationships between quarreling religious sects, and on the duties of the state to suppress these quarrels and impose a solution of justice, tolerance, and peace. The position of Voltaire this time is so strikingly similar to Spinoza's at the beginning and the end of the *Tractatus* that it is with some surprise that one notes complete silence on his part. The first thought that comes to mind is that he must not have been aware of the similarity. Ignorance in this case, though, seems an improbable hypothesis, for the deistic, clandestine treatises which derived from the *Tractatus*—the very treatises with which Voltaire was most familiar—time and time again make affirmation of a universal moral law. Nor can we propose a necessity for prudence, since the poem was a product of the Potsdam society where one would expect an open show of Spinozism when the opportunity presented

---

[13] Pomeau, however, gives Calmet as the original source for Mme du Châtelet and maintains that she does not quote Spinoza (*Religion*, p. 170). He adds that the note on Spinoza in the *Notebooks* is rather superficial. He admits, though, that Voltaire probably took from the *Tractatus* the origin of the Hebrew word "ruagh."

itself, rather than a circumspect silence. To explain Voltaire's attitude, we must turn, rather, to that side of Spinoza which Voltaire
for personal reasons did not approve. For it was precisely the atheism
of Spinoza and, more specifically still, his determinist position on
morality that kept Voltaire from approving any of his views,
whether they were similar to his own or not. Hence, he presented
a view of natural law and a theory of political tolerance in *La Loi
naturelle* which obviously had much in common with the *Tractatus,*
but he carefully refrained from invoking its assistance, preferring
to seek whatever support he needed in antiquity, in Locke, and in
Bayle.

Vernière (*Spinoza*, II, 507) notes that conditions had changed by
1762 to the point where the policy of prudence was no longer necessary. The government was now unable to combat the *Encyclopédie*
openly. In August of that year, the order of the Jesuits was suppressed in France. Voltaire elaborated his scheme for the war against
l'Infâme, beginning, Vernière adds, with the *Sermon des cinquante*.
Henceforth, according to this interpretation, in all the biblical criticism which the Patriarch poured forth in treatise after treatise, he
"ne cesse de faire appel au *Tractatus*" (II, 510). Although it is undoubtedly true that Voltaire organized a campaign against *l'Infâme,*
that his clandestine biblical treatises played an active part in its
execution, and that the *Tractatus* was an important source in the
movement, Vernière's time schedule cannot be correct. In the first
place, the *Sermon des cinquante* was surely not composed in 1762.
All the evidence shows that it dates from the Cirey period, probably
1746, certainly before 1749. It was genuinely Spinozistic, however,
as were all these Voltairean biblical tracts. There can be no doubt,
then, that Voltaire came under the influence of Spinoza at Cirey,
which, incidentally, was the normal time and, in view of Mme du
Châtelet's *Examen de la Genèse*, the normal place. If it became an
avowed influence only after 1762—(certainly by 1767 with the *Lettres sur Rabelais*, in which Voltaire openly defended Spinoza's
Tractatus against the accusation of atheism), it had long before fit
into Voltaire's critical plans—almost thirty years before, in fact. One
can agree with Vernière, however, that, for those of Voltaire's remarks which were based on the relationship of philology to biblical
criticism, Spinoza was Voltaire's only source. One can concede, also,

that Voltaire's attitude toward miracles was precisely that of Spinoza: "il n'arrive rien dans la nature qui contredise à ses lois universelles." And it is highly probable that Spinoza's solution of the authorship of the Pentateuch became Voltaire's solution. There is no reason to question Vernière's statement: "C'est avec constance que Voltaire utilise le *Tractatus* dans les limites exactes de son dessein" (II, 513). The same difficulty met earlier recurs here. In the treatises themselves, Voltaire rarely mentioned Spinoza as a source, even after his defense of 1767. Vernière concludes that Spinoza must have appeared to Voltaire a questionable ally because he was Jewish. I suspect, rather, that it was more the charge of atheism leveled against Spinoza which accounted for Voltaire's continued circumspection.

This circumspection began to wear thin around 1766, however. Indeed, from the publication of the *Philosophe ignorant* (1766) to the *Questions sur l'Encyclopédie* (1772), Voltaire was constantly preoccupied with Spinoza's treatment of the existence of God in the first part of the *Ethica* and the resultant "morale." His source was still Boulainvilliers's *Réfutation de Spinoza*, whose two parts, "L'Etre en général et en particulier" and "Des Passions," pointed up clearly the dual foundation of Spinoza's thought: a metaphysics which insisted upon a unique universal substance which is God, and a "morale" which derived the foundations of the good life from the interplay of the passions. Essentially, the work could not have been better devised to enlist Voltaire's interest. He who insisted upon the necessity of God's existence from the observation of a design in nature, he who insisted just as vigorously upon a metaphysics which could without difficulty be reduced to a morality, could have found no preceding philosopher who better answered these two needs. It was thus that he began to note that Spinoza constantly insists that the universe is ruled by a universal Intelligence. His comments frequently convey some surprise. Often, they are followed with the remark that, in spite of this insistence upon a universal principle which is a controlling Intelligence, Spinoza must be all the same an atheist. Sometimes, the refusal to believe the evidence is countered by doubt about Bayle's ability to comprehend Spinoza. The doubt finally turns into a near certainty. Voltaire, noting that there is a shift in intellectual opinion about Spinoza, gives indication that he, too, is shifting. He begins an investigation of his own, ranging from the popular presentations of the Amsterdam philosopher to the apology of Pluquet and the attack of Nieuwentyt, not to mention the elucidation of Condillac.

This turning toward Spinoza is not, however, effected without hesitations, contradictions, even much suspicion. Voltaire, having become firmly convinced that Spinoza really believed in the existence of a superior Intelligence, still refuses to believe that Bayle can be wrong in calling the author of the *Ethica* an atheist. Voltaire himself seeks reasons to impugn the position of Spinoza. The first is still drawn from Bayle: "Ce Dieu n'étant que l'immensité des choses, étant à la fois la matière et la pensée, il est absurde que Dieu soit à la fois agent et patient, cause et sujet, faisant le mal et le souffrant, s'aimant et se haïssant lui-même, se tuant, se mangeant." Voltaire as usual plays this remark in all keys. The second reason is drawn from a deficiency in Spinoza which can be found repeated by Lamy, Fénelon, Houtteville: the Amsterdam philosopher did not emphasize the marvelous design in the phenomena of the universe; he did not realize to what extent it proves the existence of a universal Providence. The world of Spinoza may have a superior Intelligence, but that Intelligence seems to act blindly and not according to a plan. Things are left to chance, rather than governed by a fixed set of mathematical laws. Voltaire appears so firmly resolved to defend the doctrine of final causes that he is willing for once to advance the Leibnizian proposal of a universal "Mathesis," a set of absolute laws presided over by a general Providence. Voltaire proposes a third reason for opposing the author of the *Ethica*; this suggestion is original with him. Spinoza supposed, as did Descartes, that the universe is a plenum, a premise which is absolutely false. If there are empty spaces, then, what happens to the infinite, universal, absolute substance which is God?

Voltaire, however, probably without being conscious of the inconsistency, had already capitulated. In the *Traité de métaphysique* (1734), it will be remembered, he had stated that the only way a reasonable interpretation could be given to Malebranche's doctrine of occasionalism would be to explain it as a type of Spinozism. He now practically reverses the formula: the only way to give a reasonable interpretation to Spinozism is to interpret it in accordance with the "tout en Dieu" theory of Malebranche. This Voltaire did in the essay *Tout en Dieu* of 1769. He was now in a position to have *his* vision. He sees a Deity from whom all things flow as rays of light from the sun. He maintains, none too clearly, that his doctrine of immanence can never be condemned as Spinozistic because God, for him, is not all phenomena but simply the source whence all phenomena flow. The distinction is a bit too subtle to have any reality. What had happened was that the old Patriarch, in the search for his own identity, could only find traces of it in a kind of Malebranchism, or a kind of Leibnizianism which fundamentally was a kind of Spinozism.

MALEBRANCHE

By his own confession, Voltaire first became acquainted with Malebranche's *Recherche de la vérité* around 1723. In a letter to the *Pour et contre* (*circa* August 1738), he wrote: "Qui peut avoir lu la *Recherche de la vérité*, sans avoir principalement remarqué le chapitre IV du L. III, de *l'Esprit pur*, seconde partie? J'en ai sous les yeux un exemplaire marginé de ma main, il y a près de quinze ans." The statement is a little ambiguous, since it is not perfectly clear whether it was the *Recherche* or the third section of the *Recherche* on *L'Esprit pur* that had received his copious commentary. At all events, the statement itself indicates that Malebranche was just about the first modern philosopher to have attracted the attention of Voltaire. Coming before Bolingbroke's famous 1724 letter, this link with Malebranche shows us a Voltaire already turning toward philosophy and—to judge by the specific reference to the section *L'Esprit pur*—to metaphysics. It is this fact, presumably, which accounts for the remarks about Malebranche and Descartes which Bolingbroke made in his letter. In the opinion of the noble lord, Malebranche might be an excellent writer and an incomparable "romancier" but was, for all that, no less a "rêveur." Voltaire could only share his English friend's opinion that the Oratorian priest was more poet than philosopher. He referred to him in a letter to Cideville as "ce rêveur de l'oratoire," while to Formont he confided that he was a "sublime fou." A bit later to the same correspondent, he stated that the Oratorian was "le romancier le plus subtil." In spite of this seemingly unfavorable comment, Voltaire had, around May 1731, borrowed from Formont the works of both Descartes and Male-branche, which he at this time returned to the owner.

His own library was well supplied with Malebranche's *Works*. There was an *Avis touchant l'Entretien d'un philosophe chrétien avec un philosophe chinois, pour servir de réponse à la critique de cet entretien*, Paris, 1708. There was, also, a copy of the *Entretien d'un philosophe chrétien, et d'un philosophe Chinois, sur l'existence et la nature de Dieu*, Paris, 1708. Voltaire had two copies of the *Recherche de la vérité, où l'on traite de la nature de l'esprit de l'homme, et de l'usage qu'il en doit faire pour éviter l'erreur dans les sciences*: the fifth edition, 3 vols., Paris, 1700; and the seventh, with the *Eclaircissements*, 4 vols., Paris, 1721. In addition, Voltaire pos-sessed the *Conversations chrétiennes dans lesquelles on justifie la vérité de la religion et de la morale de Jésus Christ*, Paris, 1733; the *Méditations chrétiennes et métaphysiques*, Lyon, 1707; the *Réfle-xions sur la prémotion physique*, Paris, 1715; the *Traité de l'amour de Dieu, en quel sens il doit être désintéressé*, Lyon, 1707; and, finally, a *Traité de morale*, 2 vols., Lyon, 1707. There were in his library as well two works often attributed to Malebranche: a *Traité de l'infini créé, avec l'explication de la possibilité de la transsubstan-tiation*, published along with a *Traité de la confession et de la com-munion*, Amsterdam, 1769. This latter work was preceded by a bi-ography of Malebranche by L. Th. Hérissant. Finally, there was the famous *Tout en Dieu, commentaire sur Malebranche*, Geneva, 1769, which was Voltaire's own work. Voltaire does not seem to have had a biography of Malebranche by the Père André. Outside of Bayle, to judge by the number of works in the library, no other seventeenth-century philosopher attracted as much of Voltaire's attention as the Oratorian priest. This attraction is not easy to explain. Pomeau (*Religion*, p. 95) attributes it to the immense popularity of the Oratorian priest, who was considered one of the outstanding Christian rational-ists. Pomeau adds that Voltaire's philosophical itinerary both began with Malebranche and, after long years of fidelity to Locke, ended with Malebranche.

The road was long, however, and on the way Voltaire encountered many more philosophers besides these two, as we have seen. In May 1731, Voltaire, on returning to his friend Formont the work of Malebranche he had borrowed, enclosed a few couplets (M. X, 267):

Je renonce au fatras obscur
Du grand rêveur de l'Oratoire,
Qui croit parler de l'esprit pur;
Ou qui veut nous le faire accroire;
Nous disant qu'on peut, à coup sûr,
Entretenir Dieu dans sa gloire.

Only shortly thereafter (1732), in some verses to Mlle de Launay, Voltaire indicated that he was now comparing Malebranche and Locke, as Bolingbroke had advised. The catalogue of writers in the *Siècle de Louis XIV* mixes respect with some harshness. Voltaire calls the Oratorian "l'un des plus profonds méditatifs qui aient jamais écrit." He attributes to him an overpowering imagination. He had, says Voltaire, many followers. He disclosed in admirable fashion the errors of the senses and of the imagination, but, when he tried to understand the nature of the soul, he went astray just as everybody else had done. Voltaire remarks casually that, like Descartes, he was a "great man" but that, when one studies him, one learns little. There is a general tendency on Voltaire's part to make light of Malebranche's more profound meditations. In the *Systèmes* (1772), for instance, Voltaire wrote (M. X, 173):

D'un air persuadé, Malebranche assura
Qu'il faut parler au verbe, et qu'il nous répondra.

In the *Dialogue de Pégase et du vieillard*, two years later, he called the philosopher "un fou" (M. X, 206) but added that the *Recherche de la vérité*, which he referred to as *Le Traité des erreurs des sens,* was a masterpiece. It seems to have been his constant opinion. Five years earlier, in the *Défense de Louis XIV* (1769), he also remarked that the *Traité des erreurs des sens et de l'imagination* was equal in value to any philosophical work of 1769 (M. XXVIII, 329). It is very difficult to strike some sort of balance between Voltaire's light mockery of the philosopher and his respect for the work. It seems that, whenever Malebranche was compared with Locke, all the defects of the dreamer emerged but that, when he was examined through his own works alone, Voltaire found much to recommend him.

What is certain is the way in which Voltaire returned to Malebranche. At the very beginning of his philosophical career, he undertook to present Malebranche's views of man. Man for him, said Voltaire, is a substance made in God's image, much spoiled by original sin but, nonetheless, more united with God than with his own body (M. XXII, 190), seeing all things in God, thinking and feeling all things through God. This problem was, of course, intimately connected with the origin of ideas. If, as Locke had maintained, we do not possess innate ideas, whence come our ideas? Locke, with Democritus and the Greek naturalists, had suggested that they come from external objects through the senses. But, when it became necessary to explain how an external object was capable of producing an idea which a sense could pick up and transmit to the mind, Locke confessed his ignorance. At the same time, he had in an essay combated Malebranche's proposal that we see all things through God.

In the *Traité de métaphysique*, Voltaire was too saturated with his three readings of Locke to revive his early acquaintance with Malebranche. He asserted that the French metaphysician had gone astray in the most sublime fashion. Malebranche's explanation that our perceptions occur in connection with external objects but are not caused by these external objects, yet do not come from ourselves either, and, consequently, must be given to us by God perplexed the author of the *Traité de métaphysique*, who quoted the famous "Dieu est le lieu des esprits." Following Locke, who had taken up Malebranche's explanation point by point only to remark time and time again that he did not himself understand either the problem or its solution, Voltaire began a whole line of puzzled inquiries. What does it mean to say that we see and feel all things in God? What advantage would we have and how much wiser would we be if this were the case? Voltaire concluded for the time being that Malebranche's explanation was a form of Spinozism, and, since he rejected Spinozism as atheism, he rejected Malebranche also, with the remark that philosophers are always trying to penetrate the impenetrable. As a fervent follower of Locke, he added that true philosophy consists in knowing its own limits.

In the *Eléments* (1740), Voltaire returned to Malebranche, this time to condemn his physics as a derivative of Cartesian physics. Voltaire would have none of his "tourbillons mous," rejected as incomprehensible his treatment of the size of objects on the horizon, and condemned, in general, all his scientific notions. It was a tactic frequently used in the Descartes-Newton quarrel. When it came to the doctrine of occasionalism, however, Voltaire showed some care in examining it (M. XXII, 424):

Il commence par supposer que l'âme ne peut avoir aucune influence sur le corps, et de là, il s'avance trop: car de ce que l'influence de l'âme sur le corps ne peut être conçue, il ne s'ensuit point du tout qu'elle soit impossible. Il suppose ensuite que la matière, comme cause occasionnelle, fait impression sur notre corps, et qu'alors Dieu produit une idée dans notre âme et que réciproquement l'homme produit un acte de volonté et Dieu agit immédiatement sur le corps en conséquence de cette volonté; ainsi l'homme n'agit, ne pense que dans Dieu, ce qui ne peut, me semble, recevoir un sens clair qu'en disant que Dieu seul agit et pense pour nous.

Voltaire was much intrigued by this explanation. There is some evidence that he understood the way in which the problem had arisen. The separation of matter and spirit, body and soul, which was a cardinal point in Cartesianism, is what had produced it. If there is no connection between the substance of matter, distinguished by extension, and the substance of the soul, distinguished by thought, how can ideas find their way from external objects (possessing only extension) to the understanding (possessing only thought)? Only three explanations had been proposed by the time of the *Traité de métaphysique*: Spinoza's single substance, Leibniz's preestablished harmony, and Malebranche's occasionalism. Voltaire had rejected Spinozism, and he had not yet, at the time of the *Traité*, come upon the Leibnizian explanation. When he did (in 1736), he declared it incomprehensible and rejected it. For the moment, only Malebranche's explanation remained. This was not very satisfactory to Voltaire either. How, he inquired, can man will by himself if he cannot think by himself? Since Voltaire was struggling in the *Traité* precisely with the problem of free will, it was necessary to give some thought to the relationships between thinking, feeling, knowing, and being, between soul and body, and between thinking, knowing, being, and action. All of a sudden, the Lockean "néophyte," like the Newtonian "néophyte," found himself in a difficult position. If God does our thinking, who does our willing? If the will controls our actions, how does it find the material from which to draw its conclusions? How free can one be if his thoughts come from a Superior

Power, if they are limited by our small capacity to experience, and if we do not know what matter is or what spirit is?

It was this situation which set up the last conversation in *Micromégas* between the little "Animalcules" and the traveler from Sirius. To the question what is the soul, the Animalcules respond with varying answers: the Cartesian offers the theory of innate ideas of Descartes ("un esprit pur qui a reçu dans le ventre de sa mère toutes les idées métaphysiques"); the follower of Malebranche, to the question what does the soul do, replies, "rien du tout . . . c'est Dieu qui fait tout pour moi"; the Leibnizian calls the soul "une aiguille qui montre les heures pendant que mon corps carillonne"; the partisan of Locke confesses that he does not know how he thinks but does know that he never has thoughts that did not come by way of the senses. For the time being, Voltaire seems to favor the Lockean explanation, since it excuses our ignorance of the nature of matter and spirit, since it relieves man from being entirely dependent upon the Deity, and since it does away with innate ideas and preestablished harmony, which Voltaire could not understand. Around the time of *Micromégas* (1739), then, Voltaire was prepared to discard Malebranche in spite of his respect for his style, which, he declared, in the *Conseils à un journaliste*, reminds one of Cicero, though it is "plus fort et plus empli d'images" (M. XXII, 265). To Maupertuis, on 10 August 1741, he wrote: "Il n'y a pas un mot de vérité, par exemple, dans tout ce que Malebranche a imaginé. . . ." Moreover, to the *Journal de politique*, Voltaire wrote (M. XXX, 393) that the Oratorian took no interest whatever in history, and at a much later date (1768) he added that, having seen the philosophy of occult qualities, Malebranche, instead of stopping on the brink of the abyss, had jumped right into it.

It was this same abyss which beckoned to Voltaire also. In a relatively long note to *Les Systèmes* (1772), Voltaire mentions that Malebranche's system is inevitably united with Spinozism. He now quotes from the *Esprit pur* section of the *Recherche* (Book III, Part II): "Dieu est le lieu des esprits, de même que l'espace est le lieu des corps. Notre âme ne peut se donner d'idées. . . . Nos idées sont efficaces, puisqu'elles agissent sur notre esprit. Or, rien ne peut agir sur notre esprit que Dieu. Donc, il est nécessaire que nos idées se trouvent dans la substance efficace de la Divinité." Voltaire reasons that, if we can have perceptions only in God, we cannot have any feeling or pursue any action except in God. Consequently, we are nothing but modifications of the Deity, and there is in the universe only one substance. This is pure Spinozism, Voltaire charges, even though the Oratorian defends these views by quoting from St. Paul and St. Augustine. Voltaire hastens to add that he is not accusing Malebranche of being Spinozistic but only thinking that his views would appeal to a follower of Spinoza.

One wonders, though, whether the Sage of Ferney had not followed his first philosopher-guide into the abyss. In the *Tout en Dieu, commentaire sur Malebranche* (1769), Voltaire gives every appearance of capitulating to the Oratorian. Beginning with Aratus's statement "In Deo vivimus, et movemur, et sumus," as it was quoted and approved by St. Paul, and supplementing it with Cato's statement "Jupiter est quodcumque vides, quocumque moveris," as quoted (and apparently approved) by Lucan, the old Patriarch remarks that, when the author of the *Recherche* attempted to comment upon that great truth that "Tout est en Dieu," everybody said that the commentary was more obscure than the text. Voltaire, however, now reasons that we cannot give our ideas to ourselves, nor can the external objects we perceive give them to us, since there is no reasonable way in which a piece of matter can produce in us a thought. Therefore, says Voltaire, God, who produces everything, produces ideas, in whatever way He chooses. But ideas, sensations, memory, imagination, and judgment are not real entities. They are only abstractions of the being who thinks, feels, recalls, imagines, and judges. We possess the faculties, not the things, which are, properly speaking, modes.

How does God produce these modes in organized beings? Certainly not by putting two sources of being in each organized body. There are not *two* beings in a deer—one which makes the other run. Obviously, a "general mathematics" directs all of nature and produces all phenomena, each specific activity being the proven effect of complicated mathematical laws. General mathematics controls all movement. The phenomena of growth are subject to more complicated mathematical laws, the phenomena of thought, sensations, ideas to more subtle mathematical laws still.

How these laws operate Voltaire now attempts to explain. God has made all actions of animals depend upon the sensations which produce the actions. He has given animals the marvelous organs of sight, of hearing, etc. These instruments have been designed to correspond in some miraculous way with the conditions which produce sight and hearing. That He has done this for animals everyone agrees; animals have no need of an intermediary something in order to feel, to see, to hear. And, if He has done so for animals, there is no reason to suppose that He has not done so for humans. Voltaire explains that man has two kinds of action, voluntary and involuntary, and that the intermediary something which might control the voluntary action has no effect upon the involuntary actions. He therefore rejects the view that man needs a soul, since he has the organs which perform the necessary tasks.

But it is God who gives the laws, the organs, the adjustments. He does everything: "Malebranche, malgré toutes ses erreurs, a donc raison de dire philosophiquement que nous sommes dans Dieu, et que nous voyons tout dans Dieu" (M. XXVIII, 96). We understand by this expression that God gives us all our ideas. God, in short, creates all ideas. "Tout est donc une action de Dieu."

Voltaire undertakes now to demonstrate how everything is an action of God. There is in nature only one universal, eternal, active principle. If there were two different principles, they would destroy each other; if there were two similar principles, they would necessarily act as one. The unity of design in the Great All, infinitely varied though it is, announces but a single universal principle. If it acts upon every being, it acts upon every mode of each being. There is, therefore, not a single movement or a single mode or a single idea which is not the effect of a universal cause. It is, and has always been, an active principle; consequently, it has no beginning, no creation, nothing beyond it. "Dieu étant le principe universel de toutes les choses, toutes existent donc en lui et par lui."

God is thus inseparable from nature: *Deus sive natura*. Voltaire denies that the principle acts by particular actions. To get an idea of what an eternally active principle can be, Voltaire compares it (though he admits readily that the comparison is very inadequate) to light from the sun. Just as particles of light emanate from the sun, so all phenomena emanate from the eternally active principle. It is true, of course, that one particle of light is a part of light, whereas an emanation of God is God, not a part of Him. Voltaire protests against those who try to give a poetic interpretation of this principle, charging that such an interpretation can never be adequate. Nevertheless, with his symbol of light in an age of enlightenment, Voltaire is doing precisely that. The laws which regulate light in this planetary system must operate in all planetary systems. The instruments which see light on this globe must exist on all globes which receive light. The laws which operate here function everywhere. If there are instruments for seeing, there must be everywhere creatures for seeing. Voltaire concludes that there are two fundamental laws: nothing is useless, and the great laws of nature are everywhere the same. "La lumière est réellement un messager rapide qui court dans le grand tout de monde en mondes. Elle a quelques propriétés de la matière, et des propriétés supérieures, et si quelque chose peut fournir une faible idée commencée, une notion imparfaite de Dieu, c'est la lumière: elle est partout comme lui; elle agit partout comme lui" (M. XXVIII, 100).

Finally, if everything is an emanation of God, truth and virtue, too, must come from Him. Truth is that which exists; virtue is an act of my will which performs some good for one of my fellow creatures. But every emanation of God is the source of what we call good and evil: "La cause universelle produit des poisons comme les aliments, la douleur comme le plaisir." We must not expect, with our limited intelligence, to understand these things. What we can do with our limited intelligence is to invent good or evil social laws, to adopt useful or harmful prejudices. We can scarcely go further than that. And Voltaire concludes, in what I believe is genuine humility for once: "Je soumets incontinent cette faible lueur aux clartés supérieures de ceux qui doivent éclairer mes pas dans les ténèbres de ce monde."

2. VOLTAIRE'S WORLD

". . . un compte que je me rends à moi-même par ordre
alphabétique, de tout ce que je dois penser sur ce monde-ci et sur
l'autre, le tout pour mon usage, et peut-être, après ma mort, pour
l'usage des honnêtes gens."

Voltaire to Mme du Deffand, 18 February 1760,
re the *Dictionnaire philosophique*

I SHOULD NOW LIKE to attempt to present a composite view of
Voltaire's world. In entering upon such a task, one must expect
to find much fluctuation and even serious contradiction, owing
in part to Voltaire's extreme intellectual mobility and in greater
part still to his clandestinity. Voltaire not only shifted rapidly in
point of view because of differing ways in which he regarded certain
problems but was also likely to modify a position clearly delineated
through a desire not to concede anything to one or two opposing groups to which he was in constant opposition. The *Désastre de
Lisbonne* provides a clear illustration. It was quite evident by the
time he set to work on the *Désastre* that he could no longer accept
Pope's "whatever is is right." A violent rejection, though, would
have played into the hands of either the theologians or the atheists.
Voltaire, in his determination to concede nothing to either party,
thus wrote one of the most involved prefaces he ever produced, in
which every assertion he makes is contradicted by some other assertion. In instances like this—and they are rather frequent—the
critic not uncommonly ends up with an idea which is either unclear,
ambiguous, or not even Voltaire's opinion at all. The usual way
of handling these contradictions is to treat them as deliberate falsi-
fications, with some effort either to excuse them because of the
peculiar exigencies of the time or to condemn not only the contradictions but the whole body of his thought.

The magnificent thing about Voltaire's universe was its order.
He was fascinated by Newton's discoveries. He was thrilled by
weighing, measuring, calculating, though he understood that these
were limits as well as achievements. He used the achievements to
justify further assumptions: God, having given attraction to matter, certainly could give it thought and, having given light to this

world, certainly could give it to other worlds; since this world, which possesses light, is inhabited, certainly other worlds possessing light could be inhabited, too.

The fundamental problem for Voltaire was the existence of God. He assumed that, if God is in His Heaven, all is right with the world —or, if not right, could be made right. The essential fact for him was that God is the supreme Maker of everything and is announced by everything He makes. Voltaire's adherence to the doctrine of final causes, as well as to the doctrine of Providence, is naïvely touching. The doctrine originated in the studies of insects as elaborated by Réaumur, but it extended to Newton's law of attraction and a well-ordered universe. Whenever Voltaire wanted proof of the existence of God, he always had recourse ultimately to the argument from design, based on the metaphor of the watch and the watchmaker or, at later times, on the metaphor of eyes and light. The perfect accord between the need for an instrument, the existence of that instrument, and its marvelous functioning is sufficient evidence, he felt, to warrant a belief in the existence of a Deity. Voltaire found no way, though, of describing His nature. Man, being finite, can never comprehend the infinite, he believed, and must content himself with some small understanding of his surroundings. At first, the creation of the universe from a void seemed to him possible; later on, under the influence of Spinoza, he found it more difficult to accept. Voltaire, like many of his deist contemporaries, flirted with the idea of the eternity of matter, but never to the point of atheism.

He did not presume to know the nature of God. He assumed, however, that He is all-good, all-wise, all-powerful. He judged that He is immense, without limits, the Great All. In all difficult circumstances, in spite of his constant assertion that God rules by general, rather than by particular, laws, Voltaire bolstered his own sense of insecurity with the feeling that Providence is friendly and will come to the rescue even in individual cases. Some of his frustration at the moment of *Candide* was caused by his discovery that this is not necessarily the way Providence operates.

The soul was something which constantly baffled him. From his early remark in the *Notebooks* (1732), that we do not know what it is and, consequently, should not admit its existence, until the very end of his life, he was constantly writing essays on the soul. The net result of all this activity was rather minimal. He could give all sorts of historical definitions—"un esprit délié," "souffle et vent"—but he seemed incapable of deciding what the relationship between the soul and the organ of thought is. He never got very far beyond the belief that humans have much the same faculties as animals, that they have similar organs for the senses and, therefore, though superior (but not exceedingly so), operate in much the same way. The distinction between body and spirit Voltaire was apparently incapable of grasping. He seems to have been genuinely committed to the solution of thinking matter.

The soul, Voltaire believed, gives the orders for action; it is the "principe d'action" (M. XXVIII, 528). For Descartes, the will is the faculty which dictates those orders, after the operation of the understanding. For Locke, it is less a function of the will to incite to action than it is of uneasiness, which finds its motive in desire. Simply put, when a person desires to do something and has the power to do it, he is free. But he is free to execute his desire; he is not free to will. The will is determined by the dominating idea, and, since we receive our ideas, we receive our will—that is, we will necessarily. There is thus a relationship between thinking and willing. Voltaire, however, admitted that he did not know what it is. He confessed that he knew no more how ideas are created than how the world was made. All we can do is to grope in our incomprehensible machine. "Free will" is a word with no meaning. It is the power to do which is the only freedom. When one says "l'homme est libre," one means only that he is free to act, not that he is free from constraints. One cannot conclude that this freedom is limitless, universal. "Freedom" is merely an abstract term, like "goodness," "beauty," "justice." Sometimes men are free, at other times they are not. Hence, one can conclude that man is no freer than the animals, since they, too, possess senses. All is but a machine, subject to universal laws. Everything is the effect of the necessary nature of things and is the result of the eternal order of the absolute Master. We are but cogs in the great machine of the world.

This abstract way of presenting the problem has undoubtedly obscured Voltaire's understanding of it. If one reverts to Collins's *Recherches philosophiques sur la liberté*, where Voltaire found clarification for Locke's more simple, but ambiguous statements, one will find that the crux of the matter is not freedom or determinism, but the analysis of the factors in man which always modify him: his opinions, his prejudices, his temperament, his habits, and the situation in which he finds himself. All of these things determine his choice, but the important thing is that he chooses as he is: that is, what he is is what he does, and what he does is what he thinks. He is not free to act, but he acts. This is doubtless what Voltaire meant when he stated that, whether man is free or not, he always acts as if he is. That does not prevent man from being, as Collins said, a "necessary agent." It is this fact precisely which permits society to hold him responsible for his action, because, if his action was not determined by pain or pleasure, society could find no way to reward or punish him for it. It is in this way that rewards and punishments became the basis and the support of society. Moreover, if man did not act necessarily, determined by pain and pleasure, he would have no conception of virtue and no reason to pursue it, since virtue consists in actions which are by their nature agreeable, vice in actions which are disagreeable. Consequently, it is false to assume that there is any injustice in punishing "necessary agents." The punishment is not inflicted because the act was necessary. One punishes, rather, those who have assumed that they were "free" agents and who have acted in accord with a "free" will. The laws are made to reward and punish, not what determines the will, but the will itself.

Good and evil must be seen first in social terms. What is useful to a society is good, what is harmful is evil. The important thing about man is that he is a social animal. He is not driven into social relationship with his fellow beings by any strong instinct, as some animals and insects are, but by needs, passions, and reason. Voltaire finds this pristine need in family life: no sooner do two people unite to begin a family than the needs of providing for the offspring and finding security become paramount. To supply those needs, man sets to work and invents some coarse forms of art. There is, however, a stronger element still in man's social tendencies: he has a natural benevolence for his species which animals do not possess. This expresses itself as pity, which is certainly not as strong as pride but is sufficiently strong to temper our attitude toward others. All the passions, though, contribute to drive us to form a social group. Voltaire accepts Mandeville's interpretation of the first beginnings of society. The prime motive was pride. But, when man learned that with the sacrifice of self to the public good one attained a superior position, everybody wanted to belong to this group. To achieve this end, all the passions were played upon, and laws were established, laws which seem arbitrary but which depend upon the interests, passions, opinions, and conditions of the people assembled. The result is a kind of moral relativism. But, whatever customs each group practices, all agree to one thing: what is in conformity with the law is virtuous, what is opposed is criminal. These laws attempt to achieve what is useful to society, and, consequently, the general rule underlying the many forms of human conduct is social utility. These laws, nonetheless, derive from more general natural laws, which are common to all.

These thoughts—the existence of God, the nature of God, the immortality or mortality of the soul, the nature of the soul, the eternity of matter, the infinity of inhabited worlds, thinking matter, free will and determinism, the nature of good and evil, vice and virtue—formed what Voltaire considered the indispensable metaphysical background of his world. Voltaire attempted to give them coherent expression in 1734-1739, with much aid from Locke, Collins, Shaftesbury, Mandeville, and Newton in the *Traité de métaphysique* and some further aid from Leibniz, Frederick, and Mme du Châtelet in the first section of the *Eléments*. He rehashed them in more or less the same way, but with more stress upon skepticism, in the *Philosophe ignorant* in 1766. The solutions he proposed in these works do not differ greatly. Their outstanding characteristic is their affinity with Locke and Newton, rather than with Pascal, Descartes, and Malebranche; that is to say, the answers are more English than French and bespeak a greater adherence to a practical, commonsense approach than to a truly philosophical, systematic approach. The influence of Leibniz seems to have distorted a bit the "English" character of this philosophy. Essentially, though, it remained Voltaire's fundamental philosophy. Its three major tenets were the existence of God, the universality of the physical law of attraction, and the necessity for a universal moral law.

The world of Voltaire was thus conceived from the first as a magic world, full of wonders, arranged in orderly fashion, and controlled by an all-wise, all-good, all-powerful Deity. It presents itself to us as an immense world, infinite in space, infinite in possibilities, because of the infinite goodness, justice, and power of God. Man's place in it is normal, reasonable, natural, and modest. What he seeks is happiness, enjoyment. What he recognizes is justice, what he craves is society and the joys which constitute it, what he shares with his fellow creatures is benevolence or, in times of need, beneficence. To achieve these ends, God has given him reason—limited, to be sure, but sufficient to penetrate his reality and his purpose.

Physically very old, Voltaire's world has undergone as many changes as the various states have experienced revolutions. Land now inhabited was once beneath the sea, the moving sands of the Sahara must once have been a seabed. One cannot be sure, according to Voltaire, that the sea has formed the mountains; the seashells found on mountains may have other explanations. It is certain, however, that, in the vast regions of the universe and over the limitless periods of time, nature has undergone gigantic cataclysms: seashores have been engulfed, stars have disappeared, whole continents have been swallowed up.

This globe is inhabited by races which are entirely different from one another. These differences can be clearly seen in the physical appearances of each. These races, especially the Asian, have existed for countless centuries. To bring a people together so that it is closely organized, powerful in war, and wise requires a prodigious amount of time. For the most part, early societies were small groups, hardly larger than family tribes. Only rarely did they turn into kingdoms. In the small groups, the arts were unknown. The tribesmen lived in huts. Those in warm climates went almost naked; those in the colder regions clothed themselves in animal skins. Some hunted, others lived on roots. None craved another existence, since it was inconceivable. Their industry never exceeded their pressing needs. Their first need was language, which at first was only gesture and only after an enormous amount of time became speech. To provide a body of laws for the group required an unconscionable amount of time. Consequently, the life of the tribe resembled over the ages the life of brutes. Given the hazards of life, the limited defense of the individual, and the loose constitution of societies, the human species must have been very small in numbers in all climates. The inhab-

itants had no conception of the soul; they were not at all philosophers. All they could do was to identify vaguely life and thinking
as the same thing.

With the passing of time, some societies, those that became better
policed, had more leisure to reflect. Certain experiences—death,
dreams—suggested immaterial things. Voltaire supposed that each
people had a religion and a "culte grossier." The members of the
group must have been too occupied with survival to have had a clear
idea of divinity. Each group, however, adopted a protector: an insect, the sun. These tutelary gods took their origin in the great disasters of the globe. With time, each group had its tutelary divinity
who protected the nation. In spite of the diversity of the cults and
divinities, almost all groups had the same customs and the same
feelings. Practically all were swayed by fables and superstitions.

Man, in general, has always been what he is: he has always had
the same instinct which urges him to esteem himself in himself,
in his companion, in his children, in his works. For thousands of
centuries, man has tilled the land. He has a mechanical instinct
which furnishes him with useful objects. And he has two sentiments which are at the basis of his society: pity and justice. God
has given him these two principles as He has given birds wings.
Around the tropics, the people submit to a ruler; further north, they
have always been independent. Nearly all ancient nations have been
organized and governed by a kind of theocracy since the earliest
times. The tutelary divinity has a corps of priests who speak in his
name and often practice human sacrifice.

In all of these respects, Voltaire's physical world did not differ
appreciably from the picture his contemporaries presented. In general, it derived from Fontenelle and Boulanger. One of the historical
problems of the time concerned the questions of origin, coherence,
and continuity. It was the attempt to find solutions to these questions that constituted, properly speaking, the Enlightenment's philosophy of history. That this was the normal way of approaching
the subject can be readily seen in Voltaire's own *Philosophie de
l'histoire*.

Voltaire, like all his contemporaries, was fascinated by the nations
of the earth. Diligently, he studied their origins, their manners and
customs, their laws, their achievements, and their rise and decline.

Those of Europe were of primary interest, and among them England, France, Sweden, Russia, and Germany attracted his attention the most. Among the ancient races, he expatiated at length upon China, India, Chaldea, Persia, Phoenicia, Greece, and Egypt. His outlook, in contrast with Bossuet's, was worldwide. Professor Perkins (*Voltaire's Concept of International Order*, p. 22) has noted that Voltaire's library contained 15 books on Africa, 24 on America, 48 on Asia, and 230 on Europe. His preoccupation in each case was characteristically with the country's arts, institutions, and laws—in short, with all factors which contributed to its civilization.

The world of Voltaire is divided into the ancient countries of Asia and Africa, the modern countries of Europe, and the savages of America. These latter are far superior to the "savages" (that is, the "rustres") of Europe because they possess the art of manufacturing all the things they need. Besides, the American communities are free, whereas the European "savages" do not even have an idea of freedom. In America they are organized under a sovereign, they have a high sense of honor, they possess a fatherland which they love and defend. It is an error to think of these American savages as two-footed creatures living as brutes, wandering solitary in the forests, and mating without creating families. Such a solitary life is rendered impossible by human nature. The savage is born, rather, with social potentialities which he develops by instinct. All animals execute without variation the law which nature gives to the species, and so does man. Had he been destined by nature to lead a solitary existence, he would never have been able to contradict the decree of nature and live in society. And had he been destined by nature to live in groups, how could he have perverted his destiny by living during countless centuries a solitary existence? It is true he is perfectible, and, therefore, we have concluded that he has been perverted. Why not conclude instead that he has perfected himself within the limits which nature has accorded him? Man has, in general, always been what he is. He has, in all probability, devoted himself over a long period of time to tilling the soil. Nonetheless, the family is the original unity of primitive life. In this organization have arisen from cries and gestures a primitive language and rudimentary, mechanical arts. It is nature who inspires in each creature useful ideas, even our way of acting, and especially pity and justice. We thus have a principle of universal reason, given to us by God.

The ancient kingdoms are those of the Chaldeans, the Indians, and the Chinese. The Chaldeans have a record of their existence in the 1903 years of celestial observations which they made. These astronomical tables extend back to the year 2234 before the Christian era. The 470,000 years of existence which they themselves counted is said by some to be excessive, and it probably is; but, when one considers that these people—or, at least, their scholars—knew the real system of the world, one must grant that they were very ancient. In fact, the first requirement of every race is to learn how to provide subsistence; the second, to form a language; the third, to build some permanent dwelling-place and to make clothing; and, finally, to forge iron and create all sorts of industry. To advance from these elementary skills to the knowledge of astronomy requires untold ages. Although there is much talk about three kingdoms—the Chaldean, the Assyrian, and the Syrian—in all probability two of them did not originally exist in the remote past. Chaldea, with its astronomical observatory, did. It was the Chaldean philosophers, not the Egyptians, who invented the Zodiac.

After the Chaldeans came the Persians under Cyrus, who, with the Medes, conquered Babylon. These Persians maintained that they had a prophet Zerduft who lived 6000 years ago and who taught them to be just and to revere the sun. Indeed, they were the first to believe in one god, in a devil, a resurrection, a hell, and a paradise. Theirs was the most ancient system taken over centuries later by the Pharisees. After them came the Syrians, so ancient that the Persians say that their Bram or Abraham came from Balk. They introduced a cult which had no relationship to the religion of the Chaldeans: a Syrian goddess served by a castrated priesthood. They, like all the ancient kingdoms, had a holy city.

The Phoenicians were also very ancient, but less ancient than the Chaldeans because their land is less fertile. It was the sterility of the land which drove them to maritime commerce. They founded Carthage and Cadiz, discovered England, and traded with India their precious cloth. They were the Venetians and the Dutch of antiquity. Their commerce required records; and this requirement, perhaps, led them to create an alphabetic writing, which they shared eventually with the Carthaginians and the Greeks. They actually gave to the Jews all their names for the Deity. Their cosmogony was the source of all the other ancient cosmogonies.

Voltaire confessed that all of these matters were problematical. When it is a question of the origin of things, they are always wrapped in obscurity. We can state who were the last comers, but never, except by revelation, can we know who were at the beginning. He nevertheless continued to organize his information upon the ancient world.

It was in Arabia that the word "garden," "paradise," signified heavenly favor. The inhabitants have never been conquered, and they have lived since time immemorial in a beautiful land unmixed with any other nation. Their religion is the simplest of all religions: a cult of God and a veneration for the stars. All these ancient nations have as a founder Bram, Abram, Abraham.

The Hindus are the most ancient people to have been organized in a solid society. Their situation was more favorable than most, since the luxuriant plants growing uncultivated in their country supplied all their needs. "Les cannes à sucre sont sous la main." In this fortunate climate, the inhabitants were naturally organized in social groups. The interesting idea invented by the Indians is the transmigration of souls. Every one of the ancient peoples, in fact, save the Chinese, believed in another life. Each country used the concept to regulate morals, but the Chinese believed that, by moral laws and severe policing, they could achieve a similar end. Nonetheless, it is clear that "la morale" is the same in all civilized nations.

Most ancient of all present countries is China, whose Empire has existed for the last 40,000 years. While other nations try to trace their origin to the beginning of the world, the Chinese look to the beginning of recorded history. They were unskilled as natural scientists but excellent in creating "la morale." The basis of their government was the family, and their religion was simple, free from all superstition and barbarity. Never were there religious quarrels, never wars between the priests and the people, and their revered Confucius taught the purest morality.

The most important part of Voltaire's historical world was neither the faraway lands of antiquity nor the contemporary savages in America but the contemporary European countries. His definition of the contemporary was, as we have seen, somewhat elastic, since it endeavored to embrace the history from Charlemagne to the present, with a few ancient countries thrown in for good measure. All the same, he was primarily interested in that period from the end of the fifteenth century to his own day. His attention was thus directed at those events which depict manners and customs, and he sought to unravel in those events the history of the human mind. The history of the arts, Voltaire proclaimed, must be given priority over the history of facts. He consistently returned to his assertion. Even in the introduction to the Nourse edition (2 vols., 1753) of the *Histoire universelle*, he had stated that his principal aim was to know as fully as possible the manners and customs of people and to study the human mind. This aim he presumed he could achieve by tracing a faithful portrait of what deserved to be known in this universe. We have already discussed elsewhere Voltaire's method of penetrating manners and customs, institutions and the arts, and the problems he had to solve. Here, where the problem is to examine what importance the unrolling of history has upon the world of Voltaire, it will suffice to note that the general method he followed was to narrate a historical event and to deduce therefrom a moral observation. Eventually, these moral observations led to a small body of general conclusions.

Voltaire's fundamental observation was that the history of the outstanding events of this world is scarcely more than the history of crimes. At times, the whole earth is the scene of massive destruction. Church affairs become so embroiled with state affairs that it is practically impossible to separate them. Voltaire returned often to the ravages of historical events, either to note that the world is full of useless cruelties or to state that at a given moment everything was in confusion, that tyranny, barbarity, and poverty were everywhere. Even those events which promised so much glory—the crusades, for instance—produced also "infâmes actions"—new kingdoms, new establishments, but likewise new miseries, and much more misfortune than glory. The one cause of these disasters is religion, which with politicians becomes the mask of politics. There are, to be sure, exceptions. Equality, natural to all men, still exists in Switzerland, insofar as it is possible. This little country would deserve to be called happy, said Voltaire, if religion did not divide the nation, which love of public affairs had united.

Into this portrait of our universe creeps another, less attractive picture. The wonderful organs of animals and insects betoken a supreme design. But what about those who, because of malformation or malfunction of these organs, disappear from the universal design? Everything reveals a world of order, in which one simple rule—attraction—keeps everything in place. But what about hurricanes, tempests, earthquakes, gigantic cataclysms? What about sickness, pain, misery, suffering, pestilence, war? The divine order is one of wisdom, justice, and power. But what about that law which provides that every animate being lives at the expense of some other living creature in this universe, where spiders eat flies, wolves eat sheep, and man eats everything, sometimes even his fellow creatures? Why is it that the wicked flourish and the innocent suffer? How can one account for the circumstance that, in this wonderful world of magic where order reigns supreme, "le mal est sur la terre"?

There begins to appear a sharp contradiction between the magnificence of the universe in all its splendor and immensity and the apparent curse which dominates our globe. Voltaire does not seem to have had any intention of repudiating the Newtonian universe, but he did have more and more inclination to question the role of man in this infinitely small portion of it. It was apparent that the earlier view that man is as happy as his nature permits had to be modified. There was now the suspicion that evil could predominate over good, that misfortunes could be terribly frustrating, and that misery is, unfortunately, a reality. The exaltation derived from the enormous increase in scientific knowledge during the two preceding centuries was tempered with some sober second thoughts on its validity and, especially, on its utility. There was certainly a time (around 1738) when Voltaire, though he already acknowledged that man, because of his natural limitations, could not know first principles, could feel some exhilaration at weighing, calculating, and measuring. It was with genuine enthusiasm that Voltaire announced that he was now occupied with weighing the sun. Micromégas's astonishment that the human mites knew so little about first principles and acted with such horrible moral irresponsibility was just as great when he learned that they could measure his height.

Gradually, however, it became apparent that natural science (knowledge of the external world) was probably an illusion.[14] Voltaire did not mention the point until later in his letters to Mme du Deffand, but he obviously became aware, as Pascal had at a previous time, that knowledge of external things does not console man for ignorance of internal things. He became more conscious, too, that philosophy, for all its vaunted power, is not worth an hour's thought when man comes face to face with his destiny. Once more, Pascal's attitude was strikingly like his own. Still, the Newtonian universe seemed to Voltaire authentic, and he subscribed to it throughout his long life. His conviction that science was not fulfilling its rosy promises to man, however, continually grew stronger. Voltaire had some reason to believe that the justification of all this scientific activity could be found in D'Alembert's remarks on the utility of science. D'Alembert had written in the *Discours préliminaire*: "It suffices that we should find real advantage in certain knowledge, where at first we had not expected any, to feel justified in regarding all research, springing from pure curiosity, as being useful to us some day. This is the origin and the cause of the progress in the study of that vast science, called in general "la physique" or study of nature which comprises so many different branches." Voltaire was prepared, with all the thinkers of his time, to accept this general proposition. Besides, it had been the central assumption of all seventeenth-century philosophy, and particularly of Cartesianism; as Gilson has pointed out, it was the very core of Descartes's thought. Consequently, in the doctrine of progress which grew out of Cartesianism and in the subsequent quarrel between the ancients and the moderns, the outstanding tenets of the doctrine—the unity of knowledge, the utility of truth, the eudaemonistic value of scientific knowledge, the conviction that human nature and human institutions are modifiable for man's comfort and enjoyment, and the belief that knowledge is a source of power—were all built around the concept of utility, for man, for society, for everything which concerns man and society.

Voltaire's physical world, which was at first so marvelous, so orderly, so legal, became in time more than a little crude, disorderly, and, in many respects, illegal—seen, at any rate, from the human point of view. He never renounced the glories of the Newtonian uni-

[14] I. Wade, "Voltaire's Quarrel with Science."

verse, though; he never failed to stress its order and regularity, and he always insisted that these traits prove eloquently the goodness, wisdom, and power of the Maker. Even in the Newtonian universe, physical evil has a place which is neither modest nor unimportant in its consequences. It can, however, be weighed against the glories of the Newtonian discoveries, and one may thereby conclude that this sort of balance between good and evil is necessary in order to preserve the order and regularity of things, that, consequently, a partial evil only contributes more reasonably to universal good. If the matter is viewed in this light, and with some naïve good will, it is even possible to agree that whatever is is right or that "tout est bien." Voltaire in time came to believe that this weighing and calculation could be carried too far. He seemed perfectly willing to accept that "tout est bien" in the sense that everything has an order, a place, an arrangement in the whole; but he was quick to deny the inference that the arrangement has been effected with human desires and human ambitions in view. Voltaire seemed to think it permissible for spiders to eat flies and wolves to eat sheep. It is less commendable, he felt, for man to eat his fellowman, although the human intelligence might even find some plausible explanation for this distasteful event. What he found impossible to understand is that syphilis should afflict humanity at the very source of life itself. Still, if one is going to weigh and calculate good and evil, one must expect "ombres au tableau." Voltaire simply found these "ombres" more and more intolerable.

This attitude was encouraged by a perfectly natural decrease in the poet's scientific enthusiasm. Since Voltaire had set out to understand the importance of Newtonian science in man's life and to transmit this understanding to his public, the achievement of his goal, which the publication of the *Eléments* consummated, left him free, if he now wished, to become an active Newtonian scientist, a role for which he had shown relatively little aptitude, or to mark time in science, the thing he would undoubtedly have liked to do, or to reduce science to "la morale," the way he handled all knowledge. The impression we get is that he intended to pursue other scientific fields as occasions presented themselves, always reducing his discoveries to "la morale." At the same time, he criticized natural science so severely for its charlatanism that we also get the impression that he believed that, natural science being practically useless for "la morale," there was no need to pursue it further. Finally, in view of his conviction that the goal of all knowledge is "la morale," we get still another impression, that he was ready now to abandon natural science for it. All three impressions are perfectly sound. As a matter of fact, the claims of "la morale" were already making themselves felt. It was no accident that the year 1738 witnessed the publication of both the *Eléments* and the *Discours en vers sur l'homme*. It was all a carefully laid plan to round out the picture of Voltaire's world. In that world, as Voltaire conceived it, the active forces are God, nature, and moral man, as they are in Pascal's world, too.

Voltaire's serious preoccupation with the nature of man dates at least from the twenty-fifth *Lettre philosophique*, where his dispute with Pascal led him to develop a reasonable, commonsense conception of man. To the deep pessimism of Pascal's view, Voltaire opposes a more normal, practical opinion. The grandeur of man, which Pascal was willing to balance against man's misery, Voltaire is inclined to ignore. As a matter of fact, Voltaire denies the inner misery of man; he rejects Pascal's picture of man's feverish search for himself and his search for amusements to ward off boredom. Voltaire will have none of Pascal's tragic portrait of man, which he considers incomprehensible. The two natures of Pascal he repudiates outright. Man's search for pleasures in the society of his time he refuses to interpret as an attempt to escape the memory of his misery; it is, rather, a perfectly normal desire to participate in moderate social pleasures. Where Pascal treated man as a condemned criminal, subject to the effects of original sin and incomprehensible to himself, Voltaire presents specific experiences to prove that Pascal was greatly exaggerating. Man, as Voltaire presents him in rebuttal to Pascal, is not unique; he is associated with other animals. He does not have two natures; nor is he in a deplorable condition. The "odieux jour" in which Pascal pictured him, wicked and unhappy, must be combated. Voltaire retorts that man is neither as wicked nor as miserable as Pascal would have us believe. He adds that explaining man's misery by the doctrine of original sin is explaining something we do not know by something we do not understand. "Un mystère ne fut jamais une explication. . . ." Man enters into this world in the same way as animals. He is sometimes badly organized, deprived of a sense or two, or bereft of the faculty of reasoning. Those who are the best organized have the keenest passions. All have the love of self, which is as necessary as the five senses; it is given to us by God for our self-preservation. Our ideas are exact or illogical according to our organs and the keenness of our passions. Each man depends for all his existence upon the air which he breathes and the food which he eats, and there is nothing mysterious in his make-up. He has his own place in nature, superior to animals, which he resembles in bodily organs, inferior to the other beings, whom he resembles perhaps in thought. He is like everything we see, a mixture of good and evil, or pleasure and pain, endowed with passions to act and with reason to regulate his action. If he were perfect, he would be God. His contradictions, therefore, are necessary ingredients which enter into the composition of things and are as they should be. Voltaire insists upon the normalcy of all life and the rule of Providence: the earth, animals, and man are all that Providence wished them to be. Moreover, self-love is absolutely necessary. Our mutual needs are what make us useful to society: our own needs are what bind us to others. If we did not possess self-love, we could not live together, nor could we have invented the arts. Voltaire concedes that God could have made creatures attentive to the welfare of others, even though He did not do so.

In several respects, Voltaire's defense of self-love, his acceptance of the right use of the passions, his belief that both passions and self-love contribute to the correct formation of the social group which is the true origin of society give a very coherent picture of man and his relationship to his fellowman. Without these personal factors, no society could in fact endure, and, without society, the arts and man's institutions could not exist. It is true that self-love can lead man astray. To prevent such deviation, society has invented laws which are, so to speak, rules for the game, and these rules direct the action of self-love while religion perfects it. It is a mistake to maintain that man should lead the contemplative life. It is incorrect to state that he thinks only of the present. It is exaggerated to presume that nothing renders us as unhappy as the necessity of living without our own inner self. All of these observations of Pascal assume that man tends to an isolated, inactive life, whereas man is actually made for action, just as it is the nature of fire to rise or stones to fall. Inactivity and death are the same thing for him. In fact, action is one of the finest ways to gratify his social instincts. Voltaire does not accept that life is a condemnation; he refuses to be despondent at his destiny when, in fact, man is, of all living creatures, the most perfect, the happiest, and the one who lives the longest. There is no reason to condemn him because he must constantly look outside of himself. It is the only way he can have sensations, and it is only through sensations that he can have ideas and only through ideas that he can act. Nor should one forget that man's nature can be modified by custom and by education; the "honnête homme" can be trained. And all men, trained and untrained alike, can be expected to agree on justice as the core of morality.

Voltaire's morality was thus a strictly libertine morality, compounded of common sense and normal living, and tending to modest pleasures, moderate actions, and social activities. It was restricted to the limited possibilities of man, devoid of ideals, and opposed to exaggerations. He was prepared to grant that, when circumstances permit the enjoyment of life in Paris or London, those who have the means, the temperament, and the place in society which permit them to enjoy it can lead a very satisfactory existence. The life of the "mondain," for one who can afford it, can be very attractive indeed. But even those less favored can find normal, modest pleasures in the context of human benevolence and social activity. There were, of course, "ombres au tableau," but for the moment they were not very deep shadows.

Voltaire, it will be recalled, looked upon Pope's *Essay on Man* as an answer to Pascal's rigorism. He admired it for this quality, but he nonetheless found that it contained some serious misconceptions about happiness. What these false premises were Voltaire seems not to have specified. It can be presumed that his own *Discours en vers* were free from the blemish in Pope. I have examined elsewhere the relationship between the two poems. Here I should like to see in what light Voltaire regarded happiness and in what way this modified his view of man.

The first poems of the *Epîtres sur le bonheur* undertake a discussion of the subject, and the theme runs throughout the seven epistles. In the first discourse it is implied that everybody seeks happiness and that everybody thinks he does not have his due share while everybody else seems to have more than he deserves. Voltaire rejects both assumptions. For him, happiness is dependent upon the five senses. They are, to be sure, imperfect, but they are the only measure of our good or our ill. All other measures—wealth, intelligence, position—are false criteria. One should not conclude, however, that each person's store of happiness is guaranteed by the five senses and that there is not intermingled with it some unhappiness. Everybody, in fact, has a measure of both. But each person is equal to his fellowman in his right to happiness, the only perfect equality we possess. Irrespective of our wealth, our position, our intelligence, that right grants us peace, sleep, energy, and health, which are true sources of happiness. Still, every position has its ills, every man has his reverses, every estate has its disadvantages. Misfortune is everywhere as present as happiness. But happiness depends upon no privilege for its existence. Then where do we seek it? Everywhere, at all times, in nature, never complete, never enduring. We are a mixture of desires and discontent, reason and folly, moments of ecstasy and days of torture. Such is the essence of man.

One thing is certain, though: happiness is the reward for wisdom. Then how do I acquire it? Am I free to strive for it, or am I merely the tool of some other force? The poet feels assured that he is free—it is a freedom granted by God. If a person can will and has the means to act, he is free. Thus, man becomes a ruler over the earth by virtue of his thought. He has only to will, and nature obeys; he commands not only the seas and the winds but thoughts and desires. It has to be this way; otherwise, we would not exercise any influence, we could not be held responsible for our actions, there could be no rewards and punishments, and we would be only the powerless creatures of a blind destiny living in a world in which the wicked would exercise their evil deeds while putting the blame on the Deity. And God would become responsible for evil. There is, however, a difficulty. If man is so free and so wise, why is there such a disproportion between his thought and his action? The reason is that man does not have unlimited freedom, any more than he has unlimited wisdom. He is in everything a finite creature. There are periods when he is sick and other times when he is healthy. Freedom is the sign of health. The passions sometimes destroy it. Every man is free, with a freedom which is given to him for his happiness. He must, however, use it wisely. Consistent in thought, simple in courage, he must respect truth, be patient with error, and love his fellowman. True happiness is a perfect devotion to the happiness of others. Thus, it was explained to Voltaire by one of the Superior Powers.

Man, in spite of his freedom, is under the sway of vices, particularly envy. This vice, born of pride, cannot tolerate the happiness of another. Ultimately, though, in spite of persecution and satirical attacks, envy proves itself incapable of destroying merit. Man also has virtues, one of the greatest being moderation—in study, in ambition, and in pleasures. He must learn to adjust his taste, his works, his pleasures, and put a limit to his desires, particularly in the study of nature, where progress can be made but where, too, it is not limitless. Man, of course, wants to know everything. Why do animals act as they do? What makes plants grow? How does man digest? How does the blood circulate? What is the shape of the earth? What is attraction? Alas, we can measure, weigh, and calculate all we want and still not know what the universe is. If we must be prudent with our knowledge, we must be especially wary of our ambitions and, above all, avoid becoming a courtier. Our pleasures, too, must be moderate. There are pleasures for all stages of life. They must alternate with work. Happiness must be cultivated, but we must offer it something in return. It must not be thought endless, nor can it last forever. Its greatest ally is friendship, which is a "félicité parfaite."

To understand well the goal of happiness, it is necessary to comprehend the nature of pleasure. The first thing to note is that pleasure is a gift of God through the senses. It is through pleasure that the Deity leads man, who owes his existence to it. He acts, he feels, he thinks through pleasure. It is, of course, allied with pain, which warns us of excesses and other dangers. The center of the pleasures is love of self, which, though long decried, is a necessary love, the soul of our soul. Indeed, with self-love go all the passions, also a gift of God, dangerous when abused, but very useful when used in moderation. The passions especially should not be given free rein, but we should not abstain from using them either.

We can return to the nature of man, now that we know the ingredients which enter into his make-up. Boileau and Pascal had satirized him, Pope and Leibniz had taken a "sage milieu." Voltaire wondered whether he dared draw the lesson from all that his predecessors had said. Of one thing he seemed certain: every creature, including man, thinks the universe was made for him. In reality, everything has been made for God. Everything is thus as it ought to be. To be sure, man does not willingly accept this verdict. He thinks he should have a long life, boundless energies, an unlimited intelligence. But the slightest reflection will make clear that he is finite and limited because God wants him that way. We must therefore be content with our pleasures, though they are restricted and fleeting. We are not capable of knowing the power of God, or even what the reality of our world is, or what it ought to be. We can know what it is only in part and profit from its fruits.

Then what is our highest virtue? Certainly not the silly ritual of the priest. Christ, when the question was put to him by a simple mortal, replied: "Love God, but also your fellowman." Voltaire approves this advice; though the world is slanderous, vain, feeble, and envious and one could be excused for shunning it, to serve it is better still. Devotion to the cult is splendid, miracles and mysteries are attractive, but to come to the aid of one's fellowman, to assist the miserable, and to pardon one's enemies are greater still. Justice is a matter of beneficence. Doing good to others is the highest virtue, since, in reality, it embraces all the other virtues.

Perhaps we should tarry a moment to understand the quality of man, as Voltaire understood him. It should be remarked that, in spite of his vaunted intention to look at man in an objective way as a traveler from some other world would regard him, he found it difficult to assume the role of that traveler. He could not think of man in general without injecting into his picture Voltaire in particular. The "mondain" is the kind of man Voltaire wanted to be. He is not representative of man but, rather, of the kind of man who attracted Voltaire. Even the little mite in *Micromégas* who followed Locke is the kind of mite Voltaire wanted to be. In addition, the analysis which Voltaire gave of man was conditioned by his own nature and interests. Consequently, his view of moral man was likely to be that of a middle-class society well immersed in middle-class philosophy: glorification of work, moderation of the passions, love of comfort, resignation to good and bad, limitation of desires and ambitions, modesty in demands, lack of ideals, for the most part, and both practical and common sense. He almost always thought of man in terms of the eighty-five percent whose lot it is to toil and the fifteen percent whose destiny it is to enjoy, and he was inclined to talk about man with only the latter group in mind. His moral code, when he spoke of moral man, was really restricted to the five or six million Frenchmen who formed the elite of France. For him, they were the makers of civilization.

There are some important exceptions to this generalization, however. Voltaire conceived of natural law as applying to all men; he conceived of it as a law of reason, better still, as a law of justice, and, best of all, as a law of human dignity. Voltaire's ideas on this point are clear and genuine. Every man may not have intelligence, but he does have a sense of what is right and wrong in his terms. Every man may not have an ideal, but he does have a sense of what constitutes his dignity. In each case, someone may be terribly limited, or his actual viewpoint may be impossibly restricted, or he may be subject to all sorts of impeding circumstances. These things are realities. Yet, on another plane, reason, justice, and dignity are also realities, and every man in Voltaire's world participates in them in some degree. Further, every individual is —and this has always been the case—a member of a social group to which he accords some allegiance. Voltaire has no interest in the solitary man or the individual savage. In his opinion, the first state of nature, where man roamed the world in solitude, is an impossible myth. The first man who met the first woman and proceeded to have his first child formed the first society, and that is the way society has been formed ever since. Voltaire did believe that man is not born wicked. Martin best expressed the idea when he said that man was not born a wolf but had become a wolf. The implication, obviously, is that society transforms the innocence of birth into something else. The further implication is more important: society, in transforming the individual, can train him for good as well as for evil. Man is thus modifiable, education is possible, civilization can be created. The simple rule to follow is that conformity to the laws is good, lack of conformity evil. Voltaire accepted Mandeville's concept of the formation of a society: a group in process of being formed always imposes upon the individual the notion that it is noble and right to sacrifice one's self for the good of the community and, by playing upon pride which is the great passion of everybody, persuades each individual to accept the sacrifice.

These ideas, which Voltaire formed for the first time in the *Traité de métaphysique*, seem not to have changed greatly. In the *Questions sur l'Encyclopédie* (M. XIX, 373-385), he attempted a general synthesis.

Man may pronounce moral exhortations, he may have pity and benevolence for his fellowman, he may learn that each acts in his own interest, and he can be taught to sacrifice himself for his fellow creatures. Each man may have in his heart a notion of justice and may recognize that virtue consists in obeying the law and in doing what is good and useful for the social group. He may have passions which drive him to nefarious action and even remorse which follows his evil conduct. There may be some correlation between his ideas, his desires, and his action, but it is not on these terms that the ordinary man lives. Only a few can discuss such metaphysical ideas as freedom and equality or the more difficult problem of the immortality of the soul. Every man may tend to happiness, but very few achieve it.

In general, man's morality can be taken from the Book of Job: "Man, born of woman, lives briefly; he is filled with miseries, he is like the flower that blossoms, withers, that one crushes; he passes as a shadow." His life span averages twenty years. Left to himself, he must have been, at the beginning, the filthiest and poorest of all God's creatures. In the first place, he is born defenseless, and he is not handsome. We like to think of him as endowed with reason, working hands, an intellect capable of conceiving general ideas, and the ability to express them clearly. In reality, only a very few can boast of these privileges. Man is the only one of God's creatures who knows from experience that he must die. If one subtracts the few who have genius, there remain an immense number occupied only with subsisting; the principal preoccupation of each is lodging, clothing, and food. Man is not born wicked, though; in fact, he is born neither good nor bad. In childhood, he is as gentle as a lamb. Education, precepts, his government, and other institutions determine whether his life follows the path of crime or of virtue. Customs and manners have an influence upon his actions. One instinct he forever carries with him is the social instinct, since he has always lived in society. It is, in fact, the social group which, after long centuries, has transformed the savage into the citizen. It is the group which has given him a chance to exercise his reason. It is the group which has given him the opportunity to gain his subsistence, acquire his lodging, and finally reach that high state of excellence where the advantages of civilization begin to be recognized. Nonetheless, more than half the habitable earth is populated with two-footed animals who still live in this horrible state of nature, having scarcely enough to eat and to wear, enjoying but little of the gift of speech, barely aware of their wretched state, living and dying without knowing it.[15]

There has always been a society of peoples, but there has never been only one people. From the *Traité de métaphysique* on, Voltaire insisted upon the plural races of men: the black, the brown, the white. There have been innumerable societies of these separate races. And an almost infinite number of centuries were needed to bring them from the barbaric primitive state to the mere semblance of civilized living. The thing to stress, however, is that there always have been social groups. It should also be remembered that each social group has its characteristic ways of living, its manners and customs which have been developed from within itself. Hence, if in one sense of the word all men are alike, in another sense there are various groups which are profoundly distinct from each other. These differences are fostered by the temperament of the members of the group, but they depend also upon climate, geographical conditions, and all kinds of attendant circumstances. As these influences make themselves felt, there develop in the group certain fixed ways of approaching life, of responding to its challenges—what we call the

---

[15] Voltaire remained an optimist. He believed there is one genius for every one hundred men, one for every five hundred women. He was certain that it takes genius to invent an art. To develop an art, he claimed, requires thousands of centuries, to perfect it thousands of centuries more.

In the article "Méchant" of the *Dictionnaire philosophique* (M. XX, 53), Voltaire rejected the view that human nature is essentially perverse. Man becomes perverse, he said, as he becomes ill. In reality, only a few ever become radically wicked— some politicians who want to stir up trouble and some vagabonds who rent their services to the politicians. Thus, only about one person in a thousand is essentially wicked. Voltaire concluded that there is less evil than people are wont to believe.

"esprit" of a nation. There is thus in Voltaire's world a history of society, as well as a history of man. The former is the record of the events which have brought a nation along its path of development or precipitated its decline; the latter is the story of the development of the human mind and the way it has fostered manners and customs and given to man his spirit. Manners, spirit, and mind all play a role in the unfolding of history, the perpetuation or destruction of nations, even of whole races. Voltaire's world is a mobile world in its political and social structures, as in its physical phenomena.

Voltaire's world, conceived at first to be extraordinarily old and infinitely large, became more and more restricted until it embraced only this little globe of ours, which he often referred to as "ce tas de boue," and the relatively short period in history extending from the fifteenth to the eighteenth century. However, though living beneath some unfathomable curse and being horribly old, composed of nations which reach back into the dark recesses of time, this "tas de boue" had an unbelievable fascination for Voltaire. The "philosophe ignorant" was convinced that one can never know the principles of things, or the origins of things, or the ultimate meaning of things, but he never let that belief stand in the way of his tremendous curiosity. He took a childish delight in weighing, measuring, and calculating the phenomena of the external world and an equal glee in pondering the intricate phenomena of the inner universe of man. For an "ignorant" philosopher, he really had an incredible amount to say in positive terms concerning the relationship of man to his universe. We have already seen his general views on morality and science. We shall now attempt to get a glimpse of his attitude toward two of man's institutions: religion and politics.

In Voltaire's world, there was an institution distinguished by its "superstition" and its fanaticism. This institution was served by "des faquins en sandale" who had spread dissension throughout the world, bathed their hands in blood, and destroyed hundreds of cities, fomenting everywhere civil war. This institution claimed to be religion, but, whether it was led by the Pope or by Luther or Calvin, it was "une erreur fatale," abuses opposed by other abuses, scandal opposed by another scandal. These disasters had despoiled Europe and wrecked the earth. Voltaire called this superstition, served by a priesthood which nourished it, created fanaticism, and laid waste this world in civil strife, *l'Infâme*. He denied that it was religion. He stated that he had always distinguished the evils of superstition from religion, which he defined as the adoration of God, the brotherhood of man, "moins de dogme avec plus de vertu," and in which philosophy, enlightening mankind, would lead all men in peace to the feet of the Master, joined in "l'heureux tolérantisme" (*Epître à l'auteur des Trois imposteurs*).

RELIGION

Voltaire tried on numerous occasions to distinguish between true religion and what passes for religion. As we have just seen, true religion should be separated from superstition and fanaticism. He makes abundantly clear, with specific illustrations, what he understands these to be. Examples of superstition are: the liquefaction of the blood of Saint Januarius, the blessing of the horses and mules in Rome at Santa Maria Maggiore, the parades of the flagellants in Spain and Italy, the display of pieces of Christ's cross, "enough to build a hundred gun warship," and all other false relics, plus all the false miracles. Voltaire condemns the ceremonies, particularly the one which took place in Saint Louis's chapel in the Sainte-Chapelle on Holy Thursday, or at Saint-Maur. Such superstitions, Voltaire concedes, can be found in other ancient religions, but he will not admit their prior acceptance as a justification for their continued existence. He argues that they have never had a good effect and that several have created great evil. They always tend to reappear: Voltaire cites in Part II of his article "Superstition" (*Questions*) a miracle which was said to have just taken place at Tréguier in 1771. Needless to say, all miracles are attributable to superstition, in his opinion.

Fanaticism, the source of persecution, particularly of outstanding men, is "insensé," "impitoyable," "abominable." Voltaire shows that, connected with religion, it is the origin, not of piety, but of persecution. It is a "folie religieuse," somber and cruel, an illness contagious like smallpox. It thrives not so much in books as on the rostrum. "Le Fanatisme est à l'enthousiasme du superstitieux, ce que le transport est à la fièvre." It leads to trances, visions; one mistakes dreams for realities, imaginings for prophecies, and these hallucinations lead to crimes. Voltaire considers all assassins fanatics. He speaks always with horror of the Saint Bartholomew Massacre, which he regards as the greatest example of fanaticism. Judges who condemn those who are not of their opinion, he declares, are guilty fanatics.

The only remedy against fanaticism is "l'esprit philosophique," which refines manners and customs and prevents the onslaughts of the evil. Indeed, religion, with its Old Testament examples of fanaticism, has a very harmful effect on those whose minds have already been affected. The Jansenist "convulsionnaires" are contemptible, since they led to the attempted assassination of the King. Fanatics are practically always led by scoundrels. The symptoms occur in all religions except the Chinese, where philosophers are a sort of antidote. But fanatics identify themselves with groups who fight other groups: Catholic against Protestant, Jesuit against Jansenist. They are also false converters, who claim to act in God's name.

That which nourishes fanaticism is enthusiasm, which begins as a commitment, continues as a vision, brings together groups which are sent to faraway places, and culminates in civil wars in which a hundred thousand men are slain. It is this holocaust of human beings which Voltaire deplores. In the second section on "Religion" in the *Dictionnaire philosophique*, he takes a trip across a desolate region amid piles of dead bones accompanied by his "Archangel." The first piles contain the remains of the 23,000 Jews who built and worshipped the Golden Calf; then come the 24,000 who were killed by Moses for having consorted with the Madianite women. He calculates that around 300,000 had been murdered for similar misdeeds. There is a third pile of those who killed each other in "metaphysical" disputes: one group consists of 12,000,000 Americans, slaughtered because they were unbaptized. Beyond the piles of bones are piles of confiscated gold and silver, for which these crimes had been committed.

What feeds superstition, fanaticism, and enthusiasm is dogma. Voltaire states, ironically, that we must accept all beliefs taught by the Church, even though some dogmas preached by the Roman Church are contradicted by the Greek. He asserts that, in view of this lack of unanimity, charity must unite us all. "C'est surtout entre les cœurs qu'il faudrait de la réunion" ("Dogmes," *Dictionnaire philosophique*). Once more, he relates a dream in which he mounts to

Heaven and witnesses the judgment of those who were the great supporters of dogma: the Cardinal of Lorraine, who was the leader at the Council of Trent; Calvin, who established the dogma of his Church; Le Tellier, with his *Unigenitus Bull*. Voltaire notes that each had conducted himself in an immoral way toward his fellowman: the Cardinal in wild orgies with the women at the Council, Calvin in his treatment of Servet, and Le Tellier with his "10,000 lettres de cachet." All three are condemned, rather uncharitably, by the dreamer: the Cardinal is thrown into a pit, Le Tellier is burned "jusqu'aux os," and Calvin is "puni plus rigoureusement." An edict is proclaimed that no inhabitant of the infinite worlds will be judged on his ideas but only on his actions. Unfortunately, Voltaire forgets this time that what we think is what we are and what we do. But his meaning is clear: religious dogma which leads to inhuman or immoral deeds must be condemned. True religion is not what we believe, for that is adoration of God and love of our fellowman. Voltaire returns to the rights of dogma in the article "Croire." This time it is Moustapha, the Mohammedan, who asserts that he believes the miracles of Mohammed. Voltaire doubts that Moustapha believes so firmly the things he asserts. "Le fonds de Moustapha est qu'il croit ce qu'il ne croit pas." He concludes that, often, to believe is to doubt and that it is criminal to persecute those who are in doubt and distrust themselves.

Still, Voltaire believes a religion to be necessary, especially for the ignorant and brutal populace. Where the elite is concerned, he wavers. He indicates that, if a society could be conceived comparable to that of the Epicureans, he would consider it satisfactory, "car leur principal dogme était l'amitié." On the other hand, Voltaire does not, in general, approve of atheism for anybody. In speaking of the ideal religion which the human mind is capable of conceiving, he chooses the one which would require the adoration of the Supreme Being, unique, infinite, eternal, the Maker of this world, who moves it and gives it life, who has no equal or second. This religion should reunite to this Supreme Being those who merit a reward for their virtues and separate from Him those who should be punished for their crimes. It would acknowledge only a few points of dogma and would teach a pure morality which would admit of no dispute. It would not make vain ceremonies the center of its cult. It would require that its members serve their neighbors through love of the Deity and refrain from persecuting them in the name of God. It would manifest itself in pompous ceremonies to impress the vulgar masses but would reject all mysteries which might offend the wise and irritate the unbelievers. It should encourage all men to pursue social virtues, rather than offer expiation for their transgressions. And, finally, it should guarantee its ministers wages which would permit them to live decently and should establish retreats for the aged and the infirm ("Religion" I, *Dictionnaire philosophique*).

What he reproves particularly is atheism, which is the vice of "quelques gens d'esprit," as opposed to superstition, which is the vice of fools. He distinguishes three groups of religious people. First, there are those who are well-off, comfortable, sophisticated, who live in peace and serenity and in friendship without need for clarifying this problem. They are a small group similar to the ancient Epicureans. Voltaire seems to feel that they should not be molested. Then there are those who have become enlightened and who, from their observation of the order and regularity in the universe, have concluded that this order supposes a superior Intelligence. From the proof of final causes, they deduce the existence of God: *Deus optimus maximus*. Finally, there are the "peuples entièrement sauvages" who have no idea of the existence of God, although they live in society. They should be trained to live in conformity with the maxim of the Golden Rule. Voltaire is convinced that no social morality is possible among the masses unless each person acts out of fear and respect for rewards and punishments. He indicates that, even among the intelligentsia, a belief in rewards and punishments is a solid foundation for social virtues. What he rejects is the modern atheism of Holbach and the biological scientists of Diderot's group, who attribute the order and regularity of the universe to chance. To counter their argument, Voltaire falls back upon his doctrine of final causes, which he supports with Plato's concept of "l'éternel Géomètre" and with Spinoza who, "lui-même, admet cette intelligence; c'est la base de son système." Voltaire confesses that he knows not where this eternal Geometer is, or whether He has formed the universe of His own substance, or whether He is immense, without quantity and quality. "Tout ce que je sais, c'est qu'il faut l'adorer et être juste." This is what Voltaire calls his "argument de bonne femme."

POLITICS

If Voltaire's onslaught against *l'Infâme* could be calculated to weaken the institution of religion as it actually existed in his day, there arises immediately the problem of what institution would undertake its function. For Voltaire, as for Bayle, what was ultimately involved was not so much religious dogma as morality. In a society in which religion had arrogated to itself the task of combating vice and fostering virtue, any diminution of its strength could jeopardize social activity. Voltaire was clear in his attitude to the problem. The elite, he thought, could be trusted to practice virtue and avoid vice, once virtue had been defined as that action which contributes to the good of the social community, and vice that which contributes to its harm. But he was enough of a realist to recognize that even the enlightened sometimes had difficulty distinguishing between the interest of the individual and the interest of the group. He decided that, in these circumstances, society must have persuaded the individual that it is noblest to sacrifice one's own interest for the interest of the group. This he was inclined to confirm by what he called the Natural Law, defined as "Adore un Dieu, sois juste, et chéris ta patrie." This adoration of God and the pursuit of justice represented for him the nucleus of religion. Simple acceptance of God's existence and social benevolence are practically the limits of religious action for the elite. The masses, on the other hand, must be persuaded that good action is rewarded and bad action punished. Who rewards and punishes in this case? Ultimately, God; provisionally, society.[16]

This line of thinking leads directly to the problem of the relationship between church and state or, rather, between politics and religion, since both are obviously concerned with morality. Voltaire started with the principle that there cannot be two powers in a state; it is very easy, therefore, to abuse the distinction between spiritual and temporal power. Voltaire proposed that the Prince must be the absolute master of all ecclesiastical policy, without any restriction,

[16] See C. Rowe, *Voltaire and the State*; P. Gay, *Voltaire's Politics*; J. Ceitac, *Voltaire et l'affaire des natifs*; E. Faguet, *La Politique comparée de Montesquieu, Rousseau et Voltaire*; and R. Pomeau, *Politique de Voltaire*. There is also an interesting article on the subject by T. Besterman in the *Studies on Voltaire and the Eighteenth Century*, Vol. XXXII.

since it is a part of government. Moreover, history shows that, when the Prince is in authority, there are no disorders or calamities, whereas, under other circumstances, there have always been strife and dissension. The Prince must, therefore, insist that the ecclesiastical power be answerable to him. He must understand that the more reason progresses, the less there will be disputes on grace, theological quarrels, and superstition. It is to be noted, however, that Voltaire did not demand, as Spinoza did, that the state grant all sects equal justice before the law. His views on the relationship of church and state were more in accord with those of Hobbes. Admitting the primacy of Catholicism as the state religion in France, he limited himself to a simple tolerance of other sects established more on sentimental than on legal grounds.

It has often been remarked that he has no work on political theory to compare with Montesquieu's *De l'Esprit des lois* and Rousseau's *Contrat social*. It is true that he never composed a theoretical work on politics and economics. He did, however, on numerous occasions, write short articles upon aspects of these subjects, and, when these are brought together, as they have been by Pomeau, they constitute a sizable document on his political thinking. We have noted elsewhere his personal interest in this subject, which went back to his school days, if we may trust Le Jay's remark. It became a great preoccupation after his relationship with Frederick and, at two or three periods of his long life, a real ambition. There is no escaping the conclusion that his correspondence with the Prussian Prince had fired in him the desire to play a role in the political scene in Europe. There can be no doubt, either, that he proceeded to train himself, under the tutelage of Frederick during the early years of his kingship, to analyze the international situation in Europe. When the War of the Austrian Succession broke out, he was actually entrusted with a mission to Berlin, and again, in the Seven Years' War, he tried to open up negotiations between Frederick and the French ministry. This active, practical entry into politics and international European relations encouraged him to prepare a body of material on the theory of social organization and the goals of political and economic power. True to the doctrine of Lenglet Dufresnoy that the best historian must also be an experienced statesman, he sought to give himself a practical as well as a theoretical view of the political world. Naturally, he refused to make of this theoretical view a system of politics, but he did much to bring his ideas on the subject together, first, in the *Dialogues entre A, B, C* (1768) and, shortly thereafter, in various articles of the *Questions sur l'Encyclopédie* (1770-1772). These attempts were always highly conditioned by the opinions of Grotius, Pufendorf, and Locke, as well as by those of Hobbes, Montesquieu, and Rousseau.

Our concern here is with the place these ideas had in Voltaire's conception of the world. Since the social organization of that world is of prime importance to Voltaire, it is well to know what political, economic, and social concepts best support it. We should note immediately that he could not conceive of a relationship which is not a reality or of a situation which is not an action. This does not mean, however, that he was devoid of an ideal. Fundamentally, like all the philosophes, he recognized the necessity of constructing a prosperous, comfortable society to sustain a refined culture. In all discussions about the way this society may be formed, he thought always of the "enlightened few," of its privileges and the ways it may be benefited. The general goal of social organization is happiness, but that can be acquired only if the right means are used to produce prosperity and the right relationships are established to produce coherence and continuity of effort. The best judges of the goal are the "happy few"; the best evidence of success in achievement is their joy of living, cultural production in the sciences and the arts, stability of the institutions, and the refinement of manners. Envisaged in practical terms, he would have been willing to accept another age of Louis XIV provided that it could be a little more enlightened, provided, also, that one could find some means of eliminating what he came to consider, even in that glorious age, as "l'envers du tableau." That aim could be achieved, he felt certain, by changing the conditions, not of human living, but of the human mind. The revolution he sought to produce was the destruction of prejudices which he, as an enlightened human being, could no longer tolerate and the establishment of a whole set of new, modern relationships to which the human mind was willing to adjust itself. The goals to which all these relationships tended were progress—intellectual progress—and freedom—freedom from constraint. Voltaire conceived of this evolution as a release of inner energy for the purpose of increasing the capacity to create (he uses the word "to cultivate").

The problem is primarily to find the best type of social organization to achieve these goals. It must be remembered that they are to be realized first and foremost for the enlightened few—what Voltaire calls "les honnêtes gens"; later on, they may be spread to the larger number. In his opinion, though, the enlightened few have a deep responsibility to the masses—not so much, it seems, to enlighten them as to satisfy their needs and to turn them from their vices and, above all, to relieve their suffering. It is this naïve concept of humanity which lay at the roots of his thinking about all matters concerning political, economic, and social organization. Fundamentally, it was a religious preoccupation—actually, that aspect of religion which consists, in addition to the adoration of God, in love of one's neighbor. His insistence that we must always remember that we are "frères," though subject to all sorts of momentary contradictions on his part, seems genuine enough. In fact, the notion of "fraternité" loomed larger in importance for him as a political concept than "égalité" or "liberté," probably because he was still deeply committed to classical humanism. At all events, although he rarely used the abstract word, he often reverted to the notion when he discussed natural law and tolerance.

Voltaire understood, then, as many political theorists of his day did, that governments are organized for the purpose of fostering culture, promoting material and spiritual progress, and thereby achieving a maximum of happiness. Like his contemporaries, he was deeply preoccupied with the question of what type of organization is best for attaining these ends. In theory, the best government is that in which everybody obeys the laws—what we now call the rule of law. Voltaire hesitated to say what organization is best for guaranteeing that rule. He was convinced that man is potentially modifiable through intellectual progress. He was impressed by the activities of Peter the Great in building a modern civilization in Russia, still more by the way Frederick and Catherine used their political powers to create a new culture. In addition, he had experienced what it was like to live under the governments of Holland, England, and the Swiss republics, and he held a high opinion of their political achievements. He admired the equality and tolerance of Holland, the public-spiritedness of England, the "democracy" of the Swiss republics. And his respect for Louis XIV and his ministers, especially Colbert, was profound.

Of the three types of government usually discussed—despotism, monarchy, democracy—Voltaire was inclined to give scant attention to despotism, which, he said, is not a natural form of government and is often related to a monarchy of which it is a perversion, just as anarchy is often related to a republic of which it, likewise, is a perversion. Voltaire did not approve of either of these excesses because he disapproved of slavery, which they foster. However, if a despotism be unavoidable, he preferred the kind in which one man rules to the kind in which there are several rulers. Still, he felt that both are bad and that this form of government is the punishment of a nation which does not have the ability to govern itself.

In practice, Voltaire seemed content to live under a monarchy. He called attention to the fact that a monarchy, or even a republic, may become a tyranny. A tyrant he defined as a sovereign who recognizes as law only his own caprice. A tyranny may be headed by one ruler or by a corps of rulers. Of course, having defined the best government as the one in which everyone obeys the laws, Voltaire had no enthusiasm for either single or plural tyrants. He did state, however, that a society is best ruled when one man is responsible (but, of course, before the law) for the administration of the state. He preferred the kind of government where the king apportions the work to his ministers but makes the final decisions. His approval of Louis XIV stemmed from the fact that he was a king who bore the burden of ruling himself; his uneasiness over Louis XV derived from the latter's tendency to leave decisions to his ministers. Still, he asserted that there is always the chance that a king, no matter what his defects, will have some good moments.

There can be no doubt, however, that, while in practice he subscribed to monarchy because it "works," in principle he tended more and more to prefer democracy because, as he said, it is nice to see freedmen make the laws by which they live. It is, also, a comfort to be free, to associate only with equals, and to know for what one pays his taxes. It is true that this form is dangerous and that it is successful only in small countries. To Bayle, who condemned Athenian democracy in favor of Macedonian monarchy, Voltaire took exception. "Le gouvernement populaire est donc par lui-même moins inique, moins abominable que le gouvernement tyrannique." The possible vice of a republic resides in the circumstance that it has too many heads and too many tails. Too many heads are harmful, and too many tails all obeying one head are ruinous. Voltaire still approved, however, a small republic happily situated, which, in spite of its defects, would never permit massacres, inquisitions, or condemnations to the galleys.

Voltaire was uncertain about the evolution of government, since he was not too sure what kind is best. He assumed that all nations in the early stage of civilization were republics. He stated that only with refinement could a government be entrusted to one ruler. But he often suggested that republics may spring from anarchy. One thing he would not accept is that governments are sustained by principles, as Montesquieu maintained. Voltaire discussed interminably whether honor is the characteristic of a monarchy, or virtue of a democracy. Since he rejected these principles, he naturally rejected the theory of transformation and corruption of governments. In his opinion, corruption is possible in all governments, regardless of principles.

In reality, though, ardent pragmatist that he was, he, like Montesquieu, accepted England as the model form of political organization. He noted that, historically, the English government until the fourteenth century followed in every respect the progression of the French. Then the two diverged. Voltaire, in his search for some explanation for this change, proposed two answers. Being an island, England did not have to maintain a large army, but it did have to maintain a navy, making life harder and the English tougher. Besides, the English have a firmer, more reflective, and more stubborn character than other peoples. Voltaire reverted to his old theory that "mœurs" and "coutumes" derive from the "esprit" of a people. Hence, as the British became more enlightened and richer, they became more lovers of freedom. But it was a freedom founded on laws and supported by a chamber of the people's representatives. Voltaire concluded that all peoples who do not establish the state upon similar principles will experience revolutions. The English by their legislation have restored to each man the rights of nature, of which he is deprived in all the other monarchies. These rights are:

freedom of person, freedom of property, freedom of speech, right to be tried by a jury and to be judged only by the precise terms of the law, and freedom to profess in peace whatever religion one wishes. The thing to remember, Voltaire emphasized, is that the ultimate purpose of political life is the adoration of God, the extension of justice to all, and the preservation of freedom as a right guaranteed to everyone. Only under these conditions can happiness be assured.

3. PHILOSOPHER, "PHILOSOPHE,"
FREE-THINKER, OR POET?

IT SHOULD by now be apparent that, contrary to the general view, Voltaire did become deeply involved with the seventeenth-century philosophers. The three who seem to have had the least impact upon him were Bacon, Hobbes, and Gassendi. Beyond the twelfth letter in the *Lettres philosophiques*, only a brief repetition of the ideas contained therein in an article in the *Dictionnaire philosophique* and some scattered references throughout Voltaire's vast work remain to show that he had any interest in Bacon at all. About the only thing which impressed Voltaire about the father of modern English philosophy was his admission that attraction was possible. Unlike D'Alembert and the *Encyclopédie*, Voltaire displayed scant enthusiasm for Bacon's classification of knowledge; indeed, he seems to have scarcely heard of it at the time of the *Lettres philosophiques*. As for any direct knowledge of Bacon's philosophy, that, too, can be ruled out. One gets the impression from Voltaire that Bacon's contribution to philosophy was completely overshadowed by Newton's. At best, Bacon was merely a "précurseur," who deserved honorable mention but no detailed study.

Hobbes was accorded only slightly better treatment by Voltaire, probably because he was reputed to be an atheist and certainly because he represented for Voltaire an a priori thinker of the Cartesian mold. Voltaire must have regarded him likewise as a "précurseur" of English philosophy, worthy to rank with Bacon but meriting no serious study. Professor Thielemann states that it is difficult to prove that Voltaire ever read Hobbes. He concludes that most of Voltaire's information concerning the author of the *De Cive* was drawn from Clarke, Bayle, or Shaftesbury, or rather from the lengthy article on Hobbes in the *Encyclopédie*. It is known that Voltaire expressed admiration for this article and that the information contained in it found its way into the *Philosophe ignorant* (1766) and the *ABC* (1768). There Voltaire was inclined to attribute to the English philosopher some importance, although the defender of the Stuarts was, in his estimation, completely overshadowed by Locke. Voltaire's silence does not occasion any great surprise, since there were so many notions in Hobbes's philosophy which ran completely counter to Voltaire's way of looking at things. In spite of his objections, though, Voltaire conceded that the "Englishman," as Descartes called him, was a "triste" philosopher whose views on political and social philosophy came close to the truth.

It is likely that Gassendi was considered by Voltaire to have played the same "précurseur" role in French philosophy that Bacon and Hobbes played in English philosophy. Voltaire may not have remained content, however, with relegating Gassendi to this position, for, in spite of his pronounced negative opinion, there is evidence that, because of Des Alleurs, who was much interested in the Aix philosopher, Voltaire himself became aware of Gassendi's importance. Indeed, on several occasions in the course of his correspondence with Des Alleurs, Voltaire encouraged him in this interest. He nevertheless stressed with distaste that Gassendi's prolixity and his tendency to avoid coming to definite conclusions were distinctly irritating. Voltaire finally decided that his only merit lay in his opposition to Descartes. Besides, he did have inclinations to naturalism, and some actually suspected him of atheistic leanings.

If these three seventeenth-century philosophers had only a minor part in turning Voltaire from poetry to philosophy and a lesser part still in giving him a philosophical foundation upon which to build his own thought, four others—Descartes, Pascal, Newton, and Locke —were all-important. The two Frenchmen he seems to have studied for the sole purpose of condemning their philosophical views. Specifically, he all but completely neglected Descartes's metaphysics; he gave no serious thought whatever to his method; he never gave any consideration to Descartes's ethics; and he condemned almost in its entirety his scientific thought. He praised him, to be sure, as a mathematician, but he deplored his refusal to use his mathematical knowledge as a means for scientific study. Voltaire never seemed to understand that Descartes should be credited with the inauguration of mechanics in modern scientific study. For him, Cartesian philosophy was a total loss because it was dogmatic, a priori, and not in conformity with observed facts. His final judgment was that, although Descartes had overthrown the nonsense of Aristotle, he had merely replaced it with his own follies.

Voltaire's estimate of Descartes tended to be so superficial and so

negative that it is only with difficulty that we can draw any significant conclusions. It is possible to state that all his reading of Descartes gave him was ample, confirmatory material to justify the
opinion Bolingbroke expressed in his letter of 1724. When it comes
to the general tendencies of Cartesianism, however, such as Brunetière presented in his "Jansénistes et Cartésiens" in the *Etudes
critiques* (doubt, identity of existence with thought, reason supreme,
break with tradition, progress, reason powerless to prove religion, relativity of morality, and immutability of the laws of nature), it must be
admitted that Voltaire was as likely to have expressed these tendencies
as his contemporaries. Indeed, Voltaire could not possibly have had
any objection to Descartes's optimism that ways could now be found
to improve indefinitely the human species. Nor could he have reasonably disapproved of his predecessor's insistence upon the rules for
evidence or the laws of motion (or, at any rate, the necessity of the
laws of motion). If he understood what was involved in Descartes's
natural science, he could not conceivably have found fault with his
mechanism, his notion of quantity, or his concept of motion. He even
came before the end of his long life to accept his occasionalism, though probably unaware that it was one of Descartes's strong
points. Thus, we are forced, according to whichever criterion we
wish to employ, to conclude either that Voltaire understood nothing
about the significant aspects of Cartesianism, or that he understood
very well that it had no significant aspects and therefore rejected
it all, or that he sincerely believed that there were no significant
aspects to it when, unaware, he was totally permeated with its consequences. What is incontestable is that Voltaire's condemnation of
Descartes's philosophy, which was full of inconsistencies, puerilities,
and false representations, could have been motivated by all the tendencies of Cartesianism, and, beyond any doubt, was motivated by
his enthusiastic acceptance of Newton.

We could say practically the same thing about Voltaire's attitude
toward Pascal. Just as Voltaire would have none of Descartes's
world, so he also would take no stock in Pascal's inner world of man.
Beginning with the doctrine of original sin, which Pascal accepted
as the only reasonable interpretation of man's duality (misery and
grandeur), Voltaire proceeded to demolish, by a common sense,
naturalistic interpretation of man's position in the universe, all the

mystery of man's existential dilemma. It is evident here that, in addition to some manifest bad faith on his part, Voltaire understood nothing about Pascal's dialectical reasoning, or about his ways to truth, or about his epistemology, or about his logic. Having rejected original sin, the immortality of the soul, and the God of Abraham, Isaac, and Jacob, Voltaire could have no basis for discussing with Pascal man's existence and nature. And yet Voltaire felt the same ambiguity, the same irony, the same paradox, the same tension in man's lot as the "illustre misanthrope" did. His emphasis on the limits of human intelligence, which both recognized, prevented Voltaire from understanding any of Pascal's transcendence but did not prevent him from seeking to acquire it. In this, as in the previous instance, the incompatibility of the two arose from Voltaire's inability to comprehend and from an external motivation.

This external motivation was Voltaire's enthusiastic infatuation with Newton's universe and with Locke's commonsense morality. Voltaire made a considerable effort to understand the philosophies of these two English philosophers. He studied both Newton's science and Locke's metaphysics point by point. What appealed to him most was their acknowledgment of limits, their acceptance of experience as the only criterion of truth, and their insistence upon the concept of weighing, measuring, calculating. Evidence is what is experienced; doubt is the accepted way of defining limits. Precisely because Newton and Locke were undogmatic, nonsystematic, and skeptical, and thought constantly in terms of specific human experience, Voltaire regarded them as masters in philosophy.

Voltaire's introduction to these four philosophers led him to express a view upon God, nature, and man which was commensurable with modern science. It was also from these four philosophers, especially Newton and Locke, that he learned to distinguish between true and false philosophy (at least, he thought he could).

There were, in addition, three other philosophers—Leibniz, Spinoza, and Malebranche—who greatly intrigued the Sage of Ferney. Voltaire's early reaction to each of these was decidedly unfavorable—Malebranche because he was a "rêveur," Spinoza because he was considered an atheist, and Leibniz because his monads, his preestablished harmony, and his "chaîne des êtres créés" were incomprehensible. In time, however, Voltaire began to understand that there was some connection between Spinoza's single substance which is God, Leibniz's monads and preestablished harmony, and Malebranche's "tout en Dieu." Indeed, Voltaire's final philosophical position was the total acceptance of Malebranche's theory, with its Leibnizian and Spinozistic implications.

Voltaire thus seems to have found through his acquaintance with the seventeenth-century philosophers a way of justifying his unremitting deism. One would say that he had sought in the philosophers a means of shoring up his defection from Catholicism and that, contrary to what one would expect, he made use of all these philosophers primarily to give a new philosophical background to the category of religion. In his own manner, he was actually continuing the task of Descartes, Pascal, and all of Descartes's followers. Even his insistence upon "la morale" as the ultimate goal of philosophical experience can now be viewed as a perfectly logical extension of these philosophies. Voltaire's philosophy was two-pronged, however, since it was both deistic-oriented and social-oriented. The former aspect can be clearly seen in his acceptance of the Newtonian universe. But what was the origin of his social philosophy? One would like to see it in his Lockean tendencies, if not in the ethics of Spinoza, and in the "morale" of Descartes and Pascal, if not in the humanitarianism of Leibniz and Malebranche. The place where all these currents met was in the *Dictionnaire* of Bayle, who likewise wanted always to reduce all things to "la morale," who was the greatest of the libertines, and whose supreme task was the union of the thinkers with the free-thinkers.

If we look closely, we can perhaps find some pattern amidst all these relationships. Voltaire made a thoroughgoing effort to bring together in one unit all the development of European thought from Montaigne to his own time. This entailed a modest background of ancient philosophical thought. The sources here were less Plato, Aristotle, and the Greek atomists than epicureanism, stoicism, and skepticism. Voltaire sought in these "philosophies" an attitude toward life, a tone, rather than a body of thought. He extracted his information and his material mostly from Horace, Lucretius, Seneca, and Cicero by way of the Horatian poets, the libertine poets, the utopian novelists, and Montaigne and his free-thinking descendents—Charron, Naudé, Patin, Sorbière, and especially Saint-Evremond. The storehouse from which he culled this material was Bayle's *Diction-naire*. The whole development of this thought consisted in giving a stoic, epicurean, skeptical tone to free-thinking as an expression and as a way of life. The characteristic of that expression was that it was free—that is, not at all formal—and, in the larger sense of the word, poetic.

To this free-thinking, which came to Voltaire via each of the movements solidly integrated in Bayle, was united the entire development of science and philosophy as it had taken place from the Renaissance to Voltaire's time. The sources here were the formal philosophers (Bacon, Gassendi, Hobbes, Descartes, Pascal, Spinoza, Leibniz, Malebranche, Locke, and Newton), the founders of modern natural science (Pomponnazzi and the Paduans, Galileo, Harvey, Mersenne, Descartes, Huyghens, Musschembrœck, Boerhaave, and Newton), and the political theorists (Machiavelli, Bodin, Grotius, Pufendorf, Hobbes, Pascal, Spinoza, and Locke). These three fountainheads of philosophy came to Voltaire through Bayle and Fontenelle, Maupertuis and Montesquieu.

Voltaire, as well as the *Encyclopédie*, gathered up all these currents of thought and responded to them more or less in the same way. His first effort was to merge formal philosophy and free-thinking; the result, however, always favored free-thinking. This inclination to free-thinking was all the more possible since Voltaire's second effort was to unite scientific with philosophical thinking. The problem here was to determine the proper proportions of metaphysics, physics, and morality. In Voltaire's opinion, the right proportions entailed restrictions in metaphysics, the adoption of the whole vast movement in science as it culminated in Newton, Locke, and the Dutch scientists, and the application of these two formal branches to the area of ethics. The integration required combination of the more systematic in philosophy with the less systematic. This was aided by Voltaire's third effort, namely, to give priority to English thought, which by nature was scientific and free-thinking, over continental philosophy, which was more formal, a priori, and systematic. Voltaire's determination to support Newton and Locke as the leaders of European thought in his time brought about a decline of metaphysical thinking and the rise of experimental, scientific, and ethical free-thought. These efforts of Voltaire fortunately could be conjugated with those of Bayle in the *Dictionnaire* and with those of D'Alembert, Diderot, and the Encyclopedists in the *Encyclopédie*. In a fundamental way, the fountainhead of all eighteenth-century thought was to be found in Bayle, Fontenelle, Voltaire, and the *Encyclopédie*. Its outstanding characteristics were its interest in science, its tendency to derive ethical consequences from that thought, and the insistence upon its encyclopedic, utilitarian nature.

The question that needs answering, therefore, is what kind of philosopher Voltaire was. There is no blinking the fact that, having turned from poetry and drama to science and philosophy, Voltaire prepared himself in a consistent fashion to become a philosopher. The nature of that preparation cannot be overstressed.

There are certain characteristics of Voltaire's thinking which may now be explained. He had a constant dislike of philosophical systems. His active distrust of all philosophers undoubtedly had its origin in this fear of philosophical systems. Usually, whether his attitude toward a particular philosopher was favorable or unfavorable depended upon the extent to which the latter had built a system of thought. He constantly extolled the less systematic philosopher to the disadvantage of the others. Voltaire's greatest approval of a philosopher was that he had no system. He accorded that approval to two philosophers—Newton and Locke—and he repeated over and over that their great merit lay in their unwillingness to construct a system. On the other hand, his strongest condemnation of Descartes, Malebranche, Leibniz, and Spinoza was based upon the rigorous systematic way in which their philosophies were organized. He indicated that the rigidity of a system devitalizes the thought and leaves no room for doubt. The ready distinction he drew between the systematic and the nonsystematic philosopher in all probability went all the way back to Montaigne, whom he constantly approved for having an "esprit primesautier" and for knowing when to doubt.

For Voltaire, this ability to doubt was likewise a criterion of the good philosopher, and he used it constantly as a touchstone in assessing the philosophical merit of his predecessors. Both Newton and Locke, for instance, he often commended on the ground that each knew when to doubt. In some way, he connected this trait as a first essential with nonsystematic philosophy; the systematizers lack this art, and, consequently, their error is to fail to stop on the brink of an abyss into which they plunge headlong. This was one of his favorite metaphors for describing the plight of such philosophers. Voltaire attributed this fault to Descartes, Malebranche, Leibniz, and Spinoza. The source of this division of philosophizing into two camps undoubtedly can be traced to the seventeenth-century struggle between the thinkers and the free-thinkers. Whereas it was not too clear where each philosopher stood in the seventeenth century, Voltaire had no hesitation whatever in clearly making his position known.

Voltaire continually expressed contempt for metaphysics and at the same time declared a corresponding approval of both physics and morality. His basic statement on metaphysics was contained in his letter of 1737 to Frederick, where he maintains that it consists of two groups of ideas: those few things which everybody with common sense knows, and a vast number of other things which nobody will ever know. His opinion on this matter seems never to have changed. In *Zadig*, for instance, he states that the protagonist knows about all that can be known in metaphysics—that is to say, very little.

Fundamental to this attitude was his oft repeated conviction that human beings can never penetrate to the first principles of reality. We can never know, for instance, what matter is, or what spirit is, or what God is. The reason for this impossibility he derived from our finiteness and the severe limitations to which each man is intellectually subjected. Voltaire became easily irritated at all philosophical attempts to pass beyond these limits. A theory, such as pre-established harmony, or occasionalism, or a definition of substance, both worried and offended him, and his usual response was to treat it as just so much jargon. A doctrine, such as the doctrine of personal interest, evoked from him immediate opposition, as if he suddenly took fright. Any attempt to define a problem in abstract terms completely upset him, to the point that he would childishly seek on the spot for all sorts of concrete examples to prove the falsity of the problem. The result of this attitude was that he proscribed all a priori methods as ineffectual in philosophy and insisted on setting forth an interminable array of concrete facts, many not at all relevant to the discussion he was presenting. The *Traité sur la tolérance*, for instance, is filled with these irrelevancies.

In spite of these adverse reactions to metaphysics, general principles, and a priori thinking, Voltaire was attracted to all these things as a moth is drawn to a lighted candle. His statement to Mme du Deffand late in life that he sought with some uneasiness the deeper meaning of things was a confession of great importance. From the *Traité de métaphysique* to the *Questions sur l'Encyclopédie* and even beyond, he discussed interminably and with an incredible superficiality, which made him such an important force in the expansion of knowledge among the masses, the existence and nature of God, the nature of the soul, the nature of matter, the question whether God can endow matter with thought, the origin of ideas, free will and determinism, the nature of good and evil, of vice and virtue, and their relationship to free will and to thought. At first, the answers to these metaphysical problems were fashioned after Locke's empiricism; where the English "métaphysicien" faltered, Voltaire borrowed from Newton, and, when the answer was not forthcoming from either, he was inclined to supply the answer himself.

Underlying Voltaire's approach was his conception of what philosophy is and what a philosopher should be. Philosophy he defined as "enlightened love of wisdom, sustained by love of God, the rewarder of virtue, and the avenger of crime." Elsewhere (M. XX, 599) he defined it as "well-conducted physical experiments, arts and trades." The wise man is he who "grinds grain, weaves cloth, makes watches, or seeks to observe the phenomena of natural history." True philosophy, he stated, consists in knowing when to stop and in never proceeding without a sure guide (M. XXII, 205). It is virtue, the health of the soul. It consoles, makes virtue admired, and fanaticism and superstition detested. It quiets the turmoil in the world caused by superstition. It has strengthened kings, prevented schisms, and allayed fears of disaster. It mellows manners and customs. It calms religious fury, works for the suppression of the Inquisition, and makes religious disputes look ridiculous. It is evident that Voltaire thought of philosophy in terms of science, art, and even trades. He deemed it useful in stabilizing the passions of men, particularly in religion. He seemed to think of it even in terms of a new religion which fosters belief in the reality of God and love of one's fellow-

men. But, most of all, he looked upon it as an activity which im-
proves the lot of mankind, relieves suffering, nurtures tolerance, and
in every respect makes living on this earth more enjoyable, more
reasonable, more endurable, and, above all, happier.

A philosopher, consequently, is a lover of wisdom and truth. He
instructs men in virtue and teaches them moral truth. He is a lover
of mankind, who holds firm against adversity and inculcates a pure
morality by instructing man in the ways of justice. The first philosophers were poets: they were seers, they pointed the way to the future. Present-day philosophers partake of the same privilege. They
are lovers of wisdom, seekers after truth, models of virtue, and they
give mankind lessons in moral truth. They are not inspired—Voltaire made a clear-cut distinction between the seer as inspired poet
and the seer as leader in public opinion. In his view, opinion governs
men's actions, and philosophers, who are in reality leaders in public
opinion, little by little change men for their own good by universally
changing their opinions. They must make the truth known and conceal their own persons (M. XLIII, 318). They all have different ideas
on the principles of things, but they have all taught the same morality.
They have all wanted to make man better and, to this end, have
provided him with examples of virtue and lessons in moral truth.
By enlightening the human mind, through the destruction of superstition, they have served the prince, the citizens, and the laws of the
land. As a result, they have transformed beasts into men, contributed
to the triumph of reason, and "adouci les mœurs."

The philosopher who would wish to achieve his goal must have a
strategy. Voltaire's strategy consisted of two separate devices: concealment and most careful planning. Voltaire was capable of concealing his thought by ambiguous and even contradictory statement,
thereby giving the impression of superficial or naïve thinking. He
was also capable of laying the most careful plans for the effective
presentation of his ideas. In this respect, he resembled Descartes,
who adopted early in life the device Larvatus prodeo. Some of this
maneuvering was undoubtedly the product of prudence in the face
of a severe censorship, but it can be traced back also to the close relationship which Voltaire wished to establish between thinking and
acting. When he stated, for instance, that Rousseau wrote only to
write while he, Voltaire, wrote to produce action, he was expressing

his conviction that the end result of thinking is doing. The point was not that Rousseau's thought was ineffective; rather, it was that, in putting his ideas on paper, Voltaire always calculated, measured, and weighed the results beforehand. Rousseau paid attention to the expression of the thought, rather than to its "portée." Voltaire concerned himself not only with the idea but with the action it would lead to.

Consequently, thought became at times for Voltaire an instrument which had been carefully designed to produce a particular result. Naturally, Voltaire was rarely frank in disclosing his plans of procedure or the results he anticipated by pursuing a particular line of thought. Nor was he very explicit about how obvious contradictions in his thought could be reconciled. On one occasion, after the turmoil of *De l'esprit* (1758), he wrote a series of letters to Helvétius, urging him to prepare short brochures on interesting subjects and suggesting that he publish them at his own expense from a clandestine press of his own and distribute them to a limited number of interested parties. Voltaire added that it was thus that the *Abrégé de Jean Meslier* had been circulated among the public. On another occasion, he outlined his views in the campaign he was conducting against *l'Infâme*. To Damilaville, he wrote in 1764: "Je crois que la meilleure méthode de tomber sur l'infâme, est de paraître n'avoir nulle envie de l'attaquer; de débrouiller un peu le chaos de l'antiquité; de tâcher de jetter quelque intérêt; de répandre quelque agrément sur l'histoire ancienne; de faire voir combien on nous a trompé en tout; de montrer combien ce qu'on croit ancien est moderne, combien ce qu'on nous a donné pour respectable est ridicule; de laisser le lecteur tirer lui-même les conséquences" (B. 11140). Brumfitt, who quotes this statement, regards it as explanatory of the intention of *La Philosophie de l'histoire*. It seems to me to be indicative of Voltaire's purpose in all his vast production after *Candide*.

Voltaire, however, had devised a more brilliant program which contained not only specific rules of action but a general declaration of intention and a broad blueprint for the organization and development of the Enlightenment. A statement of it can be found in the Miller papers at the Bibliothèque Nationale (N. Ac. fr. 4822, f. 68):

La seule vengeance qu'on puisse prendre de l'absurde insolence avec laquelle on a condamné tant de vérités en divers temps est de publier souvent ces mêmes vérités pour rendre service à ceux même qui les combattent. Il est à désirer que ceux qui sont riches veuillent bien consacrer quelque argent à faire imprimer des choses utiles. Des libraires ne doivent point les débiter; la vérité ne doit pas être vendu comme les prêtres vendent le baptême et les enterrements.

Deux ou trois cents exemplaires distribués à propos entre les mains des sages peuvent faire beaucoup de bien sans bruit et sans danger. Il paraît convenable de n'écrire que des choses simples, courtes, intelligibles aux esprits les plus grossiers; que le vrai seul et non l'envie de briller caractérise ces ouvrages; qu'ils confondent le mensonge et la superstition et qu'ils apprennent aux hommes à être justes et tolérants. Il est à souhaiter qu'on ne se jette point dans la métaphysique que peu de personnes entendent, et qui fournit toujours des armes aux ennemis. Il est à la fois plus sûr et plus agréable de jetter du ridicule et de l'horreur sur les disputes théologiques, de faire sentir aux hommes combien la moralité est belle et les dogmes impertinents, et de pouvoir éclairer à la fois et le chancelier et le cordonnier. On n'est parvenu en Angleterre à déraciner la superstition que par cette voie.

Ceux qui ont été quelquefois les victimes de la vérité en laissant débiter par des libraires des ouvrages condamnés par l'ignorance et la mauvaise foi, ont un intérêt sensible à prendre le parti qu'on propose; ils doivent sentir qu'on les a rendus odieux aux superstitieux et que les méchants se sont joints à ces superstitieux pour décréditer ceux qui rendraient service au genre humain.

Il paraît donc absolument nécessaire que les sages se déffendent, et ils ne peuvent se justifier qu'en éclairant les hommes; ils peuvent former un corps respectable au lieu d'être des membres désunis que les fanatiques et les sots hâchent en pièces.

Il est bien honteux que la philosophie ne puisse faire chez nous ce qu'elle fesait chez les anciens; elle rassemblait les hommes, et la superstition a seule chez nous ce privilège.

The short essay, the limited edition, the method of distributing copies among a carefully selected number of wise men, the avoidance of metaphysical discussion, the insistence that the language be simple and intelligible to the most uneducated, the determination to discredit theological discussions by treating them with ridicule and horror, to confound the superstitious, to show how much more important morality is than dogma, and to use these pamphlets to educate both the nobleman and the tradesman—these suggestions form altogether a total program of enlightenment. Voltaire's central concerns are how the writer can be of service to humanity, how he can defend himself against the unjust accusation of the superstitious and the wicked, how he may teach men to be just and tolerant, and how he should unite with his fellow writers in order to combat their common enemy.

4. VOLTAIREANISM AND THE
LIFE OF THE SPIRIT

IT IS NOT SUFFICIENT to try to know what kind of a philosopher Voltaire was. We have to push on and inquire also what his philosophy was. Actually, it does not help very much to assert that we are dealing with a philosopher, a free-thinker, a philosophe, and a poet. Such a statement may serve to explain the quality of Voltaire's mind, but it does little to express the nature of his philosophical thought, and it is likely to raise the suspicion that the distinctions have become so complicated that we are dealing with no philosopher at all. This is precisely the position taken by many of Voltaire's biographers and by all of the professional philosophers. Usually, the explanation given is that, although the Patriarch had some interesting ideas, he cannot be said to have developed a coherent body of thought, and his ideas cannot be arranged either systematically or logically. No one ever forgets Faguet's designation of Voltaire as a "chaos d'idées claires."

And yet we are dealing with a man who spared himself no end of trouble to become acquainted with the long line of philosophers of the preceding century. He consulted their works continually and discussed interminably what he considered their philosophy. Special aspects of each he treated with careful consideration. He balanced the thought of one against the thought of another and took up time and time again the problems which are the perennial staple of philosophy. He treated these subjects with great seriousness and honesty. When he did not understand what a particular problem was or how a preceding philosopher had tried to settle it, he, like Locke, readily confessed that it was beyond his grasp. Nearly always, such problems were beyond the limits of any human mind. Curiously, Voltaire, in spite of his avowed incomprehension, was always trying to get some deeper insight into these problems. He admitted to having an abiding interest in metaphysics and actually wrote treatises upon its problems. When philosophy became primarily physics and the science of nature, he trained himself to master its accomplishments and introduced them almost single-handedly to the French public. He proclaimed repeatedly that his aim was to reduce all thought to "la morale." And he was the first to use the term "philosophy of history." It would be grossly unfair to deny him a hearing as a bona fide philosopher just because he often expressed himself simply and unambiguously and because he refused to offer a system of philosophy. The thing to note, it would seem, is that Voltaire's inability to qualify as a philosopher derived from the simple fact that philosophy was no longer a subject of humanistic discourse but, rather, a way of looking at any vital, humanistic subject. It was, therefore, concerned with the way the mind enters upon the adventure of living as a means of grasping the inner reality of the intellectual act. Voltaire, like his contemporaries, could not resist the thrill of this dynamic activity.

It is for this reason that, whenever an attempt is made to characterize Voltaire's philosophy, it almost always is presented as a bundle of diverse ideas on all sorts of subjects, expressed with more than ordinary wit, or as an aggregation of groups of classified ideas revolving around the categories of living and thinking—science, religion, aesthetics, politics, economics, society, morality—or, finally, as a way of looking at things, an attitude toward life, a tendency, a principle, or a set of tendencies and principles—a "way of life," as we say. Since every man is subject to these unorganized reflections and since our general understanding of these things is that they lead nowhere, philosophically speaking, we are inclined to attribute to them a minor significance in Voltaire's case, too. This could be a mistake. Voltaire's way of thinking, like that of the Enlightenment as a whole, has transformed our general way of thinking and acting. After what was done to thought in the period preceding the French Revolution, it is impossible to attribute to thought a purely reflective role in the affairs of life. It must now be accorded a dynamic role in the creation of all things pertaining to the spirit of man.

In spite of these considerations, we always revert, when we are forced to discuss Voltaire's philosophy, to a set pattern. We begin by stating that Voltaire's philosophy was Voltaireanism. When it comes to designating what Voltaireanism is, we are likely to say that it is not a philosophy at all in the strict sense, since it was not built in any systematic way. It is, rather, a relatively long list of loosely constructed thoughts, which sprang from a mind marvelously alert, but chaotic and terribly disorganized. We concede, however, that on occasion these thoughts are expressed with great clarity, often very wittily and ironically, and sometimes very ambiguously. When we are pushed to give at least some sort of academic order to them, we are prone to adopt an arbitrary, abstract arrangement—under key words, for instance, or in some sort of dictionary or encyclopedic plan, or under all sorts of indiscriminate rubrics. Thus, we break this Voltaireanism up into subjects (freedom, justice, soul, state) or into categories which describe areas of philosophical interest (moral, social, scientific, historical, political, economic, aesthetic) or into the more classical divisions (metaphysics, physics, ethics, and aesthetics). Then, after we have taken all this trouble to put Voltaire's thoughts in order, we usually make some feeble attempt to prove that, whereas the thoughts are often not very original and at the present moment not very valuable, there are a certain number (such as the ideas on freedom and justice, for instance) which are still quite relevant to our concerns today. There are even some biographers of Voltaire who would submit that many of Voltaire's thoughts (on "la morale," or on history, or on drama, or on humanism) are important philosophically. There are even a few who would venture to establish some sort of consistency in that thought, though not much continuity and certainly no organicity.

At this point, we usually begin to make distinctions. Although Voltaire, we say, in the accepted definition of the word, cannot really be considered a philosopher, it would be fitting to call him an essayist, a journalist, an encyclopedist, a writer, or a free-thinker. The difference is embedded in the distinction we make between the systematic thinkers we call "philosophers" and the indiscriminate thinkers we call "philosophes." The latter we attempt to distinguish from the free-thinkers, as well as from the philosophers. To be sure, in a way they were the original free-thinkers, but for some reason they did not succeed in becoming philosophers. This way of looking at the matter complicates our understanding of the Enlightenment a good deal. If our aim is to define the philosophy of this philosophical age, it can only be disconcerting to discover that it was expounded by "Philosophes" who are Encyclopedists and who are notorious for their lack of philosophy.

When we reach this point, we become mildly frustrated. It does not seem very significant that Voltaire should have turned from a career in poetry and drama to a career in philosophy only to discover that he had no philosophy. A "philosophe" without philosophy rather resembles a poet with no poetic talent.

We therefore make some effort to improve his philosophical image. Usually, we resort to the explanation that, although he had no philosophy, he did have some general philosophical tendencies. He was interested in the activities of the mind, curious about intellectual matters, terribly critical of the ideas of others, and sometimes skeptical about his own views. Occasionally, he wondered whether valid views were even possible. He always wanted ideas to be confined within the limits of experience. What the human mind could demonstrate as existing he was prepared to accept as a fact. He granted these things validity because they conformed to common sense. Other things which could not possibly conform to common sense he relegated to the realm of faith, either ignoring them thereafter or treating them with a false piety, although he really was not too consistent in his treatment of matters of faith, as we shall see. In principle, we commend this attitude because, as we say, it separates the realm of faith from that of reason. Finally, thoughts connected with the world of facts he respected; those involving abstractions, metaphysics, or transcendence he abhorred. His philosophy was, therefore, a kind of positivism, pragmatic and common-sense, devoid of idealism, oriented toward material prosperity, happiness, and moderation in all things. In general, it is the kind of philosophy which would commend itself to a middle-class citizen.

Some of us find this way of presenting his philosophy a bit trite. Those who make this complaint usually finish by assigning to him a philosophy of some particular subject: religion (deism), art (neo-classicism), science (Newtonianism), history (historical materialism), morality (humanism). This sort of approach always creates the impression that his fame rests on his achievement in one area alone, his thoughts in the other areas being just so much deadweight. It is the kind of a philosophy which would commend itself to a modest professor of one of the humanistic disciplines.

It is obvious, in any event, that Voltaire prepared himself diligently to become either a philosopher, a free-thinker, an encyclopedic man, a "philosophe," or a poet—or all of these things. It is obvious, too, that his preparation qualified him to become a critic of previous philosophers, a historian of ideas, a defender of certain particular ideas, and an initiator of certain thoughts of great importance for the welfare of man. As a philosopher, he had a method of approaching truth, and he used his method to formulate a body of truths.

These truths are always derived from experience, they always possess a utility for man and his society, and they always concern relationships between man's inner world, the outer world of nature, the forces in control of the universe, the society of which he is a part, the institutions of that society, the things which it has created, and its ways of acting and becoming. It is in these relationships that the sources of human experience are found.

Voltaire demands for every man the right to examine with his mind the validity of each experience and to extract what is useful from it, for himself first of all and then for his fellowman. This means that the human mind has the ability and the right to pronounce upon the validity of human experience and to accept or reject that experience as useful or useless. The experience is derived from the world of God, the world of nature, and the world of man. Man, however, cannot participate to any great extent in the world of God, since He is infinite and man is by nature finite. It suffices that he can know valid reasons for God's existence and recognize that God has given him reason to conduct himself in this life. In the world of nature, which is the source of his scientific experience, he can do a little better; that is, his knowledge of nature, while not limitless by any means, is respectable. It can be augmented, and it can be useful to him and to society. However much he measures, weighs, and calculates, though, he can never expect to know the ultimate principles of nature. The closest he can come to a principle is the conviction that the universe is an orderly, stable system in which scientific laws are immutable. The world of man is unquestionably the source of his moral experience. It is a broad world, open to all sorts of human activities, intensely interesting to the individual who will use his God-given reason to penetrate it, to understand it, to use it, and to enjoy it. It, too, is a world of relationships: whenever they reach into God's world, they become obscure, uncertain and ambiguous, because of the infinity of God and man's finiteness;

whenever they reach into the world of nature, they become less obscure and ambiguous than in God's world but not, for all that, terribly clear. This is especially true when man attempts to understand the meaning, rather than the nature, of the phenomena. It is in the world of man that these relationships offer the greatest chance for understanding. Man can learn a lot about his relations with his fellowman in all the human sciences: the arts, the trades, the manners and customs of the group, the analysis of the instrument for knowing, the history of human relationships in the past and what they have produced for the good of society, what society has contributed to man's ways of thinking and acting, the institutions which have been created and what advantages they have given man and society. It is, unfortunately, true that the ultimate purpose of all these relationships cannot be fully apparent to man, because of his finiteness. It is true, also, that not everything in these relationships is useful or desirable and that they are often terribly confusing because of the human qualities of tension, contradiction, paradox, and irony. Man has it within himself to be evil or to create evil, but he likewise has the power to be good or to create good. Enlightenment in his world is a wonderful source of human power.

We know these relationships by experience, because we live them every day. The human mind applied to the arts can create beautiful things, applied to the trades can manufacture beautiful and useful objects, applied to society can produce political, economic, social, religious, and educational organizations which will be of great benefit to mankind. Progress is possible in all of these areas; it depends upon the increase of knowledge and upon the ability to reduce evil, disharmony, ignorance, superstition, and confusion. If man has the courage to act upon that knowledge, he can, provided he and his fellow citizens will unite, create a civilization which, though it may not offer an unlimited felicity, will make life quite enjoyable through the good things it produces. Happiness is possible, even if it is never perfect.

The most significant precept Voltaire deduces from this view is the necessity of action which derives from consciousness of knowing. Facts as facts are practically valueless; to be worth anything, they must be turned into ideas. But ideas as ideas are not very important either, unless they can be turned into what we call theories and doctrines, which are in reality constructs of knowledge, plans of action, structures of possibilities, blueprints for reform. Life must be understood in the light of what we know about it. We must derive from it the "Idea" of its content. This "Idea" is the generating force of the new model upon which we are permitted to build a new life. It is, in every sense of the word, an "interior" model—a vision of things which can be, but only if man has the courage to restructure, to revise, to remake that which he has hitherto accepted as his internal model. This project naturally involves rejecting old relationships, as well as establishing new relationships. "Préjugés" must be crushed before new "rapports" can be adopted. Always change is king, revision is a new sort of vision, reform is a new kind of form, revolution is the actualization of new kinds of possibilities. These things—thought, work, energy, action, cultivation of one's garden, the exercise of one's talents—are not only sure remedies for vice, boredom, and need; they are guarantees against injustice and oppression, and the only possible insurance of freedom and tolerance. But these activities, looked at in the right human perspective, are just so many steps in the creative process; they entail not only what the philosopher thinks but what the poet feels. The act of thought transformed into reflective thinking and being is as much a poetic principle as a philosophical pursuit.

What characterizes both enterprises is the creative process. Always the problem is how to pass from the raw product of existence to an understanding of the "Idea" which suffuses that raw product, to the making of an interior model which carries within itself its own inner meaning, to the restructuring of the idea and the model until they have created a new form and endowed it with the power of taking on a new and vital inner meaning. Always within the process is working that "esprit" which is "l'esprit humain," always that "esprit humain" is being expressed by that "esprit" which is the wit of man, his response to *his* life, always that "human spirit" and that "wit" are creating new interpretations of the spirit of society and of the age. We must remember, though, Voltaire constantly warns: there is no spirit of man without the existence of God, without fraternity and social responsibility, without that insignificant but somewhat admirable little monad called man, who, on occasion, can say *yes* to God-given happiness and *no* to the injustice of the universe.

CONCLUSION

IN THE LONG journey we have made from Voltaire's choice of a career to his final philosophical position, we have been able to mark the crucial moments in his intellectual life. It is certain that, intellectually, Voltaire took his origin in four movements which were inaugurated in the sixteenth century and which extended throughout the seventeenth down to his entry into the field of literature around 1719-1723.

The first of these movements was the poetic current of the seventeenth century which began with Théophile de Viau and continued throughout the century with Des Barreaux, Dehénault, Blot, Mme Deshoulières, Chaulieu, and La Fare. The verse that came from the pens of these poets was Horatian in style, genre, and mood and at the same time free-thinking in attitude. At the time Voltaire entered upon his career as a poet, this poetry was being practiced at the Temple.

The second movement was the development of a type of fiction which was initiated by Rabelais in the sixteenth century, renewed by Cyrano de Bergerac in the seventeenth, and practiced extensively between 1650 and 1720 by a long line of writers including Vairasse, Foigny, Gilbert, Lahontan, Fénelon, and Tyssot de Patot. The thrust of this fiction was twofold, concentrating, on the one hand, upon constant satire of conditions as they existed (religious, political, social, moral, scientific, and aesthetic) and, on the other, upon creation of more ideal, utopian conditions offering greater opportunities for enjoyment of the good life.

The third movement was the wave of philosophical and free-thinking activity which embraced, among the philosophers, Bacon, Gassendi, Hobbes, Descartes, Pascal, Spinoza, Leibniz, Malebranche, Locke, Newton, and Bayle, and, among the free-thinkers, Charron, Naudé, G. Patin, Lamothe le Vayer, Saint-Evremond, and Fontenelle. Contributing together to this vast outpouring of ideas were the most magnificent group of European philosophers ever assembled in a century and a corresponding group of able free-thinkers, who had adopted Montaigne's free and easy essay style, as well as his manner of refraining from dogmatic, systematic philosophy.

The fourth movement was the production of a classical, formal literature in the seventeenth century which was brought to perfection by Corneille, Molière, Racine, La Fontaine, and Boileau.

Essentially, these four currents comprised the two greatest achievements of the seventeenth century: its literary art and its philosophical thought. Each of these achievements had both a formal, rather dogmatic, somewhat arbitrary side to it and a rather informal, free and easy, unsystematic aspect as well. Free-thinking coexisted with formal, systematic philosophy in the realm of thought, and an informal, free-thinking poetry thrived alongside a more formal, systematic mode of expression in the realm of letters.

It should be observed that these four currents were all brought together by Bayle in his *Dictionnaire historique et critique*. The Rotterdam philosopher and his dictionary consequently furnish an excellent example of the attempt which was made at the turn of the century to unite not only the literature and thought of the passing age but also the two kinds of literature and thought of the period. Voltaire did not absorb these currents from Bayle at the beginning of his career, however; it was only after 1733 that he appeared to realize just how valuable Bayle could be in this respect. For the decade 1713-1723 and even for the subsequent decade 1723-1733, Voltaire made his choice among the four currents according to his own personal interests and the milieu in which he found himself. He began by adopting as his masters the Horatian poets, along with Horace and Virgil, and the great classical writers, especially Boileau and Racine. That is, he sought distinction in lyric poetry in imitation of Horace, Boileau, and La Fontaine and in the epic and drama chiefly in imitation of Corneille and Racine. The encouragement for this interest in the epic, in tragedy, and in *épîtres*, satires, and odes came initially from his Jesuit teachers at Louis-le-Grand, from his friends at the Temple, especially Chaulieu and La Fare, and from the social environment in which he moved. The other two currents did not enlist Voltaire's attention at all until the English sojourn, and really not in any profound way until the beginning of the Cirey period. Indeed, for twenty-five years, his commitment to lyric, dramatic, and epic poetry was genuine, enthusiastic, and all-embracing. During that quarter of a century, he was generally accepted as the greatest French poet of the time, and by many as the greatest French poet of all time.

The outstanding quality of that poetry was that it was Horatian in both theory and practice. Voltaire followed the precepts of the *De Arte poetica* as a means of producing superior epic and dramatic poetry, and he imitated Horace's satiric, epicurean, and stoic tone in his lyric verse. In all of this, he did just what the time was doing; he merely did it better than his contemporaries, although not so well as his predecessors.

Unfortunately, though, there were counter-forces which limited his success. The magnificent poetry and thought of the previous age in France were both menaced by a decline: geometry was killing poetry, dogma was killing thought. As a consequence, prose was replacing poetry. Voltaire refused for twenty-five years to capitulate to this fashion. He struggled hard to renew the classical, traditional genres, and he even endeavored to infuse into them a larger philosophical content. In these efforts, he was certainly not unsuccessful, whether we judge by the esteem his contemporaries accorded him or by the opinion he held of himself. There were apparent, nonetheless, moments of hesitation, too many attempts to justify his poetic production, some evidence that he was artistically uneasy.

His English experience considerably modified his perspective. In contrast with France, England appeared fundamentally a country of thinkers. Voltaire, like all who crossed the Channel from Europe, was struck by this trait. It was especially pronounced at this particular moment, since Locke and Newton had now become the outstanding philosophers of Europe. Voltaire did not find English letters, which were becoming more classic in the French sense of the term, so different from French letters. They were merely, in his opinion, of an inferior quality. The figures of the past he found only interesting, and he scanned them for what each could offer to palliate his own country's decline in letters. Shakespeare, for instance, he thought, could offer scenes and techniques which would modernize the French theatre and give it more action and spectacle. His English literary companions, though, hardly differed from him. They, too, were Horatian, satiric, epicurean with a touch of stoicism, and, above all, moralists. Voltaire surrendered completely to Locke, Newton, and Pope.

He went much further than simple imitation, for he pushed his efforts toward the penetration of this new civilization. He placed it in contrast with the civilization which he represented. At first, the comparison appeared all in favor of the newly encountered civilization. He discovered, though, that what was infinitely more important was the merging of these two civilizations, of English thought and French art, in the interest of creating a European civilization. To undertake this project seriously, however, required that he first learn more about the making of a civilization: what elements enter into its composition and what gives it consistency, coherence, continuity, and organic unity.

Voltaire set about his task in a methodical fashion. There is evidence to indicate that he first attempted a social penetration. He wanted to get to know these strange people who, in spite of, or perhaps because of their peculiar habits, had now become the leaders of Europe. His first impression was that they were full of contradictions, so that everything characteristic of them seemed to contrast with French traits. Voltaire tried to reduce their peculiarities to some dominant way of life. He decided that they were *public-spirited*—that is, they expressed a "spirit" which was social, communal, and fraternal. He assumed that there must be some relationship between this way of life and their manners and customs. Since the English were a nation of thinkers, he assumed further that there must be some relationship between their thought and their action. In some vague way, he devised two rules: what people think is the source of their manners and customs, and these latter are the determinants of their "esprit." Thought is the instrument which gives direction to life (*mœurs et coutumes*) and through the activities of a people (*manières*) produces a "spirit" which is the achieved ideal of that life. "Esprit" is, in reality, both an instrument for creating and the action created. Voltaire discovered that, in a people, it works through manners and customs, arts and sciences, political and social institutions. To get to know the inhabitants of a country, the critic must work in the same way. He must first analyze the nature of their thought, the quality of their action, the goal which their action is designed to achieve, and the modifications which are introduced into their manners, their arts, their institutions, their sciences; then he must reduce these intellectual activities with their creative results to some sort of common denominator (which, in the case of England, was freedom). This is the procedure anyone who wants to penetrate a civilization must follow.

It was a new kind of history—the history of how man thinks himself into being, how he achieves through the full use of intelligence in all the manifestations of his being the goals which he sets for himself. For instance, a *public-spirited* people motivated by constant *reflection* cannot fail to produce a freedom of thought which, in turn, will be *reflected* in every manifestation of life. It is this free-thinking which releases within man all of his pent-up possibilities for creating—in art, religion, politics, economics, society, morality. Nowhere, not even in the magnificent introductions to the *Essai sur les mœurs*, does Voltaire systematically explain the nature of "esprit" as instrument of action and "esprit" as resultant creative activity, but that is what the *Lettres philosophiques* and the *Essai sur les mœurs* are all about, as even the most cursory reading will show.

This new direction which Voltaire took following his English experience has probably been incorrectly interpreted in the past. Insistence that Voltaire tried to adapt Shakespeare or English drama to French classical tragedy, or the lyrical English poets to French lyrical poetry, or the satiric, utopian novel or the sentimental novel or the realistic novel to French fiction, while perfectly proper in its own way, distorts the real significance of his experience. There can be no doubt that Voltaire, ever alert to innovations in literature and realizing precisely the necessity of renewing French literature at that moment with foreign literary practices, did not scruple to use a Shakespearean ghost or to increase dramatic action on the French stage. The results of these experiments were rather minimal, however. More significant was Voltaire's recognition that the origin of English vitality, in all aspects of English life, lay in English thought, for it led him to suspect that his own literature could best be perfected by enriching the content of French thought with the content of English thought. Locke, Newton, and Mandeville therefore became more essential than Shakespeare, Milton, and even Pope. France, he felt, needed particularly a deeper philosophical background and, above all, awareness that a philosophical background can support all the manifestations of a vital civilization.

Hence, although we have seen that Voltaire did not return from England a "sage," he did come back with some rather well-defined notions about the necessity of transforming the underlying thought of France by introducing into it the ideas of Newton, Locke, Clarke, Shaftesbury, Mandeville, and Bolingbroke. He likewise had now a clearer view of the necessity for studying the relationships between philosophical thought and creative activity if one would penetrate the civilization of a country. Finally, he divined, though dimly, that history was the key which could open up the study of man's possibilities and at the same time make these possibilities actualities. His program for adopting philosophy as the core of his activity, rather than poetry, specifically entailed the further study of English civilization, culminating in the *Lettres philosophiques*, the elaboration of this new kind of history concerned with the activity of the human mind, the introduction of two English philosophers, and the merging of English thought with French art in the interest of promoting a European civilization.

In order to carry out his new program, Voltaire had to reeducate himself completely. That, as we have seen, was the meaning of Cirey to him. The Jesuit education at Louis-le-Grand was no longer adequate; to tackle the problems attendant upon the creation of the new intellectual world he envisioned, additional resources were required. This new education had to be scientific: natural science was to be based on empirical data and social science was to utilize the strict empirical methods of the natural sciences. Voltaire still kept, however, the conviction that physics and the moral sciences must be based upon a small number of metaphysical principles. The combination of metaphysics and physics, history and the human sciences, offered ample means for bringing together the knowledge of both the external world and the internal world of man, so that he could assume responsibility for his goals. The results were to be viewed in the context of civilization, which was now entrusted to the human mind. The simple formula underlying the program was that ideas are the source of vital, creative power, and man becomes what he knows.

It was in elaborating this new education that Voltaire entered upon an activity of the greatest diversity, embracing Newtonian physics, Lockean psychology, and a whole new approach to history, politics, economics, and sociology, all of it interpreted in terms of a new conception of moral man. One of the effects of this activity was the replacement of older, accepted philosophies by newer ones. Descartes's philosophy of science was supplanted by Newton's. Pascal's concept of the nature of man yielded to Locke's and Shaftesbury's. Bossuet's conception of the march of history and the role of Providence gave way to a more mundane point of view which regarded the human mind as a far more dynamic instrument for progress. Moral man took the place of theological man, and encyclopedic man assumed a position of preeminence. The goals of life were reduced in perspective, though not in the challenge they presented. Everything was now encompassed by limits, it is true. But these limits were by no means restrictive; they were merely more realistic. What was of the greatest significance was that everything had been consciously subjected to thought; whatever was touched became philosophical. But, in some curious way, when thought turned into moral power, it preserved some spiritual quality, which was the ability to create. Now, however, creation was within the realm of man.

The human mind has an ability to destroy equal to its ability to create. To the student preoccupied with Voltaire's activities, this ability to destroy seems to have been more readily used than the ability to create. Whatever had not been subjected to the scrutiny of the human mind had now to be tested. If it could not pass the test, it had to be rejected, since it was by definition a "préjugé," a "superstition." Voltaire attacked these beliefs with such ferocity and repeated his objections to them so many times that we might easily be persuaded that his whole work was one gigantic denial. It is certainly true that in every category of living—religion, art, government, economy, society, science—Voltaire, like his contemporaries, could find an abundance of "préjugés." But he could find an equal abundance of new, meaningful relationships. The problem was to create with these relationships a new form of life. This task required not only a rearrangement of relationships within the categories but also a realignment among the categories. Voltaire's project of reducing everything to "la morale," for instance, entailed a tremendous transformation in the relationships of the categories, which had theretofore been organized within a scheme which reduced everything to the glory of God. We look at these massive transformations these days as reforms, and we understand that they constitute ameliorations, as indeed they may; but they imply, more importantly still, changes in the way of life, a reshaping of the meaning and goals of existence, and even the creation of conditions which have never existed in these terms. In strict academic parlance, what is thus brought into being is a new "form" of life, the result of a new "esprit." And, since it is irrevocably true that one makes his life as one creates a work of art, this new life structure is equally a new art form.

We have to be extraordinarily careful here, though, or else we might leave the facile impression that Voltaire created a whole new universe with no more than a simple "fiat lux" nonchalantly expressed. I think he would have liked to have done so, but, for humans, things are not that easy. We have to "weigh, measure, calculate" our every move. We have to rearrange, readjust, revise, reaffirm, reconsider, and, finally, "relate" our rearrangements, our readjustments, our revisions, our reaffirmations, and our reconsiderations to ourselves. If, perchance, they fit together organically, we restructure them and hope they will "reform" themselves.

The meaning of Cirey to Voltaire was inseparable from his reeducation, but the ultimate importance of Cirey to his time lay in the organic way he restructured his world. Voltaire reexamined, revised, and restructured just about every category of life. In religion, to use one example, he repudiated as prejudice all dogma, all creed, all miracles, prophecies, and all the testimony of martyrs; he denied that the historical development of Christianity provided any proof of its divinity, and he questioned the morality of the Church, as well as its organization and its mission. He used the concept of a stable universe to combat the idea of miracles and all supernatural religious manifestations and brought the events of history to bear in challenging the notions of a divine Christian morality. He drew his arguments against the divinity of the Christian religion from all fields of knowledge, concluding in a commonsense, pragmatic, realistic way that the Church was "infâme" and that this expression of religion was a prejudice.

He did not conclude, though, that God was a myth. Voltaire's belief in God was genuine, sincere, passionately naïve, and as all-embracing as Spinoza's. Though it might sometimes be vague, contradictory, and self-defeating, he never abandoned his belief. In fact, he regarded the existence of God as the one absolutely necessary thing in the universe. Without God, he felt, the universe would be impossible. Curiously, though, his ideas of God and His relationship to man seem inconsistent. He wanted to think of God as being all-good, all-wise, all-powerful, and, above all, friendly to man, but, when he held this conception up to the light of human experience, he had some difficulty in affirming it. Moreover, his assumption that God acts justly and his hope that He shares with humans a small part of His freedom and power ran counter to his firm conviction that God works only through general laws. Voltaire's faith was not at all comparable to that of the great religious leaders. It was, in fact, easily shaken by human and natural events. That is not a tribute to his rational stability, though it may be a point in favor of his personal sensibility. At all events, to the extent that deism could have a philosophical foundation, Voltaire was to that extent philosophical.

His attitude toward the other philosophical problems of theology —the immortality of the soul, free will and determinism, the nature of matter and spirit, time and space—wavered in very unphilosophical fashion. He never seems to have had any clear notions concerning the soul and its mortality or immortality, and he had only one clear conception of free will, which he accommodated to the necessities of determinism. He eventually adopted the conventional philosophical opinion of his time concerning matter and created his own myth about spirit. And he had no fixed views on either time or space, both of which, he held, involve aspects of infinity that are beyond the capability of the human mind to grasp.

He did, however, claim a body of opinions on human good and evil and a fixed body of thought upon "la morale." He believed firmly in the notions of justice, freedom, and social beneficence. He accepted as essential to all morality the notion of natural law, which he defined quite succinctly as "love of God and love of one's fellowman." Love of one's fellowman he interpreted as "bienveillance" and, in times of stress, as "bienfaisance." His sympathy for others in moments of human suffering was genuine, easily irrational, sometimes to the point of revolt. This natural law he believed to be common to all men—not an innate idea, but a trait of human nature possessed by all at maturity. Good and evil, he felt, can be measured in social terms: good is what contributes to the group's welfare, evil is what contributes to its damage. The value of actions, consequently, varies according to the manners and customs of the group. Voltaire nevertheless insisted that some form of the Golden Rule is necessary for the effective life of a society. His belief in the possibility of fraternity was often irrational, but sincere and all-embracing. The brotherhood of man, he was sure, has a rational foundation in the organization of society, since it derives from the social instinct, which he held to be common to all men—so common, in fact, that he denied the possibility of a state of nature in which man lived a solitary life.

Voltaire had no illusions about the nature of man. He did not, it is true, consider that man is born evil. But he held that society may make him evil, and he found that evil rather widespread. He attributed it, much as the seventeenth-century moralists had done, either to selfishness or to the search for personal advantage. He was just as likely to ascribe it, though, to "superstition," "préjugé," ignorance, and persecution. These causes of human evil, he felt, can be modified; he constantly asserted that enlightenment can work wonders in transforming a "brute" into a cultivated man. He assumed, in other words, that human nature is modifiable, that man learns from experience, that knowledge is a source of goodness—in short, that morality can be taught. His belief in the effectiveness of enlightenment to foster morality was genuine, although alternately optimistic and pessimistic and rather irrational at times. It was not too naïve, however.

Like Bayle, Voltaire viewed man's history as a story of continuous crimes, with suffering, persecution, ignorance, and human imbecility as its constant themes. His definition of man was taken from the Book of Job, and he often likened himself to Job. Nonetheless, the conclusions to his histories are far from despairing laments; indeed, they leave the impression that the general result of history is a steady ascent, albeit over countless centuries, to a more perfect world, where pleasure and happiness abound. These two desirable ends, he believed, are attainable even now, at least for the "happy few." In time, they may even be extended to the masses, although, for the moment, he insisted, workers are needed to make luxuries available to the "happy few." When it came to the enjoyment of luxuries, Voltaire's bourgeois beneficence was somewhat deficient.

Voltaire did not mean, however, that there are two kinds of citizens in a state, the enfranchised and the disfranchised. He was opposed to all kinds of slavery—political, economic, and social. He believed that natural law is made for all, that reason is open to all, and that the social benefits of enlightenment should be extended to all. Somewhat inconsistently, though, he did not believe that an advanced education should be offered to everybody—in the first place, because he did not think that everybody could profit by such instruction and, in the second place, because he did not think that the working classes were prepared to make good use of advanced learning. Exposing them to sophisticated ideas would, he felt, only make them uneasy, and production would suffer as a result. Voltaire believed in liberty, particularly specific kinds of liberty, interpreted as rights: the right to publish, the right to property, the right of habeas corpus, etc. These rights he considered to be open to all. But equality—social, political, economic—he did not deem possible for everybody. Voltaire could not, in fact, think beyond class structures, except in terms of fraternity. His faith in that was genuine, a bit sentimental perhaps and somewhat naïve, but all-embracing, at least in theory. Consequently, his republicanism, which he came to adopt as preferable for small states, and theoretically preferable for all states when practicable, was an aristocratic republicanism which placed genuine and well-defined social responsibilities upon the aristocracy. He could not envisage anything more progressive than representational government, his models being England, Geneva, and Holland. He accepted only two possible kinds of commonwealth: a monarchy with responsible ministers, or with a representative constituted body, and a republic with a representative constituted body and elected officials. A despotism he believed to be an abuse of a monarchy, just as anarchy is an abuse of a republic.

Whatever the form of government, Voltaire held it to be important that the laws be not arbitrary, that equality before the law be an established fact, and that the judiciary be neither venal nor arbitrary (see M. Maestro, *Voltaire and Beccaria*). He insisted that obedience to the law be required of everybody, the only test of a good state being this obedience. Failure to obey must be punished —not sporadically or arbitrarily, however, but reasonably and proportionately to the offense, which is always to be regarded as having been committed against the state, that is, against society. It should be punished, therefore, to the extent that it endangers the healthy life of the community.

No opinions, beliefs, or thoughts can be criminal: only acts can be crimes. Consequently, Voltaire argued, all punishments for religious, philosophical, or even political opinions are unfair, and those for such things as heresy, sorcery, and personal idiosyncracies are ridiculous. A person should be punished, not when he is merely suspected of having committed a crime, but only when he is known to have committed it. Everyone is entitled to a fair trial; that is, the trial must be open and public, the accused must have the right to confront his accusers, and witnesses must have the right to change their testimony without being prosecuted, when they recognize that they have testified erroneously. Finally, the extent of the punishment should be fixed by law. All of these points, which we now take for granted, perhaps a little unwisely, were only beginning to be discussed in Voltaire's day. His merit consisted in giving a human, social meaning to the concept of justice and urging from particular experiences that practical solutions to judicial problems be resolved in reasonable, commonsense, human terms. It is in that respect that Voltaire has bequeathed to us a sense of justice, of which he himself found the germs in England.

If these views are scanned carefully for their inner meaning, rather than for their explicit statement, it will be seen that they express an ideal of life which carries within it the negation of past ideals as inadequate and unreasonable. The important trait of this ideal consists in the fact that it is envisaged as possible here and now. Responsibility for its existence rests squarely upon the human mind. Voltaire never tires of quoting the "Mens agitat molem" of Virgil. The assumption is flatly made that what the mind knows to be true is not only true but useful for man's and society's welfare, and organic, too. Consequently, knowledge is a unity, a totality, and it contributes to a maturity, as Kant said. Moreover, it is fully encyclopedic; that is, it penetrates all the categories of living in order to distinguish the relationships between these categories in the making of the whole man.

The human mind (*l'esprit humain*) thus becomes the important factor in shaping human life, actions, and happiness. Its role as a guide to existence is not only dominant but paramount and, indeed, unique. There is consequently no history save the history of the activities of the human mind in the shaping of human life. This history may appear to be a story of stupidities, evils, and miseries, but the result of living history consciously, willfully, and reasonably is often a positive achievement: an increase in brotherly love, a gain in "bien-être," an enjoyment of the creations of mankind. It is true that these advances are realized only after almost superhuman intellectual efforts and after the passing of countless centuries. They could be speeded up, though, if we would keep clearly before ourselves what the human mind can and cannot do. It cannot know origins or understand the initial principles of things. Nor can it penetrate the infinite and comprehend the ultimate goals of life. But it can recognize the values of experience and learn to weigh those values. It can draw moral conclusions which, when properly assayed, will make life more smooth, more pleasurable, and more satisfactory to all. Finally, it can change the present conditions of life in favor of more pleasant, more gratifying, and more rewarding conditions. Thus, it is possible to develop taste for the true, the good, the beautiful. Art, philosophy, political and social organization, justice and freedom lie within the realm of human possibilities. There are nevertheless limits to what can be achieved through the activity of the human mind. Taste, art, thought, even justice and freedom are restricted by our capacity to live these possibilities. For the "happy few"—what Voltaire is inclined to refer to always as "les honnêtes gens"—these possibilities are great, and, once they have been turned into actualities, they can fortunately be shared with others whose lives are more limited. It is at this point that Voltaire's doctrine of "bienveillance," his fraternity, becomes so very important to his final estimate of life. Not everyone can be entrusted with the making of civilization, but everyone should be able to profit in one way or another from its gifts.

Still, we must not be too arbitrary in our exclusions. Since we know nothing of ultimate goals, we cannot clearly judge ultimate contributions to those goals. In this view of life, ideas create life by creating new possibilities of living. They get their energy from the inner life of man, and they do it by releasing his inner energy. In that sense of the word, knowledge is power—power to be a given thing at any one time. It is the capacity to transcend the normal functions of living through a process of destroying and reforming. Man is in history, to be sure, and he may be crushed by its dead-weight, but he has the capacity, if he will develop it, for making history, too, by saying *no* to all those injustices which history has inflicted upon him. He may even revolt, as Voltaire did on numerous occasions, although it can never be more than a limited revolt, because we are only human and, therefore, limited. These limits are less restraints than guidelines, however. Voltaire was convinced that too often they are accepted as constraints. With careful planning, they can be enlarged, and every enlargement offers modestly new possibilities for happiness, contentment, and self-fulfillment. Since the energy for creation lies within that self-fulfillment, the ultimate happiness for man is an aesthetic pleasure, the satisfaction of a job—the job of living—well done. The only "ultimate" happiness for humanity is, therefore, civilization: the fine and beautiful things which have been created in all the categories of living—those things which contribute to the comforts and well-being of man and which release ever new powers for the creation and enjoyment of this our world.

BIBLIOGRAPHY

A. BIBLIOGRAPHICAL AND COLLECTED WORKS

Alekseev, M. P., and T. K. Kopreeva, eds., *Bibliothèque de Voltaire; catalogue des livres*, Moscow, 1961.

Barr, M. M., "Bibliographical Data on Voltaire from 1926-1930," *Modern Language Notes*, XLVIII (1933), 292-307.

——, "Bibliographical Data on Voltaire from 1931-1940," *Modern Language Notes*, LVI (1941), 563-582.

——, *A Century of Voltaire Study: A Bibliography of Writings on Voltaire (1825-1925)*, Institute of French Studies, New York, 1929.

——, *Quarante années d'études Voltairiennes: Bibliographie analytique des livres et articles sur Voltaire, 1926-1965*, Paris, 1968.

Bengesco, G., *Voltaire. Bibliographie de ses œuvres*, 4 vols., Paris, 1882-1890.

Besterman, T., ed., *Les Lettres de la Marquise du Châtelet*, 2 vols., Institut et Musée Voltaire, Geneva, 1958.

——, ed., *Studies on Voltaire and the Eighteenth Century*, 62 vols., Institut et Musée Voltaire, Geneva, 1955-1968.

——, ed., *Voltaire's Correspondence*, 107 vols., Institut et Musée Voltaire, Geneva, 1953-1965.

——, ed., *Voltaire's Notebooks*, 2 vols., Institut et Musée Voltaire, Geneva, 1952.

Beuchot, A., ed., *Œuvres de Voltaire*, 72 vols., Paris, 1829-1840.

Cabeen, D. C., *A Critical Bibliography of French Literature*, Vol. IV: *The Eighteenth Century*, Syracuse, 1956; *Supplement: The Eighteenth Century*, ed. R. A. Brooks, Syracuse, 1968.

Moland, L., ed., *Œuvres complètes de Voltaire*, 52 vols., Paris, 1877-1885.

B. CRITICAL EDITIONS OF VOLTAIRE'S WORKS

Ascoli, G., *Zadig ou la Destinée*, 2 vols., Paris, 1929.

Bourgeois, E., *Siècle de Louis XIV*, Paris, 1906.

Brumfitt, J. H., *La Philosophie de l'histoire*, Vol. XXVIII of *Studies on Voltaire and the Eighteenth Century*, Geneva, 1963.

Carcassonne, E., *Le Temple du goût*, Paris, 1938.

Crowley, F. J., *Poème sur la loi naturelle*, Berkeley, 1938.

Foulet, L., *Correspondance de Voltaire, 1726-1729*, Paris, 1913.

Jones, W. R., *L'Ingénu*, Paris, 1936.

Lanson, G., *Lettres philosophiques*, 2 vols., Paris, 1924.

Morize, A., *L'Apologie du luxe au XVIIIᵉ siècle et Le Mondain de Voltaire*, Paris, 1909.

——, *Candide ou l'Optimisme*, Paris, 1931.

Patterson, H. T., *Traité de métaphysique*, Manchester, 1937.

Pomeau, R., *Essai sur les mœurs et l'esprit des nations et sur les principaux faits de l'histoire depuis Charlemagne jusqu'à Louis XIII*, 2 vols., Paris, 1963.

Pomeau, R., *Œuvres historiques*, Pléïade edn., Paris, 1957.

Taylor, O. R., *La Henriade*, Vols. XXXVIII-XL of *Studies on Voltaire and the Eighteenth Century*, Geneva, 1966.

Wade, I., *Epître à Uranie, Publications of the Modern Language Association of America*, XLVII (1932), 1066-1112.

——, *Micromégas*, Princeton, 1950.

White, F. D., *Voltaire's Essay on Epic Poetry*, Albany, 1915.

C. BOOKS AND ARTICLES

Adam, A., *Histoire de la littérature française au XVIIe siècle*, 5 vols., Paris, 1948-1956.

——, *Théophile de Viau et la libre pensée française en 1620*, Paris, 1935.

Ascoli, G., *Poèmes philosophiques de Voltaire*, Centre de Documentation Universitaire, Paris, 1936.

——, "Voltaire," *Revue des cours et des conférences*, XXV² (1923-1924), 16-27, 128-144, 275-287, 302-315, 417-428, 616-630; XXVI¹ (1924-1925), 262-273, 501-514, 703-721.

Asse, E., ed., *Lettres de la Marquise du Châtelet*, Paris, 1877.

Baldensperger, F., "Voltaire anglophile avant son séjour en Angleterre," *Revue de littérature comparée*, IX (1929), 25-61.

Ballantyne, A., *Voltaire's Visit to England, 1726-1729*, London, 1893.

Barber, W. H., *Leibniz in France from Arnauld to Voltaire*, Oxford, 1955.

Beaune, H., *Voltaire au collège*, Paris, 1867.

Becker, C., *The Heavenly City of the Eighteenth-century Philosophers*, New Haven, 1932.

Bellessort, A., *Essai sur Voltaire*, Paris, 1925.

Bellugou, H., *Voltaire et Frédéric au temps de la Marquise du Châtelet*, Paris, 1962.

Besterman, T., "Voltaire, absolute monarchy, and the enlightened monarch," *Studies on Voltaire and the Eighteenth Century*, XXXII, 7-21, Geneva, 1965.

Bien, D., *The Calas Affair*, Princeton, 1960.

Black, J. P., *The Art of History*, London, 1926.

Bonno, G., *La Culture et la civilisation britannique devant l'opinion française au XVIIIe siècle de la paix d'Utrecht aux* Lettres philosophiques, Philadelphia, 1948.

Bottiglia, W., *Voltaire's* Candide: *Analysis of a Classic*, Vol. VII of *Studies on Voltaire and the Eighteenth Century*, Geneva, 1959.

Bramwell, H. T., *Les Idées morales et critiques de Saint-Evremond*, Paris, 1957.

Bray, R., *La Formation de la doctrine classique en France*, Paris, 1927.

Brooks, R. A., *Voltaire and Leibniz*, Geneva, 1964.

Brumfitt, J. H., *Voltaire Historian*, Oxford, 1958.

Brunet, P., *L'Introduction des théories de Newton en France au XVIIIe siècle avant 1738*, Paris, 1931.

——, *Maupertuis, Etude biographique*, Paris, 1929.

————, *Les Physiciens hollandais et la méthode expérimentale en France au XVIIIᵉ siècle*, Paris, 1926.

————, *La Vie et l'œuvre de Clairaut (1713-1765)*, Paris, 1952.

Burtt, E. A., *The Metaphysical Foundations of Modern Physical Science*, New York, 1925.

Busson, H., and F. Gohin, eds., *La Fontaine, Discours à Madame de la Sablière*, Paris, 1938.

Busson, H., "La Fontaine et l'âme des bêtes," *Revue d'histoire littéraire*, XLII (1935), 1-32; XLIII (1936), 257-286.

Carré, J. R., *La Consistance de Voltaire le philosophe*, Paris, 1939.

————, *Réflexions sur l'anti-Pascal de Voltaire*, Paris, 1935.

Ceitac, J., *Voltaire et l'affaire des natifs*, Geneva, 1956.

Charbonnaud, R., *Les Idées économiques de Voltaire*, Angoulême, 1907.

Chardonchamp, G., *La Famille de Voltaire, les Arouet*, Paris, 1911.

Chase, C. B., *The Young Voltaire*, New York, 1926.

Clarac, P., *La Fontaine par lui-même*, Paris, 1961.

Collins, J. C., *Bolingbroke, a Historical Study, and Voltaire in England*, London, 1886.

Conlon, P. M., *Voltaire's Literary Career from 1728 to 1750*, Vol. XIV of *Studies on Voltaire and the Eighteenth Century*, Geneva, 1961.

Crist, C. M., *The* Dictionnaire philosophique portatif *and the early French Deists*, Brooklyn, 1934.

Dagens, J., "La Marche de l'Histoire selon Voltaire," *Romanische Forschungen*, LXX (1958), 248-266.

Dangeau, P. de, *Journal*, 19 vols., Paris, 1854-1882.

Dargan, E. P., "The Question of Voltaire's Primacy in Establishing the English Vogue," *Mélanges Baldensperger*, I (1930), 187-198.

Decorte, M., "La Dialectique poétique de Descartes," *Archives de philosophie*, XIII (1937), 101-158.

Dédéyan, C., *Voltaire et la pensée anglaise*, Centre de Documentation Universitaire, Paris, 1956.

Delvolvé, J., *Religion, critique et philosophie positive chez P. Bayle*, Paris, 1906.

Deschanel, E., *Le Romantisme des classiques*, Vol. V: *Le Théâtre de Voltaire*, Paris, 1888.

Diaz, F., *Voltaire storico*, Turin, 1958.

Edsall, H. L., "The Ideas of History and Progress in Fontenelle and Voltaire," *Yale Romanic Studies*, XVIII (1941), 163-184.

Ehrard, J., *L'Idée de nature en France dans la première moitié du XVIIIᵉ siècle*, 2 vols., Paris, 1963.

Faguet, E., *La Politique comparée de Montesquieu, Rousseau et Voltaire*, Paris, 1902.

Fenger, H., *Voltaire et le théâtre anglais*, Copenhagen, 1950.

Fleischauer, C., ed., *L'Anti-Machiavel, par Frédéric II, roi de Prusse* (avec les remaniements de Voltaire pour les deux versions), Vol. V of *Studies on Voltaire and the Eighteenth Century*, Geneva, 1958.

Folkierski, W., *Entre le classicisme et le romantisme*, Paris, 1925.

Gassendi, 1592-1655, sa vie et son œuvre, Centre International de Synthèse, Paris, 1955.

Gay, P., *Voltaire's Politics*, Princeton, 1959.

Gazier, A., "Le Frère de Voltaire (1685-1744)," *Revue des deux mondes*, XXXII (1906), 615-639.

Gillot, H., *La Querelle des anciens et des modernes en France*, Paris, 1914.

Graffigny, F. de, *Lettres de Mme de Graffigny*, ed. E. Asse, Paris, 1883.

Grubbs, H., "Voltaire and Rime," *Studies in Philology*, XXXIX (1942), 524-544.

Guiragossian, D., *Voltaire's Facéties*, Geneva, 1963.

Hahn, J., *Voltaires Stellung zur Frage der menschlichen Freiheit in ihrem Verhältnis zu Locke und Collins*, Borna-Leipzig, 1905.

Havens, G. R., "Voltaire's Marginal Comments upon Pope's *Essay on Man*," *Modern Language Notes*, XLIII (1928), 429-439.

———, "Voltaire's Pessimistic Revision of the Conclusion of his *Poème sur le désastre de Lisbonne*," *Modern Language Notes*, XLIV (1929), 489-492.

Haxo, P., "Pierre Bayle et Voltaire avant les *Lettres philosophiques*," *Publications of the Modern Language Association of America*, XLVI (1931), 461-497.

Hazard, P., *La Crise de la conscience européenne, 1680-1715*, 3 vols., Paris, 1935.

———, *La Pensée européenne au XVIIIᵉ siècle de Montesquieu à Lessing*, 3 vols., Paris, 1946.

———, "Voltaire et Leibniz," *Bulletin de la classe de lettres*, Académie Royale de Belgique, XXIII (1937), 435-449.

———, "Voltaire et Spinoza," *Modern Philology*, XXXVIII (1940-1941), 351-364.

Hole, A., "Jean-Baptiste de Mirabaud (1675-1760): His Contribution to the Deistic Movement and His Relation to Voltaire," Ph.D. dissertation, Princeton University, 1943.

Humeston, E. J., "Voltaire, the *Examen* and *Analyse*: A Comparative Study," Ph.D. dissertation, Princeton University, 1954.

Hurn, A. S., *Voltaire et Bolingbroke*, Paris, 1915.

Jasinski, R., "Sur la philosophie de La Fontaine dans les livres VII à XII des *Fables*," *Revue d'histoire de la philosophie et d'histoire générale de la civilisation*, I (1933), 316-330; II (1934), 218-242.

Konijnenburg, J. T., *Courant pascalien et courant anti-pascalien de 1670 à 1734*, Brussels, 1932.

Lachèvre, F., *Les Derniers libertins*, Paris, 1924.

Lacombe, J., *La Poétique de M. de Voltaire*, Geneva, 1766.

Lancaster, H. C., *French Tragedy in the Time of Louis XV and Voltaire, 1715-1774*, 2 vols., Baltimore, 1950.

Lanson, G., *Esquisse d'une histoire de la tragédie française*, New York, 1920.

———, *Histoire de la littérature française*, 4th edn., Paris, 1896.

———, "Origine et premières manifestations de l'esprit philosophique dans la littérature française de 1675 à 1715," *Revue des cours et des conférences*, XVI¹ (1907-1908), 289-298, 450-460, 601-613, 721-734; XVI² (1909-1910), 1-15, 145-156, 241-254, 409-422, 481-493, 625-637, 738-752, 817-829.

———, "Questions diverses sur l'histoire de l'esprit philosophique en France avant 1715," *Revue d'histoire littéraire*, XIX (1912), 1-29, 293-317.

———, "Le Rôle de l'expérience dans la formation de la philosophie au XVIIIe siècle," *Revue du mois*, X (1910), 5-28.

———, "La Transformation des idées morales et la naissance des morales rationnelles de 1680 à 1715," *Revue du mois*, IX (1909), 409-429.

———, *Voltaire*, Paris, 1946.

———, "Voltaire et les *Lettres philosophiques*," *Revue de Paris*, IV (1908), 367-386.

Libby, M., *The Attitude of Voltaire to Magic and the Sciences*, New York, 1935.

Lion, H., *Les Tragédies et les théories dramatiques de Voltaire*, Paris, 1895.

Lombard, A., *L'Abbé Du Bos*, Paris, 1913.

Lowenstein, R., *Voltaire as an Historian of Seventeenth-century French Drama*, Baltimore, 1935.

McKee, D., *Tyssot de Patot and the Seventeenth-century Background of Critical Deism*, Baltimore, 1941.

Maestro, M., *Voltaire and Beccaria as Reformers of Criminal Law*, New York, 1942.

Marmier, J., *Horace en France au dix-septième siècle*, Paris, 1962.

Mason, H., *Pierre Bayle and Voltaire*, Oxford, 1963.

Mauzi, R., *L'Idée du bonheur dans la littérature et la pensée françaises au XVIIIe siècle*, Paris, 1960.

———, *Mme du Châtelet, Discours sur le bonheur*, Paris, 1961.

Merrill, W. H., *From Statesman to Philosopher*, New York, 1949.

Morehouse, A., *Voltaire and Jean Meslier*, New Haven, 1936.

Morley, J., *Voltaire*, London, 1886.

Mornet, D., "Bibliographie d'un certain nombre d'ouvrages philosophiques du XVIIIe siècle et particulièrement de D'Holbach," *Revue d'histoire littéraire*, XL (1933), 259-281.

———, "Les Enseignements des bibliothèques privées (1750-1780)," *Revue d'histoire littéraire*, XVII (1910), 449-496.

———, *Les Origines intellectuelles de la Révolution Française*, Paris, 1933.

Morrison, A., *Catalogue of the Collection of Autograph Letters and Historical Documents formed by Alfred Morrison*, 13 vols., London, 1883-1897.

Naves, R., *Le Goût de Voltaire*, Paris, 1938.

———, *Voltaire et l'Encyclopédie*, Paris, 1938.

———, *Voltaire, l'homme et l'œuvre*, Paris, 1942.

Noyes, A., *Voltaire*, New York, 1936.

Pellissier, G., *Voltaire philosophe*, Paris, 1908.

Perkins, M. L., "Voltaire and the Abbé de Saint-Pierre," *French Review*, XXXIV (1960-1961), 152-163.

———, *Voltaire's Concept of International Order*, Vol. XXXVI of *Studies on Voltaire and the Eighteenth Century*, Geneva, 1965.

Petit, L., *La Fontaine et Saint-Evremond*, Toulouse, 1953.

Pierron, P. A., *Voltaire et ses maîtres*, Paris, 1866.

Pintard, R., *Le Libertinage érudit dans la première moitié du XVIIe siècle*, 2 vols., Paris, 1943.

Pomeau, R., *Politique de Voltaire*, Paris, 1963.

———, *La Religion de Voltaire*, Paris, 1956.

Rex, W., *Essays on Pierre Bayle and Religious Controversy*, The Hague, 1965.

Ridgway, R. S., *La Propagande philosophique dans les tragédies de Voltaire*, Vol. XV of *Studies on Voltaire and the Eighteenth Century*, Geneva, 1961.

Rigault, H., *Histoire de la querelle des anciens et des modernes*, Paris, 1856.

Rihs, C., *Voltaire, Recherches sur les origines du matérialisme historique*, Geneva, 1962.

Rosenfield, L., *From Beast-machine to Man-machine*, New York, 1941.

Rowe, C., *Voltaire and the State*, New York, 1955.

Russell, T., *Voltaire, Dryden, and Heroic Tragedy*, New York, 1946.

Sainte-Beuve, C. A., "Une Ruelle poétique sous Louis XIV," *Revue des deux mondes*, XX (1839), 198-204.

Sakmann, P., *Voltaires Geistesart und Gedankenwelt*, Stuttgart, 1910.

Shackleton, R., *Montesquieu*, Oxford, 1961.

Siegel, J. S., "Voltaire, *Zadig* and the Problem of Evil," *Romanic Review*, L (1959), 25-34.

Sonet, E., *Voltaire et l'influence anglaise*, Rennes, 1926.

Spink, J. S., *French Free-thought from Gassendi to Voltaire*, London, 1960.

Stephen, L., *History of English Thought in the Eighteenth Century*, 2 vols., London, 1876.

Strachey, G. L., *Books and Characters, French and English*, New York, 1922.

Texte, J., *Jean-Jacques Rousseau et les origines du cosmopolitisme littéraire*, Paris, 1895.

Thielemann, L., "Voltaire and Hobbes," *Studies on Voltaire and the Eighteenth Century*, X (1959), 237-258.

Topazio, V., *Voltaire*, New York, 1967.

Torrey, N. L., *Voltaire and the English Deists*, New Haven, 1930.

———, "Voltaire's English Notebook," *Modern Philology*, XXVI (1929), 307-325.

———, *The Spirit of Voltaire*, New York, 1938.

Vernière, P., *Spinoza et la pensée française avant la Révolution*, 2 vols., Paris, 1954.

Von der Mühll, E., *Denis Veiras et son Histoire des Sévarambes, 1677-1679*, Paris, 1938.

Vrooman, J., "Voltaire's Theatre: A Study in Tragic Focus," Ph.D. dissertation, Princeton University, 1964.

Wade, I., *The Clandestine Organization and Diffusion of Philosophic Ideas in France from 1700 to 1750*, Princeton, 1938.

——, *The Search for a New Voltaire*, Philadelphia, 1958.

——, *Studies on Voltaire*, Princeton, 1947.

——, *Voltaire and* Candide, Princeton, 1959.

——, *Voltaire and Mme du Châtelet*, Princeton, 1941.

——, "Voltaire's Quarrel with Science," *Bucknell Review*, VIII (1959), 289-298.

Waldinger, R., *Voltaire and Reform in the Light of the French Revolution*, Geneva, 1959.

Walters, R., "Voltaire and the Newtonian Universe: A Study of the *Eléments de la philosophie de Newton*," Ph.D. dissertation, Princeton University, 1954.

Waterman, M., *Voltaire, Pascal, and Human Destiny*, New York, 1942.

INDEX

Abbadie, J., 121

Ablavius, 551

Adam, A., 44, 46, 60, 65, 66, 67, 68, 77, 139

Addison, J., 166, 167, 185, 232, 247

Aeschylus, 38

Aguesseau, Chancellier d', 411

Alcibiades, 296

Alembert, J. le R. d', 95, 541, 569, 732, 755, 761

Alençon, Duc d', 171

Algarotti, F., 26, 254, 263, 269, 291, 347, 358, 359, 363, 364, 411, 439, 440, 441, 442, 444, 446, 565, 618

Amelot de la Houssaye, A. N., 320, 322, 326

Anacreon, 7, 23, 90

Anaxagoras, 235

André, Père, 712

Annet, P., 518, 519, 532, 533, 534, 535, 547, 637

Apollonius of Tyana, 235

Archimedes, 235

Argens, J. B., Marquis d', 28, 95, 254, 388, 632

Argenson, R. d', 312, 315, 316, 317, 489

Argental, C. A., Comte d', 27, 40, 128, 268, 269, 323, 352, 360, 361, 364, 365, 378, 389, 411, 422

Argental, Mme d', 110, 378

Ariosto, L., 67, 102, 270, 439

Aristotle, 24, 113, 116, 125, 130, 169, 170, 197, 235, 281, 379, 380, 405, 414, 415, 420, 437, 593, 594, 595, 599, 618, 756, 759

Arnauld, A., 71

Arnold, M., 116, 156

Arouet, F. M., 7, 8

Ascoli, G., 12, 14, 97, 106, 135, 142, 143, 146, 182, 183, 184, 373, 668, 669, 671, 674

Asse, E., 439

Asselin, Abbé, 338

Atterbury, Fr., Bishop of, 151

Auger, L. S., 522

Augustus Caesar, 34, 483

Avenel, G., 522, 555

Bachelard, G., 267, 272

Bacon, F., 125, 130, 169, 172, 185, 222, 224, 230, 235, 236, 237, 291, 332, 420, 564, 595, 615, 620, 755, 756, 760, 775

Baillet, A., 233, 237, 591

Baldensperger, F., 151, 202

Balesdens, 208

Ballantyne, A., 181

Balleroy, C. M., Marquise de, 110

Barber, W. G., 651, 655, 661, 668, 669, 671, 688, 693

Barbier, E.J.F., 548

Barclay, G., see Berkeley, G.

Bardin, de, 208

Basnage de Beauval, J., 134, 633

Barral, P., 699

Bastide, J. F. de, 121

Baudelaire, C., 373

Baudouin, 208

Bayle, P., 4, 5, 6, 19, 21, 50, 78, 124, 126, 127, 131, 132, 133, 134, 136, 144, 152, 154, 181, 184, 191, 207, 208, 210, 213, 224, 225, 226, 227, 229, 232, 233, 235, 285, 291, 297, 303, 326, 346, 408, 453, 456, 457, 458, 459, 460, 461, 462, 464, 465, 467, 468, 469, 470, 473, 480, 496, 497, 509, 519, 527, 532, 533, 535, 537, 564, 567, 568, 577, 583, 625, 626, 630, 632, 633, 634, 635, 636, 638, 639, 640, 641, 642, 643, 644, 645, 646, 647, 648, 649, 650, 651, 660, 661, 662, 663, 681, 683, 689, 693, 694, 696, 700, 701, 708, 709, 710, 712, 748, 752, 755, 759, 760, 775, 776, 784

Beaune, H., 15

Beccaria, C. de, 785

Becker, C., 461

Bell, A. E., 619

Bellessort, A., 393, 684

Bellugou, H., 253

Bengesco, G., 556

Berger, G., 306, 334, 353, 356, 359, 363, 482

Berkeley, G., 154, 233, 366, 443, 466, 613

Bernard, Mlle, 195

Bernard, P. G., 190, 337

Bernier, F., 67, 68, 70, 72, 73, 77, 516, 575

Bernières, M. M. du Moutier, Mme de, 10, 145

Bernis, F. J., Cardinal de, 128

Bernouilli, J., 236, 269, 272, 276, 277, 436, 446, 617

Bertrand, G., 522, 685

Besterman, T., ix, xvi, 168, 173, 211, 273, 293, 323, 434, 695, 748

Beuchot, A., 190, 522, 523, 538, 539, 540, 541, 542, 556, 579, 615
Beverell, 232
Bignon, Abbé, 210, 213, 226
Black, J. P., 461
Blin de Sainmore, A. M., 39, 40, 41
Blot, C. de Chauvigny, Baron de, 20, 21, 53, 54, 55, 573, 775
Boccaccio, G., 67, 397
Boccage, Mme du, 95
Bodin, J., 466, 498, 760
Boerhaave, H., 365, 417, 421, 429, 443, 444, 617, 760
Boileau, N., xix, xx, 4, 7, 18, 21, 23, 27, 34, 35, 36, 37, 38, 40, 42, 44, 60, 83, 84, 86, 87, 89, 93, 102, 106, 107, 113, 116, 141, 161, 184, 196, 207, 210, 212, 214, 241, 242, 243, 249, 250, 329, 360, 362, 372, 374, 392, 665, 739, 776
Boisrobert, F., 44, 47
Bolingbroke, H. St. Jean, Lord, 110, 128, 129, 130, 132, 134, 135, 136, 141, 146, 152, 153, 165, 168, 174, 184, 189, 191, 193, 195, 196, 233, 238, 291, 304, 470, 472, 473, 515, 518, 550, 555, 556, 564, 576, 577, 589, 590, 600, 619, 620, 622, 633, 645, 651, 659, 660, 666, 669, 681, 689, 690, 692, 711, 713, 757, 780
Bonnegarde, de, 632
Bonno, G., 184, 187, 224, 225, 229, 230, 236, 519, 619, 624
Bossuet, J. B., xix, 4, 9, 212, 451, 452, 469, 470, 486, 487, 494, 496, 513, 640, 727
Bottiglia, W., ix, 397, 398, 646
Bouhier, J., 149, 208, 214, 253, 255, 256, 258, 351
Bouillier, F., 228
Bouillon, M. R. Mancini, Duchesse de, 18, 59, 67, 77, 228
Boulainvilliers, H., Comte de, 128, 452, 470, 471, 511, 514, 529, 536, 547, 585, 635, 693, 694, 697, 699, 701, 707, 709
Boulanger, N., 635, 726
Bourgeois, L., 461
Bourignon, A., 638
Boyle, R., 420
Bradley, J., 228, 285, 422, 444, 612
Brancas, M. de, Ambassador, 188, 190, 265
Bray, R., 24
Bredembourg, J., 699
Breteuil, Abbé de, 263
Brioché, P. D., 605
Brooks, R. A., 655, 672
Brossette, C., 40, 110, 111, 151, 208
Brumfitt, J. H., ix, 191, 192, 193, 461, 469,

470, 471, 473, 474, 479, 482, 490, 492, 493, 496, 509, 765
Brunet, P., 433, 601, 668
Brunetière, F., 587, 757
Bruno, G., 20, 45, 47, 373
Buffier, C., 228
Buffon, G. L., 95, 448
Bullfinger, 420, 434
Bury, R. de, 96, 103
Busson, H., 65, 72, 77
Butler, S., 247
Byssche, E., 166

Calmet, Dom A., 520, 521, 523, 536, 537, 543, 547, 556, 638, 707
Calvin, J., 743, 746
Camas, P. H. de, 323, 324
Campistron, J. G. de, 41
Caporali, C., 205
Carcassonne, E., 13, 205, 208, 209, 211, 212, 213
Cardinal de Lorraine, 746
Carré, J. R., 578, 585
Carron de Gibert, 16
Cassini, J., 228, 437
Castel, le Père, 228, 414
Cato, 717
Caumartin, L. U. de, 97, 192
Caumont, J. de Seîtres, Marquis de, 256, 338, 340, 343, 348, 349, 350, 363, 392, 441
Ceitac, J., 748
Cervantes, M. de, 205
César de Missy, 478
Chabannes de Maugris, 16
Chabanon, M. P. de, 40, 42
Chamberlayne, E., 232
Chambonin, Mme de (Gros chat), 263, 270
Chapelle (C. E. Luillier), 18, 50, 59, 60
Charbonnaud, R., 309
Charleval, C. F. du Rys de, 124
Charron, P., 123, 759, 775
Chase, C. B., 181
Châteaulyon, Aquin de, 95
Châteauneuf, Abbé de, 7, 19, 58
Châtelet, Emilie de Breteuil, Marquise du, xvii, 26, 217, 219, 220, 253, 254, 255, 258, 260, 261, 262, 263, 264, 265, 267, 268, 269, 270, 273, 275, 276, 278, 279, 281, 282, 283, 284, 285, 288, 289, 290, 291, 293, 301, 302, 303, 311, 318, 319, 320, 322, 327, 328, 336, 339, 342, 343, 344, 346, 347, 349, 352, 355, 357, 358, 359, 360, 361, 363, 364, 389, 394, 410, 412, 415, 419, 421, 422, 432, 436, 437,

439, 440, 442, 443, 445, 483, 486, 488,
517, 518, 520, 521, 522, 523, 524, 525,
535, 536, 537, 538, 539, 542, 543, 544,
546, 547, 549, 551, 554, 555, 556, 565,
566, 594, 596, 597, 598, 601, 624, 644,
655, 656, 657, 658, 660, 664, 671, 677,
678, 679, 703, 706, 707, 708, 724
Chauchat, J., 189
Chaulieu, Abbé G. A. de, xvii, xviii, xx,
5, 17, 19, 20, 21, 23, 25, 49, 57, 58,
59, 60, 61, 67, 77, 93, 121, 122, 123,
133, 138, 142, 183, 242, 373, 573, 706,
775, 776
Chauvelin, B. L., 334
Chénier, A., 159, 374
Cheselden, W., 613
Chesterfield, Lord P. D., 94
Chetwood, 154
Choisy, Abbé de, 58
Chubb, T., 224, 518, 659, 660
Cibber, C., 153, 175, 243, 247
Cicero, 12, 130, 219, 336, 357, 457, 465,
691, 716, 759
Cideville, P. R., 188, 189, 204, 208, 209,
210, 212, 213, 214, 215, 216, 217, 218,
220, 334, 338, 339, 340, 343, 344, 345,
348, 349, 350, 351, 354, 356, 363, 364,
391, 565, 711
Clairaut, A., 272, 273, 277, 290, 392, 433,
436, 437, 439, 441, 444, 445, 446, 602
Clarac, P., 65
Clarke, S., 131, 154, 219, 236, 245, 282,
285, 291, 342, 345, 346, 358, 403, 408,
421, 422, 423, 424, 433, 443, 447, 517,
534, 605, 606, 607, 608, 625, 626, 651,
653, 657, 697, 755, 780
Clément, J., 103, 231
Clermont, Comte de, 168
Cléry, M. de, 526
Cohen, I. B., 275
Colbert, J. B., 212, 257, 486, 496
Colerus, J., 694
Colletet, G., 208
Collins, A., 224, 426, 516, 517, 520, 534,
606, 607, 652, 722, 723, 724
Collins, J. C., 181
Comines, P. de, 527
Condé, Prince de, 50, 495
Condillac, E. B. de, 710
Condorcet, C. de, 96, 665
Conduit, Mme, 154
Congreve, W., 153, 185
Copernicus, 428, 615
Corneille, P., xx, 4, 21, 37, 39, 40, 41, 93,

102, 106, 110, 113, 114, 115, 212, 213,
214, 241, 242, 370, 382, 776
Coste, P., 152, 226, 227, 233, 363, 443, 622
Cotes, R., 228
Cottin, C., 208
Courtin, Abbé H., 19, 58, 242
Cramer, G., 41
Crébillon, P. G. de, 41, 208, 335, 337, 378
Cremonini, C., 20, 48
Crist, C., 536
Croese, G., 233
Croissy, M. de, Ambassador, 188, 190
Crousaz, J. P. de, 28, 228, 668, 681, 682
Crowley, F. J., ix, 631, 669
Crozat, P., 212
Curll, E., 179
Cyrano de Bergerac, S., 48, 249, 250, 388,
573, 775

Dacier, A., 16, 23, 24, 29, 92, 130
Dacier, Mme, 85
Dagens, J., 490
Damilaville, E. N., 540, 541, 542, 765
Dangeau, P., 110, 354, 480
Daniel, Père G., 131, 452, 469
Dante, 27, 33
Dargan, E. P., ix, 129, 231
Darget, C. E., 26
Darmanson, J. M., 72
Daumart, Marguerite, Voltaire's mother, 7, 8
Daumart, Voltaire's nephew, 149
De Cayrol, 478
De Corte, M., 139
Dédéyan, C., 164, 199, 201, 247, 249, 619,
625, 627
De Dominis, 613
Deffand, Mme du, 33, 40, 267, 357
Defoe, D., 226
Dehénault, J., 18, 20, 21, 50, 51, 52, 55,
56, 57, 373, 573, 775
De Lassay, A. L., 585
Delattre, P., 678
Delvolvé, J., 456, 467
Democritus, 77, 78, 282, 285, 606, 714
Denham, Sir J., 166
Denis, Mme, niece of Voltaire, 265
Denys, N., 78
De Pons, J. F., 85, 100
Derham, W., 430, 432
Désaguliers, J. T., 422, 437
Des Alleurs, P. P., 161, 162, 173, 564, 632,
636, 756
Des Barreaux, J., 20, 21, 47, 48, 49, 50, 58,
373, 374, 573, 649, 775
Descartes, R., xix, 48, 67, 68, 70, 71, 72,

73, 74, 75, 78, 89, 121, 122, 124, 125, 129, 130, 131, 133, 139, 140, 141, 169, 170, 172, 181, 214, 218, 228, 233, 235, 236, 237, 246, 277, 278, 279, 280, 281, 282, 285, 291, 330, 333, 354, 363, 401, 408, 409, 410, 413, 414, 415, 416, 417, 419, 420, 421, 427, 428, 429, 430, 431, 433, 434, 436, 438, 447, 448, 450, 452, 564, 565, 576, 577, 588, 589, 590, 591, 592, 593, 594, 595, 596, 597, 598, 599, 600, 601, 602, 603, 605, 610, 611, 612, 613, 614, 615, 618, 620, 622, 625, 626, 632, 635, 636, 644, 651, 652, 658, 678, 698, 700, 703, 711, 712, 713, 715, 716, 722, 724, 756, 757, 759, 760, 761, 762, 764, 775

Deschamps, J., 654
Deschanel, E., 375
Desfontaines, Abbé Guyot, 23, 128, 260, 263
Desforges-Maillard, P., 335, 343, 350
Deshoulières, Mme A., 18, 20, 21, 50, 55, 56, 57, 58, 59, 373, 573, 775
Desmaizeaux, P., 124, 127, 152, 154, 226, 282, 443, 516, 635, 651, 653, 654
Desnoiresterres, G., 267
Destouches, N., 225, 378
Devaux (Panpan), F. E., 360
Diagoras, 698
Diaz, F., 461
Diderot, D., 96, 378, 383, 397, 406, 430, 447, 563, 569, 685, 747, 761
Dilly, A., 69, 72
Dodington, G. B., 153, 156
Doucin, L., 354, 480
Dryden, J., 166, 185, 200, 203, 204, 229, 231, 247, 248, 249, 250, 515, 550
Dubois, Cardinal G., 152, 315
Du Bos, J. B., 97, 98, 99, 100, 105, 206, 353, 474, 479, 480, 481, 483, 498
Du Cestre d'Auvigny, 85
Duclos, C., 359
Dufay, C. F., 392
Du Hamel, J. B., 69, 72, 77, 78
Dumarsais, C. C., 511, 515, 529, 536, 537, 540, 542, 547, 635, 707
Dunoquet, 153, 163
Du Pan, Le Conseiller, 556
Dupeyrou, P. A., 541
Dupuy, P., 318, 356
Du Resnel, J. F., 175, 248, 258, 271, 357, 666
Du Saulx, J., 16
Dutens, L., 654
Dutot, 311, 312, 355, 357

Duvernet, Abbé T., 120

Echard, L., 233
Edsall, H. L., 471
Ehrard, J., 447, 448
Epicurus, 20, 58, 60, 62, 77, 78, 79, 81, 122, 125, 282, 283, 285, 575, 606, 682, 698
Espiard, F. I. d', 127, 497, 498, 499, 500, 502, 503, 504, 506, 507, 508, 509
Euclide, 25
Euripides, 7, 39, 111

Fabre, J., 674, 675
Fabrice, F. E., 173, 190, 192, 475
Fabricius, 534
Faguet, E., 371, 619, 748
Falkener, Sir E., 153, 154, 174, 175, 177, 195, 475, 583
Faret, N., 208
Fénelon, F., xix, 4, 5, 85, 121, 136, 141, 266, 311, 326, 470, 471, 527, 528, 573, 575, 576, 640, 694, 700, 701, 710, 775
Fenger, H., 375
Fielding, H., 249
Flamsteed, J., 443, 612
Fleischauer, C., 325
Fleury, Cardinal de, 239, 315
Foigny, G. de, 5, 398, 399, 573, 775
Folkes, Martin, 439
Folkierski, W., 82, 242
Fontaine, M., 202
Fontaine, Mme de, Voltaire's niece, 548
Fontaine-Martel, Mme de, 204, 214
Fontenelle, B. le B. de, xix, 4, 5, 18, 83, 84, 85, 94, 127, 135, 136, 169, 170, 181, 184, 205, 210, 228, 234, 235, 236, 237, 337, 411, 428, 439, 440, 453, 454, 455, 456, 462, 467, 469, 470, 471, 476, 480, 496, 497, 508, 509, 535, 564, 567, 589, 591, 601, 617, 618, 652, 726, 760, 775
Formey, J., 655
Formont, J., 189, 204, 209, 214, 215, 216, 217, 218, 219, 220, 333, 334, 335, 336, 338, 342, 343, 344, 345, 348, 349, 360, 388, 423, 565, 578, 590, 620, 624, 666, 711, 712
Foulet, L., 135, 150, 151, 173, 174, 176, 177, 182, 183, 184, 188, 189, 190, 195
Fouquet, N., 50
Fox, G., 551
Francheville, Du F. de, 318
Frederick II, xvii, 25, 26, 30, 31, 96, 254, 255, 259, 262, 268, 273, 274, 278, 292, 293, 294, 296, 297, 298, 299, 300, 301,

302, 303, 304, 305, 306, 307, 308, 309, 310, 315, 318, 319, 320, 321, 322, 323, 324, 325, 326, 327, 328, 336, 337, 341, 347, 351, 352, 356, 358, 359, 362, 365, 388, 389, 422, 423, 424, 425, 427, 432, 439, 446, 478, 565, 566, 571, 604, 606, 607, 628, 630, 632, 636, 652, 653, 657, 676, 724, 749, 751, 762

Fréret, N., 511, 512, 515, 529, 536, 547, 635, 649, 707

Fréron, E., 103, 231

Froidmont, L., 71

Froulay, C. F., 358

Galileo, 169, 236, 279, 408, 413, 417, 420, 428, 489, 588, 595, 597, 601, 615, 617, 760

Galland, E., 399

Garth, S., 247

Gassendi, P., 18, 19, 48, 58, 67, 68, 71, 72, 73, 77, 78, 79, 80, 122, 124, 126, 181, 235, 274, 282, 284, 285, 291, 354, 417, 429, 431, 481, 515, 516, 565, 575, 588, 594, 606, 615, 755, 756, 760, 775

Gaston d'Orléans, 53

Gauchat, G., 96

Gay, J., 153, 166, 243, 247

Gay, P., ix, 748

Gazier, A., 10, 11

Giannone, P., 470

Gibbon, E., 460, 461

Gilbert, C., 5, 398, 573, 585, 775

Gillot, H., 82

Gilson, E., 732

Goertz, Baron G. H., 190, 191

Gohin, F., 65, 72, 77

Goncourts, J. et E., 255

Gordon, T., 320, 515, 547

Graffigny, Mme de, 255, 261, 263, 266, 267, 269, 360, 400, 520, 660, 679

Gravina, G. N., 84

Gray, T., 228

Gregory, D., 228, 413, 617

Gresset, J. B., 337

Grimm, M., 522, 540, 548

Grotius, H., 131, 466, 750, 760

Grubbs, H., 4, 374

Gruber, 654

Gua, Abbé de, 436

Guébriant, Marquis de, 265

Guéret, G., 205

Guise, Mlle de, 168

Guyon, Mme J. M., 266

Haldane, E., 71

Hales, S., 228

Halley, E., 225, 228

Harel, E., 120

Hartsœker, N., 283, 285, 291

Harvey, 760

Haudent, G., 67

Hauksbee, F., 228

Havens, G. R., ix

Haxo, H., 191, 473, 633

Hazard, P., ix, 64, 655, 656, 693, 695, 696

Hegel, 490

Heinsius, 124

Helvétius, C. A., 37, 274, 630, 764, 765

Hénault, C.G.F., 15, 254, 269, 324

Henry IV, 95, 97, 98, 100, 108, 151, 193, 316

Hérault, R., 149, 150, 154

Herbert of Cherbury, Lord, 515, 516, 626

Hérissant, L. T., 712

Hervey, Lord J., 175, 474, 482, 483

Higginson, E., 154

Hobbes, T., 71, 125, 130, 146, 169, 172, 185, 209, 235, 562, 568, 588, 625, 656, 696, 749, 750, 755, 756, 760, 775

Hogguers, Dutch banker, 191

Holbach, P. H. Thiry, Baron d', 533, 563, 648, 695, 747

Hole, A., 536

Homer, 23, 33, 67, 82, 83, 84, 85, 86, 96, 97, 100, 101, 102, 107, 109, 157, 158, 508

Hooke, R., 443, 612, 617

Horace, xx, 6, 15, 16, 17, 18, 19, 20, 21, 22, 23, 24, 25, 26, 27, 28, 29, 30, 31, 32, 33, 34, 36, 37, 42, 44, 54, 60, 62, 67, 77, 81, 86, 92, 93, 94, 97, 109, 113, 116, 122, 138, 161, 195, 196, 214, 216, 218, 241, 242, 243, 249, 256, 330, 362, 372, 395, 665, 759, 776

Houtteville, Abbé d', 136, 575, 577, 701, 710

Hume, D., 233, 460, 461

Humeston, J., 536, 543, 544

Hurn, A. S., 129

Huyghens, C., 129, 130, 170, 279, 281, 285, 291, 413, 417, 420, 428, 433, 434, 443, 576, 596, 601, 617, 760

Jasinski, R., 72, 77, 78

Jaspers, K., 428

Jaucourt, C. L. de, 654

Johnson, S., 166

Joinville, Sr. de, 256

Joly, P. L., 632

Jordan, C. E., 298, 359

Jore, C. F., 216
Josse, 256
Jourdan, C. E., 95
Jouvancy, le Père, 14
Jurieu, P., 354, 480
Jurin, J., 233, 272
Juste Lipse, 326, 466
Juvenal, 15, 21, 34

Kafka, F., xviii
Kayserlingk (Césarion), 262, 306, 318, 359
Keill, J., 228, 282, 285, 413, 421, 443, 444, 617
Kepler, J., 169, 279, 280, 285, 413, 417, 420, 428, 434, 443, 589, 601, 614, 615, 617
King, W., 134, 577, 582, 605, 641, 642, 660, 661
Kircher, A., 428, 617
Kœnig, S., 254, 269, 272, 277, 446
Koyré, A., 70

La Beaumelle, L. A. de, 96, 103, 104, 548
La Bléterie, J.P.R. de, 335
La Bruyère, J. de, 4, 311, 527
La Chaussée, N. de, 259, 378
Lachèvre, F., 48, 50, 55, 58
Lacombe, J., 6, 90, 117
La Condamine, C. M. de, 333, 436, 437
Ladvocat, J. B., 699
La Fare, C. A., Marquis de, xx, 5, 19, 21, 57, 58, 77, 242, 373, 775, 776
La Fontaine, J. de, 4, 18, 19, 20, 21, 36, 50, 58, 60, 65, 66, 69, 71, 72, 73, 74, 75, 76, 77, 78, 79, 80, 81, 93, 121, 123, 207, 210, 212, 215, 372, 374, 394, 473, 573, 575, 691, 776
Lafosse, A. C., 10
Lagrange-Chancel, F. J. de, 41
La Harpe, J. F. de, 39, 42
La Hontan, L. A. de, 5, 135, 398, 399, 775
Lamarre, 198
Lamberti, G. de, 354, 480
La Mettrie, J. O. de, 429, 635, 707
La Mothe le Vayer, F. de, 181, 515, 775
La Motte, H. de, 18, 23, 36, 38, 48, 83, 84, 85, 86, 87, 94, 100, 101, 141, 142, 159, 188, 196, 197, 205, 209, 210, 212, 242
La Mottraye, A. de, 188, 227, 233, 474
Lamy, G., 69, 72, 77, 78, 694, 701, 710
Lancaster, H. C., 110, 375
Lanson, G., xvi, 9, 12, 82, 123, 135, 136, 174, 175, 176, 177, 182, 183, 184, 203, 220, 223, 224, 232, 233, 234, 235, 253, 330, 351, 371, 372, 375, 376, 377, 382,

396, 397, 427, 451, 473, 491, 511, 559, 564, 566, 577, 578, 579, 591, 633, 634, 636, 637, 642, 661, 678, 701
La Popelinière, L. V., Sieur de, 564
La Rochefoucauld, F. de, 4
Larrey, I. de, 354, 480
Launai, Mlle de, 342, 713
Launay, J. de, 68
Law, W., 642
Leclerc, J., 85, 225, 443
Lecouvreur, Mlle, 175
Ledet, E., 208, 365
Lee, N., 195
Lefèvre, 84
Lefranc de Pompignan, J., 421
Leibniz, G. W., xix, 4, 9, 122, 131, 134, 135, 140, 154, 169, 172, 207, 226, 228, 235, 268, 272, 274, 275, 276, 277, 278, 279, 280, 282, 283, 284, 285, 288, 289, 291, 297, 300, 301, 307, 346, 358, 406, 408, 420, 421, 423, 426, 428, 429, 438, 443, 448, 565, 567, 568, 569, 589, 596, 605, 606, 607, 608, 610, 611, 618, 642, 643, 644, 645, 646, 650, 652, 653, 655, 656, 657, 658, 659, 660, 661, 662, 663, 664, 665, 668, 669, 670, 671, 673, 674, 675, 676, 680, 681, 682, 683, 684, 686, 687, 688, 689, 690, 691, 692, 693, 715, 724, 739, 758, 759, 760, 761, 762, 775
Lejay, le Père, 12, 120, 384, 749
Lejeune, 104
Le Moine, le Père P., 242
Lenglet du Fresnoy, 127, 317, 461, 462, 463, 464, 465, 467, 468, 469, 472, 478, 497, 498, 664, 749
Lesage, A. R., 5
Le Tellier, le Père M., 526, 746
Leti, G., 232, 459
Leucippus, 282, 285
Leuwenhœk, A. van, 432
Le Vasseur, 121
Lévesque Champeaux, 128
Lévesque de Burigny, 128, 353, 511, 515, 547
Lévesque de Pouilly, 128, 152, 473, 632
Libby, M., 617
Lignières, F. P., Sieur de, 58
Limiers, H. P. de, 354, 480
Linant, M., 214, 216, 218, 335
Linguet, S. N., 103
Lion, H., 375, 382
Locke, J., xvii, xix, 68, 126, 130, 131, 133, 135, 136, 144, 145, 152, 184, 185, 214, 216, 218, 219, 220, 222, 224, 226, 227, 229, 230, 233, 235, 236, 237, 241, 244,

245, 246, 270, 279, 281, 282, 291, 297, 298, 299, 301, 332, 333, 335, 342, 343, 345, 346, 358, 389, 403, 404, 407, 408, 409, 414, 423, 426, 428, 429, 439, 443, 492, 506, 516, 517, 534, 564, 565, 566, 569, 576, 589, 598, 601, 606, 607, 608, 609, 610, 618, 619, 620, 621, 622, 623, 624, 625, 626, 627, 628, 629, 630, 631, 636, 651, 653, 656, 665, 669, 696, 702, 707, 708, 712, 713, 714, 716, 722, 724, 739, 750, 755, 756, 758, 760, 761, 763, 768, 775, 777, 779, 780

Lombard, A., 99, 101
Longchamp, S. G., 267
Lorme, Marion de, 48
Lounsbury, T. R., 203
Louvois, F. M., Le Tellier, Marquis de, 353
Lowenstein, R., 375
Lucan, 717
Lucas, J. M., 694
Luchet, J.P.L., Marquis de, 95
Lucretius, xx, 17, 19, 20, 21, 47, 50, 51, 58, 60, 62, 67, 77, 78, 81, 122, 130, 135, 136, 138, 142, 183, 208, 214, 218, 759
Luillier, 18, 48. *See also* Chapelle
Luther, M., 743

Mably, G. B. de, 318
MacDonald, W. L., 668
Machiavelli, N., 306, 320, 321, 324, 326, 352, 760
McKee, K., 399
MacLaurin, C., 228, 337, 444
Maestro, M., 785
Maetius, 169
Maffei, F. S. di, 216
Maillet, B. de, 521, 635
Mailly, Cardinal de, 526
Maimonides, 706
Mairan, Dortous de, 228, 268, 272, 366, 392, 421, 444, 446, 617
Maisons, M. de, 153, 163, 174, 190
Malagrida, xii, 676
Malcrais, Mlle de, 578
Malebranche, N., 129, 130, 131, 132, 133, 136, 140, 175, 218, 219, 228, 235, 282, 291, 342, 345, 346, 366, 408, 409, 420, 421, 428, 431, 438, 443, 452, 527, 564, 567, 576, 589, 600, 610, 613, 618, 622, 625, 626, 632, 640, 651, 656, 702, 710, 711, 712, 713, 715, 716, 717, 718, 724, 758, 759, 760, 761, 762, 775
Malézieu, N., 19, 58
Malherbe, F. de, 45, 47, 374, 573
Mallet, D., 132, 556

Mandeville, B. de, xvii, 126, 145, 184, 271, 302, 310, 311, 345, 346, 347, 355, 357, 423, 512, 566, 625, 665, 667, 724, 740, 779, 780
Marais, M., 94, 96, 149, 208
Marche, Fyot de la, 12, 120
Marcus Aurelius, 323
Marivaux, P., 84, 85, 463
Marlborough, Duchess of, 174
Marmier, J., 16
Marmontel, J. F., 96, 104, 231
Marot, C., 67, 210, 213
Martin, J. B., 262
Mason, H., 633, 636, 637, 638, 639, 641, 644, 646, 693, 694, 695
Maucroix, F. de, 65
Maupertuis, P. L., 31, 216, 220, 228, 230, 234, 237, 254, 268, 269, 272, 276, 277, 332, 335, 343, 363, 365, 392, 410, 411, 412, 413, 416, 418, 432, 433, 434, 435, 436, 437, 439, 440, 441, 442, 444, 446, 564, 591, 601, 602, 616, 617, 677, 716, 760
Maurepas, J.F.P., Comte de, 149, 150, 151, 154
Mauzi, R., 267, 268, 269, 270, 271, 272, 275
Maynard, F. de, 44, 58
Mazarin, Cardinal de, 53, 495
Mazarin, Duchess of, 123
Medici, 483
Melon, J. F., 310, 311, 312, 313, 335, 355, 357
Menander, 7
Menjot, Dr. A., 67, 68, 72, 73
Merrill, W. A., 130
Mersenne, M., 71, 429, 588, 760
Meslier, J., 511, 520, 525, 526, 527, 528, 529, 530, 535, 536, 546, 547, 551, 562, 563, 635, 707
Meung, J. de, 181
Meynières, Président de, 390
Mézeray, P. E. de, 190, 452, 469
Middleton, C., 518, 534, 535, 547
Miège, G., 232
Le Militaire philosophe, 511, 529, 536
Milton, J., 165, 166, 185, 224, 227, 229, 231, 243, 247, 248, 779
Mirabaud, J. B., 511, 512, 515, 529, 530, 536, 547, 707
Missy, C. de, 152
Missy, R. de, 318
Moivre, A. de, 228
Moland, L., 522, 579
Molière, J. B., xix, xx, 4, 36, 48, 50, 66,

67, 84, 86, 141, 156, 207, 210, 212, 214, 257, 262, 776
Molyneux, 443, 612, 629
Moncarville, 411
Montague, Lady M. W., 185, 215, 247
Montaigne, M. de, xvii, 45, 47, 53, 63, 65, 68, 69, 72, 77, 121, 123, 124, 126, 135, 181, 235, 396, 527, 691, 759, 761, 775
Montesquieu, C. de Secondat, Baron de, 217, 227, 229, 326, 430, 461, 496, 497, 498, 500, 504, 505, 506, 509, 749, 750, 752, 760
Montmor, H. de, 429
More, H., 71
Morehouse, A., ix, 531, 536
Morize, A., 28, 309, 311, 346, 646, 669
Morley, Lord J., 93, 180, 181, 183, 185
Mornet, D., ix, 95, 533, 633
Morrison, A., 129
Morville, C.J.B., Comte de, 153, 163
Muralt, L. B. de, 178, 224, 232
Musschembrœck, 276, 291, 337, 365, 410, 413, 420, 429, 437, 443, 444, 617, 760

Nadal, A., 129
Nagel, 422
Naudé, G., 48, 466, 515, 527, 759, 775
Naves, R., ix, 13, 15, 24, 27, 28, 29, 84, 376, 378, 382, 397
Nevelet, I. N., 67
Nevers, Duke of, 18
Newton, Sir I., xvii, xix, 129, 130, 133, 152, 154, 164, 169, 170, 172, 184, 185, 214, 218, 220, 221, 222, 224, 225, 228, 229, 230, 234, 235, 236, 237, 241, 244, 245, 246, 266, 270, 272, 274, 275, 277, 278, 279, 281, 282, 285, 288, 289, 290, 291, 297, 332, 333, 335, 338, 341, 346, 356, 358, 362, 363, 364, 365, 367, 401, 402, 404, 405, 407, 408, 409, 410, 413, 414, 415, 416, 417, 418, 419, 420, 421, 423, 426, 428, 429, 430, 431, 433, 434, 435, 437, 438, 439, 440, 442, 443, 445, 447, 448, 449, 450, 564, 565, 566, 575, 576, 577, 589, 590, 591, 592, 596, 597, 598, 600, 601, 602, 603, 604, 605, 606, 607, 608, 609, 610, 611, 612, 615, 616, 618, 619, 620, 622, 635, 636, 645, 651, 652, 653, 656, 657, 669, 715, 720, 721, 724, 755, 757, 758, 760, 761, 763, 775, 777, 779, 780
Nicéron, J. P., 175
Nicole, P., 275, 570

Nieuwentyt, B., 430, 432, 437, 441, 696, 710
Ninon de Lenclos, 19, 58, 67, 123, 212
Nollet, J. A., 429, 436, 437, 439, 441
Nordberg, J. A., 474

Oldenburg, H., 514, 704
Olivet, Abbé d', 12, 13, 40, 41, 66, 337, 349, 350, 356, 364, 388, 618, 666
Orléans, Duc d', 430
Orosius, 459
Ovid, 67, 216

Palissot, C., 231
Pallu, le Père, 666
Pardies, G., 69, 72, 77, 78
Pascal, B., 4, 59, 63, 123, 156, 171, 216, 217, 218, 219, 224, 235, 236, 237, 246, 275, 291, 311, 333, 355, 401, 404, 408, 409, 428, 429, 448, 494, 527, 551, 564, 565, 577, 578, 579, 580, 581, 582, 583, 584, 585, 587, 589, 620, 624, 625, 644, 660, 662, 676, 724, 732, 734, 736, 756, 757, 758, 759, 760, 775
Patin, G., 48, 78, 759, 775
Patot, T. de, 5, 398, 399, 573, 775
Patterson, Mrs. H. T., 342, 346, 625
Pelisson, P., 210, 213
Pemberton, H., 163, 228, 234, 277, 363, 364, 413, 422, 433, 436, 439, 441, 442, 444, 564, 590, 591, 601, 614, 617
Penn, W., 233
Pericles, 483
Periers, Bonaventure des, 67
Perkens, M., ix, 727
Perrault, C., xix, 420, 535
Perseus, 15, 21
Peterborough, Lord, 150, 151, 153
Petit, L., 65, 77
Petronius, 67
Phaedrus, 67
Philo, 637
Phlegon, 543
Picart, J., 236
Picini, J., 695
Pierron, P., 15
Pintard, R., 64, 516
Piper, Count, 190
Pitot, H., 277, 365, 366, 411, 444, 446, 564
Plato, 67, 78, 125, 300, 420, 620, 682, 747, 759
Plemp, V., 71
Pluche, N. A., 430, 431, 432, 437, 441
Pluquet, F. A., 710

Plutarch, 67, 130, 481

Pomeau, R., ix, 8, 11, 12, 15, 120, 121, 128, 129, 272, 447, 461, 476, 486, 487, 490, 509, 518, 521, 531, 535, 536, 538, 542, 554, 555, 556, 557, 560, 577, 579, 587, 600, 672, 673, 675, 676, 681, 707, 712, 739, 748, 749

Pomponazzi, P., 760

Pope, A., 33, 101, 126, 153, 161, 162, 163, 164, 166, 184, 195, 203, 205, 215, 226, 229, 231, 235, 244, 247, 248, 249, 250, 258, 271, 357, 358, 360, 362, 515, 659, 665, 666, 667, 668, 669, 670, 671, 680, 682, 689, 690, 692, 720, 736, 739, 777, 779

Porchères, de, 208

Porée, Père C., 12, 13, 110

Prault, L. T., 360, 361

Prévost, Abbé A. F., 95, 178, 179, 224

Printzen, L. von, 306

Privat de Molières, 228

Protagoras, 78

Pryor, M., 185, 247

Pufendorf, S., 131, 489, 490, 750, 760

Pyrrhon, 698

Quesnel, Père, 354, 480

Quinault, Mlle, 364

Quinault, le Père, 215

Rabelais, F., 67, 181, 249, 250, 398, 399, 573, 775

Racine, J., xix, xx, 4, 18, 21, 23, 37, 38, 39, 40, 41, 42, 44, 66, 87, 93, 95, 102, 106, 110, 111, 114, 115, 116, 118, 156, 196, 201, 207, 210, 212, 214, 241, 242, 370, 373, 376, 377, 380, 382, 776

Rameau, J. P., 354

Rapin, Père, 465

Raspe, editor of Leibniz, 654

Réaumur, R. A. de, 337, 392, 430, 432, 437, 441, 721

Régis, P. S., 366, 589

Regnier, M., 256

Renan, E., 156

Renaud, 414

Renneville, C. de, 242

Rex, W., 638

Rey, M. M., 541

Richardson, S., 249

Richelieu, Duc de, 7, 163, 263, 265, 268, 269, 339, 415, 440, 495

Richer, A., 433

Richey, 215

Ridgway, R. S., 375

Rigaud, H. F., 65

Rigault, H., 82

Rihs, C., 509

Robertson, W., 461

Roberval, J. B., 392

Rochester, J. Wilmot, Earl of, 166, 169, 185, 247

Rœmer, O., 612

Rohan, Chevalier de, 149, 151, 154, 590

Rohault, J., 276, 431, 589

Rollin, C., 337, 476, 477

Rosenfield, L., 68, 71

Ross, G., 71

Rosset, M., 34

Rothelin, Abbé, 256

Rouelle, G. F., 430

Rousseau, J. B., 15, 93, 110, 111, 116, 208, 210, 212, 213, 242, 259, 371, 374, 702

Rousseau, J. J., 430, 548, 685, 749, 750

Roussel, 354, 480

Rowe, C., 748

Roy, P. C., 205, 242

Rupelmonde, Mme de, 131

Russell, T., 204, 248

Rymer, T., 203

Sablière, Mme de la, 18, 67, 68, 74, 78

Sade, Marquis de, 220

St.-Amant, A. G., 44, 47

St.-Augustin, 717

Sainte-Beuve, C., 3, 18, 19, 21, 123, 255

St.-Evremond, C., 5, 18, 19, 20, 60, 67, 77, 81, 84, 123, 124, 126, 127, 135, 136, 152, 154, 208, 210, 213, 226, 540, 541, 542, 573, 577, 580, 759, 775

St.-Hyacinthe, J. C., 128, 511

St.-Lambert, J. F., 42, 265, 269, 273

St.-Paul, 717

St.-Pavin, 57

St.-Pierre, C. I. Castel de, xvii, 258, 312, 313, 314, 315, 316, 354, 452, 480, 483, 484, 494, 495, 496

St.-Pierre, Duchesse de, 265

St.-Réal, C. V. de, 124, 127, 475

St.-Simon, L. de R., Duc de, 7

St.-Sorlin, D. de, 4

Sallier, Abbé C., 290

Sandras, Courtilz de, 452

Saulnier, V., 673

Saunderson, 422

Sauveur, J., 392

Saxe, Maréchal de, 25

Scribe, E., 496

Segrais, J. R., 36, 210, 213

Selden, J., 131
Sélia, editor of Perseus, 16
Seneca, 20, 51, 81, 130, 183, 759
Sénécé, A. B. de, 205
Seneuze, publisher at Châlons, 259
Senez, Bishop of, 10, 120
Servet, M., 746
Servien, Abbé, 137
Sévigné, Mme de, 275
Sewel, W., 233
S'Gravesande, W. J., 276, 337, 365, 366, 410, 413, 420, 421, 429, 430, 437, 443, 444, 617, 620, 696, 702
Shackleton, R., 497
Shaftesbury, Lord, 126, 134, 184, 355, 357, 358, 515, 566, 577, 625, 645, 665, 666, 667, 669, 681, 689, 690, 692, 724, 755, 780
Shakespeare, W., 39, 42, 116, 154, 166, 168, 174, 184, 185, 188, 195, 198, 199, 200, 201, 203, 204, 227, 229, 230, 231, 243, 247, 248, 249, 370, 375, 377, 380, 383, 473, 777, 779
Sherlock, R., 130, 618
Shouvaloff, Count A. P., 478
Sidney, A., 466
Siegel, J. S., 674
Sigogne, C. T., 654
Silhon, J., 317, 465, 466
Simon, R., xix, 4, 707
Sloane, H., 226, 228
Smith, R., 443, 444, 612, 613, 617
Socrates, 25, 296
Sonet, E., 202, 203, 619
Sorbière, S., 759
Spink, J. S., 58, 511
Spinoza, B., xix, 4, 51, 86, 122, 131, 135, 140, 146, 227, 235, 345, 408, 429, 511, 513, 514, 515, 525, 527, 538, 543, 547, 561, 567, 569, 577, 580, 589, 605, 638, 639, 646, 647, 655, 656, 668, 693, 694, 695, 696, 697, 698, 699, 700, 701, 702, 703, 704, 705, 706, 707, 708, 709, 710, 715, 717, 721, 747, 749, 758, 759, 760, 761, 762, 775, 782
Staël, Mme de, 504
Stair, Lord, 151, 152
Steele, R., 167, 233, 247
Stephen, L., 516
Sterne, L., 249
Stillingfleet, Bishop of Worcester, 623, 624
Stirling, J., 228
Stone, E., 422
Straton, 698
Strowski, F., 68

Suetonius, 458
Suhm, U. F. von, 655
Suidas, 637
Sumorokov, A. P., 42
Surgère, M. de, 210, 213
Swift, J., 153, 163, 164, 166, 195, 226, 229, 244, 247, 249, 250, 398, 399, 659, 666, 675

Tabaraud, M. M., 106
Taine, H., 66, 68
Tarteron, Père, 12, 15, 23, 24, 27
Tasso, 102, 168
Taylor, O. R., 96, 97, 98, 101, 104
Terence, 7
Terrasson, J., 100, 101
Texte, J., 181
Thiériot, N. C., 27, 37, 130, 132, 150, 151, 156, 161, 162, 163, 173, 177, 188, 190, 191, 198, 214, 217, 220, 221, 249, 270, 334, 336, 338, 344, 348, 349, 351, 356, 357, 359, 360, 363, 410, 411, 412, 414, 439, 441, 479, 520, 530, 590, 601, 659, 666
Thomas, A. L., 104
Thompson (J. Thomson), 247
Thou, de, 191
Thoyras, Rapin de, 227, 233, 470
Thucydides, 464
Tillotson, J., 408
Tindal, M., 515, 518, 520, 534, 535, 536
Toland, J., 512, 516, 533, 534
Topazio, V., 370
Torrey, N. L., ix, 129, 166, 511, 515, 516, 517, 518, 519, 520, 531, 535, 578, 678
Torricelli, E., 417
Tournemine, R. J., Père, 12, 13, 298, 343, 344, 345, 347, 401, 402, 403, 404, 405, 406, 407, 408, 409, 415, 427, 441, 527, 565, 575, 592, 597, 602, 651
Towne, R., 150, 151, 163
Townsend, Lord, 175
Trenchard, J., 515
Tressan, Comte de, 168, 356
Tristan l'Hermite, 44
Trublet, Abbé N.C.J., 104
Turenne, H. de la Tour d'Auvergne, Prince de, 495
Turrettini, J. R., 149

Vairasse, D., 5, 135, 398, 573
Valdruche, lawyer at Joinville, 255, 256, 259, 263, 273, 351, 496
Valentinian, 551
Van Dale, A., 535

Van Duren, 322, 323
Vanini, L., 20, 45, 47, 649
Vauvenargues, L., 25, 41, 95
Vendôme, Duc de, 18, 57, 77
Vernet, J., 149
Vernière, P., 531, 693, 707, 708
Veronese, P., 262
Viau, T. de, xx, 5, 17, 20, 21, 44, 45, 46, 48, 49, 50, 53, 58, 67, 77, 183, 373, 374, 573, 775
Villars, Maréchal de, 308, 335
Villelongue, La Cerda de, 188, 191, 193
Virgil, 7, 17, 21, 23, 26, 27, 32, 33, 34, 37, 38, 42, 44, 86, 93, 94, 95, 97, 98, 100, 101, 105, 109, 136, 165, 196, 216, 241, 242, 336, 388, 399, 776
Vixouse, Pagès de, 96
Voisenon, C. H. de, 40
Voiture, V., 36, 208, 210, 213
Voltaire, F. M. Arouet de, xiii and passim
Von der Muehll, E., 399
Vossius, 124
Vrooman, J., 375

Wade, I., 309, 511, 655, 669

Wagnière, J. L., 556
Waller, E., 166, 247
Walpole, H., 40, 153, 156, 620
Walters, R., 440, 442
Walther, G. C., 483, 490
Warburton, W., 668
Waterman, M., 578
Watteau, A., 262
Whiston, W., 175, 430
White, F. D., 101, 158
Wicquefort, A., 317, 466
Wolff, C., 263, 284, 285, 296, 297, 298, 299, 300, 301, 337, 347, 358, 421, 423, 443, 653, 654, 655, 660, 671
Woodward, J., 228
Woolston, T., 179, 224, 512, 517, 518, 519, 520, 525, 532, 534, 535, 536, 547

Ximenez, A. L., 40

Young, E., 153, 185, 247
Yvon, Abbé, 647

Zeno, 125